上海文化发展基金会图书出版专项基金资助项目

匠心铸梦

江南造船与中国首批万吨轮的创世传奇 （汉英对照版）

胡可一（Hu Keyi）著

The Story of Great Chinese Built

A Quartet of the Finest Steamers Debuts in Kiangnan

上海交通大学出版社

SHANGHAI JIAO TONG UNIVERSITY PRESS

内容提要

　　本书聚焦于"中国第一艘万吨轮"，深度挖掘了拥有160年历史的"中国民族工业的摇篮"江南造船厂的历史。作者作为一名从事船舶行业四十多年的资深造船工程师，以专业视角对中国第一批四艘万吨轮的总布置、船体结构、动力设备等特点进行描述和分析。作者在研究这四艘万吨级运输舰设计来源的同时，结合该型船的78份设计图纸和3份"母型船"图纸，对该型船设计的深度、铆接船体和蒸汽动力船舶的特点、关键人物的评价以及四艘美国万吨级运输舰交付以后的营运生命周期内的史实等进行了补充、核实和甄别，同时对江南造船所当时的造船设计、设备设施能力，以及四艘万吨级运输舰造船合同签订的背景进行了深度分析，丰富了本书的历史感并展现承接、设计和建造过程的系统性和完整性。作者致力于还原真实历史，确保这四艘具有里程碑意义的"中国第一批万吨轮"在中国近代船舶工业史中获得应有的地位。

　　This book is a history account of the shipbuilding industry centered on "China's first 10 000-ton freighter", supplementing the history of Jiangnan Shipyard, the "cradle of China's national industry", spanning nearly 160 years. Drawing from over 40 years of experience as a senior naval architect, the author analyzes the features of the first batch of 10 000-ton freighters in China from a marine engineer's professional perspectives. While studying the design sources of these four 10 000-ton steam freighters, the author supplements and verifies the details based on 78 sets of blue-prints and 3 sets of proto-ship's drawings, highlighting the features of the riveted hull and steam-powered ship, evaluation of key persons, and historical facts of the operation life cycles. Furthermore, an in-depth analysis explores ship design, capability and facility, and the background of the signing shipbuilding contract for four 10 000-ton steam freighters by Kiangnan Dock & Engineering Works. The historical materials enrich the historical sense of the book and shows the systematic and comprehensive undertaking, design and construction process. With a commitment to truth and historical accuracy, the author establishes these four "China's first batch of 10 000-ton freighters" as landmarks in the history of China's modern shipbuilding industry.

图书在版编目（CIP）数据

　　匠心铸梦：江南造船与中国首批万吨轮的创世传奇 =
The Story of Great Chinese Built: A Quartet of the
Finest Steamers Debuts in Kiangnan：汉英对照 / 胡
可一著. — 上海：上海交通大学出版社，2025.5.
ISBN 978-7-313-32130-5

　　Ⅰ. F426. 474

　　中国国家版本馆CIP数据核字第20254ZR903号

匠心铸梦：江南造船与中国首批万吨轮的创世传奇（汉英对照版）
JIANGXIN ZHUMENG: JIANGNAN ZAOCHUAN YU ZHONGGUO SHOUPI
WANDUNLUN DE CHUANGSHI CHUANQI (HANYING DUIZHAO BAN)

著　　者：胡可一		译　　者：胡可一　王　洁　胡聆白	
出版发行：上海交通大学出版社		地　　址：上海市番禺路951号	
邮政编码：200030		电　　话：021-64071208	
印　　制：上海颛辉印刷厂有限公司		经　　销：全国新华书店	
开　　本：889mm×1194mm　1/16		印　　张：17.75	
字　　数：818千字			
版　　次：2025年5月第1版		印　　次：2025年5月第1次印刷	
书　　号：ISBN 978-7-313-32130-5			
定　　价：150.00元			

船舶设计师平时所写的船舶建造规格书
可能不是一本完美的英语书
但实实在在地描述了"要造一艘什么样的船"

THE SHIPBUILDING SPECIFICATION USUALLY WRITTEN BY A SHIP DESIGNER

MAY NOT BE A PERFECT ENGLISH TEXTBOOK,

BUT IT DOES EXACTLY DESCRIBE "WHAT KIND OF SHIP TO BE BUILT"

序一

PREFACE I

万吨级远洋货轮曾经是近现代中国船舶建造历史中的里程碑，无论是在中国造船史研究还是在中国的近现代史研究过程中，人们一直对中华人民共和国成立后交付的第一艘万吨级远洋货轮"东风"号关注得很多，但对江南造船所1921年交付的四艘蒸汽动力万吨级远洋货轮在造船合同的获得、技术资料的来源，设计的自主性方面存在许多盲点。因此，清晰地定义第一艘中国自行设计和建造的万吨轮，以及其在现代中国科学技术发展史上的地位非常必要。

本书以深邃的历史眼光和专业的技术视角，对"中国第一批万吨轮"的诞生进行了全面而深入的探索与解读。它并非单纯地记录历史，而是通过对江南造船所建造四艘万吨级运输巨擘的生动描绘，深刻揭示了中国民族工业在艰难环境中砥砺前行的坚韧精神和卓越创新能力。

作者凭借深厚的船舶设计专业知识，依托丰富且珍贵的史料，尤其是包含78份设计图纸和5份总体设计方案的档案资料，详细剖析了这批万吨轮在船体结构、舾装、舱室和动力系统等方面的独特设计与技术创新，为我们理解那个时代的造船工艺和技术进步提供了重要的参考依据。同时，作者还通过严谨的考证与分析，展示了这些万吨轮在其服役期间的实际营运情况，真实反映了江南造船所在船舶设计领域取得的杰出成就。

The 10 000-ton ocean-going freighter constitutes a milestone in the history of modern Chinese shipbuilding. In the studies of modern Chinese history and the Chinese shipbuilding industry, much scholarly attention has been focused on the first 10 000-ton general cargo ship, "Dong Feng (East Wind)", delivered by Jiangnan Shipyard in the People's Republic of China (ca. 1957–1970). Surprisingly, our knowledge about the four 10 000-ton steam-powered freighters delivered by Kiangnan Dock & Engineering Works in 1921 is alarmingly sparse. We know little about the acquisition of shipbuilding contracts, the source of technical data, and the autonomy of their design. This lack of reliable knowledge presents a fascinating research opportunity. Therefore, a thorough examination of the first 10 000-ton ship designed and built by China is crucial. Equally important is the investigation of its place in the historical development of modern Chinese science and technology. Such a study could significantly contribute to our understanding of China's technological advancements and their impact on global maritime history.

The author masterfully steers readers through the technical and historical complexities of China's first batch of 10 000-ton ocean-going freighters. Building on this in-depth archival research about the construction of four gigantic 10 000-ton transportation vessels, the author's subtle interpretation offers not only a fresh look at the birth of China's first batch of 10 000-ton ocean-going freighters at Kiangnan Dock & Engineering Works, but also a significant rethinking of the tenacity and innovative ability of China's national industry to forge technical and commercial breakthroughs in a challenging environment.

Drawing on profound ship design expertise, the author explores a set of rich and precious historical materials that contains 78 sets of design drawings and 5 general arrangements. The author analyzes in detail the unique design and technological innovation of these 10 000-ton ocean-going freighters in terms of hull structure, outfitting, cabin layout and power system. In so doing, the author provides an important reference for the readers to understand the shipbuilding technology and technological progress of that era. At the same time, the author also shows the actual operation of these 10 000-ton ocean-going freighters during their service through rigorous research and analysis. Taken together, this book truly reflects the outstanding achievements of Kiangnan Dock & Engineering Works in the field of ship design.

该书对于我国乃至全球的航运、船舶制造、机械工程、交通运输等相关行业的专业人士而言，无疑是了解中国近代工业发展历程、感受中国民族工业精神的一部极具价值的参考资料。同时，其独特的中英对照版编排，也必将吸引更多国际读者的关注，共同见证中国民族工业在世界舞台上的崛起之路。

总而言之，本书内容丰富，史料翔实，可读性强，是一本非常值得期待的佳作。

中国工程院院士

上海交通大学教授

The book is undoubtedly a valuable reference material for professionals in shipping, shipbuilding, mechanical engineering, transportation, and other related industries in China and even around the world to understand the development process of China's modern industry and feel the spirit of China's national industry. At the same time, its unique bilingual edition will also attract the attention of more international readers and witness the rise of China's national industry in the world.

All in all, this is a revealing book based on meticulous research. The author's analysis is detailed, thorough, and persuasive.

Academician of the Chinese Academy of Engineering

Professor, Shanghai Jiao Tong University

Lin Zhongqin

序二

PREFACE II

本书堪称一部融合了工业历史研究与造船技术深度剖析的典范之作。作者以精湛的笔触和严谨的学术态度，深度挖掘了"中国第一批万吨轮"背后蕴含的深厚历史内涵和卓越技术实力，展现了一幅20世纪第二个十年中国民族工业在江南造船所这一发源地上创造出的辉煌画卷。

全书的最大亮点在于，作者运用船舶设计专家的专业洞见，结合翔实丰富的史料和珍贵的图纸档案，精细梳理出万吨轮在设计环节中体现的创新思维和领先技术，如铆接船体构造、先进的燃油蒸汽动力系统的应用，这不仅揭示了20世纪初江南造船所在船舶设计领域的领先地位，更是对其所拥有的科技智慧和工业美学做出了富有说服力的诠释。作者对四艘万吨轮交付后营运状况的严谨考证，充分体现了科学研究求真务实的精神，使得该书不仅是一部关于工业遗产保护和传承的研究文献，也是对我国早期工业化进程中科技创新实践的生动记录。

通读全文，字里行间能向读者呈现中国船舶工业史的起源和发展，同时还是对具有160年历史的"中国民族工业的摇篮"江南造船厂历史研究的一个深度补充。作为中国民族工业发源地之一，江南造船厂的技术创新和科研成果对上海地区的科技进步产生了积极影响，同时也塑造了上海敢为人先、勇于创新的城市文化特质。在领略万吨轮建造的跌宕起伏和丰收喜悦中，读者也从船舶工业方面对上海城市的发展有了一个独特的解读。

This work is an exemplary blend of industrial history research and in-depth examination of shipbuilding technologies. The book is remarkably well-researched and well-written. With a rigorous academic attitude, the author thoroughly explores the profound historical significance and outstanding technical capability behind the "first batch of 10 000-ton ocean-going freighters in China". In so doing, the author also depicts a magnificent industrial landscape created by China's national industry through a detailed analysis of Kiangnan Dock & Engineering Works in the 1920s—the birthplace of Chinese national industries.

The most important novelty of the book is that the author uses his professional insights of ship design experts in combination with a detailed analysis of unique and rich historical materials. Building on the laborious examination of precious drawings from archives, the author reconstructs the innovative thinking and cutting-edge technologies embodied in the design of 10 000-ton ocean-going freighters, such as the application of riveted hull structure and advanced oil-fuelled steam power system. Consequently, the author doesn't only reveal the leading position of Kiangnan Dock & Engineering Works in the field of ship design in the early 20th century, but also makes a convincing interpretation of the scientific and technological merits and industrial aesthetics the Dock carries. The author's rigorous research on after delivery operation of the four 10 000-ton ocean-going freighters fully reflects the truth-seeking and pragmatic spirit of scientific research. Therefore, the book is an accurate documentation of industrial heritage. Moreover, it is also a vivid record of scientific and technological innovations in the early industrialization of China.

Offering a sophisticated reading of the origins of the Chinese shipbuilding industry, the author contributes to the historical studies of Jiangnan Shipyard, too. Jiangnan Shipyard is known as the "foundation of China's national industry," which has a history of 160 years. As one of the birthplaces of China's national industries, Jiangnan Shipyard spearheaded scientific and technological progress in Shanghai. As a result, Jiangnan Shipyard also shaped Shanghai's urban culture of daring to be the first and brave to innovate. In appreciating the ups and downs of the construction of the 10 000-ton ocean-going freighters and the joy of the harvest, the reader will also gain a unique interpretation of the urban development of Shanghai from the perspective of the shipbuilding industry.

综上所述，无论是对相关领域的专业人员还是广大工科背景的研究者和历史人文的爱好者来说，这部中英对照版的著作都将是他们深入了解中国民族工业发展脉络、感悟科技进步力量的重要参考，有助于在全球范围内传播和弘扬中国工业文明的独特魅力与辉煌成就。

中国船舶集团有限公司

首席专家

陈刚

In sum, the bilingual edition will be an important reference material for engineering professionals, academic historians, and enthusiasts of humanities and history. By balancing detailed descriptions of technological progress with lucid narratives about the developmental trajectory of China's national industry, the author has given us an exemplary case study of the social and historical construction of sciences and technologies. This book is a must read for readers interested in the unique charm and brilliant achievements of China's industrial civilization on a global scale.

China State Shipbuilding Corporation Limited

Chief Expert

Chen Gang

目录
CONTENT

万吨级远洋货轮曾经是中国近现代造船史上大型船舶的标志性船型，建造万吨级远洋货轮在中国近现代造船企业的发展历史上具有里程碑的意义。"官府"号、"跃进"号和"东风"号在不同的历史时期都曾拥有过"中国第一艘万吨级远洋货轮"的称号。"官府"号系列是本书所要介绍的主角，那么后两艘船是什么背景下先后被冠名"中国第一艘万吨级远洋货轮"的？

The ocean-going freighter over 10 000 deadweight tons was one of the most remarkable ship types in the history of modern Chinese shipbuilding. Constructing such large ocean-going ships was a significant milestone in the development progress of China's modern shipbuilding industry. The SS "Mandarin", MV "Yue Jin" and MV "Dong Feng" were once respectively adorned the aureole of "Chinese first" in different particular periods. The SS "Mandarin" series is the protagonist introduced in this book, and on which backgrounds the other two ships were highly praised as "the first of China"?

0.1

中国"第一艘万吨级远洋货轮"是 1958 年下水的"跃进"号？
Chinese First 10 000-ton Freighter Was MV "Yue Jin" Launched in 1958?

1962 年，大连造船厂建成了由苏联转让技术和图纸并提供设备的"567"型 15 700 载重吨远洋货轮"跃进"号。"跃进"号的建成标志着大连造船厂在大型船舶建造工艺技术上实现了重大突破。"跃进"号是中华人民共和国成立后自行建造的第一艘载重量超过万吨的远洋货轮。"跃进"号的主要参数如表 0-1 所示。

In 1962, the Dalian Shipyard delivered a 15 700 deadweight tons ocean-going freighter named "Yue Jin", she was "567" type cargo ship designed by the Soviet. The technologies, drawings and equipments were transferred and provided by the Soviet Union. Successful delivery of MV "Yue Jin" marked that Dalian Shipyard had achieved a substantial breakthrough in the technology and methodology of building a large ship. Self-built MV "Yue Jin" was the first ocean-going freighter with deadweight over ten thousand tons after the founding of the People's Republic of China. The main particulars of MV "Yue Jin" as show in Table 0-1.

表 0-1　"跃进"号的主要参数[1]
Table 0-1　Main particulars of MV "Yue Jin"

总长	LOA	169.9	m
型宽	Bmld	21.8	m
满载吃水	Scantling draught	9.7	m
载货量	Cargo capacity	13 400	t
载重量	Deadweight	15 930	t
排水量	Displacement	22 100	t
航速	Speed	18.5	kn
主机功率	M/E power	13 000	hp
续航力	Endurance	12 000	n mile

"跃进"号采用"三岛式"（tri-isle）建造工艺，自 1958 年 9 月 30 日船台铺龙骨（keel laying），同年 11 月 27 日船体建成下水，创造了 58 天船台周期的先进纪录。虽然其船台周期达到了世界造船先进水平，但由于下水完整性差，下水后舾装、设备安装和调试等工程量较大，"跃进"号直至 1960 年底才基本建成并于 1962 年交付。

"跃进"号货轮采用了当时最新的船舶技术，配置了当时最先进的自动化、电气化设备，可以中途不靠岸补充燃料直接驶抵世界各主要港口，并有一定的冰区航行能力。图 0-1 为"跃进"号货轮 1962 年交付后的航行照片。

With the help of "tri-isle" erecting technology, MV "Yue Jin" was keel laid on 30 September 1958, and launched on 27 November of the same year. She created an advanced record of 58 days on slipway erection. Although her erection period on slipway had reached world advanced level, the completeness was not so perfect. The subsequent works of outfitting, installing and commissioning were quite heavier after ship launched, so MV "Yue Jin" was substantially completed till the end of 1960 and delivered in 1962.

MV "Yue Jin" adopted novel marine technologies and equipped the most advanced automation and electric appliances, and she was able to sail to major ports of the world without bunkering. Also, she had certain ability to navigate in iced water. Figure 0-1 is a photo of MV "Yue Jin" after delivery in 1962.

图 0-1　"跃进"号货轮 1962 年交付后的航行照片 [2]
Figure 0-1　MV "Yue Jin" freighter was sailing on the sea in 1962

1963 年 4 月 30 日，"跃进"号货轮首航，载着 13 000 吨玉米从青岛港出发前往日本名古屋西港。5 月 1 日中午，"跃进"号货轮不幸触礁沉没在苏岩礁。

On 30 April 1963, MV "Yue Jin", carrying 13 000 tons corn, departed from Qingdao Port for her maiden voyage to West Port of Nagoya, Japan. MV "Yue Jin" unfortunately stranded and sunk at Suyan Reef in the noon of 1 May.

0.2

中国"第一艘万吨级远洋货轮"是 1960 年下水的"东风"号？
Chinese First 10 000-ton Freighter Was MV "Dong Feng" Launched in 1960?

在大连造船厂"跃进"号下水后不到一年半，1960 年 4 月 15 日，中国第一艘自行设计、建造的万吨级远洋货轮"东风"号（船体号：H1290）在江南造船厂的船台下水。"东风"号万吨级远洋货轮的主要参数如表 0-2 所示。为何当时会特别强调"东风"号万吨级远洋货轮是"自行设计建造"？一是万吨级远洋货轮"跃进"号由苏联提供船舶设计方案和进口设备，不是自行设计；二是由于"跃进"号在首航中触礁沉没，此后也不愿再提了。

Less than one and half year after MV "Yue Jin" launched in Dalian Shipyard, Chinese first self-designed and self-built ocean-going freighter over 10 000 deadweight tons "Dong Feng" (means "East Wind", hull number H1290) was launched in Jiangnan Shipyard on 15 April 1960. The main particulars of MV "Dong Feng" as shown in Table 0-2.Why "self-design and self-build" were specially emphasized so much? Firstly, the previous "Chinese No.1" MV "Yue Jin" was built on basis of Soviet supplied design drawings and imported equipment. The design of this vessel was provided by the design institute of former Soviet Union not by shipyard itself. Secondly, sinking incident in maiden voyage was regarded so inglorious. Thus, aureole worn on MV "Yue Jin" was no longer appeared.

2006 年 3 月 23 日下午，中国首次开展的"十大名船评选活动"在北京人民大会堂揭晓结果，以"东风"号为首的 4 艘军舰和 6 艘民用船舶荣膺"中国十大名船"（Chinese Built Ships Top Ten）称号。这十大名船均由中国自行设计建造，堪称新中国船舶工业不同历史时期的典型代表船型。图 0-2 为中国十大名船评选活动组委会授予江南造船（集团）有限责任公司的奖牌。

On the afternoon of 23 March 2006, the final winners of China's first "The Selection of Famous Ships Top Ten" were announced at the Great Hall of the People in Beijing. Four warships and six merchant ships led by MV "Dong Feng" were awarded "Chinese Built Ships Top Ten". These ten reputable ships were entirely self-designed and self-built by Chinese shipbuilding industry, and they were significant types of ship in various historical periods of the People's Republic of China. Figure 0-2 is the organizer of "The Selection of Famous Ships Top Ten" awarded "Chinese Built Famous Ships" medal of MV "Dong Feng" to Jiangnan Shipyard (Group) Co., Ltd.

表 0-2　"东风"号万吨级远洋货轮的主要参数 [3]
Table 0-2　Main particulars of MV "Dong Feng"

总长	LOA	161.4	m
两柱间长	L_{pp}	147.2	m
型宽	Bmld	20.2	m
型深	Depth	12.4	m
设计吃水	Design draught	8.46	m
载货量	Cargo capacity	10 000	t
载重量	Deadweight	11 754	t
排水量	Displacement	17 182	t
航速	Speed	17.3	kn
主机功率	M/E power	8 820	hp
	（燃油消耗 FOC: 221.1 g+4.02 g/kW·h）		
续航力	Endurance	12 000	n mile
船员	Crew	47	P
总吨	Gross tonnage	9 351	t
净吨	Net tonnage	5 321	t

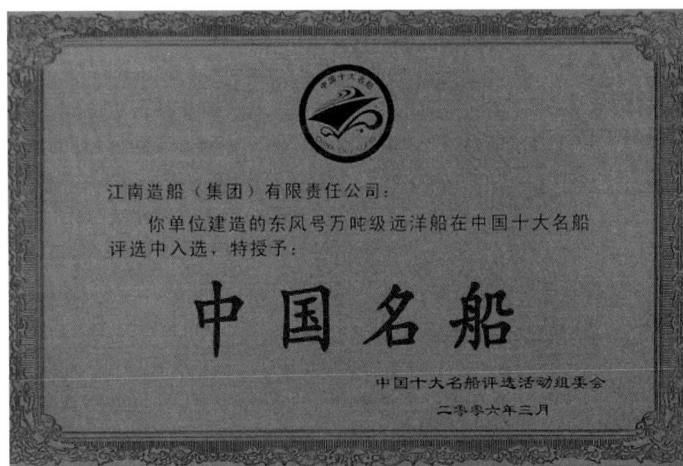

图 0-2　"东风"号万吨级远洋货轮荣膺"中国名船"的奖牌
Figure 0-2　MV "Dong Feng" awarded a medal of "Chinese Built Famous Ships"

"东风"号万吨级远洋货轮的船型为单螺旋桨柴油机驱动、双层纵通甲板、长艏楼、前倾艏柱和巡洋舰艉并具备富裕干舷的钢质远洋干货船。舯部布置有机舱和上层建筑。

"东风"号能载运各类杂货，船上设有 878 立方米的冷藏货舱及 1 145 立方米的液货舱，能载运少量的冷藏货及液货。在第二、第三货舱间设有 1 个起重能力为 60 吨的重型吊杆（heavy duty derrick），可装卸大件（project）和重型货物。在第一货舱设有防爆措施，可以装运一般易燃易爆货品。此外，在货舱内设有止移板（anti-shifting board），可减小载运散装谷物时的移动力矩（shifting moment）。"东风"号万吨级远洋货轮能在海上连续航行 40 个昼夜，可远航至欧洲、非洲和拉丁美洲。

"东风"号万吨级远洋货轮船体结构部分采用国产高强度低合金钢材料，主机采用我国自行设计制造的第一台 8 820 马力船用低速重型柴油机。船上还配置了比较新型的由废气锅炉供汽的蒸汽透平发电机组、通信导航设备和舱室内空调等。

"东风"号万吨级远洋货轮的设计建造集中反映了当时中国船舶行业设计、建造工艺水平以及船舶设备的配套生产能力，为中国批量建造万吨以上大型船舶奠定了基础。图 0-3 所示为"东风"号万吨远洋货轮在江南造船厂的船台上进行分段搭载的场景，图 0-4 所示为"东风"号万吨远洋货轮艉部分段船台大合拢的场景。

Designing and constructing MV "Dong Feng" comprehensively reflected the capabilities and abilities of Chinese shipbuilding industry in respects of ship design, building methodology and equipment. It founded a solid base for sustainably building large scale ships. Figure 0-3 is a photo showing block erection of MV "Dong Feng" cargo ship on slipway of Jiangnan Shipyard. Figure 0-4 is a photo showing stern block of MV "Dong Feng" cargo ship erected on slipway.

MV "Dong Feng" was a single propeller, diesel engine driven, B-type freeboard, steel hulled ocean-going dry cargo ship with twin continuous decks, long forecastle, inclined stem and cruiser type stern. Engine room and superstructure located amidship.

MV "Dong Feng" was able to carry various general and dry freights. She can carry certain quantity of reefer and liquid cargoes in an 878 cubic meters reefer cargo hold and an 1 145 cubic meters liquid cargo tank respectively. One set of 60-ton heavy duty derrick was arranged on upper deck in between No.3 and No.4 cargo hatches, which can handle large projects and heavier cargoes. Explosion proof measures were settled for No.1 cargo hold so that normal dangerous goods can be loaded in this cargo hold. Anti-shifting boards were supplemented in cargo holds for preventing extra shifting moments while grain loaded. MV "Dong Feng" with endurance of 40 days and nights was capable to sail to Europe, Africa and Latin America.

The hull structure of MV "Dong Feng" partially adopted the high tensile steel produced by domestic steel mills, and main engine was China first self-manufactured lower speed diesel engine with output of 8 820 hp. Novel type turbine generators, steam driven by exhaust boiler, communication and navigation instruments and air conditioning for cabin were equipped on board.

图 0-3　"东风"号万吨远洋货轮在船台上进行分段搭载的场景
Figure 0-3　Block erection of MV "Dong Feng" cargo ship on slipway

图 0-4　"东风"号艉部分段船台大合拢的场景
Figure 0-4　Stern block of MV "Dong Feng" cargo ship erected on slipway

1960 年 4 月 15 日下午，江南造船厂为国内自行设计和建造的第一艘 12 000 吨远洋货轮（H1290）举行下水盛典，交通部上海海运局局长代表交通部宣读了将新船命名为"东风"号的决定。《解放日报》《新闻日报》《文汇报》以及《人民日报》等媒体分别用头版头条醒目标题和较长篇幅报道了"东风"号胜利下水。图 0-5 所示为江南造船厂建造的"东风"号万吨远洋货轮下水的场景。

On the afternoon of 15 April 1960, Jiangnan Shipyard held a grand launching ceremony for China first, self-designed and self-built 12 000 deadweight tons ocean-going freighter. The Director of the Shanghai Maritime Transport Bureau named H1290 as MV "Dong Feng" on behalf of the Ministry of National Transportation Department. MV "Dong Feng" was then successfully launched into Huangpu (Whamgpoo) River. National major newspapers such as *Jiefang Daily*, *News Daily*, *Wenhui Daily* and *People's Daily* respectively made striking headline and long articles to report this launching event of MV "Dong Feng". Figure 0-5 shows launching ceremony of MV "Dong Feng" in Jiangnan Shipyard.

图 0-5　江南造船厂"东风"号下水的场景
Figure 0-5　Launching ceremony of MV "Dong Feng" in Jiangnan Shipyard

1965 年 12 月 31 日，"东风"号竣工交船。翌年，经中国船舶检验局检验和"东风"号国家验收委员会鉴定，其快速性、装载量、空船重量和机舱长度等指标均达到了当时国际先进水平。图 0-6 为"东风"号万吨远洋货轮试航鉴定书。图 0-7 为"东风"号万吨远洋货轮交船离厂时的航行照片。

On 31 December 1965, MV "Dong Feng" was successfully delivered. The following year, after the inspection by the China Ship Inspection and Classification Bureau (later renamed as "China Classification Society") and the National Acceptance Committee of "Dong Feng", her speed, loading capacity, light weight and length of engine room etc. had reached the advanced international level at that time. Figure 0-6 is sea trail certificate of MV "Dong Feng" issued by the National Acceptance Committee of "Dong Feng". Figure 0-7 shows MV "Dong Feng" departed from yard for her maiden voyage.

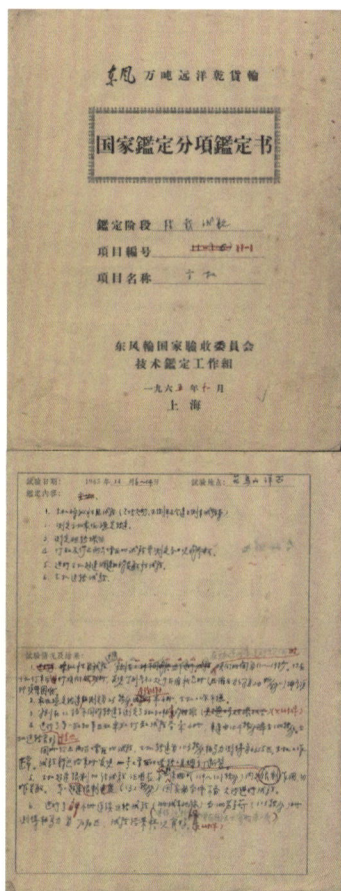

图 0-6　"东风"号万吨远洋货轮
试航鉴定书
Figure 0-6　Sea trail certificate of MV
"Dong Feng"

图 0-7　"东风"号万吨远洋货轮交船离厂时的航行照片
Figure 0-7　MV "Dong Feng" departed from yard for her maiden voyage

0.3

中国"第一艘万吨级远洋货轮"是 1921 年交付的"官府"号！
Chinese First 10 000-ton Freighter Was SS "Mandarin" Delivered in 1921!

事实上如果单纯从"自行建造"的角度来说，中国建造的"第一艘万吨级远洋货轮"既不是上文提到的"跃进"号，也不是"东风"号，而是江南造船所于 1921 年交付的"官府"号！图 0-8 为江南造船所建造的第一艘万吨级运输舰"官府"号的照片。

Simply, from the perspective of "self-built", the "Chinese First 10 000-ton ocean-going freighter" is neither the MV "Yue Jin" nor MV "Dong Feng" which were mentioned above. However it should be SS "Mandarin" which was delivered by Jiangnan Shipyard (previous English name was "Kiangnan Dock & Engineering Works") in 1921. Figure 0-8 is a photo of SS "Mandarin" built by Kiangnan Dock & Engineering Works.

图 0-8　江南造船所建造的第一艘万吨级运输舰"官府"号
Figure 0-8　SS "Mandarin" built by Kiangnan Dock & Engineering Works

在史料中通行的说法是 1920 年美国政府要求江南造船所继续履行四艘万吨级运输舰的建造合同，但实际上这四艘万吨级运输舰的建造合同的重启与当时的美国商会［American Chamber of Commerce，1915 年在上海设有分会"上海亚美商会"（AmCham Shanghai）］的创始人罗伯特·大来（Robert Dollar）决定接手这四艘万吨级运输舰并投入跨太平洋航线运输有关。他所创立的大来航运公司[4]（Dollar Steamship Company）的木材码头当时就设在黄浦江畔江南船坞的对面[5]。1918 年 11 月，由于第一次

The common statement in current historical sources is that the Government of the United States requested Kiangnan Dock & Engineering Works to resume the shipbuilding contract of four 10 000-tons steam freighters in 1920. Actually execution of the shipbuilding contract was restarted by Robert Dollar, the founder of the American Chamber of Commerce, which had a Shanghai branch named "AmCham Shanghai". Dollar Steamship Company owned by Robert Dollar decided to take over these four steam freighters for Trans-Pacific routes. The timber wharf of the Dollar Steamship Company was located just opposite of the Kiangnan along the Huangpu (Whamgpoo) River. In November 1918, the Great War was ended. Kiangnan Dock & Engineering Works disruptively redesigned these steam freighters from original purpose of

世界大战的结束，江南造船所根据美国海运委员会（United States Shipping Board, USSB）从原来侧重于战时运输变更为一般商业运输的要求进行了全新设计，因此，这四艘万吨级运输舰的最终设计是江南造船所自行完成的。

江南造船所建造的第一艘万吨级运输舰"官府"号（Mandarin）于 1920 年 6 月 3 日下水；第二艘"天朝"号（Celestial）于 1920 年 8 月 3 日下水；第三艘"东方"号（Oriental）于 1921 年 2 月 23 日下水；第四艘"国泰"号（Cathay）于 1921 年 5 月 26 日下水。四艘运输舰的载重量均超过了 10 000 吨、排水量为 14 750 吨。四艘运输舰均于 1921 年内开赴美国，交付给了美国海运委员会下属的应急船队公司（Emergency Fleet Corporation, EFC）。

本书的后续章节将对当时江南造船所的船舶设计、造船设备设施能力、造船合同签订的背景、设计图纸的来源和关键人物的评价以及铆接船体和蒸汽动力船舶进行专业解读。最后对这四艘万吨级运输舰交付以后整个营运生命周期内的史实等细节进行真实的描述和重现。

wartime transportation to normal commercial transportation as required by the United States Shipping Board (USSB). Therefore, the final design of these four steamers was completely performed by Kiangnan themselves.

The first Kiangnan built steamer SS "Mandarin" was launched on 3 June 1920, and the second steamer SS "Celestial" was launched on 3 August 1920, the third steamer SS "Oriental" was launched on 23 February 1921, and the fourth steamer SS "Cathay" was launched on 26 May 1921. The deadweight of these four steamers all exceeded 10 000 tons, and the displacement had reached 14 750 tons. All these four steamers departed to the United States within the year of 1921 and delivered to the Emergency Fleet Corporation (EFC) of the United States Shipping Board.

The subsequent chapters of this book will describe and clarify the related activities and facts of Kiangnan Dock & Engineering Works in that particular period, including the ship design, shipbuilding capabilities and facilities, the background of signing four shipbuilding contracts, the sources of design drawings and the evaluation to key persons as well as the professional explanation regarding riveted hull and steam-powered ship. Finally, the historical facts of these four steamers throughout the operational life cycle are factually described and reappeared.

作者注：

Notes:

1 "跃进"号货轮的主要参数来自网络。

2 照片选自《60 风华——中国船级社六十周年》画册。

3 技术参数摘自江南造船集团档案馆收藏的"东风"号的技术图纸。

4 资料来自：https://en.wikipedia.org/wiki/American_President_Lines#Dollar_Shipping_Company，向原作者表示敬意。

5 即后来的白莲泾码头。

"局坞分家"后的江南船坞
Kiangnan Dock after Separation

1.1

"局坞分家"、商业化运作
Commercial Operation after Separation

1885 年（光绪十一年），江南制造局在建成"保民"号铁甲巡洋舰（见图 1-1）后，清政府正式下令沪、闽两局停止造船，改为修理南北洋各省的兵轮船只[1]。后来甚至连一部分建造小型铁壳船和兵轮的修理业务也委托上海耶松、祥生等外资船厂进行。究其原因，主要是李鸿章认为"……物料匠工多为外洋购置，是以中国造船之银倍于外洋购船之价。今急欲成军，须在外国订造为省便。"

In 1885 (Guangxu 11st Year), Imperial Qing Government officially instructed Shanghai and Fujian (Fokien) Bureaus to suspect their newbuilding business respectively after Kiangnan Manufacturing Bureau completed and delivered "Pao Min" (Tribune) iron hulled cruiser (see Figure 1-1), and transformed to merely repair ships for South and North fleets and coastal provinces. Later, even for repairing works of small steel hulled ship and warship, those works were too subcontracted to foreign invested Shanghai Dock & Engineering Co. and Boyd & Co., Ltd. The main reason was that Li Hongzhang (Li Hungchang) considered: "… material and equipment mostly imported, and the cost of Chinese built ship was much higher than that purchased from foreign shipyards. In order to rapidly form the imperial navy fleet, ordering ship from foreign shipyards seems more convenient and cost effective."

图 1-1 1885 年江南制造局建造的"保民"号铁甲巡洋舰（照片摄于 1894 年 5 月旅顺附近海域，由近代海军史研究专家陈悦提供）
Figure 1-1 Iron hulled cruiser "Pao Min" (Tribune) built by Kiangnan Manufacturing Bureau in 1885 (The photo was taken in sea near Lüshun, May 1894, courtesy of Chen Yue, researcher of modern naval history)

许多近代史和史料研究把李鸿章此举的原因分析为："表面原因是经费困难，内在原因是清朝政府'崇洋媚外'思想作祟。"但客观地分析，如结合当时清朝政府的处境，财政困难加之自行建造成本高昂，又急于建设海防和北洋海军，才使造船不如买船的指导方针抬头，下令停止造船也是不得已而为之。"……查该局（江南制造局）现制枪炮火药，业必专而始精，不必再造铁甲轮船，致糜工费。"

Many historians and their papers analyzed the reason why Li Hongzhang made such decision: "Apparent cause was tight budget of Imperial Qing Government, but immanent cause was conducted by 'blindly worshiping foreign things' philosophy of government officials." At objective view point, if considering the situation of Qing Government, financial difficulties, higher cost for self-building ship, urgent needs for coastal defense and Beiyang Navy, purchasing iron cladding cruisers seems better than self-building it. Qing Government had no alternative but to decide suspending shipbuilding. "… Currently Kiangnan is manufacturing weapon and ammunition, and it should be dedicated and should keep improving and goal for perfection. It is not worth simultaneously building iron cladding cruiser at higher cost."

1862 年，祥生船厂（Boyd & Co., Ltd.）成立，其前身是英商尼柯逊（A. M. Nicolson）和鲍义德（G. M. Boyd）在上海陆家嘴开设的和记洋行（Nicolson & Boyd Co., Ltd.）。祥生船厂在苏格兰人格兰特的管理经营下，迅速发展成为拥有大型船坞和机器制造的修造船企业。1865 年，祥生船厂仅能够建造载重量为 200 吨配置 70 马力发动机的小轮船，但到了 1870 年，祥生船厂为怡和轮船公司（Indo-China Steam Navigation Co., Ltd.）建造的长 210 英尺（64.01 米）、排水量为 1 300 吨、载重量为 763 吨的货船"公和"号是当时上海地区建造的最大吨位的货船[2]。

In 1862, Boyd & Co., Ltd. was established in Shanghai, this shipyard formerly known as "Nicolson & Boyd Co., Ltd.", a British trading house, jointly founded by A.M. Nicolson and G. M. Boyd at Lujiazui of Pudong (Pootung) Shanghai. Boyd & Co., Ltd., under the management of a Scottish Galant, rapidly developed to a large scale shipbuilding and repairing yard with bigger dry dock and machinery manufacturing facility. In 1865, Boyd & Co., Ltd. was only able to build smaller ship with deadweight of 200 tons and 70 hp engine, but till 1870, Boyd & Co., Ltd. was able to deliver a large cargo ship "Kung Ho" for Indo-China Steam Navigation Co., Ltd. with hull length of 210 feet (64.01 meters), displacement of 1 300 tons and deadweight of 763 tons. She was the largest tonnage ship built in Shanghai area.

1865 年，美国人在虹口外虹桥（东大名路 378 号）创办耶松船厂（Shanghai Dock & Engineering Co.）（见图 1–2）。后由于吸收了不少英国资本，耶松船厂逐步变成英国资本为主的船舶修造厂。1895—1900 年，耶松船厂先后兼并了虹口地区的老船澳与东方船坞，建造规模更为扩大。1884 年，耶松船厂建成船长 280 英尺（85.34 米）、载重量为 2 522 吨的"源和"号，为远东最大的商船[3]。1901 年 3 月，耶松船厂和祥生船厂正式合并，总资本增至 557 万两（1 两等于 37.4 克的十足纹银，成色 93.53%）。

图 1–2　东大名路 378 号的耶松船厂办公楼铭牌
Figure 1–2　Office building of Shanghai Dock & Engineering Co.

In 1865, an American established a shipyard called Shanghai Dock & Engineering Co.(see Figure 1–2). Later by injecting British capitals, this yard progressively transformed as British controlled shipbuilding and repairing yard. During 1895 to 1900, successively acquired Shanghai Old Dock and Oriental Dock in Hongkou area, the shipyard scale was further expanded. In 1884, completed a merchant freighter SS "Yuen Ho" with hull length of 280 feet (85.34 meters) and deadweight of 2 522 tons. She was the biggest merchant ship in the Far East. In March of 1901, officially merged with Boyd & Co., Ltd., and formed a new company. The total asset of the new company was increased up to 5.57 million taels of silver (a unit of Chinese currency in Qing Dynasty, 1 tael was equal to 37.4 grams silver, and the content of pure silver was 93.35%).

合并后的耶松船厂（见图 1-3）在上海地区拥有七大修造船坞设施：祥生船坞、老船澳、引翔港船坞和丰船厂船坞、董家渡船坞、哥立尔船坞和东方船坞。该公司是远东最大的修造船企业之一，曾一度垄断上海的修造船市场[4]。

Merged totally had seven shipbuilding and repairing facilities in Shanghai: Nicolson Dock, Shanghai Old Dock, Cosmopolitan Dock, Shanghai Engineering Shipbuilding & Dock Co., Tung Ka Doo Dock, Collier's Dock and Oriental Dock. This shipyard was one of the biggest shipyards in the Far East, and it used to monopolize shipbuilding and repairing market of Shanghai (see Figure 1-3).

图 1-3　耶松船厂船坞外景
Figure 1-3　Outlook of Shanghai Dock & Engineering Co.

1904 年冬，时任两江总督的周馥奉清政府之命到江南制造局考察。对于荒废了 20 年的船坞，他认为已经到了"穷极当变之时"，要根本解决困难，就只有把船坞部分从制造局里独立出来，并采用商业化的经营模式。后经与驻沪南北洋海军兼广东水师提督叶祖珪（1852—1905）筹商，又与北洋大臣反复协商，才于 1905 年 4 月议定了改良办法，将造修船业务从江南制造局正式划分出来，成立"江南船坞"，归海军部领导。

In winter of 1904, Zhou Fu (Chou Fu), Governor-General of Liang Jiang (including Jiangsu, Jiangxi and Anhui Provinces), followed instruction of Qing Government to audit Kiangnan Manufacturing Bureau. He thought "it really is the opportunity for transformation", when he saw the dock in Kiangnan has lain idle for two decades. The mitigating solution for Kiangnan was only to separate shipbuilding segment from the manufacturing bureau and implement commercial operation. Zhu Fu then further negotiated with Ye Zugui (Yeh Tsukuei, 1852−1905), Chief of Guangdong (Canton) Naval Fleet, Shanghai Squadron of South and North Fleets, as well as Beiyang minister. A mitigating solution for Kiangnan was settled in April of 1905. The shipbuilding and repairing businesses were officially separated from Kiangnan Manufacturing Bureau and assigned newly established commercial company named "Kiangnan Dock". Kiangnan Dock would be straightly managed by the Naval Department of the Government.

以前国内近代史史料对"局坞分家"的看法，一般都局限于政治史角度的分析，把焦点都放在地方督抚如李鸿章、刘坤一、周馥、张之洞、袁世凯之间的政治合作或斗争，因而很少注意"局坞分家"在从官办企业向商业化转型上的重大意义[5]。"局坞分家"时江南船坞和江南制造局的地界划分如图 1-4 所示。

In the past, the views of modern Chinese historical researches on "Separation of Bureau and Dock" generally limited in coverage of political history, and they always focused on the political cooperation or struggle among the local governors such as Li Hongzhang, Liu Kunyi (Liu Kuni), Zhou Fu, Zhang Zhidong (Chang Chihtung) and Yuan Shikai (Yuan Shihkai). So the significance of the "Separation of Bureau and Dock" especially in the transition from government-operated enterprise to commercialization was normally ignored. Lay out of Kiangnan Manufacturing Bureau and Kiangnan Dock is shown in Figure 1-4.

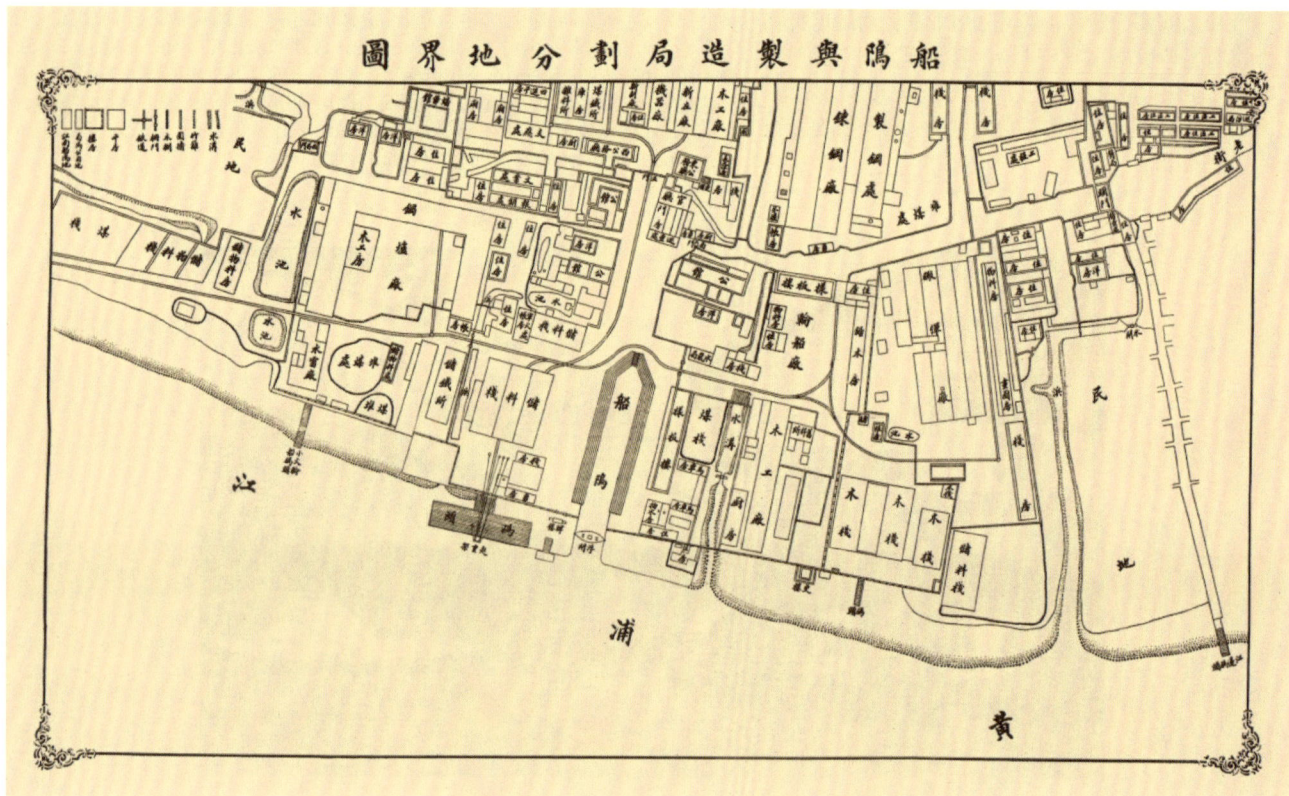

图 1-4 "局坞分家"时江南船坞和江南制造局的地界划分图
Figure 1-4 Lay out of Kiangnan Manufacturing Bureau and Kiangnan Dock

当时的上海乃至中国沿海口岸船舶运输已经有相当大的规模和运输量，修造船舶业务也日趋增长，但多由外商船厂承揽。周馥看到了这个商机，故奏请朝廷有意启用江南闲置的船坞设施。当然造船须解决资金、技术、人才等问题，对于"局坞分家"前主要靠政府补贴、官办的江南制造局而言，可谓是一个极大的挑战。因此只有将船坞部分分开独立经营，引进外商船厂的经营模式才能参与当时的市场竞争。

At that time, the marine transportation in Shanghai and even China's coastal ports had a considerable scale and quantity, and the shipbuilding and repairing businesses were also significantly increasing. However, most of them were captured by foreign invested shipyards. Zhou Fu keenly perceived this potential business opportunity, so he constructively proposed the government to intentionally re-open the idle dock in Kiangnan shipbuilding facility. Certainly, awakening shipbuilding business needed to solve the problems of capital, technology, skilled workers and experienced engineers. For the Kiangnan Manufacturing Bureau, such bureaucratic institution was completely subsidized by the government and was operated by the government. Commercial operation was really a great challenge for Kiangnan prior to "Separation of Bureau and Dock". Therefore, it was only solution that the shipbuilding segment was operated separately and independently in accordance with the commercial model and advanced philosophy from foreign shipyards. Only in this way was Kiangnan enabled to participate the market competition.

1.2

扩建设施、扁平化管理
Facility Expansion with Flat Management

1905 年"局坞分家"以后，江南船坞全面实行商业化和市场化经营，主要采取了以下几项改革举措：

第一是管理层，任命驻沪南北洋海军兼广东水师提督叶祖珪为江南船坞的督办，总兵衔候补副将吴应科为总办，另聘德国人 L. 巴斯为总稽查（Superintendent），苏格兰人毛根（Robert Buchanan Mauchan）为总工程师 [6]。

第二是精简部门并对用工制度进行改革。在辞退大量冗员的同时，生产管理采用了与工作量、责任和经济收益相关联承包的"包工制"。

第三是进行造船设施扩建和设备更新工程。把泥船坞改建为木质船坞，拓长至 385 英尺（117.30米），加宽至 75 英尺（22.90 米），挖深至 24.5 英尺（7.47 米），并修建坞东码头，填宽沿江土地，可容大型船舶停泊。此外江南船坞还添置了大量的机器设备。

第四是改变专为海军服务的封闭式经营方式，不论是官船、民船、中外军舰或商船，均可在船坞内进行维修、改建等业务。

改革后的江南船坞经营得法，呈现出新的商业化经营气象。"局坞分家"时借用的江安粮道库银 20万两开办费，原定分 10 年偿还，由于经营业绩良好，最后提前 4 年于 1911 年把全部借款还清。

"Separation of Bureau and Dock" of 1905 shortly thereafter, Kiangnan Dock commenced totally commercial and marketing operation. The following reform measures had been adopted:

The first was the management level, the Chief of Guangdong Naval Fleet, Shanghai Squadron of South and North Fleets Ye Zugui was appointed as the supervisor of Kiangnan Dock, and the Deputy General Wu Yingke (Woo Yingfo) was appointed as the General Manager. Further, the German L. Basse was nominated as Superintendent, and the Scottish Robert Buchanan Mauchan was nominated as the Chief Engineer (actually his responsibility was corresponding to "General Project Manager").

The second was to simplify the functional department as flat pattern and reform the employment system. Meanwhile dismissing a large number of redundant staffs, production management had intentionally adopted a "contracted work oriented system" that was associated with workload, responsibility and economic benefits.

The third was to expand the shipbuilding facilities and upgrade the equipment. To convert the mud walled dock to a timber walled dock, to lengthen dock to 385 feet (117.30 meters), to widen dock to 75 feet (22.90 meters), and to dredge to a depth of 24.5 feet (7.47 meters). The wharf at east side of dock was retrofitted for enabling large ship mooring. More land along the river was reclaimed. Furthermore, a lot of newly procured machineries and equipments were installed in workshops.

The fourth was to completely change the closed type business exclusively for the navy to open commercial type. All potential orders, regardless of an imperial ship, a civilian ship, a Chinese or foreign warship, or a merchant ship, it was possible to be treated as commercial business contract and to be carried out the repairs and the conversions in the dock.

After the reform of the Kiangnan Dock, the new commercial operation environment had emerged. Due to its good performance, 10 years loan of 200 000 taels of silver, which was borrowed from national treasury thereafter "Separation of Bureau and Dock", was repaid in 1911, four years in advance.

江南船坞最重要的业绩便是建造新船的数量，如表 1-1 所示。虽然每年建造交付新船数量不是很稳定，但在"局坞分家"后的 22 年间（1905—1926 年），江南船坞（1912 年改称江南造船所）共建造了 505 艘新船，总排水量达到了 165 133 吨，远远超过"局坞分家"前的 40 年只建造新船 15 艘，总排水量只有约 10 000 吨，真是不可同日而语。在上述 505 艘新造船中，排水量在 500 吨以上的中大型船舶达 62 艘，排水量总计为 112 436 吨。除了造船，1907 年至 1926 年坞修的船舶达 2 722 艘[7]，年均达 136 艘。上述数量还未包括不进坞修理的船舶。

The most important performance of Kiangnan Dock was the number of newbuildings, as shown in Table 1-1. Although the quantity of annually delivered newbuilding was unstable, during the 22 years (from 1905 to 1926) after the "Separation of Bureau and Dock", Kiangnan Dock (renamed as Kiangnan Dock & Engineering Works in 1912) had built a total of 505 new ships. The total displacement reached 165 133 tons, far more than the 15 new ships built in past 4 decades before the separation of 1905. The displacement merely aggregated approximate 10 000 tons. Among the 505 newbuildings mentioned above, there were 62 medium and large scale vessels with a displacement over 500 tons. The total displacement was 112 436 tons. In addition to shipbuilding, the number of ships repaired in the dock reached 2 722 sets from 1907 to 1926. The yearly average was 136 ships excluding the number of undocked repairs.

表 1-1　江南船坞（1912 年改称江南造船所）1905—1926 年承接的船舶数量[8]

Table 1-1　Order book of Kiangnan Dock (renamed as Kiangnan Dock & Engineering Works in 1912) from 1905 to 1926

年份 Year	艘数 Ship QTY	增加、减少 /% + & − in %	排水量 / 吨 Displ. in ton	增加、减少 /% + & − in %
1905	2	—	37	—
1906	19	+850.0	728	+1 867.6
1907	20	+5.3	5 399	+641.6
1908	39	+95.0	4 033	−25.3
1909	5	−87.2	353	−91.2
1910	11	+120.0	975	+176.2
1911	40	+263.6	9 515	+875.9
1912	16	−60.0	3 181	−66.6
1913	24	+50.0	3 474	+9.2
1914	25	+4.2	5 241	+50.9
1915	24	−4.0	5 178	−1.2
1916	50	+108.3	6 712	+29.6
1917	18	−64.0	4 471	−33.4
1918	10	−44.4	60 373	+1 250.3
1919	22	+120.0	5 398	−91.1
1920	29	+31.8	10 643	+97.2
1921	18	−37.9	8 737	−17.9
1922	26	+44.4	3 236	−63.0
1923	38	+46.2	6 281	+94.1
1924	36	−5.3	12 634	+101.1
1925	13	−63.9	2 724	−78.4
1926	20	+53.8	5 810	+113.3
总数 Total	505	—	165 133	—

江南造船所这一时期的造船修船业务还赶上并超过了在当时上海造船工业中处于垄断地位的英商耶松船厂。从造船吨位来看，耶松船厂 1910 年至 1917 年所建造船舶的总排水量达到 42 700 吨，而江南造船所在同期建造船舶的总排水量也达到了 38 747 吨，已经接近耶松船厂的。从造船的数量来看，耶松船厂为 82 艘，而江南造船所则达到了 208 艘，可见江南造船所的单船平均吨位要远远小于耶松船厂的。从单船最大吨位来看，江南造船所 1912 年 8 月竣工、招商局订造的 "江华" 号（Kiang Wah）客轮（船体号为 H124），排水量达到了 4 130 吨（载重量为 3 692 吨），打破了当时上海地区造船的吨位纪录[9]。

"江华" 号客轮长 330 英尺（100.65 米），宽 47 英尺（14.435 米），型深 14.9 英尺（4.54 米），吃水为 12 英尺（3.66 米），主机功率为 3 000 马力（2 237 千瓦），航速为 14 节。该船具有船身坚致而轻，适合在中国长江流域航行；航行稳捷而灵活，便于操纵；吃水浅，载重量大以及耗煤省等特点。该船的三缸三胀式蒸汽主机和水管锅炉也由江南造船所制造。图 1-5 为江南造船所建造的 "江华" 号客轮在码头舾装的照片，图 1-6 为 "江华" 号客轮的总布置图，图 1-7 为 "江华" 号客轮的甲板布置图。

Kiangnan's shipbuilding and repair business in this period caught up with and exceeded the British invested shipyard Shanghai Dock & Engineering Co., which had occupied a monopoly position of the Shanghai shipbuilding industry at that time. From the perspective of shipbuilding tonnage, Shanghai Dock & Engineering Co. built a total displacement of 42 700 tons from 1910 to 1917, while Kiangnan also reached a total displacement of 38 747 tons in the same period, which was close to Shanghai Dock & Engineering Co. In terms of the number of shipbuildings, the number of Shanghai Dock & Engineering Co. was 82, and that of Kiangnan had reached 208. It can be seen that the average tonnage of a single ship at Kiangnan was much smaller than that of Shanghai Dock & Engineering Co. Regarding the maximum tonnage of a single ship, Kiangnan built passenger river steamer SS "Kiang Wah" (hull number H124) for the China Merchant Bureau, was completed in August 1912. The displacement of SS "Kiang Wah" had reached to 4 130 tons (deadweight of 3 692 tons). She became a new tonnage record of shipbuilding in Shanghai at that time.

The main particulars of SS "Kiang Wah" were 330 feet (100.65 meters) in length, 47 feet (14.435 meters) in width, 14.9 feet (4.54 meters) in moulded depth, and 12 feet (3.66 meters) in draught, main engine power was 3 000 hp (2 237 kW), and speed was 14 knots. She had features of robust hull, shallow draught, suitable to navigate in Yangtze River, easy to maneuver, larger deadweight and lower coal consumption. The three cylinders, triple expansion steam engine and water tube boilers on board were manufactured by Kiangnan Dock & Engineering Works. Figure 1-5 is Kiangnan built SS "Kiang Wah" moored at quay for outfitting. Figure 1-6 is General Arrangement Plan of SS "Kiang Wah". Figure 1-7 is deck layout of SS "Kiang Wah".

图 1-5 江南造船所建造的 "江华" 号长江客轮
Figure 1-5　Kiangnan built passenger river steamer SS "Kiang Wah"

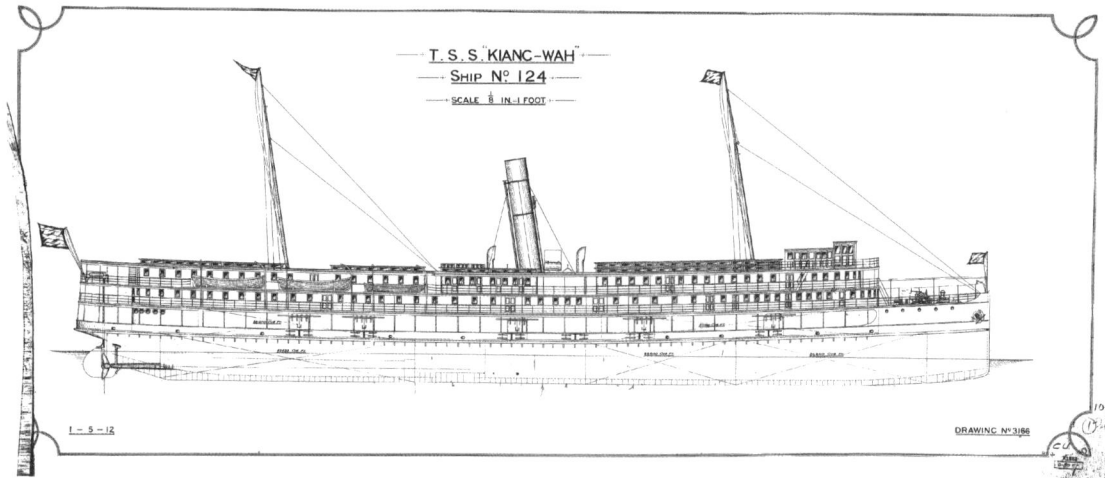

图 1-6　"江华"号客轮的总布置图
Figure 1-6　General Arrangement Plan of SS "Kiang Wah"

"江华"号客轮的船型设计颇有特色，主甲板及以上各层甲板在两舷走道处凸出主船体宽度以外以扩大甲板舱室的有效面积，这样的宽甲板设计一直在以后的长江客轮上沿用（直至 20 世纪 80 年代），成为长江客轮一种标准横剖面设计。

The hull section of SS "Kiang Wah" was quite unique. The main deck and above decks were creatively designed to protrude from moulded width for passage ways alongside, so that effective areas for deck houses were expanded accordingly. Such protruded deck design was continuously applied on Yangtze River passenger ship till 1980s and it had become a standard hull section for Yangtze River passenger ships.

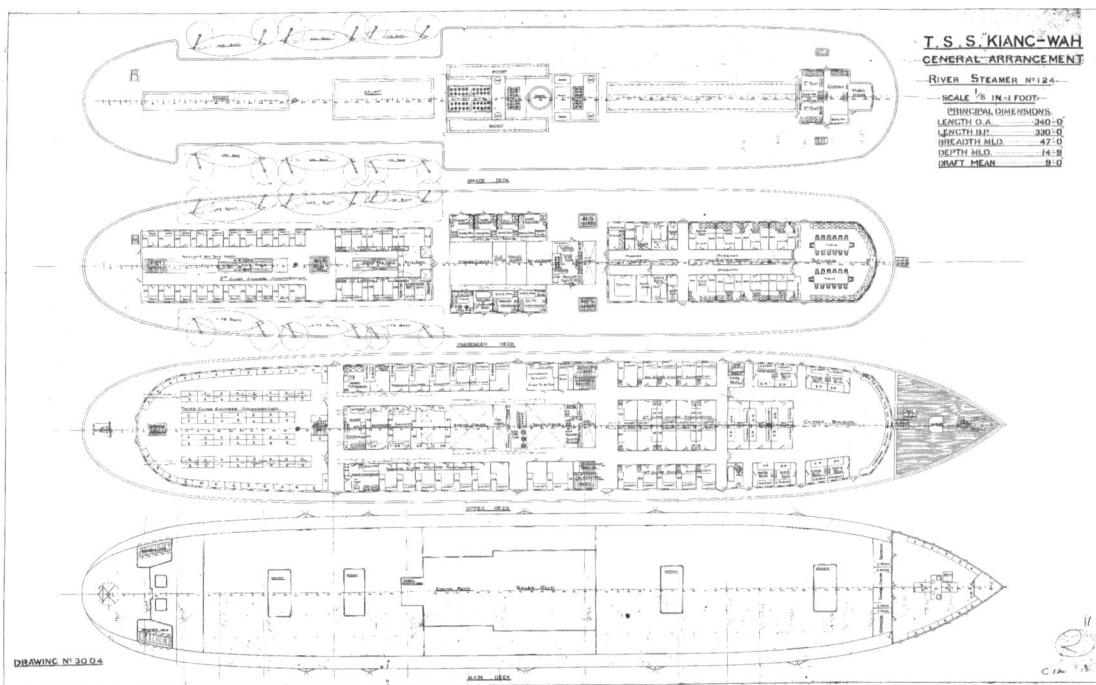

图 1-7　"江华"号客轮的甲板布置图
Figure 1-7　Deck layout of SS "Kiang Wah"

据当时的招商局总工程师张世英评价，该船比同期在英商祥生船厂建造的"江新"号和"江顺"号要坚固和实用得多。"江华"号客轮的总造价为385 000两规银。招商局在订船的时候采用了市场招标的模式，上海的外资船厂和香港的船厂串通压价竞争。由于江南船坞的报价比香港船厂的要高2 000两，招商局本来有意将此船交给香港的船厂建造。经江南船坞总办邝国华恳请邮传部尚书盛宣怀主持公道，转饬招商局不可舍近求远，以免利源外溢，招商局才决定由江南船坞建造[10]。

"江华"号客轮1949年后改名为"东方红5"号，经过改装后一直在长江客运航线营运到20世纪60年代中期。

1919年，耶松船厂下水的由英国设计的"Model 3"[11]型货船，其排水量达到了7 200吨，超过了江南造船所建造的"江华"号客轮。1918年，江南造船所承接了四艘排水量为14 750吨的美国运输舰，1921年，首制船"官府"号交付，其排水量超过耶松船厂所造大船的一倍以上。

江南船坞于1912年改名为江南造船所（Kiangnan Dock & Engineering Works），造船所大门也随着生产规模的不断扩大而屡次改建。在江南造船集团档案馆保存的图片中，仅存的大门照片是1937年江南造船所大门的照片（见图1-8），门口还有军队卫兵站岗。目前已无法找到更早期或其他江南造船所大门的照片。这扇大门从地理位置上看应该是原江南造船厂的东大门（半淞园路－江边码头轮渡）。1912年至1937年那段时期，江南造船所和江南制造局共同存在，局门和厂门共用也是有可能的。那扇大门和周围的建筑后来虽然被多次改建，但直至2008年因上海2010年世博会江南造船集团原址整体搬迁到长兴岛前还部分存在，当时为工商银行半淞园路储蓄所和一家老江南员工人人皆知的"赛乐"饭店。

As per comments from Zhang Shiying, Technical Director of China Merchant Bureau, SS "Kiang Wah" was more sturdier and durable than "Kiang Shin" and "Kiang Shun" built by Shanghai Dock & Engineering Co. The contract price of SS "Kiang Wah" was 385 000 taels of silver. China Merchant Bureau set a tender for building the ship at that time. One foreign capital invested Shanghai yard and a Hong Kong yard collaborated together to lower the building price offer. China Merchant Bureau initially intended to award the order to the Hong Kong shipyard as their offer was 2 000 taels lower than Kiangnan's. However, K. H. Kwong, Deputy Director of Kiangnan Dock, earnestly requested Sheng Xuanhuai (Sheng Hsuanhuai), Minister of Post & Transportation Department, to persuade China Merchant Bureau not come so far to a Hong Kong yard by giving up the nearby Kiangnan, which will end up with fortune overflow. Finally, China Merchant Bureau decided to put this order in Kiangnan Dock.

SS "Kiang Wah" passenger river steamer was renamed "Dong Fang Hong 5" after 1949, and she was continuously in service till middle of 1960's after retrofitted.

In 1919, Shanghai Dock & Engineering Co. launched British designed "Model 3" type freighter. The displacement of 7 200 tons had exceeded SS "Kiang Wah" built by Kiangnan. In 1918, Kiangnan secured shipbuilding contract of four American steam freighters with displacement of 14 750 tons. The first steam freighter SS "Mandarin" was delivered in 1921, whose displacement was one time more than "Model 3" freighter built by Shanghai Dock & Engineering Co.

Kiangnan Dock was renamed Kiangnan Dock & Engineering Works in 1912, and the main gate was re-built several times along with progressively developed shipyard scale. In Archives Institute of Jiangnan Shipyard Group, only one photo can be found (see Figure 1-8). It was Kiangnan main gate in 1937, and there was a soldier as guard who stood at outside of gate. No earlier photo can be found. This gate should be eastern gate of Jiangnan Shipyard as per its geometrical position (at end of Ban Song Yuan Road close to River Ferry Terminal). During the period of 1912 to 1937, this gate was most properly shared by both Kiangnan Dock and Engineering Works and the Manufacturing Bureau. This gate building later was retrofitted several times, and partially existed until Jiangnan Shipyard completely moved to Changxing Island for World EXPO 2010. It was used to be a branch of China Industrial and Commercial Bank and a restaurant named "Sai Le", which Jiangnan's old staffs quite familiarized with.

图 1-8　1937 年江南造船所大门的照片
Figure 1-8　The gate of Kiangnan Dock & Engineering Works in 1937

1.3

毛根的西式管理
Mauchan Instituted Western Philosophy

"局坞分家" 后江南船坞所实行的商业化经营和现代化管理，苏格兰总工程师[12] 毛根（Robert Buchanan Mauchan，1868—1936）（1907 年 5 月任总稽查）起了相当重要的作用。图 1-9 为江南造船集团档案馆保存的毛根的照片。

As above mentioned, Kiangnan implemented commercial operation and modern management after "Separation of Bureau and Dock", Scottish Chief Engineer (May 1907, he took the position of Superintendent) Robert Buchanan Mauchan (1868–1936) played an extremely important role in Kiangnan. Figure 1–9 is a photograph of Mauchan kept in Archives Institute of Jiangnan Shipyard Group.

图 1-9　毛根的照片
Figure 1-9　The photograph of Robert Buchanan Mauchan

1.3.1

毛根的生平
Mauchan and His Career

关于毛根的生平，特别是在他加入江南造船所之前有多种说法。法国学者柯容（Christine Cornet）写过一篇题为"Le Grand Mauchan et le chantier naval de Jiangnan (1905—1927)—Un example de coopération sino-étrangère"的论文并刊于《中国研究手册》，1990 年第 9 期，第 55～70 页。中国社会科学院近代史研究所研究员黄庆华摘译了这篇文章，并以"大毛根[13]与江南造船所（1905—1927 年）——中外合作一例"为题刊登在 1994 年的《国外中国近代史研究》第 24 辑上。黄庆华的文章又引用了《江南造船厂厂史：1865—1949》中对毛根经历的描述[14]。作者将多方资料综合后对毛根的生平做了一个比较全面的描述。

毛根 1868 年 5 月 25 日出生于苏格兰的邓巴顿（Dumbarton）附近的海伦斯堡（Helensburgh），为家中 10 个孩子中的长子，其父以贩卖家畜维持 12 口之家的生计。他的祖父母是裁缝出身，根本和造船业无缘。只有他和他的弟弟小毛根（Andrew Clark Mauchan，1877—未知）来过中国。小毛根在家中排行第五，由毛根招募到江南造船所工作[15]。

他的职业生涯很早就开始了，大约在 1882 年，当时他才 14 岁，就职于邓巴顿最大的克莱德河造船厂之一的威廉·丹尼兄弟造船公司。该公司以完成传奇的快帆船"卡蒂萨克"（短衬衫）而闻名。他先后在邓巴顿的工学院和格拉斯哥的法学院受过教育，据信在那里他学习了航海工程专业，他接受的应该是在职教育。

为了寻求自己的财富，他于 1887 年 19 岁时移居中国，定居在繁华的上海，那里有大量的法国、英国和美国人。他在李鸿章创办的招商局蒸汽轮船公司工作了 7 年。这种官商合伙经营的办法并未使招商局的业务取得预期的效益，然而毛根在这个企业的经历使他适应了中国的环境。1894 年，毛根在 1865 年创

Regarding Mauchan's personal details, there were several different versions. French historian Christine Cornet wrote a paper titled "Le Grand Mauchan et le chantier naval de Jiangnan (1905–1927)—Un example de coopération sino-étrangère" dans *Cahiers d'Etudes Chinoises* published on No. 9, Publication Paris, 1990, pp. 55–70. Huang Qinghua, Researcher of Institute of Modern History Chinese Academy of Social Sciences, translated this paper and published on a Chinese magazine. Huang Qinghua also quoted some descriptions from *History of Jiangnan Shipyard: 1865–1949* in his paper. After summarized materials collected from various channels, following paragraphs try to truly describe personal details and the career of Mauchan.

R. B. Mauchan was born on 25 May 1868 in Helensburgh, near Dumbarton, Scotland. He came from quite a large family and was the oldest of 10 children. His father maintained a livelihood of a family of twelve by selling livestock. His grandparents came from a tailor and had no any connection with the shipbuilding industry. Only he and his younger brother Andrew Clark Mauchan had been to China. Andrew Clark Mauchan (1877–unknown) ranked the fifth in the family and was recruited by R. B. Mauchan to work in Kiangnan Dock & Engineering Works.

His professional career began quite earlier, around 1882 when he was just 14 years old, with William Denny and Brothers, one of the largest River Clyde shipbuilders in Dumbarton. This shipyard was the most famous for completing the legendary clipper ship "Cutty Sark". He was educated at Dumbarton Burgh Academy and then Glasgow Athenaeum where it is believed he was taught nautical engineering as a trade, and most probably he had an on-job education.

Likely to seek his own fortune, he moved to China in 1887 at the age of 19 and settled in the bustling city of Shanghai with its large foreign population of French, British and Americans. He spent the next seven years with the China Merchant Steam Navigation Co. established by Li Hongzhang in 1872. This kind of government-commercial partnership did not boost the business of China Merchant Bureau to achieve the expected benefits. However, Mauchan's experience in this enterprise had

办的英商耶松船厂里谋得了一个机械工程师的职位。此后,他也曾在英商所办的其他船厂就职。几年之后,他被委以 1896 年设立于上海的和丰船厂经理一职(另一说法:1894 年,毛根进入英商和记洋行,向中国口岸正在兴建的新工厂推销蒸汽驱动机器。1895—1900 年,他加入上海新兴的现代纺织业推销缫丝机器。毛根后来成为上海英商耶松船厂的一员,1904 年负责修理日俄战争后破损的俄国船只)。他对修造船技术和船厂经营管理都较为熟悉。毛根加入江南船坞时已经积累了 20 多年造船业的工作经验。

1904 年 4 月 30 日,他 35 岁时在上海的圣三一基督教堂与 25 岁的珍妮·海伦娜·布鲁斯·威尔(Janey Helena Bruce Weir)结婚。威尔小姐于 1879 年出生于上海,她的父亲是招商局蒸汽轮船公司海事总监托马斯·威尔(Thomas Weir,1845—未知),母亲名叫茜茜莉亚(Cecelia)。毛根娶托马斯·威尔之女为妻,为他跻身上海航运界上层打下了基础。毛根熟悉中国传统和近代企业,曾经在上海最大的英商造船企业工作过,并在其岳父的关照下进入商界,所以他有立足上海造船界的最大的王牌——声望、技术和判断力。

assisted him to familiarize the Chinese environment. In 1894, Mauchan secured a mechanical engineer position at the British invested shipyard, Shanghai Dock & Engineering Co., founded in 1865. Since then, he had also worked in other British invested shipyards. A few years later, he was appointed as manager of Shanghai Engineering Shipbuilding & Dock Co., which was established in Shanghai in 1896 (Another saying: In 1894, Mauchan entered the British trading house Nicolson & Boyd Co., Ltd. to sell steam-driven machines to a new factory under construction at Chinese coastal cities. In years of 1895 to 1900, he joined newly booming modern textile industry in Shanghai to sell silk reeling machines. Later, Mauchan became a member of Shanghai Dock & Engineering Co., a British invested shipyard in Shanghai. In 1904, he was responsible for repairing Russian ships damaged in the Russo-Japanese War). He was familiar with shipbuilding technology and shipyard operation and management. When Mauchan joined Kiangnan Dock, he had accumulated more than 20 years of experience in shipbuilding business.

On 30 April 1904, at the age of 35, he married 25-year-old Janey Helena Bruce Weir at the Holy Trinity Church in Shanghai. Miss Weir was born in Shanghai in 1879. Her father was Thomas Weir (1845–unknown), the Marine Superintendent of the China Merchant Steam Navigation Co., and mother was Cecelia (dates unknown). Mauchan's marriage with Thomas Weir's daughter was a solid base for him to elevate to top rank of Shanghai shipping industry. Mauchan was familiar with Chinese traditional and modern enterprises. He once worked in Shanghai's largest British invested shipbuilding company and entered the business community under the care of his father-in-law. Therefore, he had the biggest trump cards in Shanghai shipbuilding industry: reputation, technology and judgment.

1.3.2

毛根和江南的不解之缘
Mauchan and Kiangnan

1905 年"局坞分家"时，北洋政府任命北洋海军主管轮机的德国人 L. 巴斯（L. Basse）为船坞的总稽查（Superintendent）。然而，巴斯只懂轮机操作并不懂造船，他到了江南船坞以后不谙造船业务的弱点很快就暴露出来了。巴斯只好请他的朋友、毛根的岳父托马斯·威尔帮忙物色一位精通造船技术的工程师。威尔趁机吹嘘他女婿的才干，并且竭力说服巴斯聘用毛根。

苏格兰人毛根于 1906 年 8 月以总工程师的身份进入了江南船坞。他身材高大、宽额头、椭圆脸，鼻子下面常蓄着浓密的胡子，身着三件套的西装，头戴一顶英格兰帽。

在 20 世纪 70—80 年代出版的近代史、江南造船厂厂史等历史文献中也有这样的描述："毛根进江南船坞时的职务是总工程师，职权是管理工程事宜兼招揽中外兵商修造生意，他的实权已经超出了作为总工程师分管的技术工作的范围。"为此，有必要再次核实 1922 年出版的文献《江南造船所纪要》中的原始记载。此书记载：

"光绪三十一年春，南、北洋大臣札委副将吴应科任江南船坞总办，二等宝星副将衔洋员巴斯为总稽查，并聘英人毛根为总工程司，管理工程事宜，兼招揽修造华洋兵、商轮船，立有合同为据。[16]"

After "Separation of Bureau and Dock" in 1905, Beiyang Government nominated a German named L. Basse, in charge of machinery in Beiyang navy, as Superintendent of Kiangnan Dock. Basse was only familiar with machinery operation and did not understand shipbuilding. When he came to Kiangnan Dock, his weakness in shipbuilding business was soon exposed. Basse had to ask his friend, Mauchan's father-in-law, Thomas Weir, to help him look for an engineer proficient in shipbuilding technology. Weir immediately took the opportunity to brag about the talents of his son-in-law and made his great efforts to persuade Basse to hire Mauchan.

Scots Mauchan entered the Kiangnan Dock in August 1906 as Chief Engineer. He was tall, with a wide forehead, an oval face, a thick beard under his nose, and often wore a three-piece suit and an English hat.

In the later modern history, the history of Jiangnan Shipyard and other historical documents published during 1970s to 1980s, Mauchan's title and his assigned responsibility were commonly described as follows: "Mauchan's position when he joined Kiangnan Dock was Chief Engineer, and his responsibility was managing project engineering and marketing shipbuilding and repairing business for Chinese and foreign ship owners. But his actual power had been beyond the scope of the technical as per his title of the Chief Engineer." For further verification, it is necessary to recheck the original description in *Summary of Kiangnan Dock & Engineering Works* published in 1922. Following describe was found in this book:

In the spring of Guangxu 31st year, the Deputy General Wu Yingke was appointed by Nanyang/Beiyang Minister as the General Manager of Kiangnan Dock. In addition, the German Basse was nominated as Superintendent, and the Scottish Mauchan was nominated as the General Project Manager, managing project engineering and marketing shipbuilding and repairing business for Chinese and foreign ship owners. Related definitions were included in employment contract.

后期的近代史、江南造船厂厂史等历史文献把毛根进江南船坞时的职务"总工程司"误写成"总工程师"了。这里的"司"应该是司职和担当的意思，相当于现代企业里的首席运营官（COO）或常务副总经理（主管生产和营销等主要事务），而不是单单管技术的总工程师。因此，作者认为在后期的近代史、江南造船厂厂史等历史文献中评价毛根"他的实权已经超出了作为总工程师分管的技术工作的范围"是不全面的。作者也核实了国外的文献，均把毛根的职务翻译成 Superintendent（总稽查）或 Manager（经理），而不是 Chief Engineer（总工程师）或 Technical Director（技术经理）。

In the later modern history, as well as the history of Jiangnan Shipyard and other historical documents, they made some misunderstanding of "General Project Manager" (in Chinese "总工程司", same pronunciation with Chief Engineer in Chinese). The "General Project Manager" is a post corresponding to "Chief Operation Officer, COO" in modern enterprise management but it is not technology oriented "Chief Engineer" or "Technical Director". In foreign published papers, the title of Mauchan was usually translated as "Superintendent" or "Manager" but not "Chief Engineer". The evaluation in Chinese historical documents, "his actual power had been beyond the scope of the technical as per his title of the chief engineer" is obviously biased. In the foreign historical documents, Mauchan's title is always translated as "Superintendent" or "Manager", but not "Chief Engineer"or "Technical Director".

江南制造局后期一直受到英国人柯尼斯等人操纵，主要的供货渠道也来自英国，是英国人的势力范围。"局坞分家"初期，德国人巴斯被委任为总稽查让英国人大为吃醋，当时代表英国利益的上海英文报纸《字林西报》[17]便曾大声疾呼"德国势力进入了江南船坞"，"克虏伯（德国的兵工厂）代替了阿姆斯特朗（英国的兵工厂）"。后来，巴斯介绍毛根进江南船坞可能也是英德势力妥协的结果。

In later period of Kiangnan Manufacturing Bureau, Kiangnan was exactly controlled by British Cronies etc., and main procurement channel was also from British. Kiangnan was the British sphere of influence for a long time. In the initial period after separation, a German was nominated as Superintendent of Kiangnan Dock, which really let British uncomfortable. An English newspaper *North China Daily News*, mainly representing British interests, shouted out "German has influenced Kiangnan Dock", "Krupp has replaced Armstrong". Basse's introduction of Mauchan's entry into Kiangnan Dock might also be the result of the compromise between the British and German forces.

毛根在加入江南船坞前曾在耶松船厂任机械工程师，在造船方面积累了丰富的经验和人际关系网。在主持江南船坞的技术和管理工作以后，他将耶松船厂的管理理念和规章制度引进江南船坞，并从耶松船厂挖来了一批工程技术人员和监造人员，同时遣散了400多名原江南制造局留用的员工。

Before joining Kiangnan Dock, Mauchan worked as a mechanical engineer at the Shanghai Dock & Engineering Co., and he has accumulated considerable shipbuilding experience and human relationship network. After presiding over the technology and management of Kiangnan Dock, he introduced the management philosophy, rules and regulations of Shanghai Dock & Engineering Co. into Kiangnan Dock. He poached a group of engineers, managers and experts from his former employer, meanwhile he decisively dismissed more than 400 former employees of Kiangnan Manufacturing Bureau.

据记载，在毛根管理下的江南船坞，"各部工程技术人员，如造船部门、造机部门、设计部门以及轮机工场、冷作间等，多数是英国人作为主导和骨干"[18]。除了毛根担任总工程师以外，还有总管洋账员戴吉士、绘图师梅根·霍伦森和罗柏逊、机器匠泰勒和迈克尔、锅炉匠格里芬，皆为英国人，均为光绪三十一年（1905年）后陆续雇佣的。毛根的月薪为1 000两，余则三四百两银不等[19]。毛根还带来了中国包工老板和工头十余人，分别管理固定工人和包工工人。毛根为了争取可靠的盟友，巩固其在造船所的地位，他把

As per historical records, in Kiangnan Dock under the management of Mauchan, "engineers and technicians in shipbuilding, machinery and design departments as well as machinery and steel workshops etc. were mostly British as leaders and cadres". Besides Mauchan as Chief Engineer, others like General Accountant (Foreign Currency) David Gist, Draftsmen Meghan Holenson and Robertson, Mechanical Fitters Tailor and Michael, Boiler Fitter Gryphon, were all British. These British were employed by Kiangnan since Guangxu 31st Year (1905). Regarding their remunerations, Mauchan was monthly paid 1 000 taels of silver, and others was 300 to 400 taels of silver per month. Mauchan also brought more than 10 subcontractors and foremen for managing permanent workers and contracted workers. In order to win reliable allies and

自己的部分权力下放给一些中国人，这些人是从毛根在耶松船厂工作时结识的中国技术人员中挑选出来的。船厂的技术能力是依托于人而存在的，人的因素无疑是最重要的。毛根的人事改组无疑是江南造船所技术能力重构的基础。

consolidate his position in Kiangnan Dock, Mauchan devolved the part of his power to some Chinese colleagues. These Chinese were selected from technicians who worked for the former employee of Mauchan. The technical capabilities of shipyard quite depend on the personnel ability in traditional shipbuilding. The human factor, therefore, was undoubtedly the most important. The personnel reformation promoted by Mauchan was undoubtedly the basis for the restructuring of the technical capabilities of Kiangnan Dock.

1907 年 5 月，德国人巴斯被调回北洋政府另有任用，总稽查一职也由毛根接任。江南船坞的一切重要事宜，包括业务经营、生产技术和行政管理均由以毛根为首的英国管理团队把持，大权独揽。当时报纸的报道均把毛根称为江南船坞 / 江南造船所的“洋经理”。江南造船所在《远东周刊》上登的广告中将毛根的职位写成“经理”。

In May 1907, Basse was transferred back to the Beiyang government for another appointment. The post of Superintendent was also replaced by Mauchan. All important decisions of Kiangnan Dock, including business operations, production technology and administrative management, were entirely controlled by the British management group. The British group led by Mauchan absolutely held sole authority. At that particular period, Mauchan was referred as the foreign “manager” of Kiangnan Dock/ Kiangnan Dock & Engineering Works in Shanghai newspaper reports. Mauchan’s position was also written as “Manager” in an advertisement published by the Kiangnan Dock & Engineering Works on *The Far Eastern Review*.

图 1-10 所示为江南造船所 1909 年在《远东周刊》5 月号上刊登的广告，广告中上面一张照片是江南造船所的西码头，下面一张照片是江南造船所建造的“津通”号（Tsin Tung）双桨拖轮配置的蒸汽主机［200 马力、145 磅力 / 英寸 ^{2}（1 兆帕）、170 转 / 分］和组合的板式冷凝器。

Figure 1–10 is an advertisement published by Kiangnan Dock & Engineering Works on *The Far Eastern Review*, May 1909. The upper photo shows West wharf of Kiangnan Dock & Engineering Works, and the lower photo shows two sets of compound surface condensers for twin screw tug boat “Tsin Tung”. Each of these engines developed 200 hp with 145 psi (1 MPa) and 170 revolutions per minute.

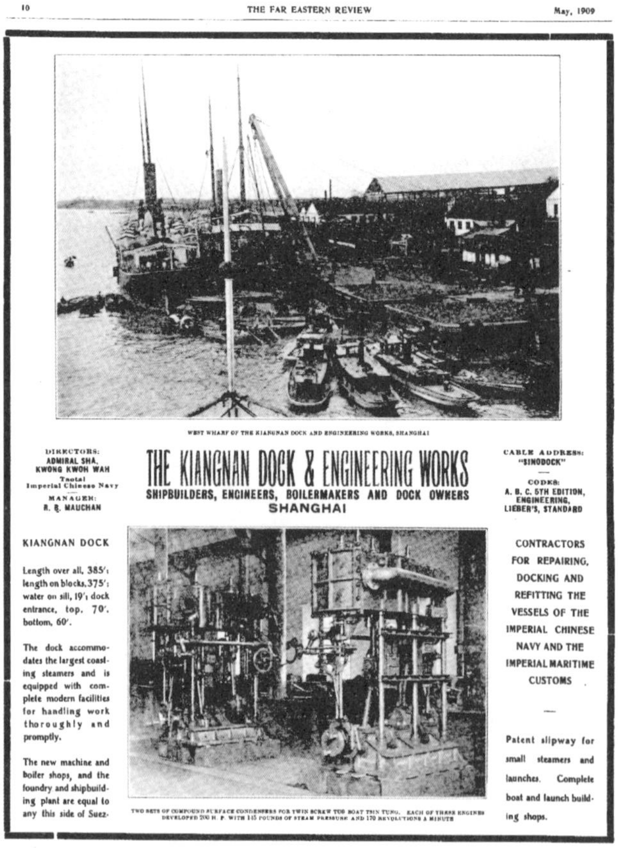
10 THE FAR EASTERN REVIEW May, 1909

WEST WHARF OF THE KIANGNAN DOCK AND ENGINEERING WORKS, SHANGHAI

DIRECTORS:
ADMIRAL SHA,
KWONG KWOH WAH
Taotai
Imperial Chinese Navy
MANAGER:
R. B. MAUCHAN

THE KIANGNAN DOCK & ENGINEERING WORKS
SHIPBUILDERS, ENGINEERS, BOILERMAKERS AND DOCK OWNERS
SHANGHAI

CABLE ADDRESS:
"SINODOCK"
CODES:
A. B. C. 5TH EDITION,
ENGINEERING,
LIEBER'S, STANDARD

KIANGNAN DOCK

Length over all, 385'; length on blocks, 375'; water on sill, 19'; dock entrance, top, 70', bottom, 60'.

The dock accommodates the largest coasting steamers and is equipped with complete modern facilities for handling work thoroughly and promptly.

The new machine and boiler shops, and the foundry and shipbuilding plant are equal to any this side of Suez.

TWO SETS OF COMPOUND SURFACE CONDENSERS FOR TWIN SCREW TUG BOAT TSIN TUNG. EACH OF THESE ENGINES DEVELOPED 200 H. P. WITH 145 POUNDS OF STEAM PRESSURE AND 170 REVOLUTIONS A MINUTE

CONTRACTORS FOR REPAIRING, DOCKING AND REFITTING THE VESSELS OF THE IMPERIAL CHINESE NAVY AND THE IMPERIAL MARITIME CUSTOMS

Patent slipway for small steamers and launches. Complete boat and launch building shops.

图 1–10　江南造船所 1909 年在《远东周刊》5 月号上登的广告
Figure 1–10　Advertisement on *The Far Eastern Review*, May 1909

图 1–11 为江南造船所 1919 年在《远东周刊》上刊登的一则广告，其中有这样一段广告词：

（江南造船所）拥有优良的设备和工具可承担各种大小工程，配置两个永久性的小型斜船台可（修理和建造）小型船舶。强大的蒸汽驱动的剪式把杆吊具有 60 吨的提升能力。554 英尺长的船台带有钢质屋顶可不受天气的影响。

Figure 1–11 is an advertisement published by Kiangnan Dock & Engineering Works on *The Far Eastern Review*, 1919. Following description is on the advertisement:

Superior Plant and Tools for the handling of all classes of heavy and light work. Two patent slips are provided for small craft. Powerful shearlegs to lift 60 tons worked by steam. Shipbuilding berth 554 feet long with iron roof, allowing work being carried on irrespective of the weather.

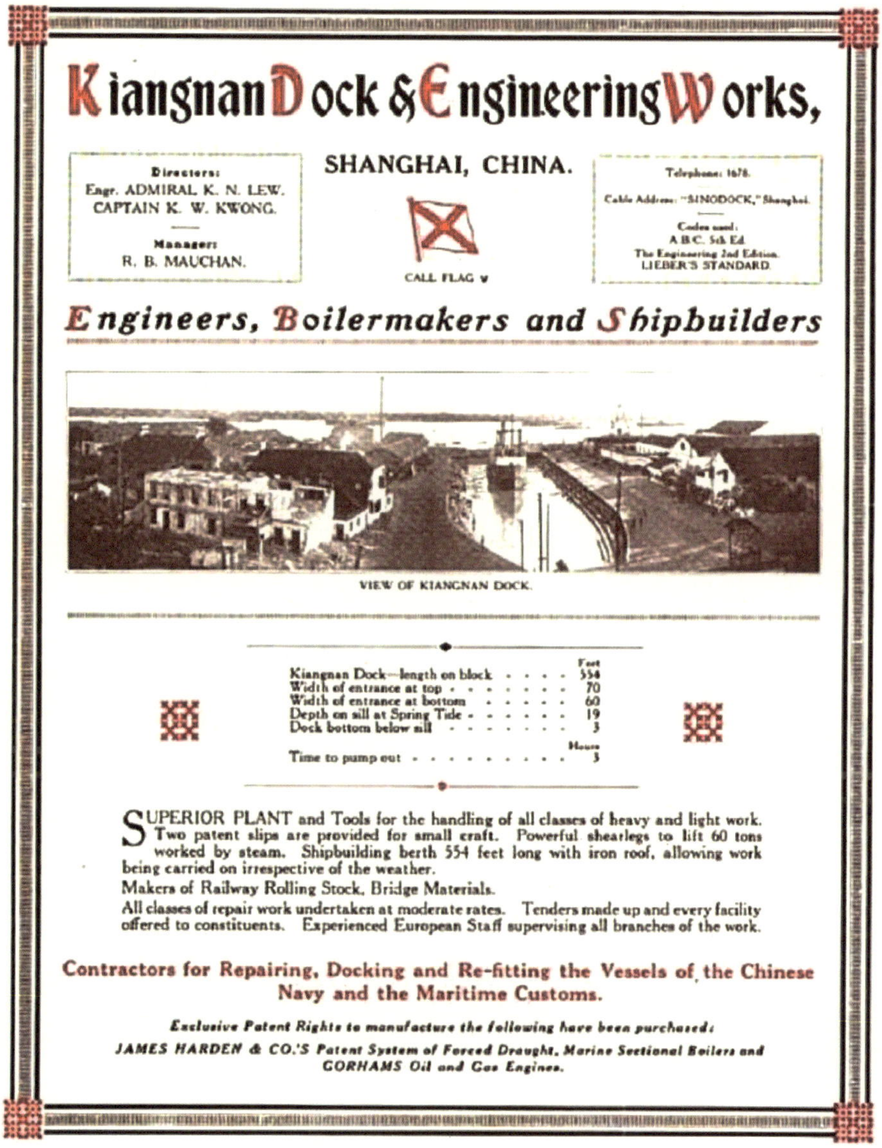

图 1–11　江南造船所 1919 年在《远东周刊》上登的广告
Figure 1–11　Advertisement on *The Far Eastern Review*, 1919

（江南造船所）是铁路车辆和桥梁材料的制造商。可以适中的价格承担各种修理工程，可提供基于各种设备的分项投标价，由有经验的欧洲雇员指导各项工程作业。

Makers of railway rolling stock, bridge materials. All classes of repair work undertaken at moderate rates. Tenders made up and every facility offered to constituents. Experienced European staff supervising all branches of the work.

除此之外，毛根还利用他在外商中建立的广泛的人脉关系，为江南造船所多方承接修造船业务。毛根对船舶市场比较了解，并且和外国的航运公司及上海的各个船厂关系密切，因此给江南造船所招揽了不少新的客户。"局坞分家"后江南船坞／江南造船所迅速扩充船厂建造设施和规模。在毛根主导下推进采用英商船厂注重"质量、进度和成本"的管理模式。他的这一能力，对于江南造船所面向市场后的快速发展有着十分重要的影响。

In addition, Mauchan also utilized his extensive relationships with foreign owners and brokers to undertake more shipbuilding and repairing contracts for Kiangnan. Mauchan had a relatively good understanding of the ship market and had close relations with foreign shipping companies and various shipyards in Shanghai, so he has attracted many new customers to Kiangnan. After the "Separation of Bureau and Dock", Kiangnan quickly expanded the construction facilities and scale as well as procurement of novel machineries and equipment. Kiangnan, under the leadership of Mauchan, strongly promoted the duplication of the operating model implemented in British owned shipyard. British owned shipyard normally paid more attention on their mission of "to quality, on schedule and to cost". His ability had an extremely important influence on market oriented operation for rapid development of Kiangnan Dock & Engineering Works.

当时英国是世界上首屈一指的海上强国，英国船东也是毛根掌管江南船坞／江南造船所时（1906—1926年）的主要客户。《江南造船厂厂史：1865—1949》的附录"江南造船厂造船一览表"中记载[20]内容和江南造船集团档案馆中保存的资料统计如下：

In that particular period, United Kingdom was the world's leading maritime country. The British shipowners were key accounts who Mauchan focused on, while he managed Kiangnan Dock/Kiangnan Dock & Engineering Works (from 1906 to 1926). According to "Delivery List of Jiangnan Shipyard" in *History of Jiangnan Shipyard: 1865–1949* and documents kept in Archives Institute of Jiangnan Shipyard Group:

1906—1926年江南船坞／江南造船所为英商船东／公司建造了许多船舶，其中，太古洋行63艘、亚细亚火油公司55艘、怡和洋行9艘。继1918年7月美国海运委员会订造的四艘美国运输舰以外，第一次世界大战结束后，美商开始到江南造船所订造船舶。大来航运公司订造了2艘柚木驳船；美孚行其及子公司最多，共订造了21艘，绝大部分都是油驳类的小型船舶；美国海军订造了7艘，其中6艘是长江浅水炮舰。

During 1906 to 1926, Kiangnan Dock/Kiangnan Dock & Engineering Works delivered a large amount of ships to British owners, including 63 sets for Butterfield & Swire Co., 55 sets for Asiatic Petroleum Co., Ltd., and 9 sets for Jardine Matheson & Co. Besides that the United States Shipping Board ordered four steam freighters, American owners started to order the ships in Kiangnan after armistice of the Great War implemented. Dollar Steamship Company ordered two teak hull barges, Mobil Petroleum Co. and subsidiary trading companies ordered 21 sets in total, and most of them were small size oil barges. U.S. Navy also ordered 7 sets, including 6 sets of Yangtze River shallow water gunboat.

尽管一些近代史学者认为毛根在承接订单时偏袒英美船东和航运公司，但从上述"江南造船厂造船一览表"中的数据也可以看出，江南造船所也为中国的官办航运公司，如轮船招商局、合营企业、海关和邮传部建造船舶。1905—1926年，轮船招商局在江南船坞／江南造船所订造了14艘船舶。一些航运公司也订造了江南造船所擅长设计建造的长江浅水船舶和破冰船。事实上这个隶属于海军部的船厂却很少为海军建造舰船。在建造合同的洽谈过程中，毛根也不是唯一的参与者和最终的决策者。

Despite some modern historians believing that Mauchan favoured British and American shipowners and shipping companies when he taking orders, it can also be seen from the above mentioned "Delivery List of Jiangnan Shipyard" that Kiangnan likewise built ships for imperial and state owned shipping companies, such as the China Merchant Bureau, joint venture companies, Customs and Post and Transportation Department From 1905 to 1926, the China Merchant Bureau ordered 14 ships at Kiangnan Dock / Kiangnan Dock & Engineering Works. Some shipping companies also put their orders of the Yangtze River shallow water ships and icebreakers since Kiangnan designed ships had excellent reputation in actual service. However, Kiangnan, as a naval shipyard under the leadership of the Navy Department, rarely built ships for the Navy. Furthermore, during the negotiation of the shipbuilding contract, Mauchan was not the only participant and final decision-maker.

毛根也因为成功说服美国海运委员会主席爱德华·N. 赫尔利签订建造四艘万吨级运输舰合同，从而获得了江南造船所刘冠南所长的进一步信任。毛根在这个合同的谈判过程中所起的作用是具有决定性意义的，特别是他充分利用了其与同是苏格兰人的罗伯特·大来船长的密切关系，请大来到美国海运委员会为江南造船所游说。1918 年 7 月，四艘万吨级运输舰合同的成功签订更加稳固了毛根在江南造船所中的地位，也赢得了所长和江南造船所全体员工对他的信任。"造万吨轮时，如果不是毛根坚持，中国人是没有胆量承接的。"[21]

毛根掌管的所内的管理事务也越来越广。他既主导财务和技术管理，又主导生产计划的制订。他引入了全套的英式管理模式，要求用英文书写通报、计划和合同，这样只有那些具有良好英语能力的员工才有机会被提拔和升迁。江南造船所的员工对他的"专横跋扈"感到不满，工人也抱怨这位苏格兰"老板"傲慢、滥用职权、目中无人。为赶工程进度他肆意要求工人加班，增加劳动强度。

在刘冠南所长的任期内，江南造船所的工人们曾经指责他对毛根言听计从。但客观地说，1918 年 5 月，刘所长指派毛根赴美和美国海运委员会洽谈并签订了四艘万吨级运输舰的合同，是出于对毛根的信任而不是什么滥用职权。此外，刘所长看重的是毛根的沟通能力和人脉关系以及在承接美国四艘万吨级运输舰过程中所起的决定性作用，特别是毛根很好地利用了同是苏格兰人的罗伯特·大来在美国政府上层的影响力。这一切都说明刘冠南所长是用人得当的。

江南造船所的老员工黄容回忆道："由于当时建造四艘万吨级运输舰的所有材料、锅炉等都由大来公司转运过来，整个造船周期长达三年。美国的首付款大部分被大来公司扣下来作为材料（采办）费（和运输费）了，因此，这段时期厂内的一切开销及工资等费用必须（由江南造船所）先行垫付，总数达 20 万两之多，超过了银行的贷款，连毛根和总办的私人存款也被提出来（贴进去了）。"[22]

澳大利亚历史学家诺曼·L. 麦凯勒（Norman L. Mckellar）在提到江南造船所得到为美国海运委员会建造四艘万吨级运输舰的合同时有这样一段描述：

Mauchan won the further trust of Liu Guannan, Director of Kiangnan Dock & Engineering Works, for successfully persuading the chairman of the United States Shipping Board, Edwards N. Hurley, to successfully secure a contract to build four 10 000 deadweight tons steam freighters. Mauchan's role in this negotiation was obviously decisive. In particular, Mauchan took full advantage of the close relationship with Captain Robert Dollar, a Scottish, and earnestly requested him to lobby the United States Shipping Board for Kiangnan. In July 1918, the successful signing of contract for four steam freighters further strengthened his position at Kiangnan, and he won the trust of the directors as well as employees of Kiangnan. "For building these 10 000-ton steam freighters, the Chinese would not have sufficient courage to take them if it was not Mauchan's insistence."

Mauchan's management of affairs in Kiangnan became wider and wider. He led both financial and technical management as well as production schedules. He introduced a full set of British style management to Kiangnan. He requested Kiangnan's staffs to write all documents like notifications, plans and contracts in English. The Kiangnan's employees quite hated his arrogance, because only the employees with good English skills had the opportunity to be promoted. Kiangnan's workers also complained that the Scottish "boss" was arrogant, abused his authority, and looked down on others. He arbitrarily required workers to work overtime to increase the labour intensity in order to catch up schedule.

During Liu Guannan's tenure of director, Kiangnan's workers once accused him of obeying Mauchan without his own idea. But objectively speaking, in May 1918, Director Liu delegated Mauchan to the United States for negotiating and signing contract of four steam freighters with the United States Shipping Board, clearly showing that Mauchan was trusted by Kiangnan's management team and not an abuse of authority. Furthermore, Director Liu quite valued Mauchan communication ability and personnel connections as well as his decisive role in securing the contract of four American steam freighters. Mauchan subtly utilized special relationship with the Scottish Robert Dollar and made his efforts in upper-level of the U.S. Government. This clearly proves that Liu Guannan made the right decision in selecting the right person.

Huang Rong, an elder employee of Kiangnan Dock & Engineering Works, stated in his reminiscence: "Since all the materials and boilers for the construction of four 10 000-ton steam freighters were transported by Robert Dollar Company, the entire construction period lasted up to three years. The most of the down payment paid by the United States Shipping Board was deducted by Robert Dollar Company for paying the material and shipping costs. Therefore, all expenses and wages in the shipyard, more than 200 000 taels of silver, prior to sequential installments had to be borne by Kiangnan themselves. Such huge fund even exceeded the bank loan. Private deposits of Mauchan and the Directors of Kiangnan were withdrawn to mitigate the financial shortage. "

Australian historian Norman L. McKellar described the shipbuilding contracts that Kiangnan Dock & Engineering Works assigned with United States Shipping Board for the construction of four 10 000-ton steam freighters:

"中国的（造船）合同源自江南造船所总稽查造访华盛顿。一个精明的苏格兰人，他口袋里带着一份由美国政府提供钢材的四艘船舶建造合同离开了美国。这被注明将会是一批优秀的船舶。"

在 1918 年 9 月号《论坛》杂志上，斯蒂芬·马歇尔（Stephen Marshall）撰写的一篇文章中提到，毛根热情洋溢地谈到了他在江南造船所的工作和与中国人民的共事经历，他说："美国航运委员会授予上海船厂的一份巨额造船合同将为美国造船业在中国产生显著的成果。"他接着说："您是否意识到在中国建造美国船舶会对中国年轻人产生影响？航运业在赢得这场世界大战中所起的作用是众所周知的，您难道看不到它在经济上的感性的一面吗？必须建立更紧密的商业关系；（这是）中美之间商业关系发展的巨大机遇。中国人是睿智的，在中国造船不是什么新事物，它的历史可以追溯到数百年前。但是在中国建造美国的船舶是新鲜的。当所有人都注视着这艘船的时候，它的魅力深深地打动了中国人。"

战争结束后，美国必须出口其多余的钢铁、机床、机械和农具等。如果不能和中国这样的国家建立大量的出口业务，美国的制造业将受到影响。但是中国造船业的发展不会对美国产生任何影响。互惠关系将远远超过平衡。

"The Chinese contracts arose from an approach to Washington by the Superintendent of the Kiangnan Dock & Engineering Works in Shanghai. A canny Scot, he left the U.S. with a contract in his pocket for the building of 4 ships from steel to be supplied by the U.S. Government. These proved to be excellent vessels."

In an article written by Stephen Marshall in the September 1918 edition of *The Forum*, Mauchan spoke passionately about his work at Kiangnan and the Chinese colleagues, saying "the action of the United States Shipping Board in awarding a huge contract to the Shanghai yard is going to produce remarkable results for America shipbuilding industry in China". He went on to state, "Do you realize the effect building American ships in China will have upon the young men of China? Knowing as they do the part shipping plays in winning this world war, can you not see the sentimental side of it as well as the economical? Closer commercial relations must result; a development of the vast opportunities for commercial relations between China and America. China is intellectually awake. Shipbuilding in China is not a new venture. It goes back hundreds of years. But building American ships there is new and novel. It has an appeal that strikes the Chinese mind with tremendous force at a time when all eyes are turned toward her."

After the war, America must have an outlet for its surplus steel and machine tools, machinery and agricultural implements. Without a large export business built up with countries like China, the manufacturing industry in America will be affected. But the development of shipbuilding in China will in no way affect America. The reciprocal relations will more than balance.

1.3.3

毛根离去的原因
Why Mauchan Left Kiangnan

毛根常常自居为江南造船所的"老板",态度蛮横。江南造船所的技术人员和工人也曾组织起来反对毛根的专制。1926 年在遍及全中国的排外罢工运动中,毛根的压力越来越大,1926 年 10 月,毛根被迫辞职。其弟小毛根则于 1927—1945 年仍就职于江南造船所,但其权位和威望远不如其兄 [23]。

毛根从 1906 年进入江南船坞当总工程师,到 1926 年离厂,前后长达 21 年。一名外国雇员在一家中国企业干了这么长的时间,这在当时的中国是不多见的。那毛根为什么要走呢?

1926 年 11 月 1 日,上海《字林西报》的载文披露了这件事。标题十分醒目:《毛根先生向江南造船所辞职反对中国军阀以政治目的挪用造船所经费》。根据这篇报道,毛根离开江南造船所是另有原因的。

自 1905 年"局坞分家"之后到 1911 年辛亥革命,江南造船所虽然遇到不少困难,但企业不断发展、经营情况较好、船厂多有盈余,这些成绩无疑有毛根的功劳。毛根亦以此自居为江南造船所的"老板",盛气凌人。

民国以后,天下大乱,各派军阀连年混战,国家财政十分困难,军阀头子不仅拼命搜刮民财,也把贪婪之手伸向江南造船所,竟勒令造船所交出 20 万两银款,还要控制造船所的财务活动和经费收支。江南造船所所长无力违抗军阀,但毛根却忍不住了。

Mauchan often considered himself as "big boss" of Kiangnan, and his attitude was very arrogant. Kiangnan's technicians and workers once stood together to oppose Mauchan's autocracy. Since the xenophobic strike movement throughout China in 1926, Mauchan felt more obvious pressure. Mauchan was forced to resign in October 1926. His younger brother, Andrew Clark Mauchan, still worked at the Kiangnan Dock & Engineering Works from 1927 to 1945, but his power and prestige were far less than his elder brother.

Mauchan joined Kiangnan Dock as Chief Engineer in 1906, and left Kiangnan in 1926. He dedicatedly work at Kiangnan for 21 years. It was extremely rare in China that a foreign employee had worked in an enterprise of China for so long. Which reason was Mauchan forced to leave Kiangnan?

On 1 November 1926, the article in *North China Daily News* in Shanghai revealed this incident. The headline would exactly be attractable: "Mr. Mauchan resigned to Kiangnan to oppose the misappropriation of shipbuilding funds by Chinese warlords for political purposes". According to this report, Mauchan might have left Kiangnan for some other reasons.

After the "Separation of Bureau and Dock" in 1905 to the Revolution of 1911, even though Kiangnan had occasionally encountered many difficulties, the shipyard had smoothly developed and operated quite well. Kiangnan maintained certain surplus. These achievements undoubtedly were the contribution of Mauchan. Based on this, Mauchan often regarded himself as the "big boss" of Kiangnan, and his attitude was very arrogant.

Since the Revolution of 1911, the warlords had tangled warfare for many years, and the national finances have been tight for maintaining. The warlords not only desperately searched the people's wealth, but also extended their greedy hands to Kiangnan. They unexpectedly ordered Kiangnan to submit 200 000 taels of silver, and they even were going to control financial activities and funds of the shipyard. The Director of Kiangnan Dock & Engineering Works was unable to defy the warlords, but Mauchan couldn't accept such unreasonable request.

毛根担任的职务是总工程师，实际上他总揽了江南造船所的经营、技术和生产大权，人称"洋总管"。早期，派驻江南造船所的政府官员基本上不干涉江南造船所的生产经营，企业在很大程度上可以自主经营。毛根不仅拥有生产技术大权，而且在经营和财务方面也有很大的支配权。如果军阀控制了江南造船所的经济命脉，随时可以取走钱款，这将使江南造船所的自主经营权受到很大的限制，对江南造船所的经营乃至他本人的利益产生很大的冲击。

在江南造船所工作二十多年的毛根，如果不是到令他实在忍无可忍的地步，是不会轻易提出辞职的。当时毛根在中国也是一个有一定影响力的人物，因此，在他提出辞呈后，北洋政府曾要他收回辞呈，江南造船所也多次挽留他。但当时毛根提出，要他留下可以，但北洋政府必须出面解决此事，唯一的条件就是让军阀归还挪用的银两。殊不知，北洋政府本身就是军阀执政，与各地军阀是一丘之貉，他们怎么可能支持毛根呢？最后，留给毛根的只有一个唯一的选择——卷铺盖走人。

《字林西报》的报道还提到："毛根的辞职使中国政府企业失去了一位忠诚的雇员，他曾经为中国企业提供极有价值的服务……。毛根离开江南造船所时还是依依不舍的。"[24] 确实，毛根在江南造船所工作了21年，对江南还是很有感情的，毛根离开江南时，他把自己使用多年的满满两箱技术书籍和绘图仪器赠送给了江南造船所的船舶设计专家叶在馥。

Mauchan worked for Kiangnan as Chief Engineer (actually acted as General Project Manager). In fact, he already took over all powers in respects of the management, technology and production, so called "Foreign General Manager". In the initial period, government delegated officials in Kiangnan normally did not interfere in the operational and financial aspects. The shipyard had sufficient flexibility for self-operating. Mauchan not only possessed great powers in production and technology, but also had a great deal of control in business and finance. If the warlords took over the control, they were able to withdraw the money as their wish at any time, which will greatly restrict financial freedoms and operating independence of Kiangnan. It would significantly impact the interests of both Kiangnan and Mauchan his own.

Mauchan, who had worked at Kiangnan for more than two decades, would not rashly make decision of resign if it was the last straw for him. In that particular period, Mauchan could be regarded prominent personage in China. After he submitted his resignation, the government, therefore, had earnestly requested him to withdraw his resignation, and the directors of Kiangnan persuaded him several times as well. However, Mauchan emphasized the precondition for abandoning his request that the government should make their efforts to force the warlords refunding the misappropriated money. Actually, the Beiyang Government itself was representing the interests of the warlords, and it was impossible to stand at same position with Mauchan. In the end, Mauchan had only one choice to "roll away".

The article of *North China Daily News* also mentioned: "Mauchan's resignation has caused Chinese government enterprise unfortunately to lose a loyal employee. He used to provide extremely valuable services to Chinese companies… When Mauchan left Kiangnan, he still was reluctant." Indeed, Mauchan had worked at Kiangnan for 21 years, and he still had a lot of gratitude for Kiangnan and his colleagues. When Mauchan left Kiangnan, he gave away two boxes of technical books and drawing instruments, which he had used for many years, to Ye Zaifu, a ship design expert of Kiangnan Dock & Engineering Works.

1.3.4

对毛根的评价
The Evaluation of Mauchan

尽管对毛根的评论多为负面的，然而他却是在中国一家官办企业中任职最长的外国人。他以一个管理者、经营者和谈判者的身份同江南造船所的历届所长相处，关系大体是和睦的。在刘冠南担任所长期间（1916—1925 年），他们彼此配合得很好，这也反映了两人之间的默契，以及权力的平衡。在促进江南造船所管理改进升级、设施现代化、承接外国造船订单和防止外国势力控制江南造船所等方面，毛根是有相当大贡献的。

1961 年，陈绍宽（1889—1969，从 1930 年 11 月到 1934 年 11 月，在前任所长马德骥称病期间担任江南造船所所长一职）在上海接受访谈时对毛根有这样一段评价[25]：

"英人毛根的政治背景不明显，但在孙传芳军队想掠夺江南造船所的资财时曾经说过要请英国派军舰来保护江南造船所，被海军当局拒绝了。毛根在技术和经营上都有一套，工作态度也很认真，对江南造船所的发展还是有贡献的，但他骄傲和专断，不大肯听中国当局的指挥，常同中国所长发生冲突。当时的所长邝国华、陈兆锵和刘冠南等都是海军大员，在技术上也都是内行，但因毛根在管理上很有一套，便将技术和经营业务都让他负责，他们自己只管理一些行政上的事务。后来毛根合同期满后未再续聘。毛根离开江南造船所后，很长一段时期仍住在上海并没有回国[26]。我在主持江南造船所的工作时，还曾经见过他。他和其弟小毛根关系很僵，他听说江南造船所任命小毛根任总工程师时，颇不以为然，说小毛根脑筋不好，根本没有能力担任这一职务。小毛根比起毛根来，

Although many comments to Mauchan from most domestic historians were quite negative, he was the foreigner who worked in a Chinese government-own enterprise for the longest period. As a manager, operator and negotiator, he got along well with previous directors of Kiangnan Dock & Engineering Works, and he was generally harmonious with Chinese directors. During Liu Guannan's tenure (1916–1925), he cooperated quite well with Director Liu, which also reflected the tacit understanding and balance of power among management members. Mauchan had made considerable contributions in promoting the management and upgrading of Kiangnan, modernizing its facilities, securing orders of foreign ship owners, and preventing foreign forces from controlling Kiangnan.

In 1961, Chen Shaokuan (1889–1969, from November 1930 to November 1934, served as Director of Kiangnan Dock & Engineering Works during the period when the former Director Ma Deji was ill) accepted an interview and expressed his evaluation to Mauchan:

"The political background of the Scottish Mauchan was not so obvious. But when Sun Chuanfang's army (a warlord of China) wanted to plunder the wealth of Kiangnan, he would ask the British Navy to send warships to protect Kiangnan. This request was rejected by the Naval Department. Mauchan had both technical and operational advantages. He had a serious working attitude and had contributed to the development of Kiangnan. However, he was quite proud and arbitrary, and was reluctant to listen to the instructions of the Chinese authorities. He often conflicts with Chinese directors. Although the directors Kuang Guohua (K. H. Kwong), Chen Zhaoqiang, and Liu Guannan were all naval officers and technical experts, they considered that Mauchan had good management skills, and confidingly assigned Mauchan to take responsibility of both technical and business operations. They only managed some administrative matters. Later, Mauchan did not intend to extend his employment contract. After Mauchan left Kiangnan, he still lived in Shanghai for a long time and did not return to Scotland. I had met him when I was in charge of Kiangnan. He had a stiff relationship with his younger brother. When talking about the appointment of his younger

无论在技术上和工作魄力上都差得多，但没有毛根武断。"

综合各方面的评价来看，陈绍宽对毛根的评价是比较客观和公正的。

brother as chief engineer by Kiangnan Dock & Engineering Works, he said that his younger brother had a bad brain and was unable to take up this position at all. Comparing with Mauchan, his younger brother was not as excellent as Mauchan especially in technical ability and decision courage, but he was not so arbitrary."

From the perspective of various evaluations, Chen Shaokuan's evaluation about Mauchan was relatively objective and fair.

1.3.5

毛根回到苏格兰
Mauchan Moved Back to Scotland

毛根辞职后并没有马上离开上海。他从心爱的上海迁出很可能是由于 1932 年 1 月 28 日至 3 月 3 日在上海发生的"一·二八事变"。当时日军企图强行占领上海。如果没有发生这场动乱,他可能会一直待在上海,直到他去世。

1933 年 5 月 26 日,毛根和他的夫人珍妮一起乘坐加拿大太平洋轮船的邮轮"里士满公爵夫人"号抵达苏格兰的格林诺克。他们与珍妮的母亲一起定居在一个名为"布林克利夫"的美丽庄园中,这个庄园位于苏格兰海伦斯堡杜希尔路的高档社区内,面朝大海。在庄园附近的拐角处是由苏格兰籍著名建筑师查尔斯·雷尼·麦金托什设计的著名的"希尔之家"。

1936 年 3 月 11 日,回到苏格兰后仅 3 年,毛根在苏格兰逝世,享年 67 岁。其夫人珍妮也于次年去世。1937 年 11 月,上海和他曾经为中国民族造船工业发展努力工作过的江南造船所沦陷。

他一生的大部分时间(67 年人生中的 46 年)都在上海度过。在那段时间里,他身处中国尤其是上海的巨大变革中的前沿。从衰落的清朝到辛亥革命、军阀混战,最后日本帝国入侵和占领的开始,上海在这个动荡的时期发展迅速。

Mauchan did not move back to Scotland after resignation. It is highly likely that his relocation from Shanghai was due to what was known as the "January 28 Incident" to the Chinese which occurred between January 28th and March 3rd 1932 when Japanese forces first attempted to take Shanghai by force. If the turmoil had not occurred, he might well have stayed in Shanghai until his dying day.

On 26 May 1933, Robert and Janey arrived in Greenock Scotland together aboard the Canadian Pacific Steamship SS "Duchess of Richmond". They settled in a beautiful estate called "Brincliffe" with Janey's mother, located on Dhuhill Drive in the exclusive upper section of Helensburgh, Scotland, facing the ocean. Just around the corner is the famous "The Hill House" designed by Scottish Architect Charles Rennie Mackintosh.

Robert passed-away three short years after their move back to Scotland, on 11 March 1936 at the age of 67. Janey is believed to have passed-away the following year. Shanghai fell to the Japanese Empire in November of 1937, and with it, Kiangnan Dock & Engineering Works he had worked so hard to develop for the Chinese national shipbuilding.

He spent the majority of his life in Shanghai, nearly 46 of his 67 years. During that time he had a front row seat to the dramatic changes China, and especially Shanghai would face. From the fall of the Qing Dynasty, to the Revolution of 1911, warlords and bandits and finally the beginning of the invasion and occupation by the Japanese Empire, Shanghai grew rapidly during this tumultuous period.

作者注：

Notes:

1　陆舸编著，《江南往事》，上海画报出版社，2005 年，第 78 页。

2　资料来自上海船厂厂史资料；王志毅著，《中国近代造船史》，海洋出版社，1986 年，第 37 页。

3　同上。

4　《上海地方志》1994 年第四期。

5　李培德，《论江南制造局"局坞分家"的经营史意义》，载于《近代史学刊》2015 年第 2 期。

6　原始文献《江南造船所纪要》中为"总工程司"，参见本书 1.3.2 节。

7　数据资料出处：上海社会科学院经济研究所编，《江南造船厂厂史：1865—1949》，江苏人民出版社，1983 年，第 106-107 页。

8　资料来自：上海社会科学院经济研究所编，《江南造船厂厂史：1865—1949》，江苏人民出版社，1983 年，第 103 页。

9　Dock Manager Dies: Well-Known Identity of Shanghai Waterfront Mr. R. B. Mauchan, South China Morning Post (1903—1941); Mar 24, 1936; ProQuest Historical Newspapers: South China Morning Post. Page 2.

10　江南造船厂志编纂委员会，《江南造船厂志：1865—1995》，上海人民出版社，1999 年，第 137-138 页。

11　《江南造船厂厂史：1865—1949》一书中将其误译为"模范 3"号。据作者了解，第一次世界大战期间，英国设计了一些标准船型，以"Modal X"命名。

12　原始文献《江南造船所纪要》为"总工程司"，参见本书 1.3.2 节。为方便阅读，后文描述沿用多数文献所记的"总工程师"。

13　"大毛根"是江南船坞送给他的雅号，因其弟也在江南船坞工作，故有大小之分。"毛根"和他的英文名字 Mauchan 的发音大相径庭，只是江南人都这么称呼他也就约定俗成了。后文中的"毛根"均指"大毛根"。

14　上海社会科学院经济研究所编，《江南造船厂厂史：1865—1949》，江苏人民出版社，1983 年，第 137 页。

15　Andrew Clark Mauchan 原来在江南造船所担任船体设计工作，被称作"小毛根"以和"毛根"区别。上海社会科学院经济研究所编，《江南造船厂厂史：1865—1949》，江苏人民出版社，1983 年，第 144 页。

16　江南造船所所长刘冠南审核、廖骎编写，《江南造船所纪要》，民国十一年四月（1922 年 4 月），第 10 页。

17　《字林西报》（North China Daily News），又称《字林报》，前身为《北华捷报》（North China Herald），曾经是在中国出版的最有影响力的英文报纸。

18　江南造船厂志编纂委员会，《江南造船厂志：1865—1995》，上海人民出版社，1999 年，第 63 页。

19　池仲祐，《海军实纪》，民国七年（1918 年）版。摘自《中国舰艇工业历史资料丛书》编辑部编纂，《中国近代舰艇工业史料集》，上海人民出版社，1994 年，第 179 页。

20　"江南造船厂造船一览表"，上海社会科学院经济研究所编，《江南造船厂厂史：1865—1949》，江苏人民出版社，1983 年，第 326-376 页。

21　江南造船所老员工黄容在《谈 1927 年以前江南造船所的生产经营情况》一文中回忆，当时他负责船坞工程。1960 年 4 月，访问于四川北路 961 弄怡兴里 6 号，许维雍整理。

22　同上。

23　（法）科尔耐，黄庆华译，《大毛根与江南造船所（1905—1927）——中外合作一例》，载于《国外中国近代史研究》1994 年第 24 辑，第 120-132 页。

24　《字林西报》扫描版，1926 年 11 月 1 日，上海图书馆藏。

25　《陈绍宽先生的访谈纪要》。1961 年 5 月 31 日于上海华东医院，蒋立记录。

26　有文献记载，毛根于次年（1927 年）回国。毛根在上海的安福路有私人房产和产业，不排除回国后再到上海的可能性。

江南造船所承造美舰的背景
The Background of EFC Contract in Kiangnan

2.1

"卢西塔尼亚"号被击沉事件
RMS "Lusitania" Attacked by U–20

皇家邮轮"卢西塔尼亚"号，是英国的一艘豪华邮轮，隶属于英国的卡纳德航运公司（Cunard Line），其主要参数如表 2-1 所示。1915 年 5 月 7 日该船在爱尔兰外海被德国潜艇 U-20 击沉，造成共 1 198 人死亡。由于伤亡者中包括大量美国人，"卢西塔尼亚"号的沉没和"齐默尔曼电报"事件一同成为美国参加第一次世界大战的导火索。

RMS "Lusitania" was a luxury cruise liner owned by Cunard Line of UK. The general characteristics of RMS "Lusitania" are shown as Table 2-1. RMS Lusitania was sunk in outer Irish Sea by attack of German submarine U-20 on 7 May 1915, and 1 198 people were killed in this attack. Since casualties include a lot of Americans, the incidents of RMS "Lusitania" sunk together with Zimmermann Telegram as trigger forced the United States into the Great War.

表 2-1 皇家邮轮"卢西塔尼亚"号的主要参数
Table 2-1 General characteristics of RMS "Lusitania"

主要参数 General characteristics[1]		
船型	Ship type	豪华邮轮 Ocean liner
吨位	Tonnage	31 550 总吨（GRT）
排水量	Displacement	44 060 长吨（long tons）（44 767 t）
船长	Length	787 ft（239.9 m）
船宽	Beam	87 ft（26.5 m）
型深	Depth	60 ft（18.3 m）至艇甲板（to boat deck），165 ft（50.3 m）空气吃水（to aerials）
吃水	Draught	33.6 ft（10.2 m）
载客甲板数	Decks	9 层旅客甲板 9 passenger decks
装船功率	Installed power	25 台锅炉，4 台直接作用蒸汽轮机，共 76 000 马力（57 兆瓦） 25 Scotch boilers, four direct-acting Parsons steam turbines producing 76 000 hp（57 MW）
推进	Propulsion	4 具三叶螺旋桨（1909 年改成四叶螺旋桨） Four triple-blade propellers (replaced by quadruple-blade propellers in 1909)
航速	Speed	25 kn (46 km/h) 26.7 kn (49.4 km/h) （最大速度，1914 年 3 月的一天）（Top speed, single day's run in March 1914）

（续表）
(continued)

主要参数 General characteristics[1]		
载客量	Passenger capacity	552 个头等舱、460 个二等舱、1 186 个三等舱，共 2 198 个客位。可装载 7 000 吨煤作为燃料 552 first class, 460 second class, 1 186 third class, 2 198 total. 7 000 tons coal as fuel
船员数	Crew	850 人

"卢西塔尼亚"号是英国卡纳德航运公司 3 艘大型客船（其余两艘是"毛里塔尼亚"号和"阿奎坦尼亚"号）中的首制船。1903 年，31 500 总吨级的"卢西塔尼亚"号（H367）在苏格兰克莱德班克的约翰·布朗船厂开工建造。1904 年，姐妹船"毛里塔尼亚"号开工建造。1907 年 8 月，"卢西塔尼亚"号顺利下水。"卢西塔尼亚"号和两艘姐妹船开创了跨大西洋邮轮航速的新纪元。图 2-1 为"卢西塔尼亚"号的航行照片；表 2-2 所示为"卢西塔尼亚"号的营运史。自此之后，大型邮轮纷纷把速度和豪华同时作为追求的目标。

RMS "Lusitania" was the first ship of Cunard's "Grand Trio", along with RMS "Mauretania" and RMS "Aquitania". In 1903, 31 500 GRT RMS "Lusitania" (H367) commenced construction in John Brown & Co., Clydebank, Scotland. In 1904, sister ship RMS "Mauretania" started steel cutting. In August of 1907, RMS "Lusitania" was successfully launched. Cunard's "Grand Trio", RMS "Lusitania" and her sister ships created a new speed era for crossing Atlantic Ocean. Figure 2-1 is RMS "Lusitania" in sailing; Table 2-2 shows operation history of RMS "Lusitania". Speed and luxury became targets of many large ocean liners after Cunard's "Grand Trio".

图 2-1 航行中的"卢西塔尼亚"号
Figure 2-1 RMS "Lusitania" in sailing

表 2-2   "卢西塔尼亚"号的营运史
Table 2-2   Operation history of RMS "Lusitania"

营运历史 Operation history[2]		
船名	Name	"卢西塔尼亚"号 RMS "Lusitania"
船东	Owner	英国卡纳德航运公司 Cunard Line
营运商	Operator	英国卡纳德航运公司 Cunard Line
登记港	Port of registry	利物浦 Liverpool
航线	Route	纽约至利物浦 New York to Liverpool
建造厂	Builder	苏格兰克莱德班克的约翰·布朗船厂 John Brown & Co., Clydebank, Scotland
船厂编号	Yard number	367 号 / No.367
铺龙骨	Laid down	1904 年 6 月 9 日 / 9 June 1904
下水	Launched	1906 年 6 月 7 日 / 7 June 1906
命名	Christened	Mary, Lady Inverclyde
首航	Maiden voyage	1907 年 9 月 7 日 / 7 September 1907
营运	In service	1907—1915 年 From 1907 to 1915
失事原因和地点 Wrecking cause and location		1915 年 5 月 7 日（星期五），德国潜艇 U-20 用鱼雷攻击了正常航行中的"卢西塔尼亚"号 [距离古金赛尔角（Old Head of Kinsale）灯塔 18 千米处]，被攻击后破损的"卢西塔尼亚"号沉入 91 米深的海底 Torpedoed by German U-boat U-20 on Friday, 7 May 1915. Wreck lies approximately 11 miles (18 km) off the Old Head of Kinsale Lighthouse in 300 ft (91 m) of water at 51°25′N 8°33′W, 51.417°N 8.550°W

第一次世界大战爆发后，英国政府曾经计划把卡纳德航运公司的"卢西塔尼亚"号和"毛里塔尼亚"号改装成武装的辅助巡洋舰。后来卡纳德航运公司的"毛里塔尼亚"号和新船"阿奎坦尼亚"号被征用改装成医院船。"卢西塔尼亚"号则被允许继续从事跨大西洋客运业务，以方便美国和英国之间的战时交通。它航行时不挂任何旗帜，船名也被遮盖掉了。当时，英国军方乐观地坚信这艘被称为"大西洋快犬"的"卢西塔尼亚"号，其 25 节的航速足以摆脱任何企图追击它的德国潜艇。

1915 年 5 月 1 日，德国大使馆在美国报纸上刊登声明，称任何乘坐悬挂英国旗帜的商船的美国旅客，其生命安全都得不到保障。但是"卢西塔尼亚"号上的乘客并没有把这则消息放在心上。因为他们相信"卢西塔尼亚"号有足够快的速度，足以摆脱德国潜艇的追击。于是，"卢西塔尼亚"号满载着 1 959 名乘客（大部分是美国人）和船员从美国纽约出发了。图 2-2 所示为"卢西塔尼亚"号从哈得孙河纽约港出发的盛况。

After Great War started, UK Government used to plan to convert RMS "Lusitania" and RMS "Mauretania" to armed merchant cruiser (AMC). Later RMS "Mauretania" and newbuilding RMS "Aquitania" were requisitioned and converted as hospital ship. RMS "Lusitania" thereafter was allowed to continuously operate the passenger business crossing Atlantic Ocean in order to provide transportation between America and Europe in wartime. She never flew any flag in voyage, and ship's name was hidden as well. The Royal Navy excessively trusted RMS "Lusitania", so called "Atlantic Ocean Cynosarges", and her 25 knots speed was able to throw off any Germen submarine which attempts to catch her.

On 1 May 1915, German embassy published a statement on the newspapers of the United States, and they announced that the life safety of American passengers can not be guaranteed if they travel with merchant ship flying Great Britain flag. But the passengers planned to travel with RMS "Lusitania" did not pay more attention on this announcement. They blithely assumed RMS "Lusitania" had such a fast speed that she was able to throw off any German submarine. Then RMS "Lusitania" carried 1 959 passengers (most of them were American) and crew departing from New York. Figure 2-2 shows the scene when RMS "Lusitania" departing from Hudson River of New York Port.

图 2-2　"卢西塔尼亚"号从哈得孙河纽约港出发的盛况
Figure 2-2　RMS "Lusitania" departing from Hudson River of New York Port

1915 年 5 月 7 日，"卢西塔尼亚"号航行到了爱尔兰外海，在那里遇到了大雾。威廉·特纳船长命令把船速降至 18 节。到了中午 11：30，大雾逐渐消散。下午 2：12，正在附近游弋的 U-20 潜艇发现了"卢西塔尼亚"号并对其发射鱼雷进行攻击。U-20 潜艇发射的第一枚鱼雷击中了"卢西塔尼亚"号桥楼下部的船体。紧接着，第二枚鱼雷击中了煤舱。弥漫的煤炭粉尘引起了猛烈的爆炸。船上的旅客在惊慌失措中纷纷挤上了救生艇甲板，秩序极为混乱。由于煤舱爆炸船体出现了一个大洞，船体急速倾斜，只有右舷的救生艇可以使用。20 分钟后，"卢西塔尼亚"号带着 1 198 名乘客和船员（许多还没来得及跑出船舱）沉入了大海。"卢西塔尼亚"号的航海生涯就此结束。不过比起 3 年前沉没的"泰坦尼克"号来说，幸运的是那些跳入水中的乘客被迅速赶来的爱尔兰渔船救起而得以幸存。

"卢西塔尼亚"号的沉没在大西洋两岸的民众中引起了极大的震惊和恐慌。美国和英国政府以及舆论纷纷指责这是一场残酷的谋杀，德国的报纸则声称"卢西塔尼亚"号是一艘军火船，否则不会沉没得这么快。美国国内政界和民众间"立刻对德国宣战"的呼吁甚嚣尘上。德国迫于国际舆论谴责的压力，宣布取消对客船和中立国船只的无限制潜艇战。

直到 1917 年，德国由于在欧洲战场西线战局不利，又恢复了无节制的潜艇猎杀作战，这种不人道的攻击行为直接导致美国对其宣战。1917 年威尔逊政府向德国宣战的决议，得到了美国民众的支持[3]。

On 7 May 1915, RMS "Lusitania" met thick fog when she sailed at outer Irish Sea. Captain William Turner ordered the ship to slow down to 18 knots. Morning fog diffused till noon time of 11：30. At PM 2：12, surrounding cruising German submarine U-20 keenly found RMS "Lusitania" and fired torpedoes to RMS "Lusitania". The first torpedo attacked on hull underneath of bridge, and the second torpedo attacked on coal fuel storage space. Pervasive coal dust caused violent explosion. The passengers disorderly crowded up to boat deck. Hull rapidly heeled due to big opening by explosion in coal fuel storage space, thus starboard life boats were merely available. After 20 minutes, RMS "Lusitania" together with 1 198 passengers and crews (a lot of people not yet got off their cabins) sunk into the sea. Navigation career of RMS "Lusitania" was terminated promptly. But comparing with RMS "Titanic" sank three years ago, fortunately, some passengers jumped into water were rescued by Irish fishing boats and survived.

The sinking of RMS "Lusitania" caused extreme astonish and scare in the people of transatlantic. The public opinion of governments of the United States and the United Kingdom censured that was a cruel murder in succession. German newspaper quibbled that RMS "Lusitania" was an ammunition ship, otherwise she did not sink so quickly. American politicians and people strongly called on "declaring war against Germany". Germany, forced by international public opinion, announced to cancel unrestricted submarine warfare to passenger ship and neutral country's ship.

Till 1917, since the situation in western European battlefield was unfavourable for Germany, German Navy desperately restarted unrestricted submarine warfare. Such barbaric action directly forced the United States to declare war against Germany. The declaration of war on Germany from President Woodrow Wilson extensively obtained the support of American people in 1917.

2.2

美国海运委员会和应急船队公司的成立
The Establishment of USSB and EFC

1914 年 8 月，第一次世界大战全面爆发后，美国明显地意识到由于战争物资运输需求的大幅增长，美国的运输商船将会出现明显的运力不足。8 月 18 日美国国会先制定了《应急船舶登记法》（*Emergency Ship Registry Act*），允许外国船厂建造的船舶登记为美国船籍，挂美国国旗。

《应急船舶登记法》颁布后，截至 1915 年 7 月 1 日共有 148 艘外国船舶登记为美国船籍。同时美国财政部成立了战争风险保险局（War Risk Insurance Bureau）为参保的美国籍商船提供保险，一旦遭到敌方水面舰艇、布设的水雷和潜艇攻击所造成的人员财产的损失将由战争风险保险局给予赔付。然而，由于战时原材料诸如造船钢材和木材紧缺，船舶机械和设备价格飞涨，加之战时运营风险过大，美国的航运企业仍不愿投资造船和将船舶投入大西洋航线营运。1915 年 5 月 7 日，英国卡纳德航运公司的皇家邮轮"卢西塔尼亚"号在爱尔兰附近海域被德国潜艇击沉后，威尔逊总统被迫决定采取更加强硬的措施。

1916 年 9 月 7 日，在威尔逊总统的反复请求下美国公布了《海上运输法案》（*Shipping Act 39, Stat. 729*），随后成立了美国海运委员会。此机构也被称为战时海运委员会（War Shipping Board）。美国海运委员会作为美国政府在战时的一个应急机构，被赋予了更大的权力，通过该机构美国政府有权租用、管理和监控所有从事国内外贸易运输的美籍船舶。在战时及其后 5 年内由美国政府统筹一切船舶事宜[4]。

On August of 1914, after the Great War broke out, the United States sensibly recognized that the marine transport capacity of American merchant ship would be obviously insufficient due to substantially increased demand of military supplies. On 18 of August, the Congress of the United States enacted the *Emergency Ship Registry Act*. This act allowed that ship built in shipyards outside of the United States can be registered in the United States with American flag.

After this *Emergency Ship Registry Act* ratified, 148 sets of foreign ship transferred to American registry till 1 July 1915. Meanwhile American Treasury Department established War Risk Insurance Bureau providing marine insurance for American merchant ships. Once property damage and personnel loss of wreck happened due to attacks by surface warship, mines and submarines, War Risk Insurance Bureau would pay proper compensation. Since the shortage of shipbuilding raw materials such as steel, timber, the cost of marine machineries and equipment increased rapidly, and big risk in wartime, American shipping companies were not willing to invest shipbuilding and put tonnage into Atlantic Ocean operation. On 7 May 1915, RMS "Lusitania" of Cunard Line was attacked by a German submarine and sunk in outer Irish Sea. President Wilson was forced to take a tougher stand against Germany.

On 7 September 1916, President Wilson repeatedly requested enactment of a *Shipping Act 39, Stat. 729*. Thereafter the United States Shipping Board was established as an emergency agency by the *Shipping Act 39, Stat. 729*. It was sometimes referred to as the War Shipping Board. As an emergency organization, American Government assigned more authorities to chart, handle and track tonnages for coastal and ocean going transportation, and American Government would manage all issues regarding ship and shipping in wartime and five years post war.

美国海运委员会的主要职能[5]：
The functions of the United States Shipping Board were to:

◆ 代表美国政府系统地管理商船、制定贸易规则、收取海运保险和洲际水运贸易的运费、负责船舶登记转让等；

◆ Regulate commercial maritime carriers and trade practices, collect marine insurance, and the rates charged in interstate waterborne commerce, be responsible for transfers of ship registry;

◆ 从政府层面调查是否有足够的码头和水上运输设施；

◆ Investigate adequacy of port and water transportation facilities;

◆ 决定必要的运输航线和在这些航线营运的船舶的技术要求；

◆ Determine the necessity for steamship lines and the characteristics of vessels on those lines;

◆ 动员军辅船和商船加入战时运输；

◆ Develop a naval auxiliary and merchant marine;

◆ 资助私有造船企业扩大产能。

◆ Subsidize private ship construction.

总统提名并经参议院同意由爱德华·N. 赫尔利（Edward N. Hurley）担任战时海运委员会主席、雷蒙德·B. 史蒂文斯（Raymond B. Stevens）担任副主席、班布里奇·科尔比（Bainbridge Colby）、约翰·A. 唐纳德（John A. Donald）和查尔斯·R. 佩奇（Charles R. Page）三人担任委员会委员。如图 2-3 所示为美国战时海运委员会的主要成员。赫尔利主席在江南造船所订造四艘万吨级运输舰的决策中起了重要作用。

Mr. Edward N. Hurley was appointed as chairman of the War Shipping Board by the President and confirmed by the Senate, Raymond B. Stevens as vice chairman, Bainbridge Colby, John A. Donald and Charles R. Page as commissioners. Refer to Figure 2-3 the major members of the War Shipping Board. Mr. Hurley, chairman of the War Shipping Board, played the most important role for Kiangnan securing four American steam freighters.

图 2-3　美国战时海运委员会的主要成员
Figure 2-3　The major members of the War Shipping Board

为应对德国于 1917 年 2 月在北大西洋和地中海实行的无节制的潜艇猎杀攻击，4 月 16 日政府在美国海运委员会的组织下根据《海上运输法》成立了应急船队公司，主要目的为调度、维持美国所有船舶运力，使国家战时防卫政策和国内外物资运输需求发展协调配合[6]。图 2-4 所示为美国海运委员会在第一次世界大战中（1917—1918 年）制作的宣传海报。

In order to defend against Germany's unrestricted submarine warfare in the North Atlantic and the Mediterranean since February of 1917, the Emergency Fleet Corporation (EFC) was established by the United States Shipping Board (USSB), sometimes referred to as the War Shipping Board, on 16 April 1917 pursuant to the *Shipping Act, 39 Stat. 729* to acquire, maintain, and operate merchant ships to meet national defense, foreign and domestic commerce during the Great War. Figure 2-4 is a poster for the United States Shipping Board and Emergency Fleet Cooperation during the Great War, 1917–1918.

美国参加第一次世界大战后，需要运送大量的军队和军事辎重到欧洲战场，但运输舰船严重不足。为此美国除采取武装商船、改装扣留的德国油轮等紧急措施外，还在 1917 年夏季拟定了建造 1 000 万载重吨远洋运输舰船的庞大造船计划。

After the United States entered the war, a huge quantity of troops and military supplies were needed to be transported to European continental, but transporting capability was obviously insufficient. In the summer of 1917, American Government even made an enormous newbuilding plan for a fleet with 10 million deadweight tons beside some emergency counter measures like armed merchant ships, conversion of detained German oil tankers, etc.

THE SHIPS ARE COMING
UNITED STATES SHIPPING BOARD ■ EMERGENCY FLEET CORPORATION

图 2-4　美国海运委员会在第一次世界大战中制作的宣传海报（1917—1918 年）
Figure 2-4　A poster for the USSB (1917–1918)

2.3

美国的目光转向远东造船
The Far East Shipbuilding Facilities Requisitioned by USA

尽管做出了巨大的努力，但美国自身和其盟友的造船能力仍满足不了他们巨大的需求。这些努力包括建造几十个新的造船厂和开发模块化船舶设计方法，这种"预制船舶"可以分段建造，并通过铁路运输到船坞进行组装后下水。但很快美国也需要向其他国家寻求帮助，比如一些远东国家，特别是日本和中国，以满足他们巨大的需求。

当时已经工业化的日本是一个合乎逻辑的选择。彼时日本的造船业已经相当成熟，而且在第一次世界大战中是英美的积极盟友。然而，日本缺乏自然资源，尤其是需要从国外进口钢铁。应急船队公司最初从日本购买了约 15 艘处于各个建造阶段的在建船，然后拟签合同约定再建造 30 艘或更多。这项协议附带的条件是美国提供日本急需的钢铁作为补偿的一部分。美国海运委员会在横滨设立了办事处，并配备了来自美国的造船方面的专家。

根据 1919 年 1 月 18 日的《航海公报》："美国航运委员会东方委员会和应急船队公司监督 8 家日本造船厂和上海的一家中国船厂建造用于组建一个钢质货轮船队的船舶。"这个委员会有特别委员约翰·A. 麦格雷戈、联合钢铁公司的前总裁、助理委员 J. 刘易斯·卢肯巴赫、卢肯巴赫轮船公司的老板 J. 刘易斯·卢肯巴赫的侄子，以及太平洋邮船公司的前秘书哈里·W. 迪恩斯。为他们工作的有几位造船专家，包括船体专家 M. A. 佩里、发动机专家克里斯托弗·C. 迈尔斯和设计师 J. W. 鲁斯特。

显而易见当时的中国并不是一个合适的选择。经过几个世纪的闭关锁国后，它只是一个新兴的共和国。中国最后一个封建王朝清朝 1912 年才灭亡。北洋政府对北京以外的地方几乎没有控制权，大部分农村地区被各地军阀控制。长江流域盗匪横行。美国在上海有一个相对较小但不断扩大的据点，美国海军和英国海军在长江上开展商业护航巡逻。

Despite a monumental effort to meet their demands, the United States was soon be operating at full capacity, as well as those of her allies. Efforts included the building of dozens of new shipyards and developing modular ship designs, called "fabricated ships" that could be built in sections and delivered by rail to dockyards for assembly and launching. Soon, America too needed to look elsewhere, to the Far East, specifically Japan and China, to supplement their enormous requirements.

Japan was a logical choice as they were already industrialized, already quite proficient at shipbuilding and were an active ally of England and America in the Great War. Japan lacked natural resources, however, especially steel which they imported largely from abroad. The EFC initially bought about 15 ships from Japan in various stages of completion, followed by contracts to build 30 ships and more. This agreement came with the condition that America provide their much needed steel as part of the compensation. The USSB set up offices in Yokohama and staffed it with American experts in their fields.

According to the January 18th, 1919 edition of *The Nautical Gazette*: "The Oriental Commission of the United States Shipping Board and Emergency Fleet Corporation to supervise the construction of a fleet of steel freighters at eight Japanese shipyards and ane Chinese shipyard at Shanghai." Leading the commission was special commissioner John A. MacGregor, former president of Union Iron Works, assistant commissioner J. Lewis Luckenbach, nephew of J.Lewis Luckenbach-owner of Luckenbach Steamship Co., and secretary Harry W. Deans, formerly with the Pacific Mail Steamship Company. Working for them were several shipbuilding experts including hull expert M.A. Perry, engine expert Christopher C. Miles, and Designer J.W. Rust.

China was not such an obvious choice. It was still emerging as a new republic, after centuries of isolation. China's last imperial dynasty, the Qing, had only ended in 1912. The Beiyang Government in Peking had little control outside of the capital, and much of the countryside was controlled by warlords. The Yangtze River basin was beset by bandits and pirates. America had a relatively small but growing foothold in Shanghai and the U.S. Navy, along with their British counterparts patrolled the Yangtze to protect commerce.

英国人自 19 世纪中叶以来已经在中国建立了相当成功的造船产业，主要是在香港和上海。然而他们的产量比较低。为什么英国人不自己在中国全面开展生产呢？问题的答案似乎是原材料，特别是钢铁的缺乏和不足。众所周知，中国拥有巨大的自然资源和商业潜力，但它们还尚待开发；当局政府也没有建立一个有效的运输系统（如铁路）将这些资源从内陆运到沿海。即使是宽阔的长江也无法在正常商业航运能力之外承受如此大的货运量。

英国人认为中国在造船方面可取的唯一优势是廉价劳动力。正如 1913 年 10 月 3 日英国月刊《工程师》在描述英商拥有的上海耶松船厂时所述："这些工作完全由中国工人在英国人的监督下完成。刚开始时中国工人觉得完成这项工作相当困难，但是管理层的耐心和毅力以及中国人的勤奋和才智造就出了一小批熟练的工人，他们的技能水平堪比欧洲的造船工匠。支付给这些熟练的工人的工资不到英国工人工资的三分之一。至此整个造船行业陷入困境。虽然原材料成本和管理费用比西方船厂的高，但是人工成本的差异仍可使中国船厂处于有利的竞争地位。"

事实上，在应急船队公司成立之前美国政府就已经涉足了中国的造船业。这主要是前文提到的与上海耶松船厂之间合作建造了一些各种类型的船舶。这些船主要在菲律宾营运。其中包括一艘 362 英尺（110.34 米）长、6 000 载重吨的单螺旋桨钢质运煤船"休伯特·L. 威格莫尔"号，以及一艘 300 英尺（91.44 米）长、排水量为 2 898 吨的双螺旋桨运输船"梅里特"号。江南造船所重新组装和舾装了长江浅水炮舰"莫诺卡西"号和"帕洛斯"号。这些长江浅水炮舰在美国加利福尼亚州瓦列霍的梅尔岛海军船厂进行建造，分解成总段后用船运到上海完成整船组装（因为长江浅水炮舰没有能力自航穿越太平洋）。中国的船厂还建造一些各种类型的小型船舶。

美国应急船队公司最初计划在战争期间从中国订购数十艘船只。根据为参加军备限制会议的美国代表团准备的有关太平洋和远东事务的文件（华盛顿，1921—1922 年，国务院出版物司。D 系列第 79 号，标注为"机密文件"，政府印刷局 1922 年 5 月 20 日出版发行）中的"XXV"节——美国加利福尼亚大学东方语言文学教授、远东事务司成员、远东事务部前部长

The British, for their part, had already established a fairly successful shipbuilding business of their own in China since the middle of the 19th century, mainly in Hong Kong and Shanghai. Production was fairly low, however, why the British simply didn't go into full production in China for themselves. The answer appears to have been raw materials, specifically steel and iron, and the lack thereof. China was known to have enormous natural resources and potential, but they had not yet been developed, nor was there an efficient transportation system (namely rail) set up to get that material from the interior to the coast. Even the mighty Yangtze River was not capable of handling that volume on top of normal commerce.

The only factor that made shipbuilding a viable option to the British in China was the advantage of inexpensive labour. As noted in the October 3rd, 1913 edition of the British monthly *The Engineer* when describing the British owned Shanghai Dock & Engineering Co. :"The work is done entirely by the Chinese under British supervision. There was considerable difficulty with labour at the commencement, but the patience and perseverance of the management, and the industry and aptitude of the Chinese, has resulted in a small group of skilled workmen whose work compares favourably with that of the European shipwright. The wages paid amount to less than a third of the rate of pay in England. It is on this point the whole industry hangs. Material and management were more expensive items than in a Western yard, but the difference in the cost of labour enabled the company to compete favourably. "

In fact, before the EFC came into existence, the United States Government dabbled in shipbuilding in China. This was mainly with the above mentioned Shanghai Dock & Engineering Co., who built a number of ships of various types mainly for the Philippines' waters. These included a 362 feet (110.34 meters) long, 6 000 deadweight tons, single screw steel collier, USAT "Hubert L. Wigmore"; a 300 feet (91.44 meters) long, displacement of 2 898 tons, twin-screw transport vessel, USAT "Merritt". Kiangnan did re-assembly and fitting out of the Yangtze River shallow water gunboats "Monocacy" and "Palos", which had been built at the Mare Island Naval Shipyard, Vallejo, California, then broken down as sections and shipped to Shanghai for completion (because the shallow water gunboats were not capable of crossing the Pacific on their own), and various other smaller crafts.

From China the American EFC initially had plans to contract dozens of ships as long as the war went on. According to papers relating to Pacific and Far Eastern Affairs prepared for the use of the American Delegation to the Conference on the Limitation of Armament, (Washington, 1921–1922, Department of State, Division of Publications. Series D, No. 79. Marked CONFIDENTIAL, Government Printing Office, printed and distributed 20 May 1922), in a section titled "XXV"—*China Builds Ships for the United States* written by Dr. E. T. Williams, professor of

E. T. 威廉斯博士撰写的《中国为美国造船》中有如下描述：

"美国对德国宣战后，美国政府立即大力推进造船以提供战争所必需的运输船队。1917 年 5 月 31 日（即应急船队公司成立一个月后），美国驻北京公使馆向美国驻华领事馆官员发出了一份机密的通函，询问有关各地区船厂设施的信息以及木船或其建材的资料。"

时任美国驻上海副总领事沃尔特·A. 亚当斯（Walter A. Adams）于 1917 年 6 月向美国政府提供了一份长达 8 页的详细报告，提到了目前上海共有 3 家有能力建造大型船舶的造船公司，分别如下：

（1）江南造船所；
（2）英商耶松船厂；
（3）英商瑞镕船厂。

3 家公司中的英商耶松船厂，据其经理称，该公司的经营"极其保守，自 1889 年以来没有建造过一艘大船"[7]。至于另一家英商瑞镕船厂则称，如果木材原料来源无虞，可造 6 艘木船。"局坞分家"后的江南造船所是一家官办企业，能造商船及军舰，当时是设备、设施齐全，具备造船能力。

这份报告详细分析了造船用的木材板材在大战爆发后价格飙升，柚木的价格却比战前便宜，但木料进口运输因大战时期十分困难，中国船厂难以保证能进口足够的木料来造船。报告中对于中国人勤快、学习效率高，又有木工技术赞誉有加。上海美孚公司的一名油轮主管就曾向亚当斯表示，在上海至少可以找到数百位能绘制轮船图的一流技术人员和熟练的木工[8]。

oriental languages and literature, University of California; member of the Conference Section of the Division of Far Eastern Affairs; formerly chief of the Division of Far Eastern Affairs:

"Immediately after the declaration of war against Germany by the United States, the American Government exerted itself most earnestly to encourage shipbuilding so as to provide the tonnage so indispensable to the prosecution of the war. On May 31, 1917 (a month after the Emergency Fleet Cooperation was formed), the American Legation at Peking sent to American Consular officers in China a confidential circular instruction asking information regarding shipyard facilities in their respective districts and materials available for the construction of wooden vessels or parts thereof. "

The American Deputy Consul Walter A. Adams in Shanghai submitted a detailed 8 pages report to American Government in June of 1917. This report mentioned that there are three shipyards with the capability to build large scale ships, i. e.,

(1) Kiangnan Dock & Engineering Works;
(2) Shanghai Dock & Engineering Co.;
(3) New Shanghai Shipbuilding & Engineering Works Ltd.

Among those three companies, the manager of the Shanghai Dock & Engineering Co. claimed "the operation of the company is ultra-conservative, never build any large ship since 1889". The New Shanghai Shipbuilding & Engineering Works Ltd. promised that they are able to build 6 sets of wooden ships if material can be supplied. Kiangnan Dock & Engineering Works was separated from Kiangnan Manufacturing Bureau. Kiangnan was a government operated enterprise, capable to build merchant ships and warships with perfect facilities. Kiangnan had available slots at that time.

This report analyzed in detail regarding the shipbuilding materials. Timber for shipbuilding purpose is extremely expensive after the war started, but teak price is cheaper than that before the war. Chinese shipyards have difficulty ensuring imported wooden materials as per requires. Chinese people have many excellent qualities, including their hard working nature, higher study efficiency, and well skilled carpenters, all of which are commended in this report. A tanker manager of Mobil Petroleum told Adams that Shanghai has at least hundreds naval architects and machinery engineers as well as skilled carpenters.

但美国驻上海副总领事亚当斯的这份报告不知何故竟被驻上海总领事忽略，并未马上送到美国国务院。江南造船所总稽查毛根于 1917 年 12 月 5 日向美国驻上海总领事自荐，表达该所对承造美国轮船的热切诚意，并陈述该所技术先进，足以承造大型轮船。毛根表示，江南造船所同时可以承造两艘 5 000 吨级或三艘 3 000 吨级的钢质船舶，中国工人足以承担这样的造船工作，而且保证建造质量优良。毛根说："如果美国政府需要 3 000 吨级的轮船，无疑江南造船所的工人可以打造出不输于世界任何一家船厂的一流船舶。"[9]毛根的这封自荐信连同前述美国驻上海副总领事的 8 页调查报告，到 1917 年 12 月 13 日才被总领事送交美国国务院[10]。

美国驻上海总领事托马斯·西蒙斯（Thomas Sammons）在转交给美国国务院关于《在上海造舰的可能性》的报告中，他推荐了江南造船所，认为江南造船所比起其他两家英国公司更适合与美国政府合作。西蒙斯在报告中陈述了他推荐江南造船所的理由：

"我在上海找到了一家伟大的现代化造船厂，由中国政府拥有和运营，但由于战争实际上切断了对中国的钢铁供应，因此该造船厂几乎无所事事。"

"该船厂名为江南造船所，拥有供中国政府海军专用的大型船坞。整个船厂由中国政府全资拥有并由海军独家控制。江南造船所成立于 1865 年。从 1905 年开始，由外资船厂的技术人员组成了核心团队，其中大部分来自苏格兰；船厂在造船大师毛根的领导下一直为中国政府服务。"

"船厂内有多个船台，每个船台都能建造出最现代化的大型钢质船舶，车间都配备了现代化的机械，并能够生产功率强大的船用发动机和所有船舶配件。这个船厂已经完成并交付了三百多艘船，全部工程都在这个船厂内完成。船厂内有一个设施完备的船坞，可以容纳长 544 英尺的船。"

But the report of Deputy Consul Adams was somehow ignored by American Consul General in Shanghai, and was not immediately submitted to State Department. Robert Buchanan Mauchan, Superintendent of Kiangnan Dock & Engineering Works, recommended himself to American Consul General for good faith of building American steamers. Mauchan emphasized Kiangnan has advanced technologies and capability for building large ships. Kiangnan can build two 5 000 tons or three 3 000 tons steel ships in parallel. Chinese workers are able to undertake these shipbuilding with good quality. Mauchan said: "Kiangnan has confidence to deliver first class ships comparing any shipyard in the world if American Government needs 3 000 tons class ship." Mauchan's cover letter together with the Deputy Consul's 8 pages report were thus submitted to American State Department by Consul General in Shanghai on 13 December 1917.

When Thomas Sammons, Consul General in Shanghai, submitted the report of *Shipbuilding Possibilities at Shanghai*, he recommended Kiangnan Dock & Engineering Works for cooperation with the United States Government rather than another two British-owned companies. Sammons stated his reasons for recommending Kiangnan in his report:

"I found a great modern shipbuilding facility at Shanghai, owned and operated by the Chinese Government, but near to idleness because the war had practically cut off the supply of iron and steel to China."

"The shipyard is known as the Kiangnan Dock & Engineering Works and includes the big naval dock exclusively for China Government. The entire works are wholly owned by the Chinese Government and are under the exclusive control of the navy. It was established in 1865. Since 1905, a technical team consisted of foreign staffs form other shipbuilders, most of them from Scotland and under the direction of R.B. Mauchan, a master ship constructor, took over the works and have been operating them ever since for the Chinese Government."

"There are several launching slipways in the shipyard, each capable of erecting large steel ships of the most modern type, and all workshops fully equipped with modern machinery and capable of producing powerful marine engines and all ship outfittings. The yard had delivered more than three hundred ships, all completed in this yard. There is a big dry dock capable of docking ships up to 544 feet in length."

但他又在报告中加上了个人观点，认为目前原料价格如此高昂，在中国造船要仰赖从美国进口木料和原料，如果造价是美国政府的主要参考因素，那么中国市场的廉价劳力和高昂的进口原料成本将两相抵消，这项交易并不划算；除非美国政府有意通过与江南造船所的合作来促进中美之间的友好关系[11]。

第一次世界大战期间，美国在海外的造船计划不仅是为了弥补其国内造船能力的不足，而且其原材料的管制和造舰需求均与国防外交联系在一起。美国选择中国船厂的初衷是为了解决战时美欧航线的运力不足才与中方有所接触的，孰料战时原材料价格一再上涨致使中方造船的劳动力成本优势荡然无存。美国政府最后同意在江南造船所建造运输舰的主要原因还是为了向中国表示友好，同时表明对中国和日本一视同仁。

But he also added his personnel view, that Chinese shipbuilding needs to import raw material and equipment from the United States, and lower labour cost will be compensated by higher cost of imported material and equipment. It is not worth to do this deal if American Government merely concerns the cost provided that American Government intentionally boost Sino-American relationship via this cooperation with Kiangnan.

During the Great War, American abroad shipbuilding plan did not only cover the shortage of domestic shipbuilding, but also relate the shipbuilding plan together with material export control to national defense and foreign affairs. Initially considering building ship in Chinese shipyard was exactly for mitigating insufficient tonnage in Atlantic routes, but increased material cost almost counteracted lower labour cost in Chinese shipyard. For sake of good relationship with China, American Government finally assigned the shipbuilding contracts of steam freighters to Kiangnan. This assignment also expressed that American Government gave fair treatment to both China and Japan.

2.4

造船合同签订始末
Whole Story of Signing Shipbuilding Contract

2.4.1

毛根代表江南赴美签约
Mauchan Was Dispatched to USA for Signing Contract

据北洋政府外交档案记载，1918 年 4 月 8 日，江南造船所所长刘冠南请示海军部将派总工程师毛根赴美与美国政府当面讨论造船合同事宜。海军部发给驻美公使顾维钧[12] 的电报如下：

美领事奉其政府来电，商嘱本所代造五千吨商轮多艘，并据美领事之意造船一事，往返电商殊难详尽，且虑迟延，不如由所总工程师毛根代祈与美政府商订承造较为便捷。[13]

受江南造船所所长刘冠南派遣，总工程师毛根于 1918 年 5 月 9 日启程赴美商谈建造万吨级运输舰事宜[14]。

1918 年 7 月初，美国海运委员会主席爱德华·N. 赫尔利请求国务院指示是否批准江南造船所建造运输舰的申请书，原因是其辖下的应急船队公司已收到江南造船所提出的在美国方面能供应所需造船钢材的前提下愿为美国政府建造数艘运输舰的申请书。

美国海运委员会表示，由于美国造船工业目前需要大量造船钢材和船用设备，美国海运委员会并不赞成在美国境外船厂建造运输舰，但是此造船合同是和中国政府的船厂增进相互关系的契机[15]。美国国务

According to diplomacy archives of Beiyang Government, on 8 April 1918, Liu Guannan, Director of Kiangnan Dock & Engineering Works, requested instruction of Naval Department to dispatch Chief Engineer Mauchan to the United States for face to face discussion of shipbuilding contracts. Naval Department of Beiyang Government sent telegraph to Gu Weijun (Vi Kyuin Wellington Koo), Minister Counselor of China in the United States:

American Consul sent a telegraph as per instruction of government that he is on behalf of American Government to express the intention for building several 5 000 tons cargo steam freighters in Kiangnan. Consul suggested to dispatch Chief Engineer Mauchan to the United States for face to face discussion of shipbuilding contracts of those steam freighters rather than communication via telegraph.

On 9 May 1918, Chief Engineer Mauchan was dispatched by Liu Guannan, Director of Kiangnan Dock & Engineering Works to the United States for discussion of shipbuilding contracts of those steam freighters.

At the beginning of July, 1918, Edward N. Hurley, Chairman of the United States Shipping Board, asked an instruction whether the State Department grants the application from Kiangnan Dock & Engineering Works for building American steam freighters, because EFC had received this application on the premise that the U.S. Government can supply the required steel materials to Kiangnan for building these steam freighters.

The United States Shipping Board considered that because the shipbuilding industry of the United States currently requires a large quantity of marine steel and equipment, the USSB does not intend to support the construction of steam freighters in the shipyards outside of

院很快批示："国务院出于政治立场方面的考虑，认为和江南造船所签订这份合同是件好事。"国务院还提及美国海运委员会目前和日本境内的船厂也有类似的合同。驻华领事的报告也显示江南造船所已经具备良好的造船设施和能力。国务院认为，"美国海运委员会应极尽可能利用此机会促成此合同的达成，并可以此为机促进中美友好关系的发展。同时借此可表明，美国在造船合同中无歧视中国之意，消除中方认为美方偏袒日本船厂的疑虑。"[16]

1918 年 7 月 13 日，美国海运委员会转请美国政府致电美国驻上海总领事："请告江南造船所，合同条款规定其可全力以赴"[17]。但美国海运委员会合同司经理莫里斯·D. 费里斯（Morris D. Ferris）显然有所顾虑，以密件的形式询问美国国务院远东司司长埃德华·T. 威廉斯（Edward T. Williams）："这份与中国签订的造船合同是否系特殊条约或外交文书（special treaty of diplomatic correspondence），国务院是否要在合同中加上特殊条款[18]？"远东司司长很快回复称："这份和中国造船厂签订的造船合同并非所谓特殊条约或外交文书，此合同由美国海运委员会代表、江南造船所毛根、大来公司代表罗斯·W. 史密斯 (Ross W. Smith) 于远东司洽谈，远东司衷心乐见此圆满的结果[19]。在这件事中美国政府扮演了一个中间协调人的角色，不仅让中美企业作为双边合作的主人发挥主导作用，且能以促成此合同展现中美邦交之好。"

纽约《布鲁克林鹰报》次日引用华府（美国政府）的善意说辞称："中国成为以造船来协助美国击溃德国的国家成员，此合同是大战以来中美关系发展最受瞩目的成果之一，中国也通过此事展现了中国试图发挥参战国一员的作用[20]。"

此后合同谈判进展顺利，7 月 25 日签订正式合同十七款（应急船队公司的合同编号为 399，共 18 页）。按照合同约定，建造材料由美国海运委员会协助购买，江南造船所按美国政府拟之价给付，限自每艘船的材料到齐上海后 6 个月内建造完工。合同规定建造载重量为 10 000 吨的运输舰 4 艘，每艘定价为 1 950 000 美元，共计 7 800 000 美元，分七期支付。第一期之款限于合同签字后 15 日内支付，余款随建

the United States. But such shipbuilding contract is an opportunity to really improve relationships with Chinese shipyards with government background. The State Department immediately responded and instructed: "The State Department, for political standpoint, considers these contracts with Kiangnan to be a positive thing." The State Department also mentioned that the United States Shipping Board currently had similar contracts with shipyards in Japan. The consular report in China also showed that Kiangnan has professional shipbuilding facilities and capabilities. The State Department believed that "the United States Shipping Board should make every possible use of this opportunity to facilitate the conclusion of these contracts, and could utilize them as an opportunity to promote friendly relationships between China and the United States. Meanwhile, it could be shown that the United States did not discriminate against China in shipbuilding contracts, and dispel doubts that the Chinese side was biased in favour of Japanese shipyards."

The United States Shipping Board requested the government to call the U.S. Consul General in Shanghai, on 13 July 1918, to "inform Kiangnan that the contract is concluded to take up full capacity of their works". But Morris D. Ferris (Manager, Contract Division of the United States Shipping Board) seems to worry about something. He inquired Edward T. Williams (Chief of Division of the Far Eastern Affairs) in a confidential document: "Does this contract mean a special treaty of diplomatic correspondence?" Division of the Far Eastern Affairs responded: "This shipbuilding contract signed with Chinese shipyard does not mean any special treaty of diplomatic correspondence. This contract will be settled by the representatives of the United States Shipping Board, Mr. Mauchan of Kiangnan Dock & Engineering Works as well as Mr. Ross W. Smith of Robert Dollar Company after negotiation at the Far Eastern Affairs. The Far Eastern Affairs felt happy to see this so perfect conclusion. Government just played as role of 'broker', the China and American companies are leading roles in bilateral cooperation, and such cooperation can promote diplomatic relationship between China and the United States."

"China has become a member of the country that helped defeat Germany by building ships, and this contract is one of the most high-profile achievements of Sino-American relations since the Great War," *Brooklyn Daily Eagle*, New York, quoted the remark of Washington official in the next day. "China has also demonstrated through this incident that it is trying to play its role as a member country of the Allies."

Since then, the contract negotiations had been proceeded smoothly, and on July 25th, the final shipbuilding contract (EFC Contract Number: 399, 18 pages in total) containing 17 articles was signed. As terms mutually agreed in contract, the materials would be purchased with the assistance of the United States Shipping Board, and Kiangnan would pay at the unit price set by the United States Government. The ship would be completed within six months after the material arrived in Shanghai. The contract specified to construct of four steam freighters with a cargo loading capacity of 10 000 tons, each priced at $1 950 000, and four vessels for a total of $7 800 000. The payment would be further divided

造进行情形续付，至船抵美时付讫。合同中第十七款"附加船舶的选择权"提到选择船事宜，即在未来两年内船东可指派合同方通过代理人续订造多至 8 艘船。值得注意的是大来公司为合同方所任命之代理人和收款方，付款支票将寄给大来公司[21]。也就是说，这份合同虽是订购 4 艘船，但日后总数有可能增加至12 艘，为未来合作预留了更大的空间。合同签订后，美国海运委员会主席赫尔利发来贺电，对中国造船工业的进步表示祝贺，并将此合同视为中国与协约国一致共同对抗敌对国家的努力，使中美传统友谊更加坚固[22]。

8 月 4 日，在北洋政府海军部给顾维钧公使的电报中，除了对顾维钧促成此事之功表示感谢外，更进一步希望毛根设法让福州船政局[23]也能接到美国的订单。顾维钧收文后批示："约毛工程师来见"，但毛根是否与其相见，因相关资料不足后续结果不得而知。从海军部的这份电报可知，中国政府希望美方能够继续向中国船厂订造船舶，不仅仅是江南造船所，福州船政局亦能胜任，希望借此扩大中国造船业在美国市场的份额。

电报原文如下：

"闻美国政府续造运船尚多，此次工程福州船政局亦能胜任，际此德奥战事方殷，我国既加入参战，凡有应监义务之处自当黾勉为之，仍请贵使鼎力赞助，向美航务部总理[24]一陈，或密饬工程师毛根设法再为招徕分归福州船政局承造，俾我国各厂均有发达[25]。"

顾维钧在其回忆录中并未提到经办江南造船所之事，但他在给中国外交部陈述这个合同之所以奏捷居功不讳。

电报原文如下：

"查该工程师抵美京后，即由钧与之晤谈，并代向美船务局[26]吹嘘，该局初尚有犹豫，嗣经向美外部示意，大致谓美拟助华各举多成画饼，未免可惜，

into seven installments. The first instalment would be paid within 15 days after the signing of the contract, and remain installments would be paid as per construction progress. The final installment would be paid upon arrival in the United States. Article 17 "Option for Additional Vessels" of the contract referred to option ships, i.e., the United States Shipping Board as ship owner might declare to build up to eight ships through broker over the next two years. The Robert Dollar Company was the agent (broker) and payee appointed by the Shipping Board, and the payment check would be sent to the Robert Dollar Company. That means that four firm ships in this contract could be possibly increased to twelve in the future. It remained more room for future cooperation. After the signing of the contract, Hurley, the Chairman of the United States Shipping Board, sent a congratulatory message for congratulating China's shipbuilding industry on its progress, and the contract could be considered as China's efforts to join forces with the allies against hostile countries. The traditional Sino-American friendship would be further reinforced.

On August 4, the Naval Department of Beiyang Government sent a telegraph to Vi Kyuin Wellington Koo, Minster Counselor of China. In this telegraph, besides expressed their gratitude for securing this shipbuilding contract, the Naval Department further expected that Mauchan tried efforts to get more orders from the United States for Foochow Arsenal. Mr. Koo commented "Please make an appointment to Mr. Mauchan" after he received telegraph. But related information is insufficient to confirm whether this meeting was realized or not. From this telegraph of the Naval Department, Beiyang Government, in order to enlarge the share of Chinese shipbuilding industry on American market, was willing to get more orders for Chinese shipyards, not only Kiangnan Dock & Engineering Works but also Foochow Arsenal.

Original massage of telegraph as follows:

"We got some information, said American Government may need to build transportation ships. Such ships can be also built by Foochow Arsenal. Since our country has already jointed the war, we should take responsibility to support allied nations. Please approach the Chairman of the United States Shipping Board, or communicate with Mr. Mauchan to discuss the possibility for building more ships in Foochow Arsenal. It can promote our shipyards to develop further. "

Vi Kyuin Wellington Koo did not mention his efforts to secure Kiangnan's shipbuilding contract in his memoirs, but he emphasized his contribution to make this success deal in the telegraph to the Ministry of the Foreign Affairs of Chinese government.

Original massage of telegraph as follows:

"I had a meeting with Mr. Mauchan after he arrived in Washington, and persuaded the United States Shipping Board to put the order in Kiangnan. Initially they quite hesitated for this deal, but later they were instructed by the Foreign Ministry of the United States. Considering

此次江南造船所特派工程师代表来美商订承造船只事宜系看重贵国领事转商托造之意，亦即中美两国彼此表示邦交敦笃之机，深望该工程师能不虚此行云云，并将此意设法间接上达白宫，钧颇动容，故旋饬船务局与毛根商订合同于本月二十五日签字该合同[27]。"

former many Assistance Programs did not be finally implemented, but this time, Kiangnan delegated their representative to the United States for negotiating newbuilding. It really concerned good faith of Chinese Minster Counselor. With the opportunity of diplomatic relationship made between China and the United States, they expressed their sincere wish that Mr. Mauchan does will not make this trip in vain. They then reported their clear intention to the White House. I was so touched by their efforts, then pushed the United States Shipping Board to sign the contract with Mr. Mauchan on 25th of this month. "

江南造船所这个案例为民国初美国协助中国实业的少数成功案例。造船合同条款中的付款方式亦格外通融，以免江南造船所筹款垫支为难。顾维钧的电报中也说明了美国官方内部文献提到的美国海运委员会正与日本洽谈订造船只事宜，而江南造船所取得的平均价格亦比美国向日本订造之船每吨多 30 美元，此外，待这批船只造好时，"如空船来美时，准其装货，更系暗中贴补美政府我感情本佳"。顾维钧认为这次优惠的合同确系展现了美国有意联络和发展中美之间的友好情谊[28]。

作者曾尝试寻找这份造船合同和其他文字技术资料，但目前在江南造船集团档案馆和原第六机械工业部七六所（现为船舶档案馆，位于陕西省兴平市）保存的江南造船所建造的四艘万吨级运输舰（船体号：H317~H320）的图纸资料中[29]已经无法找到任何相关文字资料。也许当初毛根等英国人离开时将文字性的原稿带走了？也许原件被江南造船所的职员收藏了？再也许是此类档案在几经辗转的过程中丢失了？关于这个问题的答案，目前还不得而知。

This case was one of the few successful cases which the United States aided Chinese industries during initial period of the Republic of China. The payment terms specified in the contract were quite fair. Kiangnan Dock & Engineering Works was not required to prepare additional fund during execution of the contract. Mr. Koo's telegraph further mentioned, as per American internal document, the United States Shipping Board was also negotiating with Japanese shipbuilders for newbuildings. The unit price in Kiangnan's contract was 30 U.S. dollars per ton, which was more than Japanese contracts on par. In addition, the United States Shipping Board kindly allowed these steam freighters to load the cargo in maiden voyage for the United States. Mr. Koo thought these favourable terms really expressed Government of the United States intentionally improving relationship between countries.

But it is a pity that no literal materials, such as shipbuilding contracts, specifications and calculation sheets etc., regarding those four steam freighters (hull number: H317–H320), were found in both Archives Institute of Jiangnan Shipyard Group and former No.76 Institute National Sixth Department of Machinery Industry (The Archives of CSSC, in Xingping, Shaanxi Province). Probably, these documents might be carried away by Mr. Mauchan when he left Kiangnan? Might be become private collection of former Kiangnan's staffs? Might be lost during relocation of those archives? The answer to this question remains unknown at present.

2.4.2

美国国家档案馆中的新发现
New Discoveries in the National Archives of the United States

作者在中文版《揭秘中国第一批万吨轮》的撰写初期（2017 年 6 月），曾经在网络上查询到美国国家档案馆（National Archives of the United States）保存了有关江南造船所的卷宗 RG32。RG32 卷宗中包括以下四个部分：

(1) 1919—1921 年日本和中国特别代表的记录；

(2) 1918—1921 年的（船舶建造）合同；

(3) 1919—1922 年日本和中国所建造船舶的统计表；

(4) 1919—1934 年日本建造船舶的图纸。

RG32 卷宗的前三部分保存在美国国家档案馆（华盛顿）（见图 2-5）。第四部分主要是船舶的图纸，虽然标注的是"1919—1934 年日本建造船舶的图纸"，但包括了江南造船所建造的"官府"号系列四艘万吨轮的图纸。此部分图纸现存于马里兰大学帕克分校[30]。

During initial period (about June 2017) of when I wrote the Chinese version titled *Mandarin Series and Their Entire Lives*, I checked the website of the National Archives of the United States, the archive file box RG32 (Record Group 32) contains some material and documentation regarding Kiangnan Dock & Engineering Works. RG32 includes the following four series:

(1) Records of the special representative in Japan and China, 1919–1921;

(2) Contracts, 1918–1921;

(3) Statistical tables relating to Japanese and Chinese-built vessels, 1919–1922;

(4) Plans of Japanese-built ships, 1919–1934.

The first to third series of RG32 are collected in the National Archives in Washington D.C. (700 Pennsylvania Avenue, NW, Washington, D.C. 20408-0001) (see Figure 2–5). The fourth series of RG32 is titled "Plans of Japanese-built ships, 1919–1934", but the drawings of Kiangnan Dock & Engineering Works built SS "Mandarin" quartet are integrated. This drawings are stored in University of Maryland，College Park.

图 2-5　美国国家档案馆（华盛顿）[31]
Figure 2-5　The National Archives in Washington, D.C.

2022 年 4 月，作者在美国的一位中学同学在前往华盛顿特区的途中参观了美国国家档案馆，由于事先不知道档案馆的预约流程，因此当天他无法进入档案馆的图书馆。但他在档案馆发现了一些索引，为作者完成进一步的资料搜索奠定了基础。

2023 年 10 月，作者的一位大学校友的孩子（陈语霆）在美国芝加哥大学社会学系读博士，他对民国时期的工业史和造船业的发展很感兴趣。当他得知作者想找到这些材料时，不仅热心地帮助作者在网上查找资料，而且还专程前往华盛顿特区的美国国家档案馆查找纸质实物档案。美国国家档案馆的接待大厅如图 2-6 所示。

In April 2022, a middle school classmate of mine in the United States visited the National Archives of the United States while traveling to Washington, D.C., but was unable to enter the library because he did not know the reservation process of the archives in advance. Nevertheless he found some indexes for further searches.

In October 2023, my alumni of university, his son (Yuting Chen) studying in the University of Chicago Department of Sociology as PhD student, is interested in the history of industry and the development of the shipbuilding industry during the Republic of China. When he learned that I would like to find these materials, not only was he enthusiastic about helping me find materials online, but also made a trip to the National Archives in Washington, D.C. to find paper archives. Figure 2-6 shows the reception hall of the National Archives in Washington, D.C.

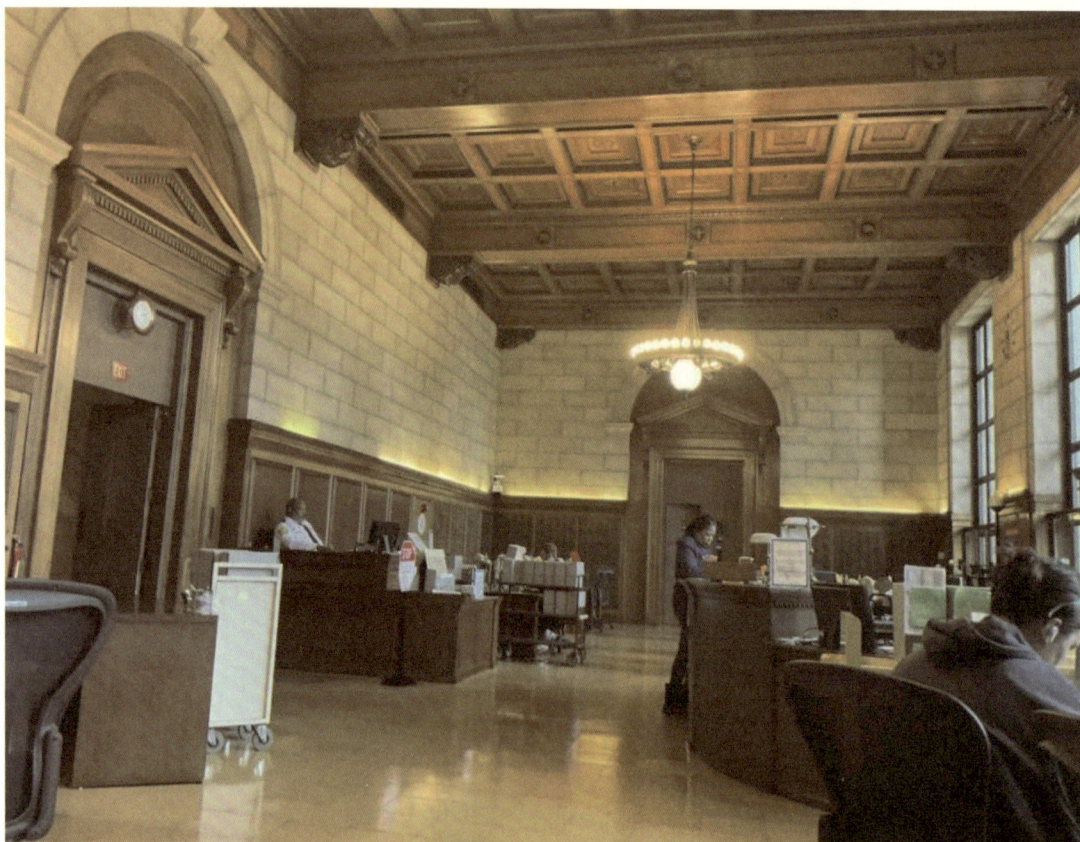

图 2-6　美国国家档案馆的接待大厅 [32]
Figure 2-6　The reception hall of the National Archives in Washington, D.C.

陈语霆查到了 RG32 卷宗中记录美国海运委员会 1914 年到 1938 年的以下相关内容：

Yuting Chen found the box of RG32. The box of RG32 recorded the United States Shipping Board's activities from 1914 to 1938 includes the following details:

RG32 卷宗的索引中还提到：

"应急船队公司于 1918 年 4 月从日本承包商那里购买了 15 艘船，并于当年 5 月与 13 家日本造船公司签订了在日本造船厂建造 30 艘船的合同。部分付款将用钢材支付。已经建造或正在建造的船舶的合同要求每载重吨船舶向日本船厂支付一吨钢材；未建造的船舶合同要求每两载重吨支付一吨钢材。1918 年 7 月，在上海与一家中国造船公司签订了建造 4 艘钢制船舶的类似合同。"

It is also mentioned in the index of RG32:

"The Emergency Fleet Corporation purchased 15 vessels from Japanese contractors in April 1918 and in May of that year signed contracts with 13 Japanese shipbuilding companies for the construction of 30 vessels in Japanese shipyards. Partial payment was to be made with steel. The contracts for vessels already built or in process of construction called for the release to Japan of one ton of steel for every dead-weight ton of ship; contracts for vessels to be built required the release of one ton of steel for every two dead-weight tons of ship. A similar contract for four steel vessels was signed with a Chinese shipbuilding company in Shanghai in July 1918."

可以确认这 4 艘钢制船就是江南造船所建造的"官府"系列万吨轮。

2024 年 1 月，陈语霆在美国国家档案馆内再次找到了 RG32 卷宗，其中的船舶建造合同和船舶规格书对进一步厘清船舶合同的条款细节、设计来源、大来公司的代理情况、材料采购等有重要意义。

美国国家档案馆中保存的船舶建造合同有两份，合同编号是 399。一份合同与日本船厂建造的 30 艘船的合同装订在一起（合同编号为 344~373，见图 2-7）。江南造船所的 399 号合同的正文共 11 页 17 部分。另一份合同上备注了"新版"，但比较下来两者在文字和格式上没有差异。

It can be confirmed that these four steel hulled ships should be the SS "Mandarin" series of 10 000-ton steam freighters built by Kiangnan Dock & Engineering Works.

In January 2024, Mr. Chen found the RG32 file in the National Archives of the United States, in which the ship construction contract and ship specification are of great research value for further clarifying the terms of shipbuilding contracts, the source of the ship design, the agency of Robert Dollar Company, and the procurement of materials.

There are two copies of shipbuilding contract preserved in the National Archives of the United States, and the contract number is 399. One copy of Kiangnan's contract was for the binding of 30 shipbuilding contracts built by Japanese shipyards (contract numbers 344−373, see Figure 2−7). The contract No. 399 for Kiangnan Dock & Engineering Works includes 11 pages with 17 articles in total. Another copy identified "New", but there is no difference in text and formatting in comparison.

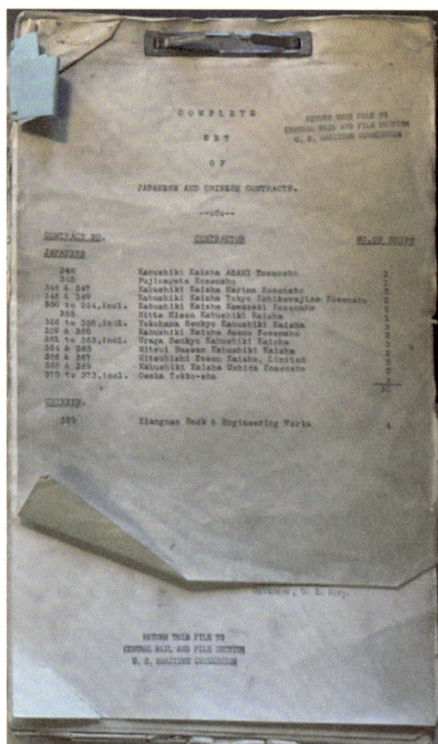

图 2-7　日本船厂和江南造船所造船合同的合订本
Figure 2−7　The bound volume of shipbuilding contracts for Japanese shipyards and Kiangnan Dock & Engineering Works

造船合同的首页注明了合同的签订日期为 1918 年 7 月 10 日，同时也备注了江南造船所是中华民国海军部下属的官办机构。

The first page of the shipbuilding contract states that the contract was signed on 10 July 1918, and that Kiangnan Dock & Engineering Works was "a commercial institution subject to exercise of control by Minister of Navy of the Republic of China".

造船合同的第二部分定义了船价，现代造船合同通常是约定船舶的总价，而本造船合同约定的是船舶完工时每载重吨的单价（195 美元 / 载重吨）。为方便计算分期付款，合同中建造船舶以载重吨 10 000 吨为假定数，即每船总价为 195 万美元。付款一共分为七期：

(1) 在合同签订 15 天内支付每船总价的 15%；
(2) 船体敷设龙骨时支付每船总价的 15%；
(3) 船体安装肋骨时支付每船总价的 15%；
(4) 船体安装外板时支付每船总价的 15%；
(5) 船舶下水并准备安装主机和锅炉时支付每船总价的 15%；
(6) 船舶完成试航并被船东有条件接收时支付每船总价的 15%；
(7) 船舶验收通过时支付剩余的尾款。船东有权保留 25 000 美元的保证金直至船舶完全被船东接收。

造船合同的第十六部分指定了位于加利福尼亚州旧金山的大来公司作为合同方（江南造船所）的代理收款人，如图 2-8 所示。

Article II of the shipbuilding contract defines the price of the ship, which is usually agreed upon in a modern shipbuilding contract as the total price of the vessel, while this shipbuilding contract stipulates the unit price per DWT of the ship at completion ($195/DWT). To facilitate the calculation of instalments, a total price of $1.95 million per vessel is assumed to be 10 000 DWT. The payment was further divided into seven instalments:

(1) 15% of total contract price of each vessel in 15 days of the contract signed;
(2) 15% of total contract price of each vessel when the keel plates thereof are laid;
(3) 15% of total contract price of each vessel when the same is in frames;
(4) 15% of total contract price of each vessel when the same is plated;
(5) 15% of total contract price of each vessel when the same is launched and the engine and boilers for same are ready for installation;
(6) 15% of total contract price of each vessel when a satisfactory trial trip for said vessel is had and said vessel is conditionally accepted;
(7) Balance due to each vessel under this contract upon the delivery and final acceptance of said vessel. Owner reserves the right to retain $25 000 until all of said vessels are finally accepted.

Article XVI of the shipbuilding contract designated the Robert Dollar Company, located in San Francisco, California, as the authorized agent for the contractor (Kiangnan Dock & Engineering Works). See Figure 2-8.

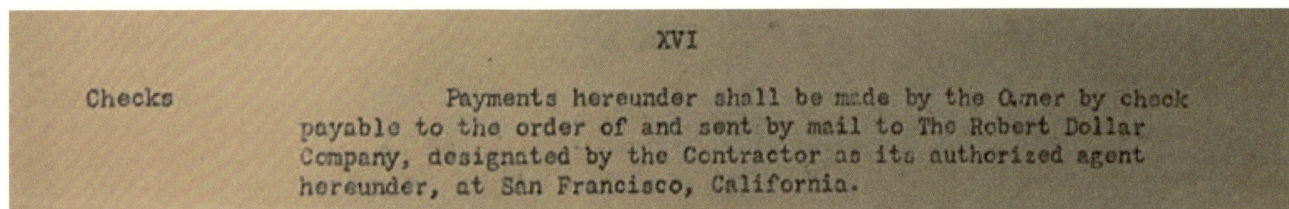

图 2-8　造船合同的第十六部分
Figure 2-8　Article XVI of the shipbuilding contract

造船合同的最后一页（第 11 页，见图 2-9）有民国政府驻美国公使顾维钧代表民国政府对毛根的签字和合同执行的授权（签名和盖章）、美国海运委员会秘书斯蒂芬·博尔内（Stephen Bourne）作为见证人（attest）的签字、江南造船所代表毛根的签字、美国海运委员会和应急船队公司主席爱德华·N. 赫尔利的签字、见证人（witness）约翰·E. 巴伯（John E. Barber）的签字[33]。

The last page of the shipbuilding contract (page 11, see Figure 2-9) shows the signature of the Minister of the Republic of China in the United States by Vi Kyuin Wellington Koo (signed and sealed) on behalf of the Government of the Republic of China to R. B. Mauchan and the authorization of the execution of the contract, the signature of Stephen Bourne, Secretary of the United States Shipping Board, as an attest, the signature of the Kiangnan Dock & Engineering Works on behalf of Mauchan, the signature of Edward N. Hurley, the Chairman of the United States Shipping Board and the Emergency Fleet Corporation, and the signature of John E. Barber, as the witness.

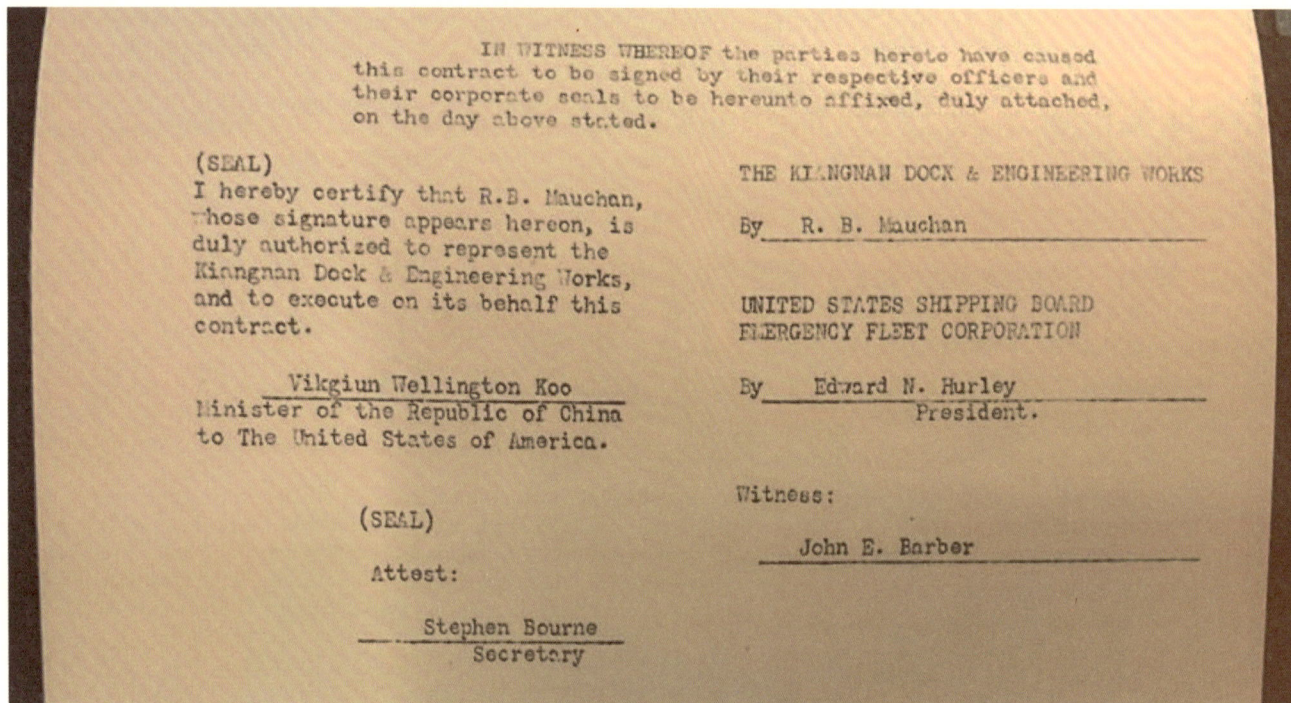

IN WITNESS WHEREOF the parties hereto have caused this contract to be signed by their respective officers and their corporate seals to be hereunto affixed, duly attached, on the day above stated.

(SEAL)
I hereby certify that R.B. Mauchan, whose signature appears hereon, is duly authorized to represent the Kiangnan Dock & Engineering Works, and to execute on its behalf this contract.

Vikgiun Wellington Koo
Minister of the Republic of China to The United States of America.

(SEAL)

Attest:

_____Stephen Bourne_____
Secretary

THE KIANGNAN DOCK & ENGINEERING WORKS

By _____R. B. Mauchan_____

UNITED STATES SHIPPING BOARD EMERGENCY FLEET CORPORATION

By _____Edward N. Hurley_____
President.

Witness:

_____John E. Barber_____

图 2-9　造船合同的最后一页（第 11 页）
Figure 2-9　The last page of the shipbuilding contract (page 11)

顾维钧在合同上的授权词如下：

"我特此证明，毛根（其签名出现在此处）被正式授权代表江南造船所，并代表该所执行本合同。"

在同一个文件夹中，还包含了一份美国海运委员会和应急船队公司副主席霍华德·孔利（Howard Coonley）写给爱德华·N. 赫尔利主席的信件，作为合同的附件、附件 B：船体钢材清单及一个关于战时人员和武备配置的附件。

合同的附件——霍华德·孔利副主席写给赫尔利主席的信件（见图 2-10）。

Vi Kyuin Wellington Koo's authorization in the contract are as follows:

"I hereby certify that R. B. Mauchan, whose signature appears hereon, is duly authorized to represent the Kiangnan Dock & Engineering Works, and to execute on its behalf this contract."

Also included in the same folder is a letter from Howard Coonley, Vice President of the USSB and EFC, to Chairman Edward N. Hurley as a supplement to the contract No.399 S. C., Schedule and Schedule B: List of hull steel material and addenda regarding military and guards requirement of wartime.

Supplement to the contract — A letter from Howard Coonley to Chairman Hurley, refer to Figure 2-10.

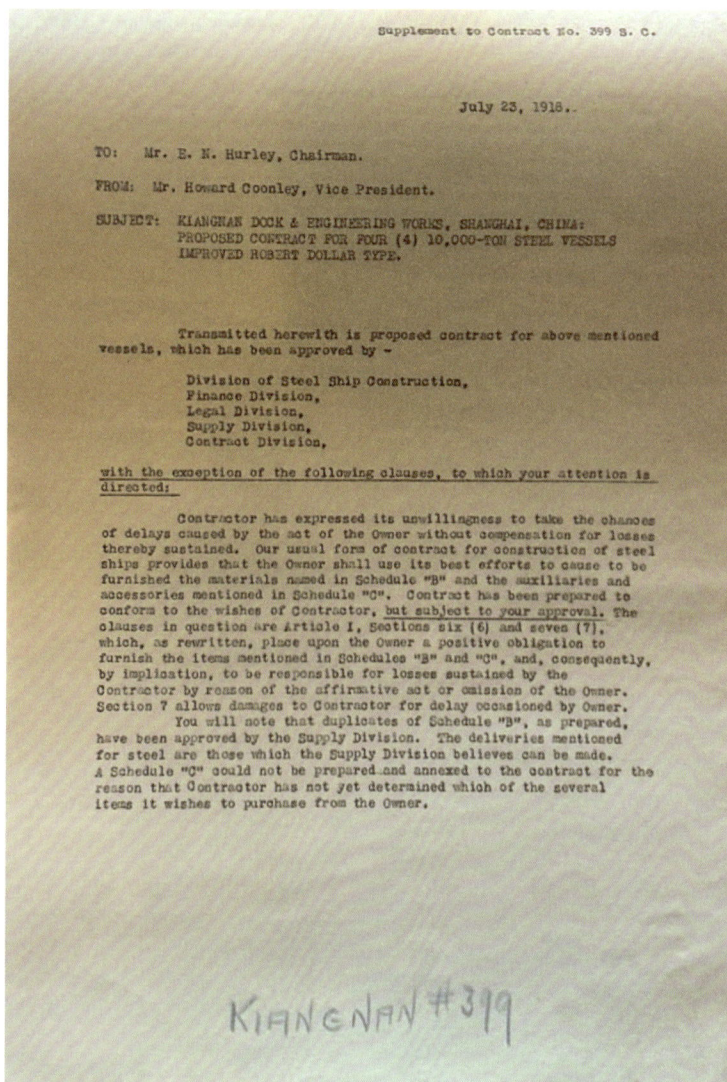

图 2-10　霍华德·孔利副主席写给赫尔利主席的信件
Figure 2-10　A letter from Vice President Howard Coonley to Chairman Hurley

这封信的落款日期是 1918 年 7 月 23 日，比合同上注明的合同签订日期差不多晚了两个星期。此信件主要报告以下几件事项。

(1) 四艘万吨轮的合同文本已经得到钢制船舶建造、财务、法务、供应和合同五个部门的认可。

(2) 但在因船东提供的材料和设备引起的脱期条款双方有争议时，提请赫尔利主席最后决策。

The letter is dated 23 July 1918, almost two weeks after the date of the contract as indicated on the contract. This letter mainly reports the following issues.

(1) The proposed text of the contract for captioned four vessels has been approved by the five departments of steel ship construction, finance, legal, supply and contract.

(2) However, there was a dispute between the two parties about the terms of the delays caused by the owner's provision of materials and equipment, and it was subjected to Chairman Hurley for final decision.

（3）合同方（船厂）表示不承担出于船东方面的原因而引起的脱期和造成的相关损失。

（4）通常我们（应急船队公司）标准格式的钢质船舶合同规定，船东应尽最大努力提供附件 B 中提到的材料以及附件 C 中提到的辅助设备和配件。

（5）合同的准备符合船厂的意愿，但须经您（赫尔利主席）的批准。有问题的条款是第一款，第 6 段和第 7 段，经重写后，船东有义务提供附件 B 和附件 C 中提到的物品。因此，这意味着船东将对船厂因船东的作为或不作为而遭受的损失负责。

值得注意的是这封信的标题：

江南造船所，中国上海：
四艘 10 000 吨钢质船舶的建造合同的建议
罗伯特·大来船型的改进型

在信件的标题中注明的四艘万吨轮是"罗伯特·大来船型的改进型"，但并没有注明是哪一型船。作者推断是"EFC Design 1013"，所谓的改进主要是增加了遮蔽甲板。参见本书第 5 章。

合同档案中包括一份材料清单（附件 C），但这份清单和应急船队公司的标准设备材料清单是不同的，清单中只列出了钢材材料。

在上述材料清单中，列出了每艘船详细的材料明细。钢板 3 250 吨、型材 1 075 吨、扁钢和圆钢 160 吨以及铆钉 200 吨，第一批 2 000 吨钢板和 500 吨型材的交付日期为 1918 年 11 月 10 日。在合同中还提到，首制船将于材料运抵船厂后 6 个月交付。

(3) The contractor (shipyard) expressed its unwillingness to take the responsibilities of delays caused by act of the owner without compensation for losses and thereby sustained.

(4) Our (EFC's) usual form of contract for construction steel ship provides that the owner shall use its best efforts to cause to be furnished the materials named in Schedule B and the auxiliaries and accessories mentioned in Schedule C.

(5) Contract has been prepared to conform to the wishes of contractor, but subject to your (Chairman Hurley) approval. The clauses in question are Article I, Section 6 and Section 7, which, as rewritten, place upon the owner a positive obligation to furnish the items mentioned in Schedules B and C, and, consequently, by implication, to be responsible for losses sustained by the contractor by reason of affirmative act or omission of the owner.

Notable is the title of this letter:

KIANGNAN DOCK & ENGINEERING WORKS, SHANGHAI, CHINA:
PROPOSED CONTRACT FOR FOUR (4) 10 000-TON STEEL VESSELS
IMPROVED ROBERT DOLLAR TYPE

In the title of the letter, clearly indicated that four (4) 10 000-ton steel vessels were "IMPROVED ROBERT DOLLAR TYPE", but they were not specified which type they were. "EFC Design 1013" might be a prototype. The so-called improvements are mainly the addition of a sheltered deck. See also Chapter 5 of this book.

There is a material list (Schedule C) together with the contract in the file box, but this schedule has deviation with the standard formatted Schedule C of EFC. Only quantity and delivery of steel material were listed.

In the above-mentioned material list, a detailed material breakdown for each vessel is listed. 3 250 tons of steel plates, 1 075 tons of shapes, 160 tons of flat and round bars, and 200 tons of rivets, the first batch of 2 000 tons of steel plates and 500 tons of shapes was scheduled to be delivered on 10 November 1918. It was also mentioned in the contract that the first ship would be delivered six months after the materials arrived at the shipyard.

合同档案中还包括一份附录，列出了适用于战时的特殊要求，包括船上配置的 24 个武装警卫和相关的舱室设施、火炮平台和瞭望台、火炮基座、常备弹药箱盒的弹药库、备用救生设备、通信设备和战时涂装要求等。

由于到了 1918 年 11 月，战争结束了，美国不再需要大量的运输船。合同中规定的材料未能如期运抵江南造船所。战时配置在后续船舶设计建造过程中也没有实施。

The contract also includes an addenda listing the special requirements applicable in wartime, including the 24 armed guards on board and associated cabin facilities, gun platforms with look-out station, gun foundations, ready service ammunition boxes and magazines, additional life-saving equipment, communications equipment and wartime painting requirements.

Since by November 1918, the war was over, and a large number of transport ships were no longer needed. The materials specified in the contract did not arrive at Kiangnan Dock & Engineering Works as scheduled. The wartime configuration was also not implemented during the subsequent ship design and construction.

2.5

造船合同的技术附件
Technical Attachments of Shipbuilding Contract

通常造船合同是带有技术附件（Technical Attachments）的，如船舶建造规格书（Shipbuilding Specification）、总布置图（General Arrangement Plan）、舯横剖面图（Midship Section）和主要设备厂商表（Maker List），这些技术附件的主要用途如下：

♦ 定义船舶的主要参数、性能；

♦ 定义船体主要结构尺寸；

♦ 定义船上设备配置规格；

♦ 定义技术和建造标准；

♦ 定义主要材料设备的供应商。

对于江南造船所的造船合同的技术附件，作者认为主要设备厂商表未必有，一是因为当年的主要设备材料都由应急船队公司指定，且当时全球处于材料和设备的短缺时期，采购到什么设备就用什么设备；二是很可能这些设备材料的规格直接定义在船舶建造规格书里而不作为单独的文件。

作者在查阅原第六机械工业部七六所（现为船舶档案馆，位于陕西省兴平市）保存的江南造船所建造的四艘万吨级运输舰（船体号：H317~H320）的图纸资料时，发现了三张最重要的图纸：总布置图和舯横剖面图。图 2-11 和图 2-12 的右下角有美国海运委员会秘书斯蒂芬·博尔内和江南造船所总工程师毛根两人的签名（标注日期为 1918 年 7 月 18 日），这两张图应该是造船合同的技术附件。图上的主尺度 [除了两柱间距离短了 4 英尺（1.22 米）之外] 和最后完工船舶的主尺度是完全一致的。另外还有一张修改过并重新绘制的总布置图（标注日期为 1918 年 8 月 8 日），与图 2-11 所示的 1918 年 7 月 18 日的总布置图相比，不仅图面描述更加详细，而且把一些结构的细节删除了，并增加了舯横剖面的尺寸定义。此外，图面上还有美国海运委员会秘书博尔内提的修改意见，

Normally, shipbuilding contract always has Technical Attachments, such as Shipbuilding Specification, General Arrangement Plan, Midship Section and Maker List. The purposes of these Technical Attachments are to:

♦ Define main particulars and performance of ship;

♦ Define scantling of major structural members;

♦ Define the specification of onboard equipments;

♦ Define technical and construction standards;

♦ Define maker or supplier of main material and equipment.

Regarding the Technical Attachments of shipbuilding contract for Kiangnan built steam freighters, it can be deduced Maker List might not exist, because main equipments and materials were directly selected by Emergency Fleet Cooperation. The shortage of supply was quite normal at wartime. Such procurement really depended on availability. Further the particulars of equipment might be directly specified in Shipbuilding Specification but not individual document.

Three most important drawings, General Arrangement Plan, Midship Section and revised General Arrangement Plan, were found in the documents of Kiangnan built four steam freighters which are stored in former No.76 Institute National Sixth Department of Machinery Industry (The Archives of CSSC, in Xingping, Shaanxi Province). Stephen Bourne, Secretary of the United States Shipping Board, and R. B. Mauchan, Chief Engineer of Kiangnan, signed on General Arrangement Plan and Midship Section dated 18 July 1918 (see Figures 2-11 and 2-12). These two drawings could confirm that they were technical attachments of the shipbuilding contract. The particulars specified on these two drawings were completely identical with the final as built particulars except that the length overall was four feet (1.22 meters) short. Another version of General Arrangement Plan dated 8 August 1918 was redrawn and modified. Comparing with last version dated 18 July 1918, this version has more details and some structural details had been deleted accordingly, and some scantling definition of Midship Section was further added. In addition, there were hand-writing comments from Bourne, Secretary of the United States Shipping Board on this General Arrangement Plan as well as the signatures of both Bourne

旁边还有两个人的确认签名。其中图上有一条手写的意见特别有价值："To be rearranged, see specification（须重新布置，见规格书）"。这说明合同附件里是有规格书的，如今只可能是散失了或毛根等人将文字性的原稿带走了而没有保存下来。

为了进一步探究图 2-11 和图 2-12 的来源以及设计、绘制时的参考资料或者母型船，作者仔细地浏览了这两张图纸并根据作者多年从事船舶初步设计的经验，对其进行了以下几点的分析判断。

总布置图（1918 年 7 月 18 日）参见图 2-11：

（1）该船的总布置充分体现了当时该船作为战时运输舰的需求，艏部和艉部各配置了一个炮塔平台以便安装一门舰炮用于自卫。

（2）该船总布置上有一个特别之处，即在上甲板上增加了一层遮蔽甲板（shelter deck），使船体内的中间甲板增加了一层，这样大大增加了战时物资（包装货）运输的舱容利用率。这在当时是一种比较新颖的设计，通常货船的船体内只有一层中间甲板。在本书的第 4 章对这种设计方案和可能的来源有详细的比较分析。

（3）该船在驾驶桥楼的后部布置了一个用于装载燃煤的深舱，说明此船的初始设计为采用燃煤锅炉。这种在舯部设置机炉舱、深舱和上层建筑在当时是一个常规的设计。

（4）这张总布置图绘制得比较粗，从图上来看，这张总布置图是根据一张船体基本结构图绘制的，在图纸名称中也标有"PROFILE AND DECKS"的字样，左上角还有结构详图和构件尺寸标注，纵中剖面绘制的也是船体内部的基本结构，螺旋桨、轴系、甲板上的舾装件和上层建筑的舱室等均没有表示出来，遮蔽甲板和上甲板基本上是个概略图。当时这样的总布置除了遮蔽甲板之外是一种十分常见的布置形式，大来公司的船队里有许多类似的船型。值得注意的是，图 2-11 的右方有一个"Yeo Y. Sharp"的签名，这个人是这张图纸的绘制者？或是毛根的随行者？作者从船舶设计者的角度考虑，这样一张粗略的总图在毛根到达美国后几天内赶工绘制出来是有可能的，况且

and R. B. Mauchan. One hand-writing comment, "To be rearranged, see specification" of Bourne was really worthy. That means technical specification should exist and be included as contract attachments, but why no any literal document was remained? Mauchan might carry these documents away when he left Kiangnan?

In order to further verify the sources, reference materials or prototype ships for these two drawings (see Figures 2–11 and 2–12), after carefully reviewing and comparing these two drawings as per normal practice of ship basic design, the following comments are summarized.

General Arrangement Plan dated 18 July 1918, see Figure 2–11:

(1) The general layout well presented the demands of transportation vessel in wartime, and there was one turret each fitted bow and stern for late retrofitting guns as self-guiding armament.

(2) The general arrangement of this type vessel had a special feature. A supplemental shelter deck was added above the upper deck, which means that one more intermediate deck was available inside hull. It would significantly increase internal spaces for parcel cargo and military appliances, especially in wartime. This was quite a novel design at that time, as normally there was one tier of intermediate deck in normal cargo steamer design. Such unique design and possible source of design will be further analyzed in Chapter 4.

(3) Originally, this type of steamer was designed to burn coal for boiler, and a deep tank for storage of coal was arranged in rear of navigation bridge. Such design with amidship located engine and boiler room, deep tank and superstructure was a quite popular design at that time.

(4) This General Arrangement Plan looks quite rough. From the content of drawing, this General Arrangement Plan was amended on basis of a general structural plan of hull, and "PROFILE AND DECKS" was also written in the title column. The structural details and scantling were indicated on the left corner of drawing. Longitudinal profile indicates internal structure of hull, and propeller, shafting, outfittings on decks and cabin layout were not indicated. Shelter and upper decks were roughly described in outline. At that time such general arrangement, except shelter deck, was quite popular layout for general cargo ships. There were many similar ships in the fleet of Robert Dollar Company. A signature of "Yeo Y. Sharp" was on this General Arrangement Plan (right side of Figure 2–11). He was draftsman of drawing? Attendant of Mauchan? From viewpoint of ship design, such a brief plan can be probably completed on basis of general structural drawing within a few days after Mauchan's delegation arrived in Washington. Comparing ink marks on drawing and signature as well as some structural details at the up right of drawing,

还可能有现成的结构图作为参考。对实图和图上签字进行比较，结合图纸左上角留有的船体结构细节来看，这张图是一张在毛根一行到达美国后在一张类似船型纵中剖面结构图的基础上赶工修改绘制出来的草图的可能性极大。

this drawing most probably was amended in a short period on basis of a general structural drawing of prototype ship after Mauchan and his colleagues arrived in Washington.

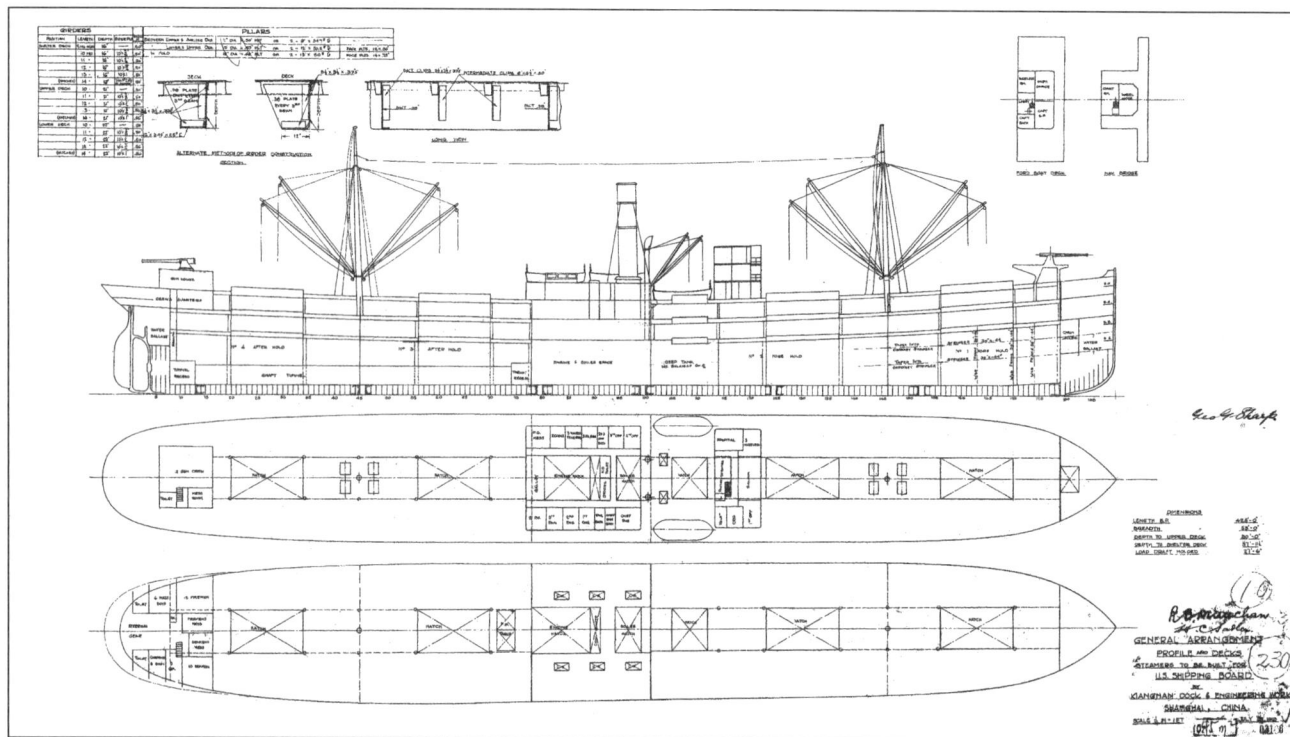

图 2-11　造船合同技术附件之一，总布置图（1918 年 7 月 18 日）
Figure 2-11　Technical Attachments of shipbuilding contract, General Arrangement Plan dated 18 July 1918

舯横剖面图参见图 2-12：

Midship Section, refer to Figure 2-12:

（1）与总布置图形成鲜明的对比，这张舯横剖面图绘制得非常详细。图上不仅有足够详细的尺寸信息，而且结构细节、舾装数、锚重、锚链长度和缆绳等信息也表达得十分详细，从这些细节来看这是一张实船的图纸。

（1）Comparing General Arrangement Plan, this Midship Section was drawn in great detail. Not only detailed scantlings were indicated on drawing, but also structural details, outfitting number, anchor weight, chain length and cable, etc. were indicated quite detailly. All these details show that it was a drawing for an existing ship.

（2）从图 2-12 右边所标注的数据来看：该图由两部分组成，一是原图的标注，二是江南造船所加上去的标注，包括用模板写的和手写的两部分，还有一些划改的痕迹。同样图 2-12 的右侧也有一个"Yeo Y. Sharp"的签名，这个人或许是这张图纸的修改和标注信息的添加者。

（2）The data indicated on Figure 2-12 consist of two parts, one was original, and the other was added by Kiangnan, including additionally written by template and hand as well as some strikethrough marks. A signature of "Yeo Y. Sharp" also appeared at the right side of Figure 2-12. It could be inferred that this person might be one who did amendments and additionally mark on the drawing.

(3) 虽然在原图"LLOYD'S NUMERALS"中标注的船宽是 55 英尺（16.76 米），但作者对图纸的标注尺寸和标注尺寸与实际尺寸间的比例关系进行了详细核对，发现图上此船的船宽是 53 英尺（16.15 米），而不是江南造船所后面加上去的船宽标注 55 英尺。这更说明此张图是借用了一张类似船型的舯横剖面图纸。

(4) 在图 2-12 上标有图号（Drawing No. 6545），并有两处日期标注：一处为 "7-5-18"（如果按照江南造船所的日期标注习惯，这个应该是英式日期标注，即图纸的完成日期在 1918 年 5 月 7 日，此时毛根应该还没有去美国）；另一处是手写的 "July 18, 1918"（这个是美式日期标注，即 1918 年 7 月 18 日），与总布置图的日期是一致的。因此作者推断这可能是借用了一张现成的图纸，这张图纸不太像是 1918 年 7 月 5 日在毛根一行抵美后绘制的[9]。

(3) Although the ship width of 55 feet (16.76 meters) was indicated on the original drawing "LLOYD'S NUMERALS", but the original ship width was 53 feet (16.15 meters), not 55 feet which was added by Kiangnan after carefully verified. It can be probably confirmed that this midship section drawing came from an existing ship.

(4) On Figure 2-12 (Drawing No. 6545), there were two dates indicated: one was "7-5-18" (if following Kiangnan practice, British date format, this drawing should be completed on 7 May 1918, at that date, Mr. Mauchan had not been to the United States); another date was hand written "July 18, 1918" (this is American date format), which was consistent with on General Arrangement Plan. It can be inferred that this Midship Section was an existing drawing and amended by Kiangnan's staff. It seems that this drawing is not like to be drafted after Mauchan's delegation arrived in Washington.

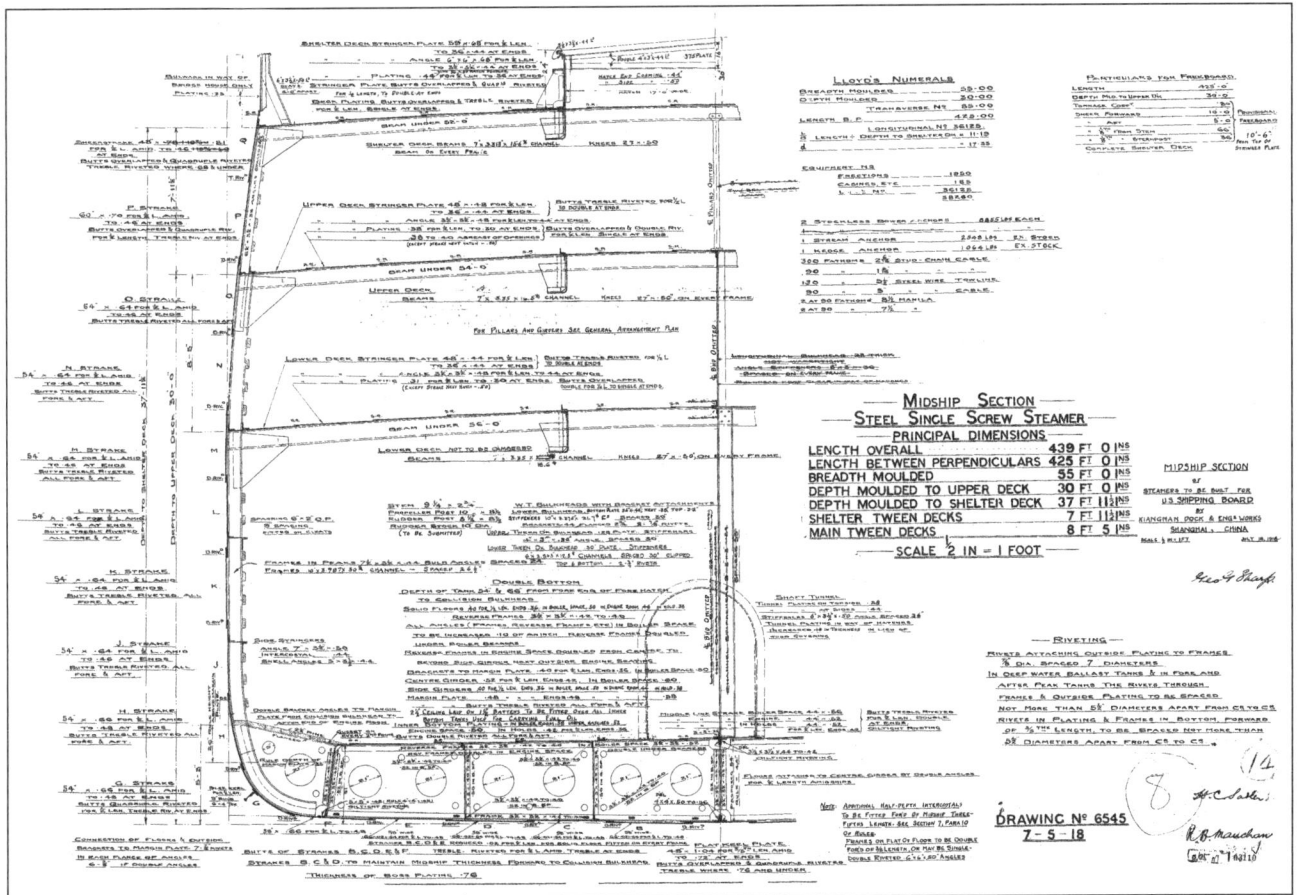

图 2-12 造船合同技术附件之二，舯横剖面图（1918 年 7 月 18 日）
Figure 2-12 Technical Attachments of shipbuilding contract, Midship Section dated 18 July 1918

根据上述判断可以得出这样一个结论：总布置图是在毛根一行到达美国后几天内在一张类似母型船的纵中剖面结构图的基础上赶工修改绘制出来作为造船合同的技术附件，图中加上了应急船队公司要求增加的一层遮蔽甲板。舯横剖面图则可能是借用了其他在制船的图纸并在上面做了一些小的修改。

母型船的来源分析对厘清江南造船所建造的四艘万吨级运输舰的设计来源是比较关键的，在本书的第 5 章将会有进一步的详细叙述。

1918 年 7 月 25 日正式的造船合同签订以后，毛根一行并没有马上离开美国，而是利用在美逗留期间，进一步了解美方对船舶设计的需求，修改、深化并重新绘制了图纸，即总布置图的修改版（1918 年 8 月 8 日）。在本书的第 4 章将对总布置图的修改版（1918 年 8 月 8 日）的设计特点进行比较详细的分析。

2024 年 1 月，陈语霆在美国国家档案馆里找到了 RG32 卷宗中的船舶建造规格书（两个版本，见图 2-13）。船舶建造规格书分为船体规格书（共 40 页，见图 2-14）和轮机规格书（共 28 页，见图 2-15）两个部分。一个版本的封面上标了"新版"字样，上面盖有江南造船所的印章。两个版本标注的日期都是 1918 年 7 月 10 日，内容上没有区别。新版上有很多铅笔手写标注，其中特别标注了战时配备的相关描述内容。

A conclusion can be made based on above judgements: General Arrangement Plan was amended on basis of "profile and decks" of a similar existing ship, and one tier of shelter deck was added to satisfy the latest requirement of Emergency Fleet Cooperation. Midship Section might directly utilize an existing ship with minor modification. These two drawings were used as Technical Attachments of the shipbuilding contract.

The source of prototype ship is key point to verify the design source of Kiangnan Dock & Engineering Works built four steam freighters. It will be further elaborated in Chapter 5.

After signing the shipbuilding contract on 25 July 1918, Mauchan and his delegation did not leave the United States immediately. They might still stay in Washington for further understanding the requirement from the United States Shipping Board. They modified, deepened and revised drawing, i.e. revised General Arrangement Plan dated 8 August 1918, during their stay in the United States. The design features of this revised General Arrangement Plan will be comprehensively verified in Chapter 4.

In January 2024, Mr. Chen found the Shipbuilding Specification was included in the RG32 file box of the National Archives of the United States (two editions, see Figure 2-13). The Shipbuilding Specification is further divided into Hull Part (40 pages in total, see Figure 2-14) and Machinery Part (28 pages in total, see Figure 2-15). One edition was labeled hand-writing "NEW" and was stamped with the seal of the Kiangnan Dock & Engineering Works. Both editions were dated 10 July 1918, and there is no obvious difference in content. The new edition has a lot of pencil handwriting, especially the description of special military requirement for wartime.

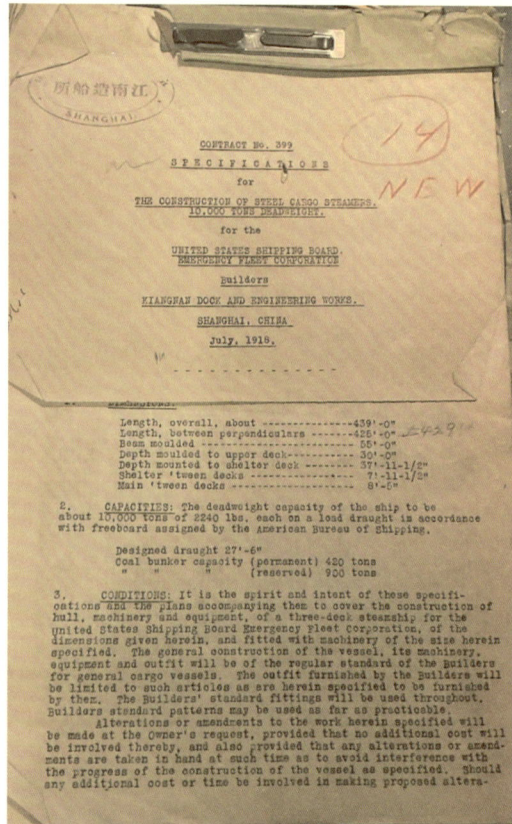

图 2-13　RG32 卷宗中的船舶建造规格书的封面
Figure 2-13　The cover of Shipbuilding Specification in RG32 file box

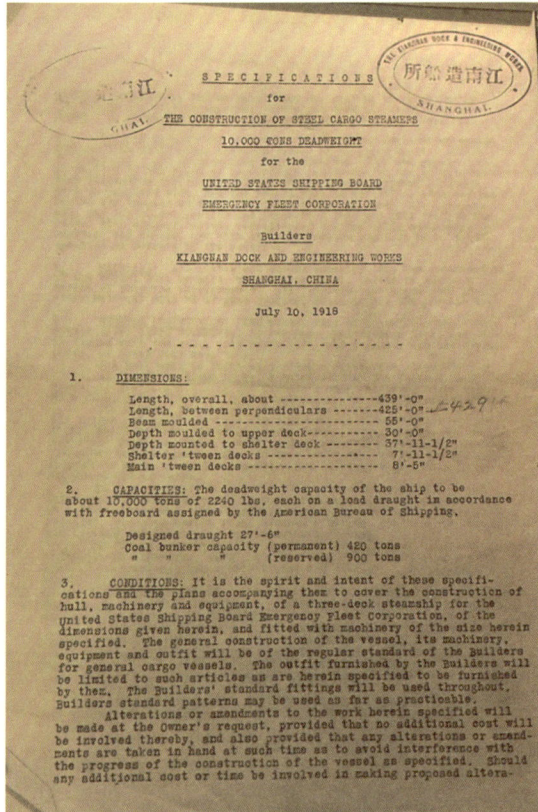

图 2-14 RG32 卷宗中的船体规格书首页
Figure 2-14 The first page of Hull Specification in RG32 file box

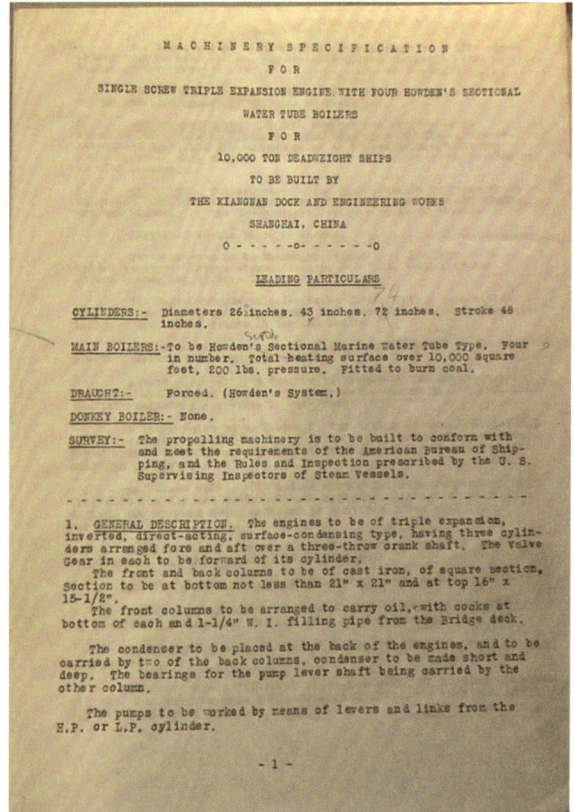

图 2-15 RG32 卷宗中的轮机规格书首页
Figure 2-15 The first page of Machinery Specification in RG32 file box

2.6

报刊对造船合同签订的报道
Newspapers Reported This Shipbuilding Contract

造船合同的签订是一个很重要的事件，合同签订的公告很快刊登在美国各地的大小报纸上并迅速传播。在 1918 年 7 月 14 日版的《西雅图周日时报》的"沿江边"专栏中有这样的报道："中国将为美国建造 12 艘船——航运委员会主席赫尔利让上海（的船厂）执行造船合同——华盛顿，7 月 13 日（星期六）——航运委员会主席赫尔利今天宣布了一项在上海的中国船厂建造 12 万载重吨船舶的合同。"

当时中国的报刊也很快刊登了江南造船所获得这份造船合同的好消息，并非像以前北洋政府一样对一些对外实业借款不予披露。上海 1918 年 8 月 9 日《申报》第三版报道了这个消息，图 2-16 为上海《申报》第三版报道的复印件。消息来源取自上海的英文报《大陆报》。

"江南造船所为承造美舰四艘现已开始筹备扩张规模，务使此船厂不为远东独一只大坞，亦当为中国造船界中之巨擘，拟在船厂西角购入新地三十亩，各方在磋商中。政府委员已由京抵沪，办理续划官地，以供厂用之事，此外复购买民地。如能有成，则厂中可得容留一万吨大船六艘之地……，全厂工事进行、先事预备，而各工厂改革尤多，……"[34]

It was a very big deal and the announcement was spread quickly through large and small newspapers around the United States. In the July 14th, 1918 edition of the *Seattle Sunday Times,* "Along the Waterfront" section they wrote: "CHINA WILL BUILD TWELVE VESSELS FOR U.S. — Chairman Hurley of Shipping Board Lets Contract to be executed in Shanghai — WASHINGTON, Saturday, July 13 — Chairman Edward N. Hurley of the Shipping Board today let a contract for the construction of 120 000 tons of ships in the Chinese yard at Shanghai."

Chinese newspapers timely too rejoiced to report Kiangnan Dock & Engineering Works secured this shipbuilding contract. It was not like that former Chinese Government always hesitated to disclose foreign loan for Chinese industries. *Shanghai Daily (Shen Bao)* of 9 August 1918 reported this news on the 3rd Page. Figure 2–16 is a copy of this page of *Shanghai Daily*. News source came from *China Press*, English newspaper of Shanghai.

"In order to build four American steamers, Kiangnan has commenced to expand shipbuilding facilities. Kiangnan has not only the biggest dry dock in the Far-East, but also it is giant of Chinese shipbuilding. Now related parties are negotiating for acquisition of 30 mu (a unit of area, 0.066 7 hectares) land in west side of shipyard. Government officials have arrived in Shanghai for dealing with some procedure of government controlled land. Remain area is needed to procure private lands. If these lands can be procured, shipyard area is able to accommodate up to six sets of steamers with ten-thousand deadweight tons … Construction preparation is orderly carried out, reformation in workshops are ubiquitous, …"

图 2-16　上海 1918 年 8 月 9 日《申报》第三版报道的复印件
Figure 2–16　Report of *Shanghai Daily* 3rd Page, 9 August 1918

合同中对于原材料和机器设备等条款提到，第一批不出 3 个月可望提用，称：

"大约再过八个月，第一艘大货船当可下水。……船各载重一万吨，此种大船固属中国境内从未造过，即美国造船局[35]所已造者，亦无如是之大。"对于这批轮船的图式、尺度、航速和设备也详加介绍："将依照美国造船局所规定之图式，并由美政府督工监造。按照图式，船长四百三十九英尺，阔五十五英尺，吃水二十六英尺，有甲板三层，皆以钢为之。船桅有四，每桅有起重机二，又有辅助起重机二，共计船上有起重机十、绞车十。船之前后皆有双底，以备装油，船之燃料非油即煤，船中亦有煤舱也。船中机械皆系最新式，有汽锅三，其作用压力约为两百磅，速率为每小时十海里半至十一海里。"又提到："此项新船系货船式，全船皆用钢制，用木之处甚少，一切装置皆须依照美国造船局与督工员之需要[36]。"

同年 8 月 30 日，上海的《申报》刊出《江南造船所成绩优美》一文（见图 2-17），文中提到江南造船所近日承揽的各家造船公司的订单，包括为中国海滨公司所造和美孚煤油公司所造，买主均大为赞赏[37]。

As per terms specified in the shipbuilding contract regarding the row material, machinery and equipment, the first batch will arrive within three months.

"*Then the first steamer can be launched after eight months. …… the deadweight of these steamers is ten thousand tons, so big ship is not ever built in China. She is also bigger than existing ships in the fleet of the United States Shipping Board.*" The newspaper mentioned, and the newspaper further introduced the specification of the ship: "*Kiangnan will build the steamers according to the specification required by the United States Shipping Board and under the supervision of American surveyors. As per the specification, ship length is 439 feet, beam is 55 feet, and draught is 26 feet respectively. There are three tiers decks, and all hull structure is made of steel. The ship is equipped four derricks, and two master lifting booms and two auxiliary lifting booms are equipped for each derrick. Ten lifting booms and ten winches are installed on shelter deck in total. Double bottom is arranged through bow to stern, fuel oil can be loaded inside double bottom. Ship's fuel is either oil or coal, and coal storage space is located amidship. All machinery on board is latest model. The ship equips three boilers with acting pressure approximate 200 psi, ship speed can reach 10.5 to 11 nautical miles per hour.*" The article additionally mentioned: "*This ship is merchant cargo ship with steel hull, and less wooden material is needed, all equipment and construction should be done in accordance with requirement of the United States Shipping Board and under the supervision of American surveyors.*"

The article captioned "Kiangnan Well Performed" reported by *Shanghai Daily* (see Figure 2-17), 30 August 1918 emphasized Kiangnan secured several shipbuilding contracts from various owners, including China Coast Shipping and Mobil Petroleum Co. The buyers would much praise for Kiangnan.

图 2-17 　《申报》刊出《江南造船所成绩优美》一文
Figure 2-17 　"Kiangnan Well Performed", *Shanghai Daily* article, 30 August 1918

江南造船所承造美国轮船一事受到了上海中外媒体的关注，且江南造船所亦借此事大肆炫耀。1918年10月9日，《申报》报道了这项造船工程的进度，"美国政府需海军运输舰十二艘由江南造船所承造，业已订立合同共约造价规银三千万两，所需材料已由该造船所向香港采购，并由刘所长商借兵工厂[38]西炮台隙地工作。"并提到"所购造船材料近日可运沪，拟先建造四艘"，即造船合同中所载明的四艘。[39]

江南造船所副所长邝国华（K. H. Kwong），为1875年10月赴美的第四批留美幼童。1918年11月23日，《密勒氏评论报》（Millard's Review）以一张半版面刊出这个价值规银3 000万两合同的新闻，并附有签约照片（见图2-18，照片中从左至右为美国海运委员会秘书斯蒂芬·博尔内，美国海运委员会主席赫尔利，中华民国驻美国公使顾维钧、江南造船所总工程师毛根）。文章标题："中国如何替美国造船"（How China Plans to Build Ships for America），强调此次造船案史无前例，美国如此海权大国竟然寻求中国来建造合乎他们需求的大船，可见江南造船所的造船技术已可媲美欧美先进国家。该文简述了江南制造局自曾国藩创立以来的变革历史，强调中国海军军舰和商船过去多购自英、美、日等国。自1912年以后，江南船坞改称江南造船所，自整顿后造船技术日进千里，不仅能够承担维修轮船的工作，还能建造军舰和商船，共计约316艘。该所不仅帮中国政府造船，中国商人及各国在华船主的订单源源不绝，甚至也为俄国人造船。该所宣称这项承造美国万吨巨轮案需再雇佣熟练和一般工人约2 500人、收购25亩地以上。这个合同从一个侧面展示"形势已转变了，证明中国人已经有能力做到以前必须仰赖外人才做得到的事。由此写下中国工业发展史的新篇章"。[40]

The news of Kiangnan building four American steamers attracted the attention of Shanghai and foreign media. Kiangnan hyped this shipbuilding contract. On 9 October 1918, *Shanghai Daily* reported the progress of shipbuilding:"American Government has decided to order up to 12 steamers in Kiangnan Dock & Engineering Works for military transportation, and the shipbuilding contract has been signed with price of 30 million taels of silver (Chinese currency, equal to approximate 7.8 million U.S. dollars). The materials for shipbuilding have been purchased by Kiangnan via Hong Kong. Director Liu of Kiangnan has negotiated with Shanghai Arsenal to rental some land space for storage of material." *Shanghai Daily* further mentioned:"Purchased materials for shipbuilding will be transported to Shanghai soon, and four steamers will be built in advance." That means the four steamers specified in the contract were firm orders, while others might be optional.

K. H. Kwong, Vice Director of Kiangnan, was the 4th batch of students studying in the United States who departed from China in October of 1875. *Millard's Review* reported this news of orders 30 million taels of silver worth of merchant ships from China in half page, Nov. 23, 1918, and the photo of signing contract was attached. The Secretary of the United States Shipping Board Stephen Bourne, Chairman E. N. Hurley, Ambassador of the Republic of China in the United States, Vi Kyuin Wellington Koo, and R. B. Mauchan, Chief Engineer of Kiangnan Dock & Engineering Works attended this contract signing (see Figure 2-18). The title of article was "How China Plans to Build Ships for America". The article emphasized that the shipbuilding contract was unprecedented. The United States, such a powerful maritime country, selected a Chinese shipyard for their "tailor-made" larger steamers. It can be proven that the shipbuilding technique of Kiangnan has been able to match the advanced shipbuilding countries in Europe and the United States. The article briefly described the transformation history since the establishment of Kiangnan Manufacturing Bureau by Zeng Guofan, and emphasized that Chinese naval and merchant ships previously built by British, American and Japanese yards. Since the republic revolution in 1912, Kiangnan Dock was renamed as Kiangnan Dock & Engineering Works, and its building technique was improved so rapid that it facilitated not only repairing the ships but also newbuilding. Kiangnan has built and delivered altogether 316 warships and merchant ships for Chinese Government, Navy, domestic and international owners, even for Russian owners. Kiangnan has planned to additionally hire 2 500 skilled and non-skilled workers and requisition over 25 mu (Chinese area unit) land. "The table is now turned. It has been proven that China is able to do something by itself which former have to be assisted by abroad. A new chapter of Chinese industry is thus begun". The article finally concluded.

494   MILLARD'S REVIEW   *November 23, 1918*

America Orders G. $30,000,000 Worth of Merchant Ships from China

The signing of contracts for G.$30,000,000 worth of merchant ships to be built at the Chinese Government's Yard at Shanghai. From left to right: S. N. Bourne, Secretary U. S. Shipping Board; E. N. Hurley, Chairman of the Board; Dr. Wellington Koo, Chinese Ambassador to the United States; and R. B. Mauchan, a British Engineer who has spent many years in China and has helped to introduce modern shipbuilding methods here.

图 2-18　江南造船所承造价值 3 000 万两规银万吨级运输舰的合同在美国华盛顿签约的照片。照片中从左至右为美国海运委员会秘书斯蒂芬·博尔内，主席赫尔利，中华民国驻美国公使顾维钧、江南造船所总工程师毛根。此照片刊登于 1918 年 11 月 23 日的《密勒氏评论报》

Figure 2-18　Contract signing in Washington, D.C. for orders G. $30 000 000 worth of merchant ships from China. From left to right in photo: USSB Secretary Stephen Bourne, Chairman E. N. Hurley, Ambassador of the Republic of China in the United States, Vi Kyuin Wellington Koo, and R. B. Mauchan, Chief Engineer of Kiangnan Dock & Engineering Works. This photo was posted in *Millard's Review*, 23 Nov. 1918

江南造船所承造美国万吨轮是中国前所未有之事，在当时引起了轰动，激发起国人的民族自豪感。上海的《申报》刊文称："诚以美国船只最多，而能不菲薄中国，请其相助造船，此乃前所未有者也。美国此举乃承认中国船业建筑力大有进步之证。""从前中国所需之军舰商船，多在美、英、日三国订造，今则情形一变，向之需求于人者，今能供人之需求。中国工业史，乃开一新纪元。"[41] 美国此举确实赢得了中国人对美国的"诚恳友睦之良感"。毛根对一家美国媒体称："（签署合同的）赫尔利主席正在中国为美国开辟一条辉煌的道路，它将是史无前例的，我了解中国，知道中国人怎么看美国。"[42]

Kiangnan Dock & Engineering Works building four steam freighters for the United States was unprecedented in China. It caused a sensation, and inspired the national pride of the people at that time. Shanghai's newspaper reported: "U.S. Government ordered steam freighters in Chinese shipyard is an unprecedented achievement. That means U.S. Government has approved the ability and capability as well as significant improvement of Chinese shipbuilding industry." "Previously China always ordered either warships or merchant ships in American, British and Japanese shipyards, but nowadays it completely changed that China can build ships for exporting. Chinese shipbuilding industry has commenced a new era in the history." "This contract has really won 'earnest goodwill' of Chinese people to the United States." "Chairman Hurley is now proving a brilliant way in China for the United States, Which is unprecedented. I fully understand China, and I am fully aware what do the Chinese think of America." Mr. Mauchan said to an American newspaper.

2.7

为造美舰扩建设施和招募工人
Expanding Facility and Hiring Working Force for Building American Steamers

2.7.1

扩张造船设施
Expansion of Shipbuilding Facilities

江南造船所原有场地和设备已不能满足建造四艘万吨级运输舰的需要。合同签订后，江南造船所立即开展大规模的造船设施扩充工作。

首先是扩充场地。美舰的交船期限异常紧迫，四艘要同时建造，为此需要新建四个大船台。所内原有场地只够建造两个船台，因此还需要大片土地。1905年"局坞分家"时，制造局原有土地一分为二，南侧沿江地方划给江南船坞，北侧土地留给江南制造局。

现在江南造船所为建造四艘万吨级运输舰要扩充场地，势必要占用上海兵工厂（1917 年后江南制造局改称为上海兵工厂）的地方。上海兵工厂对出让土地很不情愿，态度强硬，江南造船所所长刘冠南为此亲赴北京，找他任海军总长的哥哥刘冠雄出面帮忙游说。刘冠雄在国务会议上提出议案，国务会议做出决议，令陆军、海军两部派人会同办理。经过双方多次协商最后达成协议：兵工厂让出无字号栈房以东地段及处、征、往三个字号栈房所占地方，江南造船所为兵工厂另外购买同等面积的土地并承担建造新栈房的费用，另外"局坞分家"时规定由两家共用的土地现全归造船所，造船所按照市价补偿兵工厂土地款。显然，为使兵工厂让出土地，江南造船所付出了很大代价。

After the contract was signed, Kiangnan Dock & Engineering Works decided to immediately commence the expansion of shipbuilding facilities because the existing facilities and equipments cannot be expected to construct four American steam freighters.

The most crucial issue was land acquisition. Since the delivery schedule was transnormal tight, and four hulls should be erected in parallel. Four slipways, therefore, were needed to be newly constructed. Only the area for two slipways was utilized in boundary of Kiangnan Dock & Engineering Works, and additional land area was required. When the shipbuilding portion became independent in 1905, the area of Kiangnan Manufacturing Bureau was divided into two parts, the southern area along with river belonged to Kiangnan Dock, and the northern area was remained by Kiangnan Manufacturing Bureau.

In order to expand area for building four steam freighters, Kiangnan had to acquire some land which belonged to Shanghai Arsenal (Kiangnan Manufacturing Bureau was renamed as Shanghai Arsenal in 1917). The Shanghai Arsenal was very reluctant to sell the land and had a tough attitude. Liu Guannan, Director of the Kiangnan Dock & Engineering Works, went to Peking for this land acquisition, and asked his elder brother Liu Guanxiong, the Chief General of the Navy, to help lobby. Liu Guanxiong submitted this proposal at the State Council, and the State Council made a resolution to request the departments of army and navy handling this issue. The conclusion was reached after many negotiations between two departments: Shanghai Arsenal would sell the land up on request. Kiangnan Dock & Engineering Works would purchase the land of equivalent area and bear the cost of relevant buildings on those areas. All shared area as per agreement made in 1905, "Separation of Bureau and Dock", would sell to Kiangnan Dock & Engineering Works at the market price as compensation to Shanghai Arsenal. Kiangnan Dock & Engineering Works really paid great cost for acquisition of those lands.

到 1919 年江南造船所的土地又不敷使用，再次花巨资使兵工厂让出无字号栈房及其前面直通江岸的空地。此外，江南造船所还花费 22 000 余银元购买了 60 余亩民地。至此，江南造船所的土地已经比"局坞分家"时扩大了一倍以上。江南造船所新建了 4 个大船台，每个船台长 396 英尺（120.70 米），宽 36 英尺（10.97 米）[43]，高 20 英尺（6.10 米），可容纳 500 英尺（152.4 米）长的大船（含水下部分），船台两侧竖立 10 根可起吊 4 吨的起重立柱。图 2-19 所示为江南造船所扩建船台的场景。图 2-20 所示为江南造船所的干船坞（照片摄于 1920 年前后）。

In 1919, the area was insufficient for production scale, and Kiangnan Dock & Engineering Works paid significant cost again to acquire the land of Shanghai Arsenal. In addition, Kiangnan Dock & Engineering Works paid 22 000 Chinese sliver dollars to purchase civil land of 60 mu. Till that time, the area of Kiangnan had expanded more than one time comparing the year of 1905, when the dock became independent from Kiangnan Manufacturing Bureau. Kiangnan newly constructed four slipways, each of 396 feet (120.70 meters) in length, 36 feet (10.97 meters) in ramp span, and 20 feet (6.10 meters) in height. It was possible to accommodate a 500 feet (152.4 meters) long big ship including under water part of slipway. 10 sets of 4-ton derricks were arranged at both sides of slipway. Figure 2-19 is the construction scene of slipway expansion. Figure 2-20 is the main dry dock at Kiangnan Dock & Engineering Works circa 1920.

图 2-19　江南造船所扩建船台的场景
Figure 2-19　Construction sense of slipway expansion

图 2-20　江南造船所的干船坞（照片摄于 1920 年前后）

Figure 2-20　The main dry dock at Kiangnan Dock & Engineering Works circa 1920

除了扩大场地，江南造船所还新建了许多厂房，购买了大量机器设备。新建的轮机厂与旧厂连接，规模扩大了一倍以上，能容纳一千多名工人同时工作，添置各种新式机器 76 台，并将原有蒸汽动力全部改为电动，添置发动机 4 台，总马力达 425 匹，凡船厂所需的最大部件，皆能制造。新建的合拢厂，能容纳五六千匹马力的机器进行合拢试验，比旧厂产能增加了两倍。新建电力剪机厂、弯肋骨厂、舣样厂，购置了最新式的电机驱动钢板剪刀车、冲孔机、角钢冷弯机等机器设备 23 台。新建的造船铁工厂，配置有吊重在 3~5 吨的吊车 9 台和电力驱动大号弯铁板机一台。新建的压气机厂，购置大小压气机各一部及小型压气机械二百余台。此外，还新建和扩充了木模厂、打铁厂、打铜厂、铸铁厂、大库栈等厂房，并在各厂房和大库栈之间铺设铁轨，以便运输。

Besides land expansion, Kiangnan Dock & Engineering Works also newly constructed many workshops, and purchased a lot of machines and equipments. New machinery workshop connected with original one, and the scale was expanded over one time. More than one thousand workers were able to work simultaneously in this workshop. Expanded workshop replenished 76 sets of novel machines, 4 sets of motor with total power of 425 hp, and all driven power was changed from steam to electric. Any large size parts required by shipbuilding can be fabricated in this workshop. Newly completed engine assembly workshop enabled to assemble and test a 5 000 to 6 000 hp engine. Cutting workshop, frame bending workshop and curved plate workshop were newly completed with procured brand novel electric motor driven plate cutter, puncher, angle bar bender and other machines total 23 sets. Newly established iron workshop equipped 9 sets of gantry with capacity from 3 to 5 tons and electric driven plate bender. One each large and small compressor as well as more than 200 sets pneumatic machinery were procured and installed in just completed compressor workshop. In addition, workshops likes pattern making, forge iron and copper, casting and warehouses were newly established and expanded. Narrow railways were also laid in between the workshops and warehouses for easy transportation.

江南造船所原有一个 556 英尺（169.47 米）长的船坞，此次扩建又将船坞加宽，以容纳美舰进坞油漆船体，并将起重架从坞西移至坞东，起重杆长度增加三分之一，起重能力从 50 吨增至 75 吨。拆除了船坞西口的旧码头，填土造地，向江中延伸约 20 英尺（6.10 米）远，建造了可停泊大型船舶的新码头。为改善办公条件，江南造船所还新建了办公楼（见图 2-21）和洋餐楼。江南造船所为建造四艘万吨级运输舰进行的大规模扩建花费了一百数十万银元，超过了"局坞分家"时它所分得的资产总值。图 2-22 为江南造船所的码头（照片摄于 1920 年前后）。根据收藏者的信息，码头边正在修理的可能是太古洋行的客货轮（凯廷级）。码头上 A 字形的 75 吨吊车是扩建后的最大起重设备，照片右边的 A 字形吊车好像是浮吊。

Kiangnan Dock & Engineering Works had an originally 556 feet (169.47 meters) long dry dock, which was widened for accommodating American steamer to be finally painted inside. Meanwhile the derrick was moved from the western side of dock to the eastern side, the lifting beam was lengthened one third accordingly, and lifting capacity was enlarged from 50 tons to 75 tons. A new quay was constructed and extended 20 feet (6.10 meters) to the river after dismantling old quay and reclaiming land. For improving office condition, Kiangnan further constructed a new office building (see Figure 2-21) and a western style restaurant. For building four American steam freighters, Kiangnan spent more than one million Chinese silver dollars for massively expending their facility, even exceeding the total assets acquired after independence of shipbuilding segment. Figure 2-22 is a wharf of Kiangnan Dock & Engineering Works circa 1920. As per information collector, Butterfield & Swire Co. steamers (Kiating class) ware tie up in front of the Kiangnan possibly for repairs. A 75-ton shearleg was installed on wharf for hoisting material and large component for outfitting. Another shearleg shown on the right side of photo looks like a floating crane.

图 2-21 江南造船所新建的办公楼
Figure 2-21 New office building of Kiangnan Dock & Engineering Works

图 2-22 江南造船所的码头
（照片摄于 1920 年前后）
Figure 2-22 A wharf of Kiangnan Dock & Engineering Works circa 1920

2.7.2

为造舰广招人才
Hiring More Workers for Building Steamers

在船舶建造和修理技术方面，由于江南造船所为各种船东修造了各式复杂的船舶，随着生产业务的不断发展，技术人员和技术工人队伍的数量以及技术水平也在增加和提高。据《江南造船厂厂史：1865—1949》[44]记载："船坞开办初期，工程技术人员全部是外国人，达 14 名之多，而本国职员只有 20 余人"。"固定工人 60~70 人，其中熟练工人也仅是少数。随着生产的发展，本国的造船工人和技术人员队伍不断壮大。全所熟练和半熟练的技术工人有两千多人，一般工人则达六千多人。"

1920 年的《新青年》杂志（第 7 卷第 6 号，第 37 页）对当时江南造船所工人中各种技术工种的分布情况曾有下列记载："所内工人随工程的繁简而多少，无一定数额。现在总共在四千人以上，有时竟达七千人左右。其中机器匠近四百人，木模匠近百人，翻砂匠二百余人，铁匠三百余人，铜匠约一百人，木匠三百人，锅炉匠三百人，舢板匠一百多人，电镀电灯漆工约五十人，其余在船台、修船坞、煤栈、材料栈二千余人。"

关于钢板切割，江南造船所 1918 年以前一直采用冷作加工的方式，如锯和剪等。1915 年，有一位叫刘墨泉的工人在法国马赛的一家造船厂学到了一门氧乙炔切割的手艺。1918 年，刘墨泉回到江南造船所，成为国内第一位掌握气焊和气割技术的工匠。[45]

本国的工程技术人员也在逐步成长。1905 年进江南船坞的王平轩是最早的本国造船技术人员，从事轮机设计工作，后成为蒸汽机专家。1916 年以后，留学英美学习造船技术的郭锡汾、叶在馥、伍大名等陆续学成回国，由海军部派到江南造船所工作，充实所内本国技术人员的队伍[46]。

In terms of newbuilding and ship repairing technologies, since Kiangnan Dock & Engineering Works had done their business for various ship owners and complicated types ships, the quantity and proficient of technicians and skilled workers also developed and improved with the continuous growth of production business. According to the records in *History of Jiangnan Shipyard : 1865–1949*, "in the beginning of the Kiangnan Dock, there were 14 foreign engineers and technicians, while only about 20 Chinese engineers". "There were about 60 to 70 permanent workers and only a small portion of skilled workers. With the development of production, the quantity of domestic workers and technicians grew accordingly. There were more than 2 000 skilled and semi-skilled workers in Kiangnan, and more than 6 000 ordinary workers."

In 1920, the magazine *New Youth* (Vol. 7, No. 6, Page 37) wrote an article regarding the distribution of various technical jobs in workers of Kiangnan as follows: "The number of workers in Kiangnan is not stable, and it is always variable as per complexity of project. Current number of worker is more than four thousand, sometimes as many as seven thousand. Detailed breakdown is nearly four hundred machine-fitters, nearly a hundred wood-moulders, more than two hundred sand-tillers, three hundred blacksmiths, one hundred coppersmiths, three hundred carpenters, three hundred boilermakers, one hundred dinghy operators, about fifty electrician and painters respectively, remaining workers more than two thousand for building berths, repairing docks, coal stacks, and material stacks."

As for steel plate cutting, Kiangnan has been using cold work processing methods such as saw and shear until 1918. In 1915, a worker named Liu Moquan learned the oxyacetylene cutting technique at a shipyard in Marseille, France. In 1918, Liu Moquan returned to Kiangnan and became the first domestic craftsman to master gas welding and gas cutting technologies.

Meanwhile Chinese engineers and technicians were also growing. Wang Pingxuan, who entered the Kiangnan Dock in 1905, was one of the earliest domestic ship engineers, engaged in steam engine design and later became an expert in steam engines. After 1916, Guo Xifen, Ye Zaifu and Wu Daming, who studied shipbuilding technology in British and American colleges, returned to China sequentially. They were delegated by the Naval Department to join the work in Kiangnan Dock & Engineering Works and intentionally reinforce a the domestic technician team.

作者在查找资料时，偶然发现一位叫司徒梦岩的小提琴制作家和演奏家曾经在江南造船所技术部门工作过，但目前可以查到的船舶系统的史料里仅有司徒傅权（即司徒梦岩）于 1918 年 9 月作为绘图员被授予"六等文虎奖章"的记载[47]，并没有更多关于司徒梦岩的记载。更多关于司徒梦岩的记载如下（作者在文字上略做润色）：

司徒梦岩（F. C. Seetoo，1888—1954），原名司徒傅权，广东开平人。我国近代著名造船专家、小提琴制作家和演奏家。1908 年，司徒梦岩赴美留学，先在菲利普斯学院预科学习两年，后考入麻省理工学院攻读机械工程、造船工程、海军工程等专业。在美期间，始终坚持学习小提琴演奏，后又到波士顿新英格兰音乐学院学习，成为奥地利小提琴家尤根·格鲁恩贝格的学生。1914 年司徒梦岩学成回国，1915 年由海军部指派到江南造船所工作。

江南造船所是清末以来中国最著名的造船厂，当时主要的设计工作都是由总工程师毛根负责。每艘船在建造前，图纸都要经过英国劳氏船级社审核后才可开工和投保。刚回国的司徒梦岩并不知道，当时所里的每份图纸都必须经毛根签字后才寄往英国。一次，他在完成图纸设计后，按在美国工作的习惯，在图纸右下角签上了自己的名字。毛根看见有签名的图纸很生气，认为这份图纸一定会被船级社退回来，没审核图纸，便吩咐秘书直接寄往伦敦。毛根想等此图纸被拒收时再来教训这个不懂规矩的中国后生。后来船级社不但没有拒收，而是认可了这份图纸。司徒梦岩对毛根非常尊重，此后两个人还成了好朋友。后来毛根离华时，特推荐司徒梦岩为江南造船所的总工程师。司徒梦岩不但设计建造了我国第一艘通航长江上游的浅水客货船，还为美国政府成功地设计建造了万吨级运输舰，这是中国人首次设计和建造万吨巨轮。

毛根离开江南造船所时，当时的所长陈兆锵推荐了毛根的弟弟小毛根担任总工程师。司徒梦岩还是回到了他钟情的小提琴制作和小提琴演奏领域，并将小提琴融入广东音乐，开创了"洋为中用"的先河。

During searching historical information of Kiangnan, Situ Mengyan, a violin maker and player, was accidentally found. He used to work in the technical department of Kiangnan Dock. In the Chinese shipbuilding history, only a similar name Situ Fuquan (i.e. F. C. Seetoo can be found). In September 1918, Seetoo as a draftsman was awarded the "Sixth Grade Wenhu Medal". There is no more record about Situ Mengyan. More information about Situ Mengyan is recorded as follows (in italic font):

Situ Mengyan (F. C. Seetoo, 1888–1954), formerly known as Situ Fuquan, was born in Kaiping, Guangdong Province, China. China's modern famous shipbuilding expert, violin maker and performer. In 1908, Situ Mengyan went to study in the United States. Firstly he studied for two years preparatory course at Phillips College. Then he entered MIT for mechanical engineering, shipbuilding engineering, naval engineering and other majors. During his stay in the United States, he continued to study violin and later went to the Boston New England Conservatory and became a student of the Austrian violinist Jürgen Grunberg. In 1914, Situ Mengyan graduated and returned to China, and in 1915 he was assigned by Naval Department to work at Kiangnan Dock & Engineering Works.

Kiangnan Dock & Engineering Works was a most famous shipyard in China, and at that time Mauchan was in charge of all designs. Prior to construction of ship, relevant drawings had to be approved by Lloyd's Register then can commence work and take out insurance. Seetoo, who just returned the country, was not fully aware of Kiangnan's practice, i.e., every drawing should have Mauchan's signature prior to be mailed to UK. One time, he signed his name at the right corner of drawing after finishing drafting according to American practice. Mauchan was very angry when he saw the signed drawing by Seetoo. He convinced that classification society would definitely not accept this drawing. He did not check the drawing and directly instructed his assistant to send this drawing to London. Mauchan thought he would lesson this unregulated young Chinese if this drawing would be rejected. But finally Lloyd's Register approved this drawing beyond Mauchan's expectation. Seetoo really respected Mauchan, and then the two became good friends. Later, when Mauchan left China, Mauchan strongly recommended Seetoo as the Chief Engineer of Kiangnan Dock & Engineering Works. Seetoo not only involved design of Chinese first shallow water passenger-cargo ship for upper stream of Yangtze River, but also successfully designed and built four 10 000 deadweight tons American steam freighters, which were a debut of Chinese for designing and building large vessels over 10 000 tons .

When Mauchan left Kiangnan, the then Kiangnan's Director Chen Zhaoqiang recommended Mauchan's younger brother to take the position of Chief Engineer. Seetoo still returned to his favourite violin production and violin performance, and he creatively incorporated the violin into Cantonese music, and created a precedent of "integrating foreign culture into Chinese".

从上述史料来看，司徒梦岩和郭锡汾、叶在馥、伍大名等技术人员都是先期在江南造船所的中国工程技术人员，而且司徒梦岩早于他们，但为何在江南造船厂厂史和其他船舶系统的史料里没有关于司徒梦岩的记载？

Based on the above historical records, the Chinese engineers such as Situ Mengyan (F. C. Seetoo), Guo Xifen, Ye Zaifu and Wu Daming were all pioneers in Kiangnan Dock & Engineering Works, and Seetoo was even earlier than others. Why was Seetoo not recorded in the history of Jiangnan Shipyard and other historical documentation of Chinese shipbuilding?

2.7.3

包工制和包工头甘燋初 [48]
Contracted Worker System and Labour Contractor Gan Xiaochu

江南制造局初期，生产工人大都是固定的，为正式员工，局内供应员工的食宿。上海造船行业真正的包工制度是在 19 世纪末首先在外商船厂中发展起来的。这个包工制度通常是由船厂管理方把船舶修造中的某几项工程通过投标和议标的方式承包给包工头。包工头则根据工程量的大小和技术要求自行招聘劳务工人或再转包出去进行生产。凡和劳务工人相关的招聘、解雇、日常管理、薪酬支付、劳保安全、工伤抚恤等责任均由承包工程的包工头负责，船厂方和劳务工人无直接雇佣关系。[49] 江南制造局在后期阶段也开始实行以固定工人作业班组为单位计件性质的包工制度。

1905 年"局坞分家"时，江南船坞聘请了苏格兰人毛根作为总工程师，在他的主张下开始实行包工制。毛根不仅带来了英商船厂的包工制度，还带来了一批包工头，如冷作大包工头甘燋初、铸工大包工头唐友良等，都是英商祥生船厂及和丰船厂的包工队老板和匠目，也是毛根的老部下。

到了江南造船所时期，所里生产组织机构按不同工种分成两个系统：一个是点工形式，主要有车工、钳工、铜工、木模工等，约占全所工人总数的 30%；另一个是包工形式，主要有冷作工（相当于现代船厂船体加工、装配等工种）、木工、油漆工、铸工和锻工等，约占工人总数的 70%。

当时江南造船所的包工组织形式分为以下三类：

第一类是木工和油漆工，既包工又包料。当时承包江南造船所木工工程的承包商有海记、广福昌和阿德记等 6 家。木工工程包工老板们还成立了一个叫"集

During the initial era of Kiangnan Manufacturing Bureau, most workers were permanent employees. Company entirely offered dietary and accommodation for their staffs. Contracted working system was initially implemented in foreign invested shipyards in Shanghai since the end of 19th century. Such contracted work was normally that shipyard management subcontracted several working scopes of shipbuilding or repairing to subcontractors via bidding or bids discussion. Subcontractor, based on working loads and technical requirement, would decide to hire labour or out resource to perform signed labour contract. Subcontractor would take responsibility for all respects of contracted labour, such as recruitment, dismissal, daily management, salary payment, labour security, work injury pension, etc. There was no direct employment relationship between the shipyard and the workers of subcontractor individually. In later period of Kiangnan Manufacturing Bureau, Kiangnan trailed to implement working load oriented contracted working system in fixed labour teams.

In 1905, the shipbuilding segment became independent, and Kiangnan employed Scottish Mauchan as Chief Engineer. Under his suggestion, the labour contract system of British-owned shipyard was duplicated and implemented in Kiangnan Dock. Mauchan also brought serval foremen like steel work Gan Xiaochu, casting Tang Youliang etc., who were former subordinates of Mauchan when he worked in British owned shipyards, Boyd & Co., Ltd. and Shanghai Engineering Shipbuilding & Dock Co.

In era of Kiangnan Dock & Engineering Works, workers were further divided into two categories as per production organizations: one category was inserted workers, mainly including lathe operator, fitter, plumber and wooden model maker etc., and this portion was approximately 30% of the total workers; the other category was contracted workers, mainly including steel worker (corresponding to hull fabricator, assembler etc. in modern shipbuilding industry), carpenter, painter, founder and metalsmith etc., and this portion was approximately 70% of the total workers.

The organization of contracted worker was further divided into three patterns as follows:

The first pattern was for carpenter and painter, contracted for labour and materials. Six subcontractors, "Hai Ji", "Guang Fu Chang" and "Ade Ji", etc. took Kiangnan's jointing works. These subcontractors established

益会"的类似于帮会的民间团体，协调各方关系，抑制内部低价竞争；油漆工则只有楼友记一家；木工和油漆工的包工老板往往还兼做其他船厂和别的生意。

第二类是铸工和锻工，只包工不包料，材料和工具设备全部是所里的。"局坞分家"初期，铸工和锻工是固定工不是包工制。江南造船所 1918 年承接了四艘万吨级运输舰后才改为包工制，铸锻件的承包价格是按件和成品的重量计算。铸工和锻工的包工老板只做江南造船所的铸锻件生产生意。铸工的包工老板只有唐友良一人 [50]，而锻工的包工老板有张连福、丁连生和张桂福 [51] 3 个包工老板。在建造四艘万吨级运输舰时，铸件的工程量大，最多时铸工的人数达 120 多人。

第三类是冷作工（即与船体和锅炉结构制造相关的工种），也是只包工不包料，大小工具和材料均由所方供给。它与铸锻工种不同的是包工的工程量很大，工人数最多，工种也最复杂，有抹眼、捻缝、放样、冷工、火工、铆钉工等。通常一个包工老板无法承包全部工程，于是就按工种和工作量另行分包出去，形成二包；二包再分包出去形成三包，三包的工头通常也是直接劳动者。当时，冷作大包头有甘燸初、李庆祥、阮致祥、梁坤和顾梦雄等几位，其中就数甘燸初的包工范围最广，他手下的长工就有 100 多人，大小领班 20 多人，包工人数多达数千人。

当时江南造船所造船工程的包工项目，一般都经过招标的形式，由投标价最低者中标，因此包工老板之间的竞争相当激烈。而有竞争力的包工老板通常必须具备四大优势：第一，熟悉生产技术，能看懂设计图纸，熟知工程量，会安排工程项目计划；第二，经济实力雄厚，有开工前垫款的实力；第三，在生产工人、冷作行会和帮会中有一定的地位和势力；第四，要得到以毛根为首的管理层的信任。甘燸初本人是冷作工出身，有一身好手艺，懂技术，他从小包工头做起发展到大包工头，经济实力雄厚，他是当初毛根从祥生船厂带来的，两人私交甚密。甘燸初有毛根这个"后台"是他战胜其他竞争对手的最主要的原因。

a guild of "Jiyi Hui" like "Gang" for coordinating related parties, avoiding competition at lower price. Painting subcontractor was only "Louyou Ji". These subcontractors of jointing work and painting also undertook businesses for other shipyards.

The second pattern for founder and metalsmith, contracted for labour only but not material. Materials, facilities and tools were provided by the shipyard. In the initial period of independence of shipbuilding, founder and metalsmith were permanent workers but not contracted workers. Founder and metalsmith were converted into contracted worker after Kiangnan took shipbuilding contract for four American steam freighters in 1918. The contract price was accounted on the basis of piecework and weight of finalized product. The subcontractor of founder and metalsmith did production dedicatedly for Kiangnan. Foreman of founding/casing subcontractor was Tang Youliang only, smith/forging were Zhang Lianfu, Ding Lianshen and Zhang Guifu, three subcontractors/foremen. During construction of four American steam freighters, the maximum founders used to reach 120 workers due to heavier working loads of casting.

The third pattern for steel worker (hull and boiler structure related works), contracted for labour only but not material as well. Materials, required equipments and tools were provided by the shipyard. The obvious difference was that the quantity of contracted work was much heavier than casting and forging, and much more workers were needed. The working posts were also more complicated including (rivet) hole drilling, calking, lofting, steel cold work, thermal bending, rivet fitting etc. Normally single subcontractor was not able to take entire scope of hull steel work, and they would separate into working packages for secondary subcontracting; secondary subcontractor might further subcontract its sub-scope, and the foreman of such thirdly out resourcing most properly would be worker himself. At that time, bigger subcontractors of steel work were Gan Xiaochu, Li Qingxiang, Ruan Zhixiang, Liang Kun and Gu Mengxiong and so on. Gan Xiaochu covered the widest range of work, and he had more than one hundred long-term hired workers and more than 20 foremen and group leaders. The total contracted workers had reached thousands.

The contract works of the shipbuilding projects in Kiangnan Dock & Engineering Works were generally in the form of bidding. The bid was awarded by the lowest bidder, therefore, the competition in the contractor bosses was quite fierce. Competitive large-scale foremen usually should have four major advantages: First, they were familiar with production methodology, working loads and distribution, and they can understand design drawings. They were able to arrange production plans. Second, they have strong financial background and have advances prior to construction commencement. Third, they have a certain status and power in the workers, steel work guilds and gangs. Fourth, they should have the trust of management led by Mauchan. Gan Xiaochu himself used to be a steel worker. He had a good craftsmanship and knew the methodology very well. He developed from a small contractor to a large contractor with strong economic strength. He was brought by Mauchan from Boyd & Co., Ltd. at that time. Mauchan was the "backstage" of Gan Xiaochu, which was the most important factor in defeating other competitors.

1918—1921 年，江南造船所承造四艘万吨级美国运输舰，船体建造工程由甘熜初出面承包，他与李庆祥等 5 个大包工头联合组成一个公司联合承包，他们的工人人数达 3 000 余人，全部承包工程价格在 60 万 ~70 万银元（按 1920 年银元和美元的汇率 1.429：1 计算，承包工程价格为 42 万 ~49 万美元，占船价的 5.4%~6.3%。如果计入江南造船所本所的其他劳动力成本，这个比例和现代造船几乎一致）。联合承包公司整个承包工程按工作量和工作难度分成若干股，由大包工头持有大部分股份，其余的主要人员如总管事和大领班等也有部分股份。在承造四艘万吨级美国运输舰的过程中，仅甘熜初一人的收益就占了承包工程利润的 20%~40%，获利丰厚。

据江南造船所的老员工回忆，通常大包工头们一周会乘自备包车来所两三次，在造船工地上兜上一圈，看看账目，一切生产管理和事务性的工作有专人打理，过着十分逍遥自在的日子。

甘熜初在承包承造四艘万吨级美国运输舰钢结构工程的同时，还承包了多项其他船只的修造任务，这些工程的承包收入都十分可观。每当甘熜初完成一项承包工程获取高额利润时，他自然不会忘记毛根的好处，而毛根也千方百计为甘熜初承包下一个工程铺平道路。

1921 年，甘熜初完成了承造四艘万吨级美国运输舰的建造工程后，他就离开了江南造船所，到香港投资轮船公司，此后生意也越做越大。

从客观的角度来看，毛根带来的英商船厂的包工制度不仅打破了原来江南制造局的"大锅饭"现象，而且使造船工程的生产效率得到了大幅度提高。

During 1918 to 1921, Kiangnan Dock & Engineering Works (Kiangnan for short) built four American steam freighters. The hull construction scope was initially contracted by Gan Xiaochu. He and other large foremen, including Li Qingxiang, consolidated a company to take the contract. There were more than 3 000 people in this company, and the price of all contracted projects was 600 000 to 700 000 silver dollars (calculated at the exchange rate of silver dollars and U.S. dollars in 1920: 1.429 ： 1, about 420 000 to 490 000 U.S. dollars, it occupied 5.4% to 6.3% of the ship price. If considering Kiangnan's own labour cost, the labour rate was almost the same as modern shipbuilding). The entire contracted project of the consolidated company was further divided into several shares according to the workload and difficulty of the work. The majority of the shares were held by the large contractor, and the remaining shares were held by key personnel such as the general manager and the foremen. In the process of constructing four American steam freighters, only Gan Xiaochu single person was able to obtain a dividend of about 20%–40% from the contracted profits, which was really a huge profit.

According to reminiscence of elder employees of Kiangnan Dock & Engineering Works, the big bosses of the contractors usually took their own cars to shipyard two or three times per week. They took tour around the construction sites, and looked at the accounts. All production management and affairs were handled by their nominated staffs. They really had a very easy life.

While Gan Xiaochu was doing steel structural construction of four American steam freighters, he also contracted a number of other ship repairing works. The contracted revenue of these projects was considerable. Whenever Gan Xiaochu completed a contracted project to obtain high profits, naturally he never forgot to share some benefits with Mauchan, and Mauchan has done everything possible to pave the way for Gan Xiaochu to capture the next project.

In 1921, after Gan Xiaochu completed the construction of four American steam freighters, he left Kiangnan and invested in a shipping company in Hong Kong. His business grew bigger and bigger.

From an objective point of view, the contract work system duplicated from British owned shipyards by Mauchan, not only broke the original "Communal Pot" phenomenon in Kiangnan Manufacturing Bureau, but also greatly improved the production efficiency of shipbuilding process.

2.7.4

江南造船所首次颁发奖章 [52]
The First Award of Kiangnan Dock & Engineering Works

1918 年 9 月，当江南造船所正在为美国建造四艘万吨级运输舰而忙碌地进行前期准备工作之际，时任江南造船所所长的刘冠南，筹划了一次全所授勋颁奖活动，以表彰有贡献的员工，这是从 1905 年 "局坞分家" 开始的 14 年时间里从来没有过的。

刘冠南以所长的名义呈文海军部，申述颁奖的理由。呈文大意是：14 年里造船所成绩斐然，承造军舰商船 300 多艘，修理舰船 3 000 多艘，造修船水平 "沪上各洋厂莫不推崇" 并在国内外航运界产生了很大影响，以致美国政府也来下订单造船，因此请求按资劳择优奖励以酬前劳，而策效后。鼓励大家再接再厉，以便顺利地造出四艘美国万吨级运输舰。

刘冠南建议的颁奖的名单如下：

副所长邝国华等由海军总长刘冠雄呈请大总统授给勋章。

五等纹虎奖章 [53] 4 名：报销员萨景颜、绘图师洋员罗伯逊、总管洋账员戴吉士、正会计师兼庶务员邝国英。

六等纹虎奖章 11 名：翻译员陈镇桓，副报销员潘志卓，副会计员高奎光，管洋账员杜福生、管材料员李彦涵、常梅魁，缮核员温本，绘图员刘福培、司徒傅权（司徒梦岩）和余建复以及绘图司事王金生。

In September of 1918, when Kiangnan Dock & Engineering Works was working hard to prepare for the construction of four American steamers, Liu Guannan, the Director of Kiangnan Dock & Engineering Works, planned to organize an award-giving ceremony for recognizing excellent employees. This kind of award had never happened in the past 14 years, from the "Separation of the Bureau and Dock" in 1905.

Liu Guannan, as the Director of Kiangnan Dock & Engineering Works, reported to Naval Department of the Republic of China to state the reasons of award-giving. In the past 14 years, Kiangnan Dock & Engineering Works has made great achievements. They have delivered more than 300 newbuildings of naval and merchant ships, and completed repairing more than 3 000 ships. Kiangnan has been recognized by shipping companies that the technical level and quality were in line with or even higher than foreign shipyards in Shanghai. Kiangnan had elevated their reputation in the world shipping circle so that American Government had surely built up confidence to order four steam freighters. Nowadays, Kiangnan is going to honour contributors to excellent performance, and the real intention is to encourage all staffs to try their best efforts for building and delivering four American steam freighters.

Awarding list proposed by Liu Guannan was as below:

Vice Director K. H. Kwong and so on would be awarded by the President of the Republic China after reported by Liu Guanxiong, Naval General.

The Fifth Class "Wen Hu" a.k.a. "Order of the Striped Tiger", total 4 persons: Claims Officer Sa Jingyan, Draftsman Robertson, General Accountant (Foreign Currency) David Gist, and Accountant Kwong Guoying.

The Sixth Class "Wen Hu", total 11 persons: Translator Chen Zhenheng, Deputy Claims Officer Pan Zhizhuo, Vice Accountant Gao Kuiguang, Accountant (Foreign Currency) Du Fusheng, Material Manager Li Yanhan and Chang Meikui, Audit Officer Wen Ben, Draftsman Liu Fupei, F. C. Seetoo (Situ Mengyan) and Yu Jianfu as well as Draft Assistant Wang Jinsheng.

七等纹虎奖章 1 名：机器厂总匠目李国元。

The Seventh Class "Wen Hu", 1 person: Li Guoyuan, Foreman in General of Machinery Workshop.

二等奖章 1 名：锅炉厂包工匠目甘燋初。

The Second Class Medal, 1 person: Gan Xiaochu, Foreman of Boiler Workshop.

三等奖章 8 名：木工厂包工匠目何祖康、机器厂钳床副匠目徐六香、机器厂车床副匠目沈静嘉、锅炉厂包工匠目李庆祥、木样厂匠目李承、铸铁厂匠目陈爱德、打铁厂包工匠目张连福和张桂馥。

The Third Class Medal, total 8 persons: He Zukang, Foreman of Carpenter Workshop, Xu Liuxiang, Vice Fitter Foreman of Machinery Workshop, Shen Jingjia, Vice Lathe Foreman, Machinery Workshop, Li Qingxiang, Foreman of Boiler Workshop, Li Cheng, Foreman of Wooden Model Workshop, Chen Aide, Foreman of Casting Workshop, Zhang Lianfu and Zhang Guifu, Foreman of Forging Workshop.

这份名单亦见于 1918 年 9 月 27 日上海的《新闻报》。从名单中可以看出，按当时的工厂体制，有资格获奖的自然只有职员和包工头，普通工人没有。但出乎意外的是所长刘冠南和总工程师毛根未在名单上。刘冠南和毛根应该是这份名单的拟定者，也许所长刘冠南和总工程师毛根不便将自己列入嘉奖名单，把这个题目留给海军部来解了。

This name list was also reported on *The Shanghai News* on 27 September 1918. It can be seen from the list that, as per the practice at that time, only staffs and foremen were eligible for awards, but not ordinary workers. It was unexpected that Director Liu Guannan and Chief Engineer Mauchan were not on the list. Director Liu Guannan and Chief Engineer Mauchan should be key persons who finalized this list, and perhaps it might be inconvenient for them to insert their names into this list. This question could be only answered by the Naval Department itself.

作者从其他渠道的信息得知，毛根在他的职业生涯中获得过两次比较高的荣誉：

As per information from other sources, for Mauchan's service to China, he was awarded twice as follows:

（1）1914 年被授予二等纹虎勋章。

(1) The Second Class "Wen Hu"–1914.

（2）1918 年被授予三等"嘉禾"勋章，即"珍贵辉煌的金穗勋章"或"丰收"的寓意。根据这个年份，主要是表彰毛根在承接美国四艘万吨轮所做出的贡献。

(2) The Third Class "Chai Ho"–1918, a.k.a. "Order of the Precious Brilliant Golden Grain" or in English it takes the meaning of "Bountiful Harvest", based on the date, likely for his work securing the contract from the United States Shipping Board for four 10 000-ton steam freighters.

2.8

伟大的太平洋老人罗伯特·大来
Robert Dollar — Grand Old Man of the Pacific

江南造船所新购置的机器设备有很多是通过大来洋行在美国购置的。大来洋行与中国往来密切，其老板罗伯特·大来以木材生意起家，进而涉足木材运输，后来积极开拓横跨太平洋的航运和贸易，发展成为太平洋两岸最大的航运和贸易巨头。

Most of the machineries and equipments recently procured by Kiangnan Dock & Engineering Works were purchased in the United States through Dollar Company. Dollar Company had closer relationship with China. Its boss, Robert Dollar, initially started his business from lumbering, then further extended his business to timber transportation and later aggressively pioneered shipping and trade across the Pacific Ocean. Dollar Company rapidly developed and became the largest shipping and trading giant Pam Pacific.

关于罗伯特·大来的生平，在 Falkirk Cultural Center 网站上一篇以"伟大的太平洋老人"[54] 为题的文章和上海亚美商会（AmCham Shanghai）的网站上一篇以"The Dollar Family as Founding Members of AmCham Shanghai"[55] 为题的文章都做了详细的介绍：

Regarding the life of Robert Dollar, an article on the Falkirk Cultural Center website entitled "Grand Old Man of the Pacific" and the AmCham Shanghai's website also features an article entitled "The Dollar Family as Founding Members of AmCham Shanghai":

罗伯特·大来（见图 2-23）1844 年出生于苏格兰小镇福尔柯克（Falkirk）的一个贫穷家庭。1858 年，14 岁的他随家人移民到加拿大，在一个伐木场（lumber camp）里做勤杂工（chore boy）。在后续的 5 年里，他学会了法语并担任伐木场的会计，22 岁时他开始负责管理一个伐木场。

Robert Dollar (see Figure 2-23) was born in a poor family of Falkirk, a Scottish town, in 1844. In the year of 1858 when he was 14 years old, he immigrated together with his family to Canada, and then worked as a chore boy at a lumber camp (known as "shanty"). Over the next five years, he learned French and worked as an accountant for the lumber camp, and at the age of 22, he began to manage and operate a lumber camp.

图 2-23　罗伯特·大来的照片
Figure 2-23　Portrait of Robert Dollar

1872 年，他买下了第一个伐木场。虽然他入行木材行业后的初始业绩并不理想，但他先在加拿大，随后在美国密歇根半岛，最后在加利福尼亚州北部圣拉斐尔（San Rafael）购置了伐木厂，最终成为木材行业的一个最伟大的成功者。1888 年，罗伯特·大来开始收购加拿大的不列颠哥伦比亚省、美国加利福尼亚州北部的索诺马（Sonoma）、门多西诺（Mendocino）、俄勒冈州的木材加工厂和伐木场。他在美国西部设立了一个木材公司，其下有多个木材加工厂，木材年产量可达 1 500 万根英尺（board foot[56]）。

罗伯特·大来的第二个职业生涯始于 1895 年，是年他购置了一艘蒸汽动力纵帆船（SS "Newsboy"，steam schooner, 300 DWT）用于从索诺马海岸运输原木到旧金山。他的投资获得了巨大的成功，他随即又购置了多艘船舶用于原木运输。到 1900 年，他已经拥有了 4 艘船。1901 年，罗伯特·大来成立了大来航运公司（Dollar Steamship Company, American President Line 的前身）[57]。大来航运公司成为 20 世纪初最主要的跨太平洋运输的航运公司。

罗伯特·大来从 1902 年开始往返于美洲和亚洲之间拓展其公司业务，他成为在中国开展贸易的先锋和领先者。在大来 70 岁时，他在美国和远东建立了最重要的贸易业务。1920 年，他推出了严格按照船期表营运的环球货物船舶运输模式，这在当时是一个具有革命性理念的创举。1924 年，他进一步推出了按照事先公布的船期表运行的环球客运航线。这几个创举的成功使罗伯特·大来成为"伟大的太平洋老人"。他作为封面人物出现在 1928 年 3 月 19 日的《时代》周刊上，欧内斯特·普尔（Ernest Poole）曾经撰写了关于罗伯特·大来的系列文章刊登在 1929 年发行的《星期六晚报》上。

罗伯特·大来积聚了约 4 000 万美元的财富。在 1995 年的调查中，根据当时的美国国民生产总值计算的最富有的 100 人中，罗伯特·大来名列第 88 位。他从一个贫穷的移民成为一个具有远大目标、不屈不挠、机敏的商人。他前瞻性地开拓了环太平洋贸易，他一生到亚洲不下 30 次，在他 1932 年逝世前不久还访问了亚洲。当时，超过 3 000 人参加了他的葬礼，包括外国的高官、政府官员、与大来洋行有业务往来的相关人员、生前友人和他的家人。美国政府还派出

In 1872, he acquired his first lumber camp. Although initial performance was not so good, he became one of the biggest successes in the lumbering industry after he sequentially bought lumber camps in Canada, the Michigan Peninsula and San Rafael of northern California. In 1888, Robert Dollar began to acquire lumber camps and timber mills (sawmills) in British Columbia of Canada, Sonoma of northern California, Mendocino and Oregon State. He set up a timber company in the western America, with several timber mills. Annually producing timber aggregated up to 15 million board feet.

Robert Dollar began his second career since 1895. He bought a steam schooner SS "Newsboy" of 300 deadweight tons for transporting logs from the coast of Sonoma to San Francisco. His investment successfully yielded generous profits. He further purchased several ships for log transportation thereafter. He had operated four ships by 1900. In 1901, Robert Dollar founded the Dollar Steamship Company, the predecessor of American President Line. Dollar Steamship Company had become a well-deserved shipping major among trans-Pacific shipping companies in the early 20th century.

Since 1902, Robert Dollar had frequently travelled between the Americas and Asia for developing his business. He was a pioneer and leader of trade in China. At the age of seventy, he established the most important trade operations in the United States and the Far East. In 1920, he introduced an innovated shipping transportation pattern, i.e., cargo liners strictly following sailing schedule, which was a revolutionary concept at that time. In 1924, he further launched the global passenger routes, which were operated based on a pre-published sailing schedule. The success of these initiatives made Robert Dollar a "Great Old Man of the Pacific". He appeared on *Time* magazine as the cover person on 19 March 1928, and Ernest Poole wrote a series of articles about Robert Dollar on *The Saturday Evening Post* of year 1929.

Robert Dollar accumulated a fortune of about $40 million. In the statistics of the 1995, Robert Dollar ranked the 88th out of the 100 richest people in terms of gross national product of the United States at the time. He went from being a poor immigrant to an indomitable, astute businessman. He was a pioneer of Pam-Pacific trade, and frequently visited Asia more than 30 times in his lifetime. He visited Asia shortly even before he passed away in 1932. More than 3 000 people attended his funeral, including senior foreign officials, government officials, people associated with his business, friends and members of his family. The United States Government also sent a Naval dirigible to scatter roses over the church. California Governor James Rolph, Jr. said highly at

了海军的飞艇（dirigible）到教堂上空撒玫瑰花。加利福尼亚州小詹姆斯·罗尔福州长在他逝世后是这样评价他的："这个国家没有一个人像罗伯特·大来那样将美国国旗这么多次地飘扬在大洋上。"[58]

his funeral, "Robert Dollar has done more in his lifetime to spread the American flag on the high seas than any man in this country."

图 2-24　杭州灵隐寺大殿的木柱
Figure 2-24　Wooden pillars in Lingyin Temple of Hangzhou

关于罗伯特·大来促进美中木材贸易的事迹，在一些公开网站上还有一些关于天津大来木行的记载：

Regarding Robert Dollar's performance in developing the Sino-America timber trade, there are also some excerpts from public websites about the Tianjin (Tientsin) Dollar Lumber Company:

美国实业家罗伯特·大来（Robert Dollar，1844—1932）有木材大王之称，曾与亨利·福特、考尔曼、杜邦、洛克菲勒等人齐名，被誉为"创建美国的五十位伟人"之一，其影响力可见一斑。1901年开始，罗伯特·大来向中国输入北美木材，并在天津成立了大来木行。罗伯特·大来通过自伐自运自销的有利条件，以及运用各种营销手段，使大来木行很快占据了中国市场，成为当时贸易额最大的木材企业。据估算，大来木行40年的木材营业额就达20亿美元之巨，纯利为7亿美元。国内众多名人故居修缮时所使用的木料都是大来木行提供的。杭州灵隐寺大殿修缮时，选用的木材也来自大来木行，其中最重的一根达20吨之巨，图2-24所示为杭州灵隐寺大殿的木柱。

Robert Dollar (1844–1932), an American industrialist known as the Timber Giant, was listed as one of the "Fifty Great Men who Created America", along with Henry Ford, Coleman, DuPont, Rockefeller and others. Since 1901, Robert Dollar has begun his business to export North American timber to Chinese market and established Dollar Lumber Company in Tianjin (Tientsin). Robert Dollar, with help of favourable conditions of self-producing, transporting and marketing, as well as the use of flexible marketing strategies, Dollar Lumber Company quickly occupied the Chinese market, and became the largest lumber trade enterprise in the world. It is estimated that the 40-year lumber sales of the Dollar Lumber Company would reached a huge $2 billion, net profit of $700 million. The wooden materials for repairing the domestic celebrity houses in China were provided by the Dollar Lumber Company. During repairing work of Lingyin Temple in Hangzhou, required wood material was supplied by the Dollar Lumber Company as well. The weight of the heaviest wooden pillar even reached 20 tons. Figure 2-24 is the wooden pillar of the Lingyin Temple in Hangzhou.

依靠木材贸易起家后，罗伯特·大来还成立了轮船公司、无线电公司以及进出口贸易公司等，涉足领域相当广泛。大来的联合企业在中国各地的分支机构众多，但以大来木行命名的，只有天津和汉口两处，其余都以大来洋行为名。

After success of the timber trade, Robert Dollar also set up his shipping company, radio company and import and export trading company, etc. These companies were to get involved in the many different fields. Dollar's joint venture companies had many branches throughout China, but the Chinese branch companies named as "Dollar Lumber Company" were only in Tianjin (Tientsin) and Hankou (Hankow), and all rest were named as "Dollar Company".

在天津赤峰道与和平路交会处，有一栋建筑在此屹立超过了 100 年。和平路 285 号，它就是大来木行的原址。这栋建筑始建于 20 世纪第二个十年，原为协隆洋行的房产，1924 年大来木行以 50 万美元的价格买下作为办公楼。图 2-25 为天津和平路 285 号大来木行办公楼。

In Tianjin, at the intersection of Chifeng Road and Peace Road, there is a building standing there for more than 100 years. 285 Peace Road, it is the original site of the Dollar Lumber Company. Built in the 1920s, the building was originally A.J. Yaron (Xielong) Company's property and was purchased as the office building of Dollar Lumber Company in 1924 for $500 000. Figure 2-25 is the Dollar Lumber Company office building at 285 Peace Road, Tianjin (Tientsin).

图 2-25　天津和平路 285 号大来木行办公楼
Figure 2-25　Dollar Lumber Company office building at 285 Peace Road, Tianjin (Tientsin)

罗伯特·大来还在中国帮助、创建了许多公共慈善机构，如帮助建造了基督教青年会大楼，建立了一个孤儿院、一个盲童学校和一所乡村小学。他的社会责任先导作用在早年上海亚美商会的活动和运作中得到了非常好的体现。

Robert Dollar also helped and created many public charities in China, such as helping to build the YMCA house, an orphanage, a school for blind children and a primary school in countryside. His leading role in social responsibility was evident in the activities and operations of the American Chamber of Commerce in Shanghai in the early years.

大来大楼（Robert Dollar Building）现在还完好地保存在原址上海市黄浦区广东路 51 号。大来大楼 1920 年由美商大来轮船公司投资委托美籍建筑师亨利·默飞（Henry Murphy）设计，并于 1921 年竣工。这里曾经是上海亚美商会 20 世纪第二个十年初的办公楼（见图 2-26 和图 2-27）。

保罗·弗伦奇（Paul French）写的 The Old Shanghai A–Z 书中提到，上海亚美商会原先是在广东路 3 号，后来才移至 51 号。大来大楼地处上海外滩繁华的商业区，楼内商贾云集。三菱株式会社、美国无线电公司（Radio Corporation of America，RCA）、Sunmaid Raisins（总部位于美国加利福尼亚州的干果公司）、中国联合工程公司（China United Engineering Corporation）、合众国钢铁公司（United States Steel）、中国航空公司（China National Aviation Corporation，CNAC）的总部和大来航运公司的办公室都在大来大楼内[59]。

The Robert Dollar Building is now kept as intact at 51 Guangdong Road, Huangpu District, Shanghai. The Robert Dollar Building was designed in 1920 by Henry Murphy, an American architect, and completed in 1921. It was once the office building of the Asian-American Chamber of Commerce in Shanghai in the early 1920s (see Figures 2–26 and 2–27).

Paul French's book The Old Shanghai A–Z mentioned, the Asian-American Chamber of Commerce in Shanghai, originally was at 3 Guangdong Road, and later moved to No.51 of the same road. Robert Dollar Building is located in the bustling commercial district of Shanghai's Bund. Mitsubishi Corporation, Radio Corporation of America (RCA), Sunmaid Raisins, California-based dry fruits company, China United Engineering Corporation, United Nations Steel, the headquarter of China National Aviation Corporation (CNAC) and Dollar Steamship Company etc. were all rented offices in this building.

图 2-26　上海市广东路 51 号大来大楼
Figure 2-26　Robert Dollar Building in 51 Guangdong Road, Shanghai

图 2-27　上海市优秀历史建筑大来大楼的铭牌
Figure 2-27　"Heritage Architecture"awarded by Shanghai Municipal Government for Robert Dollar Building

罗伯特·大来还善于与政界人士交往，他与中国政商各界都有很深的关系。大来船长此举借以提升其企业知名度，并寻求政治方面的保护和商务方面的便利。大来船长本人多次来中国，曾组织美国太平洋沿岸商会代表团访华，并接待中华总商会访问美国。1912 年，他因代表美国政府来华，游说中国组团参加太平洋万国博览会一事而声名大噪。

1918 年，黎元洪（1864—1928）曾授予罗伯特·大来一等大绶宝光嘉禾[60]勋章（四星，Chia Ho-First Class）。图 2-28 所示为一等大绶宝光嘉禾勋章。而且罗伯特·大来每次来华，都要去看望黎元洪[61]。他多次受邀赴黎元洪的私宅商谈外交、财政等事宜。据说袁世凯去世后，黎元洪继任大总统时，发的第一个电报就是给罗伯特·大来的，可见两人关系之深厚[62]。

关于当时的中华民国总统授予罗伯特·大来一等大绶宝光嘉禾勋章一事，在旧金山的地方志中有一段记载[63]。

中国政府为表彰旧金山公民罗伯特·大来船长争取美国政府价值 1 400 万美元建造八艘运输舰[64]的合同所做出的贡献，授予其大绶宝光嘉禾勋章。授予大来船长的是一枚四星勋章，两颗金星和两颗银星重叠，中间是成熟的麦穗。

——中华民国总统黎元洪，星期三

Order of the Chia Ho, China's most prized decoration has been conferred upon Captain Robert Dollar, San Francisco capitalist, in recognition of his service during the war in securing from the United States Government for the Chinese Government a $14 000 000 contract for the construction of eight ships. Captain Dollar received the decoration–four stars, two gold and two silver overlapping, with a raised shock of wheat in the center.

—from the President of the Republic of China, Li Yuanhong, Wednesday

Robert Dollar was also good at dealing with politicians and had deep ties with Chinese politicians and businessmen. Captain Dollar intentionally utilized these personnel relationship to raise reputation of his company, and to seek political protection and business convenience. Captain Dollar himself had visited China many times, and he once organized a delegation from the U.S. Pacific Rim Chamber of Commerce to visit China, and hosted the Chinese General Chamber of Commerce to visit the United States. In 1912, he became famous for representing the U.S. Government to visit China, and lobbying China to organize a delegation to the Pacific World's EXPO.

In 1918, Robert Dollar received the First Class "Pao Kong Chia Ho" decoration (four stars) from the Republic of China President Li Yuanhong. Figure 2-28 is the First Class order of "Pao Kong Chia Ho". Every time Robert Dollar paid his visit to China, he had to see Li Yuanhong. He had been invited to discuss foreign affairs, finance and other issues at Li's private residence. It is said when Li Yuanhong succeeded as President after former Yuan Shikai passed away, the first telegram was to send this news to Robert Dollar, which really showed the depth of their relationship.

Regarding the President of the Republic of China honored Robert Dollar with the First Class order of "Pao Kong Chia Ho", a description of which is herewith given in the following excerpt from the San Francisco Chronicle:

图 2-28　一等大绶宝光嘉禾勋章
Figure 2-28　The First Class order of "Pao Kong Chia Ho"

除了与北洋政府要员交往外，民国后期，罗伯特·大来和国民政府要员也多有交往。罗伯特·大来还受到了蒋介石的接见。

烟囱上涂有巨幅"$"标志的大来航运公司的远洋巨轮（见图2-29）装载着木材、钢铁、矿石、火车机车、煤油、面粉、食品等各种货物往来于中国和美国之间，一度成为象征中美贸易的标志。大来洋行在中国的上海、天津、汉口等主要港口都设有分支机构和货栈码头，每个星期都有大来航运公司的轮船在上海停泊。它还经营川江航运，把触角深入中国的腹地——四川。

In addition to associating with key officials of the Chinese Government, Robert Dollar had also many interactions with important officials of the Republic of China. Robert Dollar was also invited a meeting with Jiang Jieshi (Chiang Kai-shek, 1887–1975).

The ocean going cargo steamers of Dollar Steamship Company. with big "$" funnel mark (Figure 2–29) sailed between China and America on Pacific Ocean for carrying various freights such as timbers, steel materials, mine, locomotives, kerosene, flour and food etc. The fleet of Dollar Steamship Company was used as an emblem of Sino-America trade. Dollar Company established branches and wharfs in major Chinese ports, for instance, Shanghai, Tianjin (Tientsin) and Hankou (Hankow) etc. The freighters of the Dollar Steamship Company scheduled to call at Shanghai every week. Dollar Company further extended shipping business to Chuan Jiang (upstream of Yangtze River), Sichuan (Szechuen) Province, the interior of China.

图 2-29　大来航运公司的远洋货轮
Figure 2-29　Cargo steamer of Dollar Steamship Company

罗伯特·大来与江南造船所总工程师毛根都是苏格兰人，有很好的私交。1918 年，大来洋行在江南造船所订造了两艘柚木驳船（船体号为 H326/327）。大来洋行的木材码头和堆场就在江南造船所的对面（即白莲泾码头靠黄浦江白莲泾入口区域。见图 2-30）。相邻区域的码头为华商中兴煤矿码头。在1928 年的内部资料中将此码头标注为"大来洋行的木材码头"（见图 2-31）。1950 年，政府征用大来码头并拨交给中国人民解放军东海舰队使用。1956 年又交归港务局，改称"白莲泾码头"。1984 年 12 月起为上海木材装卸公司管辖经营 [65]。大来洋行的船舶驶抵上海时，也指定由江南造船所进行坞修和航修。毛根很好地利用了罗伯特·大来对美国政府上层的影响力，赢得了四艘万吨级美国运输舰的建造合同。

Robert Dollar and Mauchan, Chief Engineer of Kiangnan Dock & Engineering Works, were both Scottish, and have a good personal relationship. In 1918, Dollar Company ordered two teak hull barges (Hull Nos. H326/327) at Kiangnan. The wharf and lumber yard of Dollar Company were located just opposite of Kiangnan (i.e., it fronts on the Huangpu River and Bailianjing, refer to Figure 2-30). The adjacent wharves belonged to a Chinese company, Zhong Xing (Chung Hsing) Coal Mine Terminal. The internal documents of 1928, labeled the pier "The warf of Dollar Company" (see Figure 2-31), and in 1950 the Chinese Government requisitioned the Dollar Company's wharf and handed it over to the East China Sea Fleet of Chinese Navy. In 1956, it was returned to the Port Authority and renamed "Bailianjing wharf". Since December of 1984, it has been operating under the jurisdiction of Shanghai Timber Handling Company. When the freighters of Dollar Company arrived in Shanghai, it was also designated by Kiangnan for docking and repairing. In particular, Mr. Mauchan made good use of Robert Dollar's influence at the top of the U.S. Government, winning contracts to build four 10 000-ton steam freighters.

图 2-30 大来洋行在上海白莲泾的办公楼和仓库
Figure 2-30 Robert Dollar's office and warehouse at Bailianjing

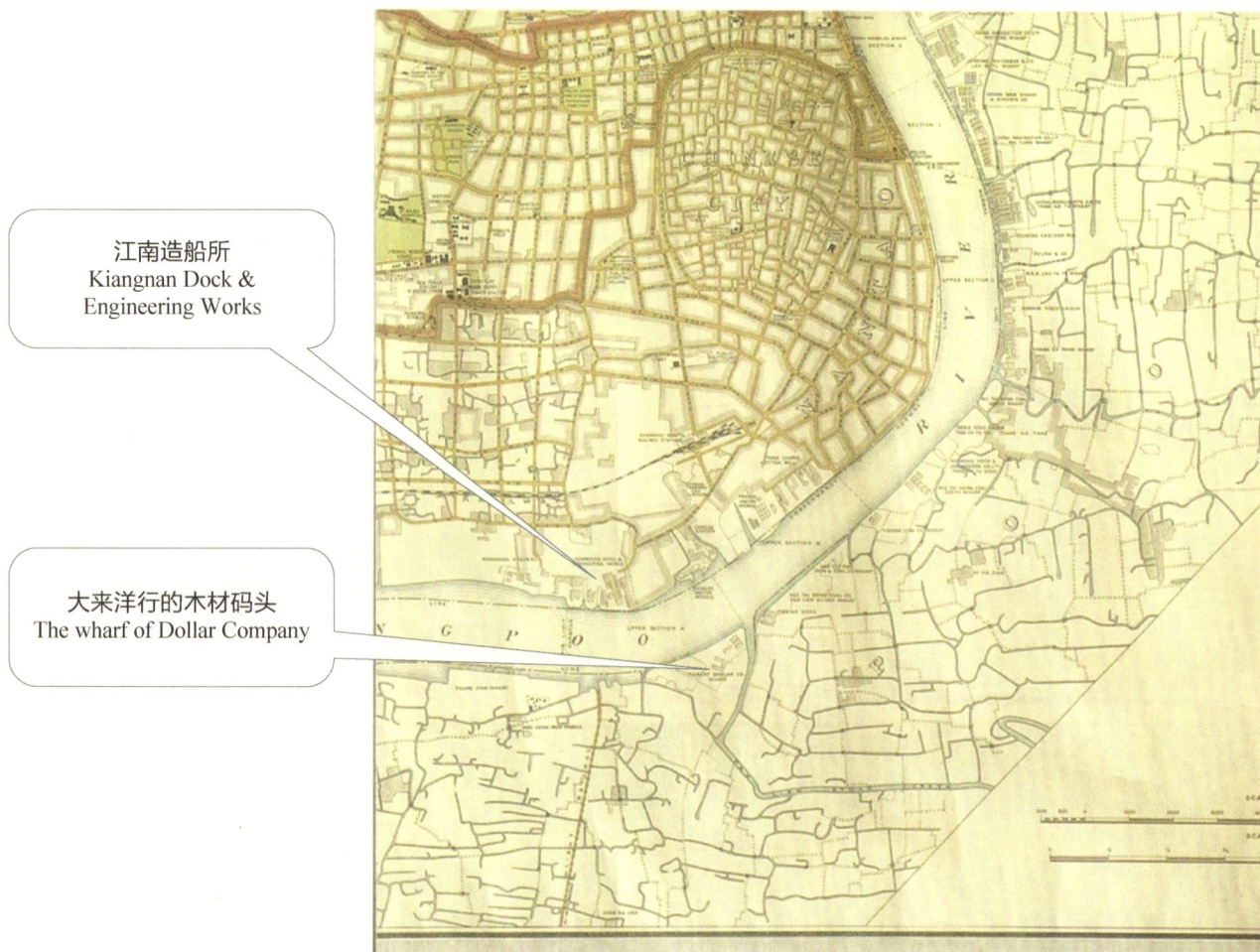

江南造船所
Kiangnan Dock &
Engineering Works

大来洋行的木材码头
The wharf of Dollar Company

图 2-31　1928 年的内部资料（局部）
Figure 2-31　The internal documents of 1928 (partial)

罗伯特·大来在签订这份合同的过程中起了决定性作用。此外，根据作者的考证，合同文本（草稿）的标注日期是 1918 年 7 月 10 日，但这并不是实际的签订日期，实际合同的签订日期为 1918 年 7 月 25 日（参见本书第 2 章 2.4 节）。

罗伯特·大来在他回忆录的第 25 页也写道：

"1918 年 8 月，我有半个月不是待在纽约就是华盛顿。那时真热，但我完成了一宗大生意，圆满地完成了中国政府（企业）为美国政府造船的合同。在合同签订完成后，中国政府通过他们的驻美大使顾维钧

It can be seen that Robert Dollar played a decisive role in the signing of this contract. As per additional verification, the date of the contract text (draft) is 10 July 1918, but not the actual date of signing on 10 July 1918, the actual contract signed on 25 July 1918 (see Section 2.4 of Chapter 2).

According to Robert Dollar's own memoir (*Memoirs of Robert Dollar*, Page 25), he wrote:

"*I spent half of August (of 1918) either in New York or Washington. It was really hot but I got through with a great deal of business, principally in connection with the consummation of the contract for the Chinese Government to build steamers for the American Government. On closing the contract the Chinese Government through their Ambassador,*

对美国海运委员会主席赫尔利提出要求美国政府将数百万的造船款通过我转交，同时不要求我提供任何担保和协议，这是对我很大的信任。我禁不住地把这个信任作为我所接受到的最高荣誉。"

大来航运公司在 20 世纪第二个十年末试图扩张时负债累累，一旦大萧条开始，公司运营艰难，无法恢复。罗伯特·大来于 1932 年去世。1938 年大来航运公司被美国政府买下，这些资产随后被用来成立美国总统航运公司，简称"APL"。后来美国总统航运公司又被法国的集装箱航运巨头达飞轮船公司收购。

Wellington Koo, conferred a very high honor on me by telling Mr. Hurley, Chairman of the ships, which would amount to many millions of dollars and not ask me to give either bond or agreement for the money. I cannot help but prize this confidence as one of the highest honors I have ever received."

The Dollar Steamship Company became heavily indebted while trying to expand in late 1920s and could not recover once the Great Depression set in. Robert Dollar passed away in 1932 and the line was bought out by the U.S. Government in 1938. Their assets were then used to establish American President Lines, known as "APL". This container line company was acquired by CMA CGM, a French container giant, which is still in business today.

2.9

赫尔利对毛根的评价
The Evaluation from Chairman Hurley to Mauchan

那么毛根到底在江南造船所承接这四艘美国运输舰的过程起了什么作用呢？作者查到了美国海运委员会主席赫尔利先生曾经写过一本回忆录（*The Bridge to France*）。书中第51页第7章"应急船队公司开始运作"（THE EMERGENCY FLEET CORPORATION BEGINS ITS WORK），有两段文字是美国海运委员会主席赫尔利对江南造船所总稽查毛根的评价。

毛根是一个在克莱德（苏格兰格拉斯哥附近的一个小镇）接受过造船工程师训练的苏格兰人，在中国上海的江南造船所担任负责人。他到华盛顿是为了说服美国海运委员会在他的船厂里使用中国的劳动力建造船舶。但此项交易取决于他的船厂能在我们提供钢材的前提下，以合适的价格建造出符合要求的船舶。最后我在中国驻美大使顾维钧和应急船队公司的官员的见证下签署了合同。这份中国造船合同的签署不仅仅意味着是对我们船队运力的充实。这更加巩固了美国和中国间的友好关系；或者说至少我判断的是中华民国据此（合同的签订）授予了罗伯特·大来先生勋章，表彰他在两国合同协商中的付出。没有其他船比这四艘由中国船厂建造的更出色。罗伯特·大来在接手购买它们之后对于江南造船所高水平的建造水平给予了最高的评价。

我非常乐意和毛根这样的人交谈。我们需要他提出很多值得考虑的想法。许多人真诚地带着想法来到海运委员会，这是显示他们勇气的机会。其中一些人已经拥有丰富的船舶经营管理经验。他们将得到大显身手的机会。这里是为那些爱国志士提供机会的地方，或者如果他们没有其他的技能，至少他们战胜了自私。有一点他们是相似的，那就是他们如何很好地利用了这些机会，如何在最困难的时候为国效力。我和那些志在成为造船者的朋友交流的经历给了我足够多值得考虑的机会来证明一个平凡人经常会认为自己什么都能干，但日积月累这种想法会造成很严重的问题。如果只是用自私自利来为自己的失败开脱是很肤浅

What kind of role did Mauchan play in the process of Kiangnan Dock & Engineering Works securing the contract for building four American steam freighters? Edward N. Hurley, Chairman of the United States Shipping Board, had written a memoir *The Bridge to France*. On page 51 of Chapter Ⅶ "THE EMERGENCY FLEET CORPORATION BEGINS ITS WORK", there are two paragraphs regarding the evaluation of Mauchan, Superintendent of Kiangnan Dock & Engineering Works.

Mr. R. B. Mauchan, a Scotchman who received his training as a marine engineer on the Clyde, a small town nearby Glasgow, and who was Superintendent of the Kiangnan Dock & Engineering Works, Shanghai, China, turned up in Washington to interest the Shipping Board in the possibilities of having vessels built in his yard with Chinese labor. It was decided that his yard could build satisfactory ships at a satisfactory price if we furnished the steel. Later I signed the contract in the presence of Wellington Koo, the Chinese Ambassador, and the leading officials of the Fleet Corporation. The signing of this Chinese contract meant more than adding to our fleet. It did much to cement the friendly relations between this country and China; or at least I judge so because of the decorations conferred by the Chinese Republic upon Mr. Robert Dollar, who aided in the negotiations. No finer ships were built than the four laid down in the Chinese yard. Dollar paid the highest possible tribute to their fine construction by buying them later.

I was, glad to talk to a man like Mauchan. If men had any ideas worth considering, we wanted them. Many came to the Shipping Board with apparently sincere arguments that this was their chance to show their mettle. Some had acquired extensive experience in operating ships. They were given a chance. Here was an opportunity for such men to demonstrate their love of country, or, if nothing else, their enlightened selfishness. How they rose to their opportunity, how they served their country in its blackest hour, is familiar to the public. My experience with would-be ship-builders gave me ample opportunity to note how common is an ordinary human trait, which in its cumulative effect may become a serious problem of administration. It would be superficial to dismiss the human failing that I have in mind with merely the word "selfishness". Such a designation would be neither adequate nor just. The situation was such that nearly every man who ever had seen a ship concluded that

的，也是不完整、不公平的。几乎每个看到过船的人总认为他自己就能造，而且觉得这对海运委员会会有帮助，如果他还能在造船上盈利，那完全是靠运气。但既然肯定有人会盈利，他会觉得他可能正好就是那个。这也不是完全不正确的，过去肯定有不专业的人造过船。绝大多数想要成为造船方的人往往忽略了这些问题：他们要不就是忽视了船舶建造过程中个人经验的价值，要不就是忽视了拥有经验丰富的船体和轮机工程师的必要性。

从上述赫尔利主席的评价来看，毛根对江南造船所赢得美国这四艘万吨级运输舰的努力和贡献是显著的，他优秀的沟通能力和充实的技术背景为在美国海运委员会面前充分展示江南造船所的技术和建造实力奠定了基础。这四艘万吨级运输舰的建造和交付对江南造船所的跨越式发展是有里程碑意义的。

he could build one; that his services would be invaluable to the Shipping Board, and that if in building ships he made money, the profit was purely incidental. Since someone must make a profit, he felt that he might just as well be the one. Perhaps the reasoning was not wholly incorrect. Ships certainly were built by men who had not been professional ship-builders. The only points overlooked by most would-be ship-builders were either the value of personal experience in ship construction, or the necessity of engaging naval architects and engineers who had the experience.

From the evaluation of Chairman Hurley, Mauchan's efforts and contribution to secure, construct and deliver these four American steam freighters were really remarkable, and his excellent communication ability and substantial technical background had fully demonstrated the technical and construction strength of Kiangnan Dock & Engineering Works to the Shipping Board. The construction and successful delivery of these four steam freighters had become a milestone of Kiangnan to realize rapid development.

作者注：

Notes:

1 https://en.wikipedia.org/wiki/RMS_Lusitania.

2 同上。

3 （英）诺曼·斯通（Norman Stone）著，王东兴、张蓉译，《一战简史：帝国幻觉》（*World War One: A Short History*），中信出版社，2014 年。

4 James D. Ciment and Thaddeus Russell eds. The Home Front Encyclopedia: United States, Britain, and Canada in World Wars Ⅰ and Ⅱ, Vol. Ⅰ, pp. 457–458.

5 http://en.wikipedia.org/wiki/United_States_Shipping_Board, 2015 年 12 月 20 日。

6 同上。

7 资料来自：吴翎君，《一次大战期间中美海运事业的合作》，发表于纪念江南造船建厂 150 周年学术研讨会。作者综合其他史料分析，应该理解为"没有造过一艘大船"。

8 Vice Consul Walter A. Adam (Shanghai), "Facilities and Materials at Shanghai for the Construction of Wooden Vessels of Standardized Parts Thereof", June 15, 1917. NA. No.893.642/8.

9 R. B. Manchan to Thomas Sammons（American Consul-General, Shanghai), 5 Dec., 1917. NA. No.893.642/8. DOCK MANAGER DIES: Well-Known Identity of Shanghai Waterfront Mr. R. B. Mauchan, South China Morning Post (1903–1941); Mar 24, 1936; ProQuest Historical Newspapers: South China Morning Post. p. 2.

10 美国国务院收到美国驻上海总领事的报告后，非常不悦，质疑总领事为何将如此重要的公文在副总领事于 6 月 16 日完成后，竟到 12 月才递交给国务院，并要他解释公文延宕的原因。此事最后不了了之。The Secretary of States to Thomas Sammons, Jan. 29, 1918. NA. No.893.642/8.

11 "Shipbuilding Possibilities at Shanghai", December 13, 1917. NA. No.893.642/8.

12 顾维钧（英文名：Vi Kyuin Wellington Koo，1888 年 1 月 29 日—1985 年 11 月 14 日），字少川，江苏省太仓州嘉定县（今上海市嘉定区）人，中华民国时期外交官。1912 年任袁世凯的英文秘书，历任中华民国北洋政府代国务总理，政府驻法国、英国大使，驻联合国首席代表，驻美大使，海牙国际法院副院长；被誉为中国现代史上最卓越的外交家之一。1985 年病逝于美国纽约。

13 海军部致驻美顾（维钧）公使函，1918 年 4 月 8 日。中国台湾研究院近代史研究所藏，《外交部档案》，03–12–010–03–001；资料来自：吴翎君，《一次大战期间中美海运事业的合作》，发表于纪念江南造船建厂 150 周年学术研讨会。

14 江南造船所所长刘冠南致驻美顾公使函，1918 年 5 月 8 日，03–12–010–03–006。

15 Edward N. Hurley to the Secretary of States, July 1, 1918, NA. No.893.642/13.

16 Alvey A. Adee (Second Assistant Secretary of the Secretary of State) to the United States Shipping Board, July 3, 1918. NA. No.893.642/13. "The Department believes that from a political standpoint it would be well to award a contract to the Kiangnan Works".

17 The United States Shipping Board to the Secretary of States, July 13, 1918, NA. No.893.642/17. "inform Kiangnan that contract is concluded to take up full capacity of their works".

18 Morris D. Ferris (Manager, Contract Division) to Edward T. Williams (Chief of Division of the Far Eastern Affairs), July 18, 1918. NA. No.893.642/21.

19 Edward T. Williams (Chief of Division of the Far Eastern Affairs) to Morris D. Ferris (Manager, Contract Division), July 20, 1918. NA. No.893.642/21.

20 "China to build Four Ships for the United States", *Brooklyn Daily Eagle*, New York, Sunday, July 14, 1918. http://bklyn. newspapers.com/image/54538122/.

21 顾维钧公使致函当时的中华民国外交部，1918 年 7 月 28 日，03–12–010–03–008，其中收有 7 月 10 日的英文合同草稿。

22 The United States Shipping Board to the Secretary of States, July 26, 1918, NA. No.893.642/19. "This happy arrangement enabled Chinese industry to become more effective in support of our splendid armies who are now advancing toward their assured victory. By making ships, China will be directly making war upon the common enemy. The occasion is one of good augury of future industrial and commercial cooperation between your great country and the United States, and confidently believed will more firmly cement the traditional friendship between the two peoples." 资料来自：吴翎君，《一次大战期间中美海运事业的合作》，发表于纪念江南造船建厂 150 周年学术研讨会。

23 1913 年 2 月 14 日，福州船政局收归当时的中华民国海军部管辖。《中国舰艇工业历史资料丛书》编纂部编纂，《中国近代舰艇工业史料集》，上海人民出版社，1994 年，第 431 页。

24 即美国海运委员会主席赫尔利。

25 中华民国海军部致驻美顾（维钧）公使函，1918 年 8 月 4 日。《外交部档案》，03-12-010-03-010。这份电报也收录于次日江南造船所所长刘冠南给美国海运委员会主席的感谢函中。资料来自：吴翎君，《一次大战期间中美海运事业的合作》，发表于纪念江南造船建厂150 周年学术研讨会。

26 即美国海运委员会。

27 中华民国外交部收顾公使函件，1919 年 1 月 6 日。但在这份电文中顾维钧的报告于 1918 年 7 月 28 日所写，03-18-103-03-001。

28 中华民国外交部收顾公使函件，1919 年 1 月 6 日，03-18-103-03-001。

29 1976 年，根据当时第六机械工业部的指示，江南造船厂保存的 1949 年以前的技术档案转至第六机械工业部七六所（现为船舶档案馆，位于陕西省兴平市）继续保存。

30 在第六机械工业部七六所（现为船舶档案馆）保存了 1979 年江南造船厂移交的四艘万吨轮的图纸档案。

31 照片由陈语霆拍摄并友情提供。

32 同上。

33 合同上顾维均的名字疑为打印之误。合同上有两个单词"attest"和"witness"，字面解释都是"见证人"，到底有什么区别呢？作者咨询了资深的英美法律专家，他们的解释是 attest 的责任更重，是针对文件内容的"证明、确认"；witness 一般只针对形式，比如签字形式上的"见证"。

34 《申报》，1918 年 8 月 9 日，第 3 版。

35 即美国海运委员会。

36 《申报》，1918 年 8 月 9 日，第 3 版。此处的描述与合同签订时的总布置图和舯横剖面图所表示的总布置是相符的。

37 《申报》，1918 年 8 月 30 日，第 3 版。"中国海滨公司所造载重一千两百吨之新船：'土海第二'号，昨日下午试验之后，购主甚为满意，该船长两百零三尺，阔二十九尺，吃水约十一尺，所用机械均系最新式者，将由赞赐公司经理，来往于香港、新加坡间。又江南造船所为美孚煤油公司所造之新式燃油船'美南'号，亦经试验，甚为顺利，日内将载煤油赴南方某海港。该船长一百四十四尺，阔二十七尺，吃水八九尺，每小时能行十海里半，造者与购者对于该船均颇得意云。"

38 即"局坞分家"以后的江南制造局，1917 年改名为"上海兵工厂"。

39 《申报》，1918 年 10 月 9 日，第 3 版。

40 K.H. Kwong , "How China Plans to Build Ships for America!", Millard Review, Nov. 23, 1918. "The table is now turned. China is to show that she is herself capable of doing what she is herself capable of doing what she has been want to get done abroad. A new chapter of her industrial is thus begun".

41 《申报》，1918 年 11 月 24 日。

42 *The Wall Street Journal*, 23 July 1918.

43 据作者分析，此为滑道间距，而非船台宽度。江南造船所建造的美国运输舰的船宽为 55 英尺（16.76 米）。

44 上海社会科学院经济研究所编，《江南造船厂厂史：1865—1949》，江苏人民出版社，1983 年，第 124-125 页。

45 陆舸编著，《江南往事》，上海画报出版社，2005 年，第 367 页。原文为"法国马赛大西洋船厂"，因为位于法国西北部圣纳泽尔的大西洋船厂是 1955 年由多家造船厂合并而成的，故作者改为刘墨泉去了"马赛的一家造船厂"，表达更加准确一些。

46 上海社会科学院经济研究所编，《江南造船厂厂史：1865—1949》，江苏人民出版社，1983 年，第 126 页。

47 参见本书 2.7.4 节造船所首次颁发奖章。

48 陆舸编著，《江南往事》，上海画报出版社，2005 年，第 226-228 页。作者核对了《江南造船厂厂史：1865—1949》（江苏人民出版社，1983 年），并对书中第 145-164 页中的相关内容在引用时进行了部分修改润色、增补和删减。

49 上海社会科学院经济研究所编，《江南造船厂厂史：1865—1949》，江苏人民出版社，1983 年，第 146 页。

50 铸铁厂匠目还有陈爱德，1918 年 9 月获三等奖章。获奖名单刊于 1918 年 9 月 27 日上海的《新闻报》，参见本书 2.74 节。

51 1918 年 9 月 27 日上海的《新闻报》所刊的获奖名单为"张桂馥"，参见本书 2.7.4 节。

52 陆舸编著，《江南往事》，上海画报出版社，2005 年，第 234-235 页。引用时作者略有修改和删减。

53 "文虎奖章"是民国时期颁发的一种勋章，寓意"文武双全"。

54 http://www.falkirkculturalcenter.org/robert-dollar/.

55 http://insight.amcham-shanghai.org/amcham-shanghai-the-early-years/.

56 木材英尺指面积为 1 平方英尺 1 英寸厚的木材的体积。

57 另据 http://insight.amcham-shanghai.org/amcham-shanghai-the-early-years/，大来航运公司成立于 1903 年 12 月 10 日。

58 原文为：California Governor James Rolph, Jr. said at the time of his death, "Robert Dollar has done more in his lifetime to spread the American flag on the high seas than any man in this country."

59 *The Old Shanghai A–Z*, Paul French, Hong Kong University Press, p. 90.

60 "The Chia Ho in English takes the meaning of Bountiful Harvest. The decoration was brought to this country by officers of one of the ships of the Dollar Steamship Company."

61 黎元洪（1864 年 10 月 19 日—1928 年 6 月 3 日），字宋卿，原籍安徽省宿松县，生于湖北省黄陂县夏店（今属孝感市大悟县），人称"黎黄陂"。清末加入海军，后担任新军协统；武昌起义后，担任湖北都督、中华民国副总统。袁世凯大总统死后，曾两次担任中华民国北洋政府大总统。

62 阮渭泾，《美商大来洋行在中国》，载于《天津的洋行与买办》一书，天津人民出版社，1987 年，第 112 页。

63 《罗伯特·大来回忆录》第 25 页。由于第一次世界大战结束了，美国不再需要大量运输舰，最后仅执行了已签订的 4 艘船的合同，剩下 8 艘选择船没有生效。

64 实际签订合同时金额为 780 万美元（4 艘船）。

65 王荣华主编，《上海大辞典》上卷，上海辞书出版社，2007 年，第 596 页。

江南造船所建造四艘万吨轮始末
The Construction of Four EFC Steam Freighters in Kiangnan

3.1

《江南造船所纪要》和万吨轮建造
Summary of Kiangnan Dock & Engineering Works and Steam Freighter Construction

图 3-1　江南造船档案馆保存的《江南造船所纪要》
　　　　的原件封面
Figure 3-1　The cover page of Summary of Kiangnan Dock &
　　　　　　Engineering Works

关于民国七年至十年（1918—1921 年）江南造船所承接和建造四艘美国万吨级运输舰的过程，江南造船厂厂志和所有中国近代史研究学者发表的论文都是引用了民国十一年四月（1922 年 4 月）由江南造船所所长刘冠南审核、廖骁编写的《江南造船所纪要》中第 65~75 页对承接和建造四艘美国万吨级运输舰的过程所做的详细记载。图 3-1 为江南造船集团档案馆保存的《江南造船所纪要》的原件封面照片。

Regarding the process of contracting and building four American steam freighters at Kiangnan Dock & Engineering Works during 1918 to 1921, all papers by researchers, who focus on modern Chinese history, and the records of local history used the primary source from *Summary of Kiangnan Dock & Engineering Works* in page 65 to 75. The document was reviewed by Liu Guannan, and edited by Liao Shen. Figure 3-1 is the cover page of *Summary of Kiangnan Dock & Engineering Works*, and the original version is kept in Archives Institute of Jiangnan Shipyard Group.

本章的 3.2 节为《江南造船所纪要》中所记载的承接和建造四艘美国万吨级运输舰过程始末。作者综合其他渠道查阅到的资料、图纸和文献对《江南造船所纪要》中有出入的描述、时间和船舶技术数据进行了修正或说明。此外，考虑到上下文的统一，作者对政府部门、机构的名称、人物的译名和船名进行了统一修改，在文字上也略有修正和润色。3.2 节中的小标题是作者添加的。

The excerpts in the Section 3.2 are the description of contracting and building four American steam freighters at Kiangnan Dock & Engineering Works. According to the available sources from other aspects such as materials, drawings and documents, some unreliable description, time, and technical data indicated in the *Summary of Kiangnan Dock & Engineering Works* have been revised and elaborated accordingly. Furthermore, the titles and wording of government departments, institutions, name of people and ships are modified in a consistent way. The subtitles in the Section 3.2 are additionally inserted.

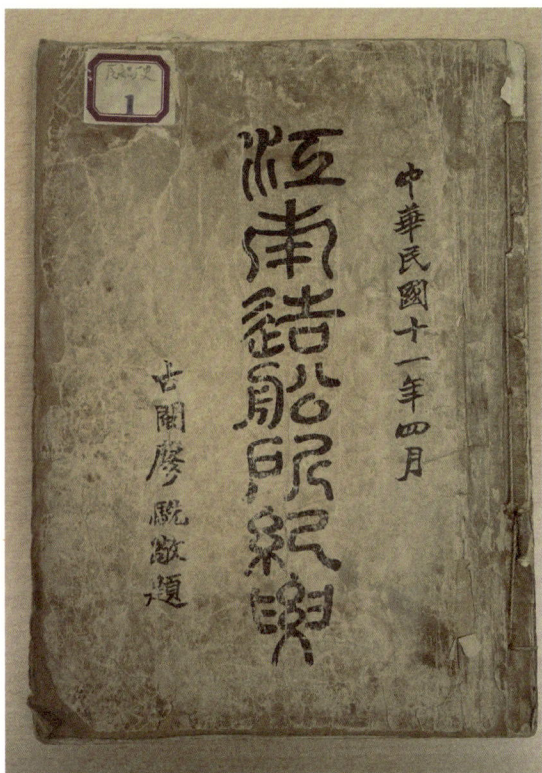

3.2

《江南造船所纪要》中所记载的万吨轮建造始末
Description of Steam Freighter Construction in *Summary of Kiangnan Dock & Engineering Works*

3.2.1

毛根赴美签约
Mauchan Departed for Signing Contract

1918 年夏，欧战正处激烈之时，美国政府以运输舰船缺乏，不敷协同助战之用，待造甚亟，特电饬美国驻上海总领事馆，商请江南造船所代为赶造五千吨运输舰多艘。本所以为我国亦为协约国之一，自应出力代为赶造以尽协同助战义务，遂由美国驻上海领事 T.W. 萨门司（T. W. Sammous）介绍于美国政府愿为代造。复据美国驻上海总领事云："订造运输舰往返电商殊难详尽，请派代表赴美商定较为妥慎。"旋派本所总工程师毛根为代表赴美接洽，经本所据情呈请海军部给予代表委任状，并由江南造船所刘冠南所长授予代表委托书，声明代表权限，摘要如下：

In the summer of 1918, fierce Great War was continuing in European continental. The Government of the United States perceived obvious shortage of marine transportation. It was urgent to speed up the shipbuilding for overcoming the ensuring shipping crisis. The United States Government intentionally telegraphed the Consulate in Shanghai regarding to quickly build several 5 000 deadweight tons freighters in Kiangnan Dock & Engineering Works. Considering China as a member of the Allies, it is duty-bound to help the United States for mitigating tonnage shortage. The American Consul, T. W. Sammous, converted the confirmation of Kiangnan to the United States Government, and he also delivered a message to Kiangnan that "…the issue of ordering freighters cannot be communicated in detail through the telegraph. It is better Kiangnan to appoint a representative to the United States for settling the project cautiously." Immediately, Kiangnan, under the permission of Naval Department, decided to appoint Robert Buchanan Mauchan as representative to the United States with a power of attorney issued by Liu Guannan, Director of Kiangnan Dock & Engineering Works. Major terms are excerpted as follows:

一、该员此次赴美商造船只，按本所力量只能承造五千吨以外一万吨以内轮船二艘。

First, for the issue of American freighters, Kiangnan only has the ability to build two steam freighters in 5 000 to 10 000 deadweight tons in the parallel.

二、到美后须将拟造之舰、所需锅炉及大宗材料价值详细考察，俟有把握致电本所查核。

Second, the cost of imported boilers and other major steel materials should be carefully reviewed and checked, and contract wording and term should be approved and finalized by headquarter of Kiangnan.

三、料价考实后估开船价，其获利至少须得成本二成办以外方为合算，因将来各料运华进口税及煤炭、人工势必贵一日，均须宽为筹算庶免吃亏。

Third, the ship price should be estimated after confirmation of materials and equipments. The benefits should be beyond 20% of the cost at least due to import tax and the costs of coal and labour, which will be increased potentially. So certain margin should be considered in the budget for avoiding risks.

四、船价估定后，须先致电本所查核斟酌，俟所长决定方为有效。

Fourth, once ship price estimated, the representative should telegraph Kiangnan for confirmation. The price will be finalized after approval of Kiangnan's Director.

五、船价由本所决定后，其承造合同由顾使与美政府议决签订之。

Fifth, in case that the price is approved by Kiangnan, Wellington Koo, on behalf of Kiangnan, will sign the shipbuilding contract with American Government.

江南造船所的总工程师毛根遂于 1918 年 5 月 9 日启程赴美接洽。7 月，毛根由美来电报告商订万吨级运输舰四艘，请赶紧筹备绘图一切。10 月回国报告经过情形，并呈交原定英文合同。摘要如下：

Thereafter, Robert Buchanan Mauchan, the Chief Engineer of Kiangnan Dock & Engineering Work, started his trip to the United States on the 9th of May. In July, Mauchan telegraphed Kiangnan that the Shipping Board intended to order four 10 000-ton transportation steamers, and asked Kiangnan immediately to prepare relevant drawings and documentation. He returned to China in October and submitted original English contract. The excerpt of contract is as below:

1918 年 7 月 10 日[1]，美国海运委员会主席赫尔利在美国首都华盛顿与我国顾公使双方签字，美国海运委员会秘书博尔内、美方官员鲍勃会同签字为证，其船身长四百二十九英尺[2]，宽五十五英尺，高三十七英尺十一寸，吃水二十七英尺六寸，速率每点钟十海里半，载重量为一万吨，每吨作价美金一百九十五元计算，四艘共四万吨，合共美金七百八十万元，分七批交付。自美国材料到厂之日起算，第一艘限期六个月交船，其余三艘均递次后五星期完工试船。保险各节亦均载明合同，至一切造法另有图单为凭。

On July 10th 1918, Chairman of the United States Shipping Board, Edward N. Hurley signed contract with Chinese Ambassador Willington Koo in Washington. Additionally, the Secretary of USSB, S. N. Bourne and American Officer Bob attended simultaneously as witness. The length of the ship was 429 feet, the width was 55 feet, and the depth was 37 feet 11 inches. The draught of the ship was 27 feet 6 inches, and the speed of ship was 10.5 nautical miles. The deadweight was 10 000 tons. The price was calculated on basis of 195 U.S. dollars per ton, so total price of the four 10 000-ton deadweight steamers was 7.8 million U.S. dollars. The payment was further divided into seven installments. The delivery of the first ship was scheduled within six months after the American materials arrived shipyard. The other three were scheduled five weeks interval. Insurance and other details were clearly specified in the contract, and all the building methods and technical details are based on attached drawings.

3.2.2

造船合同生效
Shipbuilding Contract Effected

合同签订生效之后，委托纽约大来公司代表本所收款购料一切之事。8月1日由美政府支付了第一批四舰造价首付款170万美元。由纽约大来公司代收存储于美国银行，备付购料之用，凡四舰所用之料以及关于承造该舰扩充机器等件，均由该公司代表经理购备转运，所有费用以所收船价归还。此议既成，本所赶即筹备扩充各厂、坞一切事宜，以期克日兴工。彼时美国政府及海运委员会各主要人物，咸致电海军部褒奖本所此次允为代造运输舰，实足以表示我国允为协约国出力助战之意。

After shipbuilding contract effected, Kiangnan issued delegation to Robert Dollar Company as agency for installments of contract and procurement. On August 1, U.S. Government paid 1st installment (down payment) of U.S. dollar 1.7 million for these four steam freighters. This installment was deposited into American Bank by Robert Dollar Company in New York for purchasing material and equipment. These purchased material and equipment were shipped by Dollar Steamship Company. Once the shipbuilding contract effected, Kiangnan started immediately to prepare facility expansion, such as workshops and dry docks in order to commence construction soonest. Kiangnan had received the awards for construction of those four steam freighters from key persons of U.S. Government and the Shipping Board. Chinese Admiralty had expressed their thankfulness for this achievement. It also had shown Chinese good faith for supporting the Allies.

兹摘录美国海运委员会主席赫尔利电文并海军部复文如下：

The excerpts from the telegraph of Edward N. Hurley, Chairman of the United States Shipping Board in reply to Admiralty are as below:

海军刘总长鉴：

鄙人关于上海江南造船所所订造轮船一事，现已磋商就绪，贵总长于造船之设施卓有成效，是以鄙国得与协力共作，如此佳兆促令鄙人谨申祝贺。夫船艘者能于此战中取胜也。盖无多数船只则我雄军恐难完收最后之胜利，其新近伟大之功绩已成战胜坚固之基础。今以新启得力之法建造轮船以期进取，无异携带中国参与战事也。

爱德华·N. 赫尔利
美国海运委员会主席

Dear Liu, Navy Chief of Staff:

I have finalized the shipbuilding contract for ordering four steamers in Kiangnan Dock & Engineering Works. I sincerely congratulate Kiangnan secured this contract. Since Navy Chief Liu has made great efforts to improve the facility of shipbuilding, so that United States is able to cooperate with China to build these ships. Sufficient transportation tonnage will ensure transatlantic logistics supply during the war, otherwise our army could not finally triumph in the war. Today the construction of newbuildings will commenced with more efficient technique and progressed as per schedule, it will bring China into the Allies to join the war.

Edward N. Hurley
Chairman of the United States Shipping Board

美国海运委员会主席鉴：

顷接来电，奖饰逾恒，感谢不尽。此次江南造船所承造贵国轮船，原为中国对于协约国应尽之职务，要亦借主席臂助之力，俾江南造船所得展所长，以益友邦，鄙人与有荣光，深盼将来该船辅助贵局之作用，当能收胜利之效果也。

刘冠雄
海军总长

Dear the Chairman of the United States Shipping Board:

Well received your telegraph with thanks. This time, Kiangnan building steel steamers for the United States is original obligation of China for the Allies. With the help of great supports from Mr. Chairman, Kiangnan could take this great opportunity to fulfil their potential. It is not only benefit to our friendly country, and I also get the glory. I do hope these ships can support military transportation of the United States Shipping Board to finally triumph in the War.

Liu Guanxiong
Navy Chief of Staff

3.2.3

万吨轮开工建造
The Commencement of Construction

1919 年 1 月，江南造船所第一、第二船台筑成，实行动工兴建。船壳、锅炉相关的结构、烟箱等由富有经验之匠目甘爔初、李庆祥等包工承造；木作工程由何祖康、庆瑶等包工承造；机器、轴系等件由江南造船所机器厂制造。其第一、第二两舰于 3 月安装龙骨，第三、第四两舰亦即继续兴工。是年 8 月，因第一次世界大战业已告终，此项美运输舰工程由美国政府拨交海运委员会管理，"实求坚固，毋庸着急，不必依期赶造"。江南造船所实因由美国提供的钢料未能按期到货，运输舰建造工程也相应推迟了工期。

In January 1919, once the construction work of No.1 and No.2 slipways in Kiangnan Dock & Engineering Works were completed, the construction of ship was commenced. Hull, boiler related steel structure, smoking box, etc. were sub-contracted to experienced subcontractors Gan Xiaochu and Li Qingxiang as well as their working teams; wooden interior works were subcontracted to He Zukang and Qing Yao teams; machinery and shafting were manufactured by Machinery Department of Kiangnan Dock & Engineering Works. The keel laying of No.1 and No.2 steam freighters were carried out in March, and the construction works of No.3 and No.4 steam freighters were successively started. In August 1919, the United States Shipping Board informed Kiangnan Dock & Engineering Works that these cargo steamers were transferred from the U. S. Government to the Shipping Board since the armistice had been signed last November. The construction of freighter, thus, should follow the principle of "Quality and Robust First" and not strictly follow the schedule originally defined in the contract. The real reason of postponement was that the steel material supplied by the United States can not arrive on schedule, and the construction in Kiangnan Dock & Engineering Works was been delayed accordingly.

3.2.4

首制船下水并命名
Launching and Naming Ceremony of the First Steam Freighter

1920 年 6 月 3 日，第一艘船（H317）行下水典礼，美国公使柯兰携夫人莅所行礼，并柬邀中、外官商各界观礼。先于船首架木为台，绕以万国之旗。由刘所长请美公使夫人行命名礼，致颂词云：

On 3 June 1920, the launching ceremony of the first ship (H317) was carried out in Kiangnan Dock & Engineering Works. Mr. Charles Richard Crane, the Minister Counselor of the United States, together with his wife attended this ceremony. Kiangnan Dock & Engineering Works also invited many foreign and local guests to attend this ceremony. A wooden made balcony decorated with American flags was located in front of the bow. Kiangnan's Director Liu invited Madam Cornelia Crane, the wife of America's Minister Counselor, as sponsor to deliver encomium to H317:

"余致汝于水，汝其尽汝之职，使汝主人成功，使船人平安，因而将支配汝也，余名汝曰'官府'。"

"As you sail the waters of the world, may you journeys be smooth and your tasks successful, may you be a safe haven for all who board you, and may you bring prosperity and pride to the ship owner and all. I name you 'Mandarin' ."

于是碎船首所悬香槟酒之瓶，水花四溅，欢呼者三。该舰遂缓慢下行而入黄浦江，大众又欢呼者三，一时军乐齐鸣，颇极一时之盛。图 3-2 所示为第一艘船"官府"号下水典礼的盛况。旋由刘所长引来宾入宴会厅，坐既定，举杯祝中、美两国元首之健康及来宾之惠顾。遂相继演说，末由刘所长赠美公使夫人以银器二，事茶点而散。兹将演说词摘录如下：

Then champaign bottle was broken on the bow, and splashed on shell, and all attendees were jubilant. The hull slowly slid down to Huangpu River with music played by matching band, and all attendees were jubilant again. Figure 3-2 is a photo of the launching ceremony of the first American steam freighter SS "Mandarin". After launching done, Director Liu guided the guests to walk into the banquet room and be seated, toasted the health of presidents of both countries. The representatives delivered speeches. Director Liu presented Madam Crane two silverwares with compliments of Kiangnan. The gala luncheon was finished after dessert and tea were served. The excerpts of speeches are as follows:

刘所长演说：

The Speech delivered by Mr. Liu, Director of Kiangnan:

"今日为敝所承造美国运输舰四艘之第一艘'官府'号行下水典礼，荷蒙各界诸君惠临敝所参观，至为荣幸。"

"Today we set together to celebrate launching 'Mandarin' steel steam freighter, the first ship of series for the United States. It is great honour for all guests visiting Kiangnan."

"溯中国造船历史，在西元纪元以前已有艨艟、楼船诸名称，当时构制虽有可观，究系木制所造。自近世钢铁汽船发明后，中国各船厂如福建船政局、大沽造船所及敝所等处，所造大小钢铁汽船不少，其排水量仅二三千吨而已。即敝所前代招商局造'江华'商轮，排水量四千一百余吨，彼时在中国造船界中已为仅见之事，较之今日下水之'官府'号排水量可

"If reviewing the history of Chinese shipbuilding, in pre-Christian era, China already had 'Meng Chong' (i.e., a small warship protected with cowhide, higher speed, and can accommodate approximate 20 sailors) and 'Lou Chuan' (i.e., a large scale warship with multiple decks and attack/defense weapons, and can carry 1 000 to 3 000 sailors), but they all were made of wooden structure although they had tremendous quantity. After steam driven steel hull ship was innovated in modern times, Chinese shipyards such as Fujian Shipbuilding Bureau (Fokien

一万四千七百五十吨，在今日中国造船界中不更成为空前之巨构乎？"

Shipbuilding Bureau), Dagu Shipyard (Taku Dock & Engineering Works) and Kiangnan, have built various steel steamers, but their displacements are merely in range of 2 000 to 3 000 tons. Comparing Kiangnan built 'Kiang Wah' passenger river steamer for China Merchant Bureau. Her displacement is more than 4 100 tons, which is the biggest ship at that time. 'Mandarin' with displacement of 14 750 tons launched today has really become a giant in Chinese shipbuilding industry."

图 3-2　首制船"官府"号下水典礼盛况
Figure 3-2　Launching ceremony of the first American steam freighter SS "Mandarin"

"故此次敝所得承美国政府订造此项巨舰，足征敝所工程足以见信于美国政府，而美国政府所派海运委员会代表麦格雷戈（J. A. McGregor）、卢肯巴赫（J. L. Luckenbach）及监造员艾斯勒（W. I. Eisler）诸君又皆公正和平热诚相向，甚为敝所所敬仰，实可谓敝所之良师，不特于敝所名誉能增无上之光荣，且于敝所工程方面亦增无穷之知识，从此敝所营业发达，制造日新，由万吨之船造至数万吨以上，彼时敝所同人必作饮水思源之念。"

"This time, Kiangnan could win the contract of such bigger steel steamers for American Government, it well proven that American Government trusts Kiangnan and our capability. Mr. J. A. McGregor and Mr. J. L. Luckenbach, the representatives of the Shipping Board, Mr. W. I. Eisler, site surveyor, delegated by American Government, all of them are fair, warm and sincere, rightly admired to Kiangnan. They are real teachers of Kiangnan, and they help Kiangnan to improve proficiency and supplement knowledge especially in shipbuilding engineering. Since then Kiangnan will thrive and advance with times, the ship deadweight will be raised from a decade to decades thousands. 'April showers bring May flowers', it is common vision of all colleagues of Kiangnan."

"咸额手相庆曰：本所营业发达至此，实自1918年7月25日签约承造美国万吨运输舰'官府'号始。此其感念先进国引导持携之力为何所乎！况美国大总统威尔逊、美国公使柯兰，本为吾国人民所钦慕，将来两国邦交益加亲睦，固在意中，窃望美国政府经敝所此次承造运输舰完成之后大为满意，对于敝所感情更加亲信，时予扶持，使敝所营业前途日见进步，则不但敝所同人感激不尽，且可以使中国造船界及工业、航业各界咸闻风观感，争相勤勉，以期步先进之国后尘也。所以今日特请中、外来宾参与盛典，并敬率敝所全体与在座诸君恭贺美舰'官府'号无量之幸福。"

"It is grateful that the Kiangnan achieved such success. It was originated the contract assignment of 'Mandarin' series freighter on 25 July 1918. The people of our country admire the President Wilson and Minister Counselor Crane, and we are grateful for the assistance from advanced countries like the United States. I sincerely expect that the relationship between two countries will be more harmony, more trust and support. I also do hope American Government will be quite satisfied with those four steam freighters when they are completed at Kiangnan. Business prospect is now well progressing in Kiangnan. It is not only an achievement of Kiangnan but also achievements of Chinese shipbuilding and shipping industries. Since then we shall work hard and encourage each other for following advanced countries. Today Kiangnan sincerely invites so many guests to attend this ceremony. On behalf of all Kiangnan's staffs, I would like to express our sincere thanks to all guests attended ceremony today. I wish SS 'Mandarin' bring prosperity and pride to the ship owner and all."

美公使柯兰演说：

"余素注意造船事，每次出游必研究运输方法，因此事极有趣味。"又云："彼年前曾来中国一次，见兵工厂之大进步，喜甚。"末云："世界已有五六大国皆相继破产，幸今下水之船乃一和平之船（众鼓掌）。余信太平洋可不再需要战争之船，而只驶行和平之船。吾美人极愿与中国共同合进。"

The speech delivered by Mr. Crane, Minister Counselor of the United States:

"I am so interested in shipbuilding, and I always study the transportation method before I arrange my travel plan." Mr. Crane said: "I am happy to see Kiangnan has made great progress comparing that I paid visit to this arsenal serval years ago." Finally Mr. Crane said: "Now five, six countries in the world are suffering the depression, today launched steamer is the peaceful ship (all applaud). I believe it is no longer to need warship in Pacific Ocean, only peaceful ship will sail. We will sincerely corporate with China for our common targets."

美国驻上海总领事克宁翰（E. S. Cunningham）演说：

"今日下水礼实为一极重要之机会，余愿述其要点如下：江南造船所今既能造成美国引来宾所订四大船之一，则前所云中国不能造大船之说实无根据，因一国之成功全在其出产力之大。初美国宣布参战时，急欲补足其被潜艇所沉之商船，乃当时各国船厂均已赶造新船，实无余暇，美国于是遂问中国能否代造四艘，中国立允之。吾人今日乃见此'官府'号之下水，诚盛举也。"

The speech delivered by Mr. E. S. Cunningham, Consul General of the United States:

"Today's launching is really a great opportunity, I would like to highlight: Kiangnan now can build one of these four big steamers ordered by the United States, this fact shows there is no doubt to the ability of Chinese shipyard to build large ship. The reason of achieving success is the massive productivity of the country. When the United States announced to enter the war, the government urgently wanted to overcome marine transportation crisis caused by submarine attacks, but the shipyard slots in the United States and other countries had been fully occupied. The Government of the United States, then, contacted to China to inquire the possibility of building four steamers. China immediately accepted this request. Today I experienced this launching ceremony of SS 'Mandarin', really exciting."

美臬司[3]演说：

"今日之船下水，吾人宜视为一佳兆，因此乃一和平之船，已非一战争之船矣！又逢新公使临境，更为大幸。今后余望中、美间互相扶助之事必逾多，则感情自必逾厚也。"

The speech delivered by Legal Counsel of American Government:

"Today launched steamer, I think this is good sign because she is the ship of peace but not for the war. Today new Minister Counselor can come to attend the ceremony, I feel it a great honor. I do hope the corporation between your great country and the United States will be sustainable, and the friendship between both countries will naturally become deeper."

美造船厂代表 M.A. 佩里（M. A. Perry）演说：

"本部所造之船甚多，而以工程言则'官府'号实驾乎诸船之上。吾人今日得蒙柯兰夫人驾临行礼，实大可喜之事。"

刘冠雄上将演说：

"余之来此参与典礼实为荣幸，可以代表全国之意见，因深知自此厂划分开办以来历史及其工程进展极速，足与欧、美并驾齐驱。今果能造一极大、极坚之船，实为吾人可最欣慰者。此次中国为美代造，更足以联络二国之感情，以后该厂必能为美国尽力。余见造船工人有如此新造之能力，甚望我国商船主人可向该所造新船，以与他国相竞争。余知造船所更当竭力相助，以造成我国大队之商船也。"

王正廷先生[4] 演说：

"今日之下水礼，实有两特点需说明之，美国决计做一事时必竭力为之，故其参战为保护小国之自由，使世界之共和安全，彼亦竭力为之，举其所以之利器全数牺牲，其利器即船只也。当时中欧之德、奥，若知美国亦将加入，且竭力其所有而战，则一九一四年时德、奥或不愿即宣战。吾人要知道美国能于极短时间运兵二百万登陆欧洲之岸，实一惊人之举也。夫中国为一大国，海岸线甚长，而船厂只有如此（指江南造船所）。余甚望今日之下水礼可激起华人思想，而使国人注意与研究并实行此大问题，即造船是要知商业之能力在全世界联络一气，今次美国托中国造船不亦大幸乎！"

The speech delivered by M.A. Perry, the representative of American shipyard:

"I used to involve many shipbuilding projects in our company, I really impressed the SS 'Mandarin' is exactly above our built ships in the engineering respects. It is a great pleasure for me that Madam Crane attended the ceremony and christened the ship today."

The speech delivered by Admiral Liu Guanxiong:

"I am really honored to attend this launching ceremony. I think my personal feeling is representative of Chinese people. Building such huge steamers is magnificent project since Kiangnan Dock was separated as independent. The construction of the hull is quite smooth. It is almost kept the same pace with European and American shipyards. I am so pleased to witness a large and robust hull built in Kiangnan. This time, Chinese shipyard building steam freighters for the United States will further reinforce the relationship of both countries. Kiangnan can build more ships for the United States in the future. Since Kiangnan workers have already such newbuilding capability, I would expect Chinese ship owner should have confidence to order the ship in Kiangnan. I believe Kiangnan can compete with other countries. I do hope Kiangnan shall work more hard to support merchant fleet of China."

The speech delivered by Mr. Wang Zhengting:

"For today's launching ceremony, I would like to point two facts. American will always try their upmost to do if they decided to do something. The intention of entering the war is to protect the freedom of European countries, to keep peace in the world. They mobilized all merchant ships for transporting military supplies to European continental. German and Austrian Empires would not dare to declare the war in 1914 if they known the United States would join the war and made their all efforts. It was a shocking action that the United States transported two million troops landing European continental in short period. China is a grand country with long coastline, but shipyard is merely here (means Kiangnan Dock & Engineering Works). I hope this launching ceremony can inspire affection within all Chinese people. Our people will pay more attention on rapidly developed shipbuilding capability. Shipbuilding always closely connects with world economy, this time, the United States ordered ships in China is really good opportunity for Chinese shipbuilding industry."

3.2.5

后续船下水并命名
Launching and Naming Ceremony of Sister Steam Freighters

第二艘万吨级运输舰（H318）于 1920 年 8 月 3 日下水，美国海运委员会检查员 M.A. 佩里的夫人将此船命名为"天朝"号，如图 3-3 所示。

The second steam freighter with hull number of H318 was launched on 3 August 1920 and christened "Celestial" by the wife of M.A. Perry, the Supervisor of the United States Shipping Board for Shanghai. Refer to Figure 3-3.

图 3-3　后续船下水盛况
Figure 3-3　Launching ceremony of sister steam freighter

《远东共和国》期刊描述了这一下水仪式："天朝"号的下水仪式很简短。包括领事官员、市政官员和中国官员在内的知名人士应邀参加了这次仪式。在升高的观礼台上往前看去，这艘船慢慢滑向黄浦江的江水中。下水时，一小队中国军队礼兵立正行注目礼。应

The event was described in the periodical *The Far Eastern Republic*: "The launching ceremony of the SS 'Celestial' was brief. A gathering of distinguished individuals, including consular, municipal, and Chinese officials, had been invited and from the raised platform witnessed the ship slipping down the ways into the yellow flood of the Huangpu. A detachment of Chinese troops stood at attention while the launching

江南造船所邀请出席仪式的有：美国驻上海总领事克宁翰先生、美国驻亚洲总领事埃伯哈特先生、美国航运委员会代表艾斯勒船长和 S.L. 韦尔先生、驻上海军事长官孙大德中校、司法部前部长徐少春先生、日本驻上海总领事 K. 山崎先生和美国商会会长大来洋行的 J. 哈罗德·大来（1887—1936，罗伯特·大来的小儿子）。"

在加入海运委员会之前，M.A. 佩里是马萨诸塞州福尔河造船公司的一名工程师。佩里和其他监造师最初驻扎在日本横滨。在日本的造船合同完成后，麦格雷戈和卢肯巴赫回到了美国，佩里则到了上海，并于 1920 年 4 月 17 日接手四艘船的监造工作。1922 年 1 月 15 日，他完成了他的工作回到美国。他总共在亚洲工作了 3 年。

"天朝"这个名字在四艘船中是特别有特色的。其他三艘船的名字："官府""东方"和"国泰"都与中国有着明确的联系。如在网上搜索"celestial"这个词，关联的是天空和星星，但如搜索"celestial"和"China"两个词的组合，发现中国曾被称为"天朝帝国"（根据维基百科上的资料："天朝帝国曾被用来指代中国"）。因此，"仙人"一词被用来指 19 世纪移居美国、加拿大和澳大利亚的中国移民。这两个词在当时的英语大众媒体中被广泛使用，但后来也不再使用。江南造船所曾经考虑过将"轿子"作为第四艘船的船名，最后"国泰"这个名字胜出。轿子是当时中国使用轿夫抬的一种有顶棚的椅子。

took place. Among those invited by the Kiangnan Dock & Engineering Works to witness the ceremony were E. S. Cunningham, United States Consul General; A.D. Eberhardt, United States Consul General at large; Captain Eisler and S. L. Ware, the representatives of the United States Shipping Board; Colonel T.D. Sun, representing the Military Governor at Shanghai; S. C. Hsu, former Minister of Justice; K. Yamasaki, Japanese Consul General and J. Harold Dollar (the youngest son of Robert Dollar, 1887–1936) of the Dollar Company, the President of the American Chamber of Commerce."

Prior to his assignment the Shipping Board, M.A. Perry was an engineer with the Fore River Shipbuilding Company in Massachusetts. Perry and his supervisors were originally based in Yokohama, Japan. When the contracts in Japan were completed, MacGregor and Luckenbach moved back to America, Perry moved to Shanghai, and took over the supervisory responsibilities for the completion of the four sisters on 17 April 1920. His work was considered complete by 15 January 1922, at which time he moved back to America. In all he spent three years in Asia.

Of the four names assigned to the sisters, "Celestial" stood out to me. All the other names: "Mandarin" "Oriental" and "Cathay", all had a clear connection to China. Searching on just the word "celestial" resulted in the expected references to the heavens and the stars. Searching on "celestial" in combination with "China" revealed that China was called the "Celestial Empire" in the past (According to Wikipedia.org: "The Celestial Empire was a name used to refer to China"). Accordingly, the name "Celestial" was used to refer to Chinese emigrants to the United States, Canada, and Australia during the 19th century. Both terms were widely used in the English-language popular mass media of the day, but have fallen into disuse later on. At one point, the name "Palanquin" was considered for the fourth vessel, until the name "Cathay" won out. A palanquin was a type of covered sedan chair carried by bearers   used in China at the time.

3.2.6

万吨轮完工交付
The Delivery of Steam Freighters

图 3-4　霍华德·霍勒斯·里斯船长的照片
Figure 3-4　The photo of captain Howard Horace Rees

1921 年 2 月，"官府"号完全竣工，于 15 日试轮，航速为 13 海里，比原定合同指标快了近 3 海里，实出意料之外。后双方择于 17 日赴美交船。在船长霍华德·霍勒斯·里斯（1876—1939）的指挥下，"官府"号从上海启航，于 1921 年 3 月 25 日抵达旧金山。

In February of 1921, SS "Mandarin" was fully completed, and the sea trail was performed on 15 of February. It was surprised that the trail speed reached 13 nautical miles, 3 nautical miles more than guaranteed speed defined in the shipbuilding contract. The ship was scheduled on 17 February to departure for the United States. SS "Mandarin" sailed from Shanghai under the command of captain Howard Horace Rees (1876–1939), and arrived in San Francisco on 25 March 1921.

里斯船长一直在为美国航运委员会承担接收交付船舶的工作。在第一次世界大战之前，他是科尔蒸汽船公司"波特兰"号老式蒸汽船的船长。在战争期间，他以中尉军衔指挥官的身份指挥美国海军预备役部队的"威斯布鲁克"号和"西部精神"号。图 3-4 为里斯船长的照片。

Captain Rees appears to have been working for the Shipping Board at that time for delivering ships. Before the war he was the captain of the old steamship SS "Portland" with the Kerr Steamship Company, and during the war he commanded SS "Westbrook" and SS "Western Spirit" with the United States Naval Reserve Force as a Lieutenant Commander. Figure 3–4 is a photo of captain Howard Horace Rees.

"天朝"号下水后过了 9 个月才完工。1921 年 5 月，它第一次在吴淞口外成功地进行了试航。图 3-5 是加利福尼亚大学伯克利分校班克罗夫特图书馆保存的一张"天朝"号的照片。照片上值得注意的是全宽飞桥上的遮阳篷、救生艇的数量和大小，以及甲板上不同地方可以看到的船员。

It would take another nine months after her launching before SS "Celestial" was completed. In May 1921, she made her first successful trial outside Wusong Estuary. Figure 3–5 is a photo of SS "Celestial" kept in the Bancroft Library, University of California, Berkeley, CA. This was most likely during that sea trial off Wusong Estuary. Note the awning over her full width flying bridge, the number and size of the lifeboats, and the crews that can be seen in various places along the deck.

图 3-5　加利福尼亚大学伯克利分校班克罗夫特图书馆保存的"天朝"号的照片
Figure 3-5　The photo of SS "Celestial" kept in the Bancroft Library, University of California, Berkeley, CA

"天朝"号于 1921 年 5 月 21 日左右从上海启航。它在船长弗雷德里克·E. 安德森的指挥下航行，并于 1921 年 6 月 19 日抵达旧金山。船上有 6 名美国船员、1 名苏格兰工程师和 52 名中国船员。

SS "Celestial" sailed from Shanghai on or about 21 May 1921. She sailed under the command of captain Frederick E. Anderson, and arrived in San Francisco on 19 June 1921. The complement on board were six Americans, one Scottish engineer and fifty-two Chinese crews.

船长弗雷德里克·E. 安德森 1866 年 8 月 4 日出生于瑞典的耶夫勒。据说，他在 13 岁左右时出海工作，很可能是一名服务生。图 3-6 为弗雷德里克·E. 安德森的照片。

Frederick E. Anderson was born in Gävle, Sweden on 4 August 1866. It is said, he ran away around the age of 13 and went to sea, likely as a cabin boy. Figure 3–6 is the photo of captain Frederick E. Anderson.

安德森的船长首秀是在大来航运公司为美国海运委员会管理指挥一艘 8 800 载重吨的货轮 "West Cadron" 号（EFC 1019）。据报道，他在那艘船上工作了一年，然后被转到 "Agnes Dollar" 号上继续工作。他负责指挥四艘万吨轮中的三艘 "天朝" 号、"东方" 号和 "国泰" 号从上海航渡到旧金山，交付给美国海运委员会。

Anderson's first command with Dollar Steamship Company was an 8 800 DWT freighter SS "West Cadron" of the United States Shipping Board with EFC 1019, under contract for the government. He reportedly stayed with her for a year, before being transferred to the SS "Agnes Dollar". He then ferried three sisters of the SS "Mandarin", SS "Celestial", SS "Oriental" and SS "Cathay" from Shanghai to San Francisco for delivery to the Shipping Board.

图 3-6 弗雷德里克·E. 安德森船长
Figure 3–6 Captain Frederick E. Anderson

据江南造船所的代表，大来洋行的罗伯特·大来先生由美来沪称："官府" 号、"天朝" 号 5 抵达旧金山时，经美国政府及海运委员会暨各方面详细考验，工程材料均称坚固，皆大满意，得此良誉，实属不易。云云。

Robert SS Dollar, the representative of Kiangnan Dock & Engineering Works in the United States, came to Shanghai and said: Once steamers SS "Mandarin" and SS "Celestial" arrived in San Francisco, the United States Shipping Board and related parties did inspection on board and they were fully satisfied. The results showed that hull and material were robust. The fact that Kiangnan Dock & Engineering Works soon acquired a good reputation was really not so easy, and so on.

复据美国政府派驻所监造员佩里称：8 月 12 日接到美国海运委员会主席赫尔利来函云，"余此次试验前往中国江南造船所所订造之万吨运输舰 '官府' 号、'天朝' 号两艘已经接管，成绩优美，实驾乎旧有之舰之上，工料既称坚固，其速力复溢出原定之外，殊为满意，此皆借我君认真监造与该所所长服务精勤，故能得此完美之效果。祈向刘、邝两所长并毛根总工程师代为致意申谢。"

Further as per remarks of Mr. M.A. Perry, Supervisor at Kiangnan, the representative of American Government: On August 12, I received the letter from Mr. Edward N. Hurley, Chairman of the United States Shipping Board. "Kiangnan Dock & Engineering Works built steam freighters SS 'Mandarin' and SS 'Celestial' have been taken over. The performance verified by trails was better than existing ships, the hull is robust and speed is faster than that defined in shipbuilding contract. I would be very satisfied." Hurley mentioned. "Such excellent achievement is the results of hard works of Kiangnan's staffs and suit team. Here I would like to give my sincere thanks to Directors Mr. Liu and Mr. K. H. Kwong as well as Mr. Mauchan, Chief Engineer of Kiangnan." Hurley added.

美国海运委员会决定将"天朝"号的烧煤锅炉改装成烧油的。不久该舰由旧金山 37 号码头开往旧金山的莫尔干船坞公司进行改装[6]，估装应需料费 5 000 美元。装竣之后即派交威廉姆斯·戴蒙德公司，加入行驶于欧洲航线之大新舰队。"官府"号是否将烧煤锅炉改装成烧油尚未决定[7]。唯此两舰打錾工程[8]均用手工，舰的自重为 4 750 吨，异常坚固，实于美国海运委员会中可称最优美之船舶也。云云。

"天朝"号是四艘万吨轮中第一艘在交付后进行商载航行的。1921 年 9 月 24 日，它满载着小麦、大麦和其他货物从旧金山起航前往安特卫普和其他欧洲港口。它也是四艘万吨轮中第一个通过巴拿马运河横渡大西洋的。这个航次是由威廉姆斯·戴蒙德公司租用的。"天朝"号于 1922 年 4 月 20 日通过巴尔的摩和圣佩德罗回到旧金山。

更有第三、第四两艘万吨轮，一艘名为"东方"号[9]，另一艘名为"国泰"号[10]，亦于 1921 年 10 月、12 月先后完竣。两艘船都是在船长弗雷德里克·E.安德森的指挥下赴美的。

"国泰"号于 1922 年 1 月 18 日抵达旧金山；由于"东方"号在从上海到旧金山的航程中一个汽缸产生了裂缝，尽管它于 1921 年 10 月 22 日早已到达交货地，但汽缸损坏使其无法交付，只得等到修复后，因此"国泰"号实际上是第三艘正式交付的船。

The Shipping Board had decided to convert coal fueled boilers on SS "Celestial" to oil fueled. SS "Celestial" would depart from No.37 Wharf of San Francisco to Moore Dry Dock Company, San Francisco, for converting works. Estimated converting cost would be approximately 5 000 U.S. dollars. She would be delivered to Williams Diamond & Company for jointing European route after retrofit work completed. The converting work of boiler fuel for SS "Mandarin" was not yet finalized. Since the workmanship for these two steamers was manual, the light weight was 4 750 tons, and hull structure is really robust. They could be boasted as "the best ship" among the ships ordered by the United States Shipping Board. So on.

SS "Celestial" was the first of the four sisters to make a commercial voyage after delivery. She sailed from San Francisco on 24 September 1921 for Antwerp and other European ports laden with wheat, barley and other freights. It made her the first of the four sisters to transit the Panama Canal and cross the Atlantic Ocean. This was the voyage on which she was chartered by Williams Diamond and Company. SS "Celestial" returned to San Francisco on 20 April 1922 via Baltimore and San Pedro.

Further, the third and fourth ships named "Oriental" and "Cathay" respectively, were sequentially completed in October and November of 1921. Both steam freighters sailed to the United States under the command of captain Frederick E. Anderson.

SS "Cathay" arrived in San Francisco on 18 January 1922, however, SS "Oriental" was found a crack in one cylinder on her voyage from Shanghai to San Francisco, and while making it to port earlier on 22 October 1921, the damage prevented her from being accepted until repaired, so SS "Cathay" actually became the third vessel officially delivered.

3.2.7

船舶主尺度和建造大节点
Main Particulars and Construction Milestones

江南造船所四艘美国万吨级运输舰的主尺度如表 3-1 所示，建造大节点如表 3-2 所示。

The main dimension of Kiangnan Dock & Engineering Works built four steam freighters is shown in Table 3-1. The construction milestones of Kiangnan built four steam freighters is shown in Table 3-2.

表 3-1　江南造船所四艘美国万吨级运输舰的主尺度
Table 3-1　The main dimension of Kiangnan built four steam freighters

总长	Length overall	443 英尺（feet）	（135.03 m）
两柱间长	Length PP	429 英尺（feet）	（130.76 m）
船宽	Breadth	55 英尺（feet）	（16.76 m）
型深	Depth	37 英尺（feet）11.5 英寸（inch）	（11.57 m）
型吃水	Draught moulded	27 英尺（feet）6 英寸（inch）	（8.38 m）
最大航速	Maximum speed	13 节（knots）	

主机：立式三缸三胀往复式蒸汽机一台，驱动一具四叶螺旋桨。

Main engine: one set of vertical type 3-cylinder triple reciprocating steam engine, drives single 4-blade propeller.

主机功率："官府"号为 3 430 马力；"天朝"号为 2 580 马力；"东方"号和"国泰"号均为 2 733 马力[11]。

Main engine power: SS "Mandarin", 3 430 hp; SS "Celestial", 2 580 hp; SS "Oriental" and SS "Cathay", 2 733 hp.

锅炉：燃油烟管锅炉三台。

Boilers: three sets of multi-tubular return tube single ended marine Scotch boiler, oil fueled.

空船重量为 4 750 吨，载重量实容为 10 000 吨。

The light weight of ship was approximate 4 750 tons, and the corresponding deadweight was 10 000 tons.

表 3-2　江南造船所四艘美国万吨级运输舰建造大节点[12]
Table 3-2　The construction milestones of Kiangnan built four steam freighters

船体号 Hull No.	船名 Ship name	铺龙骨 Keel laying	安（舭）板 Plate assembly	下水 Launching	竣工 Delivery
H317	官府 Mandarin	1919-3-9	1919-10-6	1920-6-3	1921-2-17
H318	天朝 Celestial	1919-3-24	1919-12-10	1920-8-3	1921-5-29
H319	东方 Oriental	1919-3-29	1920-8-3	1921-2-23	1921-10-1
H320	国泰 Cathay	1920-4-5	1920-8-3	1921-5-26	1921-12-21

江南造船所为美国建造四艘万吨级运输舰是中国造船界从来未有之大工程，被视作中国工业的巨大成就，受到世人瞩目。"每次美舰下水，来所参观者异常拥挤，道途几为之塞。"[13] 图 3-7 所示为所外拍摄的万吨级运输舰下水场景[14]。图 3-8 所示为"官府"号在江南造船所船坞内进行油漆作业[15]。

Kiangnan Dock & Engineering Works built four steam freighters for the United States Shipping Board, which was an unprecedented project never before in Chinese shipbuilding industry, and was great brilliant feat in Chinese industry. "Visitors and citizens crowed in shipyard and alongside river when ship launching, and surrounded road had heavier traffic jam." Figure 3-7 are pictures taken from outside of shipyard showing launching of Kiangnan Dock & Engineering Works built steam freighters. Figure 3-8 is a photo showing that the first steel steam freighter SS "Mandarin" was carrying out painting work in the dry dock.

图 3-7 所外拍摄的万吨级运输舰下水场景
Figure 3-7 Launching sense of Kiangnan Dock & Engineering Works built steam freighters

图 3-8 "官府"号在江南造船所的船坞内进行油漆作业
Figure 3-8 Painting work of steel steam freighter SS "Mandarin" in Kiangnan's dry dock

江南造船所所长刘冠南在下水仪式后称："本所自承造美舰工程后，营业日见畅旺，各处商轮来所订造、订修者陆续不绝，如美国海运委员会太平洋公司、提督公司、大来洋行等。凡商轮开驶来华，遇有应行维修之处，必向本所估修。此足见本所营业前途大有日渐发达之趋势也。"

Liu Guangnan, Director of Kiangnan Dock & Engineering Works, mentioned after launching:"The business of our company becomes prosperity after commencement of building American steam freighters. The orders of newbuilding and repairing from various owners, such as the Pacific Subsidiary of the United States Shipping Board, President Shipping Lines, Dollar Company, come to Kiangnan frequently. If they have some repairing work needed to do once their ships arrive in Chinese coastal, they will come to our shipyard, which will boost our business and development."

江南造船所在交付四艘美国运输舰之后，刘冠南所长打算对所内有贡献的员工进行表彰，下文为《承造美舰完竣请奖出力人员文》。

After Kiangnan Dock & Engineering Works delivered four steamers to the United States Shipping Board, Liu Guannan, the director of Kiangnan Dock & Engineering Works intended to give encourage and reward to contributors in the construction. Following wording is excerpted from "Report of Encourage and Reward for Completion of American Steamers".

"窃职所于民国七年间承造美政府万吨运舰四艘，彼时原因欧战剧烈，我国与美国有协约关系，自应勉力代造，以尽协同助战义务。惟职所向未经造此项巨舰，原有厂坞规模狭小，自非大事扩充不可，且工程浩大，责任匪轻，所有扩充厂坞、添购机器、采办材料、估计工程，当时筹划一切殊非易事，设非群策群力，一致进行，安能肩兹重任？兹幸在事各员司等，不辞劳苦，勤力同心经营构造，业已先后完全告成，陆续开美交船。"

"Kiangnan received order for American Government to build four 10 000 deadweight tons steam freighters in 1918. When intense Great War was continuing in Europe Continental, China should make the efforts to build these steam freighters in order to meet its assisting obligation during the wartime, because China and the United States have mutually signed cooperation agreement. Kiangnan has no track record to build such big ships. Shipbuilding facilities and dry docks are also needed to expend for larger ship construction. The expanding works of docks, purchasing of machine, procurement of material, estimation and planning, all these are not easy for Kiangnan, and Kiangnan really faced bigger challenges. If all staffs and workers don't make great effort together, it is not to perform the preparation works for enabling construction of larger steam freighters on schedule. Finally four steam freighters have sequentially completed and delivered with common efforts of all personnel of Kiangnan. "

"据美监造员报告，经美国海运委员会次第验收，工程既称坚固，配制又极精良，美政府大为满意等语，殊非冠南始料所及。此是职所承造此项美舰工程，对于外交既足以表当时协约之诚心，又足以答友邦眷顾之盛意，而对于我国既足以增工业进步之荣誉，又以倡航业发达之先声。此固仰赖钧部提倡维持之力，而在事各员司等皆能不惮艰苦，协力经营，苦心构造，其劳殊不可没。"

"According to the report made by American supervisors, the United States Shipping Board carried out the inspection on board. The inspection report stated: Hull is robust and outfitting is good quality, and all is quite satisfied by American Government. I am really unexpected such great achievement. These Kiangnan built steam freighters can either express good faith in foreign affairs or acknowledge great kindness of friendly country. For our country, this project will boost the progress of industry and shipping. These achievements are reached not only by the leadership of Naval Department but also by great contribution of all personnel hard working and great efforts."

"拟肯钧部特沛殊恩，准予分别优奖各员司等，以酬劳，以资激励。冠南职分应为，应请毋庸给奖。所有美舰工程完竣，拟请分别优奖在事各员司匠目缘由，理合造具请奖名册一本，履历一份，备文呈请鉴核施行，实为公便。"

"Depending on the approval of Naval Department, Kiangnan intended to give encourage and reward to contributors in the construction. I am duty-bound responsibility so I should not be given. Administration office will prepare an award list including contribution, resume and etc. after American steam freighter construction completed."

3.3

万吨轮建造是一项极其艰巨的工程
Steam Freighters Construction Was a Hard Work for Kiangnan

为完成这项在江南造船所历史上前所未有的造船大工程，江南造船所的管理人员、工程技术人员和广大工人付出了巨大的努力和艰辛的劳动。这四艘万吨级运输舰不仅尺度、吨位大，而且采用美国船级社（ABS）的规范，并要求按照美国海运委员会和应急船队公司的要求进行设计，这对习惯于采用英国劳氏船级社规范的江南造船所来说，也是一个不小的变化。好在江南造船所的设计室除了有英籍的设计人员之外，大多数中方技术人员也通晓英语，一些骨干还多为美国留学生，这个障碍很快就克服了。

关于这四艘万吨级运输舰的设计来源，据《江南造船厂厂史：1865—1949》记载，这四艘万吨级运输舰的主要设计图纸来自美国[16]，但是江南造船所的工程技术人员还是做了不少补充设计。这个说法成了国内近代史学者的基本观点。设计图纸的来源是本书所要探讨的最主要的焦点问题，也是作者考证的结果和其他史料中的结论有差异的地方，在本书的第 5 章将有详细的描述。

尽管江南造船所为建造这四艘万吨级运输舰新购置了很多机器设备，但总的来说，当时江南造船所的生产设备和工具还是比较简陋的，再加上这四艘万吨级运输舰的船体尺度大、钢板厚、设备零件重量重等诸多困难，这对靠手工完成主要作业的江南造船所的工人来说，是一个巨大的挑战。

由于这四艘万吨级运输舰的船体比以往船舶的要大得多，庞大的船体结构主要是依靠工人手工将笨重的钢板一块块铆接起来的，在缺少起重设备的情况下，很多重物都要靠人力抬上高大的船台和船上。船进出坞时，没有拖船和绞车设备，只能靠人力拖进去。特别要强调的是，由于工人工作强度大、工作环境恶劣、又缺少劳动防护设施，工伤事故经常发生。据统计，在建造四艘美国运输舰过程中因工死亡的工人达数十人之多，致伤、致残的工人数量更无法统计。

In order to complete this great project which Kiangnan had never done before, management team, engineers and technicians as well as workers made great efforts and did hard working. These four steam freighters were not only larger in scale and tonnage, but they are also designed according to the rules of American Bureau of Shipping and requirements of the Shipping Board and subsidiary Emergency Fleet Corporation. There was obvious difference comparing with rules of Lloyd's Register which Kiangnan was familiar with. Kiangnan needed to make more efforts to accustom to new rules. Fortunately, in Kiangnan's design office, besides British's designers, most Chinese designers were good at English, and some of them had experience of studying in the United States. This difficulty was accordingly overcome soon.

Regarding the design source of these four steam freighters, even though the major drawing's of these four steam freighters were provided by the United States, Kiangnan's engineers still did a lot of supplemental designs, as per description in *History of Jiangnan Shipyard: 1865–1949*. This description has become a basis and reference of Chinese historians. The source of design drawings is the most important verification of this book. There is deviation between verification results of this book and description in existing historic materials. More detailed description will be specified in Chapter 5 of this book.

Although Kiangnan newly purchased machines and equipments for building those four steam freighters, in general, the facilities and tools in Kiangnan were quite primitive at that time. In addition, building those four steam freighters had a lot of difficulty such as larger hull scale, thick steel plate, heavier equipment and parts. It was really bigger challenge for Kiangnan's workers who frequently performed their work in manual.

Because the hulls of these four steam freighters were much bigger than those they built before, huge hull structure was manually riveted piece by piece because of no adequate lifting appliances. Many heavier objects were manually lift up onto higher slipway and into hull. Docking handling can only manually carried out because there are no tug boat and winch available. During construction of four steam freighters, higher working load, abominable working environment, and less personnel protection appliance, industrial accident frequently happened. Dozens of workers died in the fatal accidents during the construction of four steam freighters, and the quantity of injured and disabled workers even cannot be counted.

这四艘万吨级运输舰所配的 3 000 马力三胀式蒸汽机也是江南造船所自行制造的。建造完工进行试航时，测得时速达到了 12.09 海里，比原合同规定的快了 1.59 海里[17]。随着工程的推展，美国驻厂专家对江南造船所的建造工作称赞不已，称"其造成之船较他国所造毫不逊色，结构艺术皆见嘉许，而中国机匠运用美国机械得心应手尤堪注意。"

图 3-9 所示为两艘万吨级运输舰系泊在江南造船所码头进行舾装工程的场景，照片估计摄于 1920 年 8 月第二艘船"天朝"号下水后。从这张照片来看，相比于下水早两个月的第一艘船"官府"号，第二艘船"天朝"号下水时的完整性比较差，上层建筑、起重桅和起重吊杆等都没有安装。有史料说，当时江南造船所的主机制造能力跟不上，下水时仅仅是船壳下水，内部的机器设备没来得及安装。在当时起重设备能力相当差的情况下，下水后安装三缸蒸汽机、锅炉和起重桅等大型设备及部件是非常困难的事。值得注意的是，照片右面的 A 字形吊杆，起重能力达到了75 吨，是下水后安装大件设备的重要设施。

Triple expansion reciprocating steam engines with 3 000 hp output were self-manufactured by Kiangnan for these four steam freighters. During speed trail after ship completed, measured speed was 12.09 nautical miles, 1.59 nautical miles faster than the guaranteed speed specified in the building contract. During building progress of steam freighters, Kiangnan construction work gained acclaim from the experts of the United States at site: "The quality of completed vessel at in the same level of other countries, structural workmanship is good, and Chinese operators adroitly running American made machines are most impressed."

Figure 3-8 shows that two steam freighters were moored at Kiangnan's wharfs for outfitting. This photo may be taken in August of 1920 just after the second steam freighter SS "Celestial" launched. Comparing the first steam freighter SS "Mandarin" launched two months earlier, the completion level of the second steam freighter SS "Celestial" was quite poor, and superstructure, post and derrick were not yet installed. Some historical material mentioned, the capability of main engine manufacture can not follow the hull construction schedule, internal equipment and machine had not yet installed when hull launched into water. It was bigger challenge to install a three-cylinder steam engine, boilers and derricks after launching. An "A" type shearleg with lifting capacity of 75 tons is noted shown on the right side of the photo. It is the most important facility for handling bigger and heavier projects after ship launched.

图 3-9　两艘万吨级运输舰在江南造船所码头进行舾装工程
Figure 3-9　Two steam freighters moored at Kiangnan's wharfs for outfitting

可惜的是，在江南造船集团的档案馆中未能找到当时江南造船所在船台上建造这四艘万吨级运输舰的照片，但作者在江南造船集团档案馆里找到了一张泥船台上造船的照片（见图 3-10）。据作者判断，这张照片摄于江南造船所为承接四艘万吨级运输舰进行船台新建工程之前，船台上正在建造的船舶也比较小，是什么船型也无从考证。从这张照片可以看出当时船台造船的方法。

船台是一块平整夯实过的泥地，没有类似于现代船台上常备的专门永久性下水滑道。

船体建造通常是先在搭建的胎架上铺设船体外板，然后安装肋骨和纵向桁材，再安装内部构件；在安装钢板构件的同时进行相应的铆接作业。

Unfortunately, there is no photo showing four steam freighters on the slipway in Archives Institute of Jiangnan Shipyard Group, but one photo showing shipbuilding scene on soil made (clayey) slipway was found, see also Figure 3-10. This photo was taken before the re-construction of slipways for four steam freighters. The ship building on this slipway was quite small, but it is difficult to verify the ship type. The shipbuilding method on slipway can be discerned based on this photo.

Slipway actually was a piece of flattening, tamped ground, and there were no permanent sliding rails, which are must-have items on modern slipway.

Hull construction procedure was normally as: laying shell plate on moulding bad, then assembling frames and girders, and finally installing internal structural members. Riveting work can be done in parallel with installation of structural members.

船台两旁的起重设备通常设置为若干根立式起重柱（俗称"把杆"），在这些立式起重柱上安装了可回转的吊杆，通过吊杆上安装的吊钩、滑轮和索具进行起重作业。这种立式起重柱（见图 3-11）一直沿用到 20 世纪 50 年代江南造船厂建造 03 级常规攻击潜艇（此型潜艇的原始设计来自苏联的 W 级常规潜艇）。

工人作业用的脚手架由垂直木架加斜向支撑铺设的水平木板组成，类似于过去码头上用单块木板搭建的"过山跳"。高空作业环境十分简陋，几乎没有什么安全防护设施。

江南造船所在承接四艘万吨级运输舰之后，对船台进行了新建工程。由于万吨级运输舰的空船重量达 4 700 吨，即便是船舶下水时舾装程度比较差，估计下水重量也会达到 3 000 吨以上。因此，如同第 2 章中的 2.7 节提到的：新建的四个大船台，每个船台长 396 英尺（120.70 米），宽 36 英尺（10.97 米）[18]，高 20 英尺（6.10 米），可容纳 500 英尺（152.40 米）长的大船（含水下部分），船台两侧竖立有 10 个可起吊 4 吨的起重立柱。从本章中两张万吨级运输舰下水的照片（见图 3-2 和图 3-7）可以看出船台上建有永久性的下水滑道，船台一侧搭有脚手架和上下船的坡道。

图 3-10　江南造船所泥船台造船的场景
Figure 3-10　Hull assembly on Kiangnan's clayey slipway

The lifting appliances along sides of slipway were practically serval derricks, a rotated lifting boom was fitted on derrick post, and lifting work was carried out via hooks, pulleys and riggings. This kind of derrick (see Figure 3-11)was continuously used for building Type 03 diesel-electric driven submarine (original design of this type submarine came from Whiskey Class of the Soviet Union).

The scaffolding for erection on slipway was a combination of vertical wooden stands and horizontal laid wooden plates, quite similar as scaffolding on the wharf with single wooden strip for loading and unloading operation. Working environment was poor and almost no safety protection appliance.

After sighing shipbuilding contract for these four steam freighters, Kiangnan started reinforcement work for slipway because the light weight of freighter was over 4 700 tons, even though considering less outfitting weight, launching weight was also heavier than 3 000 tons. As mentioned in Section 2.7 of Chapter 2, the dimensions of newly constructed four slipways were: 396 feet (120.70 meters) in length, 36 feet (10.97 meters) in width, and 20 feet (6.10 meters) in height. All of these slipways (including underwater extension) were able to accommodate 500 feet (152.40 meters) long ship. Ten derricks with lifting capacity of 4 tons stood alongside each slipway. As per photos of steam freighter launching in this chapter (see Figures 3-2 and 3-7), there were permanent sliding ramps on the top of slipway and scaffolding and access ramp to erected hull.

根据船台的位置判断，这四个船台应该是 20 世纪 80 年代还在造船的 6 号、7 号、8 号和 9 号船台，当时 6 号和 7 号船台还建造过 1 750 吨航标船和为挪威船东建造过两艘 6 000 马力供应船［UT714 supply vessel，又被称为"三用拖轮"（anchor handling, tug and supply vessel），船体号：H2151/52］。这两艘船的两柱间长为 56 米。从 6 号和 7 号船台建造现场往西侧看，当时 8 号和 9 号船台已经被作为机装车间管子材料的堆场，6 号和 7 号船台的后段已经被改建为分段组装平台。参见图 3-12 江南造船所的总布置图"最新厂坞界图"。图中标注的四个"万吨船台"为江南造船厂高雄路 2 号老厂区的 6 号、7 号、8 号和 9 号船台。

These four slipways should be No. 6, No. 7, No. 8 and No. 9 slipways of Jiangnan Shipyard in 1980s, 1 750 deadweight tons beacon vessels and two sets of 6 000 hp UT714 supply vessels for Norwegian owner (anchor handling, tug and supply vessel) used to be built on No. 6 and No. 7 slipways. To take a look over the construction site No. 6 and No. 7 slipways to further west side, No. 8 and No. 9 slipways had been converted to storage area of piping material for machinery workshop. The rear area of No. 6 and No. 7 slipways had been converted to block assembly platform. Refer to Figure 3-12 "The layout of Kiangnan Dock & Engineering Works", four slipways marked "ten thousand tons slipway" were No. 6, No. 7, No. 8 and No. 9 slipways of Jiangnan Shipyard (2 Gaoxiong Road, old site in Shanghai downtown) in 1980s.

图 3-11　20 世纪 50 年代江南造船厂船台旁的立式起重柱
Figure 3-11　Derricks along the slipway side in 1950s

在江南造船集团档案馆内保存的民国十一年四月（1922 年 4 月）由江南造船所所长刘冠南审核、廖驮编写的《江南造船所纪要》中有一张江南造船所的总布置图"最新厂坞界图"（见图 3-12）。

Summary of Kiangnan Dock & Engineering Works, which was edited by Liao Shen and reviewed by Liu Guannan, published in April of 1922, collected by Archives Institute of Jiangnan Shipyard Group, includes "The Layout of Kiangnan Dock & Engineering Works". Refer to Figure 3-12.

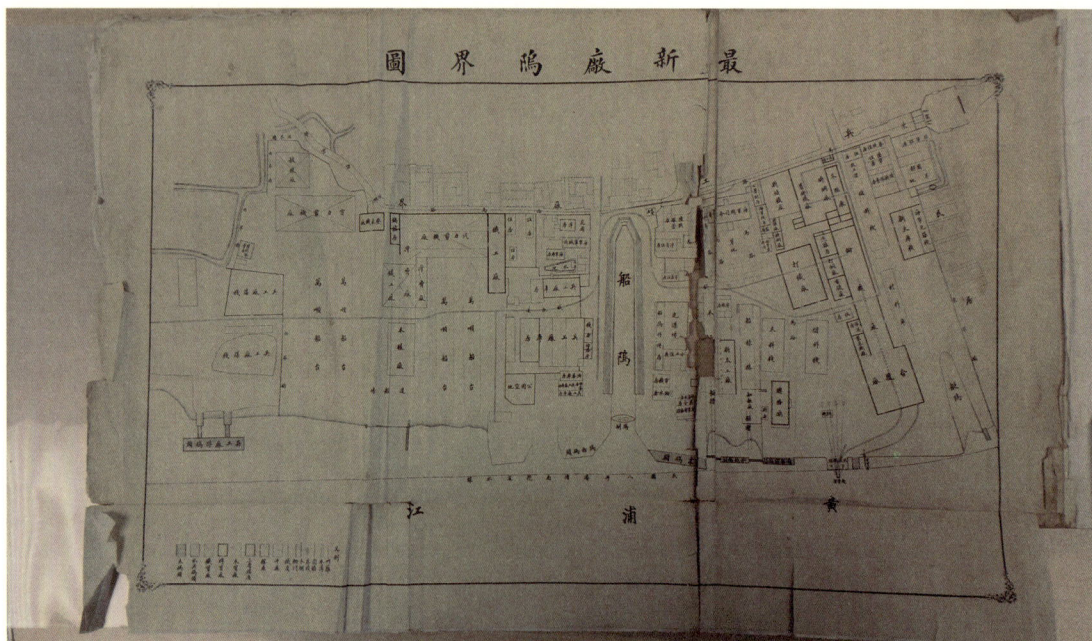

图 3-12　江南造船所的总布置图"最新厂坞界图"
Figure 3-12　The layout of Kiangnan Dock & Engineering Works

从图 3-12 可以看出，江南造船所的四个万吨船台两两一组沿黄浦江岸一字排开，中间隔了一个"木样厂""铁工厂"和两个"湾胁厂"。船台的后部还设有"铁工厂""汽力剪机厂"和"电力剪机厂"，此区域统称为"造船厂"。建造四艘万吨级运输舰的主要设施都在这个区域。图 3-13 为"最新厂坞界图"中的四个船台（放大图）。

From the above layout of Kiangnan, four slipways, two as a group, were located alongside bank of Huangpu River. Wooden template workshop, steel workshop, and two frame bending workshops were arranged between docks. Steel workshop, steam and electric driven cutting workshops were located at end of slipways, and this area was called "shipbuilding zone". The main facilities for construction of those four steam freighters were all arranged in this area. Figure 3-13 is the four slipways arrangement in "The Layout of Kiangnan Dock & Engineering Works" (zoom in).

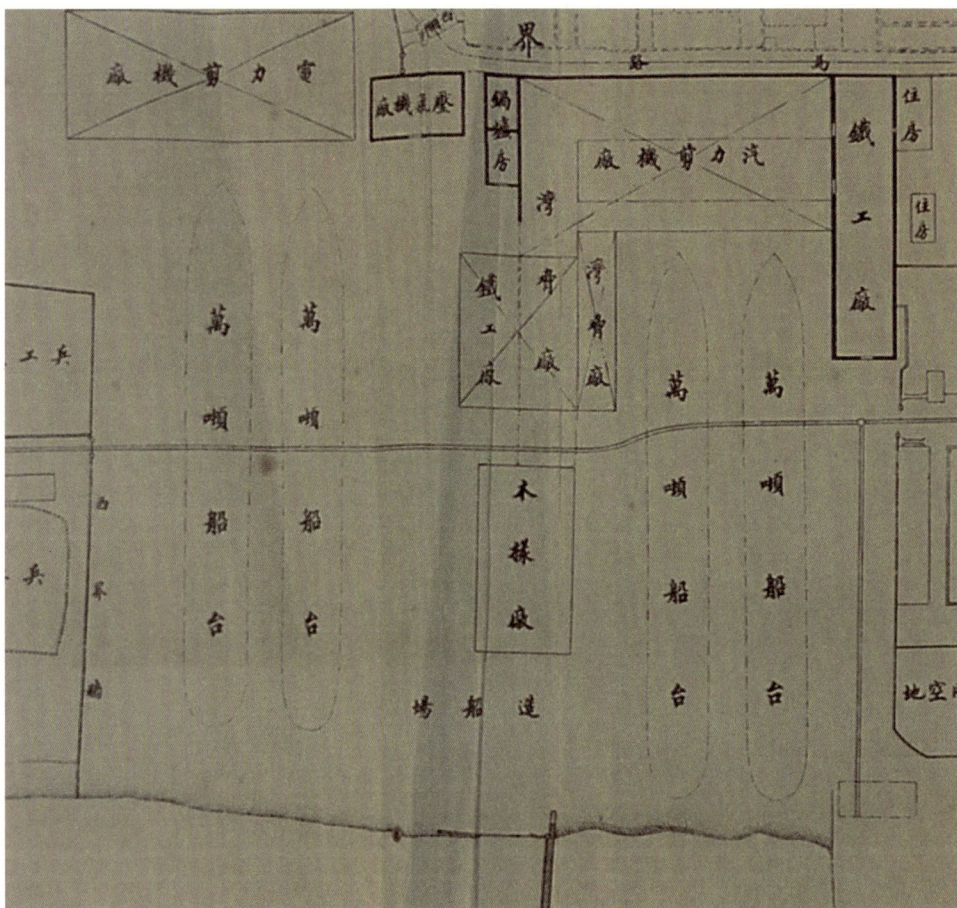

图 3-13　"最新厂坞界图"中用于建造万吨轮的四个船台
Figure 3-13　The layout of four slipways for erection of 10 000-ton steam freighter

根据当时的造船流程，"木样厂"应该是放样和制作木质样板的，但从图 3-13 上看"木样厂"的面积较大，可能还具有其他功能，如 1：1 的样台；"铁工厂"应该是钢结构加工车间；"湾胁厂"应该是型钢加工和弯制车间；"汽力剪机厂"和"电力剪机厂"应该是钢板切割车间，区别在于切割机的动力源不同。

As per shipbuilding process at that time, the purpose of wooden template workshop should be hull lines lofting and wooden template manufacturing, but wooden template workshop looks quite bigger from layout, maybe it has some other function and full scale lofting platform. Steel workshop should be mainly for steel structure fabricating. Frame bending workshop should be for the purpose of cutting and bending steel sections. Steam and electric driven cutting workshops were for cutting steel plate, and the difference was power source of cutting machine.

3.4

万吨轮建造成功的重大意义
The Significance of Steam Freighters Delivery for Kiangnan

成功建造四艘万吨级运输舰对江南造船所的跨越式发展具有十分重要的意义。从收入看，建造四艘万吨级运输舰共获得营收 780 万美元，这笔船舶建造款在 1918 年至 1922 年期间陆续支付，而以 1920 年至 1922 年的付款较为集中。

按照付款最集中的 1921 年的汇率计算，四艘运输舰的船款约合 1 700 万银元，而 1905 年至 1917 年间江南造船所的年平均收入约为 114 万银元。建造四艘万吨级运输舰获得的收入相当于此前年平均收入的 14 多倍[19]。

从江南造船所 1905 年至 1926 年的收入盈余表（见表 3-3[20]）可以看出，从四艘万吨级运输舰陆续下水的 1920 年开始，年收入几乎都超过了 300 万银元，其中 1921 年的年收入竟超过了 1 800 万银元。1918 年以前每年的盈余平均不到 18 万银元，而 1920 年至 1922 年，盈余都超过了 100 万银元，1921 年甚至超过了 216 万银元。由此可见，建造这四艘万吨级运输舰是一笔挣钱的大生意，为江南造船所创造了巨额的收益。另外一个因素是由于当时美元汇率的变化（从造船合同签订至交船这几年间银元大幅度贬值），江南造船所的效益大增，特别是 1921 年四艘万吨级运输舰集中交付时。图 3-14 所示为 1918 年至 1922 年间美元兑换银元的汇率变化曲线。

更重要的是，江南造船所利用建造美国万吨级运输舰这一契机对场地设备大规模扩充，使船厂的规模和造船能力都得到了大幅提高。江南造船所购买土地，将场地面积扩大了三分之一，并新建了许多厂房，购置了大量新式机器设备。

经历此番改造扩充，历史悠久的江南造船所"较诸昔日简陋之情形，其相去之远，诚不可以道里计。"[21] 其造船能力和设备都迈上了一个新台阶，超越上海的外资船厂而成为远东除日本之外最大的造船厂。

The successfully building four 10 000 deadweight tons steam freighters has extremely important significance for Kiangnan Dock & Engineering Works entering a stage of leaps and bounds. The total revenue of four steam freighters was 7.8 million U.S. dollars, and paid in several installments during 1918 to 1922, while these installments were concentrated in years of 1920 and 1921.

According to the exchange rate of 1921 when the installments were most concentrated in, the total amount of contract price was corresponding to 17 million silver dollars. Comparing the average annual revenue of 1.14 million silver dollars during 1905 to 1917. The revenue of Kiangnan grained from building four steamers was more than fourteen times of its annual average.

Based on "sales and balance of Kiangnan from 1905 to 1926" (see Table 3-3), since four steam freighters were sequentially launched in 1920, Kiangnan's revenue almost exceeded 3 million silver dollars every year, and the revenue of 1921 actually exceeded 18 million silver dollars. The average annual profit was less than 180 thousand silver dollars before 1918, but the annual profit exceeded 1 million silver dollars during 1920 to 1922, and the annual profit of 1921 reached peak and even exceeded 2.16 million silver dollars. This shows that building these four steam freighters was really a lucrative business for Kiangnan at that time. In addition, the exchange rate of U.S. dollar (devaluation of silver dollar from contract sign to delivery) caused extra profit of Kiangnan especially as four steam freighters were concentrated to be delivered in the year of 1921. Refer to Figure 3-14 exchange rate curve of USD vs. silver dollar in 1918 to 1922.

The great significance was that Kiangnan expanded building scale and improved capability with the opportunity of building four American steam freighters. Kiangnan purchased land and increased one third of occupied area, newly built workshops and procured a lot of machines and equipments.

After reform and expansion, venerable Kiangnan completely changed from being poor and rudimentary appearance to being modern shipyard. The shipbuilding capability and equipment of Kiangnan had reached a newer and higher stage. Except Japanese shipyards, Kiangnan had become the biggest shipyard in the Far East over foreigner invested shipyards in Shanghai.

在建造美国万吨级运输舰的过程中，江南造船所的技术人员和工人都得到了锻炼，提高了技术水平。这一点集中体现在江南造船所对长江上游川江轮的设计建造上。在建造万吨级运输舰的同一时期，江南造船所独立设计建造了适应川江险恶航运条件的"隆茂"轮。该船能在川江的激流险滩中航行自如，逆水上行时不用人工拖曳，打破了历来川江行船的惯例，赢得广泛赞誉。新订单纷至沓来，川江轮成为江南造船所的优势产品。成功建造万吨级运输舰为江南造船所赢得了声誉，对其业务开展有积极的促进作用。

By experiencing the design and construction of American steam freighters, technicians and workers of Kiangnan were well trained and raised their technical level accordingly. The technical and construction improvements of Kiangnan were well embodied in design and construction of Chuan Jiang (upstream of Yangtze River) passenger ship. Kiangnan independently designed and constructed Yangtze River suitable passenger ship SS "Long Mao" in parallel with construction of four American steam freighters. She had good performance and maneuverability in turbulent rivers and treacherous shoals, and she did not need manual assistance for navigating forward to upstream. Yangtze River suitable passenger ship had become a competitive ship type of Kiangnan, and her good reputation brought more orders to Kiangnan. In addition, successfully delivered four American steam freighters also elevated Kiangnan's reputation for further development of business.

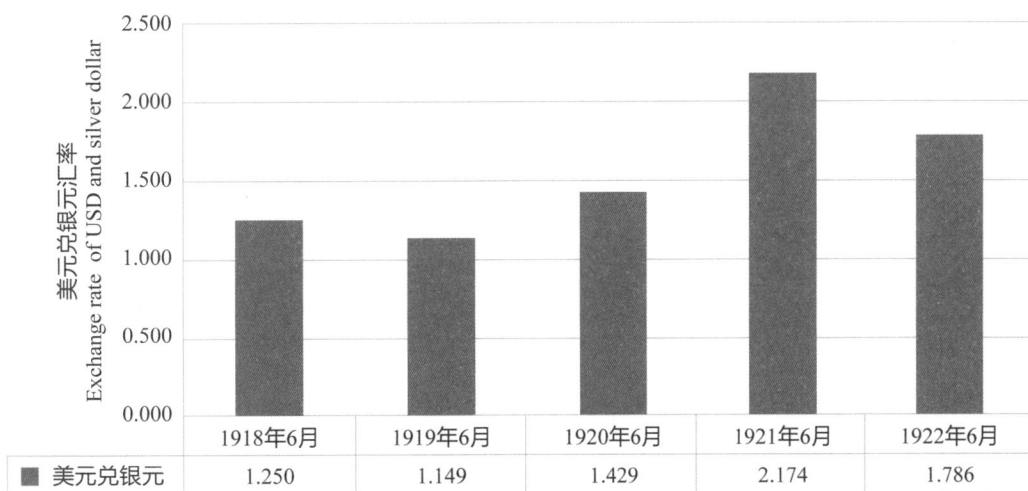

	1918年6月	1919年6月	1920年6月	1921年6月	1922年6月
美元兑银元	1.250	1.149	1.429	2.174	1.786

图 3-14　1918 年至 1922 年间美元兑换银元的汇率变化曲线
Figure 3-14　The exchange rate curve of USD vs. silver dollar in 1918 to 1922

表 3-3　江南造船所 1905 年至 1926 年营业额及盈余　　　　　　单位：银元
Table 3-3　The sales and balance of Kiangnan from 1905 to 1926　　　Unit: silver dollar

起 止 年 月 Year month	营 业 额 Sales	盈 余 Balance
1905 年 4 月—1907 年 4 月 9 日 April 1905–9 April 1907	1 691 582.37	130 280.70
1907 年 4 月 10 日—1907 年 12 月 10 April 1907–December 1907	715 379.21	107 711.92
1908 年 1 月—1908 年 12 月 January 1908–December 1908	880 694.57	116 840.86
1909 年 1 月—1909 年 12 月 January 1909–December 1909	887 600.05	85 165.47
1910 年 1 月—1910 年 12 月 January 1910–December 1910	729 709.34	45 712.54

（续表）
(continued)

起 止 年 月 Year month	营 业 额 Sales	盈 余 Balance
1911 年 1 月—1911 年 10 月 20 日 January 1911–20 October 1911	931 546.46	262 204.06
1911 年 10 月 21 日—1912 年 4 月 21 October 1911–April 1912	571 158.62	46 014.38
1912 年 5 月—1912 年 12 月 May 1912–December 1912	984 708.42	213 026.21
1913 年 1 月—1913 年 12 月 January 1913–December 1913	958 314.77	93 226.83
1914 年 1 月—1914 年 12 月 January 1914–December 1914	1 197 571.81	143 277.08
1915 年 1 月—1915 年 10 月 January 1915–October 1915	1 168 420.10	241 983.99
1915 年 11 月—1916 年 12 月 November 1915–December 1916	1 887 998.30	205 186.46
1917 年 1 月—1917 年 12 月 January 1917–December 1917	2 208 893.37	604 171.13
1905—1917 年平均 Annual average from 1905 to 1917	1 139 505.95	176 523.20
1918 年 1 月—1918 年 12 月 January 1918–December 1918	2 592 984.94	490 650.90
1919 年 1 月—1919 年 12 月 January 1919–December 1919	1 580 540.47	325 526.25
1920 年 1 月—1920 年 12 月 January 1920–December 1920	3 634 931.50	1 152 409.84
1921 年 1 月—1921 年 12 月 January 1921–December 1921	18 060 742.22	2 167 003.69
1922 年 1 月—1922 年 12 月 January 1922–December 1922	3 910 440.16	1 465 561.59
1923 年 1 月—1923 年 12 月 January 1923–December 1923	2 348 580.01	781 156.76
1924 年 1 月—1924 年 12 月 January 1924–December 1924	4 131 274.33	2 130 511.43
1925 年 1 月—1925 年 12 月 January 1925–December 1925	3 670 192.48	629 736.65
1926 年 1 月—1926 年 12 月 January 1926–December 1926	2 423 193.16	174 000.58
1918—1926 年平均 Annual average from 1918 to 1926	4 705 875.47	1 035 168.07

作者注：
Notes:

1　1918 年 7 月 10 日收到的是合同草稿，正式合同是 1918 年 7 月 25 日签署的。

2　此数据为完工时的两柱间长，签合同时的两柱间长为 425 英尺（129.54 米）。

3　"臬司"为明、清各省提刑按察使司的官职名。清朝（改称按察使司）三代设立在省一级的司法部门，主管一省的刑名、诉讼事务。《辞海》，上海辞书出版社，1999 年普及本，第 5382 页。这里应该是指美方主管法务事务的官员。

4　王正廷（1882—1961），字儒堂，浙江奉化人，著名体育领袖。14 岁即入天津北洋大学堂，毕业后曾赴日本留学，并加入同盟会。26 岁留学美国，获耶鲁大学博士学位。1911 年回国。中华民国成立后，即为内阁成员；先后担任南京临时政府参议院副议长、代理议长、代理工商部长，北京政府工商部次长、外交总长、代理内阁总理，南京国民政府外交部长、驻美国大使（1936—1938 年）等职。

5　原文译为"西勒所"号。

6　经查验江南造船所绘制的四艘船的完工图（图号：7007E，标注日期为 1921-1-27），四艘船已经取消了燃煤舱而被换为燃油舱，并相应采用了燃油锅炉。

7　同上。

8　这里所指的"打錾工程"应该理解为"钢结构金属工艺"而不是"填缝密封"（caulking）。

9　原文译为"奥连讨"号。

10　原文译为"客塞"号。

11　原文如此。美国船级社入级记录里的主机功率均为 2 600 hp。

12　由于建造方式不同，当时船体建造的大节点和现代造船的大节点是不同的。现代造船中把钢板切割（steel cutting）作为开工节点，第一个分段上船台 / 下坞作为铺龙骨。

13　刘冠南审核、廖骁编写，《江南造船所纪要》，1922 年，第 76 页。

14　照片来自网络。

15　照片来自江南造船集团档案馆。

16　原文如此。关于这四艘万吨级运输舰的设计来源参见本书第 5 章关于设计来源的分析。

17　原文如此。与《江南造船所纪要》中的记载有差异。

18　据作者分析：此为滑道间距，而非船体宽度。江南造船所建造的美国运输舰的船宽为 55 英尺（16.76 米）。

19　1921 年美元汇率较高，考虑到 1918—1922 年的美元汇率的整体情况，总船款应比 1 700 万银元略低，约为 1 500 万银元，仍为 1905—1917 年年平均收入的 10 倍以上。

20　资料来源：《江南造船所纪要》及《海军江南造船所报告书》；数据稍做修改。

21　刘冠南审核、廖骁编写，《江南造船所纪要》，1922 年，第 62 页。

剖析万吨级运输舰的设计
Analysis of EFC Design 1092

江南造船所建造的四艘万吨级运输舰（H317~H320）在设计上有什么特点？这型船的设计稿出自哪里？要对这些设计特点进行分析，必须查阅船舶的设计图纸和其他相关技术资料。

Which design features do the four steam freighters built by Kiangnan have? Where did the design of this series come from? It is necessary to verify design drawings and technical documents before identifying those design features.

按照惯例，船舶图纸应该在造船相关方处，即船厂、船东和船级社保存得最为完整，因此，作者首先从江南造船集团档案馆保存的现有资料着手进行查询。

As per normal shipbuilding practice, interested parties, i.e. shipyard, owner and classification society may perfectly keep the design drawings and technical documents. The search of existing documents in Archives Institute of Jiangnan Shipyard Group was initially carried out.

4.1

移交 1949 年以前全部底图档案
All Archives before 1949 Transferred to Shaanxi

在江南造船集团档案馆内，作者找到了第六机械工业部要求转移江南造船厂保存的 1949 年以前的技术档案的会议纪要（1978 年 11 月 24 日）；会议纪要未说明转移技术档案的具体原因。会议于 1978 年 11 月 23 日在江南造船厂工艺设计科召开，参加人员有第六机械工业部七六所（以下简称"七六所"）的赵缓响，江南造船厂的朱培生、何志诚和孙庆祥。

Through the search, Archives Institute of Jiangnan Shipyard Group still keeps a minutes of meeting dated 24 November 1978 regarding the transference of technical document before 1949. In the minutes, National Sixth Department of Machinery Industry instructed Jiangnan Shipyard to transfer all archives before May 1949. The reason of transfer was not declared in the minutes. On 23 November 1978, the meeting was held in Design Institute of Jiangnan Shipyard, and Zhao Huanxiang (No.76 Institute of National Sixth Department of Machinery Industry, hereinafter referred to as No.76 Institute), Zhu Peisheng, He Zhicheng and Sun Qingxiang (from Jiangnan Shipyard) attended this meeting.

会议纪要中的第四点是这样记录的：

The 4th paragraph of the minutes of meeting is excerpted as follows:

......

按六机部办公厅十月十八日来函：关于我厂所保存的解放前造船底图档案全部移交给部七十六所保管一事，七十六所专程派赵缓响同志来我厂联系。

...

As per Administration Office instruction of National Sixth Department of Machinery Industry: No.76 Institute has dispatched Mr. Zhao Huanxiang to Jiangnan Shipyard for coordinating transfer of old shipbuilding archives before May 1949.

移交内容：解放前的全部修造船及其他产品的底图档案（包括原来存放底图的箱子 28 个，账册 8 本）。

The contents of transferred archives: All traced drawing of shipbuilding and repairing as well as other products (including 28 pcs of traced drawing cases and 8 volumes of drawing list).

移交时间：明年（1979 年）一季度。

Transferring schedule: The 1st quarter of next year (1979).

移交办法：

Transferring procedure:

（1）江南造船厂开列清单、箱、卷（不作每份清点）。

（2）待江南造船厂一切移交工作就绪后直接与七十六所联系。

……

(1) Jiangnan Shipyard will make lists of all cases and volumes, but not check one by one.

(2) No.76 Institute will take responsibility after transferring procedure completed by Jiangnan Shipyard.

...

根据上述会议纪要，江南造船厂的档案部门于 1979 年将 1949 年以前的全部图纸档案（1905—1949 年）共计 2 423 卷，底图存放箱 24 个，账册 7 本移交给了七六所继续保存。当时江南造船厂的档案人员编制了一份档案移交清单，并将这些老图纸装箱后运往陕西省兴平市。

According to above minutes of meeting, Jiangnan's Archives Institute transferred all graphical archives (from 1905 to 1949) to No.76 Institute in 1979. These archives were total 2 423 volumes, 24 pcs of traced drawing case and 7 sets of drawing list. Jiangnan's staffs further made a detailed transferring lists, and transported these cases to Xingping city in Shaanxi Province.

图纸档案的移交清单按船体和轮机（含舾装件和设备等）分成两部分，具体如下：

The transferring list of drawing archives was further divided into two parts, hull part and machinery part (including outfitting and equipments), detail as follows:

第一部分：1905—1937 年、1946—1949 年，图纸是按照所建造的船舶以"H"开头的编号进行分卷的，从 H1"江南"号到 H854；1938—1945 年，所建造的船舶以"KS"开头的编号（"KS"为 Kiangnan Shipyard 的缩写），约 94 艘。

PART I : In the years of 1905 to 1937 and 1946 to 1949, all drawings were coded by "H" plus serial number, from H1 steam launch "Kiangnan" to H854; in years of 1938 to 1945, all Kiangnan built ships coded by "KS" ("KS" abbreviation of Kiangnan Shipyard) plus serial number, approximately 94 sets of ships.

还有编号以"KH""PS"和"KR"开头的小艇。这些船是不是江南造船所建造的呢？作者从日本三菱重工业株式会社史中查到了一些相关资料。作者的在三菱重工业株式会社工作的朋友赠送了一本 1973 年出版、由该公司"江南造船所史刊行会"编写的内部资料《江南造船所·歴史と思い出》[1]。资料中记载了江南造船所 1937—1945 年的一些史实。

In addition, some launches coded "KH" "PS" and "KR". Did Kiangnan build these launches? The corporate history of Mitsubishi Heavy Industry (MHI) and *Kiangnan Dock & Engineering Works· History & Reminiscence*, MHI published memoirs in 1973, presented by Japanese friend in MHI, described some historical facts in the years of 1937 to 1945.

1937 年 11 月 11 日，江南造船所被日本陆军占领，然后移交给日本海军并改名为"朝日工作部江南工场"。日本海军随后委托三菱重工业株式会社负责

On 11 November 1937, Japanese Army occupied Kiangnan Dock & Engineering Works, thereafter handed over to Japanese Navy and renamed as "Ashahi Works, Kiangnan Shipyard". Japanese Navy authorized MHI to take the responsibility of shipyard operation. MHI renamed

江南造船所的运行，江南造船所再次改名为"三菱重工业株式会社江南造船所"。三菱重工业株式会社在收到日本海军委托管理江南造船所一事的公文后，于1938年1月30日派遣当时的三菱重工业株式会社长崎造船所所长玉井乔介带领一个团队到江南造船所接管并开展工作。玉井乔介后来在第二次世界大战后担任三菱重工业株式会社的社长。

据玉井先生的回忆，当时的江南造船所和英商杨树浦工场（Yangtszepoo Works，即英联船厂下属的瑞镕船厂）、淑浦船渠（Sopoo Works，即英联船厂下属的和丰船厂和引翔港船坞）、求新船渠（Kiuhsin Dock，即中法合资的求新机器制造轮船厂）等造船所合并后，加上先前并入的民营鸿祥兴船厂（江南造船所浦东工场），在上海地区形成了一个很大的造船公司[2]。因此，作者推测"KH"是江南造船所浦东工场建造的船舶的船体号，"PS"是淑浦船渠建造的船舶的船体号，"KR"是英商杨树浦工场建造的船舶的船体号。

第二部分：第一部分的清单附件，主要包括舾装件、机舱布置、轮机设备如锅炉、蒸汽主机、轴系、推进器和管系等。还有一些码头趸船、浮船坞和非船舶类的结构件等。

Kiangnan to "Mitsubishi Heavy Industry Kiangnan Dock & Engineering Works". Once MHI received the instruction of Japanese Navy, January 30 of 1938, MHI dispatched Mr. Tamai Takesuke, General Manager of Nagasaki Works of MHI, as leader of team to take over Kiangnan. Mr. Tamai was appointed as President of MHI after the World War II.

As per reminiscence of Mr. Tamai, Kiangnan acquired New Shanghai Shipbuilding and Engineering Works, Cosmopolitan Dock and Internatinal Dock, Sino-France Joint Venture Nicolas Tsu's Engineering and Shipbuilding Plant (or known as "Qiu Xin Shipyard") and plus previously merged private Hung Hsiang Hsing Shipyard (i.e., Pootung Works of Kiangnan). Kiangnan became a bigger shipbuilding group. Kiangnan renamed those shipyards as Yangtszepoo Works, Sopoo Works, Kiuhsin Dock and Pootung Works respectively. "KH" may be hull number built by Pootung Works, "PS" may be hull number built by Sopoo Works, and "KR" may be hull number built by Yangtszepoo Works.

PART II : It was coded as an attachment of Part I , mainly including outfitting, engine room arrangement, machineries such as boiler, steam engine, shafting, propeller etc. In addition, Part II included some port barge, floating dock and non-ship structures etc.

4.2

寻找万吨级运输舰的图纸档案
Search for Archives of Steam Freighters

2015 年 8 月，作者的同事前往陕西省兴平市查阅了七六所保存的江南造船所建造的四艘万吨级运输舰（船体号：H317~H320）的图纸，仔细清点整理和分类后将文本资料扫描成电子版。

In August of 2015, Jiangnan's staffs went to No.76 Institute in Xingping, Shaanxi. They reviewed drawings of Kiangnan built four steam freighters with hull numbers H317 to H320, and scanned some of those drawings into electronic format.

由于江南造船所 1906—1926 年由苏格兰人毛根担任总工程师期间，船厂基本是照搬英商船厂的管理模式，所有的图纸都是英文版。七六所保存的 1979 年江南造船厂移交过去的图纸资料中，除了当时江南造船厂编制的档案移交清单以外，没有原始图纸目录。作者仔细核查了这些图纸上的编号，发现图纸编号好像是流水号，没有找出其中的规律。作者推测，1978 年档案移交会议是要求移交图纸，而一些文件性资料也许并没有移交给七六所。但作者在江南造船集团档案馆仔细查找后，也没有发现相关的图纸目录，因此无法判断目前找到的这批万吨级运输舰（H317~H320）的图纸资料是否为全部资料。

During 1906 to 1926, Scottish Mr. R. B. Mauchan was the Chief Engineer of Kiangnan. Under his insistence, Kiangnan completely followed British management pattern. Therefore, all drawings were annotated in English. There is only one document list issued by Jiangnan Shipyard in the drawing package, which transferred from Jiangnan Shipyard in 1979. However, the original list does not exist now. Personally, it seems that the codes are in the order of serial number after carefully checking these drawings. There is no coding regularity found in these numbers. Jiangnan Shipyard might only transferred graphical documents to No. 76 Institute but not literal documents. Even in the repeat search of Archives Institute of Jiangnan Shipyard Group, the drawing list does not appear. It is impossible to verify overview of drawing for these four steam freighters (H317–H320).

在七六所找到的这批万吨级运输舰（H317~H320）的全部图纸共有 78 份。这些图纸由以下几部分组成：

The searching result was 78 drawings of four steam freighters in No.76 Institute. These drawings consist of the following parts:

◆ 合同技术附件　3 份（总布置图和舯横剖面图、总布置修改图）

◆ 总体图纸　12 份

◆ 结构图纸　40 份

◆ 舾装图纸　13 份

◆ 舱室图纸　10 份（含舱室布置草图一张）

◆ Technical Attachments of contract: 3 pcs (General Arrangement Plan, Midship Section and Revised General Arrangement Plan)

◆ General drawings: 12 pcs

◆ Structural drawings: 40 pcs

◆ Outfitting drawings: 13 pcs

◆ Accommodation drawings: 10 pcs (including one sketch of cabin layout)

上述图纸中，总体图纸尽管份数较多，但包含了不同版本的总布置图，实际上展现了一个设计建造过程中逐步完善的过程。结构图纸相对比较完整，还有许多铆接结构的细节图纸。舾装部分也仅仅有舱口盖的布置图、系泊和重型吊杆的布置图，舾装专业的锚、舵、救生、桅樯信号等系统图纸一张也没有。轮机部分的图纸一张也没有。舾装件和轮机设备图纸是按照类别来分的，不是按照船体号，查找难度太大了。

这些图纸特别是总布置图为 0# 加长，长度最长的图纸为 3.6 米左右。图纸幅面非常大，纸张也很厚实。现在看来，当时第六机械工业部决定将这些图纸归到七六所保存还是有前瞻性的，这些宝贵的图纸资料在七六所得到了很好的保存和保护，没有任何的损坏和遗失。

尽管当时的船舶设计比较粗，也没有像现在船舶设计专业分得这么精细，更没有采用现代造船的船体分段建造法。但作者从一个船舶设计和建造者的角度来看，该型船的设计图纸资料至少应该包括如下内容：

◆ 用于定义船舶基本要求和配置的船舶建造规格书。

◆ 合同技术附件图纸：总布置图和舯横剖面图。

◆ 主要设备配置表或主要设备厂商表，作者认为基于下列原因主要设备厂商表未必有：
（1）一是因为当年主要设备材料都由应急船队公司指定且处于设备和材料的短缺时期，采购到什么设备就用什么设备。
（2）二是很可能这些设备材料的规格直接定义在船舶建造规格书里而不作为单独的文件。

◆ 总体、结构、舾装、内装舱室、轮机部分的图纸和相应的工艺施工要求及材料表等。但仔细看了原图，发现当时的工艺施工要求如铆接要求等主要以图面标注以及施工工人约定俗成的惯例为主。

◆ 计算书如船舶稳性、载重量、结构规范计算书和轮机方面如蒸汽平衡的计算书等。

In the above mentioned drawings, General Arrangement Plans of different versions actually showed design process with sequential amendments. Comparing the general part, structural drawing is the most completed; in addition, there are the structural details of riveted hull. In outfitting part, there is only hatch cover layout, arrangement of mooring and heavy derrick boom, but no other outfitting systems such as anchor, rudder, lifesaving, master signal etc. Meanwhile machinery drawing is out of searching. The searching was too difficult because the code system of outfitting and machinery are as per category but do not follow the hull number.

These drawings especially General Arrangement Plan is lengthened 0# size; the longest drawing is length of approximate 3.6 meters. The drawing size is very large. Paper looks quite thick. From viewpoint of now, National Sixth Machinery Department had enough foresight to decide transferring those drawings to No.76 Institute. Those drawings have been well stored and protected in No.76 Institute, with no damage or loss.

In the period of designing four steam freighters, the professionalization was not so sophisticated as modern ship design, and no block construction was adopted. The design drawings of four steam freighters, from viewpoint of ship designer, should normally include at least following:

◆ Shipbuilding Specification for defining essential requirements and equipment.

◆ Technical Attachments of contract: General Arrangement Plan and Midship Section.

◆ Major Equipment Specification or Maker List. However, they might not exist at that time with the following reasons:

（1）First, major equipments and materials were specified by the Emergency Fleet Corporation. The shortages of equipments and materials often occurred in the wartime, and the selection of equipments and materials most properly depended on the availability.
（2）Second, the particulars of major equipments might be directly inserted in the specification or specified on the drawing, but they were not formed as a separated document.

◆ Workmanship requirements and material lists for all technical parts. After carefully reviewing the drawings, there are workmanship requirements and specification directly specified on drawing, for example, requirements of rivet work, such as diameter and span of rivet bolt, etc.

◆ Calculation sheets, like stability, deadweight, scantling and steam balance etc.

从该型船 4 位数的图纸编号来看，不像是完全按专业分的，作者也未能找出其编号的规律。从目前船舶档案馆的档案保存方式和分类来看，由于没有图纸目录，图纸的分类比较乱。从编号的间隔来看，该型船的图纸数量是非常多的，但不排除和其他船混编的可能性。作者估计即便是剔除同一图纸的不同版本，全船应该有 120~150 份。20 世纪 70 年代，如果不考虑船体结构分段建造的因素，江南造船厂设计一艘万吨级的干货船的图纸数量也有 250~300 份。由此可见，当时江南造船所的船舶设计水平并不低。可惜的是，几经辗转后，相当一部分图纸早已散失了。

可以肯定的是，船舶建造规格书是有的，美国海运委员会秘书博尔内在总布置图的修改图（1918 年 8 月 8 日）上提的意见"To be rearranged, see specification"和毛根的确认签名足以证明船舶建造规格书是存在的。江南造船所中方工程师的回忆录中也提到吨位或载重量计算的问题，因此计算书应该也是有的。但不解的是，为什么文字性的资料诸如规格书、计算书、材料清册等一张也没有留下？就连图纸资料的目录也没有留下？也许是限于当时的文档复制条件？或者是文件归档的规定？再或者是文字资料已经被当事人或英国籍的管理者和技术人员作为个人资料带走了？这一切现在已经无法得知。

虽然上述几十张图纸只是该型船设计图纸的一部分，但从分析该型船的设计特点、设计来源的角度来看，还是非常有参考价值的。特别是总布置图 7007E 和 7008E（标注日期为 1921 年 1 月 21 日，从日期看，这张总图应该是首制船的完工图），图纸上的许多布置细节绘制得十分精细，比例也十分精准，线条和字形十分优美。这些精致的总图对分析鉴别船舶总布置特点、舾装专业的锚、舵、救生、系泊、桅樯信号等系统以及内装舱室布置的特点起到了非常重要的作用。此外，作者对比了江南"局坞分家"以后 1905 年至计算机辅助设计（CAD）大规模应用的 1990 年间的图面制图水准，1920—1935 年江南造船所的图面制图水准较高，后面 50 多年没有能够超越。

If checking the code on the drawing, Kiangnan used four-digit sequential coding system at that time so that it was no certain sorting method to apply. By verifying the interval of numbering, it seems huge quantity but it might be mixed with other ships. The drawing list and coding rules do not exist in the Archives of CSSC either. The total drawing quantity might be in range of 120 to 150 sets even excluding various versions in the same title of drawing. Comparing the 1970s, Jiangnan Shipyard designed 10 000-ton dry cargo ship normally had 250 to 300 sets drawings if no block erecting method applied. It is proven that Kiangnan's design level was quite advanced at that time. Unfortunately, the most literal technical documents have been lost in past decades.

A fact of which Shipbuilding Specification existed can be confirmed. Mr. Bourne, the Secretary of the Shipping Board, made his comment "To be rearranged, see specification" on the revised General Arrangement Plan dated 8 August 1918, and Mr. Mauchan also signed to confirm. This comment proved that Shipbuilding Specification existed. Chinese naval architect of Kiangnan mentioned tonnage and deadweight estimations in his memoirs. It means that such calculation sheets should exist. Inexplicable things are why no literal technical documents like specification, calculation sheet, material bill left? Even no list of drawing? It may be limited by duplicating capability? Or archiving requirement? Such textual documents may be carried away by the foreign managers and engineers when they left Kiangnan. All of these can not be confirmed now.

Although the above mentioned drawings were a small part of full scope of design drawings for constructing these steam freighters, they are very valuable for analyzing design features and finding design sources. Especially General Arrangement Plan coded 7007E and 7008E (dated 21 January 1921, this General Arrangement Plan should be "As Built" drawing of the first vessel). Many details on this drawing are presented with elaborate professional. The scales are exactly accurate, and line and font have an indescribable romantic charm. Such an exquisite General Arrangement Plan is quite helpful for analyzing the features of ship layout, outfitting arrangement of anchoring, rudder, lifesaving, mooring, mast and signal as well as cabin. In addition, comparing the drafting level of Kiangnan and Jiangnan since 1905 to 1990, the eve of when CAD system had been widely applied, it is an undeniable fact that the drafting level was the highest level in 1920 to 1935. It cannot be exceeded even in fifty-five years thereafter.

在这四艘船的整个营运生涯中（本书第 6 章有详细介绍），有许多船东经手营运。作者试图联系一家曾经在 1952—1955 年营运过该型船中的第三艘"东方"号 [当时改名为"旭光丸"号（Kyokko Maru）] 的日本航运公司三光汽船株式会社（Sanko Kisen K. K. / Sanko Steamship Co. Ltd.，创立于 1934 年），但这家航运公司已经于 2014 年重组，最终无法联系上。

在江南造船集团档案馆内，作者在江南造船厂成立 120 周年的文集中找到了一封美国船级社主席威廉·N. 约翰斯顿写给当时江南造船厂厂长赵福生的一封贺信及其赠送的一批江南造船所 1921 年建造的第一艘万吨轮的图纸资料。此外，作者还查到了1991 年上海出版的《航海》杂志第五期刊登的一篇署名"普益"的报道，报道中也提到了美国船级社主席威廉·N. 约翰斯顿在江南造船厂成立 120 周年之际发来贺信以及赠送资料一事。图 4-1 和图 4-2 所示为贺信的全文翻译稿和《航海》杂志上的报道。但作者在江南造船集团档案馆内没有发现这批美国船级社赠送的图纸。

作者联系了曾经担任过美国船级社中国区首席代表的何荣基（Wingkee Ho）先生，他 1984 年至1985 年期间曾在上海工作，并从 1997 年起担任美国船级社中国区的首席代表。何先生回忆起一个重要的细节，1985 年，他曾经代表美国船级社向江南造船厂转交过一份江南造船所 1921 年交付万吨级运输舰的载重线证书，但没有图纸。关于江南造船厂这边具体是谁接收了这份载重线证书，由于年代久远何先生已经无法确定。江南造船厂当时正在设计建造"中国江南型"65 000 吨巴拿马散货船的系列船，其中第二艘和第四艘（H2181/H2183）由美国俄勒冈州波特兰的 LASCO 航运公司订造、第三艘（H2182）由香港的泰昌祥轮船公司订造，以上三艘船均入级美国船级社。作者询问了江南造船厂与船级社有工作联系的技术、质检和外事部门的一些老前辈，但也没有找到这批赠送图纸的相应的接收人。后来何先生也到当时美国船级社在新泽西州的总部找过这些资料，但由于该批船已经被拆解多年，档案部门也几经搬迁而且还遭遇过洪水，故其档案已经不完整了，该批船的图纸资料已经没有了。

In whole operating lives of these four steam freighters (refer to Chapter 6 of this book for further detail), many ship owners operated these steam freighters. The effort was made to find the possibility to contact Sanko Kisen K. K. / Sanko Steamship Co. Ltd. (a Japanese shipping company, found in 1934), who operated the third freighter of the series (at that time renamed as "Kyokko Maru"), but unfortunately this shipping company was reorganized in 2014, and we eventually failed to contact it.

In the Archives Institute of Jiangnan Shipyard Group, a congratulatory letter from American Bureau of Shipping (ABS) was found. This letter was collected in the documentation of 120 anniversary celebration. This letter was written by Mr. William N. Johnston, Chairman of ABS and sent to Mr. Zhao Fusheng, Director of Jiangnan Shipyard. In this letter, Mr. Johnston mentioned ABS is willing to hand over to Jiangnan Shipyard some drawings and documents of 10 000-ton deadweight steam freighters delivered by Kiangnan in 1921. An article with signature of "Pu Yi" was published on *Navigation* magazine of May of 1991. In this report, it also mentioned such presentation of the old drawings and documents. Figures 4-1 and 4-2 are the congratulatory letter translated in Chinese and an article on *Navigation* magazine respectively. But unfortunately, these drawings and documents were not found in the Archives Institute of Jiangnan Shipyard Group.

I contacted Mr. Wingkee Ho, who used to work in Shanghai from 1984 to 1985, and he was appointed as the Chief Representative of ABS Great China since 1997. Mr. Ho recalled some reminiscences. He handed over a Load Line Certificate of Steamer on behalf of ABS to Jiangnan Shipyard in 1985, but not drawing. He could not confirm who received this certificate on behalf of Jiangnan. At that time, Jiangnan was building "Sino-Jiangnan" type, 65 000 DWT Panamax bulk carrier series. The second and fourth ships (H2181 and H2183) were built for LASCO Shipping, Portland, Oregon State of USA, the third (H2182) was built for Tai Chong Cheang Steamship CO., Hong Kong, and all these three bulkers were classed by ABS. I asked former Jiangnan's staffs who used to work in technical, quality control and foreign affair departments, but I did not find any further information. Mr. Ho tried to find these drawings and documents in ABS headquarter in New Jersey, but did not find any one. These steam freighters had been demolished many years ago, and the archives department used to be flooded and relocated serval times. The drawing and document of these steam freighters can not be found miraculously.

美国船检局局长兼主席
威廉·N.约翰斯顿致赵福生厂长贺信

亲爱的赵福生厂长：

在贵厂一百二十年厂庆之际，请允许我代表美国船级社向您并通过您向贵厂全体职工致以热烈的祝贺，祝贵厂不断取得成功。

自江南船厂建厂至今，她已参与了造船业中许多重大变革。她在建厂一百二十周年历程中所取得的成功应归功于她足智多谋的领导和勤劳的职工。

我们美国船检局为能与贵厂早在六十年前就开始合作而感到自豪。据我们所知，贵厂建造的"官府"号、"天国"号、"东方"号、"国泰"号是贵厂第一批出口船。这四条船的耐用性和经济性足以表明贵厂的造船质量和水平。

作为历史的见证，我们想您可能会对有关这四条船的一些文件感兴趣。所以我们想借此机会将这些船首次入ABS船级的记录（1923年版）和有关船、机和载重线检验的原始文件的拷贝及这些船的外形图、总布置图和外板展开图拷贝送给贵厂。

在此，我们再次向您和贵厂的全体职工对你们所取得的巨大成就表示祝贺。同时，我们在美国船检局（ABS）向您表示良好的祝愿，并想让您知道，我们随时准备着同您的良好船厂合作。

您忠实的
美国船检局局长兼主席威廉·N.约翰斯顿
一九八五年五月十三日

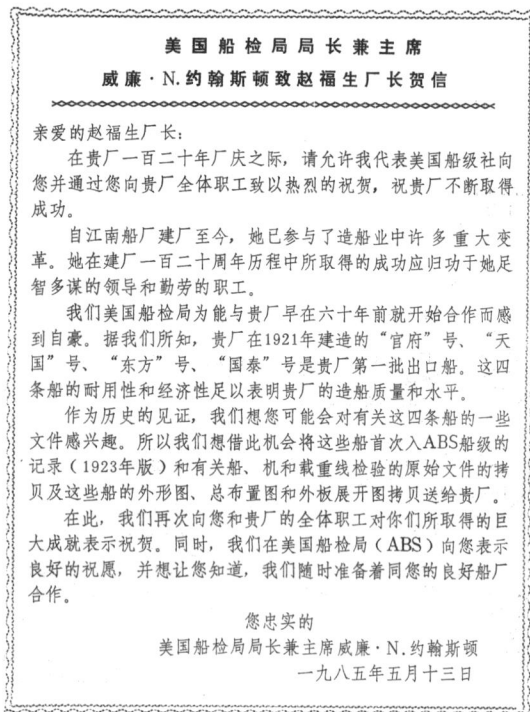

图4-1　美国船级社主席威廉·N.约翰斯顿写给
　　　　江南造船厂厂长赵福生的贺信
Figure 4-1　Congratulatory letter from Chairman of ABS to
　　　　　　Director of Jiangnan Shipyard

六十年前ABS存档的中国出口船

美国船检局局长兼主席威廉·约翰斯登，在江南造船厂120周年厂庆之际，发来了一份热情洋溢的贺信，对古今造船质量推崇备至。来信称："……我们美国船检局为能与贵厂早在60多年前就开始合作而感到自豪。据我们所知，贵厂在1921年建造的官府号第一艘万吨级出口船其耐用性和经济性足以表明贵厂的造船质量和水平。作为历史的见证，我们想您们可能会对有关这条船的一些文件感兴趣。所以我们借此机会，将这些船首次入ABS船级的记录（1923年版）和有关船、机和载重线检验的原始拷贝及这艘船的外形图、总布置图和外板展开图拷贝送给贵厂。……我们美国船检局（ABS）向您们表示良好祝愿……并随时准备同您们良好船厂合作。"

显而易见，这是我国第一艘，ABS船级社的出口船。

普登

图4-2　1991年上海出版的《航海》杂志第五期刊登的一篇报道
Figure 4-2　Article published on *Navigation* magazine, May 1991, Shanghai

2015年5月，作者在美国休斯敦参加国际海洋油气技术大会（OTC）展会期间专程到访了美国船级社休斯敦总部档案部门。作者在其收藏的 *Record of American and Foreign Shipping* 中查到了这四艘船的入级记录。遗憾的是没有查到这四艘船相关的图纸资料，图纸随着船舶的拆解而被销毁；但查到了第三艘船"旭光丸"号（Kyokko Maru）和第四艘船"Amonia"号在日本川崎重工船厂修理的图纸，以及舵杆、轴系等铸钢件的检验报告等，这也证实了第二次世界大战以后第三艘船确实在1952年转卖给了日本船东三光汽船株式会社。

In May 2015, I visited the Archives Department of ABS Headquarter in Houston during Offshore Technology Conference (OTC). The register records of these four steam freighters were found in *Record of American and Foreign Shipping*, 1922, but no related drawing was found. ABS staff explained, normally the drawing and document would be destroyed once the ship dismantled or scrapped certain years after. In Archives Department of ABS Houston, I found some repair drawings and inspection reports of "Kyokko Maru" and "Amonia", which were the third and the fourth Kiangnan built steam freighters, submitted by Kawasaki Heavy Industry. These documents provided an evidence that the third freighter was exactly resold in 1952 to Japanese owner Sanko Kisen K. K./Sanko Steamship Co. Ltd.

4.3

从图纸剖析运输舰的设计
Analysis of EFC Design 1092 by Drawings

作者基于上述在七六所查找到的图纸资料，试图从一个船舶设计者的角度对该型船的设计特点分以下几个方面进行剖析。

Based on the above mentioned drawings found in No.76 Institute, an analysis for verifying the design features of these four steam freighters has been made from view point of a ship designer.

4.3.1

总布置设计
General Arrangement

该船设计为垂直型艏（vertical bow）、巡洋舰型艉（cruiser stern）、无艏楼（no forecastle）、封闭式艉柱（close type stern frame），舯机型船型，驾驶桥楼（navigation bridge）、上层建筑（superstructure）和居住舱室（accommodation）均布置在舯部。

The vessel was so designed with vertical bow, cruiser stern, no forecastle, closed type stern frame. Steam engine, navigation bridge, superstructure and accommodation were located amidship.

主船体内设双层底（double bottom）、三层甲板：下甲板、上甲板和遮蔽甲板（lower, upper and shelter decks）、七道水密 / 油密舱壁（water/oil tight bulkhead）；货舱双层底内设燃油舱（fuel oil tank）、机炉舱（engine and boiler room），双层底内设锅炉水舱（feed water tank）。

There was a double bottom, three decks (lower, upper and shelter decks), and seven water/oil tight bulkheads inside main hull. The fuel oil tanks are located in the double bottom in way of cargo holds, and the feed water tanks were located in the double bottom in way of engine and boiler room.

主船体内部从艏至艉布置为
The sub-division inside main hull from bow to stern is:

♦ 艏尖舱（可兼作燃油舱），艏尖舱上部为木工间和储藏室，艏尖舱后面下方为锚链舱。	♦ Fore peak tank (alternately as fuel oil tank), carpenter workshop & store located on top of fore peak tank, chain lockers arranged rear of fore peak tank.
♦ 三个货舱。	♦ Three cargo holds.
♦ 舯部设置一个机炉舱。	♦ Engine and boiler rooms allocated amidship in tandem.
♦ 一个深舱（下部有纵向分隔可兼作燃油舱）。	♦ One deep tank (lower part can be used as fuel tank with longitudinal bulkhead).
♦ 三个货舱。	♦ Two cargo holds.
♦ 艉尖舱（可兼作燃油舱）。	♦ Aft peak tank alternatively used as fuel oil tank.

这种三层甲板的布置能够大大提高干货（dry cargo）和包装货（parceled cargo）的装载率及装卸效率。机炉舱上设置三层上层建筑／甲板室、机舱棚（engine casing）、烟囱和设备室。艉楼上甲板设置甲板部普通船员舱室，艉部遮蔽甲板设置艉甲板室、甲板部中级船员舱室和舵机房。表 4-1 为五个版本的总布置图的大致差异。

Such triple-deck arrangement can significantly improve space utilization, loading and unloading efficiency of dry and parceled cargoes. Three tiers superstructure/deck house, engine casing, funnel and equipment room were located above engine and boiler rooms. Seaman's cabins of deck department were located on poop upper deck, aft deck house for junior crew's cabin and steering gear room were located on aft shelter deck. Table 4-1 is a deviation in five versions of General Arrangement Plan.

艉部配置一具非平衡舵（平板式结构）、单个四叶螺旋桨、三个巴尔特无杆锚（Baldt stockless anchor，其中一个为备用锚），甲板上配置吊杆式（derrick type）起重设备。货舱内各层甲板设置铰链折叠式（folding type）舱口盖。

A non-balanced rudder (flat type structure) and a four-blade propeller were equipped at stern. There were three Baldt stockless anchors, one of them as spare. Derrick type cranes were equipped on the shelter deck. Folding type hatch covers were arranged on decks in cargo holds.

表 4-1　五个版本的总布置图的大致差异
Table 4-1　The deviation in five versions of General Arrangement Plan

图号 DWG No.	标注日期 Date	页数[3] Page	和上一版本的大致差异 Difference with last version
7007A 7008A	1919-4-24 1919-4-25	1 1	船体总长和两柱间长分别增加了 4 英尺（1.22 米）；取消了燃煤舱（驾驶室后的深舱），采用燃油锅炉；将深舱移到上层建筑后部，取消了深舱两侧的吊杆；货舱采用前三后二的布置方式；对艏部上层建筑和艉楼下的房舱做了初步布置；取消了艏艉的炮塔；对起重设备布置进行了很大的调整 Increased 4 feet(1.22 meters) to LOA and L_{pp} respectively; canceled coal storage space (deep tank behind wheel house); applied oil boilers; moved deep tank to rear of superstructure; cancelled derricks at sides of deep tank; arranged 3 cargo hatches and 2 cargo hatches in fore body and aft body respectively; re-arranged cabins in superstructure amidship and poop; cancelled gun turrets at bow and poop; modified cargo gears
7007B 7008B	1919-7-10 1919-9-01	1 1	对艏部上层建筑和艉楼下的房舱及内部家具做了进一步详细布置，修改了上层建筑内的梯道和门的布置，取消了艉楼甲板上的遮阳棚，修改了艏部通风筒布置，修改了锚链舱的布置 Further detailed cabin layout and furniture in superstructure and poop; modified staircase and door in superstructure; cancelled sun shield; modified vent arrangement at bow; modified chain locker layout
7007C	1919-9-01	1	修改了锅炉舱的天棚设计，修改了艉楼尾部的布置，细化了封闭式驾驶室的方窗设计，细化了餐厅布置。此图于 1919 年 7 月 31 日得到了美国海运委员会的认可 Modified sky light design of boiler room; modified poop deck arrangement; more detailed square windows design in the front of navigation bridge; more detailed mess room layout. This drawing was approved by USSB on 31 July 1919
7007D	1920-5-31	1	增加了木甲板的布置（救生艇甲板、驾驶室、飞行甲板、艉楼甲板和艉部遮蔽甲板），工作艇板移到了驾驶甲板，修改了无线电天线的布置，艏部锚机后移，增加了左舷舷梯，高级船员餐厅的桌子改成了圆桌（"国泰"号的完工总布置图又改成了长方形桌），内部梯道改成双向布置，修改了厨房和船员餐厅的布置，舵机改成了电动舵机，增加了锅炉烟道布置 Added wooden deck at (boat deck, navigation bridge, flying deck, poop top and shelter deck aft); dinghy moved to navigation deck; modified layout of radio antenna; moved bow windlass afterward; added portside accommodation ladder; table in officer's mess room changed rounded type (rectangle table in as built drawing of SS "Cathay"); internal stair changed to rounded type; modified layouts of galley and mess room; steering gear changed to electric motor driven; added smoke tunnel arrangement of boiler

（续表）
(continued)

图号 DWG No.	标注日期 Date	页数[3] Page	和上一版本的大致差异 Difference with last version
7007E 7008C	1921-1-21 1921-1-24	1 1	在图上标明了四艘船的船名；取消了前起重桅和后起重桅之间的天线；进一步细化了起重桅的索具布置，增加了右舷舷梯；增加了遮蔽甲板上的板缝；艉楼甲板上增加了应急人工操舵装置和舵轮；修改了遮蔽甲板的房舱布置（增加了双人床）；修改了救生艇架的布置；增加了中间甲板开口的栏杆布置；增加了机炉舱内的平台布置，并细化了各种机械和工作舱室和液舱；修改细化了桅樯信号布置。此外，因每艘船增加了一份舱容图和载重线标尺图，故去除了总布置图上液货舱内液体重量的标注 Indicated ship name; cancelled wire antenna between fore and aft posts; more detailed wire layout of derrick, added starboard accommodation ladder; added butt seams of shelter deck; added emergency steering gear on poop deck; modified cabin layout on shelter deck (added double beds); modified davit arrangement of life boat; added handrail around opening of intermediate decks; added platforms in engine and boiler rooms and more detailed working spaces and liquid tanks; modified master and signal layouts. In addition, withdrawn indications of weights in liquid tanks on General Arrangement Plan, and added independent drawings of capacity and deadweight scale

机炉舱内设三台单侧多管回焰式船用烟管锅炉[（multi-tubular return tube single ended marine smoke boiler），俗称苏格兰锅炉（Scotch boiler）]和一台三缸立式三胀式往复式蒸汽机（3-cylinder vertical type triple expansion reciprocating engine），通过布置在后半船体底部轴隧内的长轴系驱动一具四叶定距螺旋桨。

Three sets of multi-tubular return tube single ended marine smoke boilers (known as Scotch boiler) and one set of 3-cylinder vertical type triple expansion reciprocating engine were arranged in engine and boiler rooms. Engine driven directly a fixed pitch, 4-blade propeller via long shafting with trusting bearing at the front of shafting tunnel.

作者比较了同期具有应急船队公司登记号的其他船型，即使从现代船舶设计理念的角度来看，该型船的总布置设计仍是比较合理的，机炉舱布置也比较紧凑，货舱空间大，优于同期具有应急船队公司登记号的其他船型。船型设计更加接近第二次世界大战期间"自由轮"（Liberty Ship 和 Victory Ship）的设计，或者说第二次世界大战期间的"自由轮"是基于此类型船设计的。

Even though from modern shipbuilding philosophy, these four steam freighters had quite reasonable general arrangement, more compact engine and boiler rooms, and larger cargo space. Comparing other ships with EFC codes built same period, these four steam freighters were better than others. The ship design was more similar to "Liberty Ship" and "Victory Ship" in World War II. Maybe it was one of prototype of "Liberty Ship" and "Victory Ship".

在查找到的图纸资料中，江南造船所建造的四艘万吨级运输舰（H317~H320）的总布置图除了合同签字版/修改版（1918 年 7 月 18 日/1918 年 8 月 8 日）以外还有五个版本的总布置图（7007A、7007B、7007C、7007D 和 7007E，7008A、7008B 和 7008C），后续五个版本和合同签字版/修改版在船舶的总布置上有非常大的差异，比较大的几个差异如下：

In the drawings, I found the Kiangnan-built four steam freighters (H317—H320) have five versions of General Arrangement Plan (7007A, 7007B, 7007C, 7007D and 7007E, 7008A, 7008B and 7008C) besides signed version accompanying with shipbuilding contract and revised version. Subsequent five versions have obvious deviations with signed and revised versions, and major deviations are as follows:

在上层建筑下的主船体内取消了燃煤舱（深舱），将深舱移到上层建筑后部；在双层底内部和艏、艉尖舱内布置了燃油舱；采用燃油锅炉；货舱采用前三后二的布置方式。船长加长了 4 英尺，取消了艏艉的炮台，单柱式起重桅改成了双柱式的并增加了 30 吨的重型吊杆，取消了一些战时配置等。

仔细比较后续五个版本总布置图可以看出，每个版本完全是重新绘制的，图面标注和字体也不尽相同。B 版和 C 版的总布置设计根据船东的要求(USSB Requirements, 31st July, 1919）进行了修改并不断地细化。

除了上述五个版本的总布置图以外，还有一份第四艘船"国泰"号的完工总布置图（H320，图号为 8971，标注日期为 1921 年 12 月 19 日），此图和上述 7007E 绝大部分相同，只有个别舱室的内部布置有些调整和细化。图 4-3~ 图 4-6 为 7007A、7008A、7007D 和 7008C 的总布置图。

Fuel coal storage space (deep tank) underneath superstructure in main hull had been moved to rear of superstructure. Fuel oil tanks were arranged in the double bottom, fore and aft peak tanks. Fuel oil boiler was adopted. Cargo holds were arranged with 3 hatches in fore body and 2 hatches in aft body. Hull was additionally lengthened 4 feet. Gun turrets at bow and poop were cancelled. Single post derricks were changed to double post derricks with additional heavy-duty boom of 30 tons. The configuration for wartime was also cancelled accordingly.

After comparing 5 versions of general arrangement, every version was completely re-drawn, and the description and font were different. Versions B and C were modified and detailed as per owner's comments (USSB Requirements, 31 July 1919).

Besides of five versions of General Arrangement Plan, there is an "As Built" General Arrangement Plan of SS Cathay" (H320, Drawing No. 8971, dated 19 November 1921. This is mostly identical with version of 7007E except minor amendments of cabin layout. Figures 4-3-4-6 shew the General Arrangement Plan of 7007A, 7008A, 7007D and 7008C.

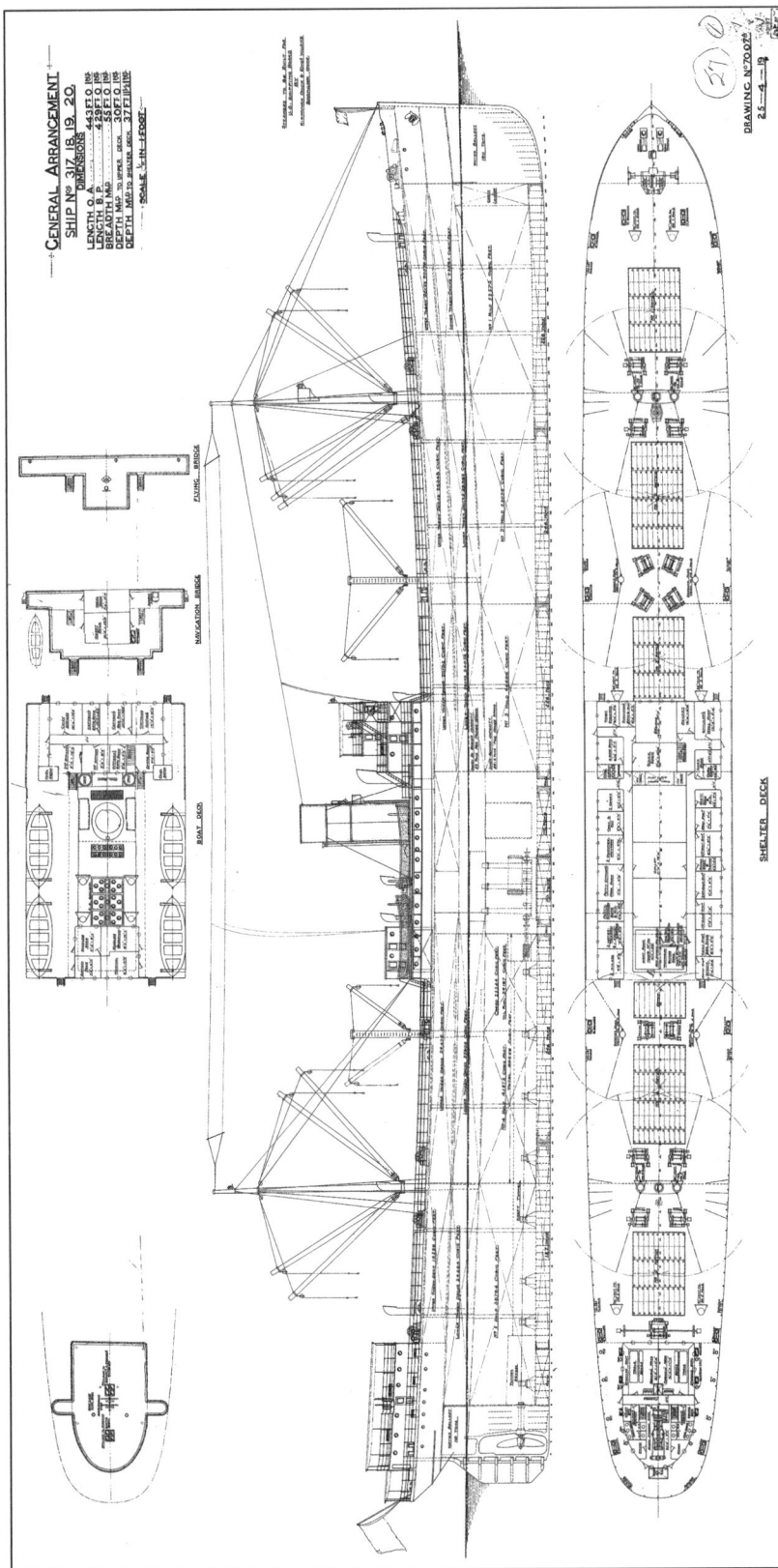

图 4-3 7007A 的总布置图，标注日期为 1919 年 4 月 25 日
Figure 4-3 General Arrangement Plan, Drawing No. 7007A dated 25 April 1919

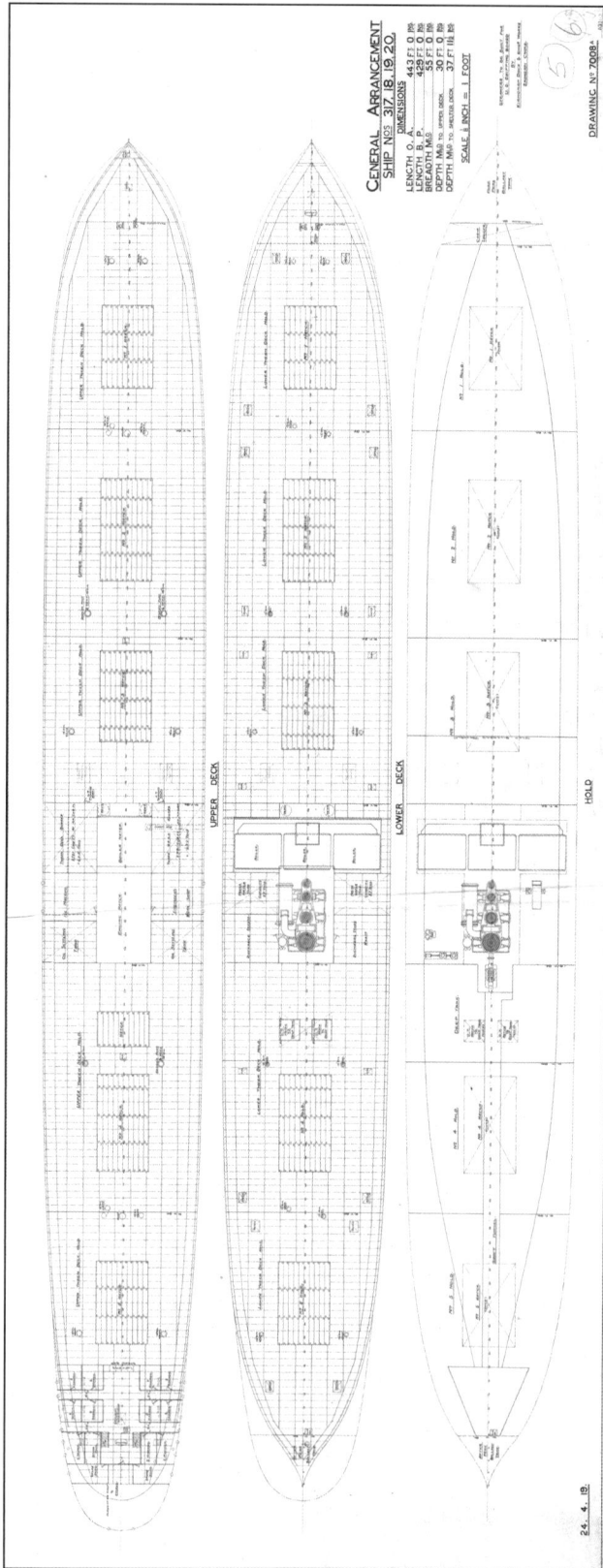

图 4-4　7008A 的总布置图，标注日期为 1919 年 4 月 24 日

Figure 4-4　General Arrangement Plan, Drawing No. 7008A dated 24 April 1919

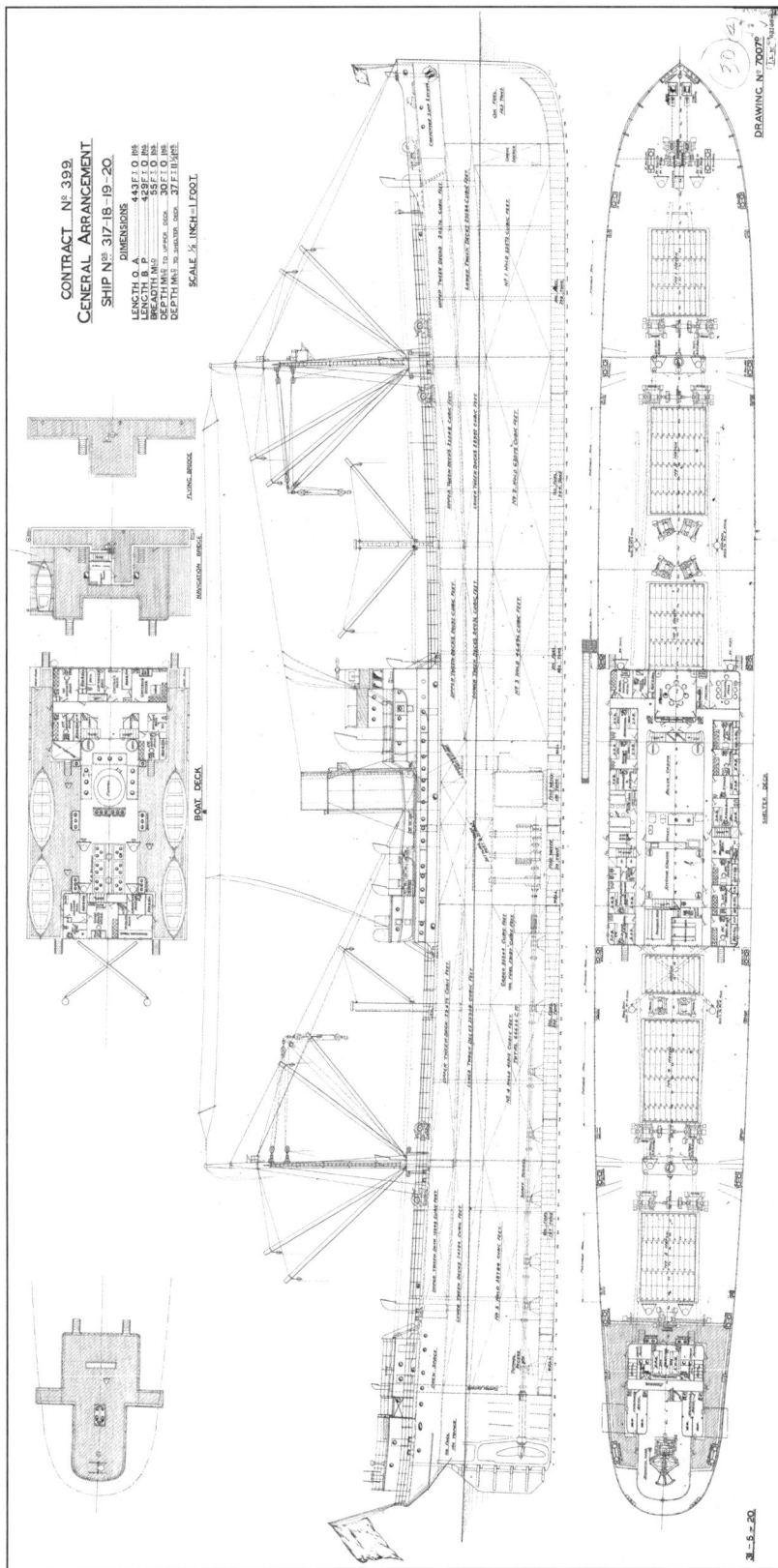

图 4-5 7007D 的总布置图，标注日期为 1920 年 5 月 31 日
Figure 4-5 General Arrangement Plan, Drawing No. 7007D dated 31 May 1920

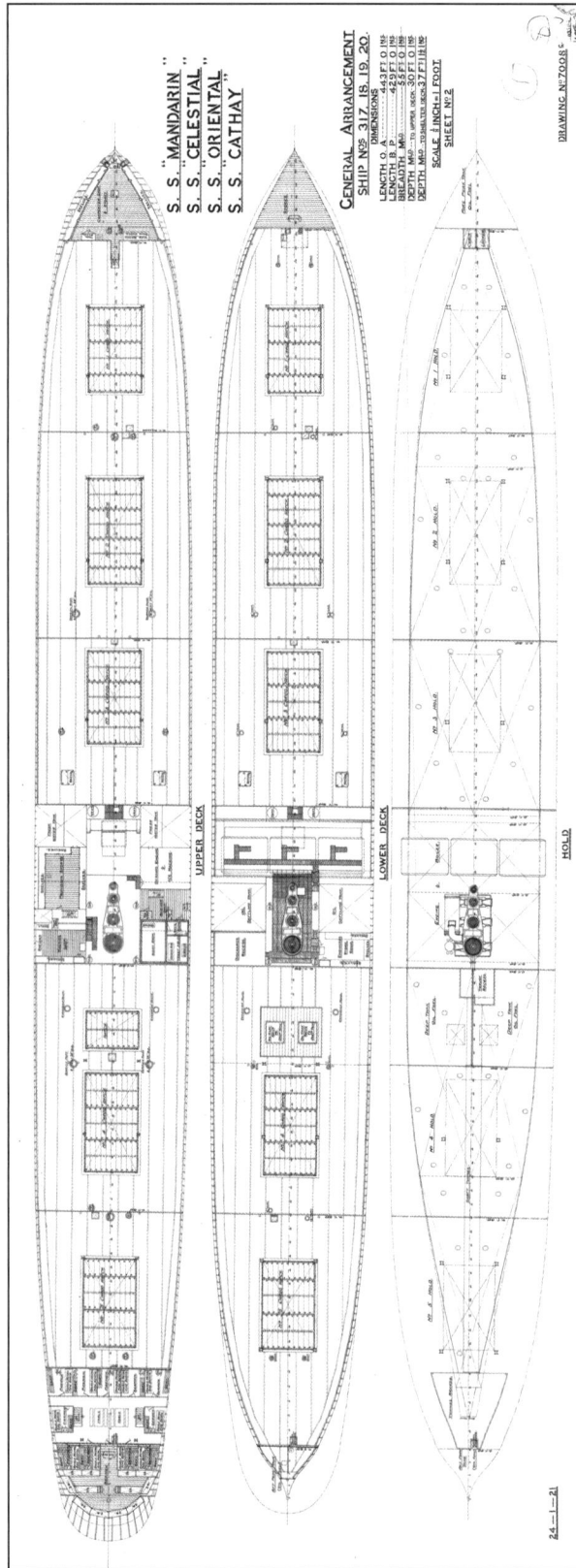

图 4-6　7008C 的总布置图 7008C，标注日期为 1921 年 1 月 24 日
Figure 4-6　General Arrangement Plan, Drawing No. 7008C dated 24 January 1921

4.3.2

主要尺度
Main Particulars

除了船体总长和两柱间长加长了 4 英尺（1.22 米）以外，从合同签字版总布置图到最终的完工总布置图，船舶的其他主尺度一直没有变化。图 4-7 为最终的完工总布置图 7007E 上标注的主尺度截图。

In addition to lengthen 4 feet (1.22 meters) in lengths overall and perpendiculars, the main dimensions of ship kept no change from contract signing till delivery. Figure 4-7 shows main particulars indicated on "As Built" General Arrangement Plan (version 7007E).

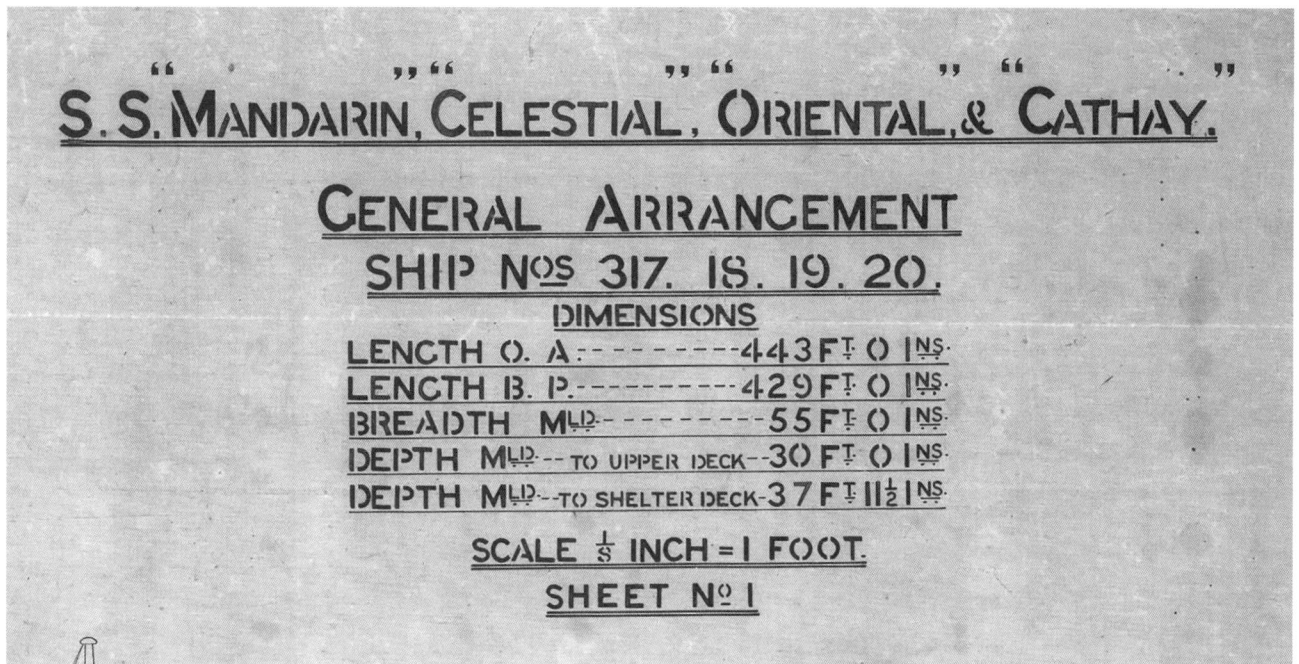

图 4-7 总布置图 7007E 上标注的船舶的主尺度
Figure 4-7 Main particulars indicated on "As Built" General Arrangement Plane (version 7007E)

在第二艘船（"天朝"号，H318）的舱容和载重量标尺图（Capacity Plan & Deadweight Scale）（见图 4-8）上，还标注了一些船舶的其他参数。图 4-9 为舱容和载重量标尺图上标注的主尺度和轮机的主要参数截图。

On Capacity Plan & Deadweight Scale drawing of SS "Celestial" (see Figure 4-8), H318, some other particulars are indicated on the drawing. Figure 4-9 shows principal and machinery particulars indicated on this drawing.

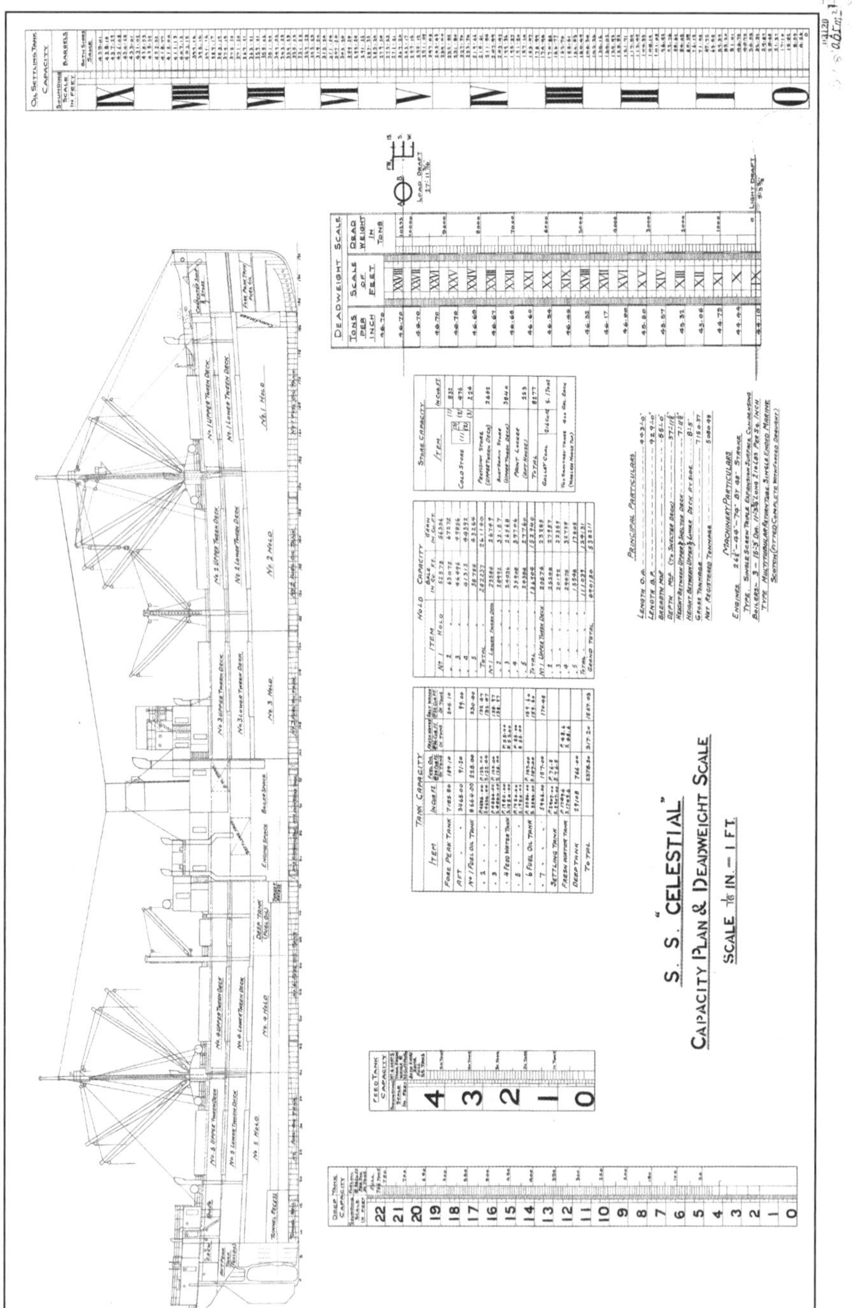

图 4-8 "天朝"号的舱容和载重标尺图，标注日期：无

Figure 4-8 SS "Celestial" Capacity Plan & Deadweight Scale

PRINCIPAL PARTICULARS

```
LENGTH O.A. --------------------------------- 443'-0"
LENGTH B.P. --------------------------------- 429'-0"
BREADTH MLD --------------------------------- 55'-0"
DEPTH MLD (TO SHELTER DECK) ----------- 37'-11½"
HEIGHT BETWEEN UPPER & SHELTER DECK ------ 7'-11½"
HEIGHT BETWEEN UPPER & LOWER DECK AT SIDE ----- 8'-5"
GROSS TONNAGE ------------------------------- 7150.37
NET REGISTERED TONNAGE ---------------------- 5080.48
```

MACHINERY PARTICULARS

```
ENGINES:- 26½"-44"-74" BY 48" STROKE
   TYPE  SINGLE SCREW TRIPLE EXPANSION SURFACE CONDENSING.
BOILERS:- 3-15'-3" DIA. 11'-3¾" LONG 210 LBS. PER SQ. INCH.
   TYPE  MULTITUBULAR RETURN TUBE SINGLE ENDED MARINE
         SCOTCH (FITTED COMPLETE WITH FORCED DRAUGHT)
```

图 4-9　舱容和载重量标尺图上标注的主尺度和轮机的主要参数
Figure 4-9　Principal and machinery particulars indicated on Capacity Plan & Deadweight Scale

在第二、第三艘船（"天朝"号，H318；"东方"号，H319）的舱容和载重量标尺图上，标注了美国船级社勘定的吃水标志和该型船的夏季吃水数据：27 英尺 11 又 3/16 英寸（8.514 米）。图 4-10 为"天朝"号的舱容数据，其他三艘姐妹船的舱容数据基本相同。

On the Capacity Plan & Deadweight Scale drawings of SS "Celestial" and SS "Oriental" (the 2nd and 3rd vessels), ABS assigned draught marks and summer draught of 27 feet and 11-3/16 inches (8.514 meters) are indicated. Figure 4-10 is capacity data of SS "Celestial". The data of other three sister ships are mostly consistent.

TANK CAPACITY

ITEM	IN CUB FT.	FUEL OIL @38 CUB.FT. IN TONS	FRESH WATER @36 CUB.FT. IN TONS	SALT WATER @35 CUB.FT. IN TONS
FORE PEAK TANK	7185.80	189.10		205.10
AFT "	3465.00	91.20		99.00
N° 1 FUEL OIL TANK	8664.00	228.00		230.40
" 2 " "	P.4636.00 S.4636.00	P.122.00 S.122.00		132.47 132.47
" 3 " "	P.4864.00 S.4864.00	P.128.00 S.128.00		138.97 138.97
" 4 FEED WATER TANK	P.1980.00 S.1980.00		P.55.00 S.55.00	
" 5 " "	P.1980.00 S.1980.00		P.55.00 S.55.00	
" 6 FUEL OIL TANK	P.5586.00 S.5586.00	P.147.00 S.147.00		159.60 159.60
" 7 " "	5966.00	157.00		170.45
SETTLING TANK	P.2907.00 S.2907.00	P.76.5 S.76.5		
FRESH WATER TANK	P.1749.6 S.1749.6		P.48.6 S.48.6	
DEEP TANK	29108	766.00		
TOTAL		2378.30	317.20	1567.03

HOLD CAPACITY

ITEM	BALE IN CU. FT.	GRAIN IN CU.FT.
N° 1 HOLD	52573	56356
" 2 "	63072	67272
" 3 "	46496	49856
" 4 "	41312	44392
" 5 "	38784	43264
TOTAL "	242237	261140
N° 1 LOWER TWEEN DECK	23584	26749
" 2 " " "	28992	32157
" 3 " " "	24036	26568
" 4 " " "	35908	39706
" 5 " " "	24384	27760
TOTAL "	136904	152940
N° 1 UPPER TWEEN DECK	20576	23285
" 2 " " "	25248	27957
" 3 " " "	20192	22359
" 4 " " "	29475	32725
" 5 " " "	15548	17805
TOTAL "	111039	124131
GRAND TOTAL	490180	538211

STORE CAPACITY

ITEM	IN CUB.FT.
COLD STORE (1) (2) (3)	(1) 832 (2) 476 (3) 224
PROVISION STORE (UPPER TWEEN DECK)	2662
BOATSWAIN STORE (UPPER TWEEN DECK)	3840
PAINT LOCKER (AFT HOUSE)	153
TOTAL	8277
GALLEY COAL	216 CU FT 5.1 TONS
TWO SANITARY TANKS (WIRELESS HOUSE TOP)	400 GAL. EACH

图 4-10　"天朝"号的舱容数据
Figure 4-10　Capacity data of SS "Celestial"

从图4-10可以看出，该型船可以装载燃油2 378.30吨［以每吨38立方英尺（1.08立方米）计算］，装载淡水317.20吨［以每吨36立方英尺（1.02立方米）计算］，压载水为1 567.03吨［以每吨35立方英尺（0.99立方米）计算］。货舱舱容：包装货（bale）为490 180立方英尺（13 880.33立方米），散装谷物为538 211立方英尺（15 240.41立方米）。备品和冷库储存空间共8 277立方英尺(234.38立方米)，厨房用煤5.1吨［储存空间为216立方英尺（6.12立方米）］。

From Figure 4-10, the vessel can load fuel oil of 2 378.30 tons [38 cubic feet (1.08 cubic meters) per ton], fresh water of 317.20 tons [36 cubic feet (1.02 cubic meters) per ton] and ballast water of 1 567.03 tons [35 cubic feet (0.99 cubic meters) per ton]. Cargo hold capacities: bale of 490 180 cubic feet (13 880.33 cubic meters), bulk grain of 538 211 cubic feet (15 240.41 cubic meters). Storage spaces of provision and refrigerating chamber of 8 277 cubic feet (234.38 cubic meters) in total, fuel coal for galley of 5.1 tons [storage space of 216 cubic feet (6.12 cubic meters)].

4.3.3

船体线型和吨位丈量
Hull Form and Tonnage Measurement

该型船的线型设计并无特别之处，是当时的一种常规设计，体现了 20 世纪初杂货船的船型特征，如垂直艏、巡洋舰艉、封闭式艉柱和舵杆组合、圆舭、中 V 剖面、舷侧列板上部内倾等。

从图 4-11 船体横剖面线型（body plan）的图面线条来看，线条非常细、水线和直剖面线的位置尺寸十分精准、横剖面曲线也十分光顺，船体底部双层底的轮廓也在图面上标出。作者曾经对图中的斜剖线进行纵向展开校验，发现纵向展开后的斜剖线也是非常光顺的。可见此图的设计者具有非常高超的技术水准，制图水平也是一流的。图 4-12 所示的船体艏艉线型（fore and aft body）进一步对艏艉线型进行定义。

The hull form was quite a normal design at that time with the features of general cargo ship in the beginning of 20 century, such as vertical stem, cruiser's stern, closed stern frame and combination of rudder post, rounded bilge, moderated V section and introversive side shell, etc.

Reviewing Figure 4-11, for the lines on the body plan, the drawn lines look quite thin with well fairing, and the accuracy of water lines and buttock lines is quite higher after the verification of slant profiles. The geometrical boundaries of double bottom were also indicated on the drawings. These drawings embodied higher professional levels in bath designer and draftsman. Figure 4-12 is a more detailed definition to the lines at fore and aft bodies.

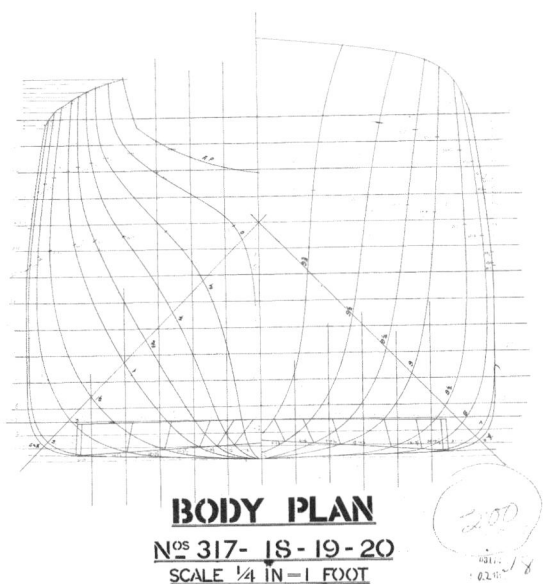

图 4-11 船体横剖面线型
Figure 4-11 Body plan of ship

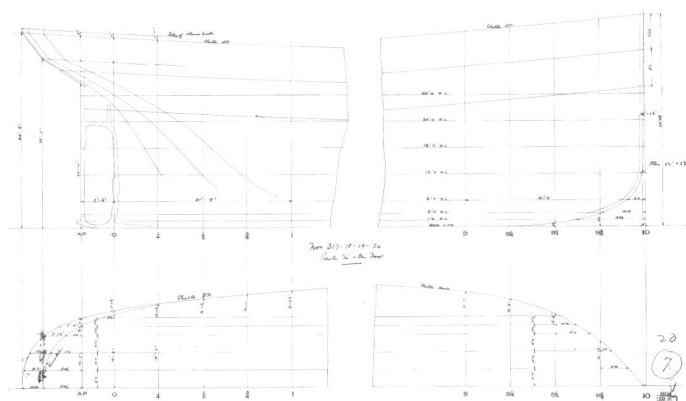

图 4-12 船体艏艉线型
Figure 4-12 Lines at fore and aft body

　　船体肋骨线型（见图4-13）已经破损，经过修补后进行了扫描。此图应该是在船体横剖面线型的基础上加密了肋骨，特别是艏艉部，同时将外板的板缝也标注上去了。此图同样绘制精细、线型光顺。但是和现在船舶设计图纸命名惯例不同的是，现在船舶设计中的"肋骨线型图"通常称为"body plan"。

The hull transverse frame plan (see Figure 4–13) had been partially damaged due to be stored for a long time. This plan was actually body plan with inserted frames especially at stem and stern, and further the seams on shell were additionally indicated on. This drawing embodied higher professional levels in bath designer and draftsman as well. But the naming practice for those two drawings was just reversed comparing modern ship design.

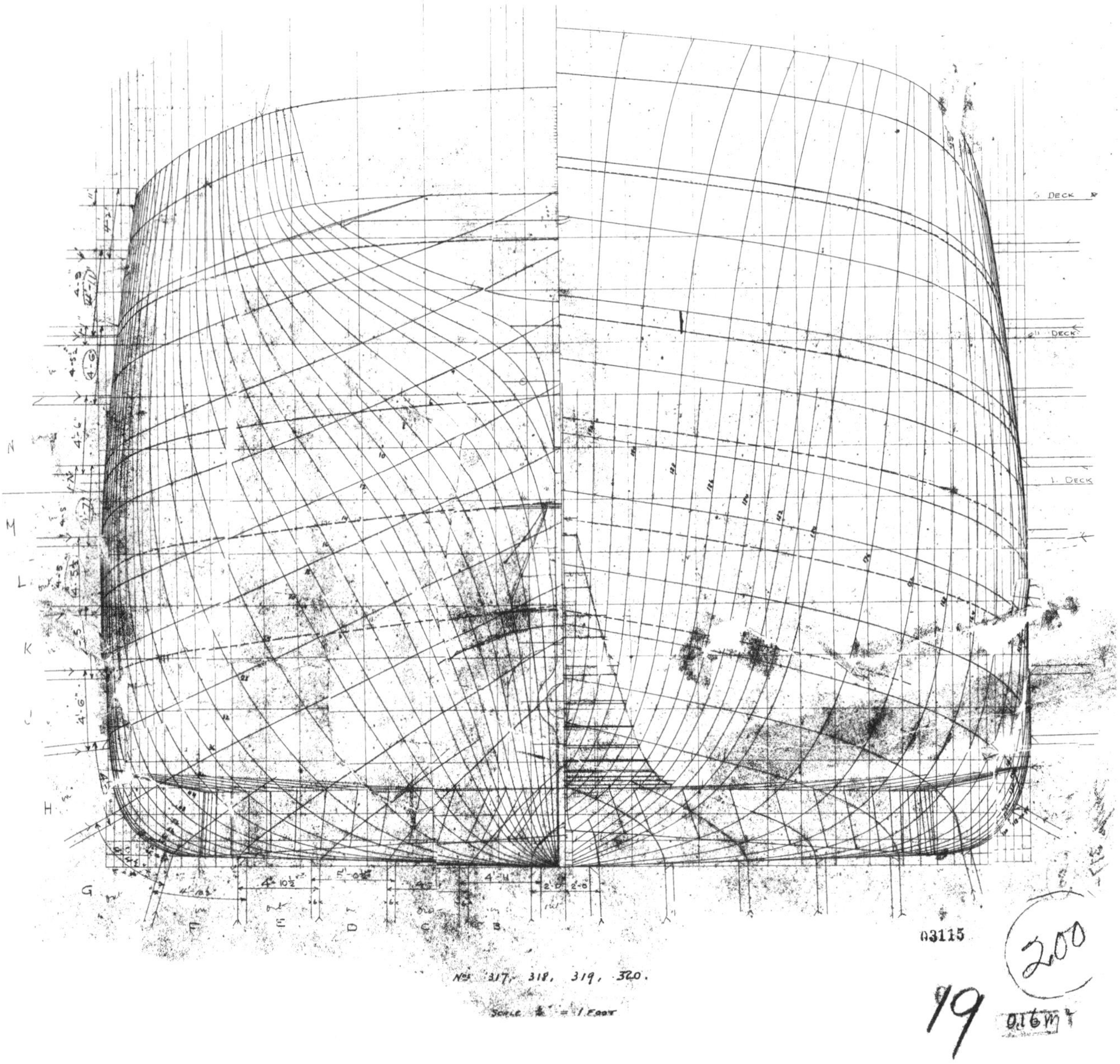

图 4-13　船体肋骨线型
Figure 4–13　The hull transverse frame plan

对船体艏部双层底的轮廓、艏柱的尺寸［10 又 1/2 英寸（26.67 厘米）× 2 又 3/4 英寸（6.99 厘米）］和艉封板的线型也专门有详图（见图 4-14）进行定义。

There was a special detailed sketch (see Figure 4-14) to define the geometrical boundaries of double bottom, the scantling of stem and cant [10-1/2 inches (26.67 centimeters) × 2-3/4 inches (6.99 centimeters)].

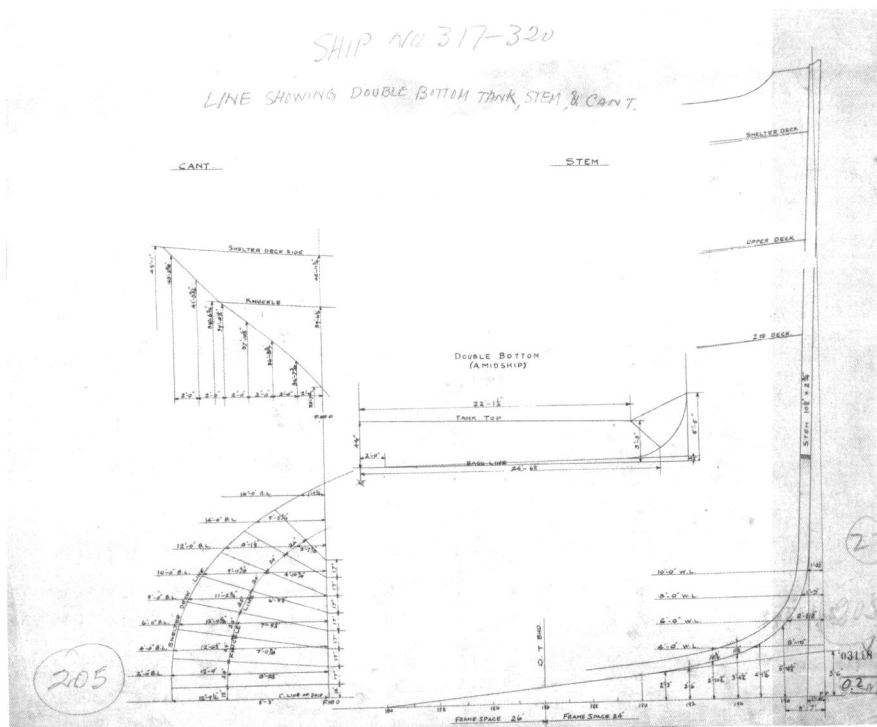

图 4-14 双层底、艏柱和艉封板线型
Figure 4-14 The geometrical definition of double bottom tank, stem and cant[4]

对总吨位和净吨位进行丈量的剖面有专门的图纸表示（Tonnage Sections，图号为 8137，标注日期为 1920 年 11 月 8 日），类似现代船舶设计中的"邦金曲线"的剖面（见图 4-15）。

For measurement of gross and net tonnages, there was a special drawing titled "Tonnage Sections" with drawing number of 8137, dated 8 November 1920. This is quite similar to "Bonjean Curve" in modern ship design, refer to Figure 4-15.

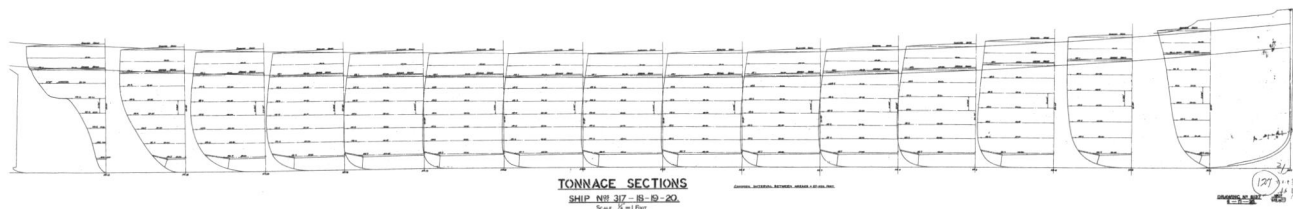

图 4-15 吨位丈量剖面
Figure 4-15 Tonnage Sections

4.3.4

入级和挂旗
Classification and Flag

2015 年 5 月，作者在美国船级社休斯敦总部档案馆内收藏的 *Record of American and Foreign Shipping* 中查到了这四艘船的入级记录（见图 4–16）。

In May of 2015, I found register records of these four ships in *Record of American and Foreign Shipping* (see Figure 4–16) while I visited the headquarter of American Bureau of Shipping (ABS) in Houston.

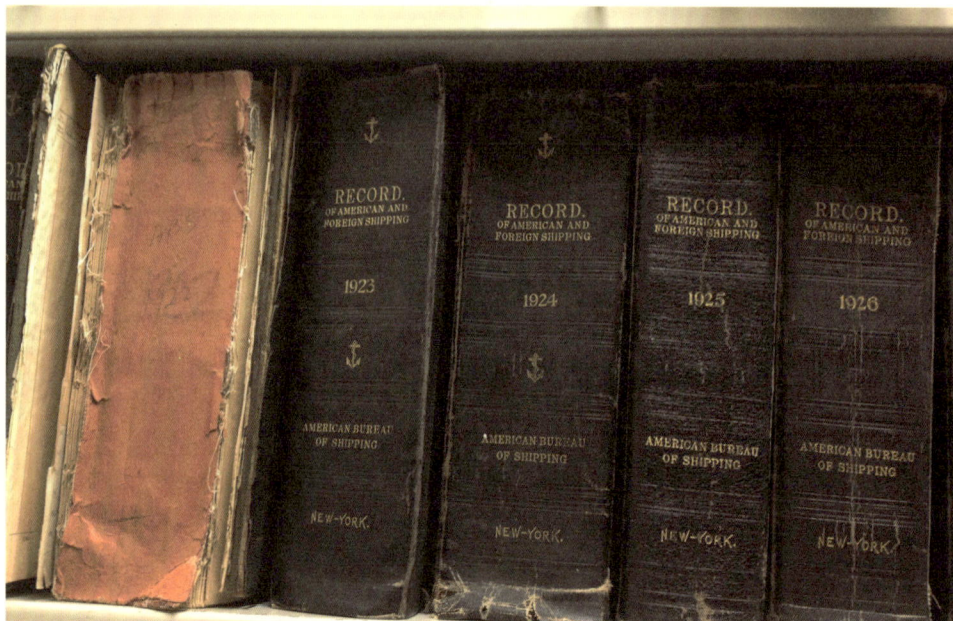

图 4–16　美国船级社休斯敦总部档案馆内收藏的船舶历年入级记录
Figure 4–16　Ship record books stored in headquarter of American Bureau of Shipping, Houston

首制船"官府"号的入级记录（1922 年的 *Record of American and Foreign Shipping*）如图 4–17 所示。

Register record of SS "Mandarin" (the first vessel) in *Record of American and Foreign Shipping*, 1922, as shown in Figure 4–17.

图 4–17　"官府"号的入级记录
Figure 4–17　Register record of SS "Mandarin"

第二艘船"天朝"号的入级记录（1922 年的 *Record of American and Foreign Shipping*）如图 4–18 所示。

Register record of SS "Celestial" (the second vessel) in *Record of American and Foreign Shipping*, 1922, as shown in Figure 4–18.

图 4–18　"天朝"号的入级记录
Figure 4–18　Register record of SS "Celestial"

第三艘船"东方"号的入级记录（1922 年的 *Record of American and Foreign Shipping*）如图 4–19 所示。

Register record of SS "Oriental" (the third vessel) in *Record of American and Foreign Shipping*, 1922, as shown in Figure 4–19.

图 4–19　"东方"号的入级记录
Figure 4–19　Register record of SS "Oriental"

遗憾的是，在 1922 年的 *Record of American and Foreign Shipping* 中未能找到第四艘船"国泰"号的入级记录，而在 1932 年的 *Record of American and Foreign Shipping* 中找到了"Diana Dollar"号（原第四艘船"国泰"号）的入级记录，如图 4–20 所示。

It was a pity that the register record of SS "Cathay" was not found in *Record of American and Foreign Shipping* of 1922, but she was found in *Record of American and Foreign Shipping* of 1932, and renamed as "Diana Dollar", as shown in Figure 4–20.

图 4–20　改名为"Diana Dollar"的"国泰"号的入级记录
Figure 4–20　Register record of SS "Cathay" renamed as "Diana Dollar"

上述完工总图（7007E）不知为何没有列出该型船的吃水数据？通常这是一个很重要的参数。作者认为这是当时制图和标注习惯所致，或船级社没有最后勘定。

Why no draught data indicated on as built General Arrangement Plan (7007E)? Normally it is quite an important figure in ship design. It may be due to the drawing practice at that time, or maybe it was not finally assigned by classification society.

根据《江南造船所纪要》中的记载和签合同时的总图上的数据来看，该型船的吃水（draught）为27英尺6英寸（8.38米），这个吃水是设计型吃水。

根据美国船级社休斯敦总部档案馆收藏的1922年的 *Record of American and Foreign Shipping* 的船舶入级记录，第一、第二和第三艘船的吃水为27英尺11英寸（8.51米），这个吃水是经过干舷勘验后的夏季吃水。

作者又复查了图纸，在第二、第三艘船（"天朝"号，H318；"东方"号，H319）的舱容和载重量标尺图上，还标注了美国船级社核定的吃水标志和该型船的夏季吃水数据：27英尺11又3/16英寸（8.51米）。

1932年的 *Record of American and Foreign Shipping* 中显示，第四艘船的吃水增加了，为28英尺1又3/4英寸（8.58米）。可能是因为局部改装空船重量增大所致。

根据上述美国船级社的入级资料，四艘船全部挂的是美国旗。虽然第三艘船未列出注册港信息，但根据其他资料分析，应该都是旧金山。

As per records in *Summary of Kiangnan Dock & Engineering Works* and GA Plan accompanied with shipbuilding contract, the draught was 27 feet and 6 inches (8.38 meters), this data was design draught.

As per registered records in *Record of American and Foreign Shipping*, 1922, the draughts of the 1st, 2nd and 3rd vessel were consistent, and the draught of 27 feet and 11 inches (8.51 meters) was summer draught after freeboard assignment.

On "Capacity Plan & Deadweight Scale" drawing of SS "Celestial", H318 and SS "Oriental", H319, ABS assigned draught mark and summer draught of 27 feet and 11–3/16 inches (8.51 meters) are indicated after double checking the drawing.

As per registered records in *Record of American and Foreign Shipping*, 1932, the draught of the 4th vessel was increased to 28 feet and 1–3/4 inches (8.58 meters). It may be caused by extra weight of locally retrofitting.

As per registered records of ABS, all four steam freighters flew American flag, and the registered port was San Francisco.

4.3.5

规范和规则
Rules and Regulations

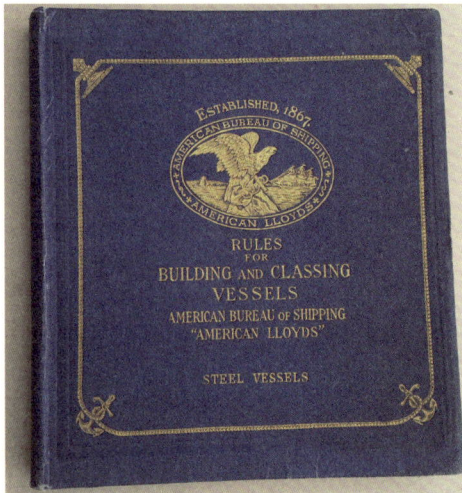

图 4-21　1917 年版的 ABS 规范的封面
Figure 4-21　The cover of ABS rules, 1917 edition

该型船当时是按照美国船级社的《钢质船舶规范》（*Rules for Building and Classing Vessels*）进行设计、入级和检验的。作者在美国船级社休斯敦总部档案馆内查到了 1917 年版的美国船级社《钢质船舶规范》（见图 4-21），并仔细翻看了规范内页（见图 4-22）以及规范中关于第 23 章"铆接船体和捻缝"的相关内容（见图 4-23）。有趣的是当时美国船级社在下面加了一个备注："American Lloyds"（美国劳埃德），可见当时"劳埃德"这个名称在海事界是享有盛名的。

This series was designed, classed and inspected according to *Rules for Building and Classing Vessels* of ABS. Original rules of 1917 are kept in Archives Department of ABS in Houston headquarter. Figure 4-21 is the cover of ABS rules, 1917 edition; Figure 4-22 is the inner pages of ABS rules, 1917 edition, Figure 4-23 is Section 23 "Riveting and Caulking". A quite interesting thing is a note of "American Lloyds" under the "American Bureau of Shipping" on the rules cover. It seems like "Lloyds", at that time, was "most famous brand in marine field.

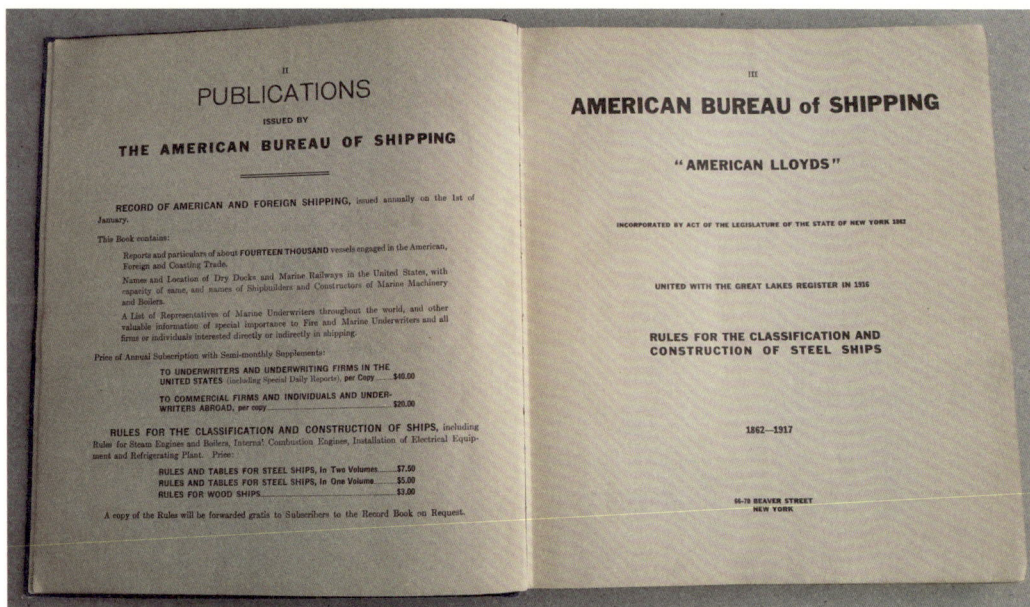

图 4-22　1917 年版的 ABS 规范的内页
Figure 4-22　Inner pages of ABS rules, 1917 edition

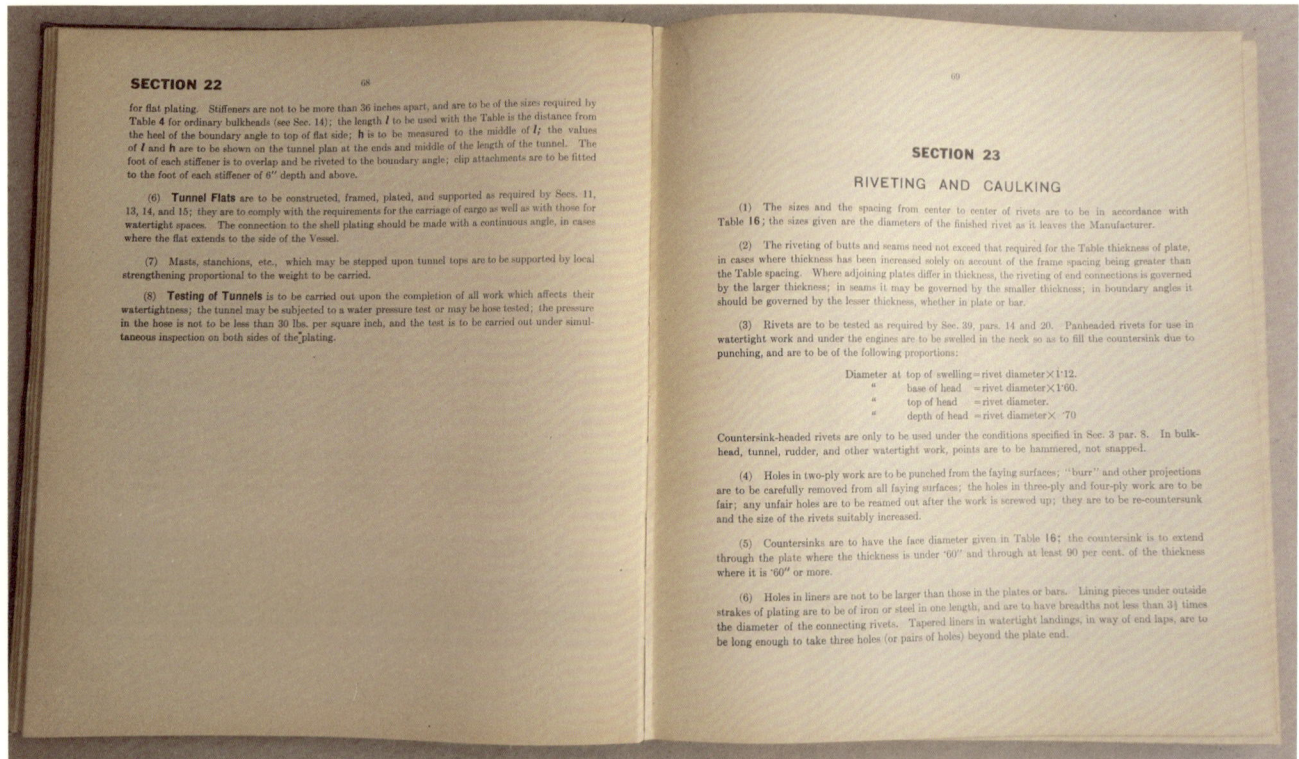

图 4-23　第 23 章 "铆接船体和捻缝"
Figure 4-23　Section 23 "Riveting and Caulking"

根据 4.3.4 节美国船级社的入级资料，四艘船全部挂的是美国旗。在现代船舶设计建造过程中，挂旗国当局有许多法定检验的规则和要求。因无法查到这四艘船的合同规格书等文字性资料，故无法判断当时挂旗国当局有哪些法定检验的规则和要求。 在现有的资料中，20 世纪 30 年代美国有一个名叫"美国海事检验和航海局"（U.S. Bureau of Marine Inspection and Navigation）的机构，不知是不是挂旗国当局的法定检验机构？

According to register records of ABS, all those four steam freighters flew American flag. In modern shipbuilding, the authorities of flag country have many statutory requirements. It is impossible to judge which requirements of flag authorities did apply because that contract specification was not found. Based on existing material, there was an authority named "U.S. Bureau of Marine Inspection and Navigation", but it's difficult to confirm whether it was statutory authority of flag country.

关于美国海事检验和航海局的功能和职能，www.crwflags.com 上有这样一段描述[5]：

Regarding the function and responsibility of U.S. Bureau of Marine Inspection and Navigation, www.crwflags.com has a description as follows:

美国海事检验和航海局是 1838 年在财政部蒸汽船舶检验服务部门的基础上成立的。1884 年改名为"航海局"，1903 年转入商务和劳工部，1932 年改名为"航海和蒸汽船舶检验局"，1936 年又改为"海事检验和航海局"。1942 年，它的职能被划转给了美国海岸警卫队和美国海关。

The U.S. Bureau of Marine Inspection and Navigation was established as the Steamboat Inspection Service on basis of the Department of the Treasury in 1838. It was renamed the Bureau of Navigation in 1884, and transferred to the Department of Commerce and Labor in 1903. It was renamed as the "Bureau of Navigation and Steamship Inspection" in 1932. It was again renamed the "Bureau of Marine Inspection and Navigation" in 1936. Its functions were respectively transferred into the Coast Guard and the Customs Service in 1942.

1936 年，这四艘船被卖给了美洲 – 夏威夷航运公司（American-Hawaiian Steamship Company），其中三艘船（"Diana Dollar" 号 / "Alabaman" 号，"Margaret" 号 / "Arkansan" 号和 "Melville" 号 / "Carolinian" 号）在旧金山和奥克兰的莫尔干船坞公司（Moore Dry Dock Company）进行了改装，另一艘船（"Stuart Dollar" 号 / "Floridian" 号）在西雅图的托德干船坞公司（Todd Dry Dock Company）进行了改装。改装的主要目的如下：

一是为了将这些船升级至可以达到美洲 – 夏威夷航运公司的公司标准（主要项目为船体结构检查、舱室的装修改装和升级，参见本书第 5 章）。

二是为了满足美国海事检验和航海局的新规范和规则的要求，例如无线电通信电报系统和内部声力电话通信系统等。

由此可见，在当时美国海事检验和航海局确实履行了船舶法定检验机构的职能。

In 1936, these four steamers were sold to American-Hawaiian Steamship Company, three of them ("Diana Dollar"/"Alabaman", "Margaret"/"Arkansan" and "Melville"/"Carolinian") were retrofitted in Moore Dry Dock Company in San Francisco and Auckland, and the other one ("Stuart Dollar"/"Floridian") was retrofitted in Todd Dry Dock Company in Seattle. The main purposes of retrofitting were:

First, to upgrade to company standard of American-Hawaiian Steamship Company. Mainly concerned hull structure investigation, renew the interior decoration of cabin. Refer to Chapter 5 for further detail.

Second, to meet new requirements of U.S. Bureau of Marine Inspection and Navigation, such as radio communication, telex systems and sound power voice tube etc.

Thus it can be seen that U.S. Bureau of Marine Inspection and Navigation really worked as role of statutory authority.

4.3.6

船体结构
Hull Structure

关于该型船的船体结构图，作者查阅了船舶档案馆保存的江南造船所建造的四艘万吨级运输舰（船体号：H317~H320）的全部图纸资料，找到以下船体结构图纸（见表 4-2，共找到 40 份，其中个别图纸是重复的，表中未列出）。

Regarding the hull structure of these four steam freighters, after checking all drawings of Kiangnan Dock & Engineering Works built four steam freighters (hull number: H317–H320) in the Archives of CSSC. The following drawings (a few of them are duplicated) were shown in Table 4–2.

表 4-2　船体结构图
Table 4–2　The hull structure of four steam freighters

序 号 Serial No.	名 称 Name	图 号 Drawing No.	标注日期 Date
1	遮蔽甲板图 Shelter Deck Plan	6861	1918 年 10 月 26 日 26 October 1918
2	舱壁图 Bulkhead Plan	6977	1919 年 1 月 9 日 9 January 1919
3	艉部斜肋骨图 Cants Plan	7029	1919 年 2 月 21 日 21 February 1919
4	艉部外板图 Stern Plating Plan	7036	1919 年 3 月 1 日 1 March 1919
5	舯横剖面图 Midship Section	7040	1919 年 3 月 6 日 6 March 1919
6	双层底舱结构图 Double Bottom Tank	7095	1919 年 4 月 23 日 23 April 1919
7	F183 防撞舱壁图 F183 Collision Bulkhead	7105	1919 年 4 月 27 日 27 April 1919
8	F8 艉尖舱舱壁图 F8 Aft Peak Bulkhead	7113	1919 年 4 月 30 日 30 April 1919
9	F153 水密舱舱壁图 F153 Water Tight Bulkhead Frame No.153	7124	1919 年 5 月 8 日 8 May 1919
10	F62 和中纵油密舱舱壁图 F62 Oil Tight Bulkhead Frame No.62 & Centre BHD	7153	缺 Missing
11	外板展开图 Shell Expansion	7154	1919 年 5 月 19 日 19 May 1919
12	轴隧结构图 Tunnel Plan	7155	1919 年 5 月 27 日 27 May 1919
13	F40 水密舱舱壁图 F40 Water Tight Bulkhead Frame No.40	7166	1919 年 6 月 4 日 4 June 1919
14	纵剖面结构图 Profile Plan	缺 Missing	缺 Missing

（续表）
(continued)

序 号 Serial No.	名 称 Name	图 号 Drawing No.	标 注 日 期 Date
15	遮蔽甲板图 Shelter Deck Plan	7173	1919 年 8 月 12 日 12 August 1919
16	上甲板结构图 Upper Deck Plan	7175	1919 年 6 月 16 日 16 June 1919
17	肋骨结构图 Frames	7201	1919 年 7 月 9 日 9 July 1919
18	肋骨结构图 Frames	7203	1919 年 7 月 9 日 9 July 1919
19	下甲板结构图 Lower Deck Plan	7208	1919 年 7 月 11 日 11 July 1919
20	边水平纵桁结构 Side Stringers	7210	1919 年 7 月 9 日 9 July 1919
21	F76 油密舱舱壁图 F76 Oil Tight Bulkhead Frame No.76	7212	1919 年 7 月 19 日 19 July 1919
22	锚链舱结构图 Chain Locker	7230	1919 年 7 月 28 日 28 July 1919
23	F99 水密舱舱壁图 F99 Water Tight Bulkhead Frame No.99	7237	1919 年 8 月 1 日 1 August 1919
24	舷墙和桥楼甲板结构图 Bulwark & Bridge Deck Plan, Revised	7533	1920 年 1 月 9 号 9 January 1920
25	艉部钢质甲板室结构图 Aft Steel Deck House	7570	1920 年 1 月 20 日 20 January 1920
26	机炉舱棚结构图 Engine & Boiler Casing Plan	7581	1920 年 1 月 20 日 20 January 1920
27	艏部舷墙图 Forward Bulwark Plan	7590	1920 年 1 月 31 日 31 January 1920
28	舯部钢质甲板室结构图 Midship Steel Deck House	7604	1920 年 2 月 5 日 5 February 1920
29	桥楼前后端壁结构图 Bridge Front & Bridge Back Plan	7689	1920 年 4 月 6 日 6 April 1920
30	桥楼甲板（前部）结构图 Bridge Deck Fore House, Revised	7702	1920 年 4 月 14 日 14 April 1920
31	F90 锅炉舱舱壁图 F90 Screen Bulkhead Frame 90	8049	1920 年 9 月 18 日 18 September 1920
32	龙骨加强板 1.04 英寸到 0.94 英寸详图 Strap for Keel Plates 1.04″ to 0.94″ Thick	6954	1918 年 12 月 20 日 20 December 1918
33	龙骨加强板 1.04 英寸到 0.94 英寸详图 Strap for Keel Plates 1.04″ to 0.94″ Thick	6954	1920 年 12 月 18 日 18 December 1920
34	龙骨加强板 0.84 英寸及以下详图 Strap for Keel Plates 0.84″ Thick & Under	6955	1918 年 12 月 18 日 18 December 1918
35	龙骨加强板 0.84 英寸及以下详图 Strap for Keel Plates 0.84″ Thick & Under	6955	1919 年 3 月 13 日 13 March 1919

该型船的船体结构全部采用横骨架式，外板和构件之间采用连结角钢铆接连接（riveted hull）。图4-24为该型船的船体结构的舯横剖面图（图号：7040，标注日期：1919年3月6日）。与合同签订时的技术附件之一中的舯横剖面图（图号：6545，标注日期：1918年5月7日，如前文所述，可以断定这是一张在制船的图纸）相比，此图已经很大程度地细化了，船体结构构件的尺度、连接节点的细节、相关剖面的连接结构、轴隧结构等也定义得非常详细，甚至连铆接的原则工艺也做了详细的定义，此外，锚、锚链和系泊索具的参数也在这张图纸上标注出来了。这说明江南造船所的船体结构工程师做了大量的设计工作，这些图才是江南造船所真正设计的图纸。当时船体的建造方式不是采用现在的分段建造方式，而是采用先铺外板后安装肋骨的散装建造模式，因此设计建造时通常不出分段结构图纸。

A transverse frame system was applied throughout the entire hull, and shell and inner structural members were connected by angle bar and rivets. Figure 4-24 is Midship Section, Drawing No. 7040, dated 6 March 1919. Comparing the contract attachment (Midship Section, Drawing No. 6545, dated 7 May 1918, which was amended from one of the existing drawings as described before), this drawing was much more detailed. In this new Midship Section, the scantling of structural members, connection details, shafting tunnel etc. even though rivet size and riveting span were finely defined. In addition, the parameters of anchor chain and mooring fitting were also indicated on this drawing. That means Kiangnan's engineers did great works for detail design of these steam freighters. These drawings were really designed by Kiangnan themselves. At that era, the hull construction method was normally "Piece-by-Piece", i.e., hull construction by "laying shell then fitting frame", block drawing, and thus, normally was not produced.

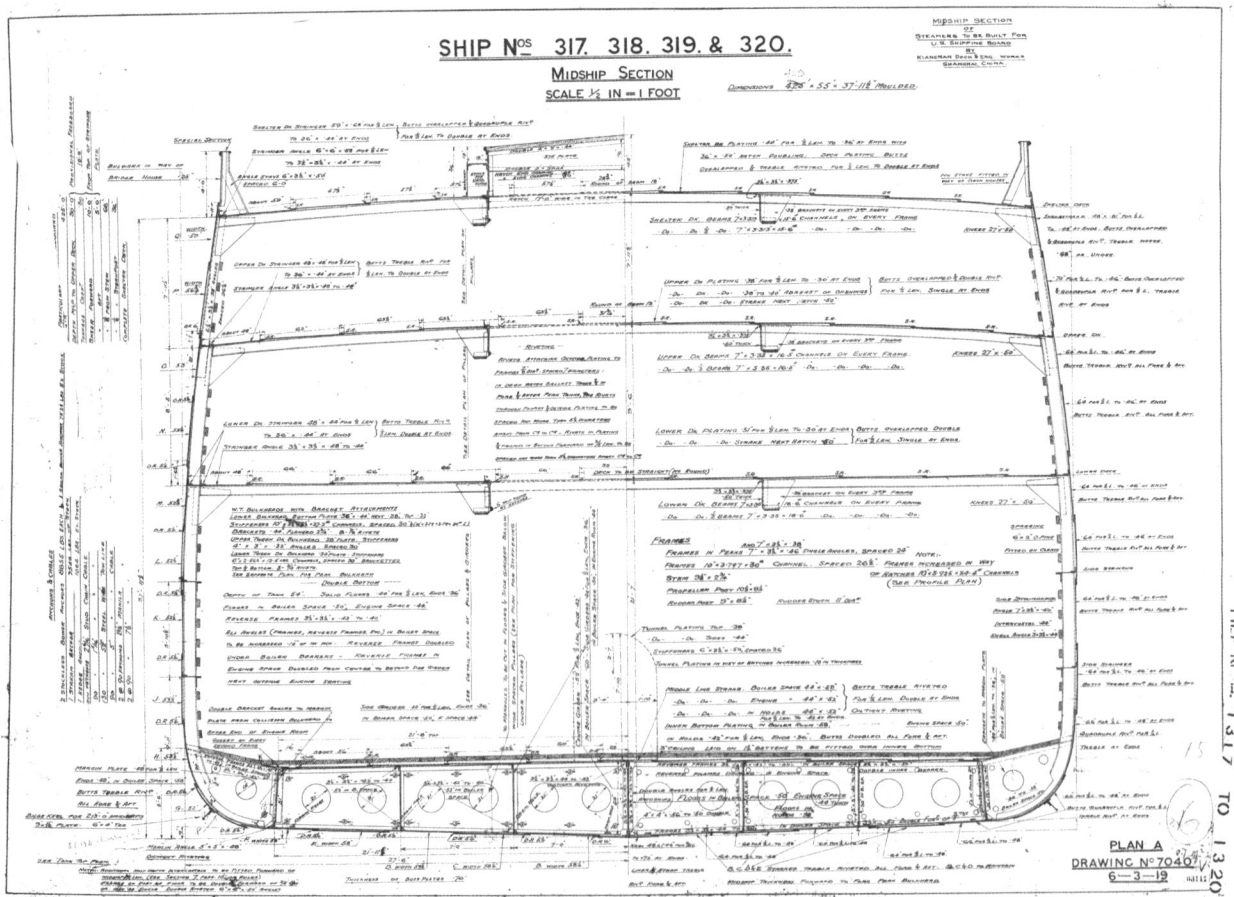

图 4-24 舯横剖面图（图号：7040，标注日期：1919 年 3 月 6 日）
Figure 4-24   Midship Section (Drawing No. 7040, dated 6 March 1919)

在上述结构图纸中有两张遮蔽甲板图，图号和标注日期都不同，结构的布置形式也不同。作者仔细地比较了这两张图纸，特别是第一张遮蔽甲板图（图号：6861，标注日期：1918 年 10 月 26 日），对该型船的设计来源分析有很大的价值，在本章的后文中有详细叙述。

双层底结构

双层底内部除了设于中心线上的龙骨外，左右舷各设置了三道纵桁，其中最外侧的为水密纵桁。双层底内每挡肋骨设置了实肋板，实肋板四周用角钢和周围结构铆接连接，实肋板上开有两个直径为 21 英寸（53.34 厘米）的圆形孔；肋板上下开有若干个流水孔和透气孔；舭部每挡设有舭肋板；内底板和舭肋板上敷设了木板条，以防止货物对钢板的冲击而造成损伤。

舭部外底板升高了 9 英寸（22.86 厘米），舭部安装有组合式舭龙骨。

舷侧结构

舷侧结构为横骨架式，从图 4-24 来看，内底板至上甲板之间的舷侧肋骨是连续的。在舭部，舷侧肋骨向下延伸相当一段长度和舭肋板连接，舷侧肋骨和甲板肋骨用肘板连接。内底板至下甲板之间的外板上还增加了两道水平纵桁。舷侧肋骨内侧安装了木板条以保护货物。在铆接船体外板的连接处通常有一定宽度的重叠。这种板重叠的结构在一定程度上增加了船体板架结构的刚度。

甲板结构

甲板结构也为横骨架式，舷侧肋骨和甲板肋骨用肘板连接。舱口两边各设了一道 L 形甲板纵桁，用肘板和甲板纵骨连接；遮蔽甲板两舷设有钢质舷墙，舱口设钢质舱口围板。遮蔽甲板和上甲板都设有梁拱，与合同附件中的舯横剖面图相比，图 4-24 中取消了下甲板的梁拱。

Two Shelter Deck Plans were found in the above drawings, drawing number and the dates are different, and structural layout has some deviation. Especially Shelter Deck Plan with number 6861, dated 26 October 1918 is quite useful for verifying design source, which will be described later in this chapter.

Double Bottom Structure

Except central girder, there were three longitudinal girders in portside and starboard respectively inside of double bottom. The most side girders were watertight. Solid floor was located every frame. Solid floor was connected with surrounded structural members by angle bar and rivets. There were two rounded opening (diameter 21 inches, 53.34 centimeters) on the solid floor, and certain drainage and air holes were arranged. Bilge bracket was located every frame. Wooden dunnage was laid on inner bottom and bilge bracket in order to avoid mechanical damage against cargo.

Bilge bottom was raised 9 inches (22.86 centimeters), and combined type bilge keel was installed at bilge area.

Side Structure

According to Figure 4-24, the side structure was a transverse type, and the side frame was continuous from the inner bottom and the upper deck. The side frame was extended down to connect with bilge bracket, and side frame and deck frame were connected by overlapped bracket. Two horizontal stringers were located on the shell between the inner bottom and lower deck. Wooden dunnages were installed inner side of side frames for protecting cargo against mechanical damage. Riveted shell plate had certain overlap, and such overlap properly increased rigidity of hull plating.

Deck Structure

Deck structure was also a transverse frame system, and the side frame and deck beam were connected by bracket. An "L" type deck girder was laid each side of hatch opening with connection with deck longitudinal by bracket. Steel bulwark was arranged at both sides of shelter deck, and hatch coaming was arranged surrounded hatch opening. Shelter and upper had a camber, but the camber of lower deck had been cancelled comparing with the last version of Midship Section (see Figure 4-24) as attachment of ship building contract.

1918 年 9 月在日本播磨造船所完工的 "Eastern Shore" 号（"Eastern Soldier" 号的同型船）的下甲板也是有梁拱的。作者认为，取消下甲板的梁拱是当时江南造船所的一个优化设计。不解的是为什么上甲板仍然设置了梁拱？通常在现代的杂货船设计中，舱内的中间甲板是不设梁拱的。有一种可能性，那就是原来母型船的设计就是没有遮蔽甲板的，遮蔽甲板是后来加上去的。第一次世界大战时期的大部分杂货船和运输舰船型（包括大来航运公司的船型）都是没有遮蔽甲板的，但将梁拱甲板改成平甲板并不是很大的设计修改。也许上甲板设置梁拱是干舷甲板规范要求的？以目前的条件来说无法将当时的规范、要求——进行比对。也许可能有其他原因？

The lower deck of Japanese Harima Dock built SS "Eastern Shore" in September 1918 (sister ship of SS "Eastern Soldier") had camber. Personally, cancellation of camber may be an optimized design of Kiangnan, but it is not clear why the upper deck was designed with camber. Normally, there is no camber applied for intermediate decks in cargo hold as per modern ship design practice. One possibility is that the original prototype design had no shelter deck, and the shelter deck was supplemented in later design stage. The most ships including those of Dollar Steamship Company had no shelter deck during the initial period of the World War I. In ship design, modification from camber deck to flat deck is not a big issue. Maybe the freeboard deck with camber was required by rules. It is currently no position to verify whether rules required or not. Maybe they had some other reasons.

船体铆接连接结构

船体构件是由大量厚度和尺度不同的钢材连接而成的，必须具备极高的连接工艺，才能保证其有足够的强度和良好的密封性。船体构件的连接方法主要有焊接（welding）和铆接（riveting）两种。

铆接是在焊接工艺普及前，船体构件的主要连接方法，甚至是 20 世纪 80 年代初在一些船舶的舷顶列板和甲板边板的连接结构上仍有用铆钉连接的。1876 年，江南制造局在建造中国第一艘 250 吨铁甲炮舰 "金瓯" 号时开始应用铆接工艺。9 年后，1885 年在建造 1 500 吨 "保民" 号钢质兵轮时铆接工艺趋于成熟。在 1918—1921 年建造四艘万吨级运输舰期间，铆接工艺运用娴熟；工人们传接烧红的铆钉时如同杂技表演一样，精湛娴熟[6]。图 4-25 为各种连接铆钉的示意图。图 4-26 为 "泰坦尼克" 号的铆接船体建造场景。

Details of Riveted Hull Structure

Hull structure consists of a lot of different scantling and size steel members with reliable connecting methods, so that sufficient strength and well tightness can be ensured. The connection of hull structural members mainly has two traditional kinds: welding and riveting.

Before welding widely applied in ship building, riveting was the main connecting method for hull structure. Even in the beginning of 1980s, riveting was applied in way of corner connection between sheer strake and upper strength deck. Kiangnan Manufacturing Bureau started to use the riveting method for building, Chinese first, 250 tons in displacement, iron hull, iron cladding gunboat, SS "King Ou" in 1876. Nine years later, the maturity of rivet methodology was improved when construction of steel hulled cruiser "Pao Min" (Tribune) of 1 500 tons. While Kiangnan Dock & Engineering Works was erecting hull of four American steam freighters, those technique and workmanship reached the highest level, and the transferring aglow rivet looked like "acrobatics" and "relay". Figure 4-25 is the illustration of various connecting rivets. Figure 4-26 is the construction scene of RMS "Titanic" riveted hull.

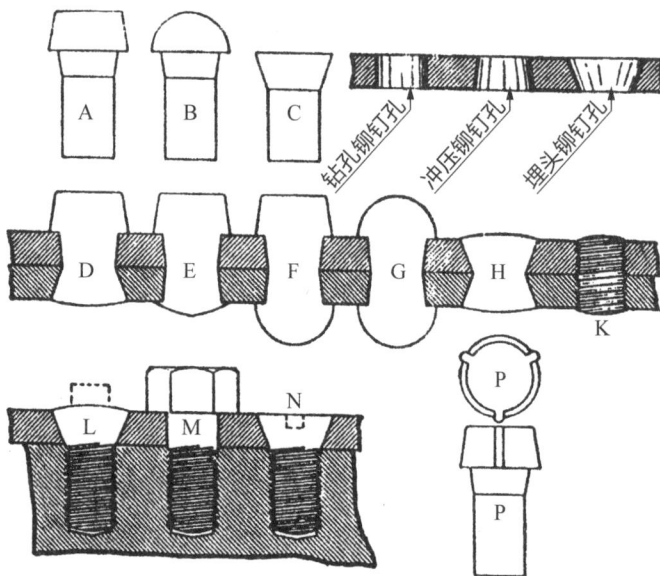

图 4-25　各种连接铆钉的示意图
Figure 4-25　The illustration of various connecting rivets

英国劳氏船级社曾向作者展示过一张关于铆接船体结构的示意图（见图 4-27），用于说明他们规范中的第 4 节"铆接和铆接工程"。

Lloyd's Register used to publish an illustration explaining Section 4 of their rules "Rivets and Riveting". Refer to Figure 4-27.

上海市鲁班路 600 号的江南造船博物馆内也曾经陈列过铆接钢板样品、一只用于加热铆钉的炉子、铆钉和夹铆钉钳子等工具（见图 4-28 和图 4-29）。

Samples of riveted plates, various rivets, heating furnace and pneumatic hammer were exhibited in Jiangnan Shipbuilding Museum. Refer to Figures 4-28 and 4-29.

图 4-26　"泰坦尼克"号的铆接船体建造场景
Figure 4-26　The construction scene of RMS "Titanic" riveted hull

图 4-28　江南造船博物馆内陈列的不同规格的铆钉
Figure 4-28　Various rivets exhibited in Jiangnan Shipbuilding Museum

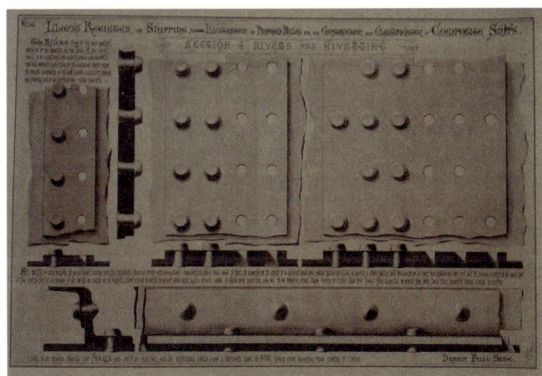

图 4-27　英国劳氏船级社的一张关于铆接船体结构的示意图
Figure 4-27　An illustration of Lloyd's Register showing rivets and riveting

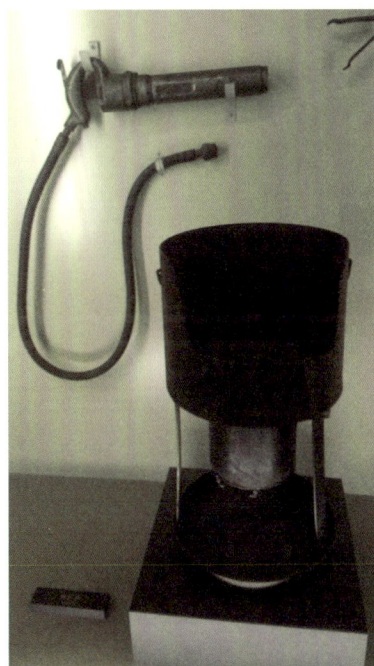

图 4-29　江南造船博物馆内陈列的加热炉和铆枪
Figure 4-29　Heating furnace and pneumatic hammer exhibited in Jiangnan Shipbuilding Museum

在德国汉堡海事博物馆内，陈列了铆钉样品和铆钉工所使用的工具以及铆接结构的样品。图 4-30 和图 4-31 所示为作者在参观德国汉堡海事博物馆时拍摄的铆钉和铆接工具、船体铆接结构模型的照片。在德国汉堡海事博物馆内还展出了铆接作业的照片和电影片段。馆内放映的电影片段再现了铆接船体的作业过程。

In Maritime Museum of Hamburg, Germany, rivets, riveting tools and model of riveted hull are exhibited. Figures 4-30 and 4-31 are photos of those samples. The riveting work is vividly recorded in the documentary film and being played in exhibition hall of museum.

图 4-30　铆钉和铆接工具
Figure 4-30　Rivets and riveting tools

图 4-31　船体铆接结构模型
Figure 4-31　Model of riveted hull

随着船舶的大型化，特别是跨大西洋邮轮的高速化，船体结构铆接技术的发展在 20 世纪 30 年代也达到了巅峰。

With larger and higher speed liners joining the fleet of crossing Atlantic Ocean, the riveting technique of hull structure had reached the peak in 1930s.

1934 年 9 月 26 日，英国卡纳德轮船公司的长 1 018 英尺（310.29 米），排水量达 80 174 吨的大型豪华邮轮"玛丽王后"号（RMS "Queen Mary"）在苏格兰克莱德班克的约翰·布朗船厂下水。

On 26 September 1934, RMS "Queen Mary", a luxury ocean liner, 1 018 feet (310.29 meters) in length with displacement of 80 174 tons, was launched in John Brown & Co., Clydebank, Scotland.

1936 年 7 月 1 日，"玛丽王后"号在拖船的环绕下缓缓离开英国南部的南安普敦港码头，开始了前往纽约的为期 4 天 12 小时 20 分钟的处女航。这艘船是当时世界上最大的铆接结构船舶。

On 1 July 1936, RMS "Queen Mary" guided by tug boats smoothly left the terminal of Southampton, and she commenced her maiden voyage for New York within the period of 4 days plus 12 hours and 20 minutes. This ship was the world's largest ship with riveted hull at that time.

1938 年，该船再次以西向 30.99 节，东向 31.69 节的平均航速从法国"诺曼底"号邮轮手中夺回了象征横渡大西洋航速度最快的"蓝飘带"奖。直到 1952 年 7 月 7 日才被美国的"合众国"号邮轮刷新了纪录 [7]。图 4-32 为大型豪华邮轮"玛丽王后"号的舷侧外板，从照片上可以清楚地看到外板上密密麻麻的铆钉，上部救生艇甲板以下的舷侧外板结构已经进行了改装和加宽，改装结构为焊接结构。

In 1938, She was recorded the average speeds of 30.99 knots (westbound) and 31.69 knots (eastbound), and won the "Blue Ribbon" Award, a speed race for crossing Atlantic Ocean, from SS "Normandy". This record was kept until 7 July, 1952 refreshed by SS "United States". Figure 4-32 shows side shell of cruiser liner RMS "Queen Mary", where a numerous rivets on side shell plating can be clearly observed. The side structure under the boat deck had been retrofitted by welding pads.

图 4-32　豪华邮轮"玛丽王后"号舷侧外板的铆接结构
Figure 4-32　Riveted side shell of cruiser liner RMS "Queen Mary"

江南造船所建造的四艘万吨级运输舰的船体结构均采用钢板铆接连接结构。在结构图纸上，不仅绘制了许多铆接结构的详图，而且标注了铆接工艺要求。在舯横剖面图和外板展开图（Shell Expansion）上也有关于铆接工艺总体要求的标注，铆接工艺要求基本上是以"铆钉直径＋铆钉间距"来表达的。图4-33为舯横剖面图上关于铆接工艺要求的标注。在一些船体结构图上，也标出了铆接结构的详图。例如在外板展开图上就画出了双层底内纵桁铆接结构的详图，如图4-34所示。

Kiangnan Dock & Engineering Works built the hull structure of those four steam freighters by riveted technology. On the aforementioned structural drawings including Midship Section and Shell Expansion, not only the details of riveted structure but also riveting specification was indicated. Normally riveting specification was expressed by "rivet diameter plus the span of rivet". Figure 4-33 shows riveting specification indicated on Midship Section. The riveting connection details were also indicated on related structural drawings. Inner girder connection details in double bottom, for instance, were indicated on Shell Expansion, see also Figure 4-34.

图4-33　舯横剖面图上关于铆接工艺要求的标注
Figure 4-33　The requirements of riveting specified on Midship Section

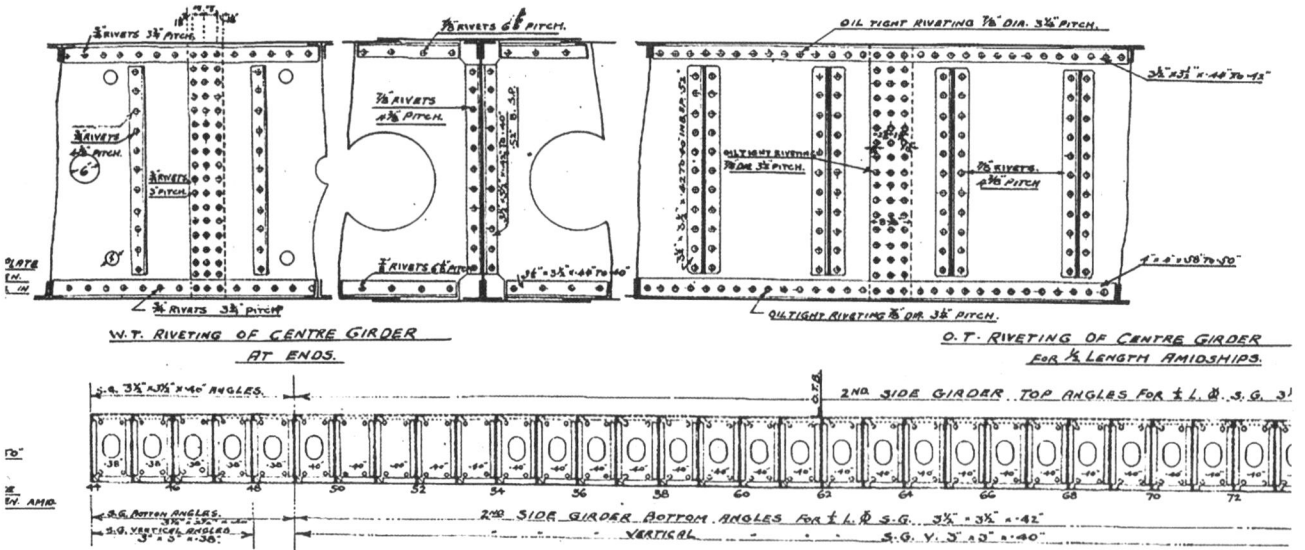

图4-34　双层底内纵桁铆接结构的详图
Figure 4-34　The details of riveted structure in way of longitudinals in double bottom

铆接船体的结构连接强度主要是根据不同的密性和受力要求按规范由铆钉间距确定。这些要求与江南造船厂20世纪70年代末和80年代初在建造铆接船体（局部）时所采用的铆钉间距标准对比，基本上是一致的。

The connection strength of riveted hull was determined by rivet span as rules requirement based on conditions of tightness and load. These requirements of rivet span were similar to those applied on riveted structure of Jiangnan Shipyard in the end of 1970s to the beginning of 1980s.

江南造船厂20世纪70年代末和80年代初在建造铆接船体时采用的铆钉间距标准[8]（*d* 为铆钉的直径）如表4-3所示。

Jiangnan's standard of rivet span in the end of 1970s to the beginning of 1980s (*d* means diameter of rivet), refer to Table 4-3.

表 4-3　江南造船厂建造铆接船体时采用的铆钉间距标准
Table 4-3　Jiangnan's standard of rivet span for building riveted hull

铆接缝的特征 Feature of the connection	油密 Oil tight	气密 Gas tight	水密 Water tight	非水密 Non water-tight	
				受力 Strength member	不受力 Non-strength member
铆钉间距 Rivet span	3~3.5*d*	4~4.5*d*	4~5*d*	5~6*d*	7~8*d*

在船底外板龙骨的部位，板与板的连接内侧加了覆板（doubling plate）。横向的加强板条（strip）有加在外侧的也有加在内侧的。此部位的铆接结构比较复杂，故针对不同厚度的龙骨加强板和不同加强板的安装方式结构工程师专门绘制了两张详图（见图4-35和图4-36）。通过这两张详图，可以清楚地看出船底龙骨板处铆接结构的连接细节。

In way of longitudinals of bottom shell, doubling plates were inserted into connected plates at the inner side. Transverse reinforce strips were supplemented either at the inner side or outer side. The riveted structures at those places were normally quite complicated. The structural designers intentionally had drawn two detailed sketches (see Figures 4-35 and 4-36) for showing different thicknesses and assembly of reinforcement plates. The riveted connection in way of bottom keel plate can be clearly verified from these two sketches.

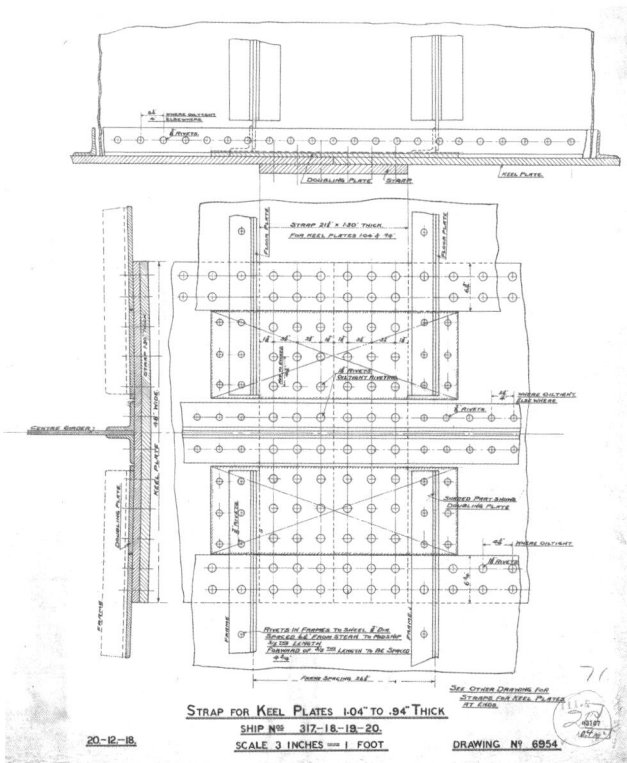

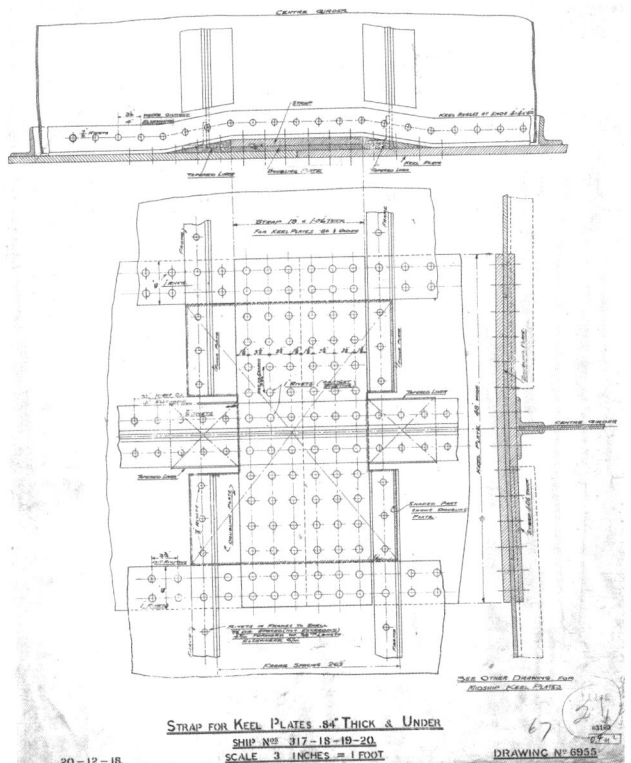

图 4-35　龙骨加强板 0.94~1.04 英寸详图
（图号：6954，标注日期：1918 年 12 月 20 日）
Figure 4-35　The details of Strap for Keel Plates 1.04" to 0.94" Thick
(Drawing No. 6954, dated 20 December 1918)

图 4-36　龙骨加强板 0.84 英寸及以下详图
（图号：6955，标注日期：1918 年 12 月 20 日）
Figure 4-36　The details of Strap for Keel Plates 0.84" Thick & Under
(Drawing No. 6955, dated 20 December 1918)

该型船货舱区域的各层甲板上均开有一个 17 英尺（5.18 米）宽的货舱开口（hatch），机炉舱内也有为安装锅炉和蒸汽机预留的开口（boiler casing and engine casing）。对于这些货舱开口，现代焊接船舶的结构设计中往往采用圆弧或椭圆形的角隅以减少应力集中，该型船的货舱开口比较小（占船宽的 31%），因此在下甲板和上甲板的货舱开口角隅处没有采取特别的加强措施，只是在遮蔽甲板货舱开口的角隅处 [3.5 英尺（1.07 米）范围内] 加了一块 0.5 英寸（1.27 厘米）厚的 L 形覆板，用于加强。图 4-37 为遮蔽甲板货舱开口角隅处的加强详图。

There were 17-foot (5.18 meters) wide hatches fitted on each deck. There were casings in engine and boiler rooms. In modern welded ship design, a rounded or elliptical corner is practically adopted to reduce the concentration of stress. Since the opening of cargo hold was quite small, 31% of ship width, no special reinforcement was applied in way of both lower and upper decks. An "L" type doubling plate with half inch (1.27 centimeters) thick was only added at the corner of the shelter deck opening. Figure 4-37 is the details of reinforcement in way of hatch opening on the shelter deck.

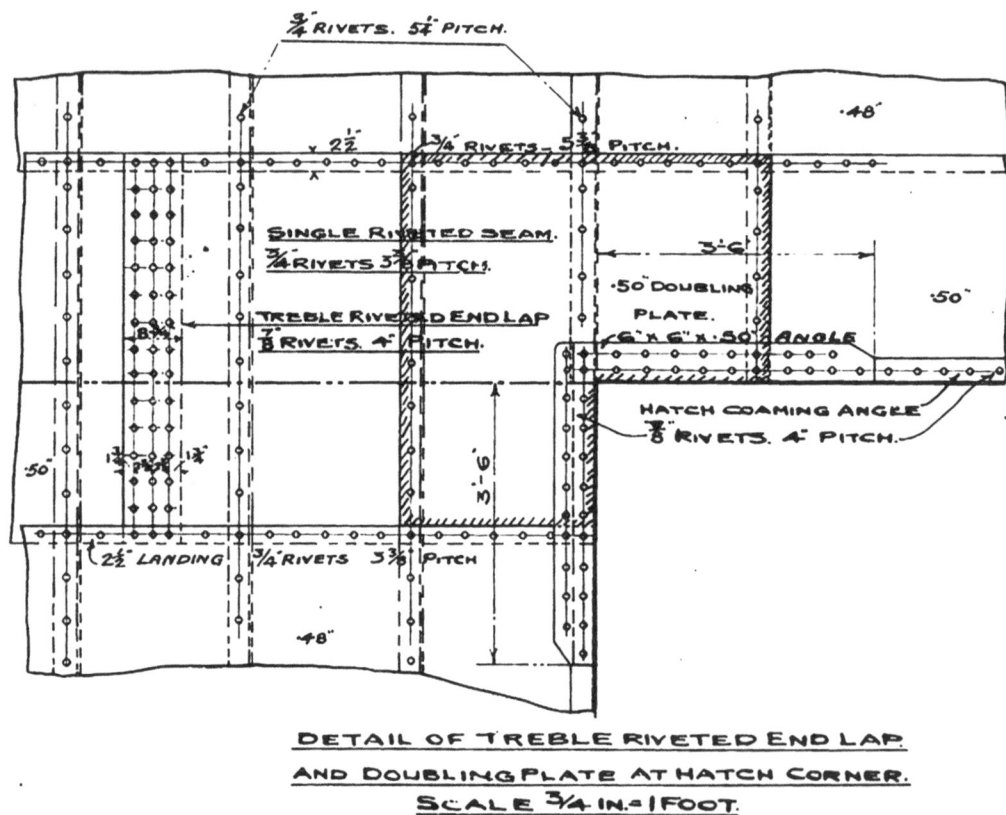

图 4-37　遮蔽甲板货舱开口角隅处的加强详图
Figure 4-37　The details of reinforcement in way of hatch opening on shelter deck

作者在江南造船集团档案馆内找到了一些铆接船体建造时的照片（见图 4-38）。此船为有"民国海军第一舰"之誉的"平海"号巡洋舰。"平海"号巡洋舰总长为 360 英尺（109.73 米）、宽为 39 英尺（11.89 米）、型深为 22 英尺（6.71 米）、吃水为 13 英尺 6 英

The photo of riveted hull erection (see Figure 4-38) was found in Archives Institute of Jiangnan Shipyard Group. She was steam powered cruiser "Ping Hai", known as "Chinese Navy No.1" of the Republic of China. The main particulars of cruiser "Ping Hai" were: length overall of 360 feet (109.73 meters), width of 39 feet (11.89 meters), depth of 22 feet (6.71 meters), draught of 13 feet 6 inches (4.11 meters), displacement

寸（4.11 米），排水量为 2 420 吨，主机为两座立式三胀四缸往复式蒸汽机，四台水管式锅炉，总功率为9 500 马力，最大航速为 22 节。

"平海"号巡洋舰于 1931 年 6 月 28 日开工建造，海军部长陈绍宽亲临船台，在龙骨上铆上了第一颗铆钉。由于受战事的影响，造舰工程时断时续，直至1936 年才竣工。1937 年 4 月，"平海"号巡洋舰交付使用，编入国民政府海军部第一舰队，列为旗舰。图 4-38 估计是在 1931 年底至 1932 年初拍摄的照片。照片上非常清晰地展现了铆接船体的结构特征和施工场景。

of 2 420 tons, main engines were of two sets of vertical type 4-cylinder triple expansion reciprocating steam engine, 4 sets of water tube boiler, total output power was 9 500 hp, and the maximum speed was 22 knots.

"Ping Hai" cruiser was commenced construction on 28 June 1931. Chen Shaokuan, Chief of Navy Department of China, inserted the first rivet into the keel plate. Construction was intermittent due to the effect of the war, and she was not completed till 1936. In April of 1937, cruiser "Ping Hai" was delivered to 1st Fleet of Chinese Navy as flagship. The photo (see Figure 4-38) might be taken in the end of 1931 to the beginning of 1932, which shows structural features of riveted hull and construction scene.

图 4-38 江南造船所建造"平海"号巡洋舰时铆接船体的场景
Figure 4-38 Kiangnan Dock & Engineering Works built "Ping Hai" cruiser with riveted hull

铆接结构的密性

铆接后水／油密结构的缝隙密封采用了铆接船体传统的捻缝密封工艺（caulking）。在英文版的维基百科中有以下一段描述[9]。

在铆接钢或铁壳船舶建造时，捻缝是一个增强接缝密性的过程。使用钝凿工具冲击邻近板材的接缝，这样做的目的是把金属与相邻的金属块紧密地结合在一起。捻缝最初是手工完成的，比如木制船体的捻缝，后来才使用气动工具。

维基百科中关于铆接船体捻缝密封工艺的描述和作者所了解到的江南造船厂老工艺技术人员所描述的捻缝工艺是一致的。

捻缝时对于水密结构，是通过在结构间塞入麻丝和红油白漆（红丹粉和厚白漆的混合物）所组成的混合填料；对于油密结构，则采用在结构间塞入铜丝布和洋干漆（虫胶清漆）所组成的混合填料[10]。

水密舱壁结构

水密舱壁（见图 4-39）和油密舱壁结构（见图 4-40）采用了板加垂直扶强材的结构，与现代船舶结构设计几乎一致。从结构的连续性来看，双层底顶板、各层甲板是连续的，而舱壁板是间断的，垂直扶强材也是间断的，扶强材的上下端用肘板连接。

Tightness of Riveted Structure

Rendering seams water/oil tight normally carried out by caulking method, following description is quoted from English version of Wikipedia.

In riveted steel or iron ship construction, caulking was a process of rendering seams watertight by driving a thick, blunt chisel-like tool into the plating adjacent to the seam. This had the effect of displacing the metal into a close fit with the adjoining piece. Originally done by hand much like wooden vessel caulking, pneumatic tools were later employed.

The description of caulking in Wikipedia is almost the same as dictated by eld staffs of Jiangnan Shipyard.

For watertight structure, it was normal to pad some mixture filler of hemp thread with red lead and thick white paint into the seams; for oiltight structure, it was practical to insert some mixture filler of wire fabric with polish.

Water Tight Structure

Plating plus vertical stiffeners were applied for the bulkheads of watertight and oiltight structure (see Figures 4-39 and 4-40), and this is quite similar as modern structural design. For viewpoint of structural continuity, tank top and intermediate decks were designed longitudinally continuous, but bulkheads and vertical stiffeners were designed discontinuous. The ends were connected by brackets.

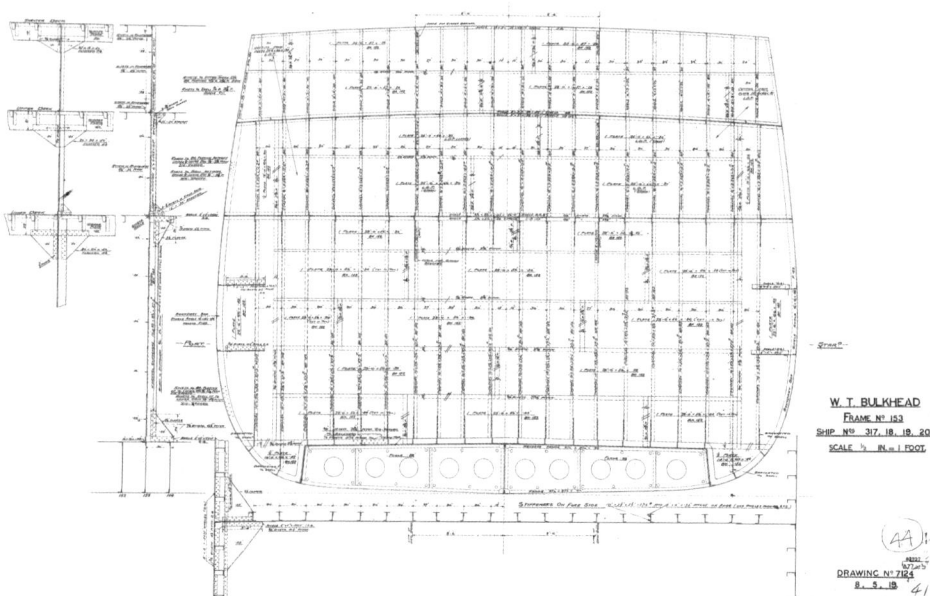

图 4-39　水密舱壁结构（图号：7124，标注日期：1918 年 5 月 8 日）
Figure 4-39　Water tight bulkhead structure (Drawing No. 7124, dated 8 May 1918)

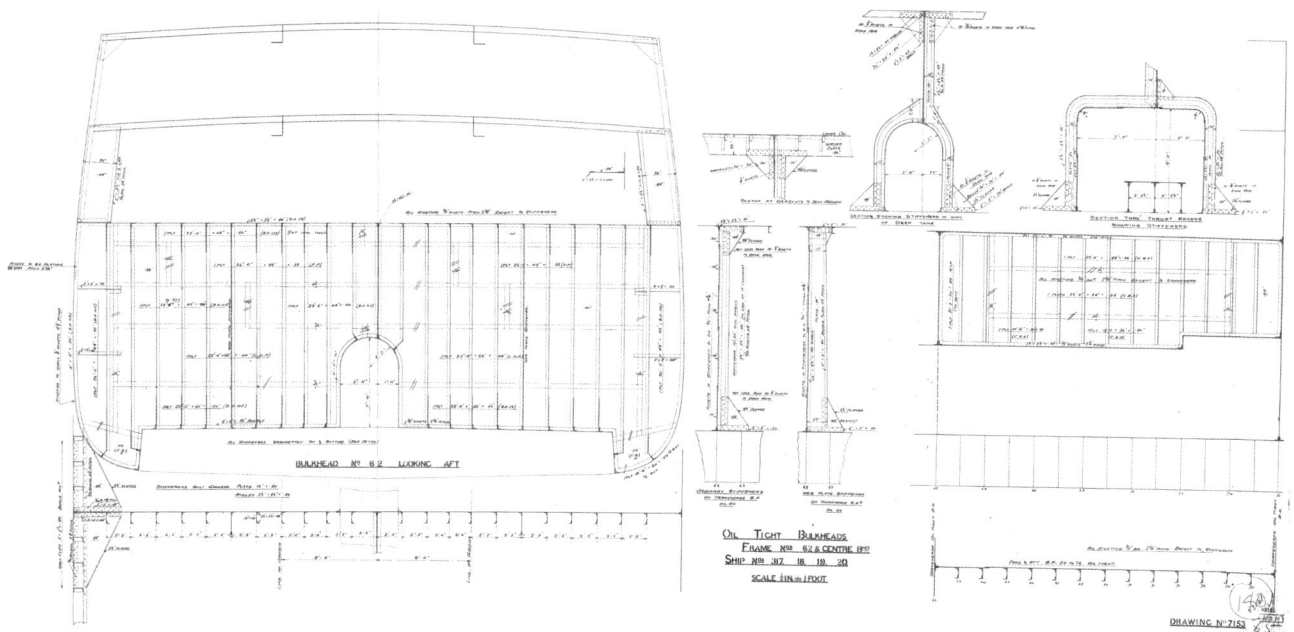

图 4-40　油密舱壁结构（图号：7153，标注日期：不详）
Figure 4-40　Oil tight bulkhead structure (Drawing No. 7153, date unknown)

船体焊接技术的推广

1931 年以前江南造船所设计建造的船舶全部采用铆接结构，1931 年以后从建造"平海"号巡洋舰开始小范围采用电焊结构。由于当时焊条和焊接工艺不完善，对电焊的质量也持有怀疑的态度，因此当时电焊主要用在次要结构和铆接困难的部位。

1937 年 11 月，江南造船所被日本海军占领。到了 1941 年 12 月太平洋战争爆发，因赶工建造新船所需，在电气熔接工场内添置了电焊设备（以交流电焊机为主）。在船体建造过程中采用"半电焊法"，即钢板对接采用电焊，钢板和肋骨相连则采用铆接。根据 1946 年 5 月 15 日中美签署的《中美造船物资借贷合约》，美国将提供价值 1 000 万美元的剩余物资给江南造船所，这批物资包括 70 台林肯（Lincoln）、哈巴特（Harpert）等品牌的焊机和电焊条等。这些设备的引进极大促进了电焊技术在江南造船所修造船舶过程中的应用。

由于应用先进焊接工艺建造的船体的质量、密性、建造效率和作业强度均明显优于传统的铆接

Welding Technology Application

Kiangnan-built ships were entirely riveted structure prior to 1931. Welding technology has been carried out as exploratory tests at selected areas during construction of cruiser "Ping Hai" since 1931. Because welding electrode and welding workmanship were not so perfect at that time, and Kiangnan was fearful of the welding quality, welding was mainly applied on secondary structures and some areas that were difficult to rivet.

In November of 1937, Kiangnan Dock & Engineering Works was occupied by Japanese Navy. With the outbreak of the Pacific War since the December of 1941, welding equipment (mainly alternating current machines) were acquired by welding workshop in order to catch the schedule of shipbuilding. "Semi-welding" method was adopted in hull construction, i.e., welding for plate butt joint, riveting for connecting frame and plating. According to terms defined in *Sino-America Loan Protocol of Shipbuilding Appliances* signed on May 15 1945, the United Sates would supply residual goods worth 10 million U.S. dollars to Kiangnan, including 70 sets of welding machine and relevant electrodes produced by Lincoln, Harpert and other makers. The introduction of those equipment significantly promoted welding technology application in Kiangnan.

Kiangnan reorganized that the quality, tightness and construction efficiency of hull as well as the working loads of workers by applying

工艺，1946 年，江南造船所为民生实业公司（Min Sung Industrical Company）建造的"民铎"号（Min To）和"民泰"号（Min Tai）全部采用了电焊造船工艺[11]。

"民铎"号和"民泰"号为钢质双桨蒸汽动力川江客货船（twin screw cargo & passenger steel steamer），该型船总长为 166 英尺（50.60 米）、两柱间长为 159 英尺（48.46 米）、船宽为 29 英尺（8.84 米）、型深为 8 英尺 6 英寸（2.59 米）、吃水为 7 英尺（2.13 米）、载重量为 270 吨、主机功率为 1 765 千瓦、试航航速为 14 节、服务航速为 12.5 节、总吨为 820 吨、净吨为 440 吨。图 4-41 为江南造船所设计建造的中国第一艘全电焊钢质双桨蒸汽动力川江客货船"民铎"号的总布置图。

advanced welding technology were obviously better than traditional riveting technology, and thus welding technology was fully adopted on SS "Min To" and SS "Min Tai" built for Min Sung Industrical Company.

SS "Min To" and SS "Min Tai" were both twin screw cargo & passenger steel steamers for Yangtze River service. SS "Min To" was the first fully welded steel steamer in China. The length overall was 166 feet (50.60 meters), the length between perpendiculars was 159 feet (48.46 meters), the width was 29 feet (8.84 meters), the depth was 8 feet and 6 inches (2.59 meters), the draught was 7 feet (2.13 meters), the deadweight was 270 tons, main engine power was 1 765 kW, the trail speed was 14 knots , the service speed was 12.5 knots, the gross tonnage was 820 tons and the net tonnage was 440 tons. Figure 4–41 is General Arrangement Plan of twin screw cargo & passenger steel steamer SS "Min To" designed and built by Kiangnan Dock & Engineering Works.

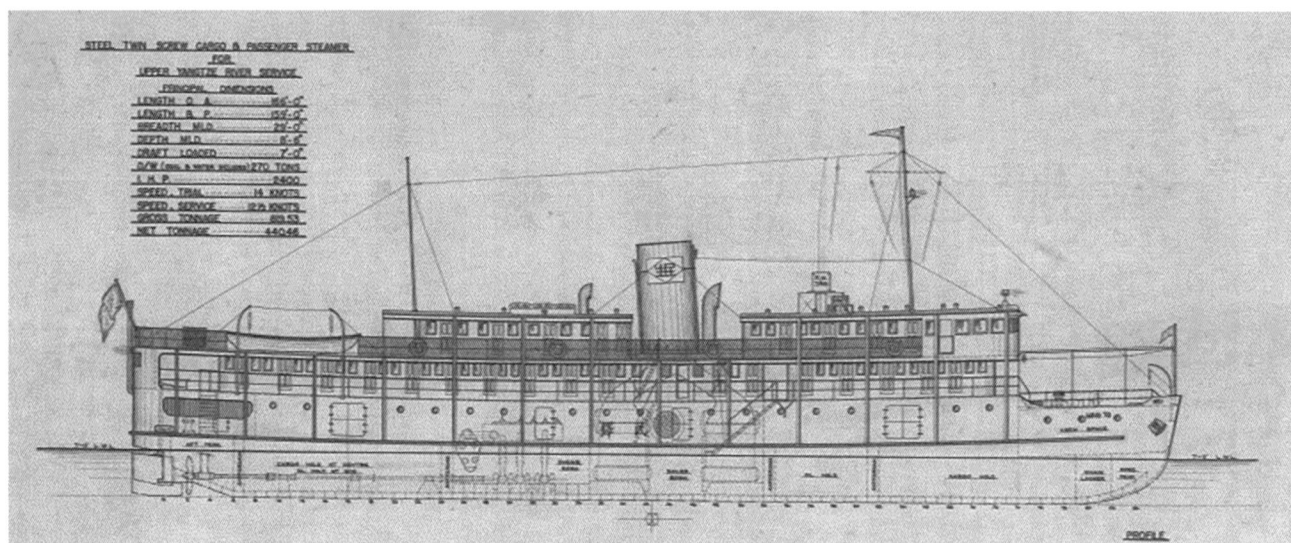

图 4-41 钢质双桨蒸汽动力川江客货船"民铎"号的总布置图
Figure 4–41 General Arrangement Plan of twin screw cargo & passenger steel steamer SS "Min To"

当时江南造船所电焊厂有焊工 200 多人。在这两艘船的建造过程中，不仅采用了电焊工艺，而且采用了当时非常先进的分段建造工艺建造船体。在"民铎"号的建造过程中，江南造船所实现了造船工艺从铆接到焊接的飞跃，这不仅是中国的第一次，在当时的全球造船业中也属于领跑性实现。图 4-42 为"民铎"号客货船在长江上航行的照片。1952 年 2 月 5 日，民生实业公司的"民铎"号在上海开往重庆的途中，在猪牙子航道（唐家沱）发生事故触礁沉没。

The welding workshop of Kiangnan Dock & Engineering Works had more than 200 welders. During the construction of these two steamers, Kiangnan adopted not only welding technology but also superior block erection technology for erecting the hull. Kiangnan realized substantial leap of ship building technology from riveting to welding. It was not only the first in China, but also in the first rank of the world shipbuilding industry. Figure 4–42 is the photo of SS "Min To" sailing in Yangtze River. On 5 February 1952, SS "Min To" sunk in Tangjiatuo due to pile up on rocks on the voyage from Shanghai to Chongqing.

图 4-42 "民铎"号客货船在长江上航行
Figure 4-42 SS "Min To" steamer sailed in Yangtze River

直到 20 世纪 80 年代，现代钢质船舶的船体建造已经全部采用焊接连接，铆接连接结构已经退出历史舞台。船体铆接连接和现代焊接连接最大的差别是铆接连接无法实现板与板的对接和角接。因此板与板在铆接连接时必须采用重叠搭接的形式，通过在铆钉孔内打入铆钉进行固定；板与板的角接必须通过附加的构件，如角钢或压制的板材，分别和不同的结构件连接。故铆接结构的船体比较重，船体外板因为有板缝的重叠，航行的阻力比较大。铆接结构的船体板与板重叠搭接的形式在一定程度上增加了船体外板的刚度。铆接船体的建造效率低，修理时工程量大。

Till 1980s, welding technology had been completely adopted in modern shipbuilding, and riveted hull had been gradually phased out. The remarkable deviation between riveting and welding connections is that riveting cannot realize butt and corner joint of plates, and therefore, the butt joint between plates is an overlap type and fixed by rivets. The corner joint between plates needs supplemental members, such as angle bars or pre-formed profiles, connected with individual structural members. Normally riveted hull is heavier and possesses more resistance in the water because of overlapped seams on shell. Such overlapped plate connection can provide additional rigidity of shell plating. Comparing with welded hull structure, the construction efficiency of riveting is quite poor, and the repairing is more difficult.

4.3.7

舾装设备
Outfittings

舵和舵机

四艘万吨级运输舰的舵柱和舵杆组合采用了闭式（closed type）结构，材料为铸钢件。艉部配置了一具非平衡舵，用舵销固定在艉框上。舵机布置在艉甲板室后部的舵机室内。舵机为电动舵机，由电动机、减速箱、制动装置、舵扇及一对缓冲弹簧组成。缓冲弹簧的作用是减少传动装置承受的冲击载荷。在艉舵机房的上方，还配置了手动的应急操舵装置，如图 4-43 和图 4-44 所示。

Rudder and Steering Gear

Rudder post and stock were designed closed type and made by casting. One set of non-balanced rudder was fixed on stern frame by pins. Steering gear was arranged steering gear room in rear of stern deck room. Steering gear was driven by electricity, which consisted of electric motor, reduction gear box, brake, rudder sector and a pair of buffer spring in between rudder plate and post. The function of buffer spring was to mitigate load impact on transmission gear. A manually emergency steering device was arranged on the top of stern steering gear room. See also Figures 4-43 and 4-44.

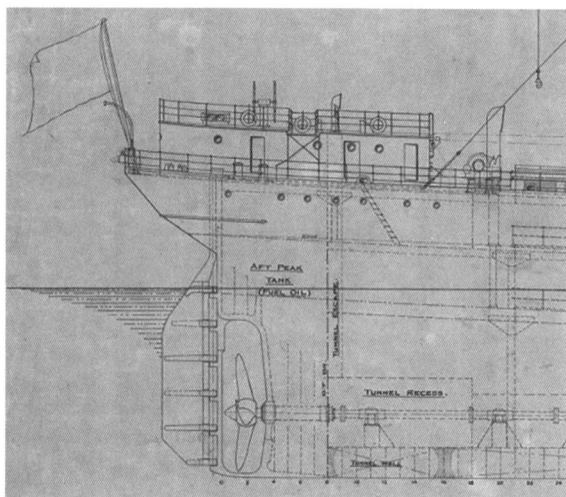

图 4-43　舵和舵机的布置（侧面）
Figure 4-43　Rudder and steering gear arrangement (side view)

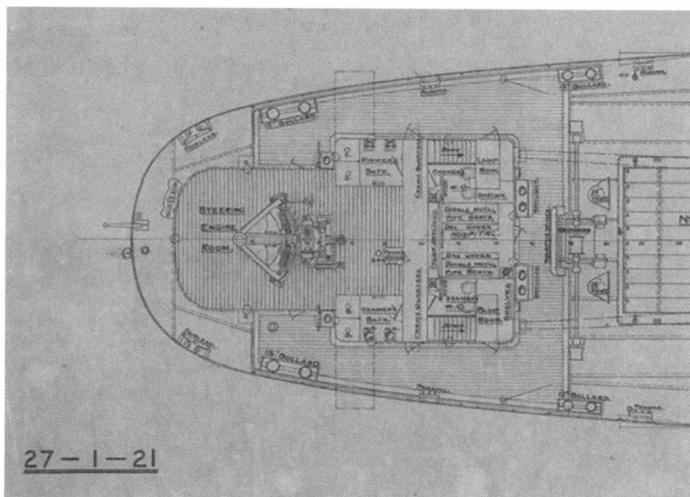

图 4-44　舵和舵机的布置（甲板）
Figure 4-44　Rudder and steering gear arrangement (deck view)

这种电动舵机结构复杂、制造精度高、体积和重量均大。现代船舶设计已经不再应用，而由电液驱动的液压舵机代替。

The electric driven steering gear is more complicated with a larger volume and a heavier weight, and it further required higher manufacturing accuracy. The electric driven steering gear has been replaced by hydro-electric driven type in modern ship design.

舾装数

在合同技术附件之一的舯横剖面图（图号：6545，标注日期：1918 年 5 月 7 日）上，标出万吨级运输舰

Equipment Number

The equipment number of 38 260 indicated on Midship Section (Technical Attachments of contract, Drawing No. 6545, dated 7 May

的舾装数（equipment number）为 38 260，这是基于两柱间长为 425 英尺（129.54 米）时的数值，未查到两柱间长加长 4 英尺（1.22 米）后的舾装数的数据。

1918) was corresponding to the length between perpendiculars of 425 feet (129.54 meters), and the equipment number based on lengthened 4 feet (1.22 meters) was not found.

锚泊设备

艏部甲板上配置了两台蒸汽驱动的组合式锚绞机（steam driven windlass），艏部甲板前部配置了两台止链器（chain stopper），后部配置了一台绳车（wire reel）。

从总布置图和舯横剖面图上标注的参数看，船首左右舷各配置了一个艏锚，形式为巴尔特无杆锚 [Baldt stockless anchor，也有可能为美国海军锚（U.S. Navy stockless anchor），因为两者外形相似]，锚重 8 855 磅（4 017 千克）（见图 4–45）。艏部甲板后部放置了一个备用锚，锚重 7 548 磅（3 424 千克）。在现代船舶设计中，通常备用锚和艏锚是一样重的。

Anchoring Equipment

Two steam driven windlasses were arranged on bow shelter deck. Two sets of chain stopper were arranged at the front of windlass and one set of wire reel was arranged at the rear of windlass.

From parameters indicated on General Arrangement Plan and Midship Section, two bow anchors were equipped on portside and starboard respectively. Anchor looks alike Baldt stockless anchor or U.S. Navy stockless anchor, because these two types of anchor are quite similar. The weight of anchor was 8 855 pounds (4 017 kilograms) (see Figure 4–45). One spare anchor was stored at aft of bow deck, and the weight of anchor was 7 548 pounds (3 424 kilograms). Spare anchor and bow anchor were normally identical as per modern ship design practice.

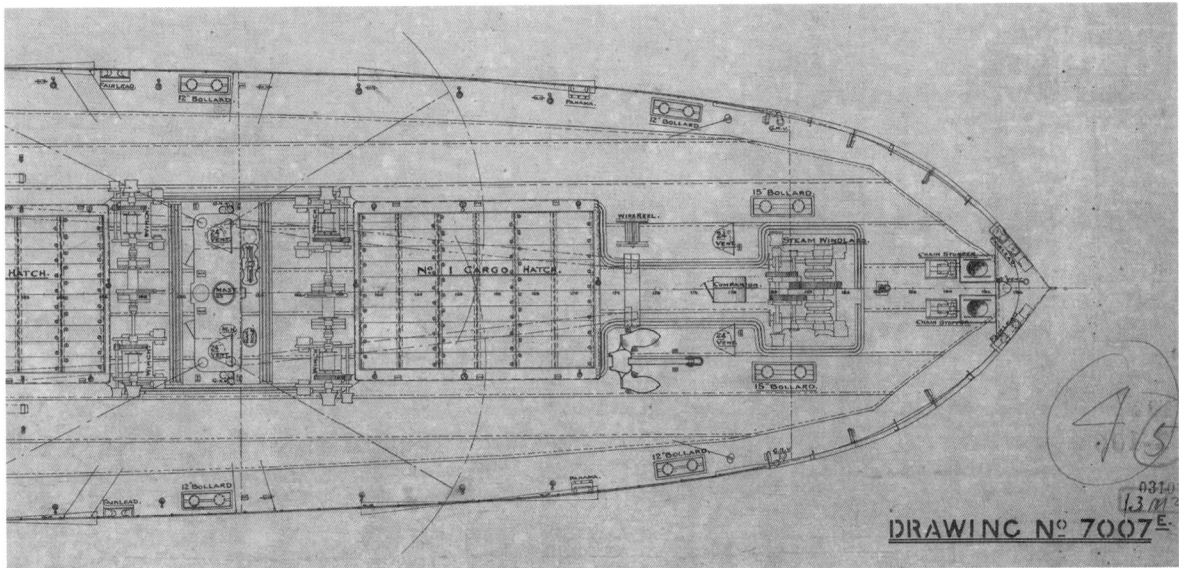

图 4-45 艏部遮蔽甲板上锚机和系泊布置
Figure 4-45 Windlass and mooring arrangement on fore shelter deck

此外，船上还配了一个 2 548 磅（1 156 千克）重的艉锚（stern anchor）和一个 1 064 磅（483 千克）重的小锚 / 移船锚（kedge anchor）。从 7007E 总布置图上看，这个艉锚布置在舵机室后部的遮蔽甲板上，小锚 / 移船锚则布置在第一货舱和第二货舱间的桅屋（deck house）前的遮蔽甲板上。

In addition, one stern anchor of 2 548 pounds (1 156 kilograms) and one kedge anchor of 1 064 pounds (483 kilograms) were equipped. On General Arrangement Plan (Drawing No. 7007E), this stern anchor was placed rear of steering gear room on shelter deck, and kedge anchor was placed on shelter deck in between deck houses of No.1 and No.2 cargo holds.

在现代船舶设计中只有在北美五大湖航行的船要求配置艉锚，小锚／移船锚的配置要求已经没有了。作者查询了维基百科英文版中关于这些锚用法的描述[12]。

船舶通常会配置一定数量的锚：艏锚（原先被称为备用锚[13]）是船舶的主锚，设在船舶的艏部。（小）艉锚（或称"小锚"，多挂在艉部）是一种较小的锚，在船舶系泊时防止船舶移动，多用于游艇在狭窄航道内快速抛锚。（大）艉锚（或称"艉锚"）通常比小锚重一些，除了用于临时系泊和防止艉部在狭窄水道（如河道和运河等）中由于潮水而引起的船舶漂移之外，还能够用于利用收锚链使船移动。

艏锚配有 300 英寻（1 英寻 =1.828 8 米）长、直径为 2.375 英寸（6.03 厘米）的有档锚链，此外还配有 90 英寻长、直径为 1.313 英寸（3.34 厘米）的有档锚链一根和 90 英寻长的钢丝绳锚链一根；另配有 130 英寻长的钢质拖索一根、4 根 90 英寻长的马尼拉麻制缆绳。马尼拉麻是一种纤维，来自一种叫"阿贝卡"（Abacá）植物的叶子，"阿贝卡"主要产于菲律宾，故以该国的首都马尼拉命名。

其他系泊设备（mooring equipment）：艏艉部中间的带缆桩（bollard）为 15 英寸（38.1 厘米）的，其他都是 12 英寸（30.48 厘米）的。在遮蔽甲板上还布置了一定数量的导缆钳（fairlead），此外遮蔽甲板上第一货舱前部和第五货舱后部两舷处还布置了巴拿马导缆孔，如图 4-46 所示。

Such stream anchor and kedge anchor are unusual in modern ship design, and only the ships sailing in Great Lakes are required to equip the stern anchor. Some description of purpose of those anchors can be found in Wikipedia.

Vessels may carry a number of anchors: bower anchors (formerly known as sheet anchors) are the main anchors used by a vessel and normally carried at the bow of the vessel. A kedge anchor is a light anchor used for warping an anchor, also known as kedging, or more commonly on yachts for mooring quickly or in benign conditions. A stern anchor, which is usually heavier than a kedge anchor, can be used for kedging or warping in addition to temporary mooring and restraining stern movement in tidal conditions or in waters where vessel movement needs to be restricted, such as rivers and channels.

A 300 fathoms (1 fathom = 1.828 8 meters) long, 2.375 inches (6.03 centimeters) in diameter chain was equipped for each bow anchor. In addition, a 90 fathoms long, 1.313 inches (3.34 centimeters) in diameter and a 90 fathoms long steel wire were equipped on board. A 130 fathoms long steel towing rope and four 90 fathoms long "Manila" hemp ropes were also equipped on board. "Manila" hemp is one kind of hemp made by leaf of plant called "Abacá". "Abacá" mainly grows in the Philippines, and so it was named "Manila", the capital of the Philippines.

Other mooring equipment: 15 inches (38.1 centimeters) bollards located in centre of bow and stern, and 12 inches (30.48 centimeters) bollards located in other areas. Certain number of fairleads located on shelter deck. In addition, Panama chocks were arranged both sides of shelter deck in way of No.1 cargo hold fore and No.5 cargo hold aft. See also Figure 4-46.

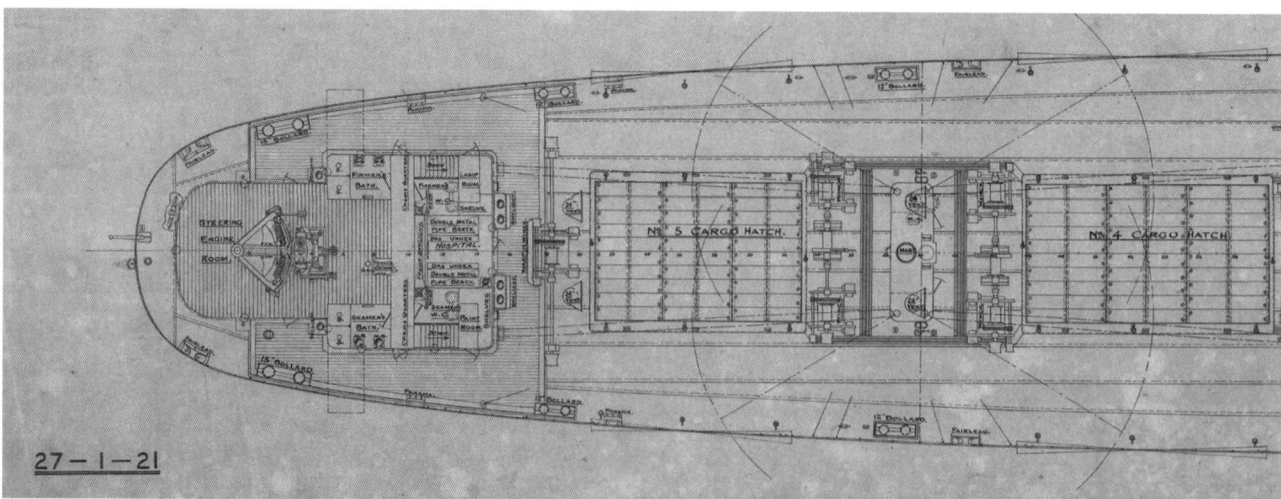

图 4-46　艉部遮蔽甲板上锚机和系泊布置
Figure 4-46　Windlass and mooring arrangement on aft shelter deck

遮蔽甲板上的系泊绞车（mooring winch）、起重绞车、锚机都带有绞缆头（warping end），可进行绞缆作业。艉系泊绞车布置在艉甲板室的前面，为了保证船尾方向的绞缆作业，绞缆头轴设计成向两舷延伸（超过了艉甲板室的宽度）。这些绞车和锚机都是由蒸汽驱动的。

救生设备

上层建筑艇甲板两侧各布置了两艘开敞式救生艇（life boat），驾驶甲板左舷还布置了一艘工作舢板（dinghy）。

起重设备

遮蔽甲板上的前桅（fore master）和后桅（aft master）各配置了四根起重能力为 3 吨的轻型吊杆（light-duty lifting boom），前桅后部还配置了一根起重能力为 30 吨的重型吊杆（heavy-duty lifting boom）（见图 4-47 和图 4-48）。前桅和上层建筑之间设置了一对"将军"柱（king post），每根"将军"柱前后各配了一根起重能力为 3 吨的轻型吊杆；上层建筑和后桅之间也设置了一对"将军"柱，每根"将军"柱后各配了一根起重能力为 3 吨的轻型吊杆。每根轻型吊杆配置了一台蒸汽驱动的起重绞车，重型吊杆的起重作业由两台绞车并车进行。

Mooring winches, derrick winches and windlasses totally equipped warping ends. They all can carry out warping operation. Aft mooring winch was arranged in front of stern deck house. Warping shaft was so designed to extend to sides (over the width of stern deck house) for warping operation aft ward. All these deck machineries were driven by steam.

Life Saving Equipment

Two open type life boats were arranged at both sides of boat deck respectively, and one set of dinghy was arranged in portside of navigation bridge.

Derrick

Four light-duty lifting booms with capacity of 3 tons were fitted at fore and aft masters on shelter deck respectively, and one heavy-duty lifting boom with capacity of 30 tons was fitted at rear of fore master (see Figures 4-47 and 4-48). A pair of king post was arranged in between fore master and superstructure; another pair of king post was arranged in between superstructure and aft master. A light-duty lifting boom with capacity of 3 tons was fitted at each king post respectively. One steam driven derrick winch was equipped for each light-duty lifting boom, and heavy-duty lifting boom was operated by two parallel running winches.

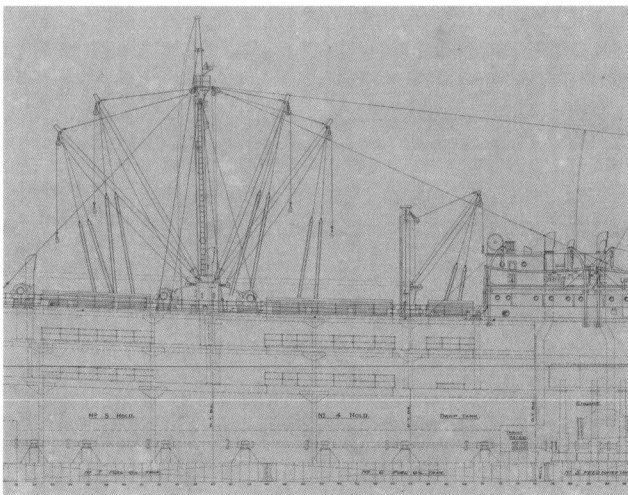

图 4-47　艉部重型吊杆布置图
Figure 4-47　Layout of heavy-duty lifting boom (aft)

图 4-48　艏部重型吊杆布置图
Figure 4-48　Layout of heavy-duty lifting boom (fore)

四艘万吨级运输舰配置的蒸汽驱动的系泊绞车、起重绞车和锚机都是由位于美国俄勒冈州波特兰的威拉米特钢铁厂（Willamette Iron and Steel Works）[14]制造的。这种蒸汽驱动的锚机、绞缆机的原型机是威拉米特钢铁厂制造的昵称为"蒸汽驴"(steam donkey)的蒸汽绞车。维基百科中有以下描述[15]：

"蒸汽驴"，或者称"驴（发动）机"，是一种蒸汽驱动的绞车的通用昵称。这种绞车也称为伐木机，曾被广泛应用但不局限于伐木作业。同样地，这种辅机也在采矿业、海事和其他所有需要动力绞车的行业中得到应用。"蒸汽驴"最初应用于海船上。在这种船上，"蒸汽驴"通常是一种小型的辅助发动机用来装卸货物，使弱小的水手可以拉起较大的船帆，或者作为驱动泵的原动机。如果通过汽缸的种类给它们分类，可分为单工式（单作用汽缸）和双工式（复合式）发动机；如果通过它们和绞车（滚轮）的连接形式分类的话，可分为三滚筒和双滚筒等；如果通过它们不同的用途来分类的话，可分为半拖式集材机、全拖式集材机、装载机、缆绳制动装置和斜提升机等。与其他早期的众多起源于商业航海的技术一样，诸多的钢索集材术语也都来源于19世纪的商业航海。

舱口盖

主船体设置了五个货舱和一个深舱，在遮蔽甲板上的每个舱配置了一个铰链折叠式（folding type）舱口盖，由布置在遮蔽甲板的绞缆机驱动开启。按照一般的船舶设计规范，遮蔽甲板上的舱口盖是风雨密的（weathertight），可惜未能在图纸上找到相关的描述。在上甲板和下甲板上的每个舱都配置了可吊离片式（panel type）舱口盖，其材质是钢制大梁加上木制舱口盖板，如图4-49所示。

The vessel equips steam driven mooring winches, derrick winches and windlass. These machineries were manufactured by Willamette Iron and Steel Works in Portland, Oregon State. The prototype of these steam driven machineries was Willamette Iron and Steel Works made steam machinery with nickname of "steam donkey". In Wikipedia, the description of "steam donkey" is as follows:

"Steam donkey", or "donkey engine", is the common nickname for a steam-powered winch, or logging engine, widely used in past logging operations, though not limited to logging. They were also found in the mining, maritime, and nearly any other industry that needed a powered winch. Steam donkeys acquired their name from their origin in sailing ships, where the "donkey engine" was typically a small secondary engine used to load and unload cargo and raise the larger sails with small crews, or to power pumps. They were classified by their cylinder type – simplex (single-acting cylinder) or duplex (a compound engine); by their connection to the winches (or "drums")–triple-drum, double-drum, etc.; and by their different uses: high-lead yarder, ground-lead yarder, loader, snubber, incline hoist, etc. A good deal of the cable-logging terminology derived from 19th-century merchant sailing, as much of the early technology originated from that industry.

Hatch Cover

Main hull was further divided into five holds and one deep tank. One set of folding type hatch cover operated by warping winch was equipped for each hold on shelter deck. As per normal ship design practice, these hatches should be weathertight but not found any description on drawing. The liftable panel type hatch covers were equipped on upper and lower decks. The structure of hatch cover was combination of steel girders and wooden panels, refer to Figure 4–49.

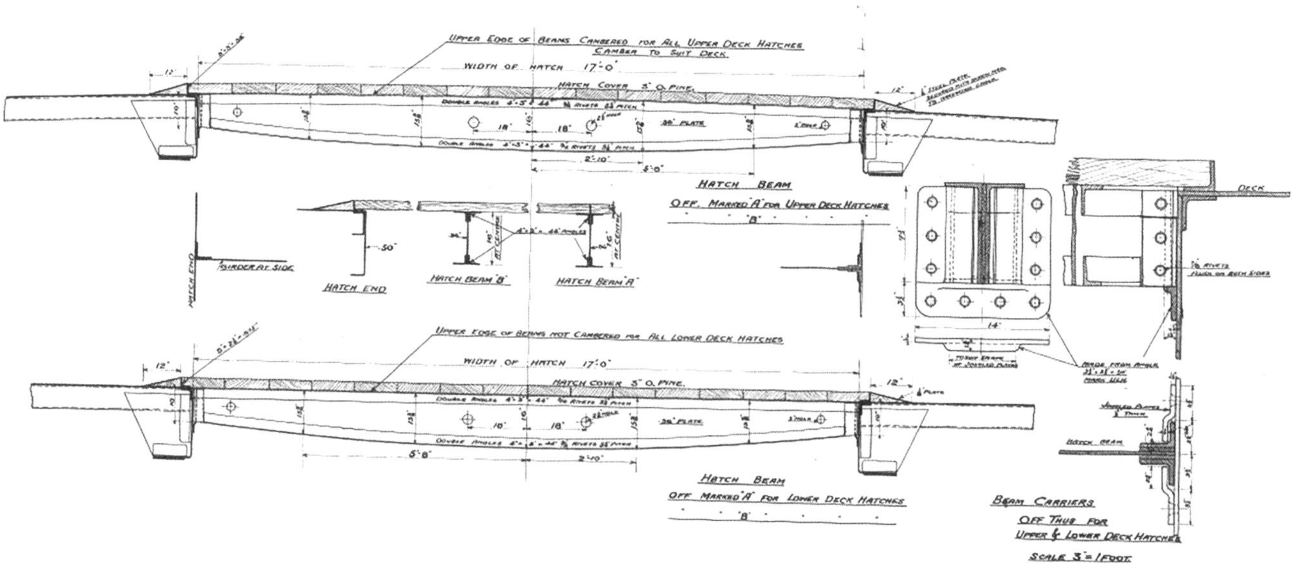

图 4-49　货舱上甲板和下甲板配置的可吊离片式舱口盖
Figure 4-49　The liftable panel type hatch cover in way of upper deck and lower deck

4.3.8

舱室布置
Accommodation Layout

舯部设置了一个机炉舱，机炉舱上有三层上层建筑、机舱棚、烟囱和甲板室。艉部上甲板设置了低级船员居住舱室，艉部遮蔽甲板设置了艉甲板室和舵机房。

船员数量配置根据航线的要求各船不尽相同，以"Margaret Dollar"号（即"天朝"号）为例，该船在1923年5月到1934年6月间主要执行"大三角贸易航线"（Great Triangular Trade Route），往返于太平洋美洲西北岸和远东地区。太平洋美洲西北岸的主要挂靠港有美国俄勒冈州的波特兰，华盛顿州的阿伯丁、贝灵哈姆、埃弗里特、安吉利斯、西雅图和塔科马；加拿大不列颠哥伦比亚省的新威斯敏斯特、艾丽斯港和温哥华。远东的主要挂靠港有中国的香港和上海、日本的大阪和横滨、菲律宾的马尼拉。

到1928年秋天为止，该型船所配置的船员平均为37人，但在1928年，最高峰时曾经配置船员多达76人。高级船员均为美国人，水手长以下低级船员均为中国人，甲板部和轮机部的低级船员为来自旧金山的华裔，服务性岗位的船员主要来自香港。这样"双岗式"的船员配置可能是出于培训后备船员的考虑[16]。

四艘万吨级运输舰的各层甲板舱室的布置和功能如下。

Engine and boiler rooms were arranged amidship, and three tiers superstructure, engine casing, funnel and deck house were arranged on top of engine and boiler rooms. Cabins for lower rank crews were arranged upper deck aft, and stern deck house and steering gear room were arranged shelter deck aft.

Complement on board was diversely dependent on different routes and ships. If taking SS "Margaret Dollar" (i.e., SS "Celestial", the second ship of series), for example she mainly operated on "Great Triangular Trade Route", and navigated between Pacific Northwest and the Far East (Orient) during May of 1923 to June of 1934. The ports of call in Pacific Northwest coast were Portland of Oregon State, Aberdeen, Bellingham, Everett, Port Angeles, Seattle and Tacoma of Washington State of the United States, as well as New Westminster, Port Alice and Vancouver of British Columbia, Canada. The ports of call in the Far East were Hong Kong and Shanghai in China, Osaka and Yokohama in Japan, as well as Manila in Philippines.

Till autumn of 1928, the complement on board was 37 persons on par, but in 1928, the complement reached 76 persons on peak. All senior officers were American, boatswain and lower rank crews were Chinese. Lower rank crews of deck and machinery departments were ethnic Chinese from San Francisco, and stewards came from Hong Kong, China. Such "double on single post" was likely to consider for training reserve crew.

The layout and function of cabins on decks are as follows.

遮蔽甲板

Shelter Deck

左舷（portside）共19人： Portside 19 persons in total:		右舷（starboard）共9人： Starboard 9 persons in total:	
事务长住舱和办公室（1人）	1 – purser office & room	高级船员餐厅	Officer's mess
学徒4人	4 – apprentice	配餐间	Pantry
舵工4人	4 – quarter master	四副1人	1 – 4th officer

左舷（portside）共 19 人： Portside 19 persons in total:		右舷（starboard）共 9 人： Starboard 9 persons in total:	
木匠 2 人	2 – carpenter	管家 1 人	1 – steward
中级船员餐厅	Petty officer's mess	服务员 4 人	4 – mess boy
面包房	Baker shop	管家盥洗室	Steward bath & W.C.
中级船员盥洗室	Petty officer's bath & W.C.	大管轮 1 人	1 – 1st assistant engineer
保管员和加水工 4 人	4 – store keeper & water tender	二管轮 1 人	1 – 2nd assistant engineer
加油工 4 人	4 – oiler	三管轮 1 人	1 – 3rd assistant engineer

舯中心 **Amidship Centre**

沙龙（大餐厅）	Saloon	机舱棚	Engine casing
梯道	Stair case	轮机部盥洗室	Engineer's bath & W.C.
锅炉舱天棚和通风管	Boiler casing & vent pipes	水手餐厅	Seamen's mess
厨房	Galley	锅炉工餐厅	Firemen's mess

从图 4-50 上看，厨房里配置了炉灶（range）、蒸汽加热桌（steam table）、蒸饭炉（rice boiler）和碗柜等厨房设备。在炉灶边上还布置了一个燃煤箱（coal box）用于放置炉灶的燃料。船员中有许多来自旧金山的华裔和香港的中国人，这也许是配置蒸饭炉的原因。

Ranges, steam tables, rice boiler, cupboards and miscellaneous cooking accessories were equipped in galley, and a coal box was located in side of range for storing coal as fuel (see Figure 4-50). The reason for equipping rice boiler maybe because of Chinese crews on board from San Francisco and Hong Kong.

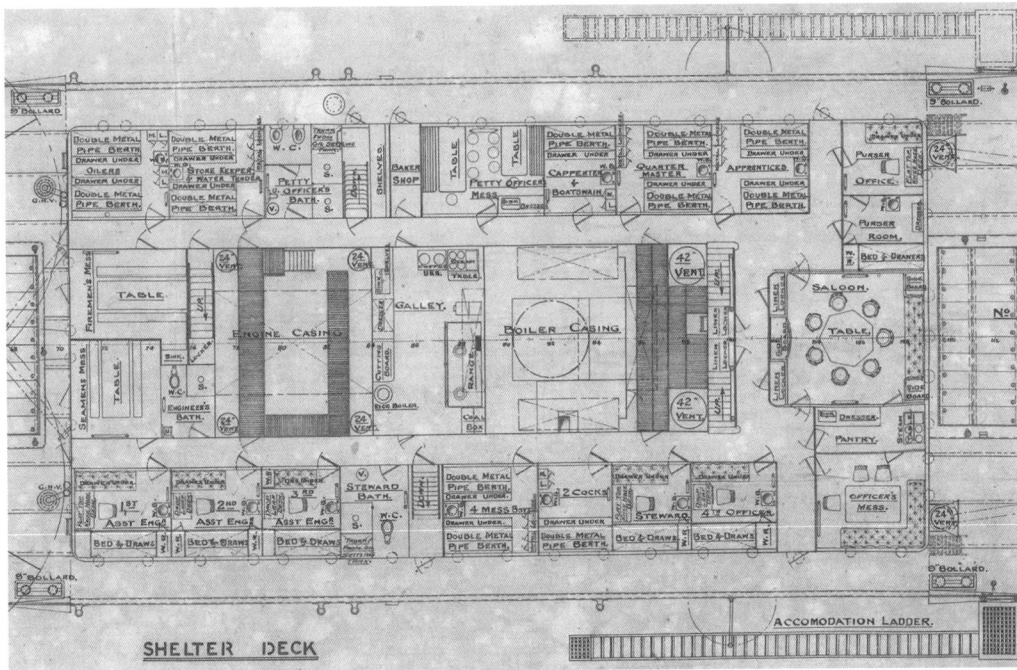

图 4-50　舯部遮蔽甲板舱室布置图
Figure 4-50　Cabin layout of shelter deck amidship

遮蔽甲板上的艉甲板室

灯间	Lamp room
油漆间	Painting room
锅炉工盥洗室	Firemen's bath & W.C.

Stern Deck House on Shelter Deck

水手盥洗室	Seamen's bath & W.C.
病房（配两张双人床）	Hospital with 2 double beds
舵机房	Steering engine room

在艉舵机房的上方，还配置了手动的应急操舵装置（见图4-51）。

A manually operated emergency steering device was located on top of stern steering engine room (see Figure 4-51).

艉部上甲板

从总布置图7008C（甲板平面）可见在艉部上甲板（upper deck）布置了11间双人房，共可住22人，其中消防员12人、水手10人（见图4-52）。艉部还有12张双人床共24人的临时铺位，估计这是战时运输舰配置武装保安的要求。

Stern Upper Deck

From General Arrangement Plan 7008C (deck plan), there were 11 double rooms, 22 persons in total including 12 firemen and 10 seamen (see Figure 4-52). In addition, 12 double beds for supplemental passengers were fitted upper deck at stern, and most properly it was a special requirement for armed guards in wartime.

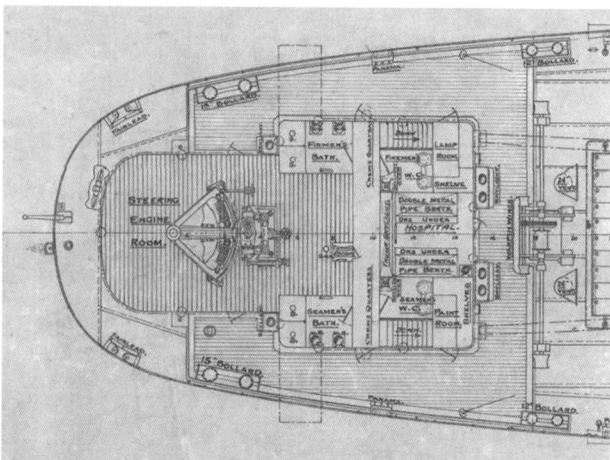

图 4-51　艉甲板室内的舱室布置
Figure 4-51　Cabin layout of stern deck house

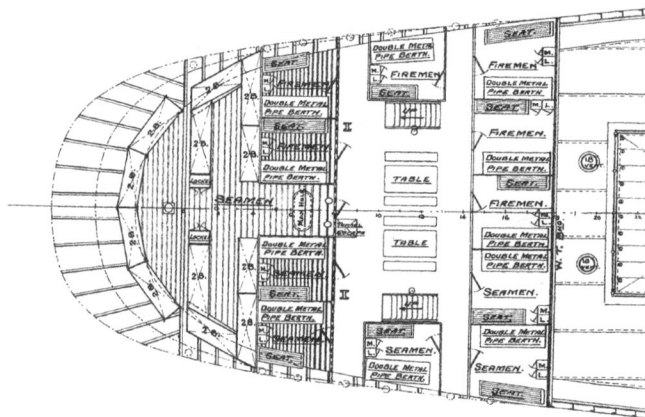

图 4-52　艉部上甲板舱室布置
Figure 4-52　Cabin layout of stern upper deck

艇甲板

舯部艇甲板舱布置如图4-53所示。

Boat Deck

Figure 4-53 shows the cabin layout of boat deck amidship.

艇甲板共布置6个单人舱室	
6 Single cabins in total on boat deck	
船长办公室、住舱和盥洗室（单人间）	1 – Captain's office, room & bath
大副单人舱室	1 – 1st Officer room

艇甲板共布置 6 个单人舱室 6 Single cabins in total on boat deck	
二副单人舱室	1 – 2nd Officer room
三副单人舱室	1 – 3rd Officer room
高级船员盥洗室	Officer's bath & W.C.
被服间	Linens
电池间	Battery room
轮机长办公室、住舱和盥洗室（单人间）	1 – Chief engineer office, room & bath
操作工单人舱室	1 – Operator's room
无线电室	Wireless room
灯间（左右舷）	Lamp rooms (P&S)
烟囱	Funnel
机炉舱天棚	Skylight of engine and boiler room

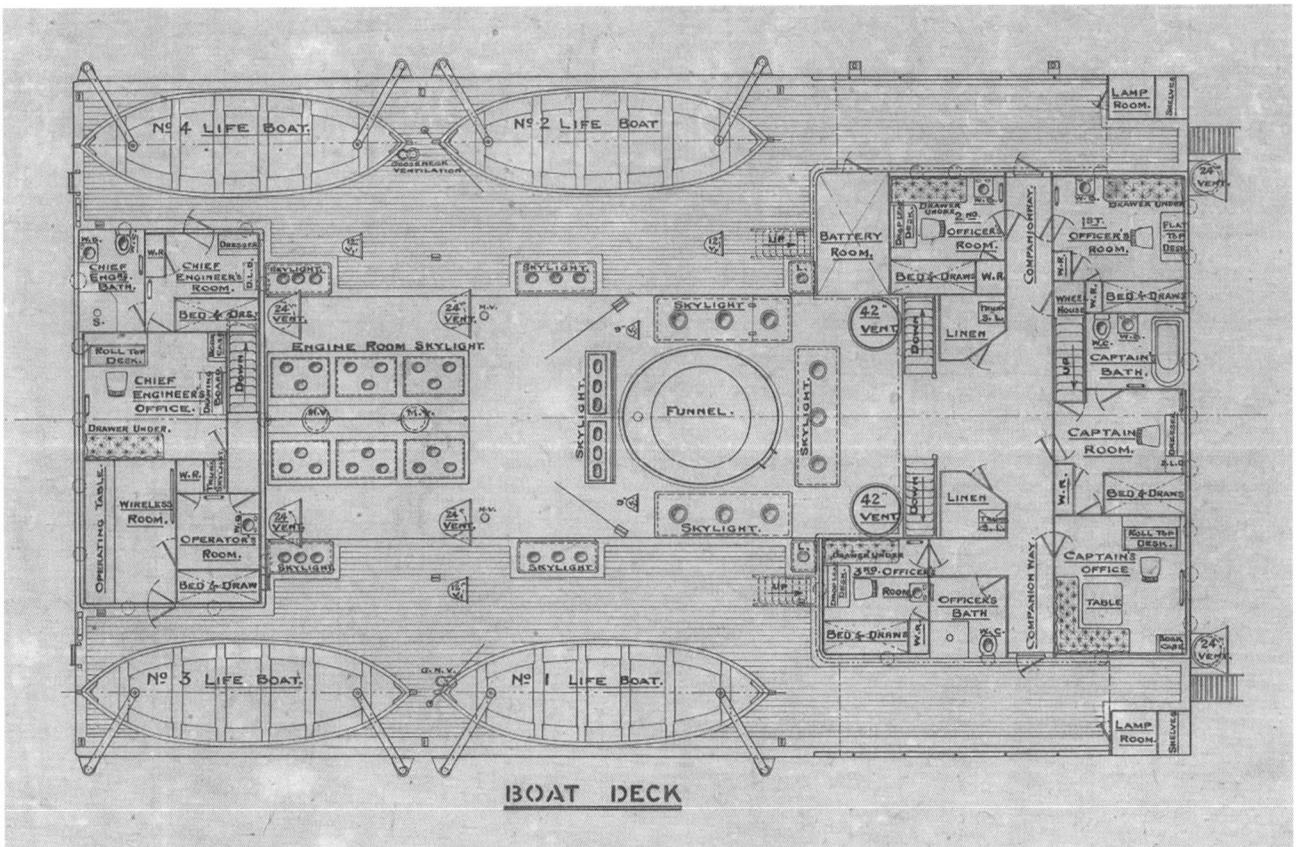

图 4–53　舯部艇甲板舱室布置
Figure 4–53　Cabin layout of boat deck amidship

驾驶甲板

辅驾驶室（封闭式）

海图室

在驾驶甲板的封闭式驾驶室内，配置了电控式辅操舵机（telemotor）、罗经复示仪（repeater of compass）和两台电报机（telegraph）。此驾驶室为备用的辅驾驶室。后部左右舷各配置了4个消防水桶（fire bucket）。海图室是独立分开的，配置了海图桌（chart table）和沙发。

顶驾驶甲板（飞桥）

主驾驶室（开敞式）

在顶驾驶甲板的开敞式驾驶室内，配置了电控式主操舵机（telemotor standard）、主罗经（compass standard）和两台电报机。此驾驶室为主驾驶室。顶上设由立柱支撑的雨篷、前面设风挡玻璃，四周不设舷窗为开敞式。驾驶室后部配置了海图桌。参见图4-54驾驶甲板和顶驾驶甲板布置图。

这种双驾驶室的布置在第一次世界大战期间使用的干杂货运输船上是一种标准布置。两个驾驶室互为备份。由于当时没有导航雷达，即使在第一次世界大战后期和战后也只配备了能够传送字符的电报机，船舶的导航和定位主要靠罗经、海图、六分仪和望远镜等目视观察仪器。由此推测两个驾驶室的主要分工是：开敞式主驾驶室主要用于进出港、复杂或狭窄航道和有敌情时的观察和驾驶；而下层封闭式的辅驾驶室则用于开敞海域和恶劣气候航行时的指挥和驾驶。

Such dual wheel house arrangement was quite popular on dry cargo ship during the World War I. Two wheel houses can backup each other. No navigation radar was available at that time, and even in later period of the World War I and post war, only telegraph was equipped on board. The navigating and positioning were mainly by means of visual instruments such as compass, chart, sextant and telescope and etc. Assumed purpose of those two wheel houses are: open primary wheel house is mainly used for port operation, narrow waters and threat from enemy; closed secondary wheel house is used for open waters, bad weather and heavier seas.

Navigation Bridge

Secondary wheel house (closed)

Chart room

Telemotor, repeater of compass and two sets of telegraph were fitted in closed wheel house on the navigation bridge, and this secondary wheel house was for backup. Four fire buckets each were fixed on navigation bridge aft, portside and starboard. Chart room was separated with chart table and sofa.

Flying Bridge

Primary wheel house (open)

The primary wheel house was open type and located on flying bridge. Telemotor standard, compass standard and two sets of telegraph were installed inside. The canopy with vertical posts was fitted on top. The wind screens were fitted in front, and no window screen was fitted at sides and rear. A chart table was arranged in aft of the primary wheel house. The layouts of navigation and flying bridge is shown in Figure 4-54.

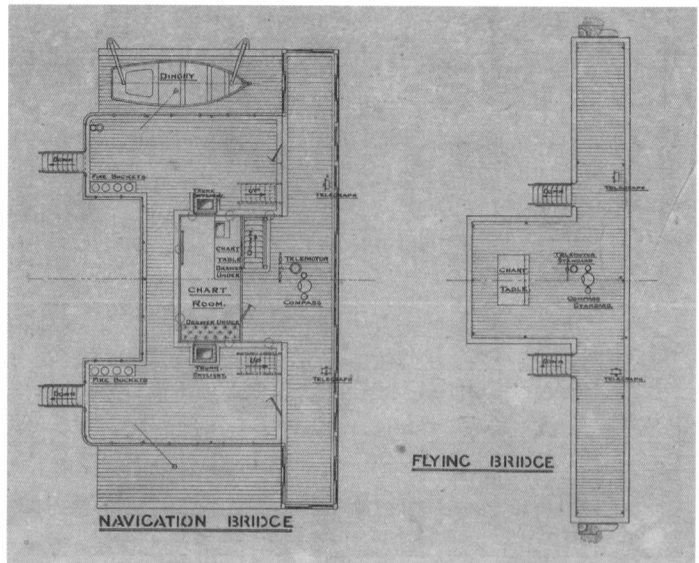

图4-54　驾驶甲板和顶驾驶甲板布置图
Figure 4-54　Layouts of navigation and flying bridge

4.3.9

冷库布置
Refrigerating Chamber

在上层建筑区域的上甲板上布置了一个冷库。冷库分为两个区域：操作间（butcher shop）和储存库。操作间内设有一条通向遮蔽甲板的梯道，另一条带舱口盖的通道则通向燃油沉淀柜。操作间内还布置了一块斩肉的砧板。储存库区域有一个缓冲间［容积为 224 立方英尺（6.91 立方米）］、一个肉库［容积为 832 立方英尺（23.56 立方米）］和一个蔬菜库［容积为 476 立方英尺（13.48 立方米）］。图 4-55 所示为冷库绝缘布置图，图 4-56 为总布置图 7008C 中的冷库布置图。

A refrigerating chamber was arranged on the upper deck in section of superstructure. Refrigerating chamber was further divided into two spaces: butcher shop and storage space. A stair connected shelter deck was arranged in butcher shop, and a trunk with hatch cover connected fuel oil settle tank. A meat cutting block was located in butcher shop. Storage space included an anteroom of 224 cubic feet (6.91 cubic meters), meat room of 832 cubic feet (23.56 cubic meters) and vegetable room of 476 cubic feet (13.48 cubic meters). Refer to Figure 4-55 for layout of refrigerating chamber and Figure 4-56 for layout of refrigerating chamber on General Arrangement Plan 7008C.

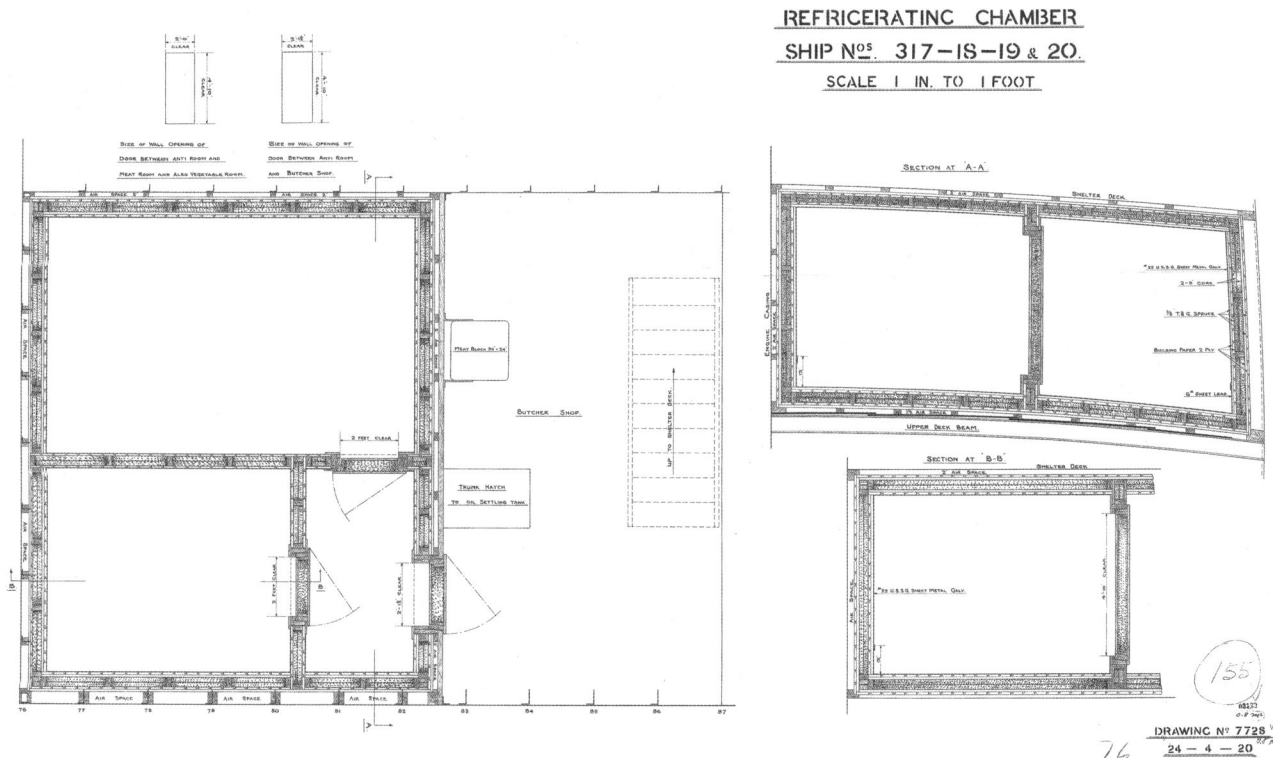

图 4-55　冷库绝缘布置图
Figure 4-55　Layout of refrigerating chamber

冷库绝缘层由以下几层结构和材料组成：

钢质围壁、空气导流通道（air space，由木条隔成）、两层防潮纸（building paper）、两层软木（cork）隔热层和镀锌钢板。

冷库制冷采用何种方式不详，但在总布置图7008C（见图4-56）中可以看到机炉舱内有发电机和制冰机间（dynamo engine & ice machine），操作间内布置有一个冰柜（ice chest）。由此可以推断，制冷方式是采用冰块。

The insulation of refrigerating chamber consisted of the following combination of materials:

Steel wall, air space made wooden batten, two tiers of building paper, two tiers of cork as thermal insulation, and galvanizing steel sheet.

The refrigeration type is not clear, but from General Arrangement Plan 7008C (refer to Figure 4-56), dynamo engine & ice machine was arranged in engine and boiler room, and ice chest was located in butcher shop. Refrigerating chamber was most probably cooled down by ice blocks.

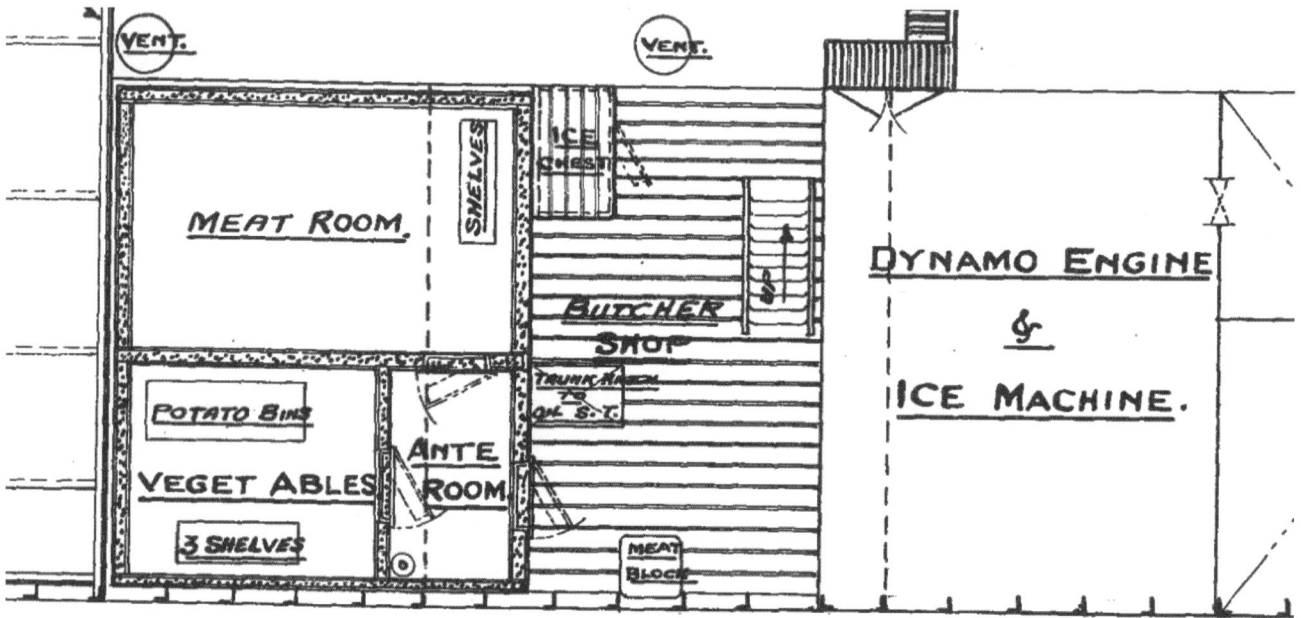

图 4-56　总布置图 7008C 中的冷库布置图
Figure 4-56　Layout of refrigerating chamber on General Arrangement Plan 7008C

4.3.10

锅炉和蒸汽主机
Boilers and Main Steam Engine

锅炉

机炉舱前部为锅炉舱，横向一字排开配置了三台圆筒形烟管锅炉（单侧多管回焰式船用烟管锅炉，俗称"苏格兰船用锅炉"，或简称"苏格兰锅炉"）。在蒸汽动力船舶上，这种苏格兰船用锅炉应用非常广泛。在第二艘船（"天朝"号，H318）的舱容和载重量标尺图上，标注了船舶蒸汽主机和锅炉的主要参数。其中锅炉的参数：直径为 15 英尺 3 英寸（4.65 米）、长度为 11 英尺 3 又 3/4 英寸（3.45 米）、压力为 210 磅力 / 英寸 ^{2}（1.45 兆帕）。图 4-57 所示为船舶轮机的主要参数。

Boilers

Three sets of multi-tubular return tube single ended marine Scotch boiler (known as "Scotch boiler") were transversely arranged in fore area of engine and boiler room. Such marine Scotch boiler was widely applied on steam powered ships at that time. On Capacity Plan & Deadweight Scale of SS "Celestial", H318, ship's machinery particulars including engines and boilers were clearly indicated. The particulars of boilers are: 15 feet and 3 inches (4.65 meters) in diameter, 11 feet and 3-3/4 inches (3.45 meters) in length, and 210 psi (1.45MPa) in pressure. Figure 4–57 is ship's machinery particulars indicated on the drawing.

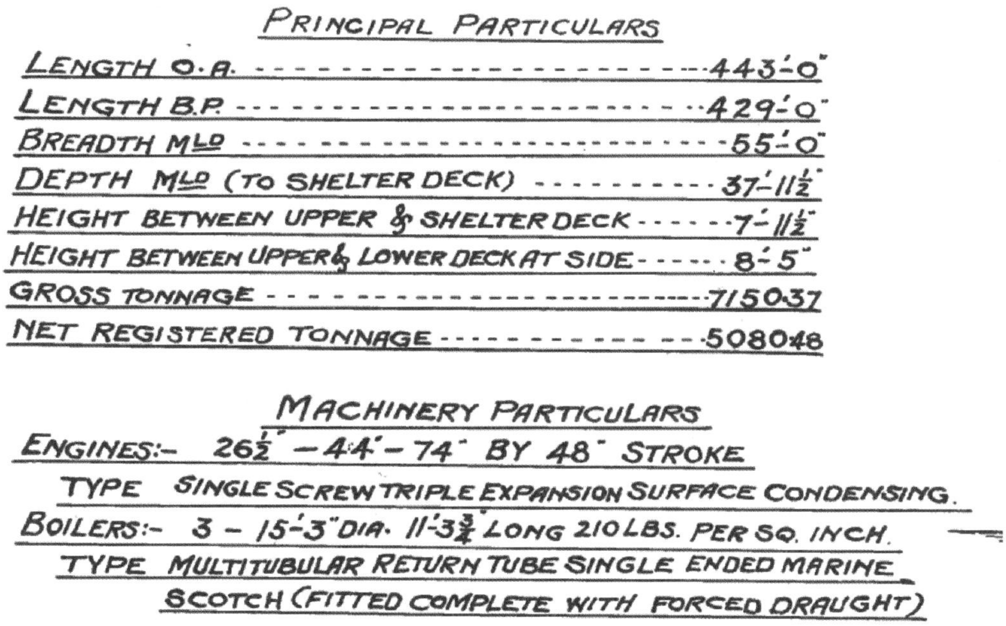

```
PRINCIPAL PARTICULARS
LENGTH O.A. ----------------------------------- 443'-0"
LENGTH B.P. ----------------------------------- 429'-0"
BREADTH MLD ---------------------------------- 55'-0"
DEPTH MLD (TO SHELTER DECK) --------- 37'-11½"
HEIGHT BETWEEN UPPER & SHELTER DECK ----- 7'-11½"
HEIGHT BETWEEN UPPER & LOWER DECK AT SIDE ------ 8'-5"
GROSS TONNAGE --------------------------- 7150.37
NET REGISTERED TONNAGE ------------- 5080.48

MACHINERY PARTICULARS
ENGINES:- 26½" - 44' - 74" BY 48" STROKE
TYPE  SINGLE SCREW TRIPLE EXPANSION SURFACE CONDENSING.
BOILERS:- 3 - 15'-3" DIA. 11'-3¾ LONG 210 LBS. PER SQ. INCH.
TYPE  MULTITUBULAR RETURN TUBE SINGLE ENDED MARINE
        SCOTCH (FITTED COMPLETE WITH FORCED DRAUGHT)
```

图 4-57 船舶轮机的主要参数
Figure 4–57 Ship's machinery particulars

注：原轮机规格书中配置的四台燃煤锅炉是苏格兰格拉斯哥 James Howden & Co., Ltd. 制造的水管锅炉。在实船设计建造过程中，采用了三台由美国波特兰威拉米特钢铁厂制造的燃油锅炉。

Note: In original machinery specification, four Howden's sectional marine water tube type boilers, manufactured by James Howden & Co., Ltd., Glasgow, Scotland, to be installed onboard, fitted to burn coal. In later actual ship design and construction, three Willamette Iron and Steel Works, Portland, USA, manufactured oil fueled boilers were adopted on board.

苏格兰锅炉，是一种火管（fire-tube）锅炉，或称烟管（smoke tube）锅炉，燃烧后的烟气通过放置在水箱里的管路时会产生蒸汽。它的外形是水平放置的圆筒形钢质容器，下部设置一个或多个圆柱形炉膛（cylindrical furnace）。炉膛是波形圆筒，炉膛可以是单侧设置（single-ended）也可以双侧设置（double-ended）。炉膛上部密密麻麻排列了小直径［通常是3英寸或4英寸（7.62厘米或10.16厘米）］的火管。炉膛里的烟气先流向锅炉的背面，经炉膛上部的火管后从烟囱（chimney）排出。在平行布置的火管段部罩着一个导烟罩（smokebox），导烟罩的上部和烟囱相接。图4-58为苏格兰锅炉的剖面和原理图[17]。图中清楚表示了炉膛（furnace）和燃烧室（combustion chamber）是两个相互连接的不同部件；图中右侧竖立的矩形部件为燃烧室，左侧为导烟罩。

Scotch boiler is one kind of fire-tubes or smoke tubes boiler. The steam is created by exhaust passing through the tubes in the cylindrical water tank. The outer shell of Scotch boiler is a steel made, horizontally placed cylindrical tank. Single or multiple cylindrical furnaces are fitted in the bottom half. Furnace is single-ended or double-ended with cylindrical corrugated shell. Dotted fire-tubes [typically 3 or 4 inches (7.62 or 10.16 centimeters) in diameter] are distributed upward furnace. Exhaust from furnace flows upward then passes through fire-tubes, finally ejects from chimney. A smokebox covers fire-tube end and connects the chimney at the upper end. Figure 4-58 shows the sectional diagram of Scotch boiler. The furnace and the combustion chamber are graphically manifested to connect each other. Components on the right and left sides are combustion chamber and smokebox respectively.

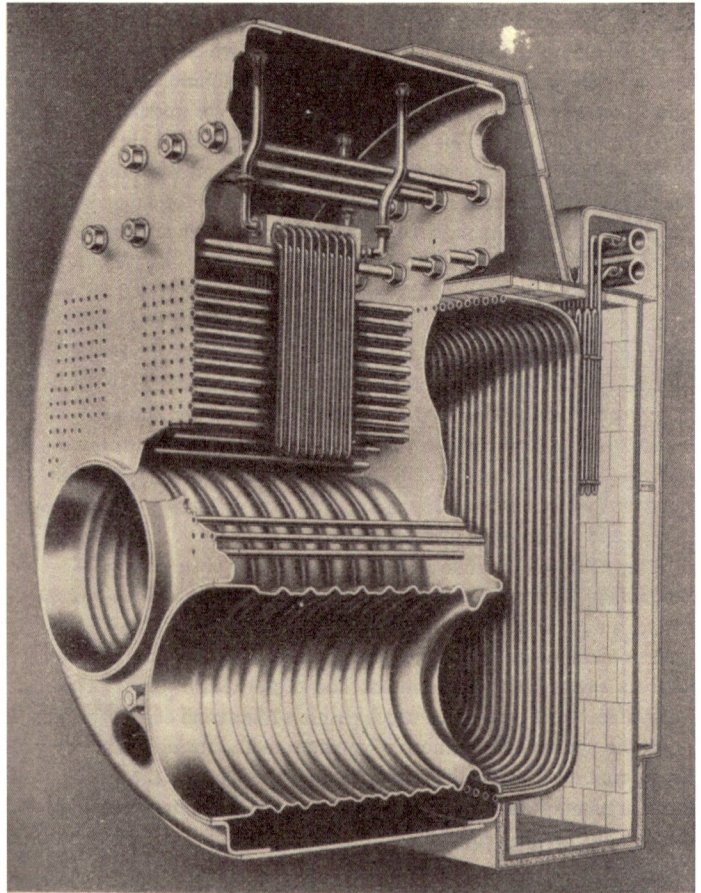

图4-58　苏格兰锅炉的剖面和原理图
Figure 4-58　Sectional diagram of Scotch boiler
（资料来源：https://paddlesteamers.org/down-to-see-the-engines/）

当时没有焊接技术，炉体外板连接用的是铆接，而火管和炉体的连接则是采用一种称为扩口（flaring，辗管）的工艺完成的。扩口工具的端部呈锥形，锥形前端有一个圆柱形的钢柱，操作时将锥形工具一边旋转一边向管内挤压，这样就把火管管体端口胀大将其牢牢地固定在炉体上。图4-59为双炉膛的苏格兰锅炉的外形照片[18]。在照片中可以清晰地看到：铆接连接的炉体外板、两个圆柱形炉膛、密密麻麻排列的火管和顶部的气室等锅炉的主要部件。

No welding technology was available at that time, and the shell plating of boiler body was connected by rivets. The fire-tube was connected with the boiler shell by the flaring method. The end of flaring tool is conical with protruded steel cylinder, which can expand the end of tube and fix on the boiler body along with rotating and pressing inward. Figure 4-59 is the outline of Scotch boiler with twin furnaces, and main components such as riveted shell plating of boiler body, two cylindrical furnaces, dotted arranged fire-tubes and dome on top of boiler body can be clearly viewed from this picture.

冷凝循环水先被引入一个叫热阱的大水柜内，然后被锅炉给水泵抽出，泵入锅炉加热蒸发成蒸汽使用。循环过程中损耗的水由机炉舱双层底内补给水舱（feed water tank）中的水进行补充。

Condensate water is guided to a bigger water tank called "hot well", and then the water is pumped into boiler by feed water pump of boiler for heating to vapour. Water loss during circulation can be replenished from feed water tank in the double bottom.

后期有些燃煤锅炉还配置了抛煤机、炉栅、出灰器等装置，尽可能用机械代替人工操作以减轻工人的劳动强度。

In order to decrease the labour intensity of the operator, some machineries were used for replacing manual operation. Spreader feeder, grate bar and ash discharger and so on were equipped for boiler in later period.

图 4-59　双炉膛苏格兰锅炉的外形照片
Figure 4-59　The outline of Scotch boiler with twin furnaces

苏格兰锅炉在蒸汽动力推进的全盛时期（heyday）几乎是一种通用标配，特别是作为三胀式蒸汽机的"黄金搭档"。大型或高速的船舶需要配置许多台锅炉。例如，皇家邮轮"卢西塔尼亚"号配置了 25 台苏格兰锅炉，参见表 2-1；邮轮"泰坦尼克"号配置

Scotch boiler was the most popular configuration in heydays of steam propulsion. It was golden mate of triple expansion reciprocating steam engine. Larger or higher speed ships needed to equip many sets of boiler. For instance, cruise liner RMS "Lusitania" equipped 25 sets of Scotch boilers, referring to Table 2-1 in this book; cruise ship RMS "Titanic" equipped 29 sets of Scotch boilers, therein, 24 sets were double

了 29 台苏格兰锅炉，其中 24 台是双侧炉膛 [直径为 15 英尺 9 英寸 (4.8 米)、长 20 英尺 (6.1 米)]，5 台是直径相同的长 11 英尺 9 英寸(3.58 米)的单侧炉膛。所有锅炉每个配置 3 个直径为 3 英尺 9 英寸(1.14 米)的莫里逊波纹炉膛（ Morrison corrugated furnace ），工作压力为 215 磅力 / 英寸^2 (1.48 兆帕)。全船共有 159 个炉膛，可以想象航行时锅炉舱内的场面非常壮观。

ended type [15 feet and 9 inches (4.8 meters) in diameter, 20 feet (6.1 meters) in length], and 5 sets were single ended type [11 feet 9 inches (3.58 meters) with identical diameter]. Three Morrison corrugated furnaces in diameter of 3 feet and 9 inches (1.14 meters) were equipped for each boiler, and the working pressure was 215 psi (1.48 MPa). Totally 159 furnaces were on board. You can imagine such grand scene in the boiler room while the ship sailing.

蒸汽主机

机炉舱的后部为蒸汽主机（ main steam engine ）舱，配置立式三缸三胀往复式蒸汽机（ vertical type 3-cylinder triple expansion reciprocating steam engine ）一座，驱动一个四叶定距螺旋桨（ fixed pitch propeller ）。立式三缸三胀往复式蒸汽机是往复式蒸汽机家族中的一种，该型机有三个不同直径的汽缸，缸径由小到大分别称为高压缸、中压缸及低压缸。从锅炉出来的高压蒸汽先引入高压缸，经膨胀做功后压力降低成中压蒸汽，再引入中压缸，然后把中压缸膨胀工作后的低压蒸汽引入低压缸工作，最后引入冷凝器冷凝成水供循环使用。

关于四艘船的主机功率（ main engine power ），《江南造船所纪要》有如下记载："官府"号为 3 430 马力，"天朝"号为 2 580 马力，"东方"号和"国泰"号均为 2 733 马力[19]。但从美国船级社总部档案室的入级记录中查到的这四艘船配置的蒸汽主机的参数都是一样的，气缸尺度和图 4-53 上的标注也是一样的。这台蒸汽主机的主要参数如表 4-4 所示[20]。

Main Steam Engine

The rear section of engine and boiler room was main steam engine room, and one set of vertical type 3-cylinder triple expansion reciprocating steam engine was arranged in engine room to drive a 4-blade fixed pitch propeller. Vertical type 3-cylinder triple expansion reciprocating steam engine is one kind of steam engines in reciprocating steam engine family. It consists of three cylinders with different diameters, sequentially from smaller one to larger one called high pressure cylinder, middle pressure cylinder and lower pressure cylinder. The higher pressure vapour from boiler injects high pressure cylinder first, after expansion and acting reduced pressure vapour injects middle pressure cylinder, then injects lower pressure cylinder. Finally, the lower pressure vapour is guided into condensator for recycling purpose.

Regarding main engine power of these four steam freighters, as per *Summary of Kiangnan Dock & Engineering Works*, 1922, SS "Mandarin" is 3 430 hp, SS "Celestial" is 2 580 hp, SS "Oriental" and SS "Cathay" are 2 733 hp, but as per registered records in Archives of ABS Headquarter, the power and engine parameters of all four steam freighters are identical, and cylinder dimensions are the same as indication on figure 4-53. Table 4-4 is the main parameters of steam power plant.

表 4-4　推进装置的主要参数
Table 4-4　The main parameters of steam power plant

主机类型	Engine type	立式三缸三胀往复式蒸汽机 Vertical type 3-cylinder triple expansion reciprocating steam engine	
气缸尺度	Cylinder dimensions	26.5 英寸（ 67.31 厘米 ），44 英寸（ 1.12 米 ），74 英寸（ 1.88 米 ）；冲程为 48 英寸（ 1.22 米 ） 26.5″(67.31 cm)，44″(1.12 m)，74″(1.88 m)；stroke is 48″(1.22 m)	
名义功率	Horsepower (nominal)	2 600 马力（ hp ）	
螺旋桨	Screw	单桨、四叶 Single, 4 blades	

自制还是进口？

这些锅炉设备是江南造船所自制的还是进口的，史料上的记载并不明确并且有互相矛盾之处。根据作者查到的美国船级社总部档案室的入级记录，这些锅炉由美国的威拉米特钢铁厂制造。关于威拉米特钢铁厂的描述，维基百科英文版有以下一段记载[21]：

威拉米特铁厂又称威拉米特钢铁公司，简称WISCO，是一家从事铸造和通用机械制造的工厂，1865 年创立于美国俄勒冈州的波特兰市，原来主要从事蒸汽动力推进船舶的锅炉和主机制造。1904 年，公司改名为威拉米特钢铁厂，一直运行到 1990 年关闭。

威拉米特钢铁厂是当时这种苏格兰锅炉的最大制造商，应急船舶公司船队里绝大多数蒸汽动力船舶上配置的锅炉都是由威拉米特钢铁厂制造的。图 4-60 为威拉米特钢铁厂在 *Pacific Marine Review* 杂志（J.S. Hines, 1918 年 5 月出版；第 140-141 页）上刊登的宣传广告[22]。

Self-manufactured or Imported?

Were these boilers self-manufactured or imported? The record in historical materials has conflicted conclusion. These boilers were made by Willamette Iron and Steel Works in the United States as per registered records in Archives of ABS Headquarter. The description of Willamette Iron and Steel Works can be found from English version of Wikipedia:

Willamette Iron Works (also known as Willamette Iron and Steel Company or WISCO) was a general foundry and machine business established in 1865 in Portland, Oregon, originally specializing in the manufacture of steamboat boilers and engines. In 1904, the company changed its name to Willamette Iron and Steel Works, under which name it operated continually until its close in 1990.

Willamette Iron and Steel Works was the world's largest manufacturer of Scotch boilers, and the most of the boilers installed on steam powered ships in EFC fleet were made by Willamette Iron and Steel Works. Figure 4-60 is advertisement on *Pacific Marine Review* (J.S. Hines, published in May 1918; pages 140–141).

图 4-60 威拉米特钢铁厂在 *Pacific Marine Review* 杂志上刊登的宣传广告
Figure 4-60 Willamette Iron and Steel Works — *Pacific Marine Review*, May 1918

《江南造船所纪要》提到：万吨级美国运输舰上的核心设备——用于主推进的蒸汽机，是由江南造船所自行制造的。图 4-61 为江南造船所自行制造的立式三缸三胀往复式蒸汽机的照片 [23]。该机系"自制三汽鼓立机，3 000 马力，机之背面附凝水管及冷水柜等"，制造完成安装后，经航行试验，"能使该舰航速比造船合同规定的每小时快 3 海里" [24]。

如前文所述，作者在美国船级社总部档案室查到的四艘船的入级记录中所记的主机功率都为 2 600 马力，工作压力为 260 巴。所有的主机（立式三缸三胀往复式蒸汽机）均由江南造船所制造，而烟管锅炉是由美国波特兰的威拉米特钢铁厂制造。那为什么首制船"官府"号主机功率的数据有上述差异呢？作者从一个船舶设计者的角度分析，可能有以下几个原因。

一是江南造船所试制蒸汽机的时间先于这四艘万吨级运输舰签合同的时间。当时毛根去美国说服美国海运委员会主席赫尔利的时候，表示江南造船所已经有能力建造三胀往复式蒸汽机了。当时这型蒸汽机没有和美国波特兰威拉米特钢铁厂制造的烟管锅炉匹配过，这里说的 3 430 马力可能是指这型蒸汽机可输出的最大功率，而不是锅炉加蒸汽机形成的推进系统能够输出的功率，所以在功率数据上存在差异。

The steam engine for propulsion, i.e., the key equipment of steam freighter, was self-manufactured by Kiangnan according to the description in *Summary of Jiangnan Dock & Engineering Works*, 1922. Figure 4-61 is a picture of Kiangnan manufactured vertical type 3-cylinder triple expansion reciprocating steam engine. "Self-made 3-cylinder vertical engine with built-in condensate pipes and water tank, output of 3 000 hp." After installation was completed and it was verified by sea trail, "the trail speed was 3 nautical miles faster than the guaranteed speed specified in the shipbuilding contract".

According to registered records of these four steam freighters in Archives of ABS Headquarter, the power of main engine is 2 600 hp with working pressure of 260 bars. All main engines (vertical type 3-cylinder triple expansion reciprocating steam engine) were manufactured by Kiangnan, but smoke boilers were made by Willamette Iron and Steel Works, Portland, USA. Why does the main power of SS "Mandarin" have such deviation? From viewpoint of a ship designer, following reasons may be possible.

First the time of Kiangnan trail-manufactured steam engine is prior to the shipbuilding contract date of these four steam freighters. When Mr. Mauchan went to Washington for persuading Mr. Hurley, Chairman of the United States Shipping Board, he expressed that Kiangnan had ability to manufacture triple expansion reciprocating steam engine. Because the steam engine built by kiangnan did not yet match the smoke-tube boiler made by Willamette Iron and Steel Works, 3 430 hp outlet was most properly the maximum power of the steam engine, but not the delivery power of the entire propulsion system (boiler plus steam engine). This may be why the power deviation exists.

图 4-61　江南造船所自行制造的立式三缸三胀往复式蒸汽机
Figure 4-61　Kiangnan manufactured 3-cylinder triple expansion reciprocating steam engine

二是可能威拉米特钢铁厂制造的燃油烟管锅炉所产生的蒸汽只能驱动江南造船所制造的蒸汽机输出 2 600 马力左右的功率,因此,后续船上的蒸汽机做了降功率的改进。

三是可能《江南造船所纪要》中对蒸汽机的最大功率和常用功率或者额定功率和指示功率的记载产生了混淆。

四是燃煤锅炉和燃油锅炉的燃烧效率可能不同,从而导致蒸汽机的输出功率存在差异。

鉴于目前可以查到的资料有限,无法判定上述推断是否合理。但从美国船级社的船舶入级资料来看,可以肯定的是这四艘船配置的蒸汽机是江南造船所制造的,燃油烟管锅炉是美国波特兰威拉米特钢铁厂制造的。江南造船所副所长邝国华在《东方杂志》1919 年 2 月号刊出的署名文章《江南造船厂承造美国万吨船四艘记》中称,首制船为该造船所制造的第 317 号船,装有三胀式蒸汽机,所有建造工程与蒸汽发动机及蒸汽锅炉均在中国制造,唯独钢材由美国供给。"除日本不计外,乃为远东以来所造最大之船四艘中之第一艘。其名称将于明年行下水礼定之。""从前中国所需军舰及商船多在美英日三国订作,今则情形一变。向之需求于人者,今能供人之需求。中国工业史乃开一新纪元。"[25]

从上述文章来看,作者对蒸汽机和锅炉均为江南造船所制造这一说法存疑。当然也不能排除江南造船所采用了威拉米特钢铁厂的图纸进行制造,类似现在的专利生产(比如现在的船用主机,中国的主机厂通常采用 MAN B&W 和 WinGD 的专利进行生产,在船级社的注册记录上一般只会登记专利拥有者的名称)。事实上江南造船所在承接这四艘万吨级运输舰之后,对其轮机制造的机械加工设备设施进行了大规模的升级和改造。比如 1918 年,扩建了轮机厂,添置了 69 台(套)进口加工设备,并将原来的蒸汽动力改成电动的,新的轮机厂可容纳千人以上作业;1919 年,新建的用于轮机制造的合拢厂配有三座 40 吨桥吊和两台大型电动钻孔机,可供五六千马力的轮机总装;同年在铸铁厂内新增了两个 6 吨铸铁炉,三座吊重 8 吨的吊车,最多可生产 15 吨的铸件;同时还新建了铸造所用的木模厂、打铁厂和打铜厂等[26]。改造后的江南造船所应该是有能力制造这些蒸汽机和锅炉的。

Second, the steam produced by the Willamette Iron and Steel Works made, oil fueled, smoke-tube boiler can only deliver 2 600 hp power on the Kiangnan-built steam engine, and the engines on sister ships were derated accordingly.

Third, the maximum power and service power or nominal power and indicated power were confused in *Summary of Kiangnan Dock & Engineering Works*, 1922.

Forth, the combustion efficiency may be different between coal and oil fueled boilers, and such deviation results in discrepancy of engine output.

It is quite difficult to verify the credibility of above mentioned possibilities because of limited available information. But based on ABS registered records, it is confirmed that steam engines for these four steam freighters were Kiangnan made and oil fueled smoke-tube boilers were Willamette Iron and Steel Works built. Mr. K. H. Kwong, Vice Director of Kiangnan Dock & Engineering Works, published a signed article titled "Kiangnan Building Four Steamers for USA" on *Oriental Magazine*, February 1919. Mr. Kwong said, the first steamer is Kiangnan built vessel with hull No.317, and triple expansion steam engine would be installed on board. All construction work, steam engine and boilers would be manufactured in China, only steel material imported from USA. "Except Japan, these four steamers are the biggest ship in the Far East. She is the first ship of series, and her name will be assigned in launch ceremony of next year." "Former Chinese warships and merchant ships were mostly ordered from USA, UK and Japan, three countries. Today's situation completely changed. China previously relied on others but now can supply to others. Chinese industry will begin a new era."

From above mentioned article, I doubt the statement that both steam engine and boiler were made by Kiangnan. Of course, it cannot exclude the likelihood that Kiangnan, like licensee, manufactured boiler according to Willamette Iron and Steel Works's drawing. Marine diesel engine, for instance, Chinese main engine makers currently produce engine under licenses of MAN B&W and WinGD. In such case, the name of licenser is normally filled in the registered book of classification society. In fact, Kiangnan massively upgraded and retrofitted machining equipment and facilities after securing shipbuilding contracts of four steamers. Machinery workshop was expanded by 69 sets of imported machining equipment in 1918, and the primer driver of steam was replaced by electric. New machinery workshop was able to accommodate more than one thousand workers; a new assembly workshop for grand assembling 5 000 to 6 000 hp engine was completed with three sets of 40-ton gantry and two sets of electric driller in 1919; in the same year, two sets of furnace of 6 tons for smelting iron and three sets of 8-ton crane were newly quipped in casting workshop, and the maximum casting up to 15 tons can be produced. A wooden pattern-making workshop for casting, forge iron workshop, forge copper workshop was newly established. Kiangnan was able to manufacture those steam engines and boilers by upgraded facilities and retrofitted equipments.

但在 1960 年江南造船所老员工黄容的访谈记录中提到："建造四艘万吨级运输舰的所有材料、锅炉等都由大来公司转运过来，……"[27] 此外，在毛根出发赴美国洽谈合同前，江南造船所刘冠南所长向毛根声明代表权限中的第二条："到美后须将拟造之舰、所需锅炉及大宗材料价值详细考察，俟有把握致电本所查核"。这说明锅炉是进口的，结合美国船级社的船舶入级记录来看，邝国华的文章是有夸大成分的，也有可能那时江南造船所能够制造的是燃煤锅炉，而后来改成较为先进的燃油锅炉以后也改成从威拉米特钢铁厂进口了。

由江南造船所建造锅炉的计划显然出于某种原因最终失败了。1918 年 10 月出版的《太平洋海洋评论》的一篇文章指出，曾经有一个计划是使用从旧金山和波特兰轮船公司的"熊"号上打捞上来的 6 台锅炉。"熊"号于 1916 年 6 月在加利福尼亚州北部海岸搁浅。这个计划也未能实现，这些锅炉最终由"阿拉巴马"号木壳轮船运到横滨。当它们被运往横滨时，可以做出的假设是，它们最终会被装配在由日本船厂建造的美国海运委员会的某些船上。

最终，一共 12 台价值 30 万美元的全新锅炉由美国俄勒冈州波特兰的威拉米特钢铁厂制造，并于 1919 年 11 月由大来轮船公司的"丰大"号货轮运至上海。1919 年 12 月 30 日，锅炉从"丰大"号货轮上被卸至江南造船所的码头。这些锅炉被描述为"苏格兰船用型，直径为 15 英尺 3 英寸（4.65 米），长 11 英尺 6 英寸（3.51 米）。它们的设计和制造的工作压力为 200 磅力 / 英寸^2（1.38 兆帕），每台锅炉重 65 吨"。每艘船上将配备 3 台这样的锅炉。

在本书的修改过程中，作者找到了三张刊登于《太平洋海洋评论》上的照片。第一张照片是威拉米特钢铁厂为江南造船所制造的锅炉准备发运的照片，刊于《太平洋海洋评论》1919 年 12 月号上。第二张和第三张是组合在一起的，分别展现了这些锅炉在江南造船所码头从大来航运公司的"丰大"号上卸下的场景和这些锅炉堆放在江南造船所厂内的场景，这两张照片刊于《太平洋海洋评论》1920 年 6 月号上。参见图 4–62 和图 4–63。

It was mentioned that "all the materials and boilers for the construction of four 10 000-ton steam freighters were transported by Robert Dollar Company…" in the interview records of Huang Rong, an old staff of Kiangnan, in 1960. In addition, before Mr. Mauchan departed to the United States for negotiating the ship building contract, Mr. Liu Guannan, the Director of Kiangnan, clearly stated his permission to Mauchan in the power of attorney. "The boilers and materials required for building steamers should be carefully verified, and wait for the approval of headquarter of Kiangnan." This shows that the boilers were imported, considering the registered record of ABS. Mr. Kwong's article might have certain exaggeration. Maybe Kiangnan was able to manufacture coal fueled boiler, and more advanced oil fueled boiler was imported from Willamette Iron and Steel Works.

As far as the boilers, the plan to have them built by Kiangnan Dock & Engineering Works apparently fell through for some reason. In an article in the October 1918 edition of the *Pacific Marine Review*, there was a plan to utilize six boilers salvaged from the San Francisco and Portland Steamship Company's SS "Bear", which had run aground on the Northern California coast in June of 1916. This plan too fell through, and the boilers were eventually brought to Yokohama on the wooden motor ship "Alabama". As they were shipped to Yokohama, the assumption is that they were eventually used in some of the Shipping Board vessels being built there.

Ultimately, twelve brand new boilers, valued at $300 000, ended up being manufactured by the Willamette Iron and Steel Works in Portland Oregon and were shipped in November of 1919 aboard the Dollar Steamship Company "Grace Dollar". The "Grace Dollar" discharged the boilers to the Kiangnan Dock & Engineering Works on 30 December 1919. The boilers were described as being "of a Scotch marine type, 15 feet 3 inches (4.65 meters) in diameter by 11 feet 6 inches (3.51 meters) long. They were designed and manufactured for a working pressure of 200 psi (1.38 MPa), and each boiler weighs 65 tons". Each ship would be equipped with three of these.

In revising process of this book, three pictures were found on *Pacific Marine Review*. The first picture on the December 1919 edition of the *Pacific Marine Review* shows the scene of Willamette Iron and Steel Works manufactured boilers for Kiangnan ready for departure. The second and third pictures on the June 1920 edition of the *Pacific Marine Review* are combined as one, showing the boiler was discharged from freighter "Grace Dollar" of Dollar Steamship Company, and the boilers arrived and stored in Kiangnan. See Figures 4–62 and 4–63.

Image of the completed Willamette Iron & Steel Works boilers staged and ready for shipment. Original caption: "A shipment of Portland-built boilers for China." From an article titled 'Direct Selling in China' by F.R. Sites, page 67 of the December 1919 edition of the Pacific Marine Review. Written on the boilers were:

UNITED STATES SHIPPING BOARD
EMERGENCY FLEET CORPORATION
c/o KIANGNAN DOCK ENGINEERING WKS.
　　SHANGHAI CHINA
　　c/o DOLLAR S.S. LINES
S.U.NO. 130　　　REQ.NO.2053-1
HULL NO. 2028　　S.I.NO.51834-B

K.D.SHANGHAI

Chinese text borders the left side. Image appears on page 69.

图 4-62　威拉米特钢铁厂为江南造船制造的锅炉准备发运
Figure 4-62　Willamette Iron and Steel Works manufactured boilers for Kiangnan ready for departure

Images of the Willamette Iron & Steel Works boilers being delivered to the Kiangnan Dock and Engineering Works in Shanghai. Per the original caption, the image above shows the 75-ton shearlegs lifting a boiler from the hold of the Dollar steamship GRACE DOLLAR. Note the Chinese translation of the vessel's name under the English spelling (Dollar standard practice), and the image below shows the boilers in the Kiangnan yard, which provides some scale with the various men and the buildings. These images were hidden in a riveting article entitled 'Electricity vs. Fuel for Heating Rivets' by F.C. Cheston discussing the merits of the new electric rivet heaters over the standard fuel burner method of the day. Oddly, the article makes no mention of the Willamette boilers produced for Kiangnan. From the June 1920 edition of the Pacific Marine Review, page 135.

图 4-63　锅炉从"丰大"号上卸下和锅炉堆放在江南造船所厂内的场景
Figure 4-63　Boiler discharged from freighter "Grace Dollar" and stored in Kiangnan

作者又查到了锅炉本体、进气道、烟道、船体上的安装基座、阀件和附件等的相关图纸，所有图纸的图面和标注都非常详细。这些部件可能是江南造船所自己设计和制造的。

记得在 20 世纪 90 年代中期，作者在德国汉堡曾经和英国白星航运公司（White Star Line）的继承人就在中国船厂重建"泰坦尼克"号进行过探讨，他们的意图是完全复造"泰坦尼克"号，不仅仅是外形和舱室保持原来的设计风格，而且包括主机和锅炉等轮机设备也要复造。当然这样的想法从现代造船技术和规范法规的角度来看，其现实性是值得商榷的。当时他们拿出了"泰坦尼克"号的锅炉等主要设备的制造图纸，从中可以看出该船配备的也是苏格兰锅炉。

与威拉米特钢铁厂提供给江南造船所的锅炉图纸相比，作者感觉"泰坦尼克"号的锅炉图纸的精细程度远抵不过威拉米特钢铁厂的，因此认为威拉米特钢铁厂这样精细程度的图纸在当时完全可以作为制造图。图 4-64 和图 4-65 为锅炉结构图纸的局部，从图面上可以看出，锅炉本体图纸是美国俄勒冈州波

Some supplemental drawings such as boiler body, inlet box, exhaust channel, foundation on hull, valves and miscellaneous fittings were unexpectedly found. All sketches and labels on drawings seem quite detailed. These components were probably designed and fabricated by Kiangnan.

In middle of 1990s, I used to discuss rebuilding RMS "Titanic" with the haeres of White Star Line in Hamburg, Germany. Their intention was completely duplicating RMS "Titanic", not only to keep the ship outline and cabin decoration as the original style, but also to duplicate steam engines and boilers as well as other machineries. The feasibility should be seriously verified from viewpoint of modern shipbuilding technology and regulatory. They brought the copy of original working drawings of boiler and main equipment and showed them to us. Scotch boiler on RMS "Titanic" was confirmed.

Comparing with Kiangnan's drawings provided by Willamette Iron and Steel Works, the boiler drawing of RMS "Titanic" looks not so detailed as Willamette Iron and Steel Works's one. Personally, it was applicable to use as working drawing for manufacturing the boiler. Figures 4-64 and 4-65 are partial drawing of boiler structure. The drawing of boiler body with drawing No. 14662 was done by Willamette Iron and Steel Works, Portland, Oregon, USA. The boiler had three

特兰威拉米特钢铁厂的，图号为14662，有三个炉膛，而且明确注明是燃油锅炉。江南造船所在此图上附加标注的图号为7171，图纸的标注日期为1918年11月21日，上面还盖有"江南造船所造机部"的印章，印章中还刻有"工程完毕原图检还"的字样。

furnaces with expository writing of "oil burning". Supplemental drawing No. of 7171 and date of 21 November 1918 were added by Kiangnan. The seals of "Machinery Department of Kiangnan" and "To be Returned after Work Completed" were stamped on the drawings.

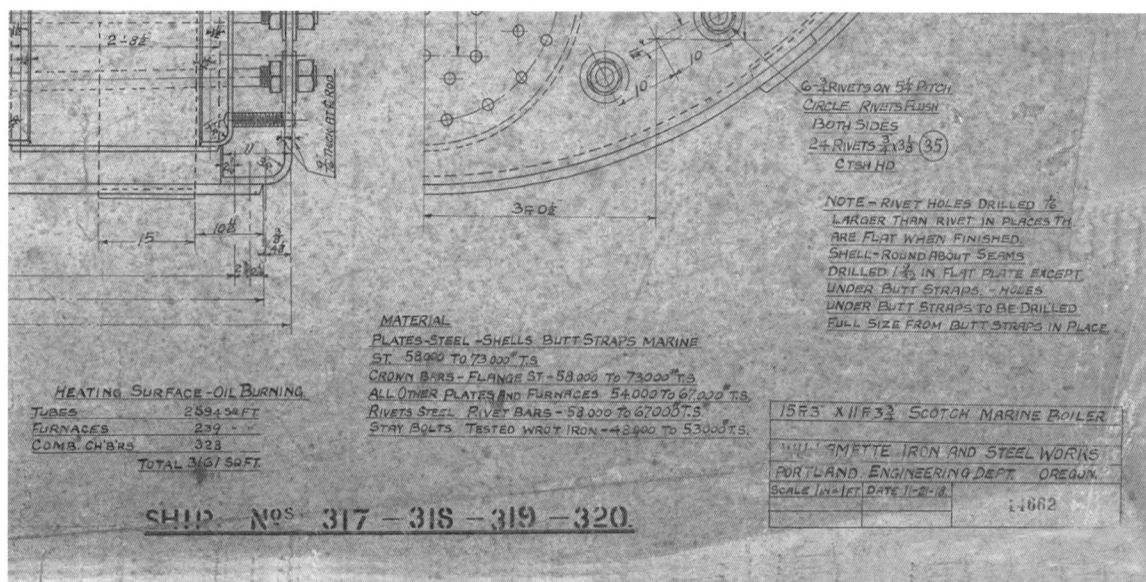

图 4-64　威拉米特钢铁厂的锅炉结构图纸（标题栏局部）
Figure 4-64　Boiler structural drawing of Willamette Iron and Steel Works (partial: title bar)

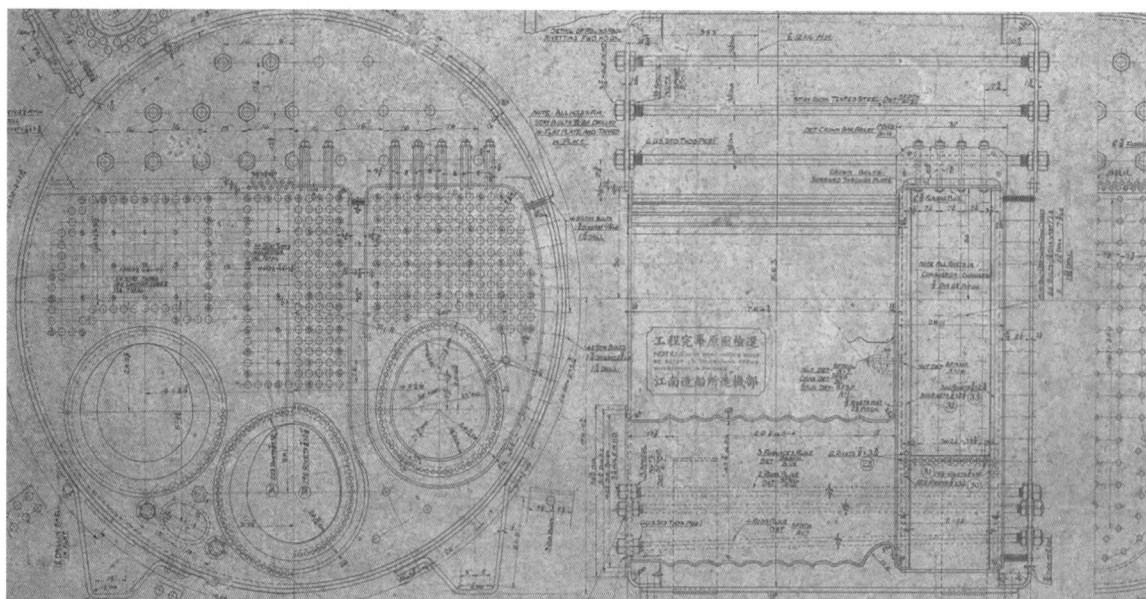

图 4-65　威拉米特钢铁厂的锅炉结构图纸（锅炉本体局部）
Figure 4-65　Boiler structural drawing of Willamette Iron and Steel Works (partial: boiler body)

使作者大惑不解的是，如果锅炉整体从威拉米特钢铁厂进口的话，为什么威拉米特钢铁厂会提供如此详细的锅炉制造图纸给江南造船所呢？如果仅仅是和锅炉安装相关的工程似乎也不需要如此详细的锅炉结构图纸。邝国华在《东方杂志》1919 年 2 月号刊出署名文章时，江南造船所已经收到了威拉米特钢铁厂提供的锅炉制造图纸而且是燃油锅炉。也许是江南造船所采用了威拉米特钢铁厂的图纸制造锅炉，类似现在的专利生产？或者是一部分船舶的锅炉是进口的，而另一部分船舶的锅炉是自行制造的？作者认为这些可能性都是存在的。

But it is extremely puzzling. If the boiler was completely imported from Willamette Iron and Steel Works, why did Willamette Iron and Steel Works provide such detailed drawings to Kiangnan? The boiler installation work does not seem to require such detail structural drawings. When the article of K. H. Kwong was published on *Oriental Magazine*, February of 1919, Kiangnan had received the working drawing of oil fueled boiler from Willamette Iron and Steel Works. Maybe Kiangnan manufactured boilers according to drawings of Willamette Iron and Steel Works, similar to manufacturing under a license? Or perhaps the boilers were partly imported and partly self-made? Both possibilities might exist.

4.3.11

机炉舱布置
Engine and Boiler Room Arrangement

机炉舱布置在船体舯部、上层建筑下方的主船体内。四艘万吨级运输舰的机炉舱布置与应急船队公司的其他船型相比是比较紧凑的，设计理念是较为先进的。同样是出于造船和造机部分图纸分别归档的原因，作者没能够查找到机炉舱的详细布置图，只能从完工版的总布置图中机炉舱各层甲板的布置进行一些概貌性的分析，这一点是比较遗憾的。

Engine and boiler room was located in hull underneath superstructure amidship. Comparing other EFC ships, design philosophy was more advanced and arrangement was more compact. Because drawings of shipbuilding part and machinery part were individually kept, it is a pity that arrangement of engine and boiler room cannot be found. Only globally analysis can be done on basis of deck arrangement of engine and boiler rooms in "As Built" drawings.

机炉舱内上甲板

机炉舱内上甲板中部为锅炉和主机开口（engine and boiler casing），前端中部布置有两个大的通风筒，主机两边各有两个通风筒。左右舷各设有一个淡水舱（fresh water tank），左舷还设有一个粮食库（provision store）、机修间（machine shop），粮食库和机修间之间布置有一部通向遮蔽甲板的扶梯；右舷还设有直流发电机室和制冰机间、冷库（肉库、蔬菜库和缓冲间）和操作间。在操作间里布置了一个冰柜和一块砧板（meat block），还布置有一部通向遮蔽甲板的扶梯，如图4-66所示。

Upper Deck in Engine and Boiler Room

Engine and boiler casings were located in centre of upper deck in top of engine and boiler rooms. Two larger vents were arranged at fore end central, and two vents were arranged at each side of main engine. One fresh water tank each was arranged portside and starboard. A provision store and machine shop were located at portside. A stair to shelter deck was arranged in between provision store and machine shop. A dynamo engine & ice machine, refrigerating chamber (including meat room, vegetable room and ante room) and butcher shop were located at starboard. An ice chest and meat block were arranged inside of butcher shop. A stair to shelter deck was also arranged inside the butcher shop. Refer to Figure 4-66 for further detail.

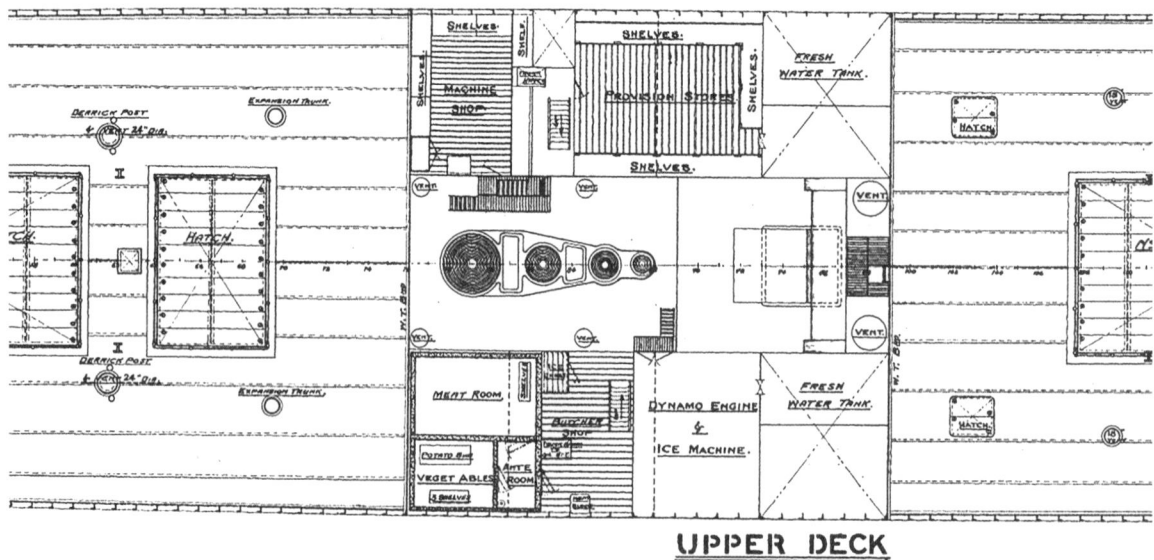

图 4-66　机炉舱内上甲板舱室布置
Figure 4-66　Layout of upper deck in engine and boiler room

机炉舱内下甲板

机炉舱内下甲板前半部为容纳三台锅炉的大开口（boiler casing），锅炉的上部布置有格栅式的走道（grating）。下甲板后半部为容纳一台三胀式蒸汽主机的大开口（engine casing），机炉舱中部左右舷各设有一个燃油沉淀舱（oil settling tank）。机炉舱后部右舷布置了工程师储藏室（engineer store room），其主要用途应该是储存备品备件，机炉舱后部左舷的空间可能被排气管占用了。机炉舱前端中部布置有两个硕大的通风筒，主机两边各有两个小的通风筒。主机的周围设置了格栅式的平台，有梯道与锅炉上部的格栅式走道相连，如图 4-67 所示。

Lower Deck in Engine and Boiler Room

There was a large boiler casing accommodating three boilers on fore part of lower deck inside of engine and boiler rooms. The passage way with grating was located at top of boilers. A large opening accommodating one set of triple expansion steam engine was arranged after part of lower deck, and oil settling tanks, portside and starboard each, were located in way of middle of engine and boiler rooms. The engineer store room was arranged in starboard aft of engine and boiler rooms, portside may be occupied by discharge recess. Two stout vents were arranged in the central of engine room front, and two smaller vents were arranged at sides of main engine respectively. Grating platform was located surrounded main engine with stair to connect upper passage way. Refer to Figure 4-67.

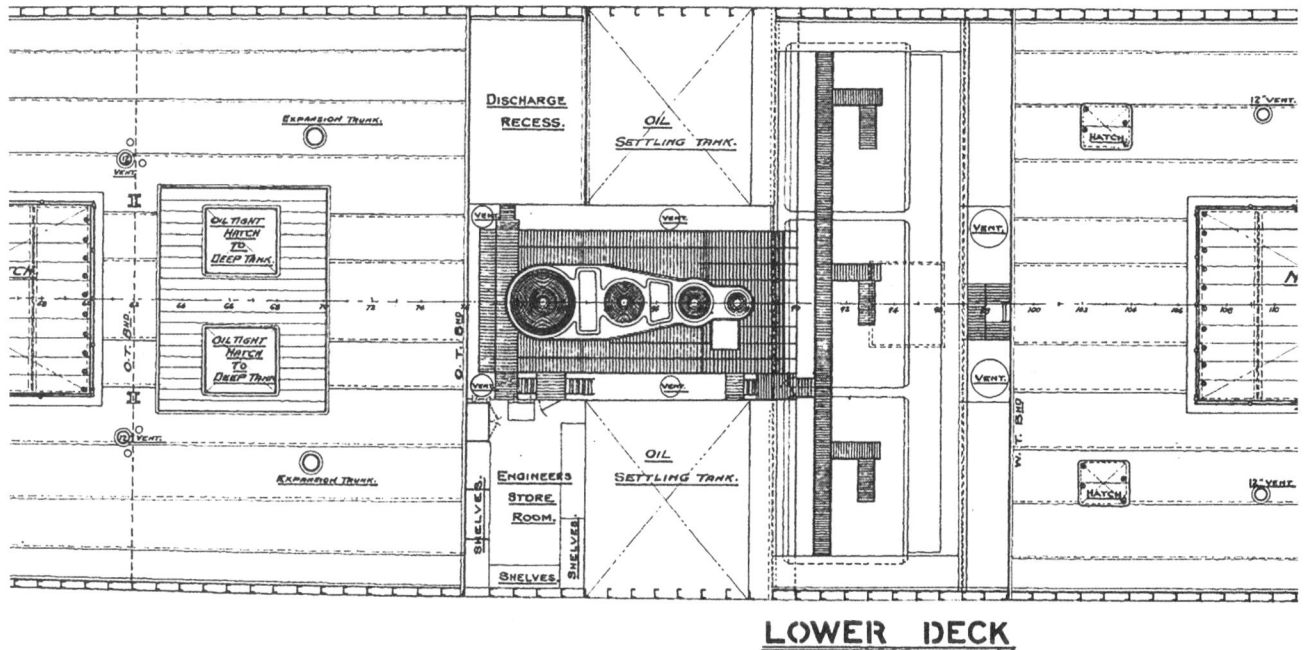

图 4-67　机炉舱内下甲板舱室和平台布置
Figure 4-67　Layout of lower deck and platform in engine and boiler room

机炉舱内双层底

机炉舱内双层底前半部布置了三台锅炉，后半部布置了一台三胀式蒸汽主机。双层底内布置有燃油舱并有纵舱壁隔开；前后设有隔离舱并与货舱底部的压载舱隔开。在机炉舱的后部、轴隧前端（燃油深舱

Double Bottom in Engine and Boiler Room

Inside the engine and boiler room, there were three sets of boilers on the double bottom fore, and one set of triple expansion steam engine on the double bottom aft. Fuel oil tanks with longitudinal bulkheads were arranged in the double bottom, and cofferdams were intentionally laid out at both ends of fuel tank for segregating ballast water tanks. A thrust

内）设有推力轴承布置空间（thrust recess），如图4-68 所示。通常在双层底上主机的左右两侧还布置有一些 小的油水柜、泵和阀件等，这些与现代船舶设计是一样的。

recess for thrust bearing was located fore end of shaft tunnel in way of aft of engine and boiler room. Refer to Figure 4-68. Some smaller oil and water tanks were arranged at both sides of main engine on double bottom as similar to modern ship design.

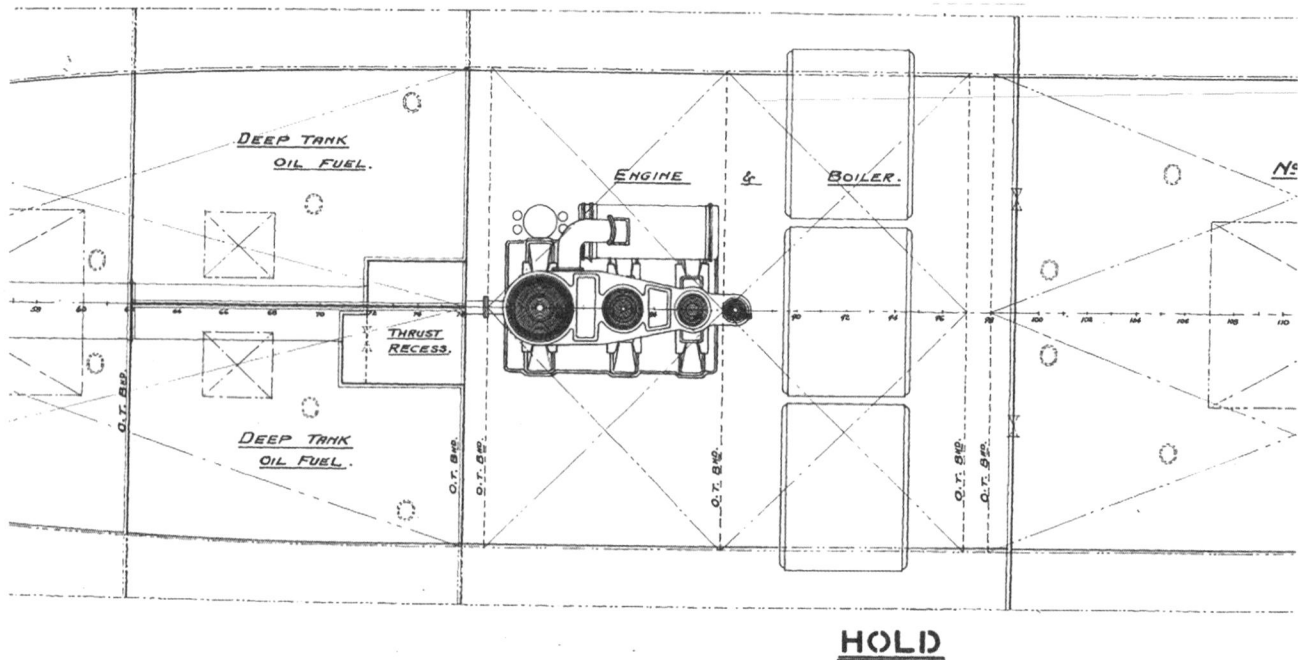

图 4-68　机炉舱内双层底布置
Figure 4-68　Layout of double bottom in engine and boiler room

4.3.12

燃煤蒸汽动力船舶的布置特点
Special Features of Coal Fueled Steamer

从 1918 年合同签订时的总布置图来看，江南造船所建造的四艘万吨级运输舰是配置燃煤锅炉的武装运输舰。1918 年 11 月由于战争结束了不再需要武装运输舰，燃油锅炉应用也越来越普遍，因此美国海运委员会决定将这四艘武装运输舰改为普通商用货船并改用当时技术比较先进的燃油锅炉。那么燃油蒸汽动力船与燃煤蒸汽动力船相比在布置上有些什么特点呢？

以煤作为燃料和以油作为燃料相比最大的不同在于煤是固体不具有流动性，因此燃煤舱不能像燃油舱一样布置在船体内的不规则部位并通过管道输送燃料。从江南造船所 1918 年的两张签字版总布置图和作者从 www.shipscribe.com 网站上查到的澳大利亚历史学家诺曼·L. 麦凯勒（Norman L. McKellar）（塔姆沃思，澳大利亚）对应急船队公司所有船型（1917—1921 年）的描述和简要总布置简图（例如第 6 章所述的 EFC 1013 和 EFC 1027）可以找到一个共同的特点，即在驾驶桥楼和机炉舱、双层底和下甲板之间布置了一个深舱（deep tank），深舱的后部布置了一对吊杆和相应的绞车（见图 4-69，1918 年 8 月 8 日签订的总布置图修改图的截图）。这个深舱上的下甲板和上甲板空间用于储存燃煤（见图 4-70，1918 年 8 月 8 日签订的总布置图修改图的截图）。

As per the General Arrangement Plan accompanied with the shipbuilding contract signed in 1918, the Kiangnan-built four steam freighters should be armed cargo ships with coal fueled boilers. Since the Great War was terminated in November of 1918, armed freighter was no longer required. Oil fueled boiler became more popular, and the United States Shipping Board, therefore decided to change these four armed steam freighters to normal merchant freighters with more advanced oil fueled boilers. Comparing these two different fuels, what special features do they have in layout of ship's sub-division?

The most obvious feature is that coal is solid and has no fluidity, and thus coal store space cannot utilize irregular space and coal can not transfer in pipeline. The common features can be found in Kiangnan's General Arrangement Plans accompanied with the shipbuilding contract and all EFC steamers under the United States Shipping Board, 1917–1921, source from www.shipscribe.com, Australian historian, Norman L. McKellar (Tamworth, Australia), i.e., deep tanks were arranged in the front of boiler room in between double bottom and lower deck, and one pair of derrick with winches was located at the rear of deep tanks (see Figure 4–69). The space on top of deep tanks was used for storing coal. Refer to Figure 4–70, showing the revised General Arrangement Plan signed on 8 August 1918.

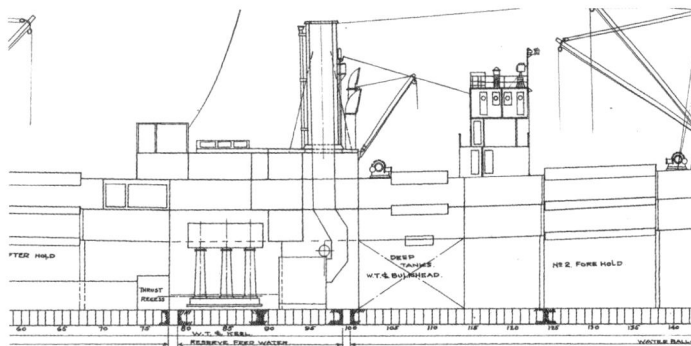

图 4-69　机炉舱和深舱侧面图
Figure 4-69　Profile of engine and boiler room and deep tank

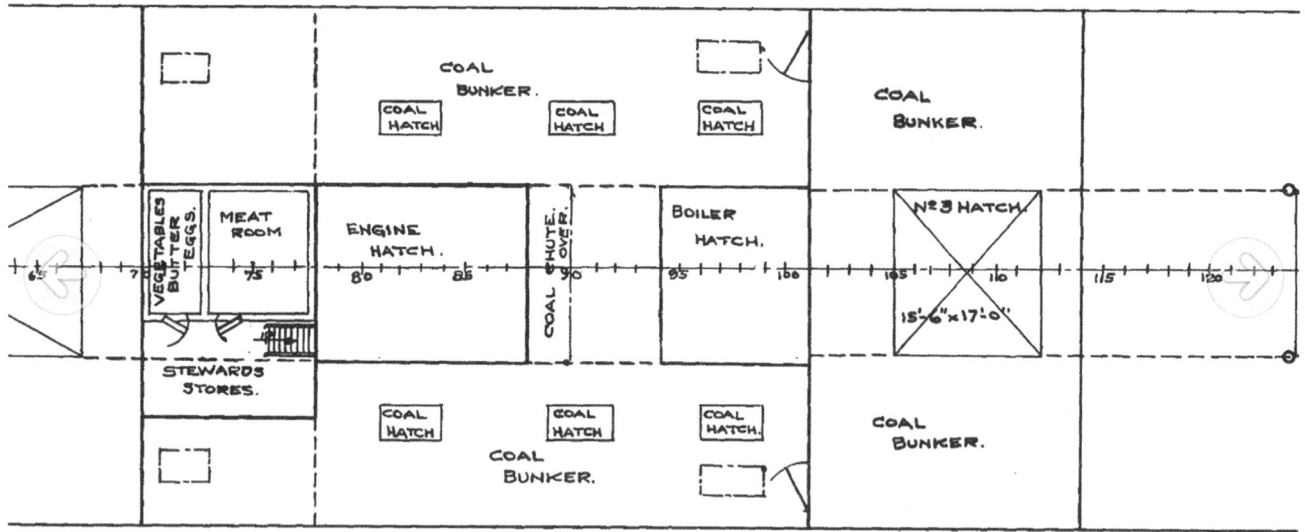

图 4-70　机炉舱和深舱上甲板图
Figure 4-70　Layout of upper deck in engine and boiler room

机炉舱内上甲板的左右舷各布置了三个燃煤舱口（coal hatch），机炉舱内上甲板的中央部位设置了燃煤槽（coal chute），机炉舱前部舱壁左右舷各设有一个舱门通向深舱上甲板区域，参见图 4-71（1918年 8 月签订的总布置图修改图的截图）。

There were three coal hatches each in way of upper deck of engine and boiler room, portside and starboard, and a coal chute was arranged at centre of upper deck in engine and boiler room. Two access doors were located on the fore bulkhead of engine and boiler room, each at portside and starboard respectively. Refer to Figure 4-71 (revised General Arrangement Plan signed in August 1918).

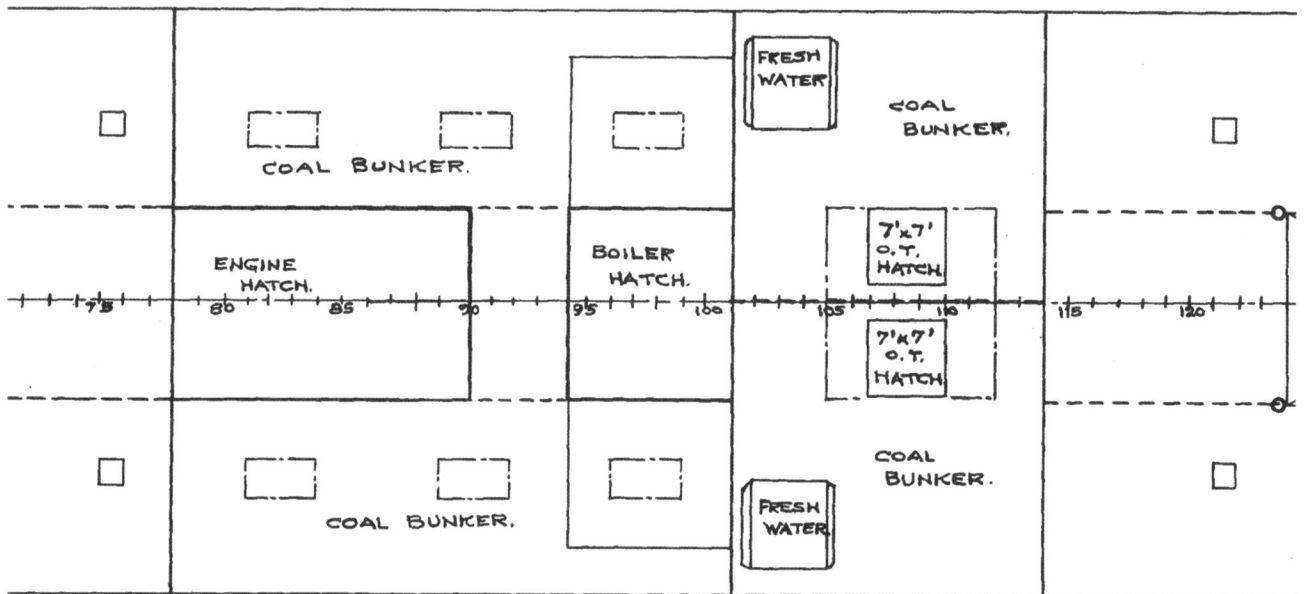

图 4-71　机炉舱和深舱下甲板图
Figure 4-71　Layout of lower deck in engine and boiler room

深舱内的下甲板左右舷各布置了一个圆形的淡水舱和 7 英尺（2.13 米）见方的油密舱口盖（oil-tight hatch）。机炉舱内下甲板中间部位为蒸汽主机和锅炉的开口，下甲板的左右两舷和深舱下甲板区域也可用于储存燃煤。

深舱下半部分（双层底和下甲板之间）是一对由水密纵中舱壁分隔的液舱，为什么在下甲板上布置了一对油密舱口盖？这对液舱到底有什么意义？根据作者推断：这个深舱应该是用于储存锅炉用水的。那为何要用油密舱口盖呢？机炉舱内锅炉和蒸汽主机的布置与后期建造的实船是一致的。图 4-72 所示为机炉舱和深舱双层底（1918 年 8 月签订的总布置图修改图的截图）。

Two cylindrical fresh water tanks and 7-foot (2.13 meters) multiple 7-foot oil-tight hatch were arranged on the lower deck of the deep tank, each at portside and starboard. Engine hatch and boiler hatch were located at the central part of the lower deck in the engine and boiler room. The portside and starboard of lower deck in both engine and boiler room as well as deep tank can be also used for storing coal.

The lower part of deep tank (in between double bottom and lower deck) was a pair of liquid tank with a central longitudinal bulkhead and oil-tight hatch cover. What purpose does this pair of liquid tank have? Maybe this deep tank is designed for storing boiler water. Why is an oil-tight hatch fitted on the lower deck? The arrangement of engine and boiler room was completely identical to that of the ship built later. Layout of double bottom in Engine and boiler room is shown in Figure 4-72 (revised General Arrangement Plan signed in August 1918).

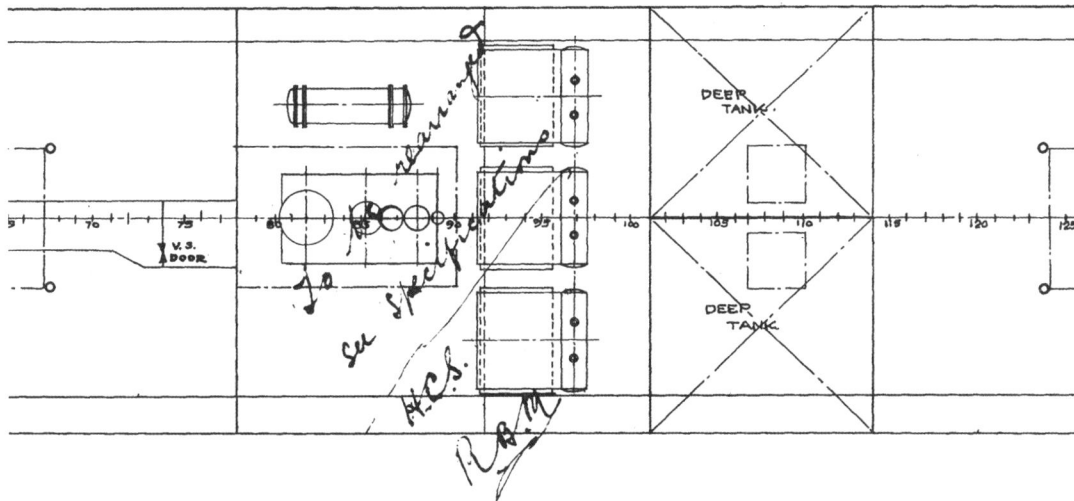

图 4-72　机炉舱和深舱双层底图
Figure 4-72　Layout of double bottom in engine and boiler room

在图 4-72 的机炉舱部位，有美国海运委员会秘书博尔内在这张总布置图的修改图（1918 年 8 月 8 日）上提的意见 "To be rearranged, see specification" 和江南造船所总工程师毛根的确认签名。这是一个非常有力的证据，说明当时在这四艘万吨级运输舰的合同中是有船舶建造规格书的，可惜这样一份重要资料却没有保存下来或被找到。

根据后续图纸，作者推测，在船舶建造规格书中，很有可能已经将燃煤锅炉改成了燃油锅炉，并取消了深舱和燃煤堆放的空间。

On the Figure 4-72, there is a comment "To be rearranged, see specification" hand written by S. N. Bourne, the Secretary of the United States Shipping Board, and confirmation signature of R. B. Mauchan. It is a powerful evidence of which Shipbuilding Specification existed, but it is pity such an important document cannot be kept or found.

As per speculation of later version of drawing, coal fueled boilers had possibly been changed to oil fueled boilers, and deep tank and coal bunker space had been cancelled accordingly.

4.3.13

推进系统布置
Shafting and Propulsion

长轴系布置在后半船体底部轴隧（shaft tunnel），整个轴系由八根中间轴通过法兰连接而成，每根中间轴有一个中间轴承支撑，参见图4-73所示的螺旋桨和中间轴系布置。靠近蒸汽主机端设有推力轴承，在燃油深舱内设有推力轴承布置空间（thrust recess），在艉尖舱内设有尾轴管前后轴承。尾轴上安装了一具四叶螺旋桨，直径约为5.3米，螺旋桨的桨毂设计成流线型。在轴隧靠近艉尖舱壁处还布置了一个逃生竖井（tunnel escape），参见图4-43、图4-44和图4-5所示的总布置图7007D。这样的布置设计在当时是比较先进的。

A long shafting system was arranged inside shaft tunnel on the aft double bottom. The whole shafting system consisted of eight intermediate shafts with flange connection, and each intermediate shaft was supported by an intermediate bearing, see also Figure 4-73. Thrust bearing was located at the rear of the steam engine, and thrust recess was arranged inside deep fuel oil tank. Fore and aft bearings of stern tube were fitted in aft peak tank. A tunnel escape for shafting tunnel was arranged in way of bulkhead of aft peak tank. Refer to Figures 4-43, 4-44 and General Arrangement Plan version 7007D (see Figure 4-5). Such a shafting arrangement was quite advanced at that time.

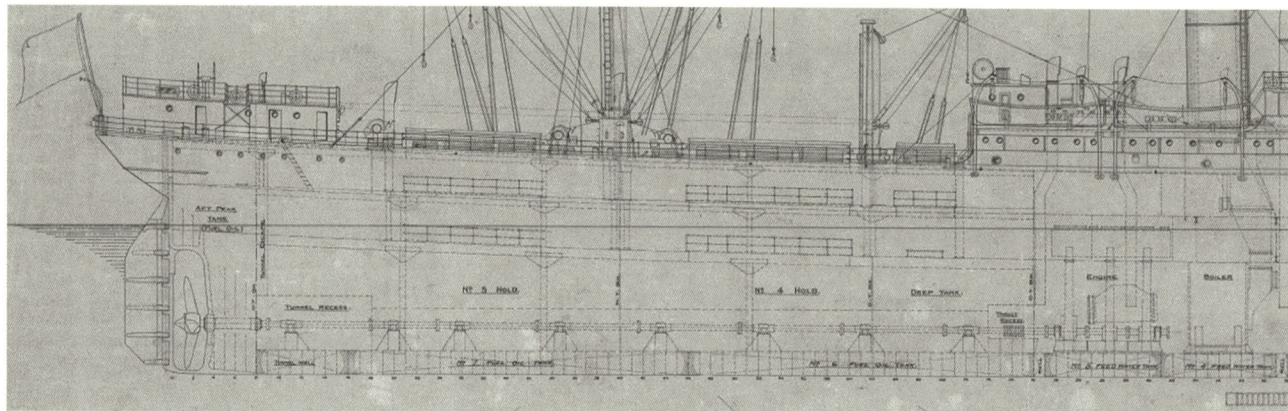

图4-73　螺旋桨和中间轴系布置
Figure 4-73　Propeller and intermediate shafting arrangement

4.3.14

通信导航设备
Communication and Navigation Equipment

与现代船舶相比，四艘万吨级运输舰的通信导航设备是十分简陋的，主、辅驾驶室内配置了仅仅能够传输字符的电报机和磁罗经，还有一些六分仪、望远镜和海图等简单的导航仪器和工具。

从不同版本的总布置图可以看出，无线电天线布置是不同的。从 7007A 到 7007D 版图上的无线电天线布置都是从前起重桅的顶部拉到后起重桅的顶部（见图 4-74），到 7007E 及以后的完工图则修改为从前起重桅的顶部拉到烟囱顶部，再从烟囱顶部拉到后起重桅的顶部（见图 4-75）。从交船后的照片来看，四艘船的天线布置除了在细节上有所不同之外，其他与完工图（7007E，见图 4-75）均是一致的。即便是 1936 年入列美洲 - 夏威夷公司前的大改装，对无线电天线布置也没有做大的修改。

Comparing with modern ships, the communication and navigation equipment of these four steam freighters are exactly simple and crude. Only telegrapher for transmitting text and magnetic compass were equipped in wheel house and flying bridge. In addition, there were navigation equipment and tools such as sextant, telescope and nautical chart equipped on board.

Radio antenna layouts were different on various versions of General Arrangement Plan. Wire type antenna was braced from fore master top to aft master top as shown in versions 7007A to 7007D of General Arrangement Plan, see also Figure 4-74. Version 7007E and as built drawing wire type antenna was modified from top of fore master top to funnel top then from funnel top to aft master top (see Figure 4-75). Reviewing the photo taken after delivery, radio antenna layouts of four steam freighters were identical to those of the built drawing (7007E, see Figure 4-75) except a few small details. Radio antenna layouts had no significant modification even though these four steam freighters were reconditioned prior to join fleet of American-Hawaiian.

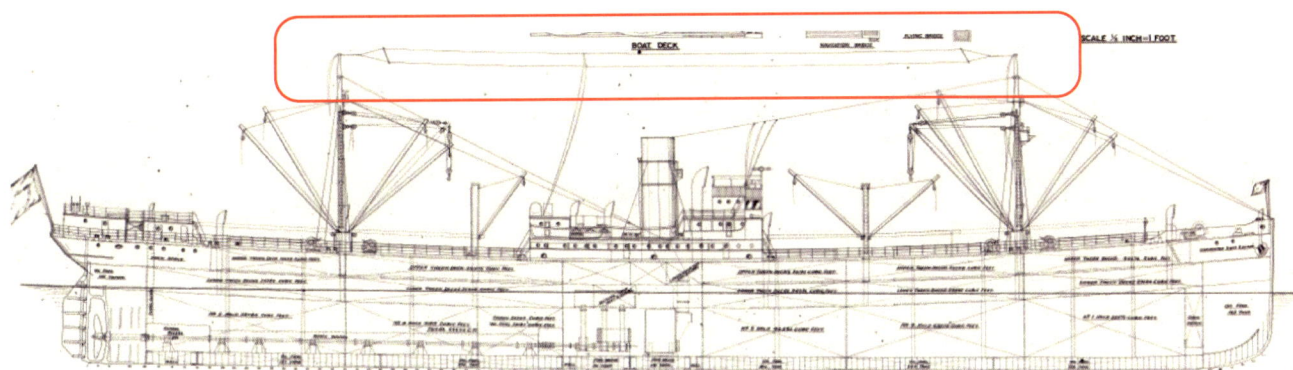

图 4-74 7007A 到 7007D 版图上的无线电天线布置
Figure 4-74 Layout of radio antenna on version 7007A to version 7007D

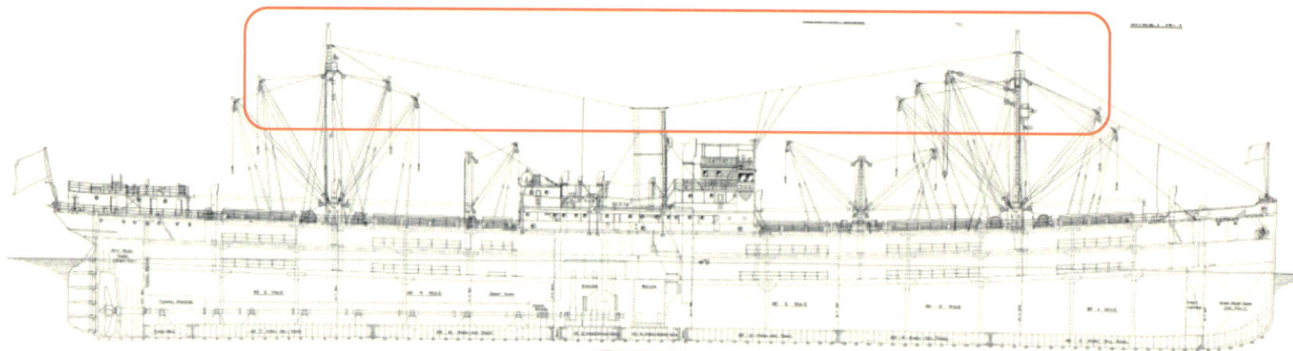

图 4-75　7007E 版图上的无线电天线布置
Figure 4-75　Layout of radio antenna on version 7007E

作者注：

Notes:

1　三菱重工业株式会社的"江南造船所史刊行会"编写，《江南造船所·歴史と思い出》，1973 年，第 25-30 页。

2　资料来自 http://news.nna.jp.edgesuite.net/free/news/20101230 cny 037 A.html。

3　总布置图为两页：第一页 7007 为船舶侧视图、遮蔽甲板布置图和上层建筑各层布置图，第二页 7008 为上甲板、下甲板和货舱的布置图。但 7007 有从 A 到 E 五个版本，而 7008 只有 A、B 和 C 三个版本。

4　cant 即"cant body"意指带有斜肋骨的船舶尾部结构。梁启康主编，《英汉双向船舶工程词典》，上海交通大学出版社，1999 年，第 76 页。

5　http://www.crwflags.com/fotw/flags/us_bmin.html#direct.

6　陆舸编著，《江南往事》。上海画报出版社，2005 年，第 367 页。

7　资料来自："玛丽王后"号的百度百科。

8　周有立、孙光二，《船舶修造中的铆接问题》，刊于《造船技术》1981 年第 2 期，第 37 页。

9　https://en.wikipedia.org/wiki/Caulking#Iron_or_steel_shipbuilding.

10　周有立、孙光二，《船舶修造中的铆接问题》，刊于《造船技术》1981 年第 2 期，第 42 页。

11　《中国舰艇工业历史资料丛书》编辑部编纂，《中国近代舰艇工业史料集》，上海人民出版社，1994 年，第 266 页。

12　https://en.wikipedia.org/wiki/Anchor.

13　此名称不确切，应该理解为备用锚和艏锚一样重。

14　关于威拉米特钢铁厂的介绍参见后文。

15　信息来自：https://en.wikipedia.org/wiki/Steam_donkey, 2015-11-17。

16　信息来自：www.ssarkansan.com，在此向原作者表示敬意。

17　图片来自：https://en.wikipedia.org/wiki/Scotch_marine_boiler。

18　同上。

19　刘冠南审核、廖驶编写，《江南造船所纪要》，1922 年，第 65-75 页。

20　数据来自：www.ssarkansan.com，向原作者表示敬意。

21　信息来自：https://en.wikipedia.org/wiki/Willamette_Iron_and_Steel_Works, 2015-11-17。

22　图片来自：https://en.wikipedia.org/wiki/Willamette_Iron_and_Steel_Works, 2015-11-17。

23　图片来自：江南造船（集团）有限责任公司档案馆。

24　刘冠南审核、廖驶编写，《江南造船所纪要》，1922 年，第 39 页。据作者考证的资料，合同规定的航速指标是基于大来公司的一艘母型船（EFC 1013）制定的，该母型船的主机功率小，航速指标相对较低。

25　《江南造船厂承造美国万吨船四艘记》，《东方杂志》第 16 卷，2 号（1919 年 2 月），第 195-197 页。

26　刘冠南审核、廖驶编写，《江南造船所纪要》，1922 年，第 35-43 页。

27　《谈 1927 年以前江南造船所的生产经营情况》，1960 年 4 月，访问于四川北路 961 弄怡兴里 6 号，许维雍整理。

5.1

国内史学家的观点
The Viewpoints of Chinese Historians

关于这四艘江南造船所建造的万吨级运输舰设计的来源，国内史学家长期以来持有以下几方面的观点。

（1）江南造船所不具备独立设计万吨级船舶的能力。"这四艘万吨级运输舰的设计图纸的主要部分都是美方提供的，江南造船所的技术人员只是为在该所建造做了一些补充设计，或是根据该所的建造工艺对原有设计进行一些修改。江南造船所只是利用其建造设备设施以及工人进行加工和总装。"

（2）《江南造船所纪要》中关于这四艘万吨级运输舰合同条款的记载："……给予保险各节亦均载明合同，至一切造法另有图单为凭。"其中"图单"一词的描述被国内史学家解释为由美方提供的图纸。

（3）以毛根为核心的外籍技术团队在主导万吨级运输舰建造时，通过技术壁垒限制中国技术人员的深度参与，客观上阻碍了企业技术体系的完整构建。"江南造船所的技术力量把持在以毛根为首的一伙外籍人员手中，他们来自上海的英资船厂，其技术水平限于船舶修理和小型船舶制造，不具备大型船舶的设计能力。更有甚者他们占据几乎所有重要职位，凌驾于刘、邝两位所长之上，把持了江南造船所的技术和经营业务，形成一个利益集团。他们为维护既得利益而故步自封，排斥中国技术人员，阻碍了江南造船所的技术进步。"

Regarding the design source of these four 10 000-ton American steam freighters built in Kiangnan Dock & Engineering Works, Chinese historians have held following viewpoints for a long time.

(1) Kiangnan didn't have the capability to design 10 000-ton class steam freighter independently. "Most design drawings were supplied by the Americans; the designers of Kiangnan only did some supplemental designs and modifications on the original design as per their own practice and workmanship. Kiangnan merely did the assembly and erection with their facilities and workers."

(2) According to *Summary of Kiangnan Dock & Engineering Works* about the contract terms of the four 10 000-ton steam freighters: "...Sections about insurance should be included in the contract, and all construction details shall comply with the supplemental drawings." Chinese historians subjectively interpreted the word "drawings" as the full set of technical drawings for shipbuilding which were supplied by the Americans.

(3) Kiangnan's Scottish Chief Engineer Mauchan, with his followers intentionally ostracized Chinese technicians, and stood in the way of Kiangnan's technical development. "Kiangnan's technical resources were in the hands of foreigners led by Mauchan. They came from a British-owned dockyards in Shanghai, and their ability was only limited to ship repairing and smaller shipbuilding. They were not qualified for designing big ships. Furthermore, they had occupied the most of key positions to override the two Directors of Mr. Liu and Mr. Kwong. They controlled the technical and commercial business and formed an interest group. In order to protect their own interest, they excluded Chinese technicians and held back Kiangnan's technical improvement."

（4）江南造船所随后没有接到大型船舶订单的主要原因是技术能力不足。"第一次世界大战期间，受德国潜艇攻击，大西洋航路上的运输船舶损失严重，特别是美国参战后，对运输船舶的需求剧增，而当时欧美各国的造船能力严重不足，使得本不具备万吨级船舶建造能力的江南造船所也意外获得四艘万吨级运输舰的大订单。这只是第一次世界大战这个特殊时期的一个特例，并且受益于这一时期美国为抑制对日本的依赖而有意扶持中国的战略。第一次世界大战结束后，世界经济进入了大萧条期，造船业从景气顶峰骤然跌落，陷入造船产能过剩、船价暴跌的困境，实力雄厚的欧美日船厂都纷纷削减产能以求生存，技术能力不足的江南造船所更难以在群雄逐鹿的世界大型船舶建造市场立足了。"

不过，也有一些媒体和历史记载基于民国时期中国工业水平客观地分析了当时江南造船所的技术水平。

随着工程的进展，美国驻厂专家对江南造船所的建造工作称赞不已，称"其造成之船较他国所造毫不逊色，结构艺术皆见嘉许，而中国机匠运用美国机械得心应手尤堪注意。"[1]

从建造方式上看，江南造船所承造美国运输舰采用了来料、来图加工的模式，美方不仅提供原材料和设计方案，还派监造员来华督工。因此，江南造船所承造美国运输舰从技术上说，较缺乏自主性。但是，由于此前江南造船所从未建造过万吨以上的巨轮，承造美舰仍然提升了该厂的技术能力。首先，尽管设计方案是从美国寄过来的，但"各部门详细设计，以及整个船舶的装配设计"，还是由江南造船所自己的设计人员着手进行的[2]。

(4) The main cause of having no further orders was due to the lack of technical capabilities of Kiangnan. "During the Great War, the Allies' transportation ships suffered huge loss in the transatlantic routes under the attack by German U-boats. Especially the United States, after joining the war, the demand for transportation was dramatically increased, while the shipbuilding slots were extremely insufficient at that time in shipyards of either Europe or the United States. Kiangnan, therefore, unexpectedly got the order of four 10 000-ton freighters even though they were not fully qualified to build such big ships. But it's just a special case during the Great War. Moreover, it was also benefited from the American strategy of supporting China to decline their dependence of Japan. After the Great War, world economic entered into the Great Depression, shipbuilding industry dropped from peak to bottom, ending up with overcapacity and a slump in newbuilding price. At that time, even the European, American and Japanese yards struggled to survive by cutting capacity, not to mention that how difficult it was for the technically incapable Kiangnan to maintain their position in the market of large scale shipbuilding."

However, there were also some other media and historical records that have objectively evaluated Kiangnan's technical level according to the Chinese industry level in the Republic of China era. The following descriptions were written:

With the progress of the project, American experts in site office complimented greatly on Kiangnan's construction work, said "The quality of completed vessel at in the same level of other countries, structural workmanship is good, and Chinese operators adroitly running American made machines are most impressed."

In view of construction methodology, Kiangnan adopted the pattern of construction with externally supplied equipment, materials and drawings, i.e., the Americans not only supplied raw material and design, but also sent the supervisors to China. Based on that, technically speaking, Kiangnan's building the freighters was lack of independency. However, as Kiangnan had never built the big ship over 10 000 tons in deadweight, building these steam freighters still improved Kiangnan's technical ability and capability. Although the design plan was mailed from the United States, "detailed design for all the parts and the outfitting design for the whole freighter" were done by Kiangnan's designers.

5.2

关于江南造船所绘图室的考证
Verification of Drawing Department

关于江南造船所设计室的历史，现有史料里的记载并不多，作者从原江南造船所设计室副主任徐振骐的回忆资料里查到这样一段描述[3]：

1905 年，局坞分家以后，江南船坞就成立了设计部门，开始的时候毛根将其称为"打样间"，以后又改称"绘图室"。1928 年成立设计处，下属造船和造机两个科室[4]。1926 年前的二十年，毛根在江南造船所时，掌握了全所的命脉，设计部门基本上由英国人主导。

"局坞分家"以后，江南造船所主要有以下五类产品。

第一类为非机动船舶和非船产品，如木筏、坞闸、救生筏、码头船、灯船、浮船、水鼓、油鼓、泥驳、货驳、浮桥、修理趸船、各种非自航挖泥船等。

第二类为长江和川江船舶，主要用于航行于上海至汉口、宜昌至重庆、重庆至叙府之间的各种客货船和拖船。

第三类为军用船舶，如双桨浅水炮舰、双桨机动警备船、保安船、小型炮艇、训练舰、一千至两千多吨排水量的巡洋舰。

第四类为海船，如万吨级远洋运输舰、三千多吨的沿海客货船、小型沿海船舶如破冰船、货船、海关船和交通船等。

Regarding the history of Kiangnan's Design Office, there are only a few records in the existing historical documents. Some descriptions from the memoir of Xu Zhenqi, the previous Deputy Director of Kiangnan Design Office, are excerpted as below:

In 1905, after the "Separation of Bureau and Dock", Kiangnan Dock set up its own design team. At the beginning, Mauchan called it as "Lofting Shop" and later renamed it as "Drafting Office". In 1928, the Design Office was established, with two departments, hull section and machinery section. In past two decades of 1926, when Mauchan was working in Kiangnan Dock & Engineering Works, he almost mastered the lifeblood of the whole shipyard, and the design department was basically dominated by the British.

After the "Separation of Bureau and Dock", Kiangnan Dock & Engineering Works mainly focused on following five categories of products.

Category Ⅰ: non-motorized ships and non-marine products, such as wooden rafts, dock gates, life rafts, floating wharf, beacon boats, pontoons, water drums, oil drums, mud barges, cargo barges, pontoon type bridges, repair barges, various non-self-propelled dredgers.

Category Ⅱ: various passenger & cargo ships and tugboats, sailing between Shanghai to Hankou, Yichang to Chongqing, and Chongqing to Xufu in the Yangtze River and Chuan Jiang (upper stream of Yangtze River).

Category Ⅲ: ships for military purpose, such as twin-propeller shallow water gunboats, twin-propeller guard boats, patrol boats, small gunboats, training ships, and cruisers with a displacement of one thousand to two thousand tons.

Category Ⅳ: seagoing ships, such as 10 000-ton ocean-going steam freighters, 3 000 tons coastal passenger & cargo ships, and small coastal ships such as icebreakers, cargo ships, revenue cutter and traffic boats.

第五类为船用机械，如往复式蒸汽机、小型水管锅炉和烟管锅炉以及蒸汽驱动的船用辅机，如舵机、锚机和各类泵等。

从承接四艘万吨级运输舰之前江南造船所设计室所设计的船舶来看，该所承造船舶的吨位也在逐步增加。如 1911 年至 1912 年设计的 4 130 吨的"江华"号长江客轮、1916 年至 1918 年设计的 1 468 吨的"祥泰"号长江客货轮、690 吨的"永健"号和"永绩"号炮舰，还有 450 吨的破冰船等，建造这些船舶有一定的难度。应该说在英国人主导下的江南造船所设计室还是有一定设计实力的。

从图纸的精细程度、图纸的数量来看，江南造船所的设计能力和产品质量也是在不断进步的。1905 年江南船坞设计的柚木船体蒸汽动力汽艇"江南"号（H1），图纸非常简单。不过从一艘长 55 英尺（16.76 米）的木质汽艇的结构和当时主要依靠工匠手工、传统工艺现场制作为主的建造模式来看，未必需要多详细的图纸。

在徐振骐的回忆资料中还提到，一艘 65 英尺（19.81 米）长的汽艇的全套船壳图纸只有十余张。在最主要的线型图上，剖面和水线比较少，绘制的线型也不太准确，因此技术人员经常到放样楼进行修改。总布置图上很多装置和设备都没有画上去；船体结构图上也只有片段、部分结构；机炉舱布置图上也只表示主机、锅炉、油舱和煤舱的位置，对一些较大的辅机设备如发电机、消防泵、冷凝柜等在可能条件下才绘制在图上，其余一些小的设备和结构的安装细节都没有定义。采用简略的图纸进行施工就需要一个拥有较强专业能力的领班。

在徐振骐的回忆资料中，没有关于四艘万吨级运输舰设计资料来源和设计图纸的详细程度的内容，而且资料中存在一个明显的错误，即他把四艘万吨级运输舰的设计工作的开展时间段说成了 1921 年以后。实际上，这四艘万吨级运输舰在 1921 年底之前已经陆续交付了。从徐振骐的回忆资料中的内容来看，他并未参与四艘万吨级运输舰的设计工作，而是主要参加了 1926 年为美国建造的六艘浅水炮舰及以后江南造船所建造船舶的相关设计工作。

Category Ⅴ: marine machinery, such as reciprocating steam engines, small water tube and fire tube boilers, and steam-driven steering gears, windlasses and various pumps as well as other marine auxiliary machines.

From the perspective of the ships designed by Kiangnan Design Office before signing the contract of four 10 000-ton American steam freighters, the tonnage had been gradually increased, for example, 4 130 tons Yangtze River passenger steamer SS "Kiang Wah", designed between 1911 and 1912; 1 468 tons Yangtze River passenger-cargo ship "Hsiang Tai", designed between 1916 and 1918; 690 tons "Yung Chien" and "Yung Chi" river gunboats, and 450 tons icebreaker etc. These ships had certain complexity. It should be admitted that the Design Office of Kiangnan under the leadership of the British did have certain strengths.

From the perspective of the fineness and the quantity of drawings, the design capability and quality of Kiangnan Dock & Engineering Works were also constantly improving. In 1905, the steam-powered teak hull launch "Kiangnan" (H1) designed by Kiangnan Dock had only a few and very simple sketches. However, for manually building the wooden structure of a 55-foot (16.76 meters) long launch with traditional craftsmanship, it was indeed unnecessary to have many detailed drawings.

In Xu Zhenqi's memoir, it is also mentioned that there were only a dozen drawings in a complete set of hull for a 65-foot (19.81 meters) long steam launch. In the most essential lines plan, the sections and waterlines were relatively in wider span, and the lines were drawn not so accurate. It was frequently adjusted and modified in the lofting shop. Many devices and equipments were missing in the General Arrangement Plan; the hull structures were only expressed partially as structural sections; the engine room plan only indicated the position of the main engine, boiler, oil tank and coal tank; and some large auxiliary equipments such as generators, fire pumps, condensing cabinets were indicated on drawing in case of that necessary information was available. Other remaining small equipments and installation details were not defined. It was thus necessary to have an experienced foreman and shipwright for construction with those sketchy drawings.

In Xu Zhenqi's memoir, nothing was mentioned about the design sources and detailed level of design drawings for the four 10 000-ton American steam freighters, and there is an obvious mistake as he said that the design work of the four 10 000-ton American steam freighters started later than 1921. In fact, the four 10 000-ton steam freighters were delivered before the end of 1921. According to Xu Zhenqi's memoir, he most properly did not participate in the design of the four 10 000-ton steam freighters. He mainly participated in the design of six shallow-water gunboats built for the United States Navy in 1926 and ships built in Kiangnan after that.

5.3

关于船舶设计来源的考证
Verification of Design Sources

国内史学家持有的第一个观点的出处大多来自《江南造船厂厂史：1865—1949》一书，书中第 121 页提到江南造船所的第一位中国工程师王平轩曾讲述过四艘美国万吨轮设计图纸的来源。

作者再次核查了 1983 年出版的《江南造船厂厂史：1865—1949》一书中的第 121 页。原文是这样写的："造这几艘美舰的图纸，主要部分虽由美国供应，但当时江南造船所的工程技术人员还是做了不少补充设计。"因编写《江南造船厂厂史：1865—1949》的原始史料是江南造船厂对老工程技术人员的访问笔录，作者又仔细核对了这些原始记录。其中有一份 1960 年 2 月 17 日王平轩的口述原始记录（记录人：许维雍）。王平轩的口述内容是这样的："造这四条大船的图纸，美国只来了一部分，有很大部分是当时江南厂的工程技术人员自行设计的。"可见，《江南造船厂厂史：1865—1949》编写组对设计来源的描述和原始口述记录相比是有偏差的，这个可能与编写组当时的立场和指导思想有关。

再从王平轩的生平和履历来看：

王平轩[5]（1880—1962）是北京人，英国格拉斯哥大学船舶机械系毕业。1905 年，江南船坞成立时进入江南船坞工作。1906—1909 年，被派往美国阿尔莎船厂实地学习。回国后又于 1910 年被派往北洋海军部工作，曾在天津北洋海军学校教轮机设计课程。1912 年，回江南造船所工作。他是江南造船所的第一位中国工程师。此后，王平轩曾先后担任民生实业公司总工程师和燕京大学教授。1947 年，王平轩担任大中华造船机器厂的总工程师，主要主持轮机设计和往复式蒸汽机设计，并著有《船舶蒸汽机》一书。

The first viewpoints held by domestic historians mainly come from the book *History of Jiangnan Shipyard: 1865–1949*. On page 121, the first Chinese engineer Wang Pingxuan mentioned the design sources of the four 10 000-ton American steam freighters.

After double-checking the wording on the page 121 of *History of Jiangnan Shipyard: 1865–1949*, 1983 edition, it reads: "Though the major drawings of these American steam freighters was supplied by the United States, but the technicians of Kiangnan still made a lot of supplementary designs." The original source of the wording was the transcript of interviewing to elder technicians of Kiangnan. One dictated original record of Wang Pingxuan on 17 February 1960 (recorder: Xu Weiyong) reads: "The United States only provided a smaller part of the drawings for the four big freighters, and a large part of the drawings were designed by the technicians of Kiangnan." It can be seen that there is a deviation between the raw records and the description in *History of Jiangnan Shipyard: 1865–1949* regarding design sources. This deviation might be due to the position and guide line of the editing team at the time.

Further reviewing the professional career of Wang Pingxuan:

Wang Pingxuan (1880–1962) was a Beijing native and graduated from the Department of Marine Mechanics at the University of Glasgow, UK. In 1905, he entered the Kiangnan Dock when it was separated from bureau. From 1906 to 1909, he was sent to the United States for practically training at Alsa Shipyard. After returning to China, he was sent to the Beiyang Naval Department in 1910. He taught engine design courses at Tianjin (Tientsin) Beiyang Naval School. In 1912, he returned to Kiangnan Dock & Engineering Works. He was the first Chinese engineer at Kiangnan. Since then, Wang Pingxuan has worked as the Technical Director of Min Sung Industrial Company and a professor at Yenching University. In 1947, Wang Pingxuan worked as the Chief Engineer of the Grand Chunghwa Shipbuilding & Machinery Plant. He was mainly responsible for the design of machinery and reciprocating steam engine, and he was the author of the book *Marine Steam Engine*.

王平轩是一位轮机工程师，按照江南造船所当时设计室的人员情况，主要管理工作基本上由英国人把持，而且船体（造船部）和轮机（造机部）是分开的，从王平轩访谈口述的原始记录来看，王平轩未必能够了解到万吨级运输舰设计来源的真实情况和细节。

Wang Pingxuan was a machinery engineer. As per the personnel situation of the Design Office of Kiangnan, the management was mainly occupied by British. The hull (Shipbuilding Department) and the machinery (Engine Department) were completely separated. From the raw record in Wang Pingxuan's interview, Wang Pingxuan might not be able to know the true situation and details of the design source of the 10 000-ton American steam freighters.

那么王平轩所说的万吨级运输舰的"一部分"设计图纸到底来自何方？作者分析有以下五种假定的来源：

So who provided Wang's mentioned "a smaller part of the drawings"? The source might be presumed in following five possibilities:

1	应急船队公司提供的设计？ Emergency Fleet Corporation provided the design?
2	美国船厂提供的设计？ American shipyard provided the design?
3	由美国船厂开发的基于"模块化设计"（modular design）组装船（pre-fabricated ships）的标准设计？ American shipyard developed "pre-fabricated ship" based on the "modular design"?
4	江南造船所自己的设计？ Kiangnan Dock & Engineering Works designed by themselves?
5	江南造船所基于类似母型船的改型设计？ Kiangnan Dock & Engineering Works designed based on modifying a prototype ship?

作者根据查到的公开资料和这四艘运输舰的图纸资料，对上述五种可能性进行逐一分析。

Based on the public information and the drawings of the four American steam freighters, personally, these five possibilities can be screened one by one.

首先，还得从美国应急船队公司的成立背景说起。根据网络上可查阅到的公开资料，应急船队公司的成立是基于以下背景：

First of all, the investigation should be started from the background of the establishment of the Emergency Fleet Corporation. According to the public information on the English version Wikipedia website, the EFC was established based on the following background:

1916 年 9 月，美国国会通过了《海上运输法案》，该法案促使美国于 1917 年 1 月 30 日成立了美国海运委员会。1917 年 4 月 6 日，美国对德国宣战，10 天后，在美国海运委员会的组织下成立了应急船队公司，旨在快速调集和协调建造船舶以满足战争物资运输的需要。虽然这是一个政府战时的协调机构，但应急船队公司对其管理的每一种船型设计图进行了编号，以便查阅和管理。

In September of 1916, the United States Congress passed the *Shipping Act 39, Stat. 729*, which directly led to the establishment of the United States Shipping Board on 30 January 1917. On 6 April 1917, the United States declared war on Germany. Ten days later, the EFC was established under the Shipping Board to quickly mobilize and coordinate the ships' construction to meet the needs of war supplies transportation. It was a coordinating institution for the government during wartime, and EFC intentionally assigned a code to each design for easy identification and management.

作者从 www.shipscribe.com 网站上查到了澳大利亚历史学家诺曼·L. 麦凯勒对美国应急船队公司所有船型（1917—1921 年）的描述，船舶的照片和简要的总布置图如表 5-1 所示（表中的缩写：SB= Shipbuilding，DSN= design）。

There are some ship photos and brief layouts of ships on the website (www.shipscribe.com) of the Australian historian Norman L. McKellar, and all EFC coded ships were listed in a tabular sheet named "Steel Shipbuilding under the U.S. Shipping Board, 1917–1921", and photos of the ship are shown in Table 5–1 (abbreviations in the table: SB=Shipbuilding, DSN=design).

表5-1 应急船队公司船型设计图列表和简述（仅列出钢质船舶）[6]
Table 5-1 List of EFC designs with descriptions (steel hull only)

Design	Material	Ship type	DWT	LOA	Descriptions
1012	Steel	Cargo	6 000	346.5	MERRILL STEVENS SB CORP DSN. (MUNRIO TYPE)
1013	Steel	Cargo	8 800	423.8	SKINNER & EDDY CORP DSN. (ROBERT DOLLAR TYPE)
1014	Steel	Cargo	7 500	396	SEATTLE CONST & DD CO DSN. (CASCADE TYPE)
1015	Steel	Cargo	9 400	416	MOORE SB CO DSN. (1015R = REFRIGERATED VARIANT)
1016	Steel	Cargo	8 800	423.8	BALTIMORE DD & SB CO DSN.
1017	Steel	Cargo	7 500	395.5	DOWNEY SB CORP DSN.
1018	Steel	Cargo	10 000	450	SUN SB CO DSN.
1019	Steel	Cargo	8 800	427	STANDARD DSN., FERRIS
1020	Steel	Cargo	3 550	261	STANDARD LAKE "A" DSN.
1021	Steel	Cargo	6 000	354.5	LONG BEACH SB CO DSN.
1022	Steel	Cargo	7 500	401	STANDARD FABRICATED TYPE "A" (HOG ISLAND)
1023	Steel	Cargo	5 075	335.5	STANDARD FABRICATED (SUBMARINE BOAT CORP)
1024	Steel	Trnsp.	8 000	448	STANDARD FABRICATED TYPE "B" (TROOPSHIP) (HOG ISLAND)
1025	Steel	Cargo	9 000	415	STANDARD FABRICATED, HARRIMAN TYPE (MERCHANT SB CORP)
1026	Steel	Cargo	7 300	385	STANDARD, FERRIS
1027	Steel	Cargo	9 500	416	STANDARD DSN. (OSCAR DANIELS SB CO)
1028	Steel	Cargo	7 500	389	WHITTLESAY PANEL DESIGN
1029	Steel	Trnsp.	13 000	535	STANDARD PASS. & CARGO (ORIG. TROOPSHIP)
1030	Steel	Tanker	10 000	444	STANDARD. SEE T1059, DESIGN NOT ORDERED
1031	Steel	Tanker	7 500	405	STANDARD TANKSHIP (BETHLEHEM SB CORP DSN.)
1032	Steel	Cargo	12 000	457	STANDARD CARGO (BETHLEHEM SB CORP DSN). ALSO TROOPSHIP, 1032-T
1033	Steel	Cargo	5 650	387.3	STANDARD. LAKER, SPLICED, DESIGN NOT ORDERED
1034	Steel	Cargo	6 000	448	REFRIG., TO T1015 REFRIG. VARIANT, DESIGN NOT ORDERED
1035	Steel	Tug-at	—	150	STANDARD 150' STEEL OCEAN TUG
1036	Steel	Tug-yt	—	100.2	STANDARD 100' STEEL HARBOR TUG
1037	Steel	Cargo	9 600	410.3	FEDERAL SB CO DSN.
1038	Steel	Cargo	5 000	335.5	JAHNCKE (LATER MOBILE) SB CO DSN.
1039	Steel	Barge	7 500	352	PANAMA CANAL COAL BARGE: ALABAMA DD & SB DSN.
1041	Steel	Tanker	10 000	425	MOORE SB CO DSN. (LENGTH IS PP)
1042	Steel	Cargo	3 350	261	STANDARD LAKE "B" DSN.
1043	Steel	Cargo	5 350	320.8	HANLON DD & SB DSN. (LENGTH IS PP). ALSO 1043-B.
1044	Steel	Cargo	3 400	261.3	MANITOWOC SB CO DSN.
1045	Steel	Tanker	9 100	431.8	BETHLEHEM SB CORP DSN.
1046	Steel	Cargo	7 400	391.8	BETHLEHEM SB CORP DSN.
1047	Steel	Tanker	10 100	435	BETHLEHEM SB CORP DSN. (LENGTH IS PP)

（续表）
(continued)

Design	Material	Ship type	DWT	LOA	Descriptions
1049	Steel	Cargo	3 700	300	ALBINA ENGINE & MACHINE WKS. DSN.
1050	Steel	Cargo	5 000	344.8	STANDARD, STRAIGHT FRAME T1023, DESIGN NOT ORDERED
1057	Steel	Cargo	11 800	427	BETHLEHEM SB CORP DSN. T1057A=11 800T, T1057B=11 700T
1058	Steel	Tanker	6 000	354.5	BALTIMORE DD & SB CO DSN.
1059	Steel	Tanker	10 300	430	BALTIMORE DD & SB CO DSN. MOD T1030
1060	Steel	Cargo	4 200	261	GREAT LAKES ENGINEERING WKS. DSN.
1063	Steel	Cargo	7 433	392.5	STANDARD SB CORP DSN.
1064	Steel	Barge	—	300	STATEN IS DSN OIL BARGE, DESIGN NOT ORDERED (LENGTH IS PP)
1066	Steel	Cargo	8 800	423.8	J.F. DUTHIE & CO DSN. (MOD T1013)
1073	Steel	Cargo	4 300	284.5	CONVERTED COMP
1074	Steel	Cargo	4 050	261	GREAT LAKES ENGINEERING WKS. DSN.
1077	Steel	Barge	5 000	372.8	TOWNSEND+DOWNEY, DESIGN NOT ORDERED
1078	Steel	Cargo	8 725	401	(LENGTH IS PP)
1079	Steel	Cargo	9 600	423.8	SKINNER & EDDY CORP DSN. (MOD T1013)
1080	Steel	Cargo	8 800	426	AMES SB & DD DSN.
1092	Steel	Cargo	10 000	443	KIANGNAN DOCK & ENGR. WKS. DSN.
1093	Steel	Cargo	4 200	361	AMERICAN SB CO DSN.
1094	Steel	Cargo	5 100	339	BETHLEHEM SB CORP DSN.
1095	Steel	Trnsp.	12 000	502	PASSENGER & CARGO (ORIG TROOPER), NEW YORK SB CORP.
1096	Steel	Barge	1 800	206	OIL BARGE (600 000 GAL.), NASHVILLE BRIDGE CO DSN.
1097	Steel	Cargo	3 200	260.8	LONG BEACH SB CO DSN.
1099	Steel	Cargo	4 050	261	AMERICAN SB CO DSN.
1103	Steel	Cargo	11 750	419.5	(LENGTH PP)
1105	Steel	Cargo	9 500	415.9	SKINNER & EDDY CORP DSN. (EDITOR TYPE)
1106	Steel	Tanker	11 375	477.8	NEWPORT NEWS SB & DD CO DSN.
1118	Steel	Cargo	5 500	330.3	JAPANESE 5 500T (LENGTH PP)
1119	Steel	Cargo	6 300	357	JAPANESE 6 300T
1105	Steel	Cargo	9 500	415.9	SKINNER & EDDY CORP DSN. (EDITOR TYPE)
1106	Steel	Tanker	11 375	477.8	NEWPORT NEWS SB & DD CO DSN.
1118	Steel	Cargo	5 500	330.3	JAPANESE 5 500T (LENGTH PP)
1119	Steel	Cargo	6 300	357	JAPANESE 6 300T
1120	Steel	Cargo	10 500	437	JAPANESE 10 500T
1121	Steel	Cargo	5 000	315	JAPANESE 5 000T
1122	Steel	Cargo	9 000	385	JAPANESE 9 000T (LENGTH PP)
1123	Steel	Cargo	5 500	315.9	JAPANESE 5 500T "B" (LENGTH PP)
1124	Steel	Cargo	12 600	461	JAPANESE 12 600T

（续表）
(continued)

Design	Material	Ship type	DWT	LOA	Descriptions
1125	Steel	Cargo	6 650	372	JAPANESE 6 650T
1126	Steel	Cargo	8 360	413	JAPANESE 8 360T
1127	Steel	Cargo	10 000	420	JAPANESE 10 000T
1128	Steel	Tanker	10 000	446	WM. CRAMP & SONS S&EB CO DSN.
1133	Steel	Cargo	11 000	431	TYPE 1013 WITH 2 DECKS AND SHELTER DECK (LENGTH PP)

从表 5-1 所列应急船队公司编号的船型设计图来看，主要有三种船型：一是干杂货船（dry cargo ship），二是油船（tanker），三是运兵船或货船兼运兵船（troopship）。其余是拖轮（tugboat）和驳船（barge）等特殊用途的船舶。所有船型设计图上均注明是哪个船厂提供的图纸，即便标准船型也是如此，有的还明确注明是针对某个特定船东的设计，如 1013 Skinner & Eddy CORP DSN. (Robert Dollar type)。由此可见，应急船队公司并不提供船舶设计。

From the design with the EFC code in Table 5-1, there are mainly three types of ships: dry cargo ship, tanker, troopship and cargo/troop combined ship. Remain is a special-purposed ship such as tugboat and barge. All ship designs are marked with the design provider, even for standard ships. Some designs even specify a particular ship owner, for instance, 1013 Skinner & Eddy Corp DSN. (Robert Dollar type). It could be concluded that EFC did not provide ship design.

在表 5-1 中明确注明了 1092 Kiangnan Dock & ENGR. WKS. DSN，可见，江南造船所建造的四艘万吨级运输舰也不是由某个美国船厂设计的，恰恰是江南造船所自己。

In Table 5-1, it clearly marked 1092 Kiangnan Dock & ENGR. WKS. DSN. It can be seen that the four 10 000-ton steam freighters built by Kiangnan were designed by Kiangnan itself but not an American shipyard and someone else.

此外，从表 5-1 中还可以看出，由美国船厂开发的基于"模块化设计"组装船的标准设计的应急船队公司的编号是 1022~1027、1029~1033 以及 1035~1036 等，可见江南造船所也没有采用这些标准设计。

In addition, from the Table 5-1, American shipyards developed prefabricated ships based on modular design were assigned EFC codes of 1022−1027, 1029−1033 and 1035−1036 and so on. It is also a proof that Kiangnan did not adopt these standard design.

那么这四艘万吨级运输舰采用的是江南造船所自己的设计吗？从美国国家档案馆特别媒体档案服务处收藏的这型船的总布置图中的说明文字（即图 5-1 下面的说明文字"Design No. 1092 for a 10 000 D.W.T. Steel Cargo Ship designed by Kiangnan Dock & Engineering Works, approved 8-1-1921"）来看，前三种假定可以被否定，这型船确实是江南造船所自己设计的。

Then, can it be concluded that the four 10 000-ton American steam freighters were designed by Kiangnan? From the description of the ship's General Arrangement Plan collected by Special Media Archives Service Division (Cartographic Section of the National Archives and Records Administration). Refer to the text description of Figure 5-1, "Design No. 1092 for a 10 000 D.W.T. Steel Cargo Ship designed by Kiangnan Dock & Engineering Works, approved 8-1-1921". All above evidences can prove that the above three assumptions can be denied, and this type of ship was indeed designed by Kiangnan itself.

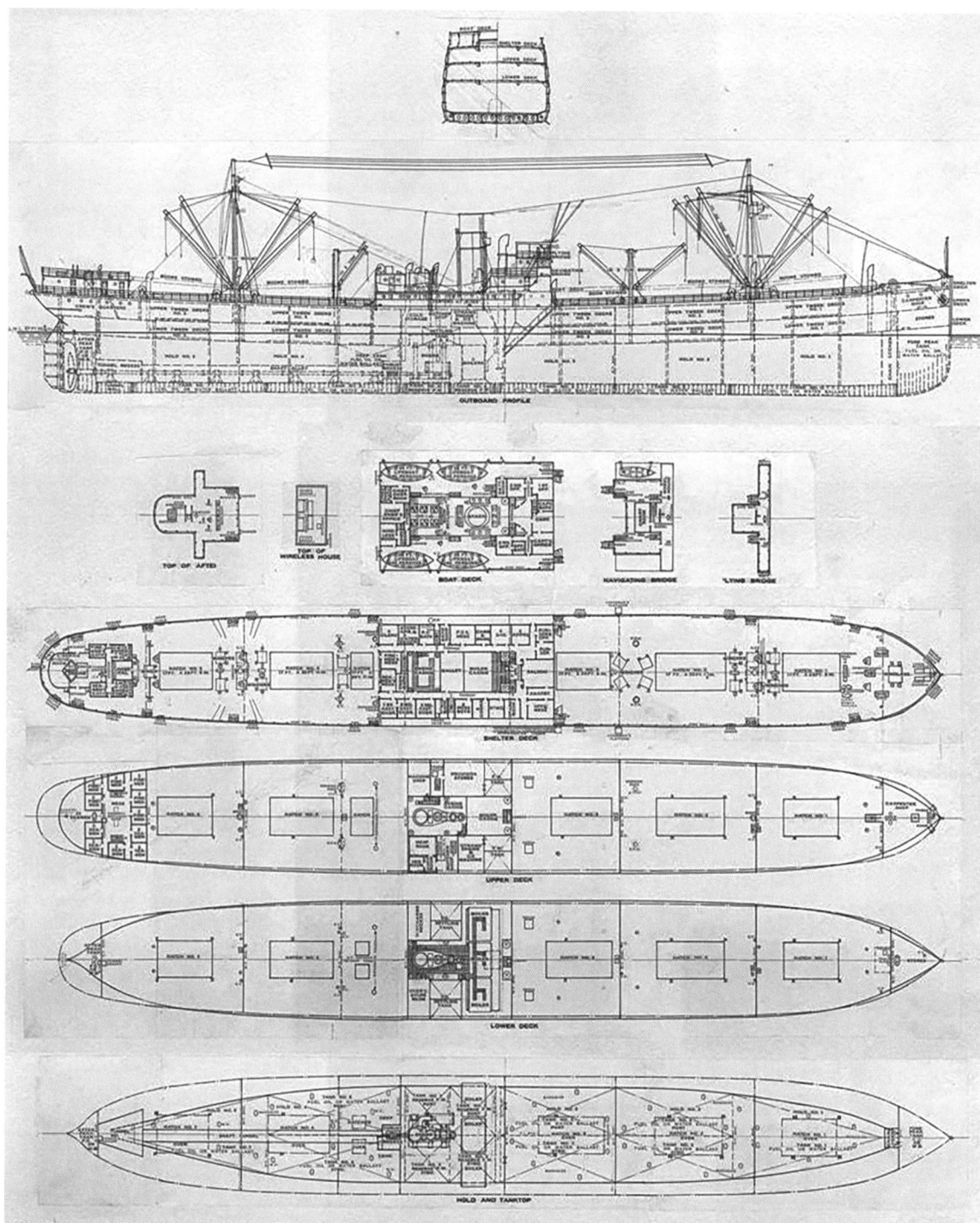

United States Shipping Board – Emergency Fleet Corporation, Records Section, Ship Construction Division, Design No. 1092 for a 10,000 D.W.T. Steel Cargo Ship designed by Kiangnan Dock & Engineering Works, approved 8-1-1921. Plans are a composite created by the editor of this website of two drawings which were paste-ups for publication mounted on cardstock, roughly 19" x 24" each. From the holdings of the Special Media Archives Services Division, Cartographic Section of the National Archives and Records Administration, College Park, Maryland. Records of the United States Shipping Board, Record Group 32, Reference NWCS: 2010M0043KK.

图 5-1　美国国家档案馆收藏的 EFC 1092 总布置图
Figure 5-1　General Arrangement Plan of EFC 1092, Cartographic Section of the National Archives and Records Administration

根据上述说明，EFC 1092 是由两张图纸拼接而成的。作者也查阅了美国国家档案馆的电子档案库中的资料，由于这些资料较老，没有相应的电子版本。作者仔细看了这张图，它是由总布置图和舯横剖面图拼接组合而成的，并对图面上的标注细节和舱室内的详细布置进行了简化。从认可日期 1921 年 8 月 1 日来看，差不多是前两艘船的交付日期，应急船队公司赋予江南造船所建造的四艘船独立的编号正说明江南造船所的设计是有别于其他船型的。从无线电天线的布置来看，这是 7007D 版以前的总布置图，参见本书第 4 章 4.3.14 节"通信导航设备"中的有关描述。

那么是否可以据此断定江南造船所建造的四艘万吨级运输舰完全是由其自己设计的呢？作者认为还不能轻易下这个结论。

第一，应该从船舶设计的特点分析着手。船舶建造通常是单艘或小批量进行的而不是根据一个标准设计大批量生产。一般商船设计采用参考母型船设计后进行修改、改型和优化设计的方式，这样做一方面设计建造的风险比较小，另一方面船舶的设计参数和所需材料的物量比较容易在合同签订之前估算出来，容易控制成本。因此，这种基于母型船的船舶设计方式哪怕到了今天仍然是一种非常普遍的设计手段，通常也称自主设计或自行设计。对母型船进行修改、改型和优化后设计出来的新船通常不存在对某方"知识产权"的侵权。

第二，从当时江南造船所的技术和建造能力来看，并不具备完全从零开始自主设计建造万吨级船舶的能力。当时江南造船所刘冠南所长给赴美代表毛根的委托书中所声明的代表权限也说明："一、该员此次赴美商造船只，按本所力量只能承造五千吨以外一万吨以内轮船二艘。"

第三，大来洋行的老板罗伯特·大来与江南造船所总工程师毛根都是苏格兰人，有很好的私人关系。烟囱上带有巨幅"$"标志的大来洋行的远洋货轮装载着木材、钢铁、矿石、火车机车、煤油、面粉、食品等各种货物往于中国和美国之间，一度成为中美贸易的象征符号。这些船舶驶抵上海时，必定由江南造船所进行维修。通过维修这些船舶，江南造船所也在一定程度上掌握了相应船型的修造技术和图纸资

According to the above description, this illustration was made up of two pieces of drawing. After checking the electronic archives of the National Archives of the United States, since these documents are outdated, there is no corresponding electronic version. This illustration is a combination of the General Arrangement Plan and the Midship Section drawing, and simplifies the marking details on the drawing and the cabin layout. The approved date of 1 August 1921 is close to the date of the first two steamers being delivered. The dedicated code of four steamers which EFC assigned to Kiangnan Dock & Engineering Works indicates that the design of Kiangnan differs from others. By verifying the features of the radio antenna, it can be explicitly determined that the version of General Arrangement Plan is earlier than 7007D, see the description in Section 4.3.14 "Communication Navigation Equipment" in Chapter 4 of this book.

Then, can it be concluded that the four 10 000-ton American steam freighters built by Kiangnan Dock & Engineering Works were completely designed by themselves? It looks still too early.

Firstly, it is necessary to clarify the features of ship design. Shipbuilding is usually "tailor-made" in single or small batches rather than massive production per a standard design. Normally, the design of commercial ship is modified and optimized on basis of the prototype ship. On one hand, the risk of design and construction is comparatively lower; on the other hand, the design parameters of the ship and the quantity of material required are relatively easy to estimate before the contract signing, hence easy to control the cost. Therefore, this kind of prototype-based design method is still widely accepted even in today's modern ship design practice, and is often referred to as "self-design". A new ship, even not entirely novel, but has been significantly modified and optimized from prototype ship, normally will not violate the "intellectual property".

Secondly, in view of the technical and construction capabilities of Kiangnan at that time, it did not have the ability to independently design and build a 10 000-ton vessel from zero. The permission in the power of attorney from Director Liu Guanan to Mauchan also states that: "For the issue of American freighters, Kiangnan only has the ability to build two steam freighters in 5 000 to 10 000 deadweight tons in the parallel."

Thirdly, Robert Dollar, the Chairman of Dollar Company, and Mauchan, the Chief Engineer of Kiangnan Dock & Engineering Works, were both Scottish and had a very good personal relationship. The ocean-going freighters, with big "$" funnel mark, carried timbers, irons, ores, locomotives, kerosene, powder and foods etc. These freighters sailing in the Trans-Pacific routes used to be the symbol of American-Sino trade. When these ships arrived in Shanghai, they always went to Kiangnan for overhauling and repairing. During those repairing and maintenance processes, Kiangnan certainly was aware of the technical drawings and

料。在江南造船所承接应急船队公司的四艘万吨级运输舰之前，大来洋行下属的航运公司的船舶已经纳入了应急船队公司的船队序列（如 EFC Design 1013）。大来航运公司对中美 / 太平洋航线上航运的实际需求和船舶的配置十分清楚，大来洋行手中拥有其在航和在建船舶的完整图纸资料。

第四，也是最重要的，罗伯特·大来和美国海运委员会的主席爱德华·N. 赫尔利的关系十分密切。罗伯特·大来向赫尔利推荐了毛根。后来，赫尔利在他的回忆录 The Bridge to France 中高度评价了毛根[7]。

基于上述各方之间的密切关系，作者从一个船舶设计者的角度有把握地做出如此推断：

前文五种假定中第五种假定的可能性最大，即大来航运公司给了毛根[8] 他们船队中 EFC Design 1013型船的部分图纸和技术资料，江南造船所当时以英国人为主的设计团队以此型船舶作为母型船进行了修改设计以满足应急船队公司的最新要求，同时又不超过江南造船所刘冠南所长设定的载重量上限（10 000吨）。江南造船所在以大来航运公司 EFC Design 1013型船的部分图纸作为参考的基础上，绘制了合同技术附件中最主要的两份图纸：总布置图和舯横剖面图，并把这两份图纸作为合同附件，有效保证了合同的签订。

根据上述分析思路，作者从 www.shipscribe.com 网站上查到了两艘 EFC Design 1013 船[9] 的相关信息。

第一艘船 "West Galoc" 号：

"West Galoc" 号 (Design 1013) 由洛杉矶造船和船坞公司建造并完工于 1918 年 8 月。该型船配置有许多战时装备，拥有战时运输船舶的特征，例如采用单柱式的起重桅代替传统的双柱式起重桅，其目的是减小被潜艇发现的概率。图 5−2 为低速航行中的 "West Galoc" 号 (Design 1013)(NHC: 19−N−14747)，照片来自 www.shipscribe.com 网站。

familiarized equipments and workmanship. Prior to Kiangnan secured order of EFC's four 10 000-ton steam freighters, the ships of Dollar Steamship Company had already been requisitioned and listed in the EFC's fleet sequence (for example, EFC Design 1013). Dollar Steamship Company knew more about the actual demands for the Trans-Pacific routes and the required specification of the ship. Dollar Company had the completed set of drawings and documents of their ships both under construction and in operation.

Fourthly, and most importantly, Robert Dollar had a very close relationship with Edward N. Hurley, Chairman of the United States Shipping Board. Robert Dollar recommended Mauchan to Hurley. Later, Hurley wrote highly comments to Mauchan in his memoir *The Bridge to France*.

Based on the aforementioned various close relationships, personally an assumption can be confidently concluded in viewpoint of a ship designer:

The fifth assumption has the biggest probability, i.e., Dollar Steamship Company provided Mauchan a part of the drawings and technical documents of the EFC Design 1013 in their fleet. Kiangnan's British-leaded design team modified the design based on EFC Design 1013 to meet the latest requirements of the EFC. Meanwhile the deadweight was maintained not exceeding the upper limit of 10 000 tons set by Director Liu Guannan. Kiangnan made the two most important drawings as contract technical attachments on basis of EFC Design 1013: the General Arrangement Plan and the Midship Section drawings. These two drawings were signed as the technical attachments of the shipbuilding contract.

Based on the above analysis, the related information of two EFC Design 1013 ships was found from www.shipscribe.com.

The first ship SS "West Galoc":

SS "West Galoc" (Design 1013) around the time of her completion in August 1918 by the Los Angeles S.B. & D.D. Co. This ship has the special rig fitted to many war-built ships in which the two topmasts on the masts were replaced by a single topmast stepped near the stack (in this case on a king post). The change supposedly made it harder for a submarine to get a torpedo firing solution. Figure 5−2 is a photo showing SS "West Galoc" (Design 1013) sailing in slow steaming (NHC: 19−N−14747), source from www. shipscribe.com.

图 5-2 正低速航行中的 "West Galoc" 号 (Design 1013)
Figure 5-2 SS "West Galoc" (Design 1013) was sailing in slow steaming

第二艘船 "West Erral" 号：

"West Erral" 号 (Design 1013) 的照片由其建造方洛杉矶造船和船坞公司拍摄，该船完工于 1919 年 2 月。鉴于第一次世界大战已经结束，许多战时装备(如艏部的炮台等) 已经不需要了，但起重桅仍然沿用单柱式的设计。图 5-3 为 "West Erral" 号 (Design 1013) 完工后停泊在洛杉矶造船和船坞公司的照片 (NARA：RG-32-S)。与 "West Galoc" 号相比，"West Erral" 号的一个明显变化是在前后起重桅的顶部增加了天线桅，以便布置无线电通信天线。而 "West Galoc" 号的天线桅仅有一个，布置在舯部左舷的起重柱上。

The second ship SS "West Erral":

SS "West Erral" (Design 1013) photographed by her builder, the Los Angeles S.B. & D.D. Co., upon completion in February 1919. The special wartime rig was no longer necessary and she and other postwar ships were completed with topmasts on each of her two single masts. Figure 5-3 is a photo showing SS "West Erral" (Design 1013) moored at quay of the Los Angeles S.B. & D.D. Co. (NARA: RG-32-S). Comparing with SS "West Galoc", an obvious change of SS "West Erral" was supplemental antennas on fore and aft derrick posts respectively for radio communication, but SS "West Galoc" had only one antenna at portside post amidship.

图 5-3　"West Erral" 号 (Design 1013) 完工后停泊在洛杉矶造船和船坞公司
Figure 5-3　SS "West Erral" (Design 1013) moored at quay of the Los Angeles S.B. & D.D. Co.

关于 EFC Design 1013- 大来船型[10]，作者在www.shipscribe.com 网站上查到了澳大利亚历史学家诺曼·L. 麦凯勒对它们主要特征的描述（见图 5-4）和船型的简要总布置图（见图 5-5）。

About EFC Design 1013-Robert Dollar type, the description by Australian historian Norman L. McKellar (see Figure 5-4) and a brief General Arrangement Plan (see Figure 5-5) can be found from www.shipscribe.com.

DESIGN 1013 - "ROBERT DOLLAR" type. 8800 tons dwt., standard dimensions 410.5 x 54 x 30. Some turbines, some triple expansion; some oil fuel, some coal. Contracts as listed under individual yards. TOTAL OUTPUT 111 - comprising 106 delivered to USSB and 5 cancelled ships later completed by yards for other account.

图 5-4　EFC Design 1013- 大来船型的主要特征说明
Figure 5-4　Main particulars of EFC Design 1013 -Robert Dollar type

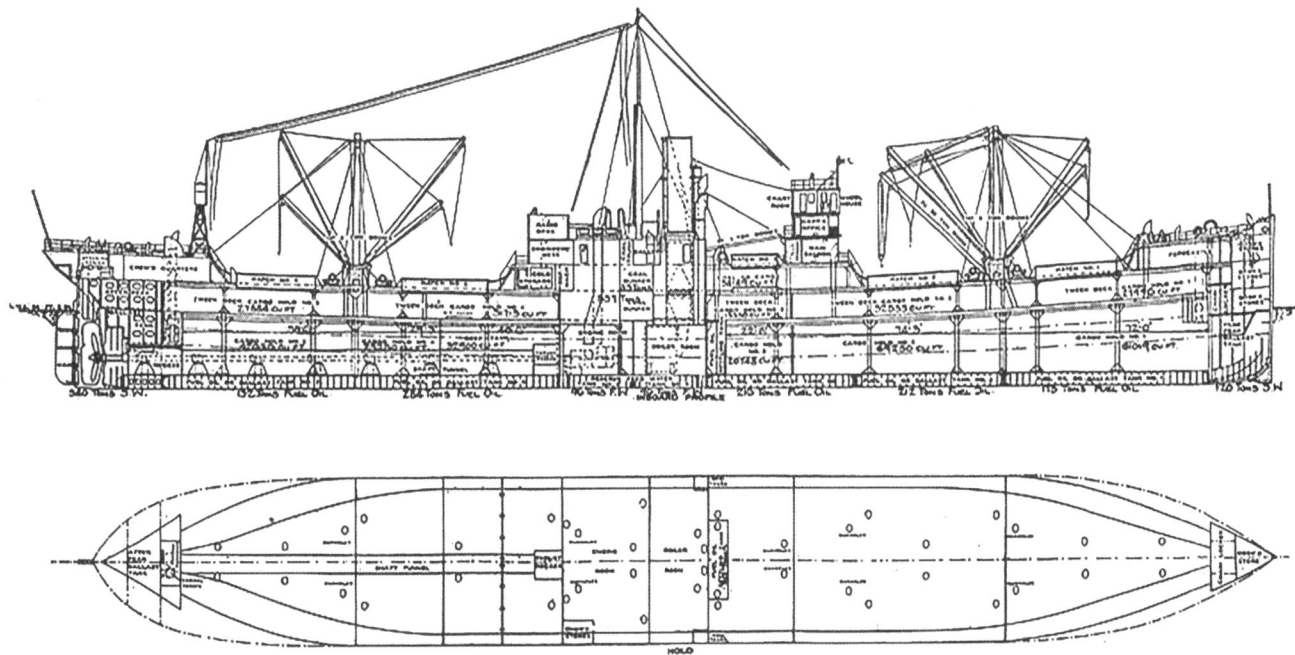

图 5-5　EFC Design 1013- 大来船型的简要总布置图
Figure 5-5　Outline General Arrangement Plan of EFC Design 1013 −Robert Dollar type

EFC Design 1013 为 8 800 载重吨的运输船，船长 410.5 英尺（125.12 米）、船宽 54 英尺（16.46 米）、型深 30 英尺（9.14 米）。该型船一共订了 111 艘，分别在五家船厂建造，一共交付了 106 艘，5 艘取消的订单后来也建造了，但没有列入应急船队公司的序列号里面。该型船主机有采用蒸汽轮机的，也有采用三联立式往复式蒸汽机的；锅炉有烧煤的，也有烧燃油的。尽管这些船都采用了相同的设计编号 EFC Design 1013，但在布置和配置的细节上还是有一定差异的。图 5-5 所示的总布置简图是 Skinner & Eddy 公司设计的，此外，从上层建筑后的深舱的布置位置来看，这是一种燃煤锅炉燃料舱的常规总布置设计。

从该型船的总布置图来看，该型船设计为垂直型船首、巡洋舰型艉、带有艏楼、封闭式艉柱、舯机型船型，上层建筑和居住舱室布置在舯部。

主船体内设双层底（double bottom）、二层甲板：下甲板和上甲板（lower and upper decks）、七道水密舱壁（water tight bulkhead）；机炉舱（engine and boiler room）双层底内设锅炉水舱（feed water tank）；

The EFC Design 1013 was a freighter with deadweight of 8 800 tons, length of 410.5 feet (125.12 meters), width of 54 feet (16.46 meters), and depth of 30 feet (9.14 meters). This type of design had a total order of 111 vessels. Totally 106 ships were built and delivered at five shipyards. The five cancelled orders were later built, but not included in the EFC sequence. The main engines of these ships were steam turbines and triple vertical reciprocating steam engines; the boilers of these ships were either coal burning or oil burning. Although they all coded the same design number of EFC Design 1013, there were some differences in the details of the arrangement and equipment. The above General Arrangement Plan (see Figure 5–5) was the design from Skinner & Eddy Company. In addition, from the position of the deep tank after the superstructure, this was a conventional fuel tank layout for a coal fueled boiler.

From the General Arrangement Plan of the ship, the ship was designed with a vertical stem, cruiser stern, with a forecastle, a closed stern frame, and engine room were located amidship. The superstructure and living accommodation were arranged amidship.

The main hull was designed with a double bottom, two decks, lower and upper decks, seven water tight bulkheads; there was a boiler feed water tank in the double bottom of engine and boiler rooms; main hull was divided into a forepeak tank and four cargo holds which were separated into fore two and aft two respectively. A deep tank located

主船体内部设艏尖舱（forepeak tank），四个货舱（cargo hold）分为前后二二设置，位于前上层建筑后的深舱，并配置了一对吊杆，这个深舱的上部应该是燃煤舱，下部则连着前面的货舱。艏部设置了一个机炉舱。艏桥楼前部设置了三层有甲板室及主辅驾驶室、机舱棚（engine casing）和烟囱；艉楼上甲板设置了船员舱室和舵机房，下部为艉尖舱（aft peak tank）。

艉部配置了一具非平衡舵（平板式结构）、单个四叶螺旋桨，甲板上配置了吊杆式起重设备。货舱内各层甲板设置了舱口盖。

机炉舱内设三台烟管锅炉（smoke boiler）和一台三缸立式往复式蒸汽机或蒸汽轮机，通过布置在后半船体底部轴隧内的轴系驱动一具四叶螺旋桨。

同样在网站 www.shipscribe.com 上，作者查到了澳大利亚历史学家诺曼·L. 麦凯勒上传的关于 EFC Design 1027 的主要特征的说明（见图 5-6）和 EFC Design 1027 的简要总布置图（见图 5-7）。

after forward superstructure and equipped with a pair of derricks. The upper part of this deep tank should be a coal storage space and the lower part was connected to the forward cargo hold. The engine and boiler rooms were located in the midship. Three-tier accommodation quarter, wheelhouse, engine casing and funnel was located in front part of the midship bridge. Crew cabin and steering gear room were arranged on the stern upper deck, and aft peak tank was arranged under the upper deck.

The stern part was equipped with an unbalanced rudder (flat structure), single four-blade propeller, and derrick type lifting device installed on deck. Hatch covers were provided on all decks including those inside cargo holds.

There were three smoke boilers and a triple-cylinder vertical reciprocating steam engine or steam turbine in engine and boiler rooms, and a four-blade propeller was driven by the shaft in tunnel of the bottom.

Moreover, on the website of www.shipscribe.com, the Australian historian Norman L. McKellar uploaded a description of EFC Design 1027 (see Figure 5–6) and a brief General Arrangement Plan of EFC Design 1027 (see Figure 5–7).

DESIGN 1027, STANDARD CARGO, "OSCAR DANIELS" type. 9500 tons dwt., standard dimensions 402 x 54 x 34.4. Triple expansion engines, oil fuel. TOTAL OUTPUT 10 ships, all built by OSCAR DANIELS SHIPBUILDING CO., TAMPA, Fla, who had contracts for EFC hulls 739-748. No cancellations.

YOMACHICHI, yard no 1, compl 1919 as O/N 219052. (USSB 19-   )/ OCELOT (US Navy, as IX 110, from -45)/ Wrecked Okinawa 9.10.1945; floated 1948,BU Shanghai.

图 5-6　EFC Design 1027 的主要特征说明
Figure 5-6　Main particulars of EFC Design 1027

这型船的总布置和 EFC Design 1013 型的比较相似，其货舱分隔、甲板的层数和机炉舱的布置都基本相同，说明它是一型标准设计。但与 EFC Design 1013 相比，该型船的船长［402 英尺（122.53 米）］较短，船宽（54 英尺）相同，型深［34.4 英尺（10.49 米）］较大，相应的吃水和载重量均较大，达到了 9 500 吨。该型船按计划总共建造了 10 艘，全部由美国佛罗里达州坦帕市的 Oscar Daniels 造船公司建造，首制船于 1919 年完工。

The layout of this type ship was quite similar to that of EFC Design 1013. The cargo hold division, the quantity of decks and the layout of the engine and boiler rooms were basically the identical. It most properly was a standard design. Comparing EFC Design 1013, the length of 402 feet (122.53 meters) was shorter, the width of 54 feet was the same, and the depth of 34.4 feet (10.49 meters) was deeper. Since the draught was much deeper, the corresponding deadweight was larger, and reached 9 500 tons. A total of 10 ships were built and no one was cancelled, all of them built by the Oscar Daniels Shipyard in Tampa, Florida, the United States. The first ship was completed in 1919.

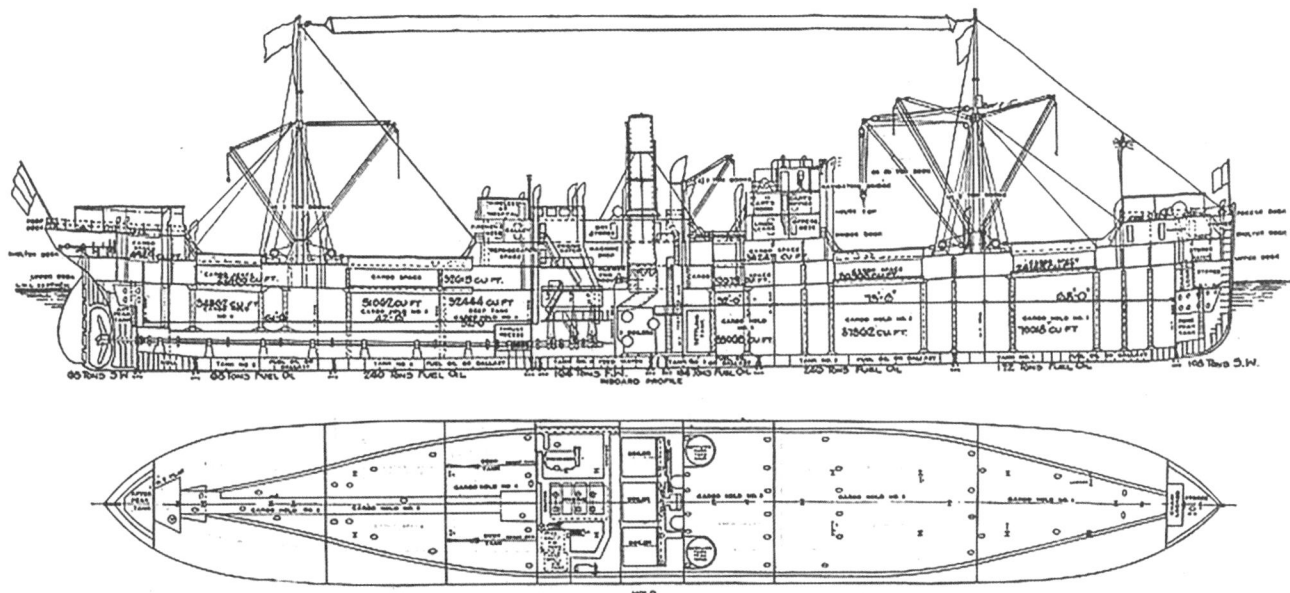

图 5-7 EFC Design 1027 的简要总布置图
Figure 5-7 Outline General Arrangement Plan of EFC Design 1027

　　这两型船的共同点是在驾驶台后部布置了一个深舱，并配置了一对吊杆，这个深舱在常规设计中上部应该是燃煤舱。深舱内设有中间甲板，如果航程短的话，只需在深舱上部装燃煤，中间甲板上还可以装货。在平面图上该型船锅炉舱前部的深舱里布置了两个圆柱形的罐子，这和江南造船所四艘万吨级运输舰合同上的总布置图的修改版一样是淡水舱，不同的是它是垂直布置的，而江南造船所的是水平布置的。此时看说明中该型船是燃油动力型的说法，显然是错误的，也许该型船是一型煤油混合动力型船舶。

　　EFC Design 1027 的天线桅设计与 "West Erral" 号的非常相似，前后起重桅上各配置了一个天线桅，两个天线桅之间架起了无线电通信天线。

　　在船舶档案馆查到的资料中，有当时（日期为 1918 年 7 月 18 日）的签字总布置图和舯横剖面图，参见本书第 2 章的图 2-11 和图 2-12。这两张图的右下角有美国海运委员会秘书博尔内和江南造船所总工程师毛根两人的签名，这两张图应该是造船合同的技术附件。图上的主尺度 [除了两柱间长短了 4 英尺（1.22 米）] 与最后完工图的主尺度是一致的。

The common feature of these two types was that a deep tank was arranged behind the bridge, and a pair of derricks was provided accordingly. The upper part of the deep tank was a coal storage space as per normal practice. The deep tank typically had an intermediate deck. Coal was able to be merely stored in the upper part of the deep tank for shorter voyage, and the space below intermediate deck can still carry cargo. In the horizontal deck view, two cylindrical drums for storing fresh water were arranged inside the deep tank in the front of the boiler room. Such layout was similar to attachment of the Kiangnan's contract. Only minor deviation was that the installing direction was vertical while that of Kiangnan's is horizontal. In the description, oil fueled ship seems an obvious mistake. Perhaps it is a coal/oil dual-fueled type? This possibility might be true at that time.

The antenna mast arrangement of the EFC Design 1027 was very similar to that of the SS "West Erral". An antenna mast each was fitted on top of the fore and aft posts, and a radio communication wires were laid in between the two masts.

Among the materials discovered in the Archives of CSSC, there are two signed General Arrangement Plan and Midship Section (refer to Figures 2–11 and 2–12 in Chapter 2). There were the signatures of S.N. Bourne, Secretary of the Shipping Board and R. B. Mauchan, Chief Engineer of Kiangnan on these two drawings. The drawings should be Technical Attachments of the shipbuilding contracts. The main dimensions on the drawing [except the length between perpendiculars was 4 feet (1.22 meters) shorter] were exactly the same as the final data on as built drawings.

从江南造船所的这张总布置图来看，与 EFC 1013 船型相比，除了为满足 10 000 吨载重量，主尺度有所增加之外，机炉舱和上层建筑的格局与 EFC 1013 船型是类似的，深舱的布置位置也相同。从深舱的布置位置来看，这型船的初步设计是采用燃煤锅炉。最大的不同点是在主甲板上增加了一层遮蔽甲板，将艉楼甲板和艏楼甲板连成一体。这张总布置图画得比较粗糙，只是大致地定义了甲板、分舱和上层建筑的布置方式，与最后的详细完工总布置图形成了鲜明的对比。如果采用现有的设计应该是比较详细的，因此从这一点来看，这张总布置图是匆忙中临时绘制的。图 5-8 为签字版总布置图的标题栏。

On this General Arrangement Plan, comparing with the EFC 1013 design, except the lengthening hull length to meet the 10 000 deadweight tons, the layout of engine and boiler rooms and superstructure look similar to those of the EFC 1013. The outline of deep tank is also the same. From the location of the deep tank, the preliminary design was with a coal fired boiler. The biggest difference is that a shelter deck is added above the main deck, connecting the poop deck and the forecastle deck. This General Arrangement Plan seems not detailed, and only roughly defined the boundaries of decks, sub-division and superstructure. It was much less detailed than final as built General Arrangement Plan. In case of existing drawing utilized, it should have more details. From this point, it can also be believed that the General Arrangement Plan most properly was drawn in a hurry. Figure 5-8 shows the drawing title of the General Arrangement Plan with the signatures.

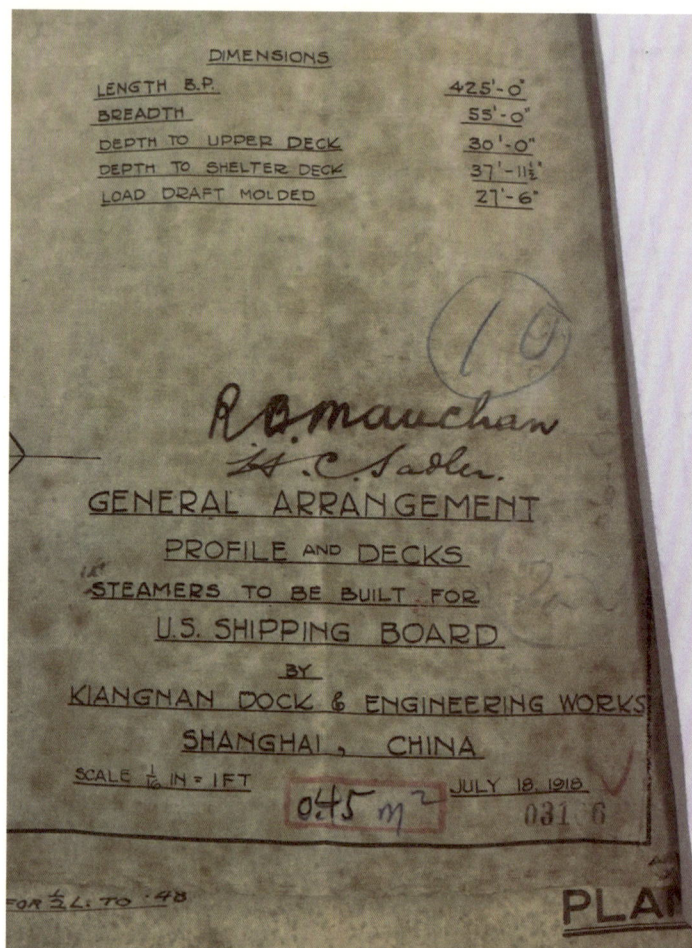

图 5-8　签字版总布置图的标题栏
Figure 5-8　Drawing title of signed General Arrangement Plan

从现有可查到的资料中无法判断毛根赴美洽谈四艘美国运输舰时是否有技术人员随行？但从合同中的总布置图的内容和手写标注[11]等迹象来看，这张图很有可能是毛根（和其随行人员？）抵达美国首都华盛顿后绘制的。

From the available information, it is impossible to judge whether Mauchan went to the United States to discuss the four American steam freighters with any Kiangnan's technicians together. But from the signatures of the contents of the drawings and handwritten notes etc., this General Arrangement Plan was probably drawn by Mauchan (and/or his followers?) after he arrived in Washington.

与简略的总布置图形成鲜明对比的是，该型船的横剖面图绘制得非常详细，正如本书第 2 章分析得出的结论：这两张图，总布置图是在毛根一行到达美国后几天内在一张类似母型船的纵中剖面结构图上赶工修改绘制出来作为造船合同技术附件的，同时根据应急船队公司提出的最新要求增加了一层遮蔽甲板。舯横剖面图则可能是借用了其他在制船的图纸。

In obvious contrast to the brief General Arrangement Plan, the Midship Section has much more details. As the conclusion in Chapter 2, these two drawings were drawn within a few days while Mauchan's team was staying in the United States. The General Arrangement Plan was amended based on the structural profile and decks of the similar ship, and the shelter deck was supplemented accordingly (the latest requirements from the Emergency Fleet Corporation). The Midship Section properly utilized a drawing of existing ship. Both drawings were accompanied with the shipbuilding contract as the Technical Attachments.

可以肯定的是，1918 年 7 月 25 日造船合同签订以后，毛根一行并没有马上离开美国，而是利用在美逗留期间，进一步了解美方对船舶设计的需求并细化图纸，即总布置图的修改版（1918 年 8 月 8 日）。

It can be confirmed that Mauchan and his followers did not immediately leave the United States after signing the shipbuilding contract on 25 July 1918. Instead, they continuously understood the requirement of the United States Shipping Board and further added more details on the drawings within their staying in the United States, i.e., the updated version of the General Arrangement Plan dated 8 August 1918.

在《江南造船所纪要》中有这样一段记载：“江南造船所的总工程师毛根遂于 5 月 9 日启程赴美接洽。7 月，毛根由美来电报告商订万吨级运输舰四艘，请赶紧筹备绘图一切。10 月回国报告经过情形，并呈交原定英文合同。”这里所谓的“绘图”应该理解为“船舶设计”而不是简单的“制图”。

In the *Summary of Kiangnan Dock & Engineering Works*, there is such a description: “Robert Buchanan Mauchan, the Chief Engineer of Kiangnan Dock & Engineering Work, started his trip to the United States on the 9th of May. In July, Mauchan telegraphed Kiangnan that the Shipping Board intended to order four 10 000-ton transportation steamers, and asked Kiangnan immediately to prepare relevant drawings and documentation. He returned to China in October and submitted original English contract.” The “drawings” specified here should mean the ship design but not simple drawing.

1918 年 7 月 16 日的上海《申报》第三版刊登的《再志江南造船所之魄力》一文中也提到“依照该所人员自制之图式起造”。图 5-9 为上海图书馆馆藏的 1918 年 7 月 16 日的《申报》第三版（电子版）。

On 16 July 1918, Page 3 of the *Shanghai Daily* published in Shanghai reads, “Restoring Kiangnan’s Courage”. It also mentioned that “(the ship) will be built in accordance with self-designed drawings”. Figure 5–9 is the Page 3 of the *Shanghai Daily* published on 16 July 1918 (electronic version) kept in the Shanghai Library.

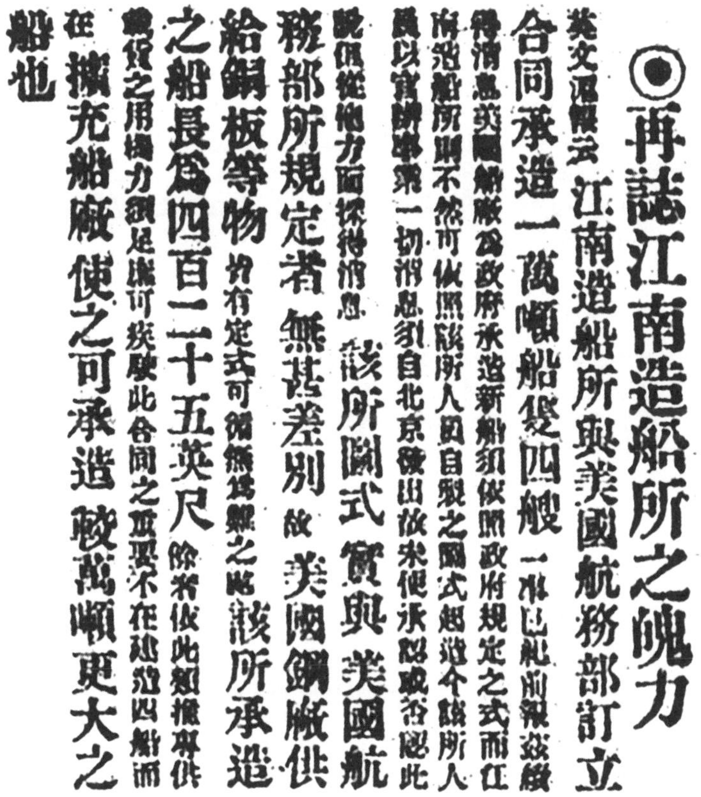
◉再誌江南造船所之魄力
美文滙報云 江南造船所與美國航務部訂立合同承造一萬噸船隻四艘 一節已紀前報茲據得消息英國船廠爲政府承造新船須依照政府規定之式而江南造船所則不然可依照該所人員自製之圖式起造今該所人員以實驗學第一切消息須自北京發出故未便承認或否認此說但從他方面探得消息 該所圖式 實與 美國航務部所規定者 無甚差別 故 美國鋼廠供給鋼板等物 均有定式可照無甚錯誤之慮 該所承造之船長爲四百二十五英尺 除將依此類推專供運貨之用機力須足駛行疾駛此合同之頂要不在建造四船而在 擴充船廠 使之可承造 較萬噸更大之船也

图 5-9 1918 年 7 月 16 日《申报》的报道
Figure 5–9 The report of *Shanghai Daily* 16 July 1918

作者在船舶档案馆查到的江南造船所建造的四艘美国万吨级运输舰（船体号：H317~H320）的图纸资料还有总体、结构、舾装和舱室等共计 81 份以及部分轮机的图纸。作者同时查阅了船舶档案馆和江南造船集团档案馆所保存的相同时期的其他船型的图纸，比对了制图风格、写字模板、日期的标注等细节，发现两者是非常相似的。结合前面的分析，作者认为可以得出的初步结论是：在合同签订后，四艘美国万吨级运输舰的设计图纸是江南造船所的技术人员自主设计完成的。

作者还在 www.shipscribe.com 网站上查到了澳大利亚历史学家诺曼·L.麦凯勒上传的关于 EFC Design 1133 的主要特征说明，如图 5-10 所示。

Totally, 81 pieces of drawing of the four 10 000-ton American steam freighters (hull number: H317—H320) were discovered in the Archives of CSSC (known as former Sixth Machinery Industry Department, No.76 Institute), including general, structure, outfitting and accommodation parts, as well as small fraction of the machinery. Comparing the contemporaneous drawings in the Archives of CSSC and Archives Institute of Jiangnan Shipyard Group, the drawing style, writing template and date marking are more comparable. Further thinking about the previous investigation, preliminary conclusion can be made: After the contract signing, the design of the four 10 000-ton American steam freighters were independently carried out by the engineers of Kiangnan Dock & Engineering Works.

On the website www.shipscribe.com, the Australian historian Norman L. McKellar uploaded a description about the EFC Design 1133, see Figure 5-10.

DESIGN 1133 - STEEL CARGO, LOS ANGELES SPECIAL TYPE. Capacity 8800 tons dwt.
Standard dimensions 431 x 54 x 26. Triple expansions, oil fuel. The "Special" characteristic was that this design had 2 decks & shelter deck. TOTAL OUTPUT 5 ships. All built by LOS ANGELES SHIPBUILDING Co., who had contracts for EFC hulls 2243-2248 and 2357-2360 - total 10 ships, of which 5 cancelled.

WEST LEWARK, yard no 31, compl 1921 as O/N 221330. (USSB 21-22)/ MEIGS (US Army transport, 22-42)/ AC/B at Darwin 19.2.1942. (NOTE: Listed by Fahey as AK 34 of USN but never handed over to Navy.)

WEST FARALON, yard no 32, compl 1921 as O/N 221385. (USSB 21-27)/ GOLDEN HIND (Oceanic & Oriental, US, 27-37)/ HONOLULAN (Amer Hawaiian, US, 37-42)/ SM/T W of Freetown 22.7.1942.

WEST GREYLOCK, Yd N°33, opl 1921, O/N 221536 (USSB 21-23)/GREYLOCK(Greylock US 23-28;SEAS, US,38-43)/SM/T E Jan Mayen Is. 3.2.43

WEST PROSPECT, Yd N°34, cpl 10.21 O/N 221603 (USSB 21-27)/GOLDEN SUN (Oc.& Or., US 27-38)/MOKIHANA (Matson,US 38-48)/FRIXOS(Cristobal,Pan,48-54)/ BU Osaka 1954

WEST CHOPAKA, Yd N°35, cpl 11.21 O/N 221666 (USSB 21-27)/GOLDEN DRAGON(Oc.& Or. US 27-38)/ MAHIMAHI (Matson,US,38-48)/MONGIBELLO(Unione,Ital,48-49) POLIFEMO (Unione,Ital, 49-59)BU Osaka 59

图 5-10　EFC Design 1133 的主要特征说明
Figure 5-10　Main particulars and explaination of EFC Design 1133

EFC Design 1133 是洛杉矶特别型（Los Angeles special type），载重量为 8 800 吨。该型船的主尺度：船长为 431 英尺（131.37 米）、船宽为 54 英尺（16.46 米）、吃水为 26 英尺（7.92 米），配备三胀式蒸汽机和燃油锅炉。所谓的"特别型"是指主船体内设置了两层甲板和遮蔽甲板。针对该型船应急船队公司共签订了 10 艘船的建造合同，其中 5 艘被取消。这履约建造的 5 艘船均在 1921 年内交付。

The EFC Design 1133 was the Los Angeles special type with deadweight of 8 800 tons. The main dimensions were: 431 feet (131.37 meters) in length, 54 feet (16.46 meters) in width, 26 feet (7.92 meters) in draught, equipped with a triple expansion steam engine and oil-fired boilers. The so-called "special type" meant that two decks and one shelter deck were provided in the main hull. The EFC signed 10 ships contracts with this special type design, 5 of which were cancelled later. The remaining 5 were all delivered in 1921.

鉴于美国洛杉矶造船公司（Los Angeles Shipbuilding Company）是一家具有丰富建造经验的船厂，曾经建造过许多类似的同型船。作者据此推断洛杉矶造船公司的造船周期短于初次涉足大型船舶建造领域的江南造船所的；再则这 5 艘船在美国船级社的入级编号（221330、221385、221536 和 221666）要晚于江南造船所建造的 4 艘船中的首制船（H317，221227）的。因此，江南造船所 EFC 1092 船型应用新的设计理念——主甲板上增加一层遮蔽甲板在先，而同样的设计理念也被应用到美国洛杉矶造船公司建造的 EFC Design 1133 型船上。

作者在船舶档案馆保存的江南造船所建造的四艘万吨级运输舰（船体号：H317~H320）的图纸资料中，发现了一张遮蔽甲板图（图号为 6861，标注日期：1918 年 10 月 26 日）（见图 5–11）。

Los Angeles Shipbuilding Company was an experienced shipyard having delivered many similar ships of the same type. It can be assumed that the construction period in the Los Angeles Shipbuilding Company was shorter than that in Kiangnan of debut. In addition, the numbers (221330, 221385, 221536 and 221666) registered by ABS of the five ships were later than the first Kiangnan-built ships (H317, 221227). Therefore, the novel concept of Kiangnan, "supplementing a shelter deck on the main deck" was creative in the EFC series. Such a design concept was later applied on the EFC Design 1133 built in the Los Angeles Shipbuilding Company.

In the Archives of CSSC, a individual Shelter Deck Plan of four American 10 000-ton steam freighters was noted. Refer to Figure 5–11, Drawing No. 6861, Dated: 26 October 1918.

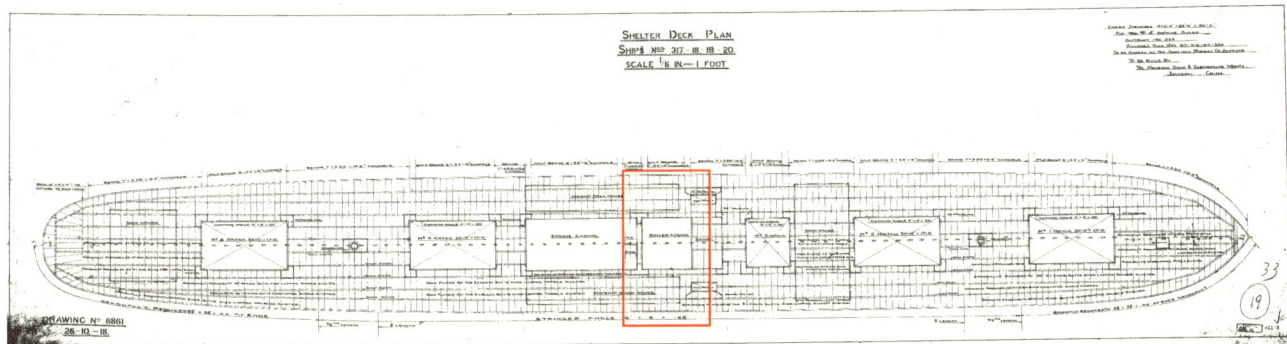

图 5–11 遮蔽甲板图
Figure 5–11 Shelter Deck Plan

作者仔细判读了这张图纸，注意到舯部的深舱位置与合同中总布置图中标注的位置是一致的（图 5–11 红框区域），而与完工的已经改成燃油锅炉的实船是不一样的。为什么会有这张图纸？作者做了如下推断。

1918 年 7 月，毛根在美国首都华盛顿和美国航运委员会签订建造四艘运输舰的合同时，总布置图（见图 2–11）如前文分析所述，极有可能是在大来航运公司的类似船型（EFC Design 1013）的基础上修改的，但 EFC Design 1013 是没有遮蔽甲板的，因此江南造船所的设计人员在合同技术附件的总布置图的基础上做了进一步的详细设计，补充绘制了这张遮蔽甲板图。但实际上这张图不是后续建造过程中采用的遮蔽甲板图。

After carefully reviewing this drawing, the deep tank location was identical to that in the General Arrangement Plan, attachment of the signed contracts (marked by red frame in Figure 5–11). It was different from the ship delivered with an oil-fired boiler. Why was this drawing specially produced? Personally, a practical ratiocination is as following.

In July 1918, when Mauchan signed the contract for four steam freighters in the Washington with the United States Shipping Board, the General Arrangement Plan (see Figure 2–11), as described in the previous investigation, was most likely to be from a similar ship of Dollar Steamship Company (EFC Design 1013). Since EFC Design 1013 has no shelter deck, the designers of Kiangnan might make further details based on the contract specification. They drafted an individual Shelter Deck Plan as supplement. However, this drawing actually was not the final one applied on the construction of these four steam freighters.

关于四艘美国万吨级运输舰船舶设计的来源，作者根据上述分析可以得出的第一个初步结论如下：

以大来公司的类似船型（EFC Design 1013）为母型船由江南造船所的技术人员进行了修改，并作为造船合同的技术附件，然后江南造船所进行了补充设计，但这个设计未做完整。最终完工的四艘美国万吨级运输舰也未采用这个设计。

Regarding the design source of the four 10 000-ton American steam freighters, the first preliminary conclusion which can be obtained based on the above analysis is:

The drawings of a similar ship, properly EFC Design 1013 of Robert Dollar Company, were amended by Kiangnan's designers as the Technical Attachments of contract specification. Kiangnan carried out the supplementary design thereafter, but this design was not fully completed. The four finally completed American 10 000-ton steam freighters also did not adopt this design.

5.4

它是第二艘母型船吗?
Is She Second Prototype Ship?

5.4.1

大战结束导致船舶改型
The Design Changed after the Great War

根据 1918 年 7 月毛根在美国首都华盛顿和美国海运委员会签订四艘万吨级运输舰建造合同的规定，在材料到达船厂后 6 个月内完工交付首制船，这个进度要求显然属于战时非常时期的要求，对初次建造万吨级大型船舶的江南造船所来说是一个极大的挑战，实际上是无法按期完成的。但 1918 年 11 月，德国宣布投降，第一次世界大战以同盟国的失败而告终。由于战争结束了，海上战略物资的运输量大幅下降，对船舶的需求也不迫切。当时江南造船所的四艘万吨级运输舰的设计工作尚在进行过程中，美方承诺提供的钢材和设备也未按期到达。随后美国海运委员会要求江南造船所"实求坚固，毋庸着急，不必依期赶造"[12]，实际上江南造船所万吨级运输舰的设计和建造工作也确实因故暂停或放缓了。

中国近代史料中的通行说法是 1920 年美国政府要求继续履行上述四艘万吨级运输舰的建造合同，但实际上建造合同的重启与当时大来航运公司有意接手这四艘万吨级运输舰投入跨太平洋航线运输有关，或者说罗伯特·大来船长和美国海运委员会主席爱德华·N. 赫尔利之间达成了某种共识。从时间上看，应该是 1919 年初而不是 1920 年。如前文所述，在整个万吨级运输舰的承接、设计、材料设备采购和建造乃至交付过程中，罗伯特·大来船长是一个非常重要的角色，他起了决定性作用。另一种说法是，江南造船所的船体建造和蒸汽机制造能力是勉强能赶上1921 年初的交船期的，从图 3-9 可以看出，船舶下

According to the contract of four 10 000-ton American steam freighters signed between Mauchan and the United States Shipping Board in Washington in July 1918, the first steam freighter should be completed within six months after the material arrived at the shipyard. Such tight schedule was definitely the special requirement in wartime. It was a huge challenge for the Kiangnan because they never built such a large ship before, and it could not be practically completed on schedule. In November 1918, the armistice was signed, and the Great War ended with the failure of the Central Powers. As the Great War was over, the marine transportation for war supplies had fallen sharply, and the demand for ships was not so urgent. At that time, the design work of four 10 000-ton steam freighters at Kiangnan was still under progress, and the steel and equipment promised by the United States did not arrive on schedule. Although the United States Sipping Board required Kiangnan to "stick to the truth and keep the pace, don't rush for time delivery". However, the design and construction work in Kiangnan had also been actually suspended or slowed down.

The common description in Chinese modern historical materials is that in 1920 American Government requested to continue the construction contract of four 10 000-ton steam freighters, but the behind pusher for restarting the construction was that Dollar Steamship Company intended to take over these four freighters and put them into the Trans-Pacific routes. Or captain Robert Dollar expressed his intension with the privity and consent of Edward N. Hurley, Chairman of the United States Shipping Board. Timewise, personally it is deduced in early 1919 instead of 1920. As mentioned before, captain Robert Dollar was a key person in the contract signing, design, purchasing, construction and delivery of steam freighters. Another explanation mentioned that, Kiangnan's capability of hull construction and engine manufacture was able to barely satisfy the delivery schedule in early 1921. From Figure 3-9, it can be seen that there was poor outfitting condition after launching, perhaps no main engine was installed before launching. Based on the above, it can be

水后的舾装完整性是比较差的，可能主机等设备未能在下水前吊装到位。因此，可以这么认为，造船合同的执行，也就是船舶建造进度是放缓了而不是暂停。

concluded that the construction progress seemed to slowly move forward but was not suspended.

在罗伯特·大来船长的回忆录中提到，罗伯特·大来在 1921 年的 12 月 12 日收到了一份"关于决定处置战时征召和订造的运输船舶"的政府急件。在这份急件中提到了美方会对第一次世界大战临近结束时过量订造的运输船舶以世界市场的平均价（on par）进行转卖这一决定。罗伯特·大来在他的回忆录中是这样写的：

Captain Robert Dollar mentioned in his memoir, that he got a government dispatch "about disposal of the ships drafted or ordered during the war" on 12 December 1921 from the United States Government. This government dispatch mentioned that a glut of merchant shipping available ordered before the end of the war, would be sold on par with market price. Robert Dollar wrote following in his memoir:

"根据旧金山航运圈得到的消息，美国海运委员会 12 月 28 日（1921 年）出售 28 艘各型货船，售价是世界市场每吨位的平均价。需要说明的是当时大来航运公司的总部在旧金山。"

"Twenty-eight cargo vessels of various types have been ordered sold by the United States Shipping Board, effective December 28. The price of the vessels will be on par with world tonnage prices, according to information received in San Francisco shipping circles. During that time, the headquarter of Dollar Steamship Company was located in San Francisco."

可见大来船长是在江南造船所的第四艘运输舰接近完工时才知道美国海运委员会有意出售这批船舶的，也许他不便将他和赫尔利之间的"默契"在其回忆录中表达出来。因此，作者判断后一种说法更加符合当年江南造船所的实际情况。那为什么 1919 年初采用了完全不同于合同签订时的设计方案呢？

It can be concluded that Captain Dollar only knew USSB's intention to sell those vessels when the forth freighter was close to completion in Kiangnan. Maybe it was inconvenient for him to disclose the privity with Mr. Hurley in his memoir. So it can be believed that the second explanation was closer to the situation of Kiangnan at that time. The question is why the design adopted in early 1919 was totally different from the Technical Attachments of contract design?

首先，再对比一下合同中签字版总布置图（1918 年 7 月 18 日），包括总布置图的修改版（1918 年 8 月 8 日）和后来实际设计并应用建造的五个版本的总布置图（7007A、7007B、7007C、7007D 和 7007E，7008A、7008B 和 7008C），其之间的最大差异：

First of all, comparing the contract signing version of General Arrangement Plan (18 July 1918) including the updated version (8 August 1918) and the General Arrangement Plan of the actual design and construction of 5 editions (7007A, 7007B, 7007C, 7007D and 7007E, 7008A, 7008B and 7008C), the obvious differences are:

在上层建筑下的主船体内取消了燃煤舱（深舱），深舱移到了上层建筑后部；在双层底内部和艏、艉尖舱内布置了燃油舱；采用燃油锅炉；货舱采用前三后二的布置方式。此外，船长加长了 4 英尺（1.22 米），取消了艏艉炮台，单柱式起重桅改成了双柱式并增加了 30 吨的重型吊杆，取消了一些战时配置等。

Coal storage space (deep tank) was cancelled in the hull part, deep tank was moved to the rear of accommodation; fuel tanks were arranged at double bottom, fore peak tank and aft peak tank; oil boiler was used; cargo holds were arranged as three tanks on fore body and two on aft body. The length of the freighter was increased by 4 feet (1.22 meters); the gun turrets on bow and stern were cancelled; the single post derrick was changed to twin-post, one 30 t heavier duty beam was added; and also some equipment only needed during wartime were cancelled.

正如 1920 年 6 月 3 日，美国公使柯兰在演说中提到的："幸今下水之船乃一和平之船。余信太平洋可不再需要战争之船，而只驶行和平之船。"此船的设计已经从运输舰改为普通远洋货船。

Just as Mr. Crane, Minister Counselor of the United States, had said on 3 June 1920: "Today launched steamer is the peaceful ship. I believe it is no longer to need warship in Pacific Ocean, only peaceful ship will sail." The design of these steamers had been changed from armed transporting vessel to merchant freighter.

再从现代船舶设计的眼光来看，和 EFC Design 1013 相比，江南造船所的完工图纸也完全是全新的设计，不是史料中所说的补充设计。这个设计是否是江南造船所自行设计的？有没有母型船？带着这样的疑问作者感觉有必要查阅一下船舶档案馆内与万吨级运输舰保存在一起的其他船舶的设计图纸。

From the view of modern ship design, compared to EFC Design 1013, Kiangnan's design was also a totally new design but not a complementary design as described in historian documents. Was it designed by Kiangnan themselves? Did it have prototype ship? With these doubt, it is necessary to review some drawings other than four 10 000-ton American steam freighters discovered in the Archives of CSSC.

5.4.2

神秘的 "Eastern Soldier" 号
Mysterious SS "Eastern Soldier"

在船舶档案馆保存的江南造船所建造的四艘万吨级运输舰（船体号：H317~H320）的图纸中作者发现了三份其他船——"Eastern Soldier" 号的图纸[13]。

Three drawings for another vessel SS "Eastern Soldier" were found among the document folders of four 10 000 DWT steam freighters (hull number: H317−H320) stored in the Archives of CSSC.

（1）"Eastern Soldier" 号的总布置图，标注日期是 1920 年 8 月 9 日，如图 5−12 所示。

(1) SS "Eastern Soldier" General Arrangement Plan, dated 9 August 1920. Refer to Figure 5−12.

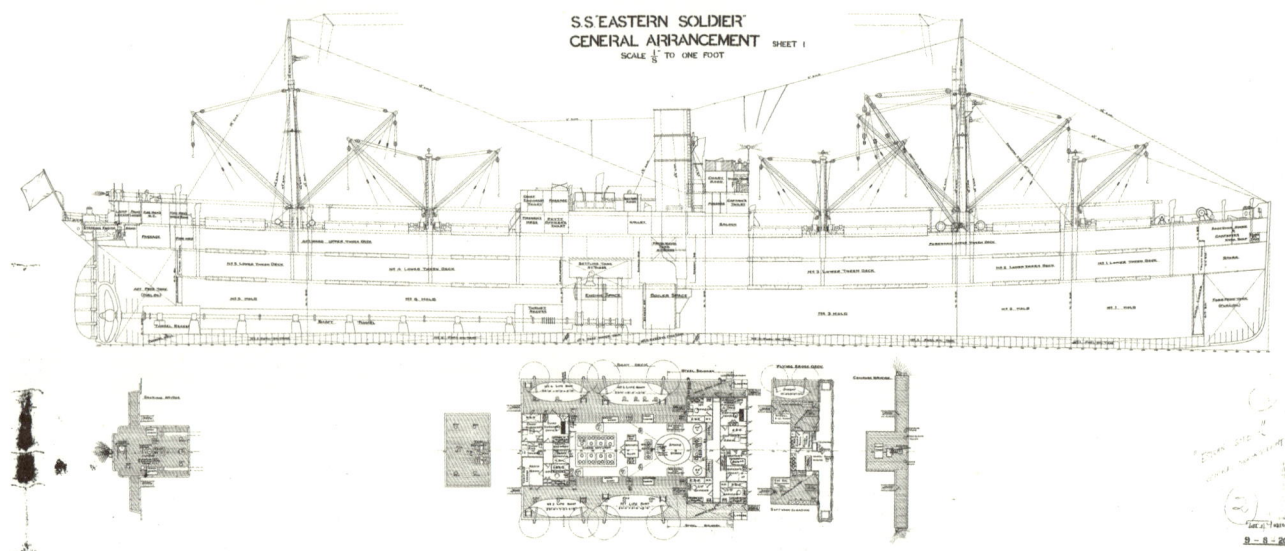

图 5−12　"Eastern Soldier" 号的总布置图
Figure 5−12　General Arrangement Plan of SS "Eastern Soldier"

（2）"Eastern Soldier" 号的舱容和载重线标尺图，标注日期不详。

(2) SS "Eastern Soldier" Capacity Plan & Deadweight Scale, unknown date.

（3）"Eastern Soldier" 号的艏部吊杆布置图，标注日期是 1921 年 3 月 4 日。

(3) SS "Eastern Soldier" Derrick Arrangement on Fore Body Plan, dated 4 March 1921.

"Eastern Soldier" 号是一艘什么船？为什么江南造船所会有这艘船的图纸？带着这样的疑问，作者开始了进一步调查。在 www.wrecksite.eu 网站上作

What kind of ship SS "Eastern Soldier" was? And why did Kiangnan Dock & Engineering Works have the drawings? With this question, the further investigation has been done, and some relative records were found

者查到了这艘船的相关记录。该船由日本 1907 年创立的播磨造船所 [Harima Dock, 1960 年与石川岛重工业株式会社合并成立石川岛播磨重工业株式会社 (Ishikawajima-Harima Heavy Industries Co., Ltd.), 2013 年并入日本造船联合公司 (Japan Marine United Corporation)] 建造。此网站的管理员阿伦·托尼 (Allen Tony) 在 2010 年 6 月 3 日添加的评注如下：

"Lena Luckenbach" 号是一艘 6 805 (总) 吨的美国货船，建造于 1918 年，当时的船名是 "Eastern Shore"，1919 年更名为 "Eastern Soldier"，1922 年再次更名为 "Lena Luckenbach"。1944 年 8 月 4 日，该船被凿沉在诺曼底奥马哈二号海滩的古斯伯里 (Gooseberry) 区域用于封锁航道。

纽约的 Luckenbach 航运公司 (1850—1974 年) 是一个历史悠久和成功的航运公司。刘易斯·卢肯巴赫 (Lewis Luckenbach) 先生在纽约以一艘拖轮开始创业，他以拖轮加驳船的创新经营模式从弗吉尼亚州的诺福克运送燃煤至新英格兰地区并获得了成功。Luckenbach 航运公司成了（美国）沿海运输的主力。[14]

该网站还提到，该船建造完工时为劳氏船级并一直保持劳氏入级直至 1952 年，这就产生了一个疑问：难道被凿沉在诺曼底奥马哈二号海滩的古斯伯里区域的 "Lena Luckenbach" 号打捞起来后修复再营运至 1952 年？作者从劳氏船级社伦敦总部档案馆查到了相关入级资料。劳氏船级社的入级资料和 www.wrecksite.eu 网站上的信息相比存在较大差异，相比之下作者更加相信劳氏船级社的入级资料。劳氏船级社的入级资料 [15] 显示，日本播磨造船所在 1918—1920 年共建造过 8 艘同型船 [425 英尺 (129.54 米) 长、53.6 英尺 (16.34 米) 宽、型深 37.6 英尺 (11.46 米)，"Eastern Soldier" 号型深为 34.9 英尺 (10.64 米)，6 750 总吨]。表 5-2 列出了播磨造船所建造的 8 艘同型船的相关资料。

on the website www.wrecksite.eu. It shows that SS "Eastern Soldier" was built by a Japanese yard named Harima Dock, which was founded in 1907 and incorporated with Ishikawajima Heavy Industries Co., Ltd. in 1960 to form as Ishikawajima-Harima Heavy Industries Co., Ltd. Ishikawajima-Harima Heavy Industries Co., Ltd. was merged by Japan Marine United Corporation in 2013. The website administrator Allen Tony added the comments on 3 June 2010 as follows:

SS "Lena Luckenbach" was an American freighter of 6 805 tons (other source said gross tonnage) built in 1918 as the "Eastern Shore". She was renamed the "Eastern Soldier" in 1919. After 1922, she returned to the original name of "Lena Luckenbach". On 4 August 1944, she was scuttled as a blockage in position Gooseberry No.2 Omaha Beach, Normandy.

Luckenbach Steamship Co. (1850–1974), New York, was one of the venerable and successful shipping companies of the United States. Mr. Lewis Luckenbach started his business with single tugboat in New York, and he built his fortune by novel tug pulled coal barge to transport coal from Norfolk, Virginia to New England. Luckenbach Steamship became later a major tonnage in the intercostal trade of the United States.

The website also mentioned that the ship was built under the Lloyd's Register and maintained her class until 1952. This raises a question: Was SS "Lena Luckenbach" scuttled in the Gooseberry area of No. 2 Omaha Beach , Normandy salvaged and operated again until 1952? After verifying the registered data kept in the headquarter of Lloyd's Register in London, the registered data have obvious deviation with the information on the website www. wrecksite. eu. Personally, it can be believed that registered data are more accurate. The registered data of the Lloyd's Register show that Harima Dock built 8 of ships this type from 1918 to 1920 with dimension of 425 feet (129.54 meters) long and 53.6 feet (16.34 meters) width, depth of 37.6 feet (11.46 meters) [SS "Eastern Soldier" depth is 34.9 feet (10.64 meters), 6 750 gross tonnage]. Table 5-2 lists the information of 8 sequential ships built by Harima Dock.

表 5-2　播磨造船所建造的 8 艘同型船的相关资料
Table 5-2　The information of 8 sequential ships built by Harima Dock

序号 No.	船体号 Hull No.	船名 Ship name	总吨 Gross tonnage	完工日期 Completion date	
1	S09	Eastern Shore	6 731	1918 年 9 月	September 1918
2	S11	Yone Maru	6 780	1919 年 3 月	March 1919
3	S10	Yaye Maru	6 781	1919 年 6 月	June 1919

（续表）
(continued)

序号 No.	船体号 Hull No.	船名 Ship name	总吨 Gross tonnage	完工日期 Completion date	
4	S29	Yuri Maru	6 787	1919 年 8 月	August 1919
5	S30	Shunko Maru	6 806	1919 年 11 月	November 1919
6	S31	Texas Maru	6 806	1920 年 2 月	February 1920
7	S17	Rocky Maru	6 806	1920 年 3 月	March 1920
8	S32	Eastern Soldier	6 750	1920 年 6 月	June 1920

在劳氏船级社的入级资料中，这 8 艘船订造时的船东是帝国航运公司（The Teikoku Steamship Co.），而船名以 "Eastern" 打头的船舶要么都卖给了美国海运委员会，要么就是为美国海运委员会建造的。"Eastern Soldier" 号 1922 年改名为 "Lena Luckenbach" 号，该船被凿沉在诺曼底区域用于封锁航道。战后被打捞出来拆解了。而 "Eastern Shore" 号则在第二次世界大战后被编入了后备船队（U.S. Reserve Fleet）一直营运到 1952 年脱离劳氏船级社，后被封锁搁置（laid-up）。显然 www.wrecksite.eu 网站的管理员阿伦·托尼把这两艘船混淆在一起了。

劳氏船级社伦敦总部档案馆内保存的 "Eastern Soldier" 号的舯横剖面图如图 5–13 所示。

Midship Section of SS "Eastern Soldier" preserved as archives in the Lloyd's Register, Headquarter, London, see Figure 5–13.

这张舯横剖面图和四艘万吨级运输舰合同签订时的技术附件中的"舯横剖面图"（第 2 章中的图 2–12）相比，总体结构格局相似，但许多结构细节是不同的。作者也比较了那个年代建造的杂货船，除了遮蔽甲板是一个主要差异点之外，其他结构格局大同小异。

In the registered records of the Lloyd's Register, the owner of the eight ships when ordered was the Teikoku Steamship Co., and the ships whose names start with "Eastern" were sold to the United States Shipping Board or just built for the United States Shipping Board. SS "Eastern Soldier" in 1922 was renamed SS "Lena Luckenbach", and the ship was scuttled in the Normandy area for channel blockage. After the World War Ⅱ, it was salvaged and dismantled thereafter. After the World War Ⅱ, the SS "Eastern Shore" was incorporated into U.S. Reserve Fleet and has been operating until 1952 under the Lloyd's Register. Later the ship was laid-up. Obviously, Allen Tony, the administrator of website, www.wrecksite.eu, made confusion for these two ships.

Overall structural layout of this drawing and "Midship Section", Technical Attachments of shipbuilding contract (Figure 2–12 in Chapter 2) are comparable except some details. Personally, comparing contemporaneous freighters, except that the shelter deck is a primary difference, the other structure arrangement looks quite similar.

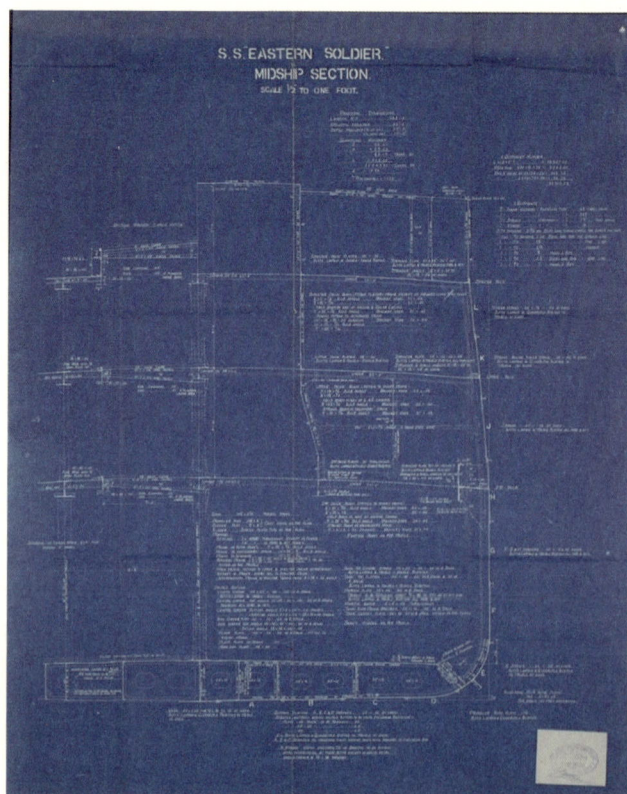

图 5–13 "Eastern Soldier" 号的舯横剖面图
Figure 5–13 Midship Section of SS "Eastern Soldier"

"Eastern Soldier" 号的总布置图和江南造船所建造的四艘万吨级运输舰（H317~H320）的 5 个版本（7007A、7007B、7007C、7007D 和 7007E）的总布置图相比，除了主尺度和载重量有差异之外，船型、结构形式和分舱布置方面相对来说是比较接近的。表 5-3 为两型船在设计方面的主要差异。

Comparing the General Arrangement Plan of SS "Eastern Soldier" with the four 10 000-ton steam freighters (H317–H320) built by Kiangnan, five editions (7007A, 7007B, 7007C, 7007D and 7007E), layout, structure and subdivision are relatively similar except the deviations of the main particulars and the deadweight. Table 5-3 shows the main difference between two types of design.

表 5-3　两型船在设计方面的主要差异
Table 5-3　The main difference between two types of design

比较项目 Comparison items	播磨造船所的设计 Harima Dock design S32		江南造船所的设计 Kiangnan design H317–H320	
船型特征 Features	干杂货船，拥有舯部上层建筑，舯机型，配置三台燃油锅炉、一台三缸往复式蒸汽机，单桨单舵 General and dry cargo, engine room and superstructure at amidship, 3 oil fueled boilers, 1 triple expansion reciprocating steam engine, single propeller with single rudder		与播磨造船所的设计相同 Same as Harima Dock's design	
主要尺度 Main dimensions	两柱间长 L_{pp} 型宽 Bmld 型深（至上甲板）D upper deck 上甲板和遮蔽甲板之间的层高 H up dk-shlt deck 吃水 Draught 载重量 Deadweight 空船重量 Light weight	425'0" 53'8" 29'0" 8'6" 28'9–1/4" 10 625 t 3 876 t	两柱间长 L_{pp} 型宽 Bmld 型深（至上甲板）D upper deck 上甲板和遮蔽甲板之间的层高 H up dk-shlt dk 吃水 Draught 载重量 Deadweight 空船重量 Light Weight	429'0" 55'0" 30'0" 7'11–1/2" 27'11–3/16" 10 293 t 4 922 t[16]
船型特征 Features	前半船体：艏尖舱、三个货舱（四个舱口盖） Fore body: fore peak tank, 3 cargo holds with 4 hatch covers 舯部：机炉舱 Amidship: engine and boiler room 后半船体：两个货舱（三个舱口盖）、艉尖舱 Aft body: 2 cargo holds with 3 hatch covers, aft peak tank		前半船体：艏尖舱、三个货舱（三个舱口盖） Fore body: fore peak tank, 3 cargo holds with 3 hatch covers 舯部：机炉舱 Amidship: engine and boiler room 后半船体：两个货舱、一个深舱（三个舱口盖）、艉尖舱 Aft body: 2 cargo holds and 1 deep tank with 3 hatch covers, aft peak tank	
起重设备 Lifting gears	前半船体：起重桅一座（配重型吊杆）、起重柱两对（艏部一对配前吊杆、舯部一对配前后吊杆） Fore body: 1 derrick post with heavy duty beam, 2 pairs of post (king post with fore lifting beam, and midship post with fore and aft lifting beams) 后半船体：起重桅一座、起重柱一对（配前后吊杆） Aft body: 1 derrick post, 1 pair of post with fore and aft lifting beams		前半船体：起重桅一座（配重型吊杆）、起重柱一对（配前后吊杆） Fore body: 1 derrick post with heavy duty beam, 1 pair of post with fore and aft lifting beams 后半船体：起重桅一座、起重柱一对（配前吊杆） Aft body: 1 derrick post, 1 pair of post with fore lifting beam	

从上述比较可以看出，播磨造船所设计的 Eastern Shore 系列（"Eastern Soldier" 号）和江南造船所的船（H317~H320）还是有差异的。作者认为：由于战争结束了，美国海运委员会认为战时运输将不再是此批船舶的职能，今后的主要任务是商业运输。因此，应急船队公司设计序列中的船舶设计图（主要是

From the above comparison, there are some difference between the Eastern Shore series designed by Harima Dock and H317–H320 of Kiangnan. Personally, it can be presumed that because the war ended, the United States Shipping Board considered that wartime transportation would no longer be the task of these ships, and instead merchant transportation would take over. Therefore, the ship designs in the EFC sequence (mainly by American shipyards) was not applicable

美国船厂的设计图）不再适用。反倒是日本船厂的设计（如不在应急船队公司设计序列编号中的播磨造船所的设计图）更加适合今后的商业运输。

那么美国海运委员会是何时向江南造船所提出修改设计以适应今后的商业运输而不是战时运输，并将燃煤锅炉改成了燃油锅炉的呢？作者没有发现进一步的佐证材料，但作者推断，鉴于本章 5.3 节中提到的江南造船所补充设计的遮蔽甲板图（见图 5–11）的标注日期是 1918 年 10 月 26 日，威拉米特钢铁厂提供给江南造船所的燃油锅炉结构图纸（见图 4–56）上标注的日期是 1918 年 11 月 21 日，因此，作者推断美国海运委员会决定修改设计应该就在 11 月第一次世界大战结束之时。因为对于威拉米特钢铁厂来说，燃油锅炉是其成熟产品，给江南造船所的图纸只是在标准型燃油锅炉的图纸上多加个船厂船舶船体号的标记而已。

此外，作者又仔细比较了后续 5 个版本的总布置图，每个版本完全是重新绘制的，图面标注和字体也不相同，图面的详细程度逐步加大。B 版和 C 版的总布置是根据船东（USSB Requirements, 31st July, 1919）的要求修改并不断地细化的。参见表 4–2。

作者认为，如果应急船队公司向江南造船所提供主要设计图纸作为参考图，从时间进度的可能性来讲，只能是"Eastern Shore"号的（此船完工于 1918 年 9 月）。如果是这样，那么江南造船所的原始档案中不可能没有一张"Eastern Shore"号的图纸。总布置图完全可以一步到位。原始档案中倒是有几张手写的技术要求和草图，疑似是美国海运委员会提出的具体要求。而"Eastern Soldier"号的两张图纸极有可能是被用来作为起重设备布置和载重线标尺计算的蓝本和参考。在江南造船所建造的四艘万吨级运输舰（H317~H320）的总布置图中，30 吨的重吊杆（heavy lifting derrick）是到了总布置图 D 版才添加上去的，这在时间上是吻合的。与常规的 5 吨吊重的吊杆相比，30 吨的重吊杆的滑轮组多、绳索布置复杂，对未涉及过类似设计的江南造船所的技术人员来说是有一定难度的。作者对比了四艘万吨级运输舰的总布置图和"Eastern Soldier"号的起重设备布置，其重吊杆的布置在细节上是十分接近的。

anymore. On the contrary, the Japanese design like Harima Dock, even though it was not in the EFC sequence, seemed more suitable for future commercial transportation.

Then, when did the United States Shipping Board request Kiangnan to modify their design from being for wartime to commercial transportation, and change the coal fueled boiler into oil fueled boiler? I did not find further evidence. But it can be concluded that the Shelter Deck Plan (see Figure 5–11) supplemented by Kiangnan mentioned in Section 5.3 of Chapter 5 was dated 26 October 1918. From Willamette Iron and Steel Works's oil boiler drawing provided to Kiangnan (see Figure 4–56), it can be seen that the date marked on the drawing was 21 November 1918. Therefore, I believe that the United States Shipping Board decision of the design modification should be finalized in November, just after the end of the Great War. For Willamette Iron and Steel Works, the oil fueled boiler was a well-proven product, and the drawings for Kiangnan were only marked with the hull number on standard drawings.

In addition, after carefully comparing the General Arrangement Plan of the next five editions, each edition was completely redrawn, the mark and font on drawings were not the same, and the level of drawing detail was gradually increased. The General Arrangement Plan of the editions B and C was modified and continually refined according to the requirements of the United States Shipping Board (USSB Requirements, 31 July 1919). See also Table 4–2.

Practically, if EFC provided the primary design drawings to Kiangnan as a reference, it can only be "Eastern Shore" as per the possibility of time schedule (this ship was completed in September 1918). However, it is impossible to have no SS "Eastern Shore" drawings in the original archives of Jiangnan Shipyard. The General Arrangement Plan can be completed in one edition. There are a few handwritten requirements and sketches in the original file, and they are suspected to be the specific requirements from the United States Shipping Board. The two drawings of SS "Eastern Soldier" are most likely to be used as a reference for the lifting appliances arrangement and free board calculation. In the General Arrangement Plan of the four 10 000-ton steam freighters (H317–H320), the 30-ton heavy lifting derrick was added to the edition D, and it is consistent in time schedule. Compared with the 5-ton derrick, the 30-ton heavy lifting derrick had many pulley sets and complicated rope arrangement, and it was difficult for the technicians of Kiangnan who had no experience. Comparing derrick arrangement of the SS "Eastern Soldier" and Kiangnan built steam freighters, the details of the arrangement of the heavy lifting derricks look very similar.

后来，作者在查阅江南造船所老员工黄容工程师的访谈回忆录时，发现了这样几段访问记录 [17]：

"日本造的船只使用了六个月就到和丰船厂进行修理。"

"当时江南造船所的英国人在计算载重量时产生了差错，载重量达不到 10 000 吨，只有 9 900 吨。后来中方的设计人员余季馥参考了相似船舶的计算资料，发现英国人的算法有误。余季馥和英国人同时进行重新计算，实际载重量超过了 10 000 吨。"

作者根据相关资料进行了核实，第三艘"东方"号和第四艘"国泰"号的载重量为 10 293 吨。这里提到的"中方的设计人员余季馥参考了相关船舶的计算资料"，这个相关船舶极有可能是"Eastern Soldier"号。联想到毛根以前曾经在和丰船厂工作过，不排除他利用其人脉关系从和丰船厂弄来了这几张图纸作为江南造船所设计吊杆布置和载重线标尺计算的参考。因此，综合以上因素，作者认为上述推断应该是成立的。

Later, when I reviewed the reminiscence of interviews with Huang Rong, an elder employee of the Kiangnan Dock & Engineering Works, such interview records were found:

"The steamers built in Japan had to repair at Shanghai Engineering Shipbuilding & Dock Co., which was only delivered six months ago."

"At that time, the British technicians of Kiangnan Dock & Engineering Works had made some mistakes in the deadweight calculation. The obtained deadweight was less than 10 000 tons, only 9 900 tons. Later, a Chinese designer named Yu Jifu referred to the calculation data of the similar ship and found some mistakes in the algorithm. Yu Jifu and the British colleague did simultaneously recalculation and the actual deadweight finally exceeded 10 000 tons."

According to my verification, the deadweights of the third SS "Oriental" and the fourth named "Cathay" freighters were an identical figure of 10 293 tons. As mentioned before, "Chinese designer named Yu Jifu referred to the calculation data of the similar ship". This "similar ship" most properly would be named "Eastern Soldier". Thinking about Mauchan's previous career at Shanghai Engineering Shipbuilding & Dock Co., possibly, he might take advantage of connections to bring these drawings from Shanghai Engineering Shipbuilding & Dock Co., as a reference for the lifting appliances arrangement and free board calculation for Kiangnan. Therefore, I believe that the above inference should be reasonable.

5.5

关于设计来源的结论
The Conclusion of Design Source

基于上述分析和推断，关于江南造船所建造的四艘美国万吨级运输舰的船舶设计来源，可以得出以下结论：

造船合同技术附件中的总布置图是以大来航运公司的类似船型（例如 EFC Design 1013）[18] 为母型船由江南造船所的技术人员进行修改和设计的，主要是增加了遮蔽甲板；舯横剖面图有可能是江南造船所的技术人员参照大来航运公司的类似船型设计绘制的，也有可能是直接在一张现成的舯横剖面图纸上修改而成的。此外，江南造船所的技术人员在合同签订后还做了一些补充设计，主要是补充了遮蔽甲板图。但这个设计没有应用到后来的实船建造中。

1918 年 11 月及以后的设计，江南造船所的技术人员根据美国海运委员会提出的船舶须适应今后的商业运输而不是战时运输和将燃煤锅炉改成燃油锅炉等要求进行了全新的设计并取消了原来的战时装备，但是否有参考 "Eastern Shore" 号的图纸不能完全确定。将 "Eastern Soldier" 号的图纸用来作为起重设备布置和载重线标尺计算的蓝本和参考，这一点基本可以肯定，其他的图纸都是江南造船所自主设计的。有一点可以肯定，正因为此型船是一型全新的设计，美国海运委员会授予江南造船所设计建造的四艘万吨级运输舰的编号为 EFC Design 1092。

根据以上分析，作者认为关于设计来源完全可以得出这样一个结论：

通过细致分析和甄别，作者认为尽管建造所用的钢材、锅炉（部分锅炉由江南造船所采用威拉米特钢铁厂的图纸进行仿制的可能性不能完全排除）等设备是从美国进口的，但认定江南造船所建造的四艘万吨级运输舰是自行设计的是符合船舶设计惯例的，其证据是比较充分的。"东风"号万吨轮不仅是我国自

Based on the above verification and inference, the following conclusions can be made about the primary design sources of four 10 000-ton steamers built by Kiangnan Dock & Engineering Works:

The General Arrangement Plan in the Technical Attachments of the shipbuilding contract was modified by Kiangnan's technicians on basis of a similar ship type (EFC Design 1013, for instance) of the Dollar Steamship Company, mainly adding a shelter deck; the Midship Section may be drawn by Kiangnan's technicians according to a similar ship of Dollar Steamship Company, or modified directly on a drawing of existing ship. In addition, Kiangnan's technicians also made some supplementary designs after signing the contract, mainly the Shelter Deck Plan. But this design was not applied to the actual ship construction later on.

As for the design after November 1918 and later, the Kiangnan's technicians, as per the requirements of the United States Shipping Board did a brand new design for future commercial transportation instead of wartime transportation, and simultaneously converted coal fueled boilers to oil fueled boilers. This novel design had completely removed the original wartime appliances. Whether the design of SS "Eastern Shore" was taken into Kiangnan's design as reference, it cannot be completely determined now, but it can be confirmed that the lifting appliances arrangement and free board calculation of SS "Eastern Soldier" were utilized as a reference for Kiangnan's design. Other drawings were designed independently by Kiangnan. Another key issue can be confirmed as well, because a new design, the United States Shipping Board assigned independent new code "EFC Design 1092" to Kiangnan designed 10 000-ton steam freighter.

Based on the above analysis, I am firmly convinced that the conclusion of the primary design sources is as follows:

According to the analysis and verification in this book, personally, the steel materials, boilers and other equipments were imported from the United States (the possibilities on the part of the boilers intimated by Kiangnan through Willamette Iron and Steel Works's drawings should not be avoided). However, I think an affirmation of four 10 000-ton steam freighters self-designed by Kiangnan is complying with the practice of ship design, and the evidence can fully prove it. MV "Dong Feng"

行设计的，而且船上所用的钢材、主机和设备都是国产的。在 20 世纪 50 年代末至 60 年代初，中国要自力更生打破技术封锁，"东风"号万吨轮的成功建造是有重大现实意义的。相比之下，四艘万吨级运输舰的承接建造虽然也有一些中美两国政治上的考虑，但更多是江南造船所外籍管理人员从企业经营角度上的考虑，并力求提高本国船舶建造的质量和水平，追求最大的经济效益。在现代船舶建造的通行惯例中，自行设计和采用国产材料设备是不完全挂钩的，即便是在中国造船业已经跻身世界前列的今天，中国船舶配套设备仍然没有实现完全的国产化。

正如本书所述，作者认为江南造船所的苏格兰总工程师毛根在承接、设计和建造四艘万吨级运输舰的过程中起了决定性作用。在自行设计这四艘万吨级运输舰的过程中，江南造船所的外籍设计团队和一批年轻的中方技术人员的努力也是值得赞誉和肯定的。作者认为，应该本着还原真实、尊重史实的宗旨，让这四艘具有里程碑意义的"中国第一批万吨轮"的设计建造在中国近代船舶工业史中有其应有的地位。

was not only self-designed, and the steel materials, main engine and equipments were all made in China. During the late 1950s to the early 1960s period, China used its own design, self-manufactured equipment and materials in order to break the technological blockade. The successful construction of MV "Dong Feng" had a great realistic significance. Compared with MV "Dong Feng", although signing the contract of four 10 000-ton steam freighters had some consideration on Sino-American political standpoint, and moreover, Kiangnan's foreign management team would try its efforts to upgrade the product mix and improve the shipbuilding skill as well as maximize economic profits. In the normal practice of modern shipbuilding, self-design and using domestic material and equipments are not linked with each other. Even in today's Chinese shipbuilding industry, some equipments are still not domestically provided.

As described in this book, personally, Scottish Chief Engineer of Kiangnan, Robert Buchanan Mauchan, played a crucial role in securing, designing and building four 10 000-ton steam freighters. In the process of self-designed four 10 000-ton steam freighters, the foreign designer team and some young Chinese engineers of Kiangnan paid great efforts, and these efforts should be highly remarkable. Personally, with the core of respecting truth and fact, the design and construction of these four 10 000-ton steam freighters should have proper position as a milestone in Chinese modern shipping industry.

作者注：

Notes:

1 《大陆报》，转引自 1919 年 12 月 15 日的《申报》。

2 《江南造船厂的回忆》，《新世界》1944 年第 5 期，第 43 页。

3 《中国舰艇工业历史资料丛书》编辑部编纂，《中国近代舰艇工业史料集》，上海人民出版社，1994 年，第 263-267 页。作者对名称和人名以及时间做了统一和修改。

4 作者对锅炉图纸上的印章（江南造船所造机部）和图纸的分类进行分析后推测，绘图室分设造船和造机两部估计是在 1918 年而不是 1928 年。

5 资料来自：《上海船舶工业志》，第十一篇"人物"中的第一章"人物传略"。

6 资料来自：http://shipscribe.com/shiprefs/efc/DsnList 2. html，但仅列出了钢质船部分和有建造实绩的部分。

7 Chapter Ⅶ, the Emergency Fleet Corporation Begins its Work, *The Bridge to France*, Edward N. Hurley, Kessinger Legacy Reprints.

8 目前能够查阅到的公开资料中无法证实毛根赴美时是否有技术人员或其他人员随行。

9 数据来自：www.ssarkansan.com，向原作者表示敬意。

10 数据来自：www.ssarkansan.com，向原作者表示敬意。

11 当时江南造船所设计图纸上的英文标注已经普遍采用写字模板。

12 刘冠南审核、廖驲编写，《江南造船所纪要》，1922 年，第 70 页。

13 作者认为可能还有更多的图纸，但由于图纸编号方式无规可循，最终未能找到更多的图纸。

14 资料来自：http://www.wrecksite.eu/wreck.aspx? 180541。

15 *Lloyd's Register Book: 1919—1920.*

16 根据 TPI=44.1 吨和空船吃水 9′3−5/8″ 推算而得。

17 江南造船所老员工黄容回忆，当时（1927 年）他负责船坞工程。1960 年 4 月，访问于四川北路 961 弄怡兴里 6 号，许维雍整理。

18 在美国海运委员会和应急船队公司副主席霍华德·孔利写给赫尔利主席的信件的标题中注明的是"IMPROVED ROBERT DOLLAR TYPE"，但并没有注明是哪一型船。参见图 2-10。"EFC Design 1013"是作者比较过具体参数后做的推论。

揭秘四艘万吨轮的营运史
Searching for Fleet Operation of Mandarin Series

6.1

"Arkansan" 号引出了营运史研究
More Studies Induced by SS "Arkansan"

从可查阅到的中国近代船舶工业史料和论文中一直没有发现关于江南造船所建造的四艘万吨级运输舰交付后的营运记录和相关描述。

一个非常偶然的机会作者在一个纪念第二次世界大战中牺牲和失踪船员（多数在跨大西洋物资运输过程中被德国的 U 型潜艇击沉）的网站上发现：1942 年 6 月 15 日被德国 U-126 潜艇击沉的 "Arkansan" 号就是江南造船所 1921 年交付的四艘万吨级运输舰中的第二艘 "天朝" 号。顺着这个线索，作者随即以 "Arkansan" 号为主线对中国第一批万吨级运输舰的订造背景、船舶设计来源、船舶建造过程和整个营运生命周期进行了深度发掘和分析。

2015 年 5 月，作者访问了美国船级社休斯敦总部，查阅了这四艘船在 1922—1932 年的船舶入级记录和钢质铆接船体的规范。2015 年 11 月，作者的同事赴陕西省兴平市查阅了船舶档案馆保存的江南造船所建造的四艘美国万吨级运输舰（船体号：H317 ~ H320）的图纸资料。随后又查阅了澳大利亚历史学家关于美国海运委员会应急船队公司的相关记载和美国加利福尼亚州立大学北岭分校图书馆内收藏的美国国家档案馆关于美国海运委员会的记录文件以及其他相关文献和资料。此外，在劳氏船级社（中国）公司的大力协助下，在其伦敦总部档案馆内查找到了有关疑似 "母型船" 的图纸资料。

The operation record and description after delivery of Kiangnan-built four steam freighters were not found in available historical studies and papers of Chinese shipbuilding industry.

Some additional information regarding Kiangnan-built steam freighters was accidentally explored on a memorial website of wreck crews (mainly attacked by German U-boats during transportation crossing Atlantic Ocean in the World War II). SS "Arkansan", sunk by attack of German U-126 on 15 June 1942, is Kiangnan built SS "Celestial", the second vessel of series, delivered in 1921. Followed this clue, further study and investigation regarding to the background of shipbuilding contract, design source, construction process and whole life circle were commenced to carried out.

In May 2015, I visited Houston Headquarter of American Bureau of Shipping (ABS) and reviewed record books from 1922 to 1932 and riveted steel hull rules. In November 2015, my colleagues visited the Archives of CSSC to review the technical documents and drawings of Kiangnan-built four steam freighters for the United States Shipping Board (hull number: H317–H320). I subsequently reviewed the records of the Emergency Fleet Cooperation under the United States Shipping Board from Australian historian as well as archives and documents of the National Archives of the United States, stored in the Library of California State University, Northridge. Furthermore, the drawings of suspected "prototype ship" were found in archives of Lloyd's Register Head Office, London, UK, with help of Lloyd's Register China.

在江南造船厂厂史和中国近代船舶工业史料中，关于四艘美国万吨级运输舰交付以后的营运情况几乎是空白，只是笼统地提到"直至第二次世界大战期间还在营运"。因此，作者着重对四艘美国万吨级运输舰交付以后的营运情况做了大量的拓展研究后，特意写了本章。

在这四艘美国万吨级运输舰中，"Arkansan"号（原"天朝"号）是最有名的一艘船，资料中该船的记录资料比较完整，相比之下，其他三艘船的信息比较少，也比较零散。为此作者以"Arkansan"号为主线对这四艘万吨级运输舰交付以后的营运史实等进行了核实、甄别和补充。

The operation records after delivery of these four steam freighters are almost blank in modern shipbuilding history of China and corporate history of Jiangnan Shipyard. It was mentioned generally as "these ships were operated until the World War II". This chapter was specially added after studying the materials of these four steamers after delivery.

In these four steam freighters, SS "Arkansan" (originally was SS "Celestial") was the most famous one with more records and archives, but the information of the other three was quite scattered. SS "Arkansan", thus, becomes the mainline for verifying, discriminating and supplementing the operation history after these four steam freighters were delivered.

6.2

入列大来航运公司营运
Serviced for Dollar Steamship Company

罗伯特·大来船长的回忆录中提到，他曾于 1921 年 12 月 12 日收到了一份"关于决定处置战时征召和订造的运输船舶"的政府急件。急件中提到了美方关于第一次世界大战临近结束时过量订造运输船舶的处理意见（参见本书 5.4.1 节）。

当时江南造船所建造的前三艘船已经交付，第四艘也接近完工。一起被处置出售的还有五艘日本朝野船厂（Asano Shipyards）建造的 12 500 载重吨的蒸汽动力货船［由东方商船（Eastern Merchant）订造，应急船队公司的编号可能是 1124 ］。"官府"号自 1921 年 3 月交付以后一直停泊（tied up）在旧金山的莫尔干船坞公司（Moore Dry Dock Company）码头，"东方"号也停泊在该码头进行维护保养。这两艘船交付以后从来没有投入过营运。由于"天朝"号被 Williams & Diamond Company 租用在欧洲执行运输任务，因此一开始并没有将其列入美国海运委员会的出售计划。

在美国有相当多的船舶在交付时实际上是有争议的。尽管合同被授予是在 1918 年，而龙骨铺设是在 1919 年，但船舶交付是在 1920 年的《商船法》（也称为《琼斯法案》，由参议员韦斯利·琼斯提出）实施之后。《琼斯法案》是一项保护性的立法，旨在保护美国造船业。《琼斯法案》"要求所有通过水路在美国港口之间运输的货物都必须由挂美国国旗的船舶完成，这些船必须在美国建造、由美国公民拥有并由美国公民或美国永久居民操作"。

江南造船所建造的四艘船显然在建造地上不符合上述法案要求，这导致一帮律师要求这些船舶只能用于对外贸易。实际上建造这些船舶所用的钢材和大部分主要设备是由美国提供的，它们是在战争期间出于美国政府的意愿被建造的，而且它们的龙骨铺设是在法案通过之前进行的，最终这些事实似乎占了上风。罗伯特·大来的影响可能并没有那么大，他渴望广泛宣传这四艘在这一时期里建造的优秀船舶以及

As mentioned in the memoirs of captain Robert Dollar, he learnt a government dispatch, dated 12 December 1921, regarding the disposition of merchant ships recruited and ordered in wartime. It was also mentioned in this dispatch that a glut of merchant shipping available would be resold on a par with world market (refer to the Section 5.4.1 of this book).

At that time, three steam freighters of series built by Kiangnan had been delivered and the fourth was closely completed. In addition, five 12 500 deadweight steamers built by Japanese Asano Shipyards (ordered by Eastern Merchant with EFC code 1124) were planned for resale. Kiangnan-built SS "Mandarin" had been tied up at the quay of Moore Dry Dock Company since delivery of March, 1921, and SS "Oriental" also had been tied up at the quay of Moore Dry Dock Company for maintenance. These two steam freighters did not carry out any cargo transportation after delivery. SS "Celestial" initially was not listed in resale list of USSB because she was chartered by Williams & Diamond Company for European regional operation.

In the United States there was actually quite a bit of controversy when the ships were delivered. As although the contracts were awarded in 1918 and the keels laid in 1919, they were delivered after the passage of the *Merchant Marine Act* of 1920 (also known as the *Jones Act*, as it was introduced by Senator Wesley Jones). The *Jones Act* was a protectionist piece of legislation designed to safeguard the U.S. Shipbuilding Industry. The Jones Act "requires that all goods transported by water between U.S. ports have to be carried on American flag ships, constructed in the United States, owned by American citizens, and crewed by American citizens and American permanent residents".

These four Kiangnan-built freighters obviously failed at construction place. This caused a group of attorneys to claim that the vessels should only be used in foreign trade. The fact that the steel and most major components were supplied by the United States, that they were built on behalf of the U.S. Government during a time of war and that their keels were laid before the act was passed eventually seemed to prevail. Robert Dollar's influence probably did not hurt as well as he was keen to get his hands on what were widely reported to be the four finest steam freighters built during this period and for decades thereafter. To be fair, Robert Dollar did intend to use them primarily in his transpacific trade, but the

之后几十年里的营运情况。说句公道话，罗伯特·大来的确打算主要在他的跨太平洋贸易中使用这些船舶，但美国航运委员会也确实证明了这些船舶也可用于沿海贸易。从大来公司的航线服务可以看出，公司需要两者兼顾。虽然大来的船只跨太平洋航行，但也航行于美国西海岸的各个港口，从中国运来成品，并为最终返回中国的航程装满待售的原材料。大来公司是当时中国造船业和建筑业木材的主要供应商之一。

United States Shipping Board did certify them for use in the coastwise trade as well. As you can see Dollar Line service, Dollar Steamship Company required both. Although his vessels sailed Trans-Pacific voyages they also ran coastwise voyages up and down various ports on the west coast dropping off finished goods from China and picking up raw material for their eventual return to China. Robert Dollar Company was one of the primary sources of lumber for the Chinese shipbuilding and construction industries at that time.

尽管“天朝”号执行了一个到欧洲的航次，但它和它姐妹船的命运和战争期间建造的其他成千上万吨的船只一样被闲置着。20 世纪 20 年代，航运业并没有那么兴旺发达。尽管美国新建了一些客船、油轮和其他特种船舶，并设法将船只从战时使用转为民用，但还是有许多造船厂被关闭导致数千人失业。

Despite the one voyage by the SS “Celestial” to Europe, she and her sisters suffered the same fate as hundreds of thousands of tons of other vessels built during the war, and all were sitting idle. The 1920s were not so roaring for the shipping industry. Despite building some passenger vessels, tankers and other specialized vessels, and making great efforts to convert vessels from wartime purpose to civilian use, many shipyards were closed and thousands of men were out of work.

对于货船来说，尽管已经面向世界市场出售和转卖多余的船舶，但直到第二次世界大战结束，供给从未如此之大，需求从未如此之低。在 1921 年间，美国政府曾多次试图拍卖这些船舶。图 6-1 是 1921 年 12 月 10 日在《航海公报》上刊登的一则拍卖广告。值得注意的是，此时第四艘万吨级运输舰“国泰”号还没有建造完成。

For freighters, the supply had never been greater and the demand never lower until the end of the World War Ⅱ, despite opening the sale of the surplus vessels to the world-wide market. On several occasions during 1921 the American Government tried to auction off the vessels. Figure 6–1, is an advertisement appearing on 10 December 1921 in *The Nautical Gazette*. It is worth noting that the SS “Cathay” had not yet even been completed at this moment.

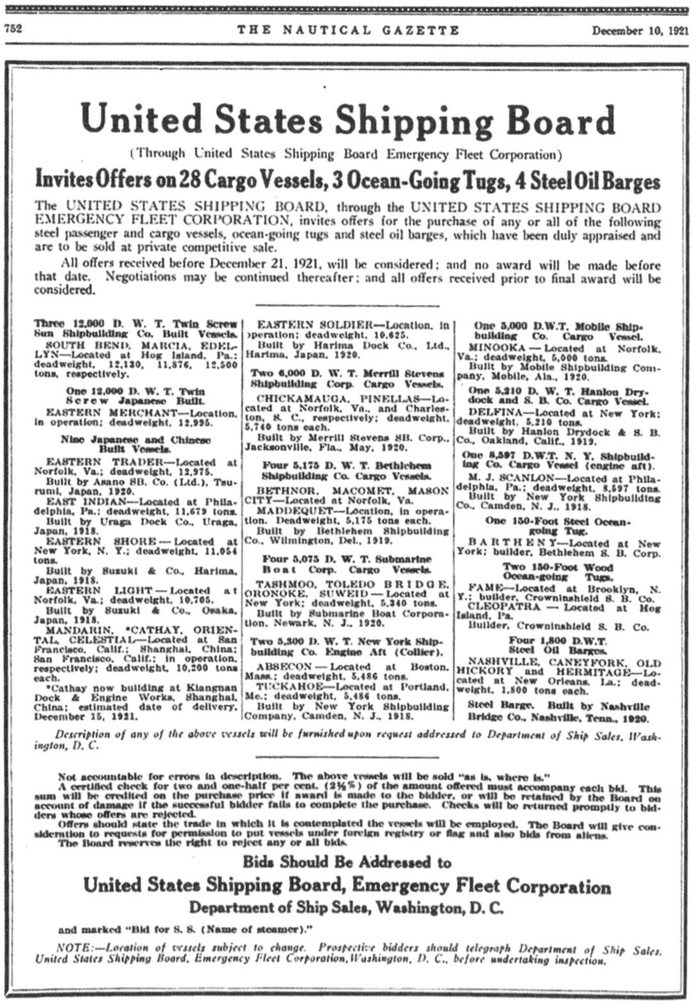
752 THE NAUTICAL GAZETTE December 10, 1921

United States Shipping Board

(Through United States Shipping Board Emergency Fleet Corporation)

Invites Offers on 28 Cargo Vessels, 3 Ocean-Going Tugs, 4 Steel Oil Barges

The UNITED STATES SHIPPING BOARD, through the UNITED STATES SHIPPING BOARD EMERGENCY FLEET CORPORATION, invites offers for the purchase of any or all of the following steel passenger and cargo vessels, ocean-going tugs and steel oil barges, which have been duly appraised and are to be sold at private competitive sale.

All offers received before December 21, 1921, will be considered; and no award will be made before that date. Negotiations may be continued thereafter; and all offers received prior to final award will be considered.

Three 12,000 D. W. T. Twin Screw Sun Shipbuilding Co. Built Vessels.

SOUTH BEND, MARCIA, EDELLYN—Located at Hog Island, Pa.; deadweight, 12,130, 11,876, 12,500 tons, respectively.

One 12,000 D. W. T. Twin Screw Japanese Built.

EASTERN MERCHANT—Location, in operation; deadweight, 12,995.

Nine Japanese and Chinese Built Vessels.

EASTERN TRADER—Located at Norfolk, Va.; deadweight, 12,975.

Built by Asano SB. Co. (Ltd.), Tsurumi, Japan, 1920.

EAST INDIAN—Located at Philadelphia, Pa.; deadweight, 11,679 tons.

Built by Uraga Dock Co., Uraga, Japan, 1918.

EASTERN SHORE—Located at New York, N. Y.; deadweight, 11,054 tons.

Built by Suzuki & Co., Harima, Japan, 1918.

EASTERN LIGHT—Located at Norfolk, Va.; deadweight, 10,705.

Built by Suzuki & Co., Osaka, Japan, 1918.

MANDARIN, *CATHAY, ORIENTAL, CELESTIAL—Located at San Francisco, Calif.; Shanghai, China; San Francisco, Calif.; in operation, respectively; deadweight, 10,200 tons each.

*Cathay now building at Kiangnan Dock & Engine Works, Shanghai, China; estimated date of delivery, December 15, 1921.

EASTERN SOLDIER—Location, in operation; deadweight, 10,625.

Built by Harima Dock Co., Ltd., Harima, Japan, 1920.

Two 6,000 D. W. T. Merrill Stevens Shipbuilding Corp. Cargo Vessels.

CHICKAMAUGA, PINELLAS—Located at Norfolk, Va., and Charleston, S. C., respectively; deadweight, 5,740 tons each.

Built by Merrill Stevens SB. Corp., Jacksonville, Fla., May, 1920.

Four 5,175 D. W. T. Bethlehem Shipbuilding Co. Cargo Vessels.

BETHNOR, MACOMET, MASON CITY—Located at Norfolk, Va.

MADDEQUET—Location, in operation. Deadweight, 5,175 tons each.

Built by Bethlehem Shipbuilding Co., Wilmington, Del., 1919.

Four 5,075 D. W. T. Submarine Boat Corp. Cargo Vessels.

TASHMOO, TOLEDO BRIDGE, ORONOKE, SUWEID—Located at New York; deadweight, 5,240 tons.

Built by Submarine Boat Corporation, Newark, N. J., 1920.

Two 5,300 D. W. T. New York Shipbuilding Co. Engine Aft (Collier).

ABSECON—Located at Boston, Mass.; deadweight, 5,486 tons.

TUCKAHOE—Located at Portland, Me.; deadweight, 5,486 tons.

Built by New York Shipbuilding Company, Camden, N. J., 1918.

One 5,000 D.W.T. Mobile Shipbuilding Co. Cargo Vessel.

MINOOKA—Located at Norfolk, Va.; deadweight, 5,000 tons.

Built by Mobile Shipbuilding Company, Mobile, Ala., 1920.

One 5,210 D. W. T. Hanlon Drydock and S. B. Co. Cargo Vessel.

DELFINA—Located at New York; deadweight, 5,210 tons.

Built by Hanlon Drydock & S. B. Co., Oakland, Calif., 1919.

One 8,597 D.W.T. N. Y. Shipbuilding Co. Cargo Vessel (engine aft).

M. J. SCANLON—Located at Philadelphia, Pa.; deadweight, 8,597 tons.

Built by New York Shipbuilding Co., Camden, N. J., 1918.

One 150-Foot Steel Ocean-going Tug.

BARTHENY—Located at New York; builder, Bethlehem S. B. Corp.

Two 150-Foot Wood Ocean-going Tugs.

FAME—Located at Brooklyn, N. Y.; builder, Crowninshield S. B. Co.

CLEOPATRA—Located at Hog Island, Pa.

Builder, Crowninshield S. B. Co.

Four 1,800 D.W.T. Steel Oil Barges.

NASHVILLE, CANEYFORK, OLD HICKORY and HERMITAGE—Located at New Orleans, La.; deadweight, 1,800 tons each.

Steel Barge. Built by Nashville Bridge Co., Nashville, Tenn., 1920.

Description of any of the above vessels will be furnished upon request addressed to Department of Ship Sales, Washington, D. C.

Not accountable for errors in description. The above vessels will be sold “as is, where is.”

A certified check for two and one-half per cent. (2½%) of the amount offered must accompany each bid. This sum will be credited on the purchase price if award is made to the bidder, or will be retained by the Board on account of damage if the successful bidder fails to complete the purchase. Checks will be returned promptly to bidders whose offers are rejected.

Offers should state the trade in which it is contemplated the vessels will be employed. The Board will give consideration to requests for permission to put vessels under foreign registry or flag and also bids from aliens.

The Board reserves the right to reject any or all bids.

Bids Should Be Addressed to

United States Shipping Board, Emergency Fleet Corporation

Department of Ship Sales, Washington, D. C.

and marked “Bid for S. S. (Name of steamer).”

NOTE:—Location of vessels subject to change. Prospective bidders should telegraph Department of Ship Sales, United States Shipping Board, Emergency Fleet Corporation, Washington, D. C., before undertaking inspection.

图 6–1　1921 年 12 月 10 日在《航海公报》上刊登的一则拍卖广告

Figure 6–1　Auction advertisement appearing on 10 December 1921, in *The Nautical Gazette*

美国航运业放缓导致美方取消了再建造八艘"官府"系列万吨轮的选择船订单，但江南造船所的工作仍在继续，只是规模较小。美国信守承诺，让江南造船所为美国海军的长江巡防队建造 6 艘长江炮艇。这些长江炮艇采用一些太平洋岛屿的名字命名，它们是关岛（PG-43）、土土伊拉岛（PG-44）、班乃岛（PG-45）、瓦胡岛（PG-46）、吕宋岛（PG-47）和棉兰老岛（PG-48）。然而，当时的中国局势比较混乱，尤其是在上海，导致许多工程延误，这些炮艇直到 1928 年才全部完成建造。图 6-2 为艺术家绘制的长江炮艇效果图。

Although there was a slow-down in the shipping industry of the United States, and the option to build eight more of the Mandarin series freighters with identical design was withdrawn, the construction work was continued at Kiangnan, just on a smaller scale. American kept its commitment to have Kiangnan build six river gunboats for the United States Navy's Yangtze Patrol. These gunboats were named as the island in the Pacific Ocean. They were the Guam (PG-43), Tutuila (PG-44), Panay (PG-45), Oahu (PG-46), Luzon (PG-47), and Mindanao (PG-48). Turmoil in China at this time, however, and especially in Shanghai, resulted in many delays and these gunboats would not be completed until 1928. Figure 6-2 is an artist's picture of Yangtze River gunboat.

图 6-2　艺术家绘制的长江炮艇效果图
Figure 6-2　Artist's picture of Yangtze River gunboat

根据上述《航海公报》的同一篇文章，当这一切都尘埃落定之时，即船舶订造时，美国纳税人支付了约每载重吨 200 美元，即为 1 万载重吨的货轮支付了近 200 万美元。大来航运公司以每吨 30 美元，或者说每艘约 30 万美元的价格买下，里面有 85% 惊人的折扣。经通胀率修正后（1922—2024 年），大来航运公司购买时每艘船仅仅支付了 420 万美元而不是约 3 690 万美元。

这笔交易引起了一些人的关注。1922 年 3 月号的《太平洋海洋评论》在一个题为"深海航运"的定期专栏上刊登了一篇题为"大来收购"的文章，文章表示：

"当这支庞大的船队被出售时，罗伯特·大来船长收购了由上海江南造船所为美国海运委员会建造的四艘一万载重吨的'国泰'号、'东方'号、'官府'号和'天朝'号货轮，引起了不小的轰动。在这次收购中，通常被认为是美国所有船东中最精明的大来船长，对中国船厂给予了很高的评价，其他人和他一起赞美了这些船。它们的工艺质量无人能及，部分原因是它们不完全是在战争压力下建造的，且建造过程中使用了大量的手工劳动。大来船长非常清楚这些船是什么，因为他的公司是江南造船所与美国政府交易和处理船舶交付业务的代理者。其中三艘已经交付，'国泰'号已于 2 月 1 日由大来公司交付给美国海运委员会。'东方'号在赴美航程中一个汽缸产生了裂缝，目前正在奥克兰的莫尔干船坞公司修理。因此在所有交付给美国海运委员会的四艘货船中，它将是最后一艘而不是'国泰'号。这四艘船将继续挂美国国旗。"

虽然美国航运委员会没有透露最终的成交价格，但相关报告显示，大来船长在这笔交易中为每载重吨支付了 32 美元。考虑到这些船的质量，毫无疑问他捡了个大便宜。

1922 年 4 月号的《太平洋海洋评论》刊登了一篇题为"美国海运委员会的工作接近尾声"的短文。文中记载："1921 年经济不景气时，对造船业的一项重要的扶持即将消失。海运委员会的工作即将结束。在太平洋沿岸，3 月中旬还剩下一艘中国建造的货轮'东方'号，它在赴旧金山的航程中裂了一个气缸，直到裂纹修复后才被海运委员会接收。莫尔干船坞公司完成修理工作后，大来公司作为江南造船所的代理人，将船正式交付给了海运委员会。海运委员会也同

According to the same article in *The Nautical Gazette* above, when it was all said and done, the American taxpayer paid roughly $200 per deadweight ton for each of the 10 000 deadweight tons vessels or $2 000 000 each in shipbuilding contract signing. Dollar Steamship Company bought them for $30 per deadweight ton for each, or $300 000 each vessel, an astonishing 85% discount. Adjusted for inflation of 1922 to 2024, Dollar Steamship Company paid $4.2 million per ship rather than about $36.9 million.

The purchase raised a few eyebrows. In the March 1922 edition of the *Pacific Marine Review* in a sub-section titled "The Dollar Purchase" under a regular article titled "Deep-Sea Shipping", this article wrote:

"While this enormous fleet is being offered, captain Robert Dollar has created more than a little stir by purchasing the four 10 000-ton deadweight freighters, SS 'Cathay', SS 'Oriental', SS 'Mandarin' and SS 'Celestial', built for the United States Shipping Board by the Kiangnan Dock & Engineering Works, Shanghai. In this purchase, captain Dollar, who is generally regarded as the shrewdest of all American shipowners, has paid a high compliment to the Chinese builder. Others join him in praising the vessels. They are second to none in quality of workmanship, partly because they were not built under stress of war but also because of the truly immense amount of hand labor that went into them. Captain Dollar knew full well what the vessels were, because his company acted as agent of the Kiangnan in its dealings with the government and in delivering the vessels. Three have been delivered, the SS 'Cathay' having been turned over to the Shipping Board by the Robert Dollar Company February 1st. The SS 'Oriental', cracked a cylinder on her voyage to the United States and is at the Moore Dry Dock Company, Oakland, for repairs. She, therefore, and not the SS 'Cathay', will be the last of all cargo vessels to be delivered to the board. The four will remain under the United States flag."

Although the United States Shipping Board has not disclosed the price, report has it that captain Dollar paid $32 per deadweight ton. When the quality of the vessels is considered, there is no doubt that he got a real bargain.

In a brief article in April 1922 edition of the *Pacific Marine Review* titled "USSB Work Nears End": "One substantial support of shipbuilding during the lean year of 1921 is about to disappear. The Shipping Board program is near an end. On the Pacific coast the one vessel that remained to be delivered at the middle of March was the Chinese-built freighter SS 'Oriental', which cracked a cylinder on her voyage to San Francisco and could not be accepted by the board until the damage was repaired. When the Moore Dry Dock Company has completed the work, the Robert Dollar Company, acting as agent of the Kiangnan, the builder, will solemnly hand the vessel over to the Shipping Board, which quite as solemnly will accept her; and when a decent interval of a few minutes

样庄严地接收了它，仅仅间隔几分钟后，海运委员会将船交还给以买方身份出现的大来公司。"

1922 年，总部设在旧金山的大来航运公司买下了这四艘江南造船所建造的万吨轮。大来航运公司将它们改名为"Stuart Dollar"号（H317，原名："官府"号）、"Margaret Dollar"号（H318，原名："天朝"号）、"Melville Dollar"号（H319，原名："东方"号）和"Diana Dollar"号（H320，原名："国泰"号）。大来航运公司将这四艘船用于北美至远东的木材运输。图 6-3 为 1923 年 6 月 25 日"Margaret Dollar"号在加拿大不列颠哥伦比亚省的温哥华港从驳船上装运木材的照片[1]。

has elapsed, the Shipping Board will hand the vessel back to the Robert Dollar Company in its capacity as purchaser."

In 1922, Dollar Steamship Company, headquarter in San Francisco, purchased these four Kiangnan-built steam freighters. Dollar Steamship Company changed their names to "Stuart Dollar" (H317, originally was "Mandarin"), "Margaret Dollar" (H318, originally was "Celestial"), "Melville Dollar" (H319, originally was "Oriental") and "Diana Dollar" (H320, originally was "Cathay") respectively. Dollar Steamship Company put these four steam freighters into timber transportation from North America to the Far East. Figure 6-3 shows SS "Margaret Dollar" loaded timber from barge at Vancouver Port, British Columbia of Canada on 25 June 1923.

图 6-3　"Margaret Dollar"号在加拿大的温哥华港从驳船上装运木材（1923 年 6 月 25 日）
Figure 6-3　SS "Margaret Dollar" loaded timber from barge at Vancouver Port (25 June 1923)

以 "Margaret Dollar" 号（即第二艘船 "天朝" 号）为例，该船在 1923 年 5 月到 1934 年 6 月营运期间，长期承担 "大三角贸易航线" 的运输任务。该贸轮以太平洋美洲西北岸与远东地区为主要服务范围，其航行网络覆盖美国俄勒冈州的波特兰，华盛顿州的阿伯丁、贝灵哈姆、埃弗里特、安吉利斯、西雅图和塔科马；加拿大不列颠哥伦比亚省的新威斯敏斯特、艾丽斯港和温哥华等重要港口。在远东地区其常规停靠港包括中国的香港和上海、日本的大阪和横滨、菲律宾的马尼拉。该船在此跨洋贸易中主要承担大宗木材运输任务。

1935 年，这四艘船被转到了大来公司的另外一个子公司大来码头轮船公司（Dollar Terminal Steamship Co. Inc.）的名下。

Taking SS "Margaret Dollar" (i.e., SS "Celestial") as an example, she mainly sailed in Great Triangular Trade Route during May of 1923 to June of 1934 with round trip between Pacific Northwest and the Far East (Orient). Main call ports in Pacific Northwest coast were: Portland of Oregon State, Aberdeen, Bellingham, Everett, Port Angeles, Seattle and Tacoma of Washington State, USA; New Westminster, Port Alice and Vancouver, British Colombia Province of Canada. Main call ports in the Far East were: Hong Kong and Shanghai of China, Osaka and Yokohama of Japan, as well as Manila of Philippines. Main cargo was timber.

In 1935, these four steamers were resold to Dollar Terminal Steamship Co. Inc., a subsidiary of Robert Dollar Company.

6.3

入列美洲－夏威夷航运公司营运
Jointed American-Hawaiian Service

6.3.1

转卖至美洲－夏威夷航运公司
Purchased by American-Hawaiian

1936 年，大来码头轮船公司将这四艘船转卖给了美洲－夏威夷航运公司（American-Hawaiian Steamship Company），其总部设在旧金山和纽约，该公司的两幢建筑至今还保存着。图 6-4 为美洲－夏威夷航运公司的帽徽。图 6-5 为美洲－夏威夷航运公司船舶烟囱上的标志。

In 1936, Dollar Terminal Steamship Co., Inc. resold these four steam freighters to American-Hawaiian Steamship Company. The Headquarter of American-Hawaiian Steamship Company San Francisco (215 Market Street in the Matson Building) and New York (East Coast Office, 90 Broad Street in lower Manhattan), these two buildings are well preserved now. Figure 6–4 is the hat badge of American-Hawaiian Steamship Company, and Figure 6–5 is the funnel mark of American-Hawaiian Steamship Company.

图 6-4　美洲－夏威夷航运公司的帽徽
Figure 6–4　The hat badge of American–Hawaiian Steamship Company

图 6-5　美洲－夏威夷航运公司船舶烟囱上的标志
Figure 6–5　The funnel mark of American–Hawaiian Steamship Company

美洲－夏威夷航运公司根据其采用美国州名命名船舶的规则将四艘船更名为："Floridian"号（H317，原名："官府"号）、"Arkansan"号（H318，原名："天朝"号）、"Carolinian"号（H319，原名："东方"号）和"Alabaman"号（H320，原名："国泰"号）。这四艘船的加盟，使美洲－夏威夷航运公司的船队总数达到了41艘，其中33艘用于沿海运输（inter-coastal service）、8艘用于跨太平洋运输（oriental service）[2]。

American-Hawaiian Steamship Company, as per their naming principle of state name of the United States, renamed "Floridian" (H317, originally was "Mandarin"/"Stuart Dollar"), "Arkansan" (H318, originally was "Celestial"/"Margaret Dollar"), "Carolinian" (H319, originally was "Oriental"/"Melville Dollar") and "Alabaman" (H320, originally was "Cathay"/"Diana Dollar"). The fleet of American-Hawaiian Steamship Company reached 41 ships in total after these four ships joined its fleet, 33 ships were put into inter-coastal service, and 8 ships were put into oriental service, respectively.

美洲－夏威夷航运公司为了将这四艘船升级到公司的标准并满足当局［美国海事检验和航海局（U.S. Bureau of Marine Inspection and Navigation）］的规范，对这四艘船进行了改装，总金额为40万~50万美元。这对大萧条时代太平洋沿岸的船厂来说是一个金额很大的改装合同。图6-6为莫尔干船坞公司的广告，从坞内船舶密集排列的盛况可见早先船厂的繁忙景象[3]，但在大萧条时代这已是过去的辉煌了。位于加利福尼亚州旧金山和奥克兰的莫尔干船坞公司（Moore Dry Dock Company）拿到了三艘船的改装合同，即"Diana Dollar"/"Alabaman"号、"Margaret Dollar"/"Arkansan"号、"Melville Dollar"/"Carolinian"号；而位于华盛顿州西雅图的托德干船坞公司（Todd Dry Dock Company）则拿到了剩下一艘船的改装合同，即"Stuart Dollar"/"Floridian"号。

In order to satisfy company standards and rules of authority (U.S. Bureau of Marine Inspection and Navigation), American-Hawaiian Steamship Company decided to retrofit these four steam freighters (reconditioning) with the cost of 400 000 to 500 000 U.S. dollar in total. It was really a big retrofitting contract for the shipyards along the pacific coast especially in the Great Depression period. Figure 6-6 shows many ships undergoing repairs at Moore Dry Dock Company "the yard that's always busy", but it was pasted glorious situation not in period of the Great Depression. Finally Moore Dry Dock Company in San Francisco and Oakland, California, secured retrofit contracts of three steam freighters, "Diana Dollar"/"Alabaman", "Margaret Dollar"/"Arkansan", and "Melville Dollar"/"Carolinian", and Todd Dry Dock Company in Seattle, Washington, secured a retrofit contract of one steam freighter, "Stuart Dollar"/"Floridian".

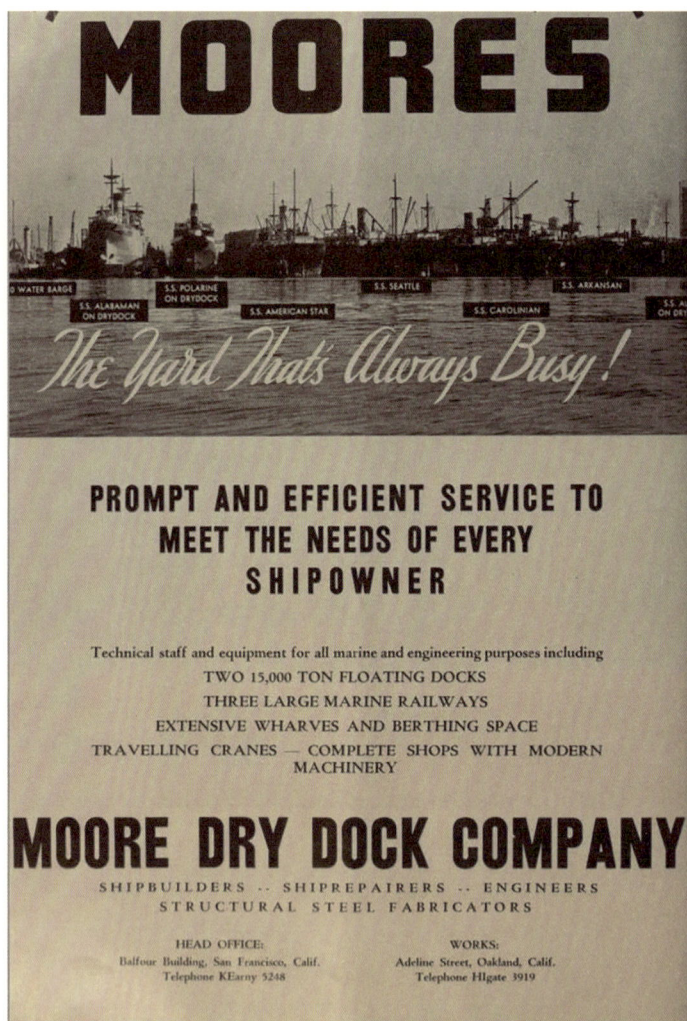

图6-6　莫尔干船坞公司坞内船舶密集靠泊的盛况
Figure 6-6　Many ships under repairing in Moore Dry Dock Company

6.3.2

莫尔干船坞公司改装
Reconditioning in Moore Dry Dock Company

莫尔干船坞公司和美洲－夏威夷航运公司签订了三艘船的改装合同，并由船厂实施了改装工程。

第一，检查船体结构。船舶进坞以后，清除了船壳上附着的海洋生物和不好的油漆，并对 26 000 平方英尺（2 415.48 平方米）的船壳板进行了喷砂处理；平均每艘船有 14 000~15 000 个铆钉进行了紧固或焊接处理。

第二，修理甲板。甲板上的敷料全部被去除以便检查甲板钢板的腐蚀情况。对上层建筑区域腐蚀严重的部位采用了焊接补丁或换板的方式进行修补。

第三，美洲－夏威夷航运公司十分注重船员的舒适性，莫尔干船坞公司根据船东的要求对船员的居住舱室进行了大规模的改造（virtually rebuilt）。比较改造前后的布置图，这些舱室格局上的改造主要集中在艉部遮蔽甲板下的船员舱室，而舯部舱室的改造主要集中在内部的装饰材料和舒适性设备设施的升级。如前文所述，从总布置图 7008C（甲板平面）可见在艉部上甲板布置了 11 个双人房间，共 22 人，艉部还有 12 张双人床共 24 人的临时铺位。估计这是战时运输舰的配置要求。

在这次改造过程中将这个甲板区域改成左右舷一共 8 个房舱，其中 5 个双人间、3 个三人间，中间是一个很大的起居室。所有这些房舱都配置了床头灯、镜面灯和通风装置以及蒸汽加热器。围壁板和天花板上包覆了塑料材质的软饰（plastic cork），这不仅可以有效地保温而且可消除钢板上的结露。起居室内配置了一张大桌子、舒适的椅子和书架以及其他一些舒适性设施。低级船员房间和卫生间的地面都敷设了瓷砖，上层建筑顶部露天甲板都敷设了防水防滑的甲板敷料。所有这些装饰材料都是旧金山的 L. S. Case 公司提供并安装的。

Moore Dry Dock Company signed retrofitting contracts of these three steam freighters with American-Hawaiian Steamship Company, and then the reconditioning works were commenced to be carried out at its dockyards.

Firstly, hull structure survey was carried out by shipyard. Sea growth and poor quality painting were removed, and shell plating of approximately 26 000 square feet (2 415.48 square meters) were treated by sand blasting. Average 14 000 to 15 000 rivets were fastened or welded.

Secondly, deck repairing was performed, and all deck covering was removed in order to inspect corrosion of deck plating. Welded patches or inserted plates were applied in way of seriously corroded places in superstructure area.

Thirdly, American-Hawaiian Steamship Company was quite concerned about the crew's comfortability. Moore Dry Dock Company virtually rebuilt accommodation according to owner's requirements. Comparing arrangement before and after rebuilding work, the layout of cabin was mainly rearranged in stern area under shelter deck, and decorating materials and comfortable facilities were mostly upgraded in superstructure and accommodation amidship. As per fore chapter described, 11 double rooms and 22 persons in total, were arranged on aft upper deck, and 12 temporary double beds and 24 persons were arranged at stern as shown as General Arrangement Plan of 7008C (deck plans). Such arrangement might be requirement for armed transportation ship.

In this reconditioning, this area was modified into 8 cabins, 5 double rooms and 3 triple rooms, and a large living room was formed in between. Bed lamp, mirror light, ventilation spreader and steam heater were equipped in those rooms. Walls and ceiling plate were covered by plastic cork for improving thermal insulation and reducing condensation. A large table, easy chairs, bookracks and other comfortable facilities were equipped in living room. Tiles were laid on deck in crew's cabins and lavatories and water proof and anti-slip deck covering were applied on top of superstructure. All these decorating materials were provided and installed by L. S. Case Inc. in San Francisco.

第四，对所有机械设备进行了彻底性的检查，主要蒸汽管路也大部分换新。货物起重绞车也换成了 Lidgerwood 公司生产的 8.5 英寸（21.59 厘米）× 8 英寸（20.32 厘米）蒸汽绞车并增加了相应的铸钢阀件，所有绞车的采购是通过旧金山的 Thos. J. Baird 公司操作的。船上的备用桨轴是通过旧金山的 General Engineering Company 采购的，备用桨是由莫尔干船坞公司自行铸造和加工的。

第五，在艏部舱口盖前端增加了一对起重柱，并为起重柱上的货物吊杆增加了两台绞车。在艏部设置一对起重柱是当时干货船上比较流行的吊杆布置形式，但不知为什么在 1919 年江南造船所设计这型船时省略了这对起重柱。从图纸上分析，原来一舱和二舱之间吊杆的工作半径完全可以覆盖，增加这对起重柱是为了双杆联合作业增加吊重还是提高小件货物的装卸效率？

第六，所有的电气布线、电气设备、发电机和电机的检修工作是由旧金山的一家名叫 Toumey Electric & Engineering 的公司分包的。对所有的电缆进行了更新并安装了许多新的电气设备。除了前面提到的船员舱室内的灯具和通风装置的更新之外，Toumey Electric & Engineering 公司还在遮蔽甲板上加装了甲板照明灯以改善安全作业环境，在货舱里也加装了固定照明灯具；在机炉舱和储藏室里增加了照明灯具。此外还检查了机械舱室内的电气系统、电报系统，以及为满足美国海事检验和航海局的新规定安装了 Bendix 声力电话系统。

第七，在改装和修理过程中，莫尔干船坞公司更换了船上的所有救生艇，船每侧配置了一艘救生艇，且救生艇的容量增加了，单一侧的救生艇可以容纳全部正常配置的船员，这已经达到了现代船舶救生规范的要求。从图 6–7 可以看出，"Arkansan" 号的一侧只配置了一艘救生艇，全船共两艘救生艇。

第八，船体的涂装也改成美洲－夏威夷航运公司的标准涂装：水线以下为暗红色，水线以上为黑色，上层建筑为白色，烟囱上的标志如图 6–5 所示。

虽然没有查到关于托德干船坞公司改装的 "Stuart Dollar"/"Floridian" 号的信息，但相信改装内容是一

Fourthly, all machinery and equipments were completely overhauled, and main steam pipes were mostly replaced by new components. Derrick winches were replaced by 8.5-inch (21.59 centimeters) × 8-inch (20.32 centimeters) steam driven winches made by Lidgerwood Company, and relevant steel casting valves were also added. These winches were purchased via a trading firm called "Thos. J. Baird", and spare propeller shaft was purchased via General Engineering Company, both in San Francisco. Spare propeller was cast and machined by Moore Dry Dock Company themselves.

Fifthly, one pair of king post was added on fore body in front of hatch cover, and two supplemental winches were added dedicated for cargo booms on post. One pair of king post was popular derrick layout of dry cargo ship at that time, but why was such king post ignored in Kiangnan's design in 1919? The working radius of derrick in between No.1 and No.2 cargo holds can fully cover after double checking drawings. Was the purpose of king posts considered for co-operation of two booms or improving the efficiency of handling small parcels and pallets?

Sixthly, all retrofitting works of cable laying, electric equipment, generators and motors were subcontracted by Toumey Electric & Engineering Company in San Francisco. All cables were renewed and new electric equipments were additionally installed. Besides renew works for light and vent in crew's cabins mentioned before, Toumey Electric & Engineering Company specially installed deck light on shelter deck for improving safety operation and fixed lamps in cargo holds, additional lamps in boiler and engine room as well as storage spaces. Further shipyard inspected electric systems in machinery spaces and telegraph system, and installed Bendix sound power phone system for satisfying new requirement of U. S. Bureau of Marine Inspection and Navigation.

Seventhly, Moore Dry Dock Company replaced all lifeboats on board during reconditioning. One each fitted at sides, but the capacities of life boats were enlarged for accommodating all crews and passengers on board in normal duty. Such arrangement has been in line with lifesaving requirement of modern ship. As shown as Figure 6–7, one set of life boat equipped on one side of SS "Arkansan", two sets in total.

Eighthly, exterior coating was changed to standard coating scheme of American-Hawaiian Shipping Company, i.e., under the water line, dull red; above water line, black; superstructure, white; funnel mark as shown as Figure 6–5.

Although no information was found regarding SS "Stuart Dollar"/ "Floridian" retrofitted in Todd Dry Dock Company, reconditioning scope was

样的，如有差别也只会体现在施工细节和选择的供应
商不同方面。

most properly identical, and maybe some deviations were in construction details and different suppliers.

图 6-7 "Arkansan" 号改装完成后的航行照片[4]
Figure 6-7　SS "Arkansan" trailed after reconditioning

　　作者凑齐了一张江南造船所建造的四艘船的全家福照片（见图 6-8）[5]，非常珍贵。左上为摄于 1939 年 4 月 3 日的 "Alabaman" 号；右上为摄于 1938 年 11 月 15 日的 "Arkansan" 号；右下为摄于 1939 年 1 月 17 日的 "Carolinian" 号，从码头仓库的屋顶上可以看到积雪；左下为 "Floridian" 号，拍摄日期不详，但推测应该和其他三艘船的拍摄日期相近。

　　A precious photo (see Figure 6-8) shows Kiangnan's quadruple. Upper left is SS "Alabaman", 3 April 1939；upper right is SS "Arkansan", 15 November 1938; lower right is SS "Carolinian", 17 January 1939, and snow was on the roof of warehouse on quay；lower left is SS "Floridian", the date is not clear, but it should be taken in the date close to that of the other three ships.

对比这些照片可以看出，"Arkansan"号和其他三艘船在外观上是有差异的：一是"Arkansan"号艏部和上层建筑区域的舷墙以及船体均为黑色，而其他三艘船则为白色；二是"Arkansan"号的驾驶桥楼为全宽封闭式的，而其他三艘船驾驶室的两翼是开放式的。

Comparing these photos, the appearance of SS "Arkansan" had some difference with the other three steamers: first, the bulwarks in way of bow and superstructure of SS "Arkansan" were painted black the same as hull shell, but the other three were white; second, the navigation bridge of SS "Arkansan" was a fully closed type, but the bridge wings of the other three were open type.

图 6-8　江南造船所建造的四艘船入列美洲－夏威夷航运公司后的照片
Figure 6-8　Kiangnan-built 4 steam freighters in American-Hawaiian's Fleet

6.4

四艘万吨轮的营运史
Fleet Operation History of Four Steam Freighters

作者综合了收集到的关于江南造船所建造的四艘万吨轮的信息和资料，将四艘船的营运历史汇总如下：

Based on collected information of Kiangnan-built four steam freighters, operation history was summarized as follows:

首制船"官府"号（H317）

The First Steam Freighter SS "Mandarin" (H317)

建造时的船体号：	H317	Hull number of construction:	H317
美国船级社的入级编号：	221227	Register ID of ABS:	221227
总吨：	7 038	Gross tonnage:	7 038

船舶营运史：

Operating history:

♦ 1920 年 6 月 3 日下水时被命名为"官府"号。1921 年 2 月 17 日完工离开江南造船所码头赴美交付给美国海运委员会下属的应急船队公司。

♦ H317 was launched on 3 June 1920 and named as SS "Mandarin" on the same day. On 17 February 1921, SS "Mandarin" departed from quay of Kiangnan for delivering to EFC of USSB.

♦ 1922 年，美国海运委员会将此船出售给总部位于旧金山的大来公司下属的大来航运公司。大来航运公司将其更名为"Stuart Dollar"号。

♦ In 1922, USSB sold SS "Mandarin" to Dollar Steamship Company (Robert Dollar Company, parent company), San Francisco, CA, USA, and she was renamed as SS "Stuart Dollar" by Dollar Steamship Company.

♦ 1935 年，大来航运公司将该船转让给大来公司下属的大来码头轮船公司。

♦ In 1935, Dollar Steamship Company transferred SS "Stuart Dollar" to Dollar Terminal Steamship Co., Inc., a subsidiary of Robert Dollar Company, San Francisco, CA, USA.

♦ 1936 年，大来码头轮船公司将该船转卖给总部位于纽约和旧金山的美洲－夏威夷航运公司，后该船在位于西雅图的托德干船坞公司进行修理改装。美洲－夏威夷航运公司将其更名为"Floridian"号。

♦ In 1936, Dollar Terminal Steamship Co., Inc. sold SS "Stuart Dollar" to American-Hawaiian Steamship Company, New York and San Francisco, USA. She was re-conditioned in Todd Dry Dock Company, Seattle, Washington State, USA. She was renamed as SS "Floridian" by American-Hawaiian Steamship Company.

♦ 1947 年，该船转卖给总部位于纽约的 Naess Mejlaender & Co., Inc. 下属注册在巴拿马的 Nortuna Shipping 公司，并更名为"Norbella"号。

♦ In 1947, She was sold to Nortuna Shipping Co., Inc., Panama, a subsidiary of Naess Mejlaender & Co., Inc., New York, NY, USA. She was renamed as SS "Norbella".

♦ 1948 年 8 月 1 日，"Norbella"号从挪威的纳尔维克（Narvik）装载铁矿石运至美国马里兰州的巴尔的摩（Baltimore）的途中在挪威许斯塔维卡（Hustadvika）的 Myrgrunden 水域搁浅。

♦ On 1 August 1948, SS "Norbella" grounded at Myrgrunden, Hustadvika, Norway on a voyage from Narvik, Norway to Baltimore, MD, USA with iron ore.

♦ 1948 年 8 月 16 日，"Norbella"号打捞起浮后，被判定为结构性全损并被送往拆解。同年 12 月 24 日，在比利时的安特卫普交付给比利时烈日（Liège）的 Ets. Dohmen & Habets 公司进行拆解。

♦ After re-floating on 16 August 1948, she was declared a constructive total loss and sold for scrapping, and delivered on 24 December 1948 at Antwerp, Belgium to Ets. Dohmen & Habets, Liège, Belgium.

第二艘"天朝"号（H318）

The Second Steam Freighter SS "Celestial" (H318)

建造时的船体号：	H318	Hull number of construction:	H318
美国船级社的入级编号：	221479	Register ID of ABS:	221479
总吨：	7 030	Gross tonnage:	7 030

船舶营运史：

Operating history:

◆ 1920 年 8 月 3 日下水时被命名为"天朝"号。1921 年 5 月 21 日完工离开江南造船所码头赴美交付给美国海运委员会下属的应急船队公司。

◆ H318 was launched on 3 August 1920 and named as SS "Celestial" on the same day. On 21 May 1921, SS "Celestial" departed from quay of Kiangnan for delivering to EFC of USSB.

◆ 1922 年，美国海运委员会将此船出售给总部位于旧金山的大来公司下属的大来航运公司。大来航运公司将其更名为"Margaret Dollar"号。"Margaret"是罗伯特·大来妻子所取的名字。

◆ In 1922, USSB sold SS "Celestial" to Dollar Steamship Company. (Robert Dollar Company, parent company), San Francisco, CA, USA, and she was renamed as SS "Margaret Dollar" by Dollar Steamship Company. "Margaret" was the given name by Robert Dollar's wife.

◆ 1935 年，大来航运公司将该船转让给大来公司下属的大来码头轮船公司。

◆ In 1935, Dollar Steamship Company. transferred SS "Margaret Dollar" to Dollar Terminal Steamship Co., Inc., a subsidiary of Robert Dollar Company, San Francisco, CA, USA.

◆ 1936年，该船被转卖给总部位于纽约和旧金山的美洲－夏威夷航运公司，后该船在位于加利福尼亚州旧金山和奥克兰的莫尔干船坞公司进行修理改装。美洲－夏威夷航运公司将其更名为"Arkansan"号。

◆ In 1936, Dollar Terminal Steamship Co., Inc. sold SS "Margaret Dollar" to American-Hawaiian Steamship Company, New York and San Francisco, USA. She was re-conditioned in Moore Dry Dock Company, San Francisco and Oakland, CA, USA. She was renamed as SS "Arkansan" by American-Hawaiian Steamship Company.

◆ 1942 年 6 月 15 日晚上 8：31，在"Arkansan"号从特立尼达和多巴哥的西班牙港出发前往路易斯安那州的新奥尔良的途中，在加勒比海的格林纳达西部海域（12.07°N, 62.51°W）被德国 U–126 潜艇 [艇长恩斯特·鲍尔（Ernst Bauer）] 用鱼雷击沉。

◆ At 8：31 PM, 15 June 1942, SS "Arkansan" was in the voyage from Port of Spain of Trinidad and Tobago to New Orleans of Louisiana. She was attacked by U–126 German submarine (captain Ernst Bauer) and sank in the area of west Grenada, Caribbean Sea (12.07°N, 62.51°W).

历史事件回顾 [6]

"Arkansan" 号装载约 9 000 吨杂货（大部分是咖啡豆）在船长保罗·R. 琼斯（Paul R. Jones）的指挥下于 1942 年 6 月 15 日凌晨从特立尼达和多巴哥的西班牙港出发驶向美国路易斯安那州的新奥尔良。船上有 10 位高级船员、1 位无线电报务员、27 位普通船员和 2 位旅客。

当时在近岸的航段可以得到驻扎在特立尼达的瓦勒基地（Waller Field）的陆军航空兵（Army Air Corps）第一轰炸机中队（Bombardment Squadron）的 B–18 "大刀" 式轰炸机和驻扎在帕里亚湾（Gulf of Paria）的海军 PBY–5 卡塔琳娜（Catalina）水上飞机的空中掩护。B–18A 因未装备雷达不能夜航，而 PBY–5 装备有雷达可夜航巡逻。

Recall of Attack Incident

SS "Arkansan" loaded approximately 9 000 tons cargo (most are coffee beans). On the morning of 15 June 1942, SS "Arkansan" commanded by captain Paul R. Jones departed from Port of Spain of Trinidad and Tobago to New Orleans of Louisiana, USA. 10 officers, 1 radio officer, 27 crews and 2 passengers were on board in total.

The coastal areas could be escorted by B–18 Bolo medium bomber, the 1st Bombardment Squadron of Army Air Corps quartered at Waller Field of Trinidad and PBY–5 Catalina seaplane of Navy, quartered at Gulf of Paria. B–18A was not able to flight in the night because no radar was equipped, but PBY–5 equipped radar enabled to patrol in the night.

背景资料一[7]:"大刀"式轰炸机

道格拉斯 B-18 "大刀"式(Douglas B-18 Bolo)是一型第二次世界大战期间服务于美国陆军航空兵及加拿大皇家空军的轰炸机。B-18 由道格拉斯飞机公司按 DC-2 型运输机为蓝本设计而成,于 1942 年首飞。虽然该机型不是当时最新、最先进的设计,但是首批在第二次世界大战期间用于战斗巡逻的轰炸机。该机除各机翼控制面用布蒙皮包覆以外,其余部分都由金属制成,该机还将装甲融入机身结构内。图 6-9 和图 6-10 分别为 B-18A 和 B-18B 轰炸机。

B-18 "大刀"式轰炸机的机组成员共 6 人,包括驾驶员、无线电操作员、后射手、观察员、投弹手和前射手。座舱盖偏向机身轴线左侧,机头为花房式,可以为观察员提供良好的视野。该机可载弹 2 000 千克。该机的自卫火力比较弱,仅装有 3 挺 7.62 毫米口径的机枪(每挺机枪备弹 300 发)。

Background Information 1: Bolo Bomber

Douglas B-18 Bolo was a medium bomber severed for the U.S. Army Air Corps and Royal Canadian Air Force in the World War II. Design of B-18 was based on the prototype of civilian passenger aircraft Douglas DC-2, and flew for the first time in 1942. Although B-18 was not the most new and advanced design, B-18 was the first batch of bomber to be transferred to patrol duties in the World War II. Except the controlling surfaces were skined by taut fabric, other parts of wing surfaces were covered by metallic material. Further plat type armour was integrated into structure of fuselage. Figures 6-9 and 6-10 are B-18A and B-18B respectively.

The completed aircrew unit of B-18 Bolo bomber consisted of six persons: pilot, radio operator, tail shooter, observer, bomber thrower and front shooter. Canopy for pilot was located on portside of centre line of fuselage, and the bow was specially designed as "greenhouse" in order to provide wider view for observer. B-18 can carry 2 000 kg-weigh bombs. The self-defense weapon of B-18 was quite weak, and only 3 sets of 7.62 mm machine gun were equipped with 300 bullets each.

B-18 "大刀"式轰炸机的主尺度:

The main particulars of B-18 Bolo bomber:

机长:17.63 米	Length:	17.63 m
翼展:27.30 米	Wing span:	27.30 m
机身高:4.62 米	Height:	4.62 m
空载重量:7 403 千克	Light weight:	7 403 kg
发动机:配置两台 Wright 746 千瓦 R-1820-53 发动机	Engines:	Two sets of Wright R-1820-53 with output of 746 kW each
最大起飞重量:12 552 千克	Maximum takeoff weight:	12 552 kg
最大飞行速度:348 千米/时	Maximum speed:	348 km/h
巡航飞行速度:269 千米/时	Cruising speed:	269 km/h
最大飞行高度:7 285 米	Maximum flying altitude:	7 285 m
最大作战半径:1 450 千米	Maximum operational radius:	1 450 km
最大转场航程:3 380 千米	Maximum endurance:	3 380 km

比较图 6-9 和图 6-10 中的机头外形可以看出,B-18B 在机头上部装备了雷达,应该是具备了夜航能力。

Comparing the bow shape on Figures 6-9 and 6-10, B-18B, equipped radar at upper part of the bow, should have the ability of night flight.

图 6-9　部署在阿瓜杜尔塞巴拿马基地的美国陆军航空兵的道格拉斯 B-18A 轰炸机
Figure 6-9　Douglas B-18A Bolo bomber of Army Air Corps in Aguadulce of Panama

背景资料二 [8]：卡塔琳娜水上飞机

PBY-5A 卡塔琳娜水上飞机，是美国联合飞机公司研制的一型水上飞机。该机在第二次世界大战期间广泛装备于美、英海军航空兵以及苏联航空兵。PBY-5A 型是在 PBY-4 水上飞机的基础上改装的水陆两用型号，改型机采用可收放前三点式起落架。PBY-5A 飞机空载重量增加了 1 043 千克，原型机在

Background Information 2: Catalina Seaplane

PBY-5A Catalina seaplane was an American flying boat developed and produced by Consolidated Aircraft Company of the United States. Naval Air Forces of U.S. and UK as well as Air Force of the Soviet Union widely equipped these kinds of seaplanes. PBY-5A was an amphibious aircraft retrofitted on basis of PBY-4 seaplane: retrofitted plane adopted tricycle landing gear. The light weight of PBY-5A was increased by 1 043 kg, and the prototype performed her first flight on 22 November 1939. PBY-5A Catalina seaplane was utmost yield in the history, the

图 6-10　陈列在美国亚利桑那州图森皮马航空博物馆内的道格拉斯 B-18B 轰炸机
Figure 6-10　Douglas B-18B Bolo bomber in Pima Air Museum, Tucson, Arizona, USA

1939 年 11 月 22 日首飞。PBY-5A 卡塔琳娜水上飞机因其卓越战绩成了历史上产量最大、用途最为广泛、最为著名的水上飞机，多用于反潜、轰炸、侦察、反舰、人员运输等。图 6-11 为 PBY-5A 卡塔琳娜水上飞机。

most famous and the multi-task due to their excellent records. PBY-5A Catalina seaplane was mainly used for anti-submarine, bombing, reconnaissance, anti-warship and personnel transportation etc. Figure 6-11 is PBY-5A Catalina seaplane.

图 6-11　PBY-5A 卡塔琳娜水上飞机
Figure 6-11　PBY-5A Catalina seaplane

　　PBY-5A 卡塔琳娜水上飞机的机组成员由 10 人组成。该机长 19.46 米、翼展为 31.70 米、机身高 6.15 米，空载重量为 9 485 千克、最大起飞重量为 16 066 千克，配置两台普惠公司（Pratt & Whitney Company）895 千瓦 R-1830-92 活塞式星型发动机，最大航速为 314 千米 / 时，巡航速度为 201 千米 / 时，最大航程为 4 030 千米，最大飞行高度为 4 000 米。该机装备有 7.62 毫米口径机枪 3 挺、12.7 毫米口径机枪 2 挺，可携带 4 000 磅（1 814 千克）航空炸弹、深水炸弹或鱼雷等武备。

The aircrew of PBY-5A Catalina seaplane consisted of 10 persons. The overall length was 19.46 m, wing span was 31.70 m, height was 6.15 m, light weight was 9 485 kg, and the maximum takeoff weight was 16 066 kg. 2 sets of star type piston engines (R-1830-92) made by Pratt & Whitney Company with output 895 kW were equipped on board. Maximum speed was 314 km/h, cruising speed was 201 km/h, maximum endurance can reach 4 030 km, and maximum flying altitude was 4 000 m. 3 sets of 7.62 mm machine gun and 2 sets of 12.7 mm machine gun were quipped on board. Air bombs, depth bombs or torpedoes in total weight of 4 000 pounds (1 814 kg) can be carried.

"Arkansan" 号的船长保罗·R. 琼斯在太阳落山一个小时后决定停止原来的 Z 形机动航线改为直线航行，期望在夜色的掩护下加快航速，补回一些前面耽搁的时间。船长保罗·R. 琼斯派出了三个瞭望岗并对全船进行灯火管制，但是他并不知道，一艘德国 U–126 潜艇正悄然从侧面接近 "Arkansan" 号。

Paul R. Jones, captain of SS "Arkansan" decided to sail the ship in straight instead of zig-zag maneuvering after one hour of sunset, and he expected to speed up in the night for capturing postponed time. Captain Paul R. Jones arranged three observation posts on board and instructed blackout of whole ship, but he was not aware that a German submarine U–126 quietly approached to SS "Arkansan".

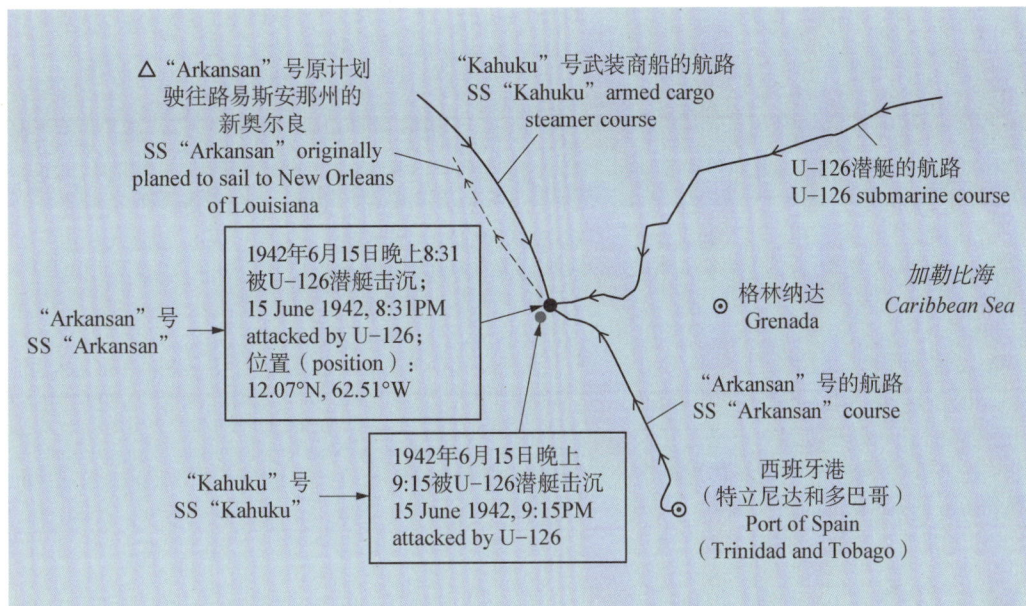

图 6–12 "Arkansan" 号和 U–126 潜艇的航行轨迹 [9]
Figure 6–12 Navigation tracks of SS "Arkansan" and U–126

1942 年 6 月 15 日晚上 8：31，无武装、无护航的 "Arkansan" 号在加勒比海的格林纳达西部海域被德国 U–126 潜艇（艇长恩斯特·鲍尔）用鱼雷击沉。参见图 6–12。

At 8：31 PM, 15 June 1942, non-armed and non-escorted SS "Arkansan" was sunken at west sea area of Grenada, Caribbean Sea, by torpedo attack of German U–126 submarine (captain was Ernst Bauer). Refer to Figure 6–12.

击沉 "Arkansan" 号的德国 U–126 潜艇是一种 IXC 型的大型潜艇，艇首和艇尾共装备六具鱼雷发射管，可发射 G7e 电动鱼雷，其战斗部装药量为 617 磅（279.87 千克）。甲板上指挥台前装备有一门 105 毫米口径的火炮，指挥台后装备有一门 37 毫米口径的机关炮，是一型水面水下火力均比较强大的潜艇。参见图 6–13。

German U–126 submarine was a kind of type IXC large scale submarine, equipped six torpedo tubes at bow and stern which can shoot G7e electric driven torpedo with warhead of 617 pounds (279.87 kilogrammes). One set of 105 millimeters cannon was located on front deck of conning tower, and one set of 37 millimeters machine gun was located on rear deck of conning tower. The firepower of U–126 submarine was violent on surface and under water. Refer to Figure 6–13.

图 6–13　U–126 潜艇的外形效果图 [10]
Figure 6–13　Artist's image of U–126 submarine

U–126 潜艇的艇长恩斯特·鲍尔是一名 28 岁经验丰富的军官，当时正指挥 U–126 潜艇在附近海域巡逻。该艇已经出航 53 天，曾在 6 月 3 日击沉了大型挪威油轮"Høegh Giant"号，6 月 14 日用火炮击沉了英国双桅帆船（twin-mast schooner）。

U–126 潜艇在潜望镜深度（periscope depth）以 210° 的航向以纯电机推进 2.5 节的航速悄然接近"Arkansan"号并从其艉部 315 米处通过。"Arkansan"号正在以 300° 的航向、11 节航速航行。潜艇上的第一瞭望长（first watch officer，同时负责水面攻击时的鱼雷发射）汉斯 – 阿道夫·施魏歇尔（Hans-Adolf Schweichel）判定"Arkansan"号是一艘无武装的货船，便下令开火；晚上 8∶31 U–126 潜艇从其艉部第五、第六号鱼雷发射管齐射了两枚 G7e 电动鱼雷。

"Arkansan"号的船长保罗·R. 琼斯发现了潜艇发射的鱼雷的航迹，他随即拉响了全船警报，加速至 13 节并操右满舵实施规避。按照当时的距离，以 30 节的速度高速航行的鱼雷从发射到命中仅仅需要 22 秒，这些规避动作显然已经无济于事。两枚 G7e 电动鱼雷击中了"Arkansan"号的舯部船体左舷。第一枚鱼雷击中了桥楼部位约水线以下 10 英尺（3.05 米）的船体，第二枚鱼雷几秒后击中了上层建筑尾端水线下的船体。"Arkansan"号受到了毁灭性的重击，船体出现了大幅度的倾斜。船长保罗·R. 琼斯下令弃船，36 名幸存船员登上了救生艇。在被击中 38 分钟后"Arkansan"号沉没。

Captain Ernst Bauer of U–126 submarine was 28 years old, an experienced officer. He was conducting U–126 submarine to patrol in that sea area. U–126 had departed her mother port for 53 days, she attacked and sank a large scale Norwegian tanker "Høegh Giant" on 3 June, and sank a British twin-mast schooner by the cannon on 14 June.

U–126 quietly approached to SS "Arkansan" in direction of 210 degrees with 2.5 knots pure electric propulsion at periscope depth, and passed through 315 meters off the stern of SS "Arkansan". SS "Arkansan" was sailing in 300 degrees with 11 knots. Hans-Adolf Schweichel, the first watch officer of U–126, also in charge of launching torpedo, affirmed that SS "Arkansan" was non-armed cargo steamer. He commanded to launch the torpedoes. At 8∶31 PM, two G7e electric driven torpedoes were launched simultaneously from No.5 and No. 6 stern tubes.

Captain Paul R. Jones of SS "Arkansan" observed the tracks of torpedo launched by submarine, he raised the alarm on board, and speeded the ship up to 13 knots with steering hard-a-starboard to avoid. Torpedo with speed of 30 knots needed only 22 seconds from launching to hitting the target, and such avoiding movement was useless. Two G7e electric driven torpedoes attacked portside hull amidship of SS "Arkansan". The first torpedo attacked hull at 10 feet (3.05 meters) below the waterline underneath of bridge, after seconds the second torpedo attacked underwater hull at end of superstructure. SS "Arkansan" suffered fatal attack, and hull had large angle heel. Captain Paul R. Jones ordered abandonment of the ship, and 36 surviving crews embarked on life boats. SS "Arkansan" sank 38 minutes after being attacked.

当日晚上 9：15，也就是袭击 "Arkansan" 号 44 分钟以后，U-126 潜艇又从其艏部的第一、第三号鱼雷发射管齐射了两枚 G7e 电动鱼雷击沉了武装商船 "Kahuku" 号（见图 6-14）。当时，"Kahuku" 号也在附近水域自北向南航行，船上载有前些天被 U-502 击沉的 "Scottburg" 号和 "Cold Harbor" 号上的 63 名幸存者。船长埃里克·赫伯特·约翰松（Eric Herbert Johanson）由于知晓附近有德国潜艇活动，因此即便在晚上还是一直以 12 节的航速进行 Z 形机动。本来 "Kahuku" 号可以借助夜色的掩护脱离这个危险区域，但船长埃里克·赫伯特·约翰松还是决定留下来救助 "Arkansan" 号上的幸存船员。船长埃里克·赫伯特·约翰松的义举使 "Kahuku" 号也未能逃脱被击沉的厄运。

At 9：15 PM of that evening, i.e., 44 minutes after attacking SS "Arkansan", U-126 launched two G7e electric driven torpedoes from No.1 and No.3 bow tubes and attacked and sank armed cargo steamer SS "Kahuku" (refer to Figure 6-14). At that time, SS "Kahuku" sailed nearby toward north. 63 survived crews from SS "Scottburg" and SS "Cold Harbor", which were sunken by U-502 serval days ago, were on board. Captain Eric Herbert Johanson was aware of German submarine actively cruising surrounded, and SS "Kahuku" kept zig-zag maneuvering in 12 knots even in night. Originally SS "Kahuku" had an opportunity to escape away from this dangerous area with the help of darkness, but captain Eric Herbert Johanson decided to help the surviving crews of SS "Arkansan", finally SS "Kahuku" did not escape the misfortune due to such humanitarian aid of captain Eric Herbert Johanson.

图 6-14　Matson 航运公司的武装货船 "Kahuku" 号 [11]
Figure 6-14　Armed SS "Kahuku" of Matson Steamship Company

第二艘船"天朝"号（H318）的外观涂装 [12]

四艘万吨轮从交付以后服务于不同的航运公司时，其外观涂装就是不同的。作者未能找到"东方"号（H319）和"国泰"号（H320）在第二次世界大战结束以后的相关照片，但在 www.ssarkansan.com 网站上发现一组不同年份"Arkansan"号船体外观涂装的变化图（见图 6–15）。图中的五个涂装方案可以清晰展现这四艘万吨轮从江南造船所完工交付以后至转卖给美洲–夏威夷航运公司乃至第二次世界大战期间被征用以后的涂装变化。

第一张图：江南造船所 1921 年交付给应急船队公司时的涂装。船体水线以上为黑色，水线以下为暗红色，水线用白色线条勾出，艏部舷墙为白色，上层建筑和艉楼为白色，烟囱为黑灰色没有涂装公司标志。这种涂装风格完全是一种商用运输船的风格，这从一个侧面说明江南造船所 1919 年完全已经将此型船修改设计成了商用型运输船，而不是 1918 年 7 月签合同时的运输舰。

第二张图：1922 年至 1936 年间服务于大来航运公司和大来码头轮船公司时的涂装。整体涂装风格和江南造船所交付时的没有太大的变化，只是取消了白色线条的水线。烟囱改成了黑色并增加了公司标志"$"和红色的环。

第三张图：1936 年至 1941 年 9 月服务于美洲–夏威夷航运公司时的涂装。艏部、上层建筑舷墙以及艉楼均改为黑色，烟囱和驾驶室后的大通风筒均改成了黄色并增加了公司标志性蓝带和"A–H"。从图 6–8 所示的江南造船所建造的四艘船入列美洲–夏威夷航运公司后的照片可以看出，上述涂装修改仅仅是针对"Arkansan"号的，而其他三艘船的艏部和上层建筑舷墙未改为黑色，仍然是白色。

美洲–夏威夷航运公司接手这四艘船后，第一艘船"Stuart Dollar"号在位于华盛顿州西雅图的托德干船坞公司进行修理改装，其余三艘船均在位于加利福尼亚州旧金山和奥克兰的莫尔干船坞公司进行修理改装。同一航运公司的同型船在同一船厂进行修理改装却采用了不同的涂装风格，这十分令人费解。如本书 6.3.2 节所述，在莫尔干船坞公司进行改装的过

External Coating Schemes of 2nd Steam Freighter SS "Celestial"(H318)

The external coating scheme was different while these four steam freighters served for different shipping companies after delivery. The pictures of SS "Oriental" (H319) and SS "Cathay" (H320) after the World War Ⅱ were not found, but pictures showing external coating scheme of SS "Arkansan" named "Arkansan Through Years" were found on website of www.ssarkansan.com (see Figure 6–15). This set of illustration consists of five external coating schemes and exhibits coating variation since being delivered from Kiangnan to American-Hawaiian Steamship Company as well requisitioned in wartime.

The first picture: this coating scheme was applied in 1921 when Kiangnan delivered the second steam freighter (SS "Celestial", H318) to EFC. Hull above waterline was painted in black, below waterline was painted in kermesinus (dark red), full load waterline was painted by white line, bow bulwark was painted in white, superstructure and poop were painted white as well, and funnel was painted in dark gray without company logo. This kind of coating scheme was completely merchant ship style. That meant that the design had been modified to merchant transport cargo ship since 1919 instead of armed transportation ship as described in shipbuilding contract signed in July 1918.

The second picture: this coating scheme was applied in 1922 to 1936, while she served for Dollar Steamship Company. and Dollar Terminal Steamship. Co., Inc. The global coating style had no big change comparing with delivery time of Kiangnan. Only white waterline was cancelled, funnel repainted black and company mark "$" and red strip added.

The third picture: this coating scheme was applied in 1936 to September 1941, while she served for American-Hawaiian Steamship Company. The bow and bulwark of superstructure section as well as poop had been repainted in black. The funnel and two large vent tubes in rear of wheel house were repainted in yellow with blue strip and "A-H". From Figure 6–8 Kiangnan-built 4 steam freighters in American-Hawaiian's Fleet, above new painting scheme was only applied on SS "Arkansan" but not the other three. The bulwark in way of bow and superstructure areas was kept white not black.

After American-Hawaiian Steamship Company took over these four steam freighters, SS "Stuart Dollar", the first steam freighter of series was carried out re-conditioning works in Todd Dry Dock Company, Seattle, Washington, USA. The retrofit for the other three steam freighters were done in Moore Dry Dock Company in San Francisco and Oakland, California, USA. It is hard to understand why different painting scheme were applied for these three identical steam freighters in the same shipyard for the same shipping company. As described in Section 6.3.2, a pair of king post was added on fore end of shelter deck, life boat arrangement

程中，艏部增加了一对起重柱，救生艇改成左右各一艘，艇的容量增大。这些改装过程中的变化在图 6-15 上已经展现出来了。

第四张图：1941 年 9 月至 12 月，上层建筑整体涂成了暗灰色，只有烟囱仍然保持了美洲－夏威夷航运公司的标准涂装。此时第二次世界大战的阴云正笼罩着欧洲大陆，但美国还未正式宣布参战。

The fourth picture: September to November of 1941, whole superstructure re-painted dark gray, only funnel was still kept as standard painting scheme of American-Hawaiian Steamship Company. At that time, the World War II was in full swing on European Continent, but the United States did not announce to enter the war.

第五张图：1942 年，美国已经正式参战。美洲－夏威夷航运公司的绝大部分船舶被征用投入战时运输。船体、上层建筑包括烟囱被统统涂成暗灰色，以利于海上隐蔽，减少被潜艇发现的概率。"Arkansan" 号被击沉时也是这个涂装。

The fifth picture: in 1942, the United States had participated in the war. Most ships of American-Hawaiian Steamship Company were requisitioned for military transportation. Hull shell, superstructure including funnel were entirely painted in dark gray in order to reduce probability detected by submarine. SS "Arkansan" was coated in this scheme when she was attacked and sunken.

was changed each for portside and starboard, and the capacity of life boat was enlarged accordingly. These modifications had been indicated on the Figure 6-15.

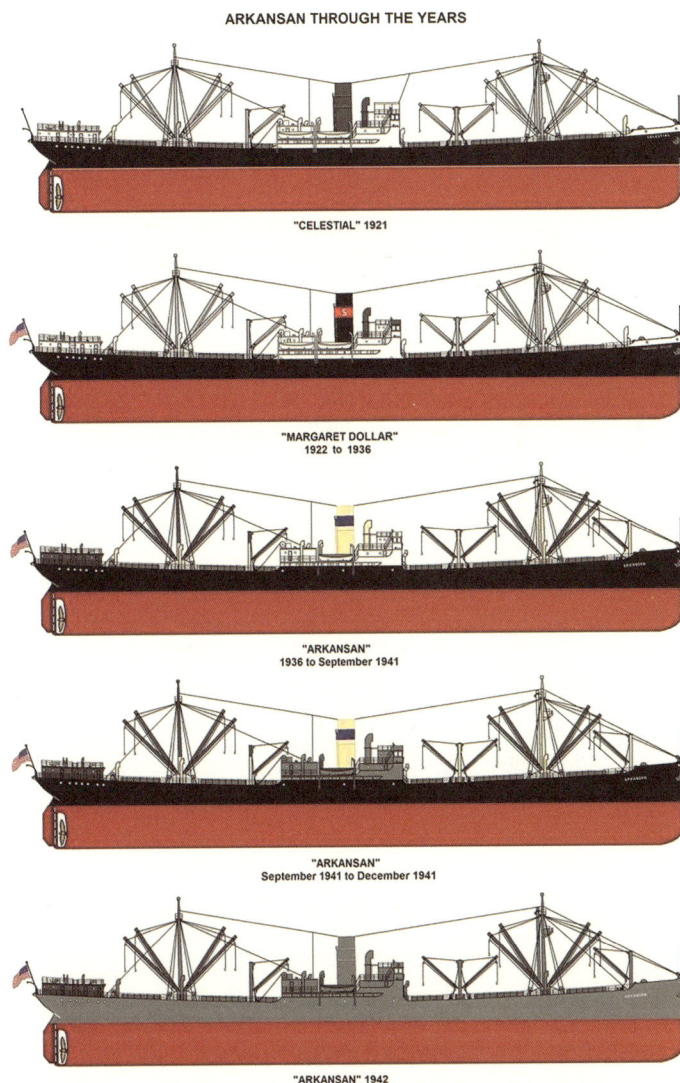

图 6-15 不同年份 "Arkansan" 号船体外观涂装变化
Figure 6-15 SS "Arkansan" coating scheme through the years

第三艘 "东方" 号（H319）

The Third Steam Freighter SS "Oriental" (H319)

建造时的船体号：	H319	Hull number of construction:	H319
美国船级社的入级编号：	221728	Register ID of ABS:	221728
总吨：	7 032	Gross tonnage:	7 032

船舶营运史：

- H319 被命名为"东方"号。1921 年 10 月 1 日完工离开江南造船所码头赴美交付给美国海运委员会下属的应急船队公司。

- 1922 年，美国海运委员会将此船出售给总部位于旧金山的大来公司下属的大来航运公司。大来航运公司将其更名为"Melville Dollar"号。

- 1935 年，大来航运公司将该船转让给大来公司下属的大来码头轮船公司。

- 1936 年，该船被转卖给总部位于纽约和旧金山的美洲－夏威夷航运公司，后该船在位于加利福尼亚州旧金山和奥克兰的莫尔干船坞公司进行修理改装。美洲－夏威夷航运公司将其更名为"Carolinian"号。

- 根据维基百科中关于的第二次世界大战期间美洲－夏威夷航运公司船队的记载，"Carolinian"号被征用参与战时运输，具体何时被征用不详。图 6-16 为 1944 年 7 月 10 日"Carolinian"号航行时的照片。从照片中可以看出，艏楼上加装了一门大口径的舰炮和两门小口径的舰炮，艉楼上也加装了一门大口径的舰炮和两门小口径的舰炮，驾驶室桥楼两端也加装了两门小口径的舰炮。1936 年改装时艏部加装的一对吊杆被拆除了。图 6-16 虽然是一幅黑白照片，但可以看出"Carolinian"号采用的是战时暗灰色的涂装。在前后桅屋的左右舷，各加装了一块倾斜挡板，不知是什么用途。2018 年底，作者访问台北长荣海事博物馆时看到馆中陈列的第二次世界大战中承担运输任务的武装商船"Lane Victory"号的模型（见图 6-17）。该船在前后桅屋的左右舷加装的倾斜挡板上放置了一艘舢板，可见这块倾斜挡板是舢板的存放和释放装置。

Operating history:

- H319 was named as "Oriental". On 1 October 1921, SS "Oriental" departed from quay of Kiangnan for delivering to EFC of USSB.

- In 1922, USSB sold SS "Oriental" to Dollar Steamship Company (Robert Dollar Company, parent company), San Francisco, CA, USA, and she was renamed as SS "Melville Dollar" by Dollar Steamship Company.

- In 1935, Dollar Steamship Company transferred SS "Melville Dollar" to Dollar Terminal Steamship Co., Inc., a subsidiary of Robert Dollar Company, San Francisco, CA, USA.

- In 1936, Dollar Terminal Steamship Co., sold SS "Melville Dollar" to American-Hawaiian Steamship Company, New York and San Francisco, USA. She was re-conditioned in Moore Dry Dock Company, San Francisco and Oakland, CA, USA. She was renamed as SS "Carolinian" by American-Hawaiian Steamship Company.

- SS "Carolinian" was requisitioned for military transportation according to description of American-Hawaiian Steamship Company during the World War Ⅱ in English version of Wikipedia, but the exact time period of requisition is not clear. Figure 6-16 is SS "Carolinian" on voyage on 10 July 1944. One set of large-caliber naval cannon and two sets of small-caliber naval gun were added on forecastle deck, and the consistent armaments were installed on poop deck as well, further two sets of small-caliber naval gun were complemented on bridge wings. A pair of king post, installed during reconditioning in 1936, was dismantled accordingly. Although Figure 6-16 is a black-white photo, dark-gray coating scheme for wartime can be verified. A steel slant plate was fitted on each side of fore and aft master houses, but what were the purpose of those plates? The answer was found in Evergreen Maritime Museum, Taipei, at end of 2018. A model of armed cargo ship SS "Lane Victory" is exhibited in this museum (see Figure 6-17), and this sloped plate was used for storing and launching the dinghy.

图 6-16　1944 年 7 月 10 日航行中的"Carolinian"号
Figure 6-16　SS "Carolinian" on voyage on 10 July 1944

图 6-17　台北长荣海事博物馆中陈列的武装商船 "Lane Victory" 号的模型
Figure 6-17　A model of armed freighter SS "Lane Victory" in Evergreen Maritime Museum, Taipei

◆ 1946 年，"Carolinian" 号被转卖给了乌拉圭蒙得维的亚的 Compania Uruguaya de Navegacion Y Transportes Aereos S. A.，并更名为 "Atlantida" 号。作者相信在转卖前该船进行了改装，拆除了原先加装的战时武备。曾被拆除的艏部的一对吊杆是否再次加装也不得而知。

◆ 1951 年，该船被转卖给了注册于巴拿马的 Shore Haven Steamship Corp.，该公司为美国纽约的 T. J. Stevenson & Co., Inc. 属下的单船公司。

◆ 1952 年，该船被转卖给了日本尼崎的三光汽船株式会社（Sanko Kisen K. K.），并更名为 "旭光丸" 号。

◆ 1955 年，"旭光丸" 号被转卖给了日本大洋冷冻母船株式会社（Taiyo Reito Bosen K. K.）。

◆ 1959 年，"旭光丸" 号被转卖给了日本日鲁渔业株式会社（Nichiro Gyogyo K. K.）。

◆ 1960 年，"旭光丸" 号在日本横须贺的东洋棉花株式会社（Toyo Menka K. K.）被拆解。

◆ In 1946, SS "Carolinian" was resold to Compania Uruguaya de Navegacion Y Transportes Aereos S. A. Montevideo, Uruguay, and renamed as SS "Atlantida". It was confirmed that all weapon for wartime was dismantled, but it was not sure that the king post was re-installed or not.

◆ In 1951, she was resold to Shore Haven Steamship Corp. registered in Panama, which was a special purpose vehicle belong to T. J. Stevenson & Co., Inc. New York, USA.

◆ In 1952, she was resold to Sanko Kisen K. K. Amagasaki, Japan, and renamed as SS "Kyokko Maru".

◆ In 1955, she was resold to Taiyo Reito Bosen K. K., Japan.

◆ In 1959, she was resold to Nichiro Gyogyo K. K., Japan.

◆ In 1960, SS "Kyokko Maru" was scrapped by Toyo Menka K. K. in Yokosuka, Japan.

第四艘"国泰"号（H320）

The Fourth Steam Freighter SS "Cathay" (H320)

建造时的船体号：	H320
美国船级社的入级编号：	221907
总吨：	7 033

Hull number of construction:	H320
Register ID of ABS:	221907
Gross tonnage:	7 033

船舶营运史：

Operating history:

◆ H320 被命名为"国泰"号。1921 年 12 月 21 日完工离开江南造船所码头赴美交付给美国海运委员会下属的应急船队公司。

◆ 1922 年，美国海运委员会将"国泰"号出售给总部位于旧金山的大来公司下属的大来航运公司。大来航运公司将其更名为 "Diana Dollar" 号。

◆ 1935 年，大来航运公司将该船转让给大来公司下属的大来码头轮船公司。

◆ 1936 年，该船被转卖给总部位于纽约和旧金山的美洲－夏威夷航运公司，后该船在位于加利福尼亚州旧金山和奥克兰的莫尔干船坞公司进行修理改装。美洲－夏威夷航运公司将其更名为 "Alabaman" 号。

◆ 根据维基百科相关内容的记载，第二次世界大战期间，美洲－夏威夷航运公司的 "Alabaman" 号和 "Carolinian" 号一样都被征用参与战时运输，具体何时被征用不详。

◆ 1947 年，该船被转卖给了注册于巴拿马的 Nortuna Shipping 公司，并改名为 "Norega" 号。该公司是位于纽约的 Naess Mejlaender & Co., Inc. 下属的单船公司。图 6–18 为 "Norega" 号在丹麦哥本哈根附近水域航行的照片。从照片可以看出，1936 年改装时加装的一对吊杆仍然被保留着，而 "Carolinian" 号的则被拆除了。也许第二次世界大战期间 "Alabaman" 号并未加装武备？

◆ 1949 年，该船被转卖给了意大利萨沃纳的 Societa Anonima Importazione Carbonie Navegazione 公司，并改名为 "Armonia" 号。

◆ 1959 年 3 月 3 日，该船抵达日本大阪，在大阪的 Rinko 公司被拆解。

◆ H320 was named as SS "Cathay". On 21 November 1921, SS "Cathay" departed from quay of Kiangnan for delivering to EFC of USSB.

◆ In 1922, USSB sold SS "Cathay" to Dollar Steamship Company (Robert Dollar Company, parent company), San Francisco, CA, USA, and she was renamed as SS "Diana Dollar" by Dollar Steamship Company.

◆ In 1935, Dollar Steamship Company transferred SS "Cathay Dollar" to Dollar Terminal Steamship Co., Inc., a subsidiary of Robert Dollar Company, San Francisco, CA, USA.

◆ In 1936, Dollar Terminal Steamship Co., Inc. sold SS "Cathay Dollar" to American-Hawaiian Steamship Company, New York and San Francisco, USA. She was re-conditioned in Moore Dry Dock Company, San Francisco and Oakland, CA, USA. She was renamed as SS "Alabaman" by American-Hawaiian Steamship Company.

◆ Both SS "Alabaman" and SS "Carolinian" were requisitioned for military transportation according to description of American-Hawaiian Steamship Company, during the World War Ⅱ in English version of Wikipedia, but the exact time period of requisition is not clear.

◆ In 1947, SS "Alabaman" was sold to Nortuna Shipping Co., Inc. registered in Panama, and renamed as SS "Norega". This company was a special purpose vehicle which belonged to Naess Mejlaender & Co., Inc. of New York. Figure 6–18 is a photo when SS "Norega" navigated in waters near Copenhagen of Denmark. Form this photo, king posts installed in 1936 were kept, but those on SS "Carolinian" were dismantled. Possibly SS "Alabaman" was not armed during the World War Ⅱ?

◆ In 1949, SS "Alabaman" was sold to Societa Anonima Importazione Carbonie Navegazione of Savona Co., Italy, and renamed as SS "Armonia".

◆ SS "Armonia" was scrapped by Rinko Company after arriving in Osaka, Japan on 3 March 1959.

　　"东方"号和"国泰"号是这四艘船中使用寿命最长的，分别长达 39 年和 38 年，这说明当时江南造船所建造的船舶的质量还是不错的，当然这和船东方良好的保养维护、入列美洲－夏威夷航运公司前的大修和改装以及第二次世界大战后运输船舶数量上的不足也有一定的关系。

　　SS "Oriental" and SS "Cathay" were the longest two in the series of four, and the operation life reached 39 years and 40 years respectively. That meant even though it was the first time for kiangnan to build such big ships, the quality was quite good. Of course, the maintenance provided by ship owners, reconditioning before joining fleet of American-Hawaiian Steamship Company and tonnage shortage after the World War Ⅱ are also reasons for longer operation.

图 6–18 "Norega" 号在丹麦哥本哈根附近水域航行
Figure 6–18　SS "Norega" navigated in water near Copenhagen of Denmark

作者注：
Notes:

1　照片来自：加拿大温哥华海事博物馆（Vancouver Maritime Museum）。

2　*Pacific Marine Review*, February 1937.

3　莫尔干船坞公司的广告图来自互联网，向上在传者表示敬意。

4　这张照片是 1941 年美国旧金山国际新闻局在 "Arkansan" 号于苏伊士受到攻击后提供给报社的。

5　照片来自：www.tugboatpainter.net。

6　综合网络上的公开信息编译而成。

7　图片和资料来自：https://en.wikipedia.org。

8　同上。

9　根据世界地图相关地区的地理位置绘制。

10　图片来自：www.ssarkansan.com，效果图由安迪·霍尔（Andy Hall）提供，向原作者表示敬意。

11　照片来自：www.marinersmuseum.org，向上传者表示敬意。

12　图片来自：www.ssarkansan.com，向原作者表示敬意。

后 记
POSTSCRIPT

在经典著作《伯罗奔尼撒战争史》中，古希腊历史学家修昔底德曾经记录了米诺斯是第一个创立海军的人。我用此事例作为开场白是因为无论个人还是集体都是将第一个创造、发现任何事物的行为作为历史中的重要事件来记录的，就像中国的一句俗话："第一个吃螃蟹的人"。不容置疑，从古至今"第一人"对于任何人来说都是一项巨大的荣誉，值得去争取和看齐。确实，"还原真实"通常是历史学家"义不容辞"的责任，但由于各种因素的制约很难做到这一点。无论是海军、海事行业还是其他工业领域，第一和第二都应该仔细地定义和研究。以船舶行业为例，万吨轮不仅是船舶工业史中一种标志性的船型，而且对于近现代中国造船工业来说，这种船型也是具有里程碑意义、非常值得关注和探究。辛亥革命以后，面临内忧外患的中国工业化是相当艰难和曲折的，回顾这个过程中的"第一"是近代工业史研究中不容忽视的一个部分。同时，在中国工业化的曲折过程中，近现代中国造船工业不应该成为一个被遗忘的"角落"。

正如史景迁所说："没有一个国家，在经历几个世纪后，可以从混乱和惨剧中解放出来。"与其将我们自己看作受害者和失败者的后代，不如用这些苦难所产生的阵痛去激励中国人民在实践中反思、重建和新生，哪怕实践的结果不一定是成功。我们不应一味谴责过去，这种观点或许使我们能够更正面、更积极地对待和认识那段历史。

虽然万吨轮是近现代中国船舶建造历史中的里程碑，但对于如何定义第一艘自行建造的万吨轮来说，总是显示出一种无奈和困扰，如同许多历史研究中的其他谜团一样。在这种现状下，清楚定义第一艘中国自行建造的万吨轮，以及它在现代中国科学技术发展史中的地位变得非常有必要。

In the masterpiece *History of the Peloponnesian War*, the ancient Greek historian Thucydides used to record that the first one who founded the Greek Navy was Minos. Personally, I choose this as a reasonable hook, because that people including individuals and groups as the first to create, discover any issues are always crucial in most history, like Chinese phrase: "The first to eat a crab". A fortiori, it seems the first from past to future is a great honor for people to pursue and achieve. Exactly, to make out the facts clearly is normally regarded as a hard task for historians to carry on. Regardless navy, marine and other industries, often, the first and the next should be defined and researched carefully. Exempligratia, 10 000-ton deadweight freighter is one of the symbolistic types not only in Chinese history of modern shipbuilding. However, to the historical development of modern Chinese shipbuilding, it is extremely treasurable and significant. Because the process of industrialization in modern China is quite rough and bumpy, facing the inner problems and outside foreign powers, any tiny progress is memorable and great. Also, through the twists and turns of Chinese modern industrialization, contemporaneous shipbuilding should not become a "dead angle" in modern Chinese industrial history to forget and miss.

Like Jonathan D. Spence commented, "No country, over the past few centuries, has been free of turmoil and tragedy." What is more necessary to see ourselves as the descendants of victims and losers through the past hundred years, the hardship and roughness of twinge invoke Chinese people to rethink, rebuild and regenerate, though some of the result of practice may be hard to label as "successful". It is a more positive and effective view to redefine the history.

Meanwhile, as a milestone in the modern shipbuilding history of Chinese shipyards, the affirmation and definition on the first self-built 10 000-ton deadweight freighter of China always shows an unwillingness and confusion as it usually occurred in many mysteries of historical research. In this status quo, a research on the first self-built 10 000-ton deadweight freighter becomes necessary and essential to every history research on modern Chinese history of science and technology.

第一艘获得此项殊荣的是大连造船厂建造的"跃进"号万吨级货轮。但是，这个桂冠只在它头上停留了一年半。发生在日本海的首航沉船事故使得当时各界对真相不得不"三缄其口"。首先，苏联和中国，两个曾经像兄弟一样友爱的邻国，关系逐渐紧张。"跃进"号的图纸是由苏联专家提供的，在那个特殊时期，沉船事件是不宜再次被提及的。事实上，"跃进"号是 1949 年后第一艘自行建造的万吨轮，但是当时我们试图弱化这一事实来减少苏联的影响。所以，顺理成章地，一年半以后在江南造船厂下水的"东风"号代替"跃进"号作为第一艘自行建造的万吨轮出现在公众的视野中。

我从读小学开始直到现在在江南造船厂工作这么多年，一直笃信中国第一艘万吨轮就是"东风"号。从来没有想到我自己有一天会去揭秘中国第一艘万吨轮。2014 年上半年，我在浏览一个记录第二次世界大战失踪和死亡船员的网站时偶然发现，被德国潜艇击沉的万吨轮"Arkansan"号就是江南造船所 1921 年建造的"天朝"号。该船是四艘万吨轮中的第二艘，第一艘为"官府"号。以此为线索我进一步找到了与这四艘万吨轮相关的海量资料。这四艘万吨轮的建造时间远远早于"跃进"号和"东风"号。

如果"官府"号系列不仅仅是依"美方来图来料加工"，而是江南造船所自行设计的，那么我们是否可以把它们当作是中国自行设计建造的第一批万吨轮呢？在好奇心的驱使下，我开始"第一艘万吨轮究竟是哪一艘"的研究活动。2015 年 5 月，在美国船级社休斯敦总部查找到了四艘万吨轮的入级资料。此外，船舶档案馆保存的四艘万吨轮的图纸资料也有力地证明了我的观点。当这些调查完成以后，我得到了一个清晰的事实："官府"号是第一艘中国自行设计建造的万吨轮。作为一项原创性发现，我认为四艘万吨轮的设计建造过程以及它们的整个营运过程是一个值得在书中详细阐述的话题，本书的写作也给我的造船职业生涯平添了一些乐趣和动力。

正是由于这些海量的第一手和第二手资料，以及我执意揭开和还原一些历史真相的初心，再加上一个船舶设计者的敏感性，我提出了书中所述的关于自行

The one, earned as the first 10 000-ton deadweight freighter is MV "Yue Jin"(known as "Leap"). However, the vessel worn the laurel only for one and a half year. The accident which led to the sink in Japan Sea became a zip on public's mouths and sensitive issue for the government propaganda. First, there was a large diplomatic tense between Soviet Union and the People's Republic of China, though these two countries used to be close as brotherhood. Actually, the drawings of MV "Yue Jin" were provided by Soviet experts, and this is hard to be mentioned again in such special period. Although it is a truth that MV "Yue Jin" was the first self-built 10 000-ton deadweight freighter, according to these circumstances, government tried to weaken any influence from Soviet Union. Therefore, they naturally used MV "Dong Feng" (known as "East Wind") to replace MV "Yue Jin" as the first self-designed and built 10 000-ton deadweight freighter in the propaganda towards public. Through the strong dissemination, MV "Dong Feng" became the well-known symbol of the rise of national industry, and it follows a logic train of thought.

I devoutly believed that the first 10 000-ton freighter in China is MV "Dong Feng" from studying in elementary school to working for Jiangnan Shipyard so many years. When the things would come to the closer, I never thought the work to unveil the secret of the First Chinese self-built 10 000-ton deadweight freighter will fall on me. The issue happened in such accident and surprise. In early 2014, when checking the list of lost and wreck crew during the World War II, I had a finding that the sunk 10 000-ton deadweight freighter SS "Arkansan", which attacked by German U-boat, is the same vessel which retrofitted from steam freighter SS "Celestial" built by Kiangnan Dock & Engineering Works in 1921. This fact attracts me to start my research for exploring more resources. SS "Celestial" is the second in the series, and the first is SS "Mandarin", which construction time was much earlier than MV "Yue Jin" and MV "Dong Feng".

If the Mandarin series is not only built by "American furnished drawing and material", but also self-designed by Kiangnan themselves, could we regard it as the first 10 000-ton deadweight freighter self-built in China? There are many questions I would like to ask and research on it to get answers. I, with the strong curiosity, started to research based on my technical background. In May 2015, I visited Huston Headquarter of American Bureau of Shipping in order to discover more useful materials of these four steam freighter. Furthermore, the resources from the Archives of CSSC also strongly prove my points during my visiting in the same month of 2015. After finishing these works, the fact is distinct: it is no dispute that the SS "Mandarin" is the first Chinese self-designed and self-built 10 000-ton deadweight freighter by Kiangnan Dock & Engineering Works (today known as Jiangnan Shipyard Group). As an original discovery, I think this is a topic worth elaborating in a book and which inspires me a lot in whatever life and work.

After unveiling the history facts from some primary sources and secondary sources, I raise several outstanding questions above, kindly hoping that I can solve them in this book in order to reach the aim of research. One thing can be quite meaningful and let me gain a lot of

设计的几个关键问题，希望我自己能够在本书的撰写过程中解答这些问题，并达到研究目的。可以揭秘当时传统的造船流程、所造的船和造船行业的林林总总是一件我自己觉得相当有意义且成就感满满的事情。1949 年以前，基于政治环境和外界对我们的有限认知，这个时段的中国通常被认为是黑暗和落后的。有时，在这一时期取得的科学技术方面的进步和成果都被低估了。但这是中国工业发展的一部分，也是国家发展的缩影，尽管国家的发展往往会经历一些曲折和磨难。如同巨大银河系中的一颗渺小的星星，民国的船舶建造行业不应该仅仅因为政治原因而被忽视。客观来说，任何一段历史的真相都不应该被隐藏。

我怀着热情深入研究这个问题的第二个原因是这四艘船的图纸仍旧是宝贵的第一手资料，值得分析与确认。读者可以通过我的专业解析对当时的船舶工业的技术沿革与发展脉络有一个清晰的认识。我对我工作的船厂有很深的感情。江南造船厂就像我的家一样，介绍和探索江南造船厂过去的历史，还原真相，这是我的荣幸。

为了深入研究和分析这些发生在这四艘中国建造的万吨轮上的历史事件和时间点，我收集了大量相关信息和资料并仔细比较和对照。在本书中，我也用自己的工作经验和专业技术分析了一些问题。希望我陈述的这些不仅展现了我个人的想法和研究内容，同时也给那些从没有接触过这个领域的读者留下深刻印象，让他们对这个领域有新的和不同的见解。

2017 年 2 月，《揭秘中国第一批万吨轮》一书出版后，受到了造船界专业读者的好评。海事界的一些外国朋友也对"中国第一批万吨轮"这个话题产生了浓厚的兴趣。我和一位年长的希腊船东谈起蒸汽动力的货船时，他激动地说："我小时候就是坐这种船横渡大西洋去美国的。"我当时就萌生了一个想法，要把此书翻译成英文，让海事界的外国朋友也了解中国建造的第一批万吨轮。

本书不仅修正了《揭秘中国第一批万吨轮》一书中的一些差错，而且补充了一些新的资料和内容。在翻译过程中，尽管得到了朋友和同事的帮助，但还是遇到了很大的挑战和困难。鉴于本人英语水平有限，书中的差错或表述不当的地方，希望读者能够包容和理解。

achievements is to reveal the traditional shipbuilding process, ships delivered and shipping industry in that particular time. The old China, which points at the China after Qing and before founding of the People's Republic of China, was usually to be defined as laggard and dark based on political environment and limited cognition. Sometimes, the progress and achievements in science and technologies are largely underestimated. However, it is a part of developing of China, though they are always including a lot of twists and hardships. As a little star in this large galaxy, the shipbuilding industry in the Republic of China should not be ignored just because the political factors. To be obvious, the truth should not be hidden in any parts of the history.

As the second reason for me to deeply research on this topic with strong passion is the drawings of these four ships are still valuable primary sources to analyze and affirm. Using my professional technology background, readers will make a clear expression on the shipbuilding industry at that time. Meanwhile, I have a deep attachment to the shipyard where I work. Jiangnan Shipyard is just like my home, and it is my pleasure to introduce and explore its history from past.

In order to conduct in-deep research and analysis on these history events and moments happened on these four 10 000-ton deadweight freighters built by China, I gathered these information and resources to compare and contrast in this book. In my study, I also make analysis on several outstanding issues with my working experience and technology. Hope the issue I state not only express my own ideas and research clearly, but also impressive to these people who had not reached the field and make them have new and different connection with it.

In February 2017, after the publication of the *Mandarin Series and Their Entire Lives* (Chinese Edition), the book was well received by professional readers in the shipbuilding industry. Some foreign friends in the maritime field have also taken a keen interest in the topic of "China's first 10 000-ton freighter". When I talked to an elderly Greek shipowner about steam powered freighters, he excitedly told me: "When I was a child, I took this kind of steamer crossing the Atlantic Ocean for the Unites States." At that time, I had an idea to translate the book into English, so that foreign friends in the maritime industry could also know more about the first batch of China's 10 000-ton freighter.

This book not only corrects some minor errors in the book *Mandarin Series and Their Entire Lives* (Chinese Edition), but also supplements some new materials and information. In the translation process, despite the help from my friends and colleagues, I still encountered great challenges and difficulties. In view of my limited English proficiency, the book will inevitably have some misunderstandings or improper expressions. I sincerely hope that readers can accept this with understanding and an open mind.

就像船舶设计师平时所写的船舶建造规格书，它可能不是一本完美的英语书，但实实在在地描述了"要造一艘什么样的船"。

上海市船舶与海洋工程学会对本书的翻译工作给予了全力支持，并将其作为国际交流工作委员会的一个研究项目。作者在此深表感谢！

在中国工程院院士、上海交通大学原校长林忠钦及上海交通大学中国海洋装备工程科技发展战略研究院和上海交通大学出版社的大力支持下，本书得以出版发行。这段发生在 20 世纪第二个十年被尘封了百余年的民族工业史终于得以重见天日。作为在造船行业工作了四十余年、见证了改革开放给船舶工业带来巨变的一名船舶人，喜悦之余，更有一种欣慰。

最后要特别感谢陈语霆，他不仅热心地帮助我在网上查找资料，而且还专程前往华盛顿特区的美国国家档案馆查找纸质实物档案。这些珍贵的纸质实物档案，特别是在造船合同和船舶建造规格书中的详细记载，大大提升了本书史料的运用维度。

Usually, the Shipbuilding Specification usually written by a ship designer may not be a perfect English textbook, but it does exactly describe "what kind of ship is to be built".

The Shanghai Society of Naval Architects and Ocean Engineers has given its full support to the translation of this book, which was enlisted as a research project of the International Exchange Committee. I hereinto would like to express my sincere thanks to them.

With the substantive supports of Lin Zhongqin, Academician of Chinese Academy of Engineering, former president of Shanghai Jiao Tong University, the China Strategy Institute of Ocean Engineering of Shanghai Jiao Tong University and Shanghai Jiao Tong University Press, this book was able to be published. The national shipbuilding industry in 1920s which has been immersed more one hundred years substantially discovered. As a practitioner who has worked in Chinese shipbuilding industry for more than 40 years and witnessed the great changes brought about by the reform and opening up of the shipbuilding industry, it is not only a joy, but also a kind of gratification.

Last but not least, I would like to specially thank Chen Yuting, who not only enthusiastically helped me find materials on the Internet, but also made a special trip to the National Archives of the United States in Washington, D.C. to find paper archives. These precious paper archives, especially the detailed descriptions in shipbuilding contract and specifications, greatly enhanced the multidimensional application of archival materials of this book.

2020 年 1 月 30 日翻译稿完成于上海

2024 年 2 月 18 日修订稿完成于上海

The translation was completed on 30 January 2020 at Shanghai

The revised version was finalized on 18 February 2024 at Shanghai

1. 《江南制造局记》，魏允恭辑录，光绪三十一年（1905年），江南造船集团档案馆藏。

2. 《江南造船所纪要》，江南造船所所长刘冠南审核、廖骕编写，民国十一年四月（1922年4月），江南造船集团档案馆藏。

3. 《海军江南造船所报告书》，民国二十年十二月（1931年12月），江南造船集团档案馆藏。

4. 《江南造船厂厂史：1865—1949》，上海社会科学院经济研究所，江苏人民出版社出版，1983年。

5. 《中国近代舰艇工业史料集》，《中国舰艇工业历史资料丛书》编辑部编纂，上海人民出版社出版，1994年。

6. 《江南造船厂志：1865—1995》，江南造船厂志编纂委员会，上海人民出版社出版，1999年。

7. 《中国近代造船史》，王志毅著，海洋出版社出版，1986年。

8. 《中国近代船舶工业史》，辛元欧著，上海古籍出版社出版，1999年。

9. 《中国第一厂风采录》，江南造船厂本书编写组编写，上海文艺出版社出版，1995年。

1. *The Record of Kiangnan Manufacture Bureau*, edited by Wei Yungong, 31st Year of Guangxu (1905), collected archive of Archives Institute of Jiangnan Shipyard (Group) Co., Ltd.

2. *Summary of Kiangnan Dock & Engineering Works*, edited by Liao Shen, audited by Liu Guannan, Director of Kiangnan Dock & Engineering Works, April, 11th Year of the Republic of China (1922), collected archive of Archives Institute of Jiangnan Shipyard (Group) Co., Ltd.

3. *The Reports of Naval of Kiangnan Dock & Engineering Works*, December, 20th Year of the Republic of China (1931), collected archive of Archives Institute of Jiangnan Shipyard (Group) Co., Ltd. Collected archive in Archives Institute of Jiangnan Shipyard (Group) Co., Ltd.

4. *The History of Jiangnan Shipyard: 1865–1949*, Institute of Economics, Shanghai Academy of Social Sciences, published by Jiangsu People's Publishing House, 1983.

5. *A Collection of Historical Materials on Chinese Modern Marine Industry*, edited by the editorial department of the *Series of Historical Materials on China's Shipbuilding Industry,* published by Shanghai People's Publishing House, 1994.

6. *The Chronicles of Jiangnan Shipyard: 1865–1995*, Editing Committee of the Chronicles of Jiangnan Shipyard, published by Shanghai People's Publishing House, 1999.

7. *Modern Shipbuilding History of China*, edited by Wang Zhiyi, published by China Ocean Press, 1986.

8. *The History of Chinese Modern Shipbuilding Industry*, edited by Xing Yuanou, published by Shanghai Chinese Classics Publishing House, 1999.

9. *The Mien of Chinese No.1 Enterprise*, Editing Group of Jiangnan Shipyard, published by Shanghai Literature & Art Publishing House, 1995.

10. 《自强之路：从江南造船厂看中国造船业百年历程》，叶宝园著，中央文献出版社出版，2008 年。

10. *Self-strengthen Roadmap: from Jiangnan to Review Hundred History of Chinese Shipbuilding Industry*, edited by Ye Baoyuan, published by Central Party Literature Press, 2008.

11. 《江南往事》，陆舸编著，上海画报出版社出版，2005 年。

11. *The Past of Jiangnan*, edited by Lu Ke, published by Shanghai Pictorial Press, 2005.

12. 《英国皇家海军战舰设计发展史》，卷 3，大舰队，（英）大卫·K. 布朗著，张宇翔译，江苏凤凰文艺出版社出版，2019 年。

12. *The Grand Fleet: Warship Design and Development 1906–1922*, Volume 3, edited by David K. Brown, translated by Zhang Yuxiang, published by Jiangsu Phoenix Literature and Art Publishing, Ltd., 2019.

13. 《一战简史：帝国幻觉》，（英）诺曼·斯通著，王东兴、张蓉译，中信出版社出版，2014。

13. *World War One: A Short History*, Norman Stone, translated by Wang Dongxing and Zhang Rong, published by China CITIC Press, 2014.

14. *The Bridge to France*, Edward N. Hurley, published by Kessinger Legacy Reprints.

15. *Memoirs of Robert Dollar*, December 1921, Second Edition, April 1922, by Robert Dollar, published by W. S. Van Cott. & Co., San Francisco, California, USA.

16. *The Rise and Decline of U.S. Merchant Shipping in the Twentieth Century*, René De La Pedraja, published by Twayne Publishers, New York, USA.

17. *Chinese History, A New Manual*, Fourth Edition, Endymion Wilkinson, published by the Harvard University Asia Center.

18. *The Search for Modern China*, Jonathan D. Spence, published by W. W. Norton & Company.

19. *The Old Shanghai A-Z*, Paul French, Hong Kong University Press, 2010.